Empires of the Dead

For
Hannah,
Curtis,
and
Jack

Andean people have not spent their history closed up in an impossible museum.

　　　　　　　　　　—Alberto Flores Galindo, *In Search of an Inca* (1986)

CONTENTS

PART 3: HEALING, 1863–1965

A NOTE ON IMAGES

The earliest known visual depictions of Inca and Andean ancestors were made by an Indigenous chronicler named Felipe Guaman Poma de Ayala, who in 1616 sent his richly illustrated manuscript *El primer nveva corónica I bven gobierno* to the king of Spain. That Guaman Poma wanted the king to see the mummified or skeletal forms of the Incas and their Andean subjects is clear. Guaman Poma was not Inca. He was a descendant of Chinchasuyu lords of the Inca empire, Tawantinsuyu, and had previously painted several illustrations for Basque friar Martín de Murúa's *Historia general del Piru*. While Murúa commissioned portraits of the Inca emperors for his *Historia*, there were no depictions of actual Andean ancestors. With *El primer nveva corónica*, Guaman Poma rectified that absence. Among his goals was the depiction of the Andean dead's variety, showing that differences in their physical preservation demanded nuance when it came to understanding the many ways that Inca and Andean peoples loved, cured, venerated, and feared the unbreathing relatives they kept close.

This book contains numerous visual depictions of Inca and Andean remains, beginning with its cover, *Yachaya*, a mixed-media sculpture by the Cuban-German artist Nancy Torres that uses paint, textiles, glass, wood, feathers, plaster, straw, wire mesh, and objects over canvas to evoke an ancestor under colonial assault. Most of the other images in this book likewise outstrip anything that Felipe Guaman Poma de Ayala intended for his royal audience of one. The mortuary culture of Inca and Andean Tawantinsuyu—where the unbreathing could look upon the living, and the living might sometimes look back—is a far cry from the nineteenth- and twentieth-century museum cultures in which non-Andean curators and anthropologists unwrapped "Inca mummies" and de-fleshed Andean crania to depict them as racialized "specimens" of wider human history. Many of these later images and photographs are—to my eyes, at least—shattering. They have contributed to a culture of displaying non-European human remains still with us today, a practice that Indigenous North Americans, in particular, have worked to end. Yet Andean ancestors are often excepted from that care. Nearly every week, I receive news alerts for articles illustrated by new photos of Andean mummies, a dead made "scientific" by their supposed distance from the present, Europe, and the United States. Some of these depictions are so artistic that they encourage casual viewers to forget that their subjects were disinterred.

Others, like *Yachaya*, a sculpture that Nancy Torres has shown in Peru, Cuba, and Germany, make that violence impossible to ignore. I chose Torres's meditation on Spanish looting of Andean bodies and wealth for this book's cover because, as Torres intended, viewers who deny the history of European assaults upon Indigenous bodies and sovereignty lose the privilege of looking away. It also inducts those viewers into a visual culture, in Peru and the Andes, that remains far more comfortable with their display. To that end, this book selectively reproduces other depictions of Andean ancestors within its pages not to titillate, but to explain why four centuries of looting Andean ancestors, skulls, and bones made them foundational to the field of human research known today as anthropology—and why thousands reached museums around the world, where they have been used to represent all human history and have inspired some of its most existential art .

This forgotten visual genealogy of Inca and Andean mummies and ancestors matters for two reasons. First, it demands that we see what museums often instruct us to unsee: their role as gathering places of the supposedly dead and inert, human and nonhuman, from whom science is made. And second, because it reminds us of how looking can also become an act of care. This book shows why the belief that looking upon the remains of the dead disrepects them, in and out of scientific settings, is not universal. For Guaman Poma, his ancestors, and some of his modern Andean intellectual heirs—some of them Peruvian anthropologists—seeing and being seen by a dead that embodied history, or healed the sick, induced respect. It could also be a demand for recognition—that ancestors be appreciated for their differing cultures of mourning, science, and care. Museums have sometimes used that fact to justify their display of Andean ancestors still sought by their original communities. But other professionals are returning that dead, working with communities to store or display them respectfully, or, in Peru, are considering places within and outside of museums for their mourning.

All of this is to say that we cannot ignore the fact that museums collected and displayed Andean ancestors in a way that extended violence. But limiting that story to violence is to ignore how the culture of their display across time and space meant radically different things. By selectively including some of these Inca and Andean ancestors in these pages, this book hopes to extend their challenging gaze. But it is also an archive of their care. Engaging with their animacy—seeing them see us if only in the pages of a book—broadens our understanding of their loss and recognizes their possibility of healing.

A NOTE ON ORTHOGRAPHY

Because this is also a book about how embodied Andean ancestors and knowledges were inscribed, an explanation of how it uses words is in order. When Spain's conquistadors invaded the Incas' realms, they met peoples who conveyed history in many ways, none of which were written on fragile paper. The Spanish praised the "Inca historians" nevertheless, singling out the *khipukamayuq*, the keepers of *khipus*, the knotted and pendant cords that kept track of labor and tribute obligations, but also the lives and accomplishments of the Inca rulers. By 1559 the Spanish seem to have confiscated some of the most important historical khipus, transcribing some of the stories recounted by their khipukamayuqs. But Castilian ears and the Latin alphabet were a poor match for Quechua (and other Andean languages like Aymara and Puquina), and the transmission of their knowledges to Europe further garbled and misrepresented the details and names of Inca history. Republished sources can reference a supposed tyrant named "Atabalica" or "Atabalipa"—actually the ruler Atahualpa or Atahuallpa, the *Sapa Inka* (Peerless Inca) whose murder by the Spanish lastingly colored his reputation.

Historians and anthropologists have worked to complicate those reputations, but imperfect transcriptions and orthographies—the spellings of words—remain a kind of colonization, as Andean linguists have noted for half a century. The Spanish inscribed the Inca capital as Cuzco, for example, while more faithful modern transcription render the Inka capital as *Qosko* or *Cusco*. Removing Spanish influences from written Andean languages has allowed their nuanced inflections of time, space, and knowledge to glow. Even the term "Inca Empire" has been questioned: to the Incas, their realm was Tawantinsuyu, "The Four Parts Bound Together."

For these reasons, this book uses modern spellings for key Inca and Andean figures and terms. However, because it is a work of history written mostly from pre-1970 texts, it preserves original spellings in primary sources, and carries some—like Inca or Cuzco—into the text itself. While unsatisfying as a solution, it allows readers searching for more conventional terms to engage with their history.

Empires of the Dead

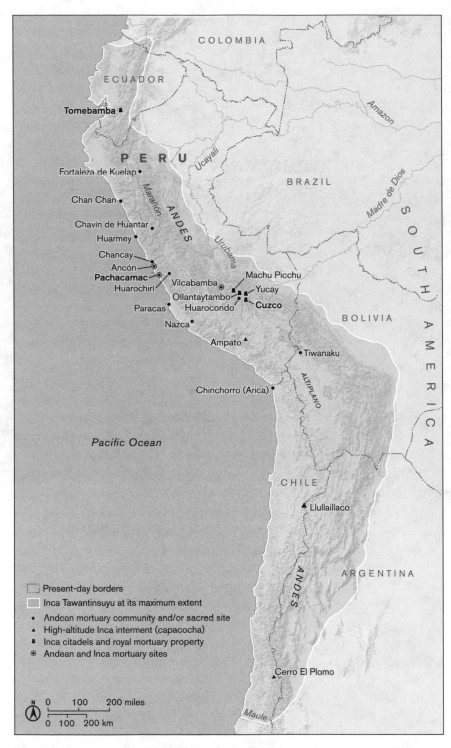

COLOMBIA

ECUADOR

Tomebamba ▲

P E R U

Fortaleza de Kuelap •

Chan Chan •

Chavín de Huantar •

Huarmey •

Chancay •

Ancón ◎

Pachacamac ◎

Huarochiri •

Vilcabamba

Machu Picchu

Ollantaytambo •

Yucay

Huarocondo

Cuzco

Paracas •

Nazca •

Ampato ▲

Tiwanaku •

Chinchorro (Arica) •

Marañón

Ucayali

Urubamba

ANDES

BRAZIL

Amazon

Madre de Dios

S O U T H

A M E R I C A

BOLIVIA

ALTIPLANO

Pacific Ocean

CHILE

Llullaillaco ▲

ANDES

ARGENTINA

Cerro El Plomo ▲

Maule

▢ Present-day borders

▢ Inca Tawantinsuyu at its maximum extent

• Andean mortuary community and/or sacred site

▲ High-altitude Inca interment (capacocha)

▲ Inca citadels and royal mortuary property

◎ Andean and Inca mortuary sites

N

0   100   200 miles

0   100   200 km

Pre-Hispanic mortuary landscapes of the Andes and Tawantinsuyu, the Inca empire, mentioned in *Empires of the Dead*. Map by Ben Pease.

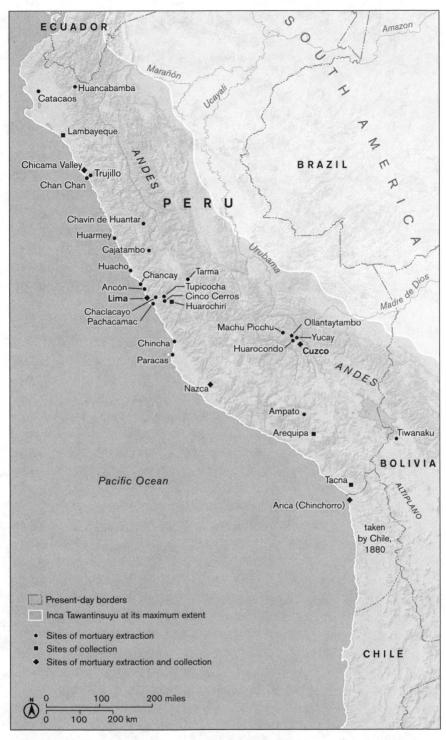

ECUADOR

Amazon

SOUTH AMERICA

Marañón

•Huancabamba
Catacaos•

Ucayali

■ Lambayeque

BRAZIL

Chicama Valley
◆ •Trujillo
Chan Chan

ANDES

PERU

Chavin de Huantar •
Huarmey •
Cajatambo •
Huacho •
Chancay •   • Tarma
Ancón —•   • Tupicocha
Lima —◆ •Cinco Cerros
Chaclacayo —•   ■ Huarochiri
Pachacamac —◆

Urubamba

Machu Picchu •   Ollantaytambo •
Huarocondo •   • Yucay
                   ◆ Cuzco

Madre de Dios

ANDES

Chincha •
Paracas •

Nazca ◆

Ampato •
Arequipa ■

Tiwanaku •

BOLIVIA

Pacific Ocean

ALTIPLANO

Tacna ■

Arica (Chinchorro) ■

taken
by Chile,
1880

☐ Present-day borders
☐ Inca Tawantinsuyu at its maximum extent
• Sites of mortuary extraction
■ Sites of collection
◆ Sites of mortuary extraction and collection

CHILE

N
0   100   200 miles
0   100   200 km

Landscape of extraction of pre-Hispanic Andean human remains and their collection in
Peru, nineteenth and twentieth centuries. Map by Ben Pease.

Global destinations of Andean ancestors and human remains, nineteenth and twentieth centuries, as mentioned in *Empires of the Dead*. Map by Ben Pease.

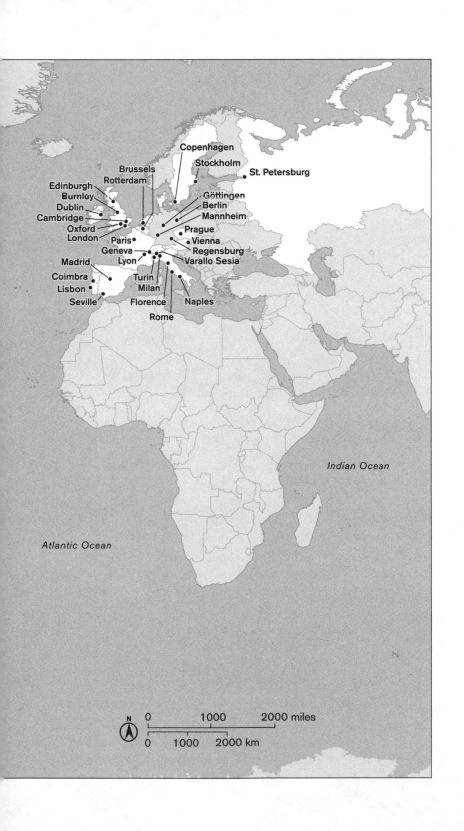

Copenhagen
Stockholm
St. Petersburg
Brussels
Rotterdam
Göttingen
Edinburgh
Burnley
Berlin
Dublin
Mannheim
Cambridge
Oxford
Prague
London
Vienna
Paris
Geneva
Regensburg
Madrid
Lyon
Varallo Sesia
Coimbra
Turin
Lisbon
Milan
Seville
Florence
Naples
Rome

Indian Ocean

Atlantic Ocean

N

0   1000   2000 miles

0   1000   2000 km

Introduction

Death's Heads: The Peruvian Ancestors at the Smithsonian

When the Hall of Physical Anthropology at the Smithsonian Institution (SI) opened in Washington, DC, in 1965, its visitors met a wall of florid death: the skulls of 160 "Ancient Peruvians," arranged like a lopsided mushroom cloud. The anthropologists at the National Museum of Natural History (NMNH) had fixed them to the wall to visualize how the "world's human population has literally 'exploded' in historic times." Every three crania represented 100 million people. At the bottom, nine skulls represented the 300 million people believed to constitute the world's human population in AD 1, the "Beginning of the Christian Era." The row above was fifteen skulls long, the 500 million people supposed alive in 1560, which the exhibit's designers labeled "Beginning Settlements in America." Thirty more crania in two rows represented the 1 billion people estimated for 1860, the eve of "The Civil War." And at the top, a thunderhead of 106 skulls represented the 3.5 billion human beings alive in 1960, "The Space Age" (see plate 1). According to the *Washington Post*, the new hall's "overall theme—man's supremacy over all other primates—[was] eerily demonstrated by the grinning skulls of the ancient Peruvians." This dual display of mortality and fertility was also a monument to a sweepingly American history of humanity, made legible via the accumulation, measurement, and concentration of the dead. Its designers called it the "Skull Wall."[1]

The *Post*'s reporter acknowledged the obvious questions. Why had these "sun-bleached Peruvian Indian skulls" come from South America to the Smithsonian? And why had the anthropologists chosen them, of all the many other peoples the institution had collected, to stand for the biggest possible thing they could say about the recent history of humanity? On this point, museum director T. Dale Stewart—also the Smithsonian's senior physical anthropologist—was both forthcoming and vague. "The death's heads," the reporter was told, "were found

Empires of the Dead. Christopher Heaney, Oxford University Press. © Oxford University Press 2023.
DOI: 10.1093/oso/9780197542552.003.0001

about 60 years ago after being uncovered by gold miners," but there was "no particular significance in their use."

"We used Peruvian skulls," Stewart explained, "because we had so many of them."

Stewart wasn't wrong. Skulls and bones from "ancient Peru" had long been the largest historical population at the Smithsonian—itself the largest scientific collection of skeletal remains in the world. When the institution's founding ethnological collection was first catalogued, the first eleven objects listed were three Peruvian mummies and eight Peruvian skulls. The early Smithsonian otherwise avoided the collection of human remains—ceding that work to the Army Medical Museum—but Stewart's predecessor Aleš Hrdlička in the 1910s more than doubled the institution's collection of human remains, mostly due to his addition of more than ten thousand "ancient Peruvian" crania, bones, and mummified remains.[2] Their use in the Skull Wall reflected that fact, given that to do otherwise would deplete more crania, proportionally, from groups less well represented in the research collection.[3]

The use of Andean remains in the hall's other displays, though, suggested that their importance at the Smithsonian went beyond numbers. The exhibit employed bones from the Peruvian Andes to show how anthropologists read skeletons for evidence of fractures, explaining that "Diseases of prehistoric man are sometimes recorded in skeletons." In another display, Andean crania demonstrated how diverse Indigenous Americans used bundle boards and bandages to modify the shape of their children's crania to embody and display group belonging. Peru's dead were also a prime example of physical anthropologists' understanding of the mutability of human "forms," the word the exhibit used instead of "race." One display illustrated how populations' phenotypes—skin color, height, cranial size and shape—changed over time owing to individual variability and the prevalence of some traits over others. It did so by highlighting the only human skeletal feature named after an ethnic group: "The 'Inca' bone," or *os incae*—an interparietal bone in the skull whose "high frequency among Inca Indians of Peru"—was the product of gradual changes and convergences in a population's traits. The larger cranial variety of Peruvians was then used to assert that "generalized Asiatic mongoloids" became the "first Americans" after crossing the Bering Land Bridge, when their physical characteristics diverged.[4]

The hall's two most memorable displays after the Skull Wall, however, suggested that the ancient Peruvians were not just an illustrative branch of American anthropology; they were part of its trunk. Unit 20 was the most jaw-dropping. It explained that "Ancient Peruvians excelled in Skull Surgery." Western doctors called this operation "trepanation," which relieved pressure on an individual's brain by cutting away sections of crania. In the Andes, the operation addressed fractures caused by everyday life and war. A case in Unit 20 thus presented the heavy metal and stone weapons that gave Andean healers so many skulls to heal. It also displayed "surgical implements" they used to lift the scalp and cut away damaged bone. Skulls with five, even seven holes made over an individual's lifetime suggested a pre-Hispanic Andean skill in this high-risk maneuver unrivaled worldwide until the late nineteenth century.[5] It was all dramatized in a massive walnut-frame painting by a Connecticut artist named Alton S. Tobey. The Smithsonian had sent Tobey to South America to study trepanation's most famed Peruvian practitioners, the Incas, whose empire, Tawantinsuyu, spanned the Andes before the Spanish invaded in 1532. The resulting painting depicted an Inca surgeon at work, opening a patient's blood-smeared skull at the Inca royal estate of Huayna Picchu, today known as Machu Picchu. This was Indigenous Americans' most ambitious medical technique, framed by their most iconic architectural site (see plate 2).[6]

Softened by Inca surgeons' ability to extend their patients' lives, visitors gazed upon Andean peoples' accomplishments at curing death itself. A display on "Mummies" was included "partly to appease the public's morbid curiosity and partly to explain how bodies get preserved" after death "due to various causes," the exhibit's script explained. Visitors likely expected to find the ancient Egyptian lying supine. But they first saw a "Peruvian," a woman from the coastal Chancay culture whose pose challenged expectations of what mummies were supposed to be. She sat upright, wrapped in a textile, her arms tucked beneath her head. The display made no mention of what her preservation meant: how Andean peoples had mummified their ancestors and children to extend their social and sacred being for eight millennia, which made the South Americans' artificial "mummies" the world's oldest (see plate 3). But more than any other display in the exhibit, this seated Andean individual reminded museumgoers that every other skull in the hall was once similarly embodied.

To be sure, Hall 25 contained the remains of other peoples besides the Peruvians. Its language was that of anthropology and its vocabulary was migration, "form," bodily modification, and pathology. Yet the Peruvians' use throughout the exhibit—to embody physical anthropology's biggest questions and most sensational subjects, as well as the "ancient" knowledges that expanded science's frame—encouraged explanations of their prominence beyond their sheer volume. The exhibit showed that anthropologists had found Andean bodies particularly important to collect and think with. It suggested that Incas and "ancient Peruvians" felt similarly—crafting and curing their living and dead in ways that later would be important to anthropology's interest in bodies, health, and mortuary rituals. Most affectingly, their extraordinary numbers hinted that Hall 25 was mostly *their* tomb, only begrudgingly shared with the visitors that

vanished when the lights went out. In the words of the *Washington Post*, they
were "death's heads."

Empires of the Dead is a history of how they got there. It shows how imperial,
colonial, and national encounters with "Inca mummies" and "ancient Peruvian"
skulls inspired five centuries of debate over Andean methods of thwarting
death. Those encounters began with the Incas, whose empire Tawantinsuyu
cured both living and dead as a sacred logic of rule. To sap that power, Spanish
conquistadors, natural historians, and priests subjected Andean ancestors to a
violent science of disinterment, dispossession, and description—an "imperial
body collecting" that rewrote Inca history.[7] Their descriptions of the Inca dead
nonetheless traveled the world, and when independence came to Peru in 1821,
foreign collectors sought these famed mummies and crania to read as specimens
of race, extinction, and the "pre-historic" Americas as a whole. So many entered
nineteenth- and twentieth-century North and South American museums—
where they were unwrapped, de-fleshed, and measured—that their display
was taken for granted, as in the Skull Wall. They seem to confirm archaeologist
Alexander Herrera's observation that the "history of Peruvian archaeology may
quickly be summarized as a history of material and intellectual pillage, which
mirrors the country's colonized position as an exporter of raw materials for foreign consumption."[8] This book suggests that these exports were highly consequential. As Hall 25 also suggests, "Inca mummies," "ancient Peruvian" skulls,
and the subsumed knowledges of the people who knew those bodies first became *materia prima* for American anthropology—the "first matter" of a field
whose subject became the culture, history, rituals, languages, and bodies of all
Indigenous American peoples.[9]

This claim recharts an anthropology whose origins are sometimes traced to
the study of Native North Americans by late-nineteenth-century white American
men.[10] Scholars have complicated the celebratory aspect of that genealogy, which
narrates an intellectual shift from claims of fixed races and social hierarchies to
explorations of changing, relative cultures. Instead, historians have shown how
anthropological actors inherited a museum-based ethnology that predicted the
disappearance of Indigenous peoples in the face of European expansion and that
sought to "salvage" their languages, looted bodies, and sacred objects.[11] Scholars
have also identified Americanist anthropology and archaeology's indebted-
ness to imperial interest in Latin American landscapes and scholarship, which
in the nineteenth century were taken as providing uniquely embedded Native
knowledges and contexts for museum collection and study.[12]

Hall 25 reveals an even earlier and specifically Peruvian frame, one that signals Andean ancestors' longstanding importance to anthropology beyond the Smithsonian. Had the *Washington Post*'s reporter traveled to Philadelphia, for example, he might have learned about the cranial collection of Samuel George Morton, whom Stewart's predecessor deemed the "father of American anthropology," and whose supremacist theorizations of separate human creations shaped the early field. When Morton died in 1851, the first and largest population in his collection—today held by the University of Pennsylvania—was also "ancient Peruvian."[13] Had the reporter gone to the Americas' first dedicated anthropology museum, Harvard's Peabody Museum of Archaeology and Ethnology in Cambridge, he might have learned that the largest original population when it opened in 1866 was Peru's dead, who composed nearly two-thirds of the collection by the museum's eighth year.[14] And had he delved into the archives of Chicago's Columbian Exposition of 1893, he might have learned that the largest and most popular display in the field-defining anthropology exhibit of the famed World's Fair were some fifty bundled mummies removed from Peru's "Necropolis" of Ancón, whose excavation was the subject of the first PhD dissertation in anthropology written by a US citizen.[15]

This book attends to the Peruvian history propelling the near-ubiquitous collection, curation, and display of the Andean dead. These Andean origins illustrate why Indigenous and Iberian encounters over bodies, knowledges, and the sacred shaped the Renaissance- and Enlightenment-era ethnologies and histories that yielded nineteenth-century anthropology.[16] The Andes were particularly important to that process because of how the Incas taught the Spanish to read their imperial bodies, and those of their subjects, for lessons of sacred ancestry, historical priority, and cultural difference and superiority. In linking this early Andean lesson in ethnology to its reapplication in the nineteenth century, this book demonstrates how Indigenous and Latin American knowledges of empire shaped later fields of racialized study and bodily control. "Peruvian" anthropology and archaeology weren't inventions of the early to mid-twentieth century; they were embedded in early Americanist anthropology itself.[17]

That science emerged from a colonial approach to the Andean dead in which to know them was to loot them. Yet this is also a history of how the Andean and Peruvian living used grave-opening's knowledges to heal. These Peruvians remembered their ancestors as more than skulls. They sought their historical and spiritual efficacy, including their ability to reach across time and space to cure or curse the living and the museums that sought to contain them. This is also a history of Inca and Andean individuals who became Christian—in part to avoid disinterment—but remembered ancestors as "little grandparents" or "Inca Kings." They crafted new stories, in which remains encountered in coastal sands or *chullpas* (houses for the dead) indicted the colonial present. Following their lead, patriotic Peruvian scholars insisted that the dead embodied "sciences" like Inca mummification and trepanation, challenging European hierarchies of knowledge and civilization. And as they learned of the importance that outsiders accorded these remains, individuals of Andean descent became archaeologists to argue for non-Inca histories of healing ancestors—a past deeper and more diverse than that of the Americas' largest Indigenous empire, or its oldest "race."[18]

As such, this is a history of not one empire but many. It is also the history of ancestors who preceded those empires' rise and survived their fall. To that end, these chapters use sixteenth- and seventeenth-century chronicles, eighteenth-century natural histories, nineteenth-century anthropological treatises, twentieth-century museum records, and archives on three continents to trace the long arc of how Incas, Spaniards, Peruvians, and North Americans made and unmade the Andean dead as ancestral subjects and scientific objects. This temporal range shows how violence, science, and care compound over time, undoing spiritually active Andean ancestors and antecessors to present them as "scientific" objects like mummies or trepanned crania. This wider scope also catches these practices' ripples across geographies—a "Peruvian" way of knowing that shaped the violent sciences directed at the Americas' many Indigenous peoples.[19] Finally, it respects the longevity of these ancestors, whose afterlives in museums across Peru and its Americas are ongoing.

————

This book's three parts follow Hall 25's three most attention-getting displays— Peru's uncanny mummies, superabundant skulls, and trepanning surgeons— back to the colonial and republican map of their science in the Andes, and forward to their itineraries abroad. The chapters follow specific bodies' transformation from sacred ancestors to forsaken "gentiles," national icons, or specimens of particular knowledges. These bodies' afterlives were often cut short. Others were extended by their collection and display.[20]

The "Inca mummy" came first. Part One, "Opening, 1525–1795," is the history of two spoils of the Spanish invasion of Tawantinsuyu: the perception that the Andean landscape was rife with human remains and hidden knowledges— such as Inca skill at "embalming" their dead—and the suggestion that Peru was thus an ideal place to approach and racialize the preserved Indigenous American past.[21] These expectations were the result of pointed Spanish investigations into the nature of Andean death, which claimed that Inca and Andean ancestors were preserved by medical "embalming" or the climate. These claims moved throughout the Atlantic world, leaving the impression that "ancient Peruvians" entombed "mummies" like the Egyptians—key context for other European encounters with Indigenous bodies and "deathways."[22] But admission to "mummyhood" denied the ancestors' sacred present, demoting Inca and Andean ways of knowing their universe into objects of global rule, science, medicine, and religion.[23] Broken apart, Andean mummies yielded "ancient" skulls that the Spanish were first to measure, shaping subsequent imperial projects of studying and regulating bodies. Inca mummies thus illuminate how the Americas became "a key protagonist in the history of modern knowledge."[24]

Yet these colonial conversions of sacred ancestors inadvertently extended their power.[25] In the preexisting Inca empire of the dead, human remains were sacred, partible, and powerful. They were carried around, capable of curing and communicating with other bodies, landscapes, and rains—much like the Catholic cult of the saints.[26] Those similarities gave Andean peoples time and space to adapt prior meanings to seemingly colonial acts, from burying themselves as Christians to engaging in *huaqueo,* the bureaucratized mining of *huacas*—sacred and spiritually active places, burials, or things.[27] Engagement with the healing powers of ancestors also survived. "Little grandparents" were still left offerings. Former ancestors became toxic "gentiles," but their sacrality diffused to mountains and egalitarian Andean Christian communities. Even Peruvian-born Spaniards and Africans adopted skulls of "Inca" forefathers to call up a superior precolonial past.[28] These grave-openings generated interpretations of the past more challenging than race or mummification. In colonial Peruvian hands, the "ancient" dead even became victims of the conquest itself.

Part Two, "Exporting, 1780–1893," shows how these competing knowledges of Andean ancestors shaped the disinterment, study, and display of Indigenous bodies worldwide. Shortly after South American revolutionary José de San Martín declared Peru's independence in 1821, he sent King George IV of England an "Inca mummy" for the British Museum. This "liberation" and display of "embalmed" American sovereignty was emblematic of other elite projects of patriotic identity formation and led to the founding of Peru's National Museum. Other "Inca mummies" and "artifacts" followed, and their display and export by late colonial and early republican Peruvians and foreigners revises the history of anthropology more generally.[29] Anatomist Samuel George Morton cast the "ancient Peruvians" as an ideal population for racial study, since this seemingly plentiful population possessed ancient "American" skulls to compare to both living Native Americans as well as the Incas' three-century-old reputation.[30] By making "ancient Peruvians" the largest population in his influential first book, *Crania Americana* (1830), Morton also clarified the use of statistically large series of remains, forcing other scholars to follow his lead, if only to dispute his racist conclusions. This was why the Peruvian dead became the largest original population of human remains in Harvard's Peabody, the American Museum of Natural History, and the Smithsonian. Around their core, museums built large collections of other Indigenous remains, entangling Andean grave-opening with settler violence and anthropology in the United States.[31]

American anthropology's interest in Indigenous ancestors as subjects of culture also benefitted from Andean tombs. For much of their history, studying the mummified Andean dead often destroyed them, like the Egyptian dead that were dissected for mid-nineteenth-century crowds.[32] But their preservation became a goal in itself, reaching its apotheosis at the late-nineteenth-century's world's fairs, where Peruvian, North American, and European collectors "mummy mined" Andean remains and staged them as "ancient Peruvian," "American," and "pre-Columbian" bodies of knowledge. These displays helped move Americanist archaeology's interest from objects to rituals, and disproved evolutionary models of civilization by showing that the Incas were only the most recent complex society in the Andes, where human habitation is at least fifteen millennia old.[33] Anthropology was also shaped by Andean understandings of the dead as still capable of shaping the health and fortunes of the living. While Indigenous grave-openers guided foreign collectors in coastal areas, some highland communities returned to ritualizing the "little grandparents," parading them to control the rains once again.[34] When collectors moved inland and, with the support of the Peruvian state, pressed highland communities to reveal bodies they still claimed as distant ancestors and antecessors, those communities' distress itself became anthropology's subject.

Part Three, "Healing, 1868–1965," shows how the Peruvian collection of ancestral Andean healing sought to remedy Americanist anthropology and redefine what a museum could be. It begins with the late-nineteenth-century "discovery" and circulation of Andean trepanation as a form of curing that the Spanish missed. While some Peruvian and American surgeons heralded trepanation as an "ancient" and lasting Andean medical skill, and traded their skulls to that end, others disputed the evidence, arguing that it was faith healing at best.[35] Through this debate Peruvian anthropologists came to see their North American counterparts in imperial terms: as exporting the remains of whole sites and cemeteries while rejecting their Peruvian counterparts' own expertise. Those counterparts' claim to know Andean mummies and skulls in more nationalist and personal terms, as "scientific ancestors," challenged American anthropology's more racialist hierarchies of medicine, science, and history.[36] As Peruvian anthropologist and surgeon Julio César Tello crowed to his colleagues, "With trepanation, Peru achieves first place in prehistoric surgery throughout the world."[37]

Part Three concludes by considering how Tello attempted to use the dead to remake American anthropology in a more Peruvian image. Tello has been celebrated as "America's First Indigenous Archaeologist," who founded Peru's first three anthropological museums. As such, he was a bundle of contradictions. Harvard-trained, he held out hope for true collaboration with his North American colleagues, but also shaped a more nationalist archaeology,

culminating in a law that claimed outright ownership of "ancient" Andean remains for the state.[38] One white Peruvian colleague claimed that Tello's anti-
racist anthropology and museum projects threatened to "crush the history of
colonial and independent Peru" under the "folkloric weight of a ridiculous imperialism exercised by mummies"—an imperialism Tello extended by sometimes sending those remains abroad.[39] Though uncredited, Tello's research
was responsible for the trepanning Peruvians' representation in Hall 25 of the
Smithsonian. But in Tello's hands, these scientific ancestors—and not the Inca
or Spanish empires—were the founders of a Peru in which anthropology was
an Andean inheritance, vouchsafing respect for "Indians" like himself. Tello
believed so fervently in this project of digging up and curating pre-Inca scientific ancestors that he had his own dead body interred alongside them. Andean
countrymen, however, believed that those very mummies killed him.[40]

If Andean mummies are a forgotten origin of anthropology in the Americas,
then the stories told of Tello's death suggest the high stakes of their recall. This
book shows how centuries of grave-opening practices claimed ancestral bodies
as objects of science. That claiming illustrates the importance of Latin American
history to knowledges of healing and colonialism, and science and the sacred.
This book's conclusion surveys the lasting presence of Andean ancestors in scientific museums and collections worldwide—the knowledge they continue to
create, the relationships they engender or deny.

In doing so, the conclusion highlights two conversations running along parallel tracks.[41] The first centers on Peru, where laws and norms have claimed the
Indigenous past for the nation since independence. The state and its actors have
sometimes exercised those claims imperiously, to manipulate and even export
the human remains they purport to protect. This means that the most legally
empowered voice in discussions of possession is that of the Peruvian state, which
since the 1980s has acted as an agent for the return of looted artifacts and high-
profile collections. Communities and archaeologists have pioneered *museos de
sitio*, or site museums, to keep what is excavated local—but the state can side-
line Indigenous communities whose resources are deemed inadequate for curation and display. Complicating matters, some communities reject outsiders'
presumption that they are descended from the "Indian" dead. Others instead
focus on the remains of loved ones who disappeared during the armed conflict
of the 1980s and 1990s.[42]

The second conversation is more apparent outside of Peru, where over
the last four decades some museums have become responsive to Indigenous
demands for the return of ancestral remains, or at least their retirement from

display. That work tends to find traction in countries with better-documented nineteenth-century policies of Indigenous dispersal and genocide, such as Argentina, Australia, and the United States, whose Native American Grave Protection and Repatriation Act (NAGPRA) remains the chief point of reference. Although some museums use laws and policies to deny affiliations between the dead and descendant groups, others are examining their collections and thinking broadly—not just about Indigenous remains, but about African-descended ancestors and the remains or sacred objects of any other country toward which a museum might have enjoyed a colonial relationship.[43]

This book shows how these conversations have fed each other for two centuries or more.[44] It argues that American anthropology's approach to Indigenous ancestors in general benefitted from the five-hundred-year arc of the extirpation, collection, and study of "Inca mummies" and "ancient Peruvian" skulls as historic beings. Ironically, retiring Andean remains from display outside of Peru while still allowing their study has muffled their public knowledge in the name of respect while maintaining them as a population for bioanthropological investigation.

That forgetting also hides the scientific descendants who first shaped their discussion. As Peruvian historian Alberto Flores Galindo observed, Andean peoples made surprising choices to escape their confinement in the "impossible museum" of their history.[45] This book shows how that "impossible museum" proved so extraordinarily literal that its escape included embracing the dead's study to make *possible* museums of one's own. These surprising choices help explain how Julio Tello could wax poetic regarding "this favorite science of unearthing cadavers interred centuries back"—wielding grave-opening for, in his mind, a more worthy end.[46]

Last, those ends suggest new beginnings for Andean ancestors and the fields they shaped. Using examples drawn from European and colonial history, historians like Thomas Laqueur have observed that dead bodies are "active agents in history," whose collapsing materiality shapes and confronts the immediate society around them.[47] The surviving Andean dead take us still further, to reflect upon how the *preservation* of ancestral and acolonial understandings of time, space, and reciprocity influence peoples yet unseen, complicating the dead's past-ness altogether.[48] Those who study them, including myself, remain entangled in their temporalities and connected to the places affected by their departure. This historical power retained by the unbreathing—ancestral or not, Peruvian or not—blurs the line between science and the sacred, between the Andes and the places its peoples' remains have reached. It suggests a Skull Wall that is less an explosion, and more a tree, rooted and ready to bloom.

PART 1

OPENING, 1525–1795

According to the Andean chronicler Felipe Guaman Poma de Ayala, November was *Aya Marq'ay Killa* in the Inca calendar, the festival of ancestors and the dead, in which they were brought out, carried, and feted by their descendants. Here he depicts his own preserved (but not embalmed) Chinchaysuyo ancestors. Guaman Poma de Ayala, *El Primer Nueva Corónica y Buen Gobierno*, ca. 1600–1615, 256 [258]. Royal Danish Library, GKS 2232 4°.

Curing Incas

Andean Lifeways and the Pre-Hispanic Imperial Dead

In older times—before Christians came to the empire that the Incas called Tawantinsuyu, before they called that empire Peru—men and women healed the living with knives, and they cured the dead with air. They hadn't always done so. The Yauyo people remembered a time when the dead "came back to life on the fifth day exactly" and were welcomed by their people with prepared food and drinks. "Now I'll never die again forever!" they would say. This was not a good thing. The people so "swiftly increased in number" that they hungrily crowded the land. One day a man returned to life a day late and his wife, enraged, threw a corncob at him. "Why are you so damn lazy?" she shouted. "Other people never let us down by failing to come. But you, yesterday, you made us wait for you, and all for nothing." The man's spirit flew back to their ancestral source, never to return.[1] Ever after, the dead made way for the living, yielding their present fertility, and the living, in grateful grief, devised new ways to keep their loved ones close.

Here is a story about them.

High in the Andes, in a region that the Spanish would call Huarochirí, a Yauyo man visited a healer. He was in pain, likely grimacing at the tender, fractured spot left of his crown where the mountain had hit him with a rock, or where he had been injured while warring for the Inca.[2] Despite that pain, he had walked to this healer on his own two legs, strong from climbing to maintain the canals of his *ayllu*—the clan group that included the living, the dead, and other beings and plants they cared for. Or, if the pain was too much to bear, his ayllu members would have born him there on their shoulders.

The healer laid him in a soft place, possibly in the open air, where the light was clear. She likely took a seat above his shoulders and took his head in her lap.[3] Centuries later, a Yauyo-descended anthropologist who held that same head would call healers like her "surgeons"—an estimation that captures her expertise

Empires of the Dead. Christopher Heaney, Oxford University Press. © Oxford University Press 2023.
DOI: 10.1093/oso/9780197542552.003.0002

in this preoperative examination, though not the more cosmic knowledges she brought to bear when observing his breathing and the pallor in his cheeks.[4] She was experienced in these injuries. Sometimes there was obvious fracture and blood. Other times, a soft swelling indicating a traumatic lesion below. The harm could also be invisible, and she had to palpate where it hurt, take a patient's pain on faith, and act to keep him from becoming *huañuc*, a dying one. In this case, she weighed his injury against her skill and decided to operate. A prayer and offering to the snowy mountain being Pariacaca, the sacred *paqarisqa* or ancestral font to which this man's spirit would someday return, would have been in order.[5]

A tourniquet around her patient's crown would cut off the blood flow from his scalp. Securing his head with one hand, she used her other to reach for the tools of her trade, perhaps arrayed on a piece of hide. Surgeons like her sometimes used bronze chisels or rods, but they relied more often on obsidian knives. She chose one, parted his hair with a thumb, and laid the blade against her patient's scalp. Breathing in and out, she pressed down through skin and flesh until she felt the blade hit bone, a few inches to the side of the trauma. She deftly moved the blade in a semicircle, expanding the incision to prepare a circular flap in the scalp. She may have daubed it with a natural antiseptic before preceding; to steady himself, the patient may have chewed a quid of coca, the sacred green leaf that suppressed hunger and pain. She edged her blade beneath the flap and gently peeled it back, exposing the skull to the air. The hill of bone was pink with blood, its smooth curve possibly cratered by a trauma endangering the delicate dura mater and brain beneath. The surgeon set her blade upon the skull at a safe distance from the wound or malady. Then with slow strokes she abraded the bone, beginning the surgical operation that the Yauyo anthropologist would call trepanation.[6]

Woman and man, surgeon and patient, were bound in a covenant of care. From his distant peak Pariacaca—who had expelled the sacrifice-hungry fire-monster Huallallo Caruincho and brought about this age of knowledge and plenty—may have watched, approving of her work. As always, that work would be temporary. The next time her patient experienced a cranial injury, the damage would be too great; in the midst of surgery he would die. This was the way of death, which uncrowded the land to support loved ones' survival.

But the care mattered and would continue when he was breathless. His loved ones would seat him as he had sat in life. They would bind his knees and arms to his empty chest, cradling his head in his hands, making his new seedlike, rooting self. They would keep vigil into the night and would mourn until the moment that his essence flew away—"Sio!"—in the shape of a fly. "Now he's going away to see Pariacaca, our maker and our sustainer," they would say.[7]

Something of his spirit would then come back. A female family member would tend his body at home, giving that returned spirit something to eat. In the coming year, his ayllu would take him to Pariacaca, or a more local shrine site where he would be mourned. In one of these caves or high houses of the dead, the cold and dry air would preserve him. His face would remain recognizable, his bundled body becoming like a *mallki*, a seedling or young tree from which the ayllu's future prosperity would grow. If he had been a leader, a *curaca* who represented his people to the Inca, his ayllu might keep him particularly active. Along with other mummified ancestors he might periodically be brought down to the community's *kayan*, a flat space or sometimes plaza where ayllus sorted out labor obligations and argued over justice. Via a *mallkipvillac*, a speaker for the ancestors, they would hear his desires. Periodically redressing, feting, and parading him, his descendants would care for their ancestral lands and canals in his name, asking him to help bring rains and food to sustain them.[8]

Or he might travel. If he became truly *huaca*—a sacred thing who spoke to Pariacaca and could therefore command offerings—he might attract the attention of the Incas' priests. They might seize him, taking him to Cuzco, the imperial capital, to join the collections of the Inca emperors' own mummified dead. His good treatment would command Yauyo loyalty. The Inca emperor could draw on his power, sending him into war, and his people could celebrate his successes or grieve his distance. If they reserved a piece of him before he left, one of them could wear him like a *huayo*, a re-embodying mask, to dance his presence. Someday, if the Inca returned him, his interment would become permanent—or so his descendants imagined.[9]

But not now. Not yet. The Yauyo surgeon succeeded, as she likely had many times before. Her steady scraping at the cranium yielded a platform of bone that she elevated and removed to reduce pressure on his swollen brain. She smoothed the rough edges of the resulting hole. She closed the scalp, allowing the bone to heal. He had survived. Someday he would stop breathing, as would she, and his cured body would preserve her skill for centuries to come. Today, they lived.

⸻

Animating the preceding passage are at least two people whose existence and expertise were as real as the sacred mountain and distant empire they connected. We know that they existed because of two bodies of knowledge generated by imperial encounters between Andean, Inca, and European sciences of history, ancestor-making, and healing. These bodies bear that encounter's marks and prevarications, which include the colonizers' disdain for those they claimed to rule. Yet historians, anthropologists, and Andean-descended peoples nonetheless use their knowledges to try to understand the world before. Although the colonial creation of these bodies of knowledge is the subject of chapters to come, they are used here to introduce this chapter's subject: what we can say of Andean and Inca peoples' curations of life and death before the Spanish invaded.[10]

The first body of knowledge was crafted by peoples in the Andes, and Huarochirí in particular, to explain the venerable ancestor-making world around them. Because the Spanish ultimately tried to eliminate those venerations, their description by an early-seventeenth-century Indigenous intellectual in Huarochirí has been crucial for their reconstruction. The exact timing, purpose, and writing of that intellectual's manuscript, composed in the Andean language Quechua, is a matter of some debate. It was once assumed to have been produced at the prodding of a cleric, Father Francisco de Ávila, who used it after 1607 to identify and extirpate Huarochirí's surviving "idolatries" of ancestor-making. Yet it was also the project of don Cristóbal Choquecasa, a converted Andean leader who had his own reasons to detail his former beliefs, and those of his Yauyo neighbors. Both contexts make the manuscript hard to read as an unbiased reflection of life before the Spanish. Yet the pride with which the Andean compiler set "forth the lives of the ancestors of the Huaro Cheri people, who all descend from one forefather," from their "dawning age" on, is reflected in the text that follows. This wonderful manuscript renders Yauyo relations with creator beings, the Inca Empire, and Christianity with nobility, humor, and nuance. This was the exact landscape traveled by the Yauyo man and his surgeon, and lines of its interpretation—by writers, scholars, and communities, Peruvian and foreign—combine to create this sketch, however blurry, of the world their descendants remembered.[11]

The second body animating that sketch is the handiwork of at least two further Indigenous intellectuals: the skull of a male individual trepanned by a Yauyo surgeon and collected by the Huarochirí anthropologist Julio César Tello from a house of the dead or burial cavern named Cushula sometime in the early 1900s. Tello understood himself as a descendant of and professional heir to the Yauyo surgeon who healed this man and others like him. He sought their trepanations to understand the medical and scientific knowledges that religiously oriented sources like the Huarochirí manuscript left out, and that the Spanish misunderstood, misrepresented, or missed altogether. In doing so, Tello hoped to recover the lives of healing ancestors otherwise lost to colonialism's lies and fires. How Tello and his predecessors then used these mummies and crania is as much this book's subject as the larger structural processes that brought this Yauyo man to Harvard's Peabody Museum of Archaeology and Ethnology, whose catalogue labels him 56-42-30/N7936.0.[12]

The rest of this chapter explores how, prior to Spain's invasion, Yauyo surgeons were already part of an empire interested in the diverse curing practices of Andean peoples. Tawantinsuyu, the Incas' empire, extended from Cuzco well beyond present-day Peru, across Bolivia and Ecuador, and into Argentina, Chile, and Colombia. These curing practices they claimed to rule healed the living and preserved the dead. As embodiments of community history, the resulting ancestors helped descendants manipulate *pacha*—both time and space in Quechua, whose location of the past upon the visible landscape, or in visible bodies, allowed descendants to care for their origins and reshape the present.

The ancestors' embodiment of time, healing, violence, and the sacred made them objects of Inca interest as well. Understanding these imperial relations in Andean terms, and not those of the Spanish, means grappling with the records generated by Europe's subsequent disruption and appropriation of the Indigenous dead. Rereading colonial records in light of recent archaeology, ethnology, and bioanthropology makes clear the contrasts between how Europeans later described these sacred worlds, and how Inca and Andean converts to Christianity described them decades after invasion. It underscores how the compounded impact of Inca and Spanish empire was experienced by actual Andean subjects, alive and dead: how geographical displacement, nutrition and the lack thereof, and the pressure of work, weapons, and class left their mark on surviving flesh and bone.[13] The Incas crafted imperial histories in which some sacred dead were older, harder, more lifelike, and more powerful than others.[14] In centuries to come, many of these ancestors would shape anthropology as "Inca" or "Peruvian" or "Andean" mummies—but their diversity requires that they be given their due.

———

The pre-Hispanic curation of ancestors in South America relied upon a variety of preserving mechanisms, from the use of a dry climate to mummify the dead "naturally," to increasingly invasive "artificial" treatments of the body's organs, skeletal remains, and skin. The cultural implications of these differing methods are overblown—later mummy scholars used them as a proxy for differing levels of civilization, rather than as more or less resource-intensive methods of achieving the same preservation. But Andean peoples' innovation of techniques for "natural" mummification helps explain how ancestor curation and preserved tombs became so widespread in Andean society—and why outsiders later cast Peru, and the many places the Inca Empire reached, as a necropolis to study and loot.[15]

The oldest artificially preserved human remains in the world belong to a South American people that archaeologists call "Chinchorro," who began mummifying their dead around 6000 BCE, about two millennia before ancient Egyptians did. Chinchorro peoples lived near what is today the port city of Arica, and archaeologists believe that they preserved their dead to engage the climates and geographies that make life both difficult and productive along South America's Peruvian Andes and Pacific Coast, where rivers fed by Andean icecaps flow westward through otherwise dry mountains, becoming alluvial fans that support vegetation amid nitrate-rich sands. Chinchorro peoples used

those fans, as well as the rich Pacific fisheries of the Humboldt Current, to support larger populations among the living, while the surrounding desert "naturally" supported larger populations of their beloved dead. An awareness of those
conditions may have encouraged the Chinchorro to understand that the dead's
dryness committed the living to their care, and that the continued inclusion of
the dead in society yielded a community's growth. Perhaps to encourage that fertility, they began mummifying the dead in a more elaborate manner: removing
their organs, stretching their skin over plant-based ligatures, and giving them
mud masks to make them ever more permanent beings. The first loved ones
given this treatment were infants and children. By replanting them, the living
turned their mourning to hope, marked the group's presence, and seeded growth
in an uncertain environment.[16]

Chinchorro peoples stopped making mummies around 2500 BCE, but subsequent South American peoples took advantage of the preserving conditions of
a dry Pacific coast and icy Andes to remake this technology of curating the dead
to survive a difficult environment.[17] Some two thousand years later, Andean
peoples far to Arica's north began bringing their dead to the neck of the sandy
peninsula of Paracas, which juts out into the Pacific. From about 150 BCE to 200
CE, they interred more than 450 bodies in cavern and shaft tombs; when Julio
C. Tello uncovered them, he believed that their number included the earliest-
known cranial surgeons in the Americas. This culture seated the dead inside a
basket with sometimes gender-specific items and wrapped them in long textiles
until they resembled large kernel-like bundles to be planted in the ground. Not
all Paracas bodies received the same treatment; these ancestors were more male
than female, were mostly elders, and were in possession of a range of grave-
goods, among them the finest textiles ever made in the Americas. But their care
was the work of the larger community, which periodically revisited these curing
ancestors to disinter and rewrap them in new and still more elaborate textiles.
They may have been community emissaries to an ocean whose waters, the Incas
much later understood, were recycled by the sun and deposited in mountains, to
the east, to support the living's agriculture.[18]

The stories told as these ancestors were unwrapped and rewrapped may have
reflected a past that was geographically, corporeally, and personally accessible,
full of celebrated ancestors who still acted upon the present.[19] In the millennium
after the tombs of Paracas were closed, these means of ancestor-making went in
many directions. After 100 CE, the northern coast of present-day Peru saw the
development of a number of societies whose leaders' construction and control
of ceremonial centers and elaborate irrigation systems allowed them to develop
centralized, territorially expansive, and exceedingly hierarchical states. The most
famous of these were the Moche and Chimú leaders (circa 100 CE to 800 CE,
and 900 CE to 1600 CE, respectively) whose interment in temple and palace

complexes distinguished them as sacred beings with origins distinct from those of subjects. While most commoners went directly into the soil, the elite were dried above ground before being installed in pyramidlike palaces, accompanied by silver and gold objects, ceremonial ceramic art, and attendants and captives whose ritual death or transformation into trophy heads magnified elite power and, seedlike, contributed to the polity's fertility.[20]

These coastal tombs were not entirely sealed. Like the interments of Paracas, they were opened and added to, subtracted from, and kept alive by withdrawing ancestors' body parts to increase the powers of the living.[21] This made them similar to the open mortuary developments of the Andean *sierras*, where, after 500 CE, less stratified communities developed society-organizing relationships with semiaccessible ancestors. For these societies, becoming an ancestor began while one was still alive—a condensation of the aged into smaller and wizened beings that concentrated one's life essence. As closer to death than the young, the elderly were also more powerful—healers, diviners, and mediators of the supernatural world.[22]

Expiration therefore was less of a conclusion than a seeding of power, watered by the tears of the living. Dried or defleshed, some dead were rendered by communities into ancestors, sometimes called *mallkis*—a desiccated plant ready to replant that required liquids and sustenance. This was *ayni* in action: a reciprocity by which the ayllu, in feeding and watering the dead, maintained the collective canals and lands that also supported the living. The agricultural metaphor was key. After about 1000 CE, across Andean highlands, ancestors were increasingly maintained in open tombs—*machays* (caves) and *chullpas* (stone mortuary towers) that linked earth and sky, where they could be easily offered the corn beer that lubricated their goodwill toward the living. Chullpas in particular permitted the dead to dry like freeze-dried potatoes (*chuño*) that millennia of experimentation had turned into a durable and perennial community resource. Like a potato cut up for replanting, an accessible ancestor might be fruitfully divided, broken apart to duplicate ancestors or craft new ones from the bones of multiple individuals. Ritual specialists who curated these ancestors might ask them to heal the living, plying them with liquid offerings so that they might intervene on the community's behalf with their *paqarisqa*, a shared sacred source responsible for rain, fertility, and the community's future growth.[23] A body, bundle, or huaca was a sacred and spiritually active place, burial, or thing.

The logic behind such a lively, partible, and healing dead, and the geography and architecture they made, meant that Andean cultures sometimes had to interact with the efficacious ancestors of others. Some communities seem to have avoided the dead of prior groups—occupying their living quarters but leaving burials alone, perhaps perceiving their potentially jealous power. Other groups occupied, transformed, or added to prior burial spaces—enlarging their own presence in the past, colonizing that of their neighbors and predecessors,

Fig. 1.1 Aymara-speaking peoples built these stone chullpas, funerary towers at the pre-Inca mortuary site of Sillustani, in the Puno region of present-day Peru. These towers housed their seated ancestral dead, where the cold altitude (over twelve thousand feet) and dry air preserved them for generations. Photographer: Milagros Mosqueira. Creative Commons ShareAlike 4.0 International License (CC BY-SA 4.0).

thereby extending their ancestry and dependent descendants in the present. The curation of stolen ancestors or trophy heads could even allow a new community to claim another group as fictive descendants, justifying their claim to work the dead's lands and command the labor of their new relatives.[24] Mingling ancestors also created community. Between what archaeologists call the Late Intermediate Period, just prior to the Inca Empire expansion, and that expansion itself, some highland communities stored their ancestors in *colca*, tiny storehouselike lodgings surrounding the *kayan*, the flat, leveling space at the heart of a community where multiple ayllus met to negotiate their obligations with each other. It was the communing of these multiple ayllus' ancestors that created a common pacha, a space-time, committing the living to a shared present.[25]

The Inca Empire that exploded across the Andes from its heartland in Cuzco in the fifteenth century CE magnified these mortuary technologies as tools of imperial history. By preserving dead leaders in the powerful, royal postures that embodied their historic authority while alive—seated, grounded like rock and stone—and commissioning commemorative songs, possibly recorded on knotted cord records, khipus, they inscribed that history for future generations. Like any historical sources, these inscriptions and embodiments could be edited by the Incas' royal ayllus: descendants updated the clothes of the dead, re-sang their deeds, and thereby jockeyed for position across landscapes of time.[26] Inca royal houses were thus as strategic in their use of history as any empire.

Spanish writers in the decades after their invasion found that even the most foundational histories were up for debate. According to some accounts, the dynasty began when an exceptional lord or creator deity named Viracocha, son of the Sun, called forth the original Inca couple, Manco Capac and Mama Ocllo, from the Isles of the Sun and the Moon in Lake Titicaca, near what archaeologists recognize as the prior monumental polity of Tiwanaku. They traveled northwest to Cuzco to found an empire whose conquests began some four generations before the Spanish invaded. Another origin tale said Manco Capac and Mama Ocllo emerged with three other pairs of brother-husbands and sister-wives from the cave of Pacariqtambo. Two brothers became empowered stone beings, while Manco and two women, Mama Ocllo and Mama Huaco, completed the migration to Cuzco. There, Mama Huaco expelled the original inhabitants, and Manco plunged his golden solar rod into the soil, founding their dynasty. These origin stories expressed important religious and social values: solar and telluric origins, gender complementarity, migrations through pacha (time and space), and the power to reorder the world. Archaeologists and ethnohistorians underscore the Inca use of these stories to rationalize their conquest, colonization, and claim of difference from the people they ruled.[27]

Archaeologists have used material and linguistic evidence to complicate that mythologized history. The original Incas seem to have had some linguistic connection to the Titicaca region, but they were otherwise just one of many groups competing within the Cuzco basin following the decline of the Wari polity, around 1000 CE. For the next four centuries or so, they engaged in long-term processes of state formation within that heartland. They used their plentiful corn production to build political and marriage alliances, making neighbors into honorary Incas. Sometimes they asserted direct political control. In other instances, they engaged in warfare that eliminated rivals. Cuzco's well-integrated heartland and toolkit of state-building patterns was a basis for their expansion after 1400 over much of the Andes, from Peru into Bolivia, Argentina, Chile, Ecuador, and southernmost Colombia. Their temples, provincial centers, way stations, storehouses, and forty thousand kilometers of roads made them one of the world's largest empires.[28]

In the mid-sixteenth century, some Incas credited their expansion across the Andes solely to Inca Yupanqui, a fifteenth-century emperor or *Sapa Inka* (peerless lord). But archaeology and careful rereading of the chronicles written from the Incas' own histories suggests that this narrative could have been authored by Inca Yupanqui himself, who wrested control of the empire from his father Viracocha and drew a line between their reigns by taking the name Pachacutic, meaning "Turning of Time/Space." Pachacutic then redrafted the histories of his predecessors. According to one account, he destroyed and remade the khipu cord records of prior Sapa Inkas, reorganizing their properties, and commissioning other renderings of their lives. He also seems to have inaugurated a more formal imperial architecture that projected Inca origin stories into new landscapes, such as at his sacred royal estate of Huayna Picchu (Machu Picchu). These strategies delivered clear statements of antiquity that were fuzzy on chronology but asserted the Incas' cosmic priority, realigning the past to match their powerful present.[29]

Sapa Inkas and close Inca kin extended these strategies of imperial history to their dead. Pachacutic's reign may also have been a watershed for mummification in the Andes (or, like other Inca historical practices, this could have been an innovation that his descendants claimed). Prior to his accession, the royal dead were apparently interred—possibly with their possessions—in the Incas' chief temple, the Coricancha, the Golden Enclosure of the Sun. These interments may have once been semipermanent, in which the dead and their inalienable sumptuary goods were placed out of reach while an icon of the dead represented them to the living.[30] At some point, however, the dead began to move—an event that Pachacutic's descendants attributed to his reign but may have been informed by encounters with more mobile mortuary cultures. Pachacutic's religious reforms included "disinterring the bodies of the seven past Incas" who preceded himself and his father, and fabricating hardened *wawqis*—smaller brother effigies—to contain their hair, fingernails, and other exuviae, thereby extending their social presence.[31] These wawqis re-embodied the *camaquen* or life force of the original body, condensing it, making it even more generative. Under Pachacutic, the dead and their wawqis were adorned with gold and bundled with textiles, awarded land and wealth for the support of their descendants, and reintroduced to Inca society, reoccupying their own former palaces.[32]

This curation of imperial history was a family affair, in which Inca women and men played key roles in renegotiating royal ayllus' relative hierarchies. Leading them were the houses whose male leaders oversaw the widest imperial expansions: Viracocha, his son Pachacutic, and Pachacutic's son Tupa Inca Yupanqui and grandson Huayna Capac, who all wore the *maskapaycha*, the royal fringe of Inca sovereignty. Yet in delineating these genealogies to the Spanish, who were fixated upon male inheritance, male Incas deemphasized the Sapa Inkas' female counterparts, the *Coyas*, their principal wives. It was the marriage of Sapa Inka and Coya that made a new royal ayllu, the ramified clan group of which they were the ancestors. This gave principal wives considerable power. If the male Sapa Inka drew his powers from *Inti*, the sacred sun from whom they descended, the Coya managed the empire's cult of *Quilla*, the moon. Their complementarity also meant the Coya ruled Cuzco when the Sapa Inka was indisposed, as did

Tupa Inca Yupanqui's wife Mama Ocllo, who ruled Tawantinsuyu for her young son Huayna Capac. For a decade, writes archaeologist R. Alan Covey, she was "the most powerful person in the Americas."[33]

If the planting of Inca ancestry began with marriage, it flowered upon the achievement and historical inscription of a "good death," according to the mortuary rituals that Pachacutic was also credited with rewriting.[34] Ideally, the Sapa Inka lived to an extraordinarily old age, only slowly becoming *huañuc*, a dying one. He then assembled his *khipukamayuq*, who kept the knotted cord records that managed the empire's affairs and recalled its royal histories. To them he would dictate his life history and the commemorative actions he wanted carried out in his name. He would name his *huañucpa rantin*, a dying one's substitute, who would succeed him as Sapa Inka. Via the life histories that his khipus may have recorded, he exhorted that heir to attend to his example.[35] Once dead, the Sapa Inka may have traveled with these records—the Spanish found Pachacutic's with his body when he was seized. In historical terms, the body and its khipus were primary and secondary sources of ancestry, ownership, and belonging— founding documents of a uniquely Andean library of sovereignty.[36]

At the empire's height, the Sapa Inka's last breath initiated a yearlong mourning process, during which he was returned to life as a still and stony ancestor. Incas told the earliest Spaniards that they were thereby rendered *ylla*—a treasured, sacred, and light-flashing thing—becoming *Yllapa*, which was also the name of the Incas' deity of thunder, lightning, and rain. Preserved Inca rulers thereby became cosmic beings capable of destruction and overabundance, who could be carried by litter across the landscape to begin or halt the seasonal rains. Hardened, flashing, an Inca's Yllapa was more similar to his *wawqi*, his hard brother effigies, than to the ancestral mallkis of subjects—dried plants to his animate, shining stone.[37] The apogee of Inca mummification may not have been the yllapa but the wawqi made before their death: Pachacutic's wawqi was Inti Illapa, made of gold, the "Sun incarnate on earth."[38]

The connection to wawqi was strengthened by the specific process of being made an yllapa—a method of bodily curing that worked and altered anatomy to maintain and magnify ancestral presence. According to early chroniclers, after Pachacutic and his descendant Sapa Inka died, they were moved to their royal estates outside Cuzco, where their viscera were extracted "without breaking a single bone." In this most perfect death, their intestines would have been buried in an adjacent "cemetery, called Tampu," while their hearts were dried or incinerated and added to those of their ancestors, amassed in the interior of the *Punchao*, the child-shaped golden sun icon that sat in the Coricancha. The remaining corpse was then "adorned" or "seasoned" with a secondary substance (one tradition held that it was with the antibacterial resin of the Peruvian pepper tree *schinus molle*, which the Incas used as an antibacterial salve). Next they were "cured" by the sun

Fig. 1.2 This "Secretary and Counselor of the Inca" or Khipukamayuq kept the knotted cord records that managed the empire's affairs and recalled its royal histories. According to chroniclers, he would have been responsible for recording the dying Inca emperor's dictation of his life history and the commemorative actions he wanted carried out with his mummification. Felipe Guaman Poma de Ayala, *El primer nueva corónica y buen gobierno* (1615/1616), 360 [362], Royal Danish Library, GKS 2232 4°.

and dry, cold air; according to one nineteenth-century descendant, this occurred at the snow-covered peak of Pachatusan northeast of Cuzco.[39] Later investigations suggest still more internal interventions: cotton to plug the orifices, and a "calabash rind beneath each cheek over which, as the flesh dried, the skin stayed tight, with a nice gloss." The face of a mummified person thereby remained "so full, with such a good color and complexion, that it did not appear to be dead."[40]

Centuries later, some scholars would cast doubt upon Incas' abilities at curing the dead. The yllapa's specific treatment by the Spanish made their later examination impossible. Yet their skill in trepanation suggests reason to credit their anatomical knowledge. Under the Incas and their subjects, like the Yauyos of Huarochirí, trepanation seems to have undergone a global renaissance. At Pachacutic's royal estate of Ollantaytambo, in the Sacred Valley north of Cuzco, 75.3 percent of the skulls of trepanation patients show signs of long-term healing. A remarkable three out of four who went under the knife in this heartland of Inca rule saw their life extended by their surgeon's skill with a blade—a success rate that Europeans only approached in the late nineteenth century.[41] Given these abilities, the extension of curing to the "life" of the unbreathing may have been no great leap. Recent studies of mummified Andeans subjected by the Incas indicate that their skin was treated with scented balms made of animal or plant fat, wax, or resins with antidecaying, antimicrobial properties.[42]

A year after the Sapa Inka's expiration, Cuzco mourned him in a monthlong ceremony. For the first fifteen days, the lords and ladies would visit the places on the landscape important to his history, weeping, and called out to him. "*Maypin kanki?*" (Where are you?). Next came a fifteen-day celebration of his victories and lament at his loss, which ended when participants threw their mourning clothes into a fire.[43]

And then he returned. Set on a litter, adorned with feathers and gold, the preserved yllapa of the Sapa Inka was carried into Cuzco's great plaza, the Huacaypata. This was his joyful social reintroduction, a ceremony called the *purucaya*, in which he and his fellow mummified emperors paraded in new orders and hierarchies of antiquity alongside their female counterparts, who were likewise mummified and duplicated with shining icons (one of which was said to have contained a powerful Coya's womb). These imperial couples reinhabited the palaces they built in life, with the sumptuary goods—vessels, jewelry, clothing—that would sustain their cult and the royal ayllu of their descendants, who reciprocally cared for their founding ancestors. Underscoring women's specific powers within larger Inca society, *mamakuna*, priestesses, maintained these married yllapa. They interpreted their will, wearing gold masks that likened them to the solar ancestors. They—and possibly a male counterpart—dressed and redressed the stony imperial couple, presenting them *aqha*, corn beer, and burning the food that they "ate." They waved away flies and unwelcome supplicants who sought to marry into their dynasties. By mothering the mummies—curating their preservation and selective display—the women at the heart of royal rule projected the Incas' overwhelming power into the cosmically imperial realm, sweetening death's sadness, though never quite defeating it altogether.[44]

The Inca embodiment of hardened and shining sovereignty in their sacred dead did not stay in Cuzco. It inflected their expansion across the Andes. It has been suggested that the Incas' system of split inheritance spurred expansion; because a new Sapa Inka received only the imperial title and the maskapaycha from his predecessor, whose estate went to the maintenance of his royal ayllu, the political heir could only provide for their own future mummy cult by making conquests and subjects of his own.[45] More likely were the spurs common to other empires—ideologies of cosmic order and political dominance, a hunger for resources and defenses that only grew. But because ancestral concerns were still a factor—if only as jealousy at other royal ayllu's estates—Inca mortuary practices were transformed by conquest itself. For example, the dressing of both living and dead in the finery of gold, silver, and marine spondylus shells would have been difficult before the Incas' incorporation of Chimú's coastal lords in the mid-fifteenth century, around the time of Pachacutic; by observing the Chimú's mortuary practices and requiring tribute from the coastal artisans who crafted that finery, the Incas could enter their afterlife with even greater material style. The death of a family member could also spur conquest. Upon the death of Mama Ocllo, her son Huayna Capac went to war against the people of Chachapoyas in northern Peru, seemingly for the feathers, "coca leaf, ceremonial foods, plunder, and captives who would become servants of Mama Ocllo's mummy."[46]

These encounters also reshaped the mortuary practices of imperial subjects. The Incas flexed their muscles by relocating resistant peoples to serve as unfree labor, sometimes thousands of kilometers from the ancestral lands they called home. These *yanakuna*, permanently detached and resettled servants, had to dispatch with their own dead where they labored, such as at Huayna Picchu. This proximity to Inca royal power could give them prestige goods, like Inca ceramics with which their dead could be interred—but they lost autonomy and were permanently separated from their independent origins, family crypts, and dead grandparents.[47]

Even more dramatic was the empire's denial of good afterlives. In the final years of the empire, Sapa Incas had trophies made from the bodies of enemies, such as skulls to drink from and drums that forced the skin of the defeated to beat the song of their own conquest. The ancestors of rebellious subjects could be burned "alive" or buried in the earth, which was considered an extraordinary assault, decomposing ancestors and desecrating their lineage.[48] Among themselves, the Incas made ancestral violence into a revisionist spectacle. During the Inca war of succession that preceded the Spaniards' arrival, an Inca faction burned a rival royal ayllu's ancestral founder and killed the khipukamayuqs who read that body's life histories. These bonfires reordered elite Inca lineages, inaugurating new historical programs whose explanation of present dominance demanded the consent of other Inca ayllus.[49] The conquered received no better treatment. On occasion, writes bioanthropologist Jacob Bongers, the empire "selectively destroyed local mortuary sites to establish new foundations of political autonomy and territorial rights," dismantling local chullpas, even burning the dead.[50]

The sacred ancestors of subjects who acceded to Inca rule, however, may have become more permanently visible. The Indigenous chronicler Felipe Guaman Poma de Ayala later claimed that the Incas prohibited the interment of the dead in family homes, instead ordering them interred in open funerary constructions in the Andean style, "with their pots and food and drink and clothes."[51] Guaman Poma may have emphasized this point as part of his case that the Incas thereby introduced "idolatry." And the prohibition was certainly not uniform: the Chimú kept interring their dead in palaces while in Guaman Poma's homeland, which the Incas incorporated as Chinchasuyu, the dead indeed moved from subterranean cists to chullpas. Bongers suggests this move could have been an imperial imposition, but also a way that subjects flagged allegiance to the Inca.[52]

The more elaborate preservation of the dead may have also been included in the imperial "package" that the Incas assembled from some subjects' knowledges to then transfer to others. The men chosen to carry the Inca's litter, for example, were Kallawaya, an incorporated people known for opening roads and, later, being healers who built their pharmacopeia using plants collected during their travels throughout the Andes.[53] The bioanthropologist Sonia Guillén has found that in the empire's northern reaches—including Chachapoyas, where Huayna Capac went to war for resources for his mother's preservation—some dead are significantly better preserved after the Inca conquest. Although preserved bodies before and after that event were originally positioned in the typical highland fashion—knees hyperflexed to chest, hands at chin—those interred before Inca rule ended up as more bone than body. Some interred after the Incas' arrival, however, remain intact through the present day. They show signs of "deliberate mummification": the dead's preparers inserted cotton in their mouth, cheeks, and nose; they removed their abdominal organs through the anus or vagina, which they then plugged with cotton; they dried the flesh in such a way that the typically musky odor of mummies was absent, even replaced by the smell of what could have been a natural antiseptic, an "organic preservative."[54]

This sort of heightened preservation was not universal under the empire; bodies in Inca funerary interments on Peru's central and northern coast are "naturally" mummified and bundled up with abundant textiles. But this very contrast may help explain why firm and semipermanent mummification practices prevailed in specific settings. On the one hand, it may have been a form of imperial control. By "curing" their elite subjects' dead, "providing hardened, mummified ancestors more durable than dry bones," the Inca Empire may have helped fix those elites' imperial incorporation in time and space, making the relationship between the Inca and the preserved ancestor permanent.[55] Or it may have been a sharpening of preexisting mortuary practices, literally hardening an elite subject's authority over the groups they claimed to belong to, but whose labor they had to redirect to the Incas.[56] That leader's descendants may have found it useful to point to that hardened dead to explain the greater labor required by the Inca, which local elites and Inca administrators kept track of on the khipus that were sometimes interred with them.[57] These hardened mortuary practices helped make Inca accounting practices sacred, and by tying them to the claim that the Sapa Inka was the solar ancestor of their subjects, the empire could claim credit for any resulting rise in productivity or fertility—and demand still more veneration and tribute.

In turn, this sort of mortuary intervention committed the Incas to care for their new subjects and their sacred ancestors and huacas. The Incas gave offerings to these sacred ancestors and spaces—including the sacred cosmic metals that underlined local lords' honorary or marital relationship to the Incas—to assist in the agricultural cycle.[58] Guaman Poma de Ayala, for example, identified November as the Incas' time of year for feting and processing the ancestors, local and imperial.[59] Given that this was also the time of waiting and praying for rain, a Sapa Inka could claim credit for having assisted in the reciprocal relationship with local huacas and ancestors, and could therefore claim credit for—and benefit from—the ensuing rains and resultant fertility.

These reciprocal honors retained an imperial edge. Sapa Inkas sometimes took physical possession of movable mallkis and sacred things. A contributor to the Huarochirí manuscript, for example, remembered that one of the Yauyo huacas, Ñan Sapa, "was a human being"—meaning that he was almost certainly a mummified ancestor—and that "the Inca took away the waka himself." This was a practice the Yauyo understood—huacas moved—but this was certainly an imperial elevation of the practice.[60] Sapa Inkas sometimes brought huacas and mallkis of those they subjected to Cuzco, where they were stored near his yllapa after they died. Local ancestors were thereby turned into honored hostages, guaranteeing a people's good behavior toward the Inca. And by making their own sacrifices to these captive huacas and mallkis, the Incas asserted control "over the past of the kin groups that these local heroes parented," grafting them onto the life history of the yllapa who incorporated them.[61] This manner of "collecting" bodies as trophies and huacas, sacred things, archaeologist George Lau suggests, was "not unlike that of many colonial projects in world history which filled the treasuries, museums . . . zoos"—and archives—"of expanding nations."[62]

The cosmic pinnacle of the Incas' inventions upon their subjects' deathways may have been the *capacocha*, the "opulent prestation" of *acllas* (sacred women), Inca children, and the children of local lords whom the Incas ritually buried alive in Cuzco and its valley, or on distant mountain peaks. They did so cyclically, but also in times of cosmic imbalance, such as natural disasters or the

Fig. 1.3 Huayna Capac's father, the emperor Tupa Inca, commands the ancestral huacas he conquered and collected, among which would have been some of the most sacred and powerful ancestors, or mallkis, of subjects like the Yauyos of Huarochirí. Felipe Guaman Poma de Ayala, *El Primer Nueva Corónica y Buen Gobierno,* ca. 1600–1615, 261 [263]. Royal Danish Library, GKS 2232 4°.

passing of a Sapa Inka. The Incas cast the capacocha ritual as an honor, binding subject families to the empire by raising their children in Cuzco, "treasuring" them, before sending the most flawless—"humanity's best"—to die in earthly or skybound ancestral places, thereby repairing breaches between the Inca polity and the cosmos. Traveling two thousand kilometers or more, they climbed the empire's highest mountains—Ampato, Llullaillaco, Cerro El Plomo. At elevations of twenty-two thousand feet they were put to sleep with corn beer or swiftly knocked out by their imperial guides. They then froze, dying of exposure—their small size inversely proportional to the work they did on the empire's behalf, repairing the cosmos.[63]

Some communities may have embraced the imperial message that the capacocha regenerated the cosmos on behalf of all, indebting the Incas to their parents at a moment of royal sadness and redistributive gratitude. On other occasions, the capacocha gained local meanings of their own. For example, an interred capacocha named Tanta Carhua was locally celebrated as a fertile huaca with lands and herds to her name through the seventeenth century. In late-twentieth-century Argentina and Peru, communities have claimed capacocha found on nearby mountains as sacred beings of their own.[64]

But scholars also emphasize how capacocha were still subject children who were taken away, killed, and preserved. They made explicit the Incas' cosmic power to take away life, but "not let die"—a freezing of power along a spectrum with the Incas' other methods of mortuary violence, like piling enemies' bodies near the summit of snowy volcanos.[65] This use of the Andean environment to cure and archive other peoples' dead elevated Inca mortuary strength to its maximum height, curating subjects as specimens of sacred and imperial history. This was not the sort of "artificial" mummification that made the dead Sapa Inkas into permanent, shining, and mobile beings—but these frozen capacocha would survive as "Inca mummies" in ways the yllapa did not.

The loss of ancestors and children to these methods of mortuary rule did not stop Inca subjects from telling counter-histories of their own, finding ways to cure and magnify the powers of ancestors taken by the Incas, if only at a distance. Tanta Carhua's memory would survive the Incas' fall, as would Ñan Sapa, the mallki the Inca took from the Yauyos. The Yauyos, however, were not so easily separated from the mallki they loved. They made "another to be his proxy"—another Ñan Sapa, who seems to have been represented by a huayo—a bone mask that could have been cut, trepanation-like, from Ñan Sapa's face. Like the mamakuna who wore gold masks and spoke for the yllapa, a Yauyo community member wore Ñan Sapa's huayo to re-embody him in dances for Pariacaca in which the Sapa Inka or his proxy also participated.[66]

In this way, Incas and their subjects used ancestors to make, enforce, and soften imperial rule in the Andes—a project millennia in the making, in which obligation, violence, and fertility remained as much a matter for the dead as for the grieving. By the 1520s, when Pachacutic's grandson Huayna Capac ruled, mortuary politics were imperial politics, in which the dead could be commanded as well as heal, bring down the thunder, and go into hiding. Any empire that hoped to succeed the Incas would have to recognize that power.

Embalming Incas

Huayna Capac's Yllapa and the Spanish Collection of Empire

Huayna Capac had been breathless for about half a decade when he met the invaders. The Inca emperor would not have been impressed.

His death had shaken his empire, Tawantinsuyu, but he had survived it. He had been on the Ecuadorian frontier for a decade or more, pumping tribute and treasure to the empire's heart in Cuzco and his new northern capital Tomebamba, in Quito, when an outbreak "like leprosy" swept the land. The disease, likely brought by the invaders, made no distinction in status.[1] Yet Huayna Capac had the means to extend his existence. When the malady laid Tomebamba low, he put his affairs in order. Becoming violently ill, he assembled his khipukamayuqs, his recordkeepers, and dictated the course of his posthumous procession back to Cuzco with his trophies of conquest. He named one son his huañucpa rantin, his dying one's substitute, to succeed him as Sapa Inka, the emperor. When he released his final breath, he became as quiet as the stone house around him.[2]

Songs of mourning then mingled with the work of making him an yllapa, a stony and shining ancestor. A Spaniard who later married into Huayna Capac's family wrote that the emperor was "opened, and all his flesh removed, seasoning him without breaking a single bone. They seasoned and cured him in the sun and the air." His entrails were added to one of two wawqis, the brother icons that duplicated his essence; his heart may have joined those of his ancestors in the golden sun icon in Cuzco, the Punchao. His cured corpse was then dressed in a fine tunic and mantle and seated on a litter adorned with feathers and gold, where he might have been joined by the yllapa of his recently deceased wife Raua Ocllo and one of his wawqis. They then processed back to Cuzco, a trip of over a thousand miles ritually prolonged to last a year. Once in Cuzco, the empire's mourning reached its peak. Huayna Capac processed into the great plaza to join his fellow yllapa. He reoccupied his palace and country estate, Yucay, and was

Empires of the Dead. Christopher Heaney, Oxford University Press. © Oxford University Press 2023.
DOI: 10.1093/oso/9780197542552.003.0003

Fig. 2.1 This drawing by the Andean chronicler Felipe Guaman Poma de Ayala depicts the yllapa, the preserved and lightning-flashing body of the former Inca emperor Huayna Capac with his principal wife (left) and what was likely his wawqi (right), a statue that contained his hair, fingernails, or (after embalming) his organs. "The dead Huayna Capac Inca, Yllapa / They carry him to Cuzco to inter him." Felipe Guaman Poma de Ayala, from the *El Primer Nueva Corónica y Buen Gobierno* (1615), 377 [379]. Royal Danish Library, GKS 2232 4°.

likely reunited with the preserved body of his first wife, Coya Cusirimay, who had predeceased him. Attended by mamakunas, gold-masked priestesses, he became "the old Cuzco," a sacred source of the current Inca universe. His yllapa, khipukamayuqs, and songs transmitted his embodied and inscribed history to descendants—his empire without end.[3]

The problem was that those descendants disagreed over his final intentions. Huayna Capac's first huañucpa rantin, the infant Ninancoyuchi—and that child's mother, Raua Ocllo, whom Huayna Capac may have actually designated his functional heir—died of the same illness. Huayan Capac's bodily preservation and slow procession to Cuzco may have also been an attempt to hide his expiration while his allies worked out the problem of deciding his successor.[4] In the coming years, two of his surviving sons and heirs, Atahuallpa (in Ecuador) and Huascar (in Cuzco), went to war for the maskapaycha, the royal fringe, each claiming a relationship to their father's person—his yllapa in Cuzco with Huascar, and one of his wawqis in Ecuador with Atahuallpa.[5]

Atahuallpa defeated Huascar, but a new faction entered the fray. Invaders from across the water landed on Tawantinsuyu's coast. In the Inca settlement of Cajamarca, they took Atahuallpa hostage. Atahuallpa tried to turn this upset to his advantage. He sent a few of his Spanish and African captors to Cuzco in litters—a privilege reserved for sacred ancestors like himself—with permission to strip the gold from the exterior of the Coricancha, the sun temple, for his ransom. His warning to these "conquistadors" that they could not loot the palace of his father, Huayna Capac, was quickly forgotten, and the intruders pushed into the palace's innermost sanctum, tempted by the gold-lidded pots within. One of Huayna Capac and Cusirimay's gold-masked mamakuna tried to stop them, but only succeeded in getting the ingrates to remove their shoes before they robbed her charges' sacred forms. But then the interlopers departed, eager to return to their comrades with tales of having looted "two Indians in the manner of *embalsamados*"—embalmed ones, adorned with gold.[6]

That desecration of Huayna Capac and Cusirimay's sacred estate stung. Yet the loss also revealed the intruders' ignorance of how to do more than plunder; they did not know how to conquer like an Inca. The invaders understood themselves to have looted the embalmed bodies of royalty, whose spirit had long before departed—an action that could anger the living, but the dead could hardly protest, they thought. This was a crucial miscalculation. In Inca terms, the right display of force and understanding of Inca sovereignty would have been to take Huayna Capac hostage or, more dramatically, to burn his corpse "alive," as Atahuallpa had just done to the yllapa of Huayna Capac's father, Tupa Inca, for supporting Huascar.[7] Instead, the invaders left Huayna Capac free, animate, and likely angry—still capable of bringing down the rains.

―――――

This retelling of how Huayna Capac's yllapa first met the conquistadors was designed to provoke. The more storied event of Spain's invasion of the Inca empire of Tawantinsuyu tends to be Francisco Pizarro's capture and judicial murder of Atahuallpa at Cajamarca, which Pizarro's secretaries presented as evidence of Christian domination of the kingdom they called Peru. For some popular historians, Atahuallpa's fall symbolizes rapid European conquest in the Americas: a moment a millennium in the making, in which Old World differences of environment, disease immunity, technology, culture, religion, and tactics immediately tipped the scales.[8]

Historians of the Spanish invasion of Tawantinsuyu have shown how false that narrative is, beginning with misrepresentations of Cajamarca itself.[9] Far from heralding a rapidly concluded military conquest, the event triggered four to five decades of negotiation and contest. Andean peoples resisted and extended conquistador violence, taking sides in a military conflict that lasted through 1572. They disputed religious and legal frameworks. They navigated and suffered consensual and forced relationships with Spanish men. They found ways to survive and even profit from Spanish extractions of Peruvian labor and the silver that made their empire. By 1600 the Crown's bureaucratic control of the world's most valuable colony was secure, but Spanish dominance was far from inevitable, and in many places it remained incomplete.[10]

Huayna Capac's independence, for example, highlights continuities of Inca power that placed some of the empire's most sacred and sovereign bodies outside of Spanish hands from 1532 to the early 1570s. This chapter explores those continuities via the Inca yllapa and the negotiations their bodies inspired.[11] It begins from the proposition that Atahuallpa's capture and execution was not the transformative event for the Incas that Pizarro claimed it was, in part because the most cosmically powerful Incas—the "old Cuzco" Huayna Capac and his fellow yllapa—remained at large. It then argues that Spain's slow domination of the Inca hierarchy included a failure to learn these mortuary terms of Andean empire. The Spanish had to learn that they could never win the empire simply by killing. They had to attend to Andean ancestors as a matter of sacred control, governing and "editing" their histories like the Incas before them.

This chapter further argues that Spaniards then investigated the Incas' sacred body politics to depict their yllapas in a more "natural" light. Colonial writers and officials sought Indigenous testimonies and knowledges of the dead, and marshaled a more historical, botanical and anatomical approach to their description. These efforts to master the histories, customs, laws, resources, and knowledges of their subjects and sovereign predecessors were part of an empire-wide experiment in practical ethnography and natural history, which some scholars present as an imperial, Iberian origin for comparative ethnography and more experiential sciences.[12] In that vein, this chapter examines a series of encounters in the half-century after Spain's invasion of Tawantinsuyu in which colonial actors sought to assert the putatively "natural" and historical foundations of the Inca ancestors' claim to be sacred, speaking, and shining beings. After finally confiscating the yllapa, Spanish officials even put them on limited display, as evidence of their nonsacred preservation. Given that this was likely the first European-led collection and exhibition of Indigenous remains in the Americas, this chapter offers this process as a sixteenth-century origin for the Peru-centric American anthropology the rest of this book explores.

This framing points to this chapter's third contention: that there was something "Inca" in the colonial science that followed. Inca emperors had themselves displayed subjugated bodies as testaments to their power, while claiming to honor them. In Spanish hands, the yllapas' display signaled an understanding of Inca sovereignty and its transfer, but colonized them, inverting their cosmic claim. By presenting these sovereigns as wonders of preservation while defining them as "dead," the Spanish "embalmed" Inca rule, denying their ability to call to down the lightning. It likewise denied the power of the women who originally curated, maintained, and spoke for these ancestors, eliminating a key religious role for Andean women in the colony to come. Most devastatingly, this "science" heralded the ancestors' material dissipation: dissection, extirpation, rot, and the bonfire. Atahuallpa's execution could become a false emblem of European conquest in the Americas because hostile witnesses like Huayna Capac were studied to death.

And yet the Incas' mark on colonialism's ways of knowing and judging the Indigenous past was profound.[13] The empire's "most thoroughgoing ideological coup" was to get "distinctive, non-Inca, subordinate cultures to claim Incas as their ancestors," historian Irene Silverblatt proposed.[14] If judged by the non-Inca nations and Andean peoples who in colonial and republican times claimed Atahuallpa or Huayna Capac as lost ancestors or benevolent kings, the Incas succeeded, if belatedly. But they also inspired an anthropology in which Inca and Andean mummies became the embodied ancients of the Americas—as soaring an imperial apex as Huayna Capac could have imagined.

Spain's agents had paid attention to the mortuary practices of the Americas' Indigenous peoples since November 1492, when Christopher Columbus's sailors opened a Taíno funerary basket on the island of Cuba. In subsequent invasions, they painted Caribbean and Mesoamerican deathways as diabolic sacrifice and cannibalism, marking its practitioners as fit for conquest or enslavement.[15] Upon invading the highlands of Tawantinsuyu in May 1532, some conquistadors likewise presented themselves as good Christians out to topple an empire in which "filthy" sacrifices of children were made upon the tombs or "sepulchers of the dead."[16] But the resemblance of Inca ancestors to Europeans' treatment of their own most elite dead at first made space for Inca descendants to parade and defend their rule.

Viewed from Cuzco, the Spaniards' arrival promised the restoration of ancestor cults disrupted by Atahuallpa's and Huascar's war. During that conflict,

Huascar told the royal houses that he was confiscating the "lands of coca and maize dedicated to the Sun and the bodies of dead lords, and those of his father, Huayna Capac," claiming that "neither the Sun nor the dead nor his now-dead father ate." Huascar's "abhorrent" challenge, which may have threatened to bury those ancestors, was followed by Atahuallpa's mortuary retribution.[17] When his general Chalcochima took Cuzco in 1532, he confiscated the yllapa of Atahuallpa's grandfather Tupa Inca Yuapanqui, whose royal ayllu supported Huascar. Chalcochima punished Tupa Inca by taking the yllapa to Cuzco's outskirts and "reducing him to ashes." Atahuallpa then proceeded on a course of mortuary revisionism. He declared himself a new "Pachacutic," destroyed competing khipus, and killed their keepers, attempting to inaugurate "a new historical program."[18]

On November 15, 1532, during the month in the Inca calendar dedicated to the dead, a delegation of conquistadors met Atahuallpa at Cajamarca; the aspiring Sapa Inka refused to answer their questions, staying as stony as his wawqi and that of Huayna Capac, with whom he traveled.[19] As in Cuzco, "where spokesmen literally put words in the mouths of the mummies of past emperors or the great regional oracles of the empire," notes historian Susan Elizabeth Ramírez, "a delegate standing beside Atahuallpa responded for him when an answer to the translated Spanish queries was required."[20] The following day, however, the Spanish toppled his litter and slaughtered thousands of his retinue. The ensuing bloodbath, looting, and rape were terrifying. But holding Atahuallpa hostage also underlined his claim to *be* Sapa Inka. From captivity Atahuallpa ordered Huascar's assassination. And by sending three Spanish and at least one Black conquistador to Cuzco as *Viracocha*—powerful beings from afar, carried on Atahuallpa's own litter like sacred things—he demanded tribute befitting an Inca and asserted his own power over the city that had supported his brother.[21]

The return to Cajamarca of those conquistadors with gold from Coricancha and Huayna Capac's yllapa brought three messages to those who awaited them. First, there was more treasure to come. Second, they had left Huayna Capac and his consort's body intact, which respected the spirit if not the letter of Atahualpa's request. And third, these were no minor lords they were looting, but a dynasty of rulers whose center of power, bodily treatment, and royal history were potentially as complex as their own. Describing them "in the manner of embalmed dead" and "bultos secos" (dry effigies) implied that they were like some of Spain's elite dead.[22] Although the Spanish monarchy had recently abandoned embalming, believing it showed vain concern for the earthly form, it remained a complex and even wondrous anatomical art associated with monarchs and heroes.[23] In Iberia, Juan Cromberger was publishing his second edition of the *Crónica del muy efforçado cavallero el Cid Ruy Diaz campeador*, in which El Cid's followers embalmed him after death and mounted him on horseback for one last charge against the Muslims.[24]

The Spanish inadvertently contributed to Atahuallpa's ability to do likewise. In July 1533 a fearful Pizarro tried the self-proclaimed Sapa Inka on charges of machinating against the Spanish, amassing armies, and assassinating his brother, Huascar.[25] Found "guilty," Atahuallpa elected to be baptized before dying— a choice that saved him from being burned alive. Atahuallpa was not simply avoiding pain. This was also ancestral strategy, averting the desecration of his own supernaturally ancestral form and the cult that would tend it—the very punishment he had inflicted upon Tupa Inca Yupanqui's yllapa the previous year.[26] Incas interviewed in the 1540s claimed that Atahuallpa told those present that he would return as a serpent.[27]

Seen from Europe, the execution seemed to be an extraordinary domination. King Charles, who later gave Pizarro a coat of arms depicting Atahuallpa in chains, at first lamented the killing of a fellow monarch.[28] He may have been assuaged by how the conquistadors wrapped that killing in Christian ritual: they recited the Apostles' Creed before Atahuallpa died and gave him a solemn funeral. These were mercies granted to "the greatest and cruelest butcher that men had ever seen," claimed Pizarro's secretary, Francisco de Xerez. The friars, Pizarro, and the other conquistadors "carried [Atahuallpa] to be buried" in a makeshift "church," "with much solemnity, with all the honor that they could offer," wearing signs of mourning.[29] This was Spanish Peru's imagined foundation in a funeral: three centuries later, an artist named Luis Montero mythologized that moment in a massive painting, *Los funerales de Atahualpa* (1867)—in which Atahuallpa's distraught and mourning wives attempt to throw themselves upon a corpse guarded by dignified conquistadors and friars in a Christianized Inca temple.[30] (See plate 4)

Left invisible was how decisively this Spanish "victory" was undercut by Atahuallpa himself. Although the conquistadors had collected their first dead Inca and inscribed him as Christian, his decision to convert and save his body enabled the continuation of Inca deathways. After Atahuallpa's Spanish funeral, Pizarro marched to Cuzco with Huayna Capac's eldest remaining son, Tupa Huallpa, to install him as a sovereign vassal of "the Emperor our Lord."[31] As they did so, however, Atahuallpa's partisans disinterred his body, "because it seemed to them indecent to the Majesty of their Inca, and against the custom of his ancestors, to be given such a poor tomb below the earth," wrote chronicler Garcilaso de la Vega Inca. They then carried Atahuallpa to Quito, where his captain Rumiñahui attempted to "embalm" him. Whether or not he was successful, a royal ayllu at least temporarily grew, in which Atahuallpa—or those who claimed him as sacred ancestor—retained his empire.[32]

In traveling to Cuzco, Pizarro's column met that empire's other claimants, alive and dead. After Atahuallpa's brother and brief successor Tupa Huallpa died on the road, their sibling Manco Inca Yupanqui swore fealty to King Charles before continuing his people's most important ancestor-making rituals. In March 1534 the Spanish watched Manco's investiture as Sapa Inka in Cuzco's most sacred plaza, accompanied by eleven to fifteen pairs of male and female yllapas and wawqis—the dead sovereigns and their sibling icons. Their ayllus paraded them, singing their deeds to remind Manco of his antecedents. Pizarro's other secretary, Sancho de la Hoz, ended his sequel to Xerez's account with this uncanny experience. Manco had become a subject of the Spanish Crown, but his royal legitimacy was evidenced by the preserved non-Christian ancestors who sat by him, like his father, Huayna Capac, who was "very entire, wrapped in rich vestments, only lacking the tip of his nose." Sancho noted that people were with Huayna Capac "day and night, keeping away the flies," and that when other lords came to salute Manco, they greeted his ancestors first. Sancho warned that the Incas venerated wawqis "as if they were gods," but he was more ambivalent about the yllapas, whom he described as an impressively preserved royal dead whose incorporation burnished Spanish rule.[33]

During that first year in Cuzco, some Spaniards even reinforced the ancestor system that Atahuallpa and Huascar had threatened. Pedro Pizarro at one point brokered a marriage between one of Manco Inca's captains and an Inca noblewoman. "I thought that I was going to speak to some living Indian," Pedro later wrote, "but they took me to the figure of one of these dead men, where he was sitting inside the kind of litter they have, on one side the Indian designated to speak for him, and on the other side the woman, seated next to the dead man." Pedro's translator delivered the message, and "for a moment the two of them remained surprised and silent; then the man looked at the woman, I believe so as to know her desire and then they both answered together saying that their lord the dead man agreed, and that the captain should take the lady since the *Apo*, the great lord, wished it thus."[34] In delivering that message, Pedro transmitted the will of the yllapa and the women who kept him alive.

Yet other conquistadors burned both ancestors and heirs to reveal their wealth, wicking away those women's power. After Francisco Pizarro founded Spanish Cuzco atop the former capital, his brother Gonzalo went hunting for Manco's great-great-grandfather, Viracocha Inca, whose ayllu had taken his rich yllapa to his estate at Jaquijahuana, south of the Sacred Valley. Gonzalo Pizarro burned "Indians, men and women," torturing them into revealing Viracocha, whom Gonzalo then looted and burned "alive." Viracocha's ayllu gathered his ashes to continue their secret veneration, but his female counterparts were less fortunate.[35] At one point the conquistadors smelted ten or twelve figures of women made of gold, "as beautiful and well made as if they were alive." If these

Fig. 2.2 Following Atahuallpa's death, his brother Manco Inca became Tawantinsuyu's Sapa Inka before rebelling against the Spanish. Here he sits in Cuzco like the mummified yllapa he would one day become. Felipe Guaman Poma de Ayala, *El Primer Nueva Corónica y Buen Gobierno,* ca. 1600–1615, 398 [400]. Royal Danish Library, GKS 2232 4°.

figures were duplicates of the Inca queens, the hardened aspect of their bodies, this would have been an extraordinary assault to the power of Inca women, whose transmutation into gold specie helped occlude their historical importance.[36] Back in Peru, Gonzalo and his cohort occupied the yllapas' palaces, murdering and marrying their female kin, and cloistering their daughters. Inca women made their own alliances to survive these assaults of their imperial and religious power.[37]

When Manco Inca's own female family members were targeted, when he too was tortured, he and Huayna Capac pushed back. In April 1536 Manco attended a ceremony for Huayna Capac's yllapa in the Yucay Valley, promising Hernando Pizarro that he would return with his father's own gold statue. Instead, likely in Huayna Capac's golden presence, Manco launched a war to take back the empire.[38] His armies besieged Lima and Spanish-controlled Cuzco and undertook mortuary violence of their own, delivering the heads of decapitated "Christians."[39] The siege failed, but Manco successfully fled to the eastern slopes of the Andes. At a place named Vilcabamba, several days' travel beyond his great-grandfather Pachacutic's estate at Huayna Picchu, he made a new hearth of independent Inca rule. From there he would deny the conquest in the presence of Punchao, the golden sun icon that contained the hearts of the Inca imperial line.

Over the next decade, the conquistadors would war among themselves and against the Crown, rejecting the "New Laws" that curtailed their claims to Indigenous labor. But through it all, Manco survived. He outlasted the Pizarros' execution of Francisco's partner Diego de Almagro in 1538. He outlasted Francisco's own assassination in 1541 by partisans of Almagro's son "El Mozo." He even outlasted his own assassination in 1544 by a few Almagristas who sought refuge in Vilcabamba. Manco's men killed the assassins and made Manco Inca into an yllapa. As an yllapa, Manco outlasted Gonzalo Pizarro's rebellion against the Crown, which ended with the conquistador's execution in 1548.[40] Spain's royal officials asserted their rule over Peru, but Manco Inca's three sons still in Vilcabamba—Sayri Tupa, Titu Cusi, and Tupa Amaru—heard their father's voice, as did the other royal ayllus who took their yllapa on the run.

———

Confronted with such a metaphysical challenge, Spain's bureaucrats, writers, and clergy tried an intellectual solution: they would learn about the sacred and ancestral bodies they faced. By doing so, they might explain away their opponents' power before giving them "ends" that respected their status as past sovereigns. This process was religious in the sense that it spoke to the goal of encouraging Christian burial and denying the Incas' sacrality. But it was also "scientific" in that it sought to identify and even monetize the yllapas' means of preservation. The Crown thereby attempted to know Andean sovereignty from the inside out.

This process began soon after the 1534 European publication of that early account of Huayna Capac and his consort as being "in the manner of *embalsamados*."[41] Describing yllapas as "embalmed ones" rendered Inca knowledge as an interesting anatomical art rather than a sacred one. As any conquistador knew, in the sixteenth-century Catholic church, a deceased person's incorruptibility might reflect a sanctity worthy of sainthood.[42] But embalming the nonsaintly dead retained the ancient, medical, and royal associations of Egypt in Greek and Hellenistic sources, as well as Joseph's care for his father, Jacob, in the final pages of the first book of the Christian Bible. In the sixteenth century, this means of curing the dead required Near Eastern *materia medica*: spices, myrrhs, bitumens, resins, aloes, and liquor from the balsam tree, whose "hot" nature slowed corruption and time and was believed to have been used by the ancient Egyptians. Embalming was also expensive, since Egypt's balsam was in short supply and was priced accordingly.[43]

The Incas' embalming of their dead thus provided anatomical and botanical intelligence for the Spanish Crown, which was at that moment testing its Indigenous subjects' botanical cures and cosmographical knowledges—a process sometimes called the Indigenous and Iberian American–led "Early Scientific Revolution."[44] The Crown had already found one profitable replacement for balsam on the island of Hispaniola in the 1520s, when a Taino noblewoman revealed a tree with healing properties to her Spanish husband. Charles V ordered physicians to make "experiences," experimental trials, to show that this "balsam" was commensurate to that of Egypt and to encourage its sale.[45] Around the same time, the Crown directed Francisco Pizarro to bring a *boticario*, an apothecary, with him to Peru.[46] And in 1536 Charles or his advisers requested and received a sample of "balsam of Peru."[47]

The Crown's bioprospecting was aided by Iberian writers who elaborated on Peru's embalming reputation. In 1555 Agustín de Zárate, who during the 1540s enforced the Crown's claimed fifth of the gold, silver, and other treasures taken from the Incas, published a chronicle advertising Peru's other resources. Among other items, Zárate wrote of a "liquor" from a sweet-smelling wood, "whose odor is so transcendent that it is overwhelming, and if one covers a dead body with it and pours it down that body's throat, never will it corrupt."[48] The following year, Portuguese Jewish physician Amato Lusitano attributed amazing powers to *oppobalsamo ex peru*. By 1586 Balsam of Peru was in Florentine apothecary Stefano Rosselli's museum—one of the last, essential ingredients necessary for the European recovery of theriac, "antidote of antidotes." By 1612, European embalmers used Balsam of Peru as well.[49]

In the 1540s, however, understanding the reasons for Inca embalming was as urgent as how they did so. The Spanish had realized that the Inca ancestors were venerated, which they took as idolatry. In 1541 ecclesiastical judge Luis de Morales proposed the ancestors' burial, believing it would facilitate conversion and remove the temptation of their looting. As evidence, he pointed to how he had convinced Paullo, a son of Huayna Capac—whose loyalty to the Crown had earned him the royal Inca fringe—to yield his non-Christian father for church interment. Morales believed Paullo was satisfied by the dignity of Huayna Capac's dispatch, but the tears of his "mother and other lords and ladies" foreshadowed the measure's failure.[50] Like Atahuallpa, Huayna Capac was smuggled from his tomb. Three years later he was possessed by Crown administrator Cristóbal Vaca de Castro, who charged fees from noble Incas who wanted to "visit" and likely venerate the former emperor's yllapa.[51] The transaction may have made sense to those Incas. It replicated how they took possession of subjects' sacred ancestors to ensure good behavior and the flow of tribute.[52] But exploiting sacred Inca ancestry also reinforced it, and Dominican friars threatened Vaca de Castro's excommunication if he didn't return the body. He seems to have yielded because by 1551 conquistador Juan Díez de Betanzos—who had married Atahuallpa's former betrothed, doña Angelina Yupanqui—reported that Huayna Capac and his fellow yllapa were again at large, hidden behind textiles in wall niches or storage bins for dried maize.[53]

To re-approach these sacred fugitives, Díez de Betanzos and his fellow conquistador and chronicler Pedro Cieza de León took a crucial step. They interviewed the yllapas' descendants—in Díez de Betanzos's case, his own relatives—regarding the history the ancestors carried, as well as the means and meanings of their preservation. In 1549 Paullo died, having been baptized don Cristóbal, but his interment in a jointly Inca and Christian space, in one of Cuzco's churches built atop Inca temples and palaces, encouraged his purucaya. For this social reintroduction a year later, his relatives made a wawqi, his sacred double.[54] Díez de Betanzos and Cieza de León took the event as a chance to interview Paullo's relatives, as well as those of Huayna Capac. Cieza de León was impressed by the genealogical songs of the occasions, comparing them to Spain's historical poetry. But his *Crónica del Perú* (1554) also offered a worried analysis of the accompanying mortuary practices. He recorded how Inca bodies were bundled in a mantle that their descendants, "in their blindness, canonized as saints, and their bones were honored by those who did not comprehend that their souls were burning in hell, thinking that they were in heaven." It was Cieza who learned that they "call this manner of canonization *ylla*, which means 'body of he that was good in life'; and in another sense, *yllapa*, which means thunder or lightning; and in this way the Indians call the shots of artillery *yllapa*, by the bang that they make."[55] In the manuscript *Suma y narración de los Incas*, which Díez de Betanzos delivered to the viceroy—the Spanish Crown's representative—in 1557, he agreed that this idolatrous "canonization" was a problem, whose solution included laying out the recipe by which Pachacutic and Huayna Capac were "seasoned" and "cured." By insisting upon the natural and artificial means of their bodily preservation, Díez de Betanzos and Cieza argued against interpreting the yllapa's solidity as saintlike. Rather, it was an invitation to idolatry.[56]

Because it was the Incas who needed convincing, the Spanish sought to convert their ancestors into retiring monarchs. They began with Manco Inca's line in Vilcabamba. In 1557 the Crown sent Huayna Capac's daughter Quispe Quipe—baptized doña Beatriz Manco Capac Yupanqui—and Díez de Betanzos to negotiate with Manco's son, Sayri Tupa. The delegation admitted Manco had been provoked into war. They offered generous terms to end Sayri Tupa's exile: his uncle Atahuallpa's royal fringe, his grandfather Huayna Capac's royal estates in the Yucay Valley, and an extraordinary dispensation to marry his sister Cusi Huarcay as his *coya*, his principal wife, in a Christian ceremony in Cuzco. Sayri Tupa agreed and was carried to Lima by litter. In Cuzco he took communion in the church of Santo Domingo, atop the sun temple where his ancestors were once interred. Once baptized, he and Cusi Huarcay occupied Yucay. These Inca heirs had founded a new royal Christian ayllu, whose first heir would be their daughter, doña Beatriz Coya, born in 1558.[57]

Amid this optimism, the Spaniards' documentation of their dynasty's historic roots finally brought Huyana Capac's yllapa in from the cold. Cuzco's royal magistrate, its *corregidor*, was Polo Ondegardo, a subtle "ethnographer" who advocated learning Inca legal precedents to facilitate Spanish rule. Ondegardo began interviewing "all of the old Indians who had survived from the pagan era, including the principal Incas"—likely including Sayri Tupa—"as well as the priests and *quipucamayos* or Inca historians." Using their responses he drafted a report on the lives and sequences of their ayllus' founders: apparently thirteen male Sapa Inkas, substantiated by his informants' resort to "the memorials of their *quipus* and their paintings that were still at hand."[58]

To make his forensic accounting of Inca rule complete, Ondegardo sought out its most primary sources. In the countryside, he hunted down the hidden yllapas of Pachacutic Inca Yupanqui, Huayna Capac, and Huayna Capac's mother Mama Ocllo; the jarred ashes of Viracocha, whom Gonzalo Pizarro burned; and possibly the yllapas of Pachacutic's son Amaru Tupa Inca and Pachacutic's mother, Mama Runtucaua, or wife, Mama Anahuarque. To those six he added the wawqi and less well-preserved remains of the other prior Sapa Inkas, all of which Ondegardo brought to his Cuzco home.[59]

This collection of these Inca ancestors—flesh, ash, stone—was a gateway moment for Spanish rule. Ondegardo portrayed it as a conquest. In spiritual terms, gathering the sacred Inca dead removed them from active ritual use as "idols." His report on these practices went to the archbishop of Lima to inform deliberations on the efficacy of Andean conversion thus far.[60] For those still loyal to these specific ancestors, such a confiscation was likely shattering. Scholars have even proposed that it revealed or seeded lasting divisions between Inca families, as Ondegardo could have learned the yllapas' location by leaning on rival ayllus.[61]

Yet when considered in light of how the royal ayllus themselves were trying to improve their circumstances, more complicated possibilities emerge. Historians of religion warn against assuming Inca and Andean understandings of the sacred were resistant or static. Decades of disease and civil war had killed many of the yllapas and wawqis' interpreters, priestesses, and retainers, likely muting their memory.[62] Spanish missionaries were also encouraging Andean converts to turn their mobile ancestors into permanently retiring lords. In 1560 the Dominican friar Domingo de Santo Tómas published the first *Lexicon* of the empire's lingua franca, Quechua, which gave missionaries a vocabulary to encourage the transformation of religious habits via subtle changes to Quechua meanings. His readers learned that *Ayácta,pampani.gui* and *Ayácta,çurcuni.gui* meant *enterrar muertos* and *disenterrar muertos*: to bury or inter and to unearth or disinter the dead. This was inexact, to say the least. These Quechua phrases actually meant "to bring the dead to a flat (common) place" and "to remove the dead from a flat (common) place"—the ritual actions of temporarily congregating royal or sacred ancestors in communal plazas. By encouraging missionaries to use this Quechua phrase to instead promote interment in a cemetery or church, Santo Tomás sought to ease Inca and Andean converts toward Christian practices. It implied that bringing royal or sacred ancestors for permanent burial was a substitute for prior practices of parading and communing the dead—but that "disinterment" was inappropriate.[63]

In Domingo de Santo Tómas's reflection, it is possible to imagine how some Incas may have reacted to the loss of the yllapa to Ondegardo. It could have been experienced as a final forced "bringing in" of ancestors to still-sacred Inca ground in Cuzco, but one that still validated an ayllu's royalty. They could have referred to the prior interments of Huayna Capac and Paullo, whose bodies re-Incanized the church tombs built atop their former temples and palaces.[64] And for those loyal to Vilcabamba, this was hardly the end. Sayri Topa had left behind the yllapa of his father, Manco Inca, and the Punchao containing the Sapa Inkas' hearts, to be cared for by his brothers Titu Cusi and Tupa Amaru and their subjects.

Finally, Ondegardo's collection may have functioned as a legitimation and transfer of Inca sovereignty in colonial and Andean terms. Ondegardo—who as corregidor was like the Crown's wawqi in Cuzco—honored the Sapa Inkas by paying them the attention they themselves had paid to some of their subjects' most sacred ancestors, collecting them to guarantee good behavior and learn their history. Ondegardo explained that the most important yllapas of Pachacutic and Huayna Capac were found with the khipus or "registers" that "recounted [their] deeds, and celebrations and idolatries."[65] In coming years, descendants of these Sapa Inkas and their attendants presented notarized genealogies that were validated by witnesses who confirmed that they had seen their ancestor—as if attesting to that ayllu's primary source and sources, archived by Spanish rule.[66]

Evidence that Ondegardo projected at least accidental competence in the mortuary politics of Inca and Andean rule lies in what happened next. The yllapa were not burned like Viracocha. They were not destroyed like comparable "relics" of the Buddha seized by the Portuguese in Goa two years later.[67] Rather,

Ondegardo "secretly buried" all the less well-preserved ancestors, possibly in the former Temple of the Sun.[68] More surprisingly, he allowed the best preserved of the yllapas to circulate in Cuzco. Chronicler Garcilaso de la Vega Inca—whose parents were a Spanish conquistador and one of Huayna Capac's nieces—remembered that Polo had "Indians" carry the yllapa "from house to house of the gentlemen who asked to see them." They were "wrapped in white sheets, and the Indians knelt in the streets and bowed with tears and groans as they passed. Many Spaniards took off their caps, since they were the bodies of Kings, and the Indians were more grateful than they could express for this attention."[69]

This was a display of dominance. The yllapa were carried by "Indians" rather than "Inca" heirs. Their "tears and groans" surpass translation. This was Cuzco's final reading and mourning of the most primary sources of Inca Empire before outsiders filed them away.

Yet it was also ambivalently respectful, if Garcilaso's memories can be trusted. Wrapped in white sheets. Bows permitted. Hats removed. Public and private farewells. Knowing that Garcilaso was headed to Spain to seek his father's family, Ondegardo even invited him into his home's inner chamber to "see some of your own whom I have brought to light; this way you will bring something to tell when you arrive." In that inner chamber Garcilaso reached out for the hand of the yllapa of his great-uncle Huayna Capac, who had been breathless for some three decades. Huayna Capac's finger remained "like that of a wooden statue, it was so hard and strong."[70]

If Huayna Capac was engaged as an yllapa after this collection, the Spaniards denied it. Instead, Ondegardo curated them in what scholars have called a "cabinet of curiosities" or even a "mummy museum," where Huayna Capac and his cohort were undone by their medical, historical, and religious autopsy as "embalmed" bodies.[71] These desecrations produced an "archaeology of the living"—a comparison of Indigenous sacralities to Old World pasts that made American peoples a matter of natural history, with the Incas at their head.[72] These paeans to Inca "embalming" made their other practices of life extension hard to see and fueled the bonfires of stricter religious rule.

These curations began with the corregidor himself. Ondegardo's account of each Sapa Inka's life ended with where he found his "body" and its relative preservation in flesh, plaster, or stone. He described those of Pachacutic and Huayna Capac as flatly "embalmed." The Jesuit Bernabé Cobo, who worked from Ondegardo's report, described the still-silver-haired Pachacutic as "completely preserved, as if he had died the same day"; Huayna Capac was so well "cured" that he "did not seem to be dead," wrote Cobo.[73]

How the Incas specifically achieved that effect became the subject of the next wave of Spanish research. The ancestors whom Ondegardo kept in his house—the five best preserved yllapa and the ashes of Viracocha—were carried down old Inca roads from Cuzco to the coast. Once in Lima, the yllapas were given to the Crown's utmost representative in Peru, viceroy Andrés Hurtado de Mendoza, who installed them in a hospital, which in this era in Europe was a place of physical and spiritual healing as well as a site of learning where cures were crafted, discussed, and demonstrated—what historian Paula Findlen likens to a "Museum of Medicine."[74] The Hospital of San Andrés, established in 1545 as the first European-led center of healing and natural learning in the Spanish capital, fit the bill.[75]

Once they entered the hospital, the yllapa were made to yield multiple lessons. One may have been their example as unbaptized, idolatrous souls. San Andrés's founder had preached to patients using a skull on a stick, an end-of-life encounter that encouraged the unbaptized to convert and save their souls. Who that skull specifically belonged to is unclear, but given Christianity's message of the damnation of the unconverted, it could well have come from one of the many Andean funerary monuments surrounding the city that were looted for treasure.[76] The Inca yllapas could have been employed in a similar manner.

There is more evidence that they taught wonder at the fact of their "embalming." According to the Jesuit José de Acosta, who arrived in Peru in 1572, "many Spaniards" viewed the "very embalmed" Incas in their medical purgatory. "It caused such admiration to see human bodies so many years old and with such a beautiful complexion and so intact."[77] This interest in the Inca dead was an aspect of Acosta's contribution to the development of comparative ethnology in the Americas, in which the idolization of the dead was a "barbaric" characteristic that revealed the Incas' religious and civilizational rank.[78] Yet the Jesuit was also a natural historian, and Spaniards' admiration for the material reality of the yllapa in the hospital prompted his speculation as to the knowledge behind Inca embalming's achievement.[79] Acosta examined them, and his *Historia natural y moral de las Indias* (1590) pondered how the Incas had harnessed Peruvian nature "to conserve the bodies of their Kings and Lords, which remained whole, with neither foul smell, nor corruption for more than two hundred years." Believing that the Incas' "great men" had access to considerable medical skills and unknown natural cures comparable to those of Old World ancients, Acosta proposed that Pachacutic Inca Yupanqui's body, for example, was "so well preserved, and adorned with a certain *betún* that it seemed alive." "Its eyes were a thin cloth of gold so well placed that Pachacutic had no need of natural ones. On his head a *pedrada,* received in a certain battle, was still visible. He was missing none of his gray hair. It was as if he had died that same day, and not sixty or eighty years before."[80]

The words *betún* and *pedrada* are worth lingering upon. The former reveals that Acosta was making a chain of informed associations. Betún may be translated as "resin," but the context of embalming suggests a substance with a more elevated history: "bitumen" or "asphalt," as one Spaniard glossed betún in 1615. In Arabic, bitumen was *mumiya*, the substance that the Egyptians used on their dead and that gave mummies their name.[81]

The *pedrada* may be even more consequential: the blow of a stone, a head wound that Pachacutic had received in battle. A large but successfully healed trepanation can leave what looks like a divot in the head. The scalp valleys over the crater made by the extraction of damaged skull.[82] Pachacutic's pedrada may have been evidence that he had been healed by an Inca surgeon. If so, this is trepanation's only trace in the colonial historical record. In Pachacuti's body, Acosta may have witnessed two life-extending methods of Andean curing. The Spaniard understood that which touched upon matters of death—embalming—but the surgical procedure may have defeated his own knowledge and expectations.

After all, he and his fellow Jesuits imagined themselves the knife-wielders. Since the fifteenth century, anatomists of Iberia and southern Europe had sharpened their skills by practicing upon foreign, criminal, and poor bodies.[83] In the late sixteenth century, the Catholic Church applied those skills to evaluating saints. Using eyewitness testimony, autopsy, and other scientific ways of knowing, the church dismissed proposed saints whose preservation could be credited to human intervention.[84] This seems to have been the case in the Andes as well, where the Counter-Reformation Church targeted the ancestral "idols" and "superstitions" supposedly tolerated by earlier missionaries.[85] Acosta noted that by 1590 the *embalsamados* were "ill-treated and worn out," which has led scholars to propose that rough handling and Lima's damp climate hastened the decay of Huayna Capac and his family.[86] Yet they, like Acosta, may have missed knowledge's mark. Decades later, praising how Inca embalming prevented both deterioration and odor, the Jesuit Bernabé Cobo wrote of a body "taken away from certain idolaters" whose "face was so full, with such a good color and complexion, that it did not appear to be dead." The reason why, Cobo explained, was the calabash rind beneath each cheek—"over which, as the flesh dried, the skin stayed tight, with a nice gloss."[87] The clearest way the Jesuits could have known this ancestor was preserved this way would have been to cut them open. In other words, by the seventeenth century, the display and extirpation of sacred Andean ancestry had become an "autoptic" project that may have disarticulated the bodies of the yllapas themselves.[88]

Colonial authorities were certainly capable of such measures after the 1560s, which culminated in a thorough deconstruction of Inca sovereignty. In 1561 Sayri Tupa, who had emerged from the independent kingdom of Vilcabamba to marry and settle in Yucay, suddenly died, and the Spanish became aware that his brothers, Titu Cusi and Tupa Amaru, remained at large. By the late 1560s, after a spate of Andean religious revivals, the ritual independence of Vilcabamba began to feel like a more existential threat to colonial Peru and its empire-making silver mines. King Philip II tasked a new viceroy, Francisco de Toledo, with drawing Manco Inca's line back to the fold. Toledo had other plans. After arriving in 1569 he reviewed the extant histories of the Incas and decided that Inca sovereignty it-self was the problem. Toledo interviewed more distant Inca nobles, as well as the Incas' most bitter former subjects. While admiring aspects of Inca rule, Toledo commissioned new histories and chronicles that claimed Manco's line was ille-gitimate and denigrated the Incas as tyrants whose rule was recent, shallow, and "God's punishment for the demonically-inspired religious practices of Andean peoples."[89]

This revisionist project addressed the Incas' history through their still-extant remains. Toledo's interviewees were asked about Inca mortuary practices, about supposed cannibalism and sacrifices that accompanied the death of emperors.[90] This was no antiquarian issue. Toledo claimed that he had hidden the bodies of Huayna Capac and his cohort within hospitals because the Incas were con-tinuing to "idolize" them.[91] More actively, Manco Inca's yllapa remained in Vilcabamba with his sons Titu Cusi—who had recently died and likely also be-came an yllapa—and Tupa Amaru, Vilcabamba's current heir. Also at large was the Punchao, the child-sized golden sun icon, which contained the hearts of past Inca rulers.

Toledo collected and disarticulated them all. In 1572 he ordered Vilcabamba's destruction. An expedition of Spaniards, Afro-Peruvians, and Andean soldiers invaded; captured Manco Inca's last surviving son, Tupa Amaru; and marched him to Cuzco in chains with the Punchao and Manco Inca's yllapa. In Cuzco's plaza, where the yllapas once paraded, Toledo decapitated Tupa Amaru and displayed his head as a warning to the thousands of mourning Incas in attend-ance. When he learned that the Incas' former subjects were venerating that head, Toledo had it buried with its body in the city's Dominican convent. Toledo was even more firm with Manco Inca's yllapa, burning him in Sacsayhuaman, the for-tress from which the Sapa Inka had besieged Cuzco in 1536.[92]

Finally, Toledo turned the Punchao into a museum piece, literally dissecting this sacred amalgam of Inca flesh and Andean metallurgy. In October 1572 he wrote to King Philip II to share what he had learned. He explained that the icon was already partly dismantled—that the soldiers who had participated in Vilcabamba's conquest had been paid with the gold plaque that had shimmered from behind the image. He described the body itself as "made of cast gold," and that "inside the body of the idol" was a box (*caxica*) containing a "heart of paste . . . now dust," made "from the hearts of the past Inca kings," which he

Fig. 2.3 The "collection" of Manco Inca's surviving son Tupa Amaru (left) and the Punchao containing the hearts of the former sapa inkas (right, in the soldier's hand) in 1572. The decapitation of Tupa Amaru, the collection and immolation of Manco Inca's yllapa, and the Punchao's disarticulation by Viceroy Francisco de Toledo were a dissection of the sacred embodiments of Inca rule. Felipe Guaman Poma de Ayala, *El Primer Nueva Corónica y Buen Gobierno,* ca. 1600–1615, 449 [451]. Royal Danish Library, GKS 2232 4°.

hoped Philip would see for himself. Toledo sent a number of specimens of Inca history and idolatry to Madrid—possibly including the Punchao—where they joined Philip's palace cabinet of "idols" and curiosities from Spain's increasingly global empire.[93]

It was not just the Incas, then, who took possession of their subjects' sacred ancestors. Philip was at that moment engaged in the collection of seventy-five hundred remains of Christian saints for the Escorial, his palace and eventual tomb outside Madrid.[94] The ancestral Inca forms in the Hospital of San Andrés and Philip's cabinet, however, were put to very different ends. These were the first European collections whose specific goal was the desecration of Indigenous human remains and their display as historical artifacts, asserting that these sacred Indigenous ancestors were lively no longer. They were now mute specimens, dissected and preserved—an empire in a cabinet.

Despite these enclosures, Inca ancestry survived, as did the former Andean subjects who rebundled it into new forms. In part, this was because Toledo was less interested in ending the Inca Empire than remaking it to support a royal, Christian, and Spanish rule that presumed Andean peoples could not govern themselves. Toledo's massive resettlement of Andean communities in new towns based on a supposedly Spanish model (reducción) functioned as some Inca settlements once had—as occasional spaces of interaction with the exploiting state, above which "old towns," with their plazas of ancestral encounter, could still be visited.[95] The health of Andean populations under this "reformed" colonial rule was worse than under the Incas, whose subjects worked hard but lived longer. But by arguing for their rights and plotting new marriages, Peru's Andean men and women led the viceroyalty's population to a late-seventeenth-century rebound.[96] Andean ancestries were also no longer exclusively located in an yllapa or mallqui; instead, Inca leaders and Andean community members sought notaries to transcribe oral genealogies and khipu records to paper. Communities maintained these hybrid archives through the nineteenth century and beyond, carrying them to viceroys in Lima to argue for reducing tribute obligations to the Crown or to challenge the demands of elite Spanish and Andean men. To support their claims of nobility, lords pointed to the good behavior of more recent ancestors, whose burials in churches and last wills and testaments kept material legacies in the family. Inca descendants even carried these archives to Spain to seek confirmation of their nobility.[97]

The cult of the dead also Andeanized Christianity. In Catholic festivals, Andean nobles and commoners dressed icons of Jesus, Mary, and the saints in Andean cloth, like the ancestors they once paraded. On the feast of St. James (Santiago)—who was associated with the thundering yllapa—the surviving Inca houses paraded in Inca tunics with sleeves of Spanish lace; their leader wore the maskaypacha, the Sapa Inka's royal fringe, while carrying the Crown's royal standard.[98] In early November, rural communities celebrated All Saints and All Souls' Days by bringing food and clothes to churches and cemeteries, where they fed and redressed the baptized and unbaptized dead as they had before.

More venerable ancestors were smuggled out of churches like Atahuallpa, to be interred in hidden tombs from which they could be accessed for veneration or care. Anthropologist Peter Gose has suggested that these moving bodies be seen as a sign of interculturation, whereby churches became more Andean, and the wider mortuary landscape became more Christian. Archaeologists have since found the dead interred with both Andean and Christian objects, in flexed Andean positions; in the 1890s, one ancestor was found bundled and interred with a papal bull.[99]

By the late sixteenth century, however, these transfers risked the ancestors' destruction. Toledo's dissections of sacred Inca rule had paved the way for active persecutions of non-imperial ancestors—a Counter-Reformation science of religious difference that asserted that Andean peoples were not just mistaken in their care for their dead, but actively idolatrous, requiring that dead's extirpation.[100] In the 1580s, the idolatry-hunting cleric Cristóbal de Albornoz gathered up 160 "yllapas, which are embalmed dead bodies of some of their past lords," in the plaza of Chinchero, north of Cuzco, and set them aflame.[101] Priest Bartolomé Álvarez subsequently called for "all the deceased in the countryside and fields to be burned."[102]

His call particularly resonated in the hearth of Spanish power. In 1599, Jesuits ventured outside Lima to dig up "many skeletons and bodies of Indians intact and dry taken from the ancient tombs." Back in their college, they used the bones and preserved bodies to stage "a dramatic presentation on the Last Judgment" and the Antichrist for the viceroy, so "to reenact more realistically the resurrection of the dead." The sight "astonished all who were present," the Jesuit Bernabé Cobo remembered.[103] Given that one of Judgment's most spectacular conclusions was the eternal damnation of idolaters, it seems likely that the Jesuits gave these unearthed Andean "gentiles" the same fiery end as Albornoz had.[104]

In the seventeenth century, the bonfires swept back into the countryside. Religious orders grew their knowledge of mortuary practices, learning regional names for the venerated dead—mallkis in the sierras, *munaos* on the northern coast—to assist their proselytizing. In 1609 secular clerics of the Archbishopric of Lima used these sorts of knowledges to take more permanent actions against the ancestral dead. To distract from parishioners' protests of his own corruptions, Francisco de Avila, the curate of San Damián in Huarochirí, presided over one of the first large roundups. In the plazas of concentrated settlements, ayllus brought the "dry and entire bodies of their ancestors," including those smuggled out of the church, "such that it seemed like the living and the dead were coming for judgment"—a reenactment of what the Jesuits staged in Lima. The clerics placed ancestors and fellow huacas (sacred things) on bonfires, smashed them to pieces, or, in Avila's case, carted these mummies "800 years old" back to Lima. There, thousands of Andean subjects watched as Avila directed "a giant auto-da-fé in Lima's great cathedral square," in which music, Quechua sermons, and the whipping and exile of the ancestors' adherents culminated in the mummies' inferno. By 1619 Peru's viceroy bragged that 1,365 ancestors had been burned.[105] Some Christian converts may have been complicit in these fires, taking them as a chance to assault the authority of old leaders or settle scores with rival communities.[106] But for those descendants who believed the ancestors were still present, it was a massacre.

The remains of Huayna Capac and his cohort—dissected or not—do not seem to have survived this era. The last credible glimpse dates to 1638, when an Augustinian friar named Antonio de la Calancha wrote that the bodies of Pachacutic Inca Yupanqui and his fellow Incas were "in a corral of the Hospital of San Andrés." Archaeologist Brian Bauer and historian Antonio Coello suggest they may have then "deteriorated to such an extent that they had lost any value as relics or curiosities," at which point they were interred somewhere in the hospital.[107] The Punchao, the golden sun icon containing the hearts of the Sapa Inkas, likewise disappeared. In 1598 Philip II died in the Escorial, and the cataloguing of his estate revealed that his cabinet of curiosities in Madrid's royal palace included various golden Inca icons. Whether they specifically included the Punchao is unclear, as Toledo had recommended that Philip send it to the pope and the original collection no longer exists. In 1734 the palace was consumed by fire, and anything that remained of this museum became slag.[108]

Like Atahuallpa's seizure, it is tempting to take these fires as signs of total conquest, the particularly burnt pages of a Black Legend of abusive Spanish rule that Northern Europeans would use to contest the legitimacy of Spanish American sovereignty.[109] Yet how these fires began, and what they could not destroy, matters. Colonial actors had gathered the yllapas and mallkis to defeat the Inca and Andean terms of sacred rule, but also to know them. In translating those terms into European modes—from yllapas to embalsamados—they sought to bury their cosmic powers and present them instead as ancient bodies, knowable in settings of healing and study. Yet in doing so, their imperial logic—by which all Inca ancestors were superior to those of their Indigenous subjects—transferred like camaquen, the charging, making, ancestral energy that could survive division, and could inhere in new forms.[110] As "embalmed" Inca bodies and gold-wrapped hearts became Peruvian soil and Spanish ash, the memory of their stolid bodies—Huayna Capac's finger resembling "that of a wooden statue, it was so hard and strong"—remained. Andean and European authors used that memory to mummify the Indigenous history of the wider Americas—and to measure their dead.

Mummifying Incas

Colonial Grave-Opening and the Racialization of Ancient Peru

In the year 1687, thirty pirates from the English privateer *Batchelors Delight* came ashore at Puerto Bermejo, where Peru's Huarmey River flowed into the Pacific Ocean. The buccaneers sought "sweet water," provisions, and if they were lucky, booty—silver from Potosí, mined by Native Andeans and minted by the Spanish viceroyalty into the specie that kept the world's economy spinning.[1]

Instead, they entered an empire of death. "We marched about four Miles up a Sandy Bay," wrote their Welsh surgeon, Lionel Wafer, "all which we found covered with the Bodies of Men, Women and Children; which lay so thick, that a Man might, if he would, have walked half a Mile, and never trod a Step off a dead human Body." The bodies, once buried, were disinterred, still clutching their possessions. The men had "broken Bows," Wafer believed, and the women had "Spinning-wheels, and Distaffs with Cotton-yarn upon them."[2]

Wafer was no stranger to the uncanny. As a castaway in Panama, he had survived by impressing Kuna shamans with his own surgical skills.[3] He now investigated the Peruvian afterlife. He hefted the bodies, felt their skin, touched their tools. He took their measure. "These Bodies to appearance, seem'd as if they had not been above a Week dead," he told his later readers, "but if you handled them, they proved as dry and light as a Spunge or piece of Cork."

Who were these people? How had they died? Why were they exposed? Wafer walked on, looking for someone to narrate the lives of those he had held in his hands. "After we had been some time ashore, we espyed a Smoak," he told later readers. In the distance, "an old Man, a *Spanish Indian*" fisherman stood working, "ranging along the Sea-side, to find some Sea-weeds to dress some Fish which his Company had caught; for he belong'd to a Fishing-boat hard by." Curious, Wafer walked in the fisherman's direction.

Empires of the Dead. Christopher Heaney, Oxford University Press. © Oxford University Press 2023.
DOI: 10.1093/oso/9780197542552.003.0004

This chapter meditates on the implications of the old man's answer. It follows the ripples of the Spanish-led looting, collection, and extirpation of the preserved Inca and Andean ancestors into three intellectual traditions that shaped the disinterment of the Indigenous dead in the Americas in centuries to come. The first knew the non-Christian dead as important past actors, significant less for their potential ancestral relationship than for the history their preservation maintained: a superior Inca past killed and disinterred by colonialism. Ironically, grave-opening and tomb-raiding, huaqueo, extended and transformed that power. For some Peruvians—Andean, Spanish, Afro-Peruvian—the human remains of the "Inca" and "gentile" dead even became tools of curing and harm.[4] What Spain's inherited mortuary empire yielded in Peru, then, was an everyday culture of encountering, valuing, using, abusing, and healing with the non-Christian dead and their possessions that, by the late eighteenth century, sometimes supported more transportable knowledges.[5]

The second tradition was that of outsiders like Wafer, who by the eighteenth century traveled to Peru expecting to find a preserved and "civilized" Indigenous American dead. This was because of published descriptions of Inca "embalming," which in the seventeenth century spread throughout the Atlantic world via translations of Jesuit José de Acosta and Peruvian chronicler Garcilaso de la Vega el Inca. Not all European readers believed these claims, but their discussion yielded an important outcome in the wider history of knowledge: the claim that embalmed Incas were in fact "mummies" like those of Egypt and the Near East. As such, "Inca mummies" became a New World anatomical tradition lost during the Spanish conquest, whose material absence allowed even grander claims of Inca civilization to be debated. By the mid-eighteenth century, some Europeans celebrated the Incas as Indigenous Americans at their most elite and complex— much as Inca heirs might have wanted—while others denigrated them.[6]

New material evidence for that debate came from the third intellectual tradition resulting from the Inca and Andean ancestors' exposure: a more elite Peruvian and Spanish American use of the dead to test prior claims for their identity, preservation, and civilization.[7] By the mid-seventeenth century those practices invented the "ancient Peruvian" as a subject of study. Three questions were asked of their remains: whether their material possessions showed greater or lesser development than that which had been claimed for the Incas; who was responsible for the death; and whether their skeletal remains were identical to those of the Indigenous present—a question that in the eighteenth century yielded the first European measurements of the racialized skulls of the American dead. Further, these questions took Inca and "ancient Peruvian" embalming as a "science" that Spanish American colonial elites claimed for themselves.[8]

The constellation of these mentalities, and the new questions they asked of varied material, textual, and embodied sources, reveal the "Peruvian" contexts of what became anthropology, archaeology, and its museums. There are many origins for those fields: sixteenth-century Roman antiquarianism, eighteenth-century Spanish American re-encounters with Aztec and Maya writing and sculptures, and nineteenth-century nationalism and professionalization.[9] Yet in Peru their global, colonial, and national hierarchies of power, knowledge, and practice arrived almost fully formed. Future chapters show how these mentalities shaped wider nineteenth-century Americanist anthropology after Peruvian independence. This chapter accounts for the bodies that these new knowledges weighed, stepped on, and drowned along the way.

Wafer waylaid the old man, the "*Spanish* Indian" searching for seaweed to dress his fish, and proceeded to ask him "many Questions, in *Spanish,* about the Place, and how those dead Bodies came there."[10]

An archaeologist would have shrugged. The once-green drainage of the Huarmey River was where many productive environments met: agricultural valleys and the fertile Callejón de Huaylas basin to the north; further coastal valleys and the highland lakes and *puna* (grass and shrublands) of highland Junín to the south; and west, out to sea, the continental shelf whose plentiful marine life this fisherman knew by heart. These resources made Huarmey a crossroads of many Andean pasts. Human presence has been dated to 2850 BCE, but is likely significantly older. There were links to the Norte Chico or Caral-Supe culture, sometimes called the Americas' oldest civilization, as well as to the wealthy Chimú lords who fought and married the Incas before Spain invaded. Archaeologists have found in these sands hundreds of individuals killed by Chimú soldiers or priests. That the bodies Wafer weighed were gripping possessions suggests more intentional burials—perhaps plantings of clan members beside the life-giving ocean—but they could have belonged to any number of cultures, dying in any number of ways.[11]

The "*Spanish* Indian," though, had a more pointed answer. Wafer recorded it without editorialization: "That in his Fathers time," the fisherman said,

> the Soil there, which now yielded nothing, was green, well culti-
> vated and fruitful: that the City of Wormia [Huarmey] had been well
> inhabited with *Indians*: And that they were so numerous, that they
> could have handed a Fish, from Hand to Hand, 20 Leagues from the
> Sea, until it come to the Kings or *Ynca's* Hand: That the River was very

deep, and the Current strong: and that the reason of those dead Bodies was, That when the *Spaniards* came, and block'd and lay'd Siege to the City, the *Indians,* rather than lie at the *Spaniards* Mercy, dug Holes in the Sand, and buried themselves alive.

In other words, Huarmey's once-populous "Indians" had been urbane cultivators and Inca subjects. They killed themselves rather than submit to Spain, and afterward the land became barren. Huarmey's sands were thus a testament to the inferiority of the colonial present, and the exposed dead around them were precisely those "Indians" whose self-sacrifice served as a reminder of the injustice of Spanish rule.

The fisherman's tale is perhaps the earliest recorded instance of a narrative later observed throughout the Andes: that the preserved and numerous dead whom archaeologists could assign a range of pre-Hispanic cultures, some millennia old, were all "Indians" or Incas alive either just before, during, or after the conquest, whose deaths revealed Spanish violence or misrule. The English paid attention to this narrative, given how well it fit with the larger Black Legend of their imperial Spanish rivals. A few years before Wafer, a fellow English buccaneer named Waggoner described the nearby remains of an "old decayed Indian fort . . . of Linga" as a place "where the Spaniards have Massacred thousands of the Poor natives as by some Sculls seen there to this day."[12] By the early eighteenth century, some one thousand miles to the south, tales of self-sacrifice in the face of Spanish invasion were being told of cemeteries surrounding the port city of Arica, whose sands later revealed the world's oldest mummies.[13] And today, in Huarochirí, near Lima, some villagers take open tombs and the remains they contain as evidence of the "Indians" who committed suicide to protest Spanish taxes and secure the rights of the present community.[14]

Rather than taking these explanations as archaeologically "wrong," it is more productive to consider how they were right. From the eighteenth century to the present, grave-openers in Peru have been periodically confronted by the fact that Andean tombs presumed to be precolonial can turn out to contain artifacts of Spanish or Christian origin. Archaeologists confirm that Andean peoples did not cease their long-held funerary practices at the first flush of colonialism. By marrying and adapting and resettling, they developed new ways to make sense of the mass death of the sixteenth century, in which virgin soil epidemics of Old World diseases like smallpox laid waste to communities and left behind interments both colonial and Andean.[15] For that reason, there is little reason to dismiss out of hand the claim that the bodies surrounding the Huarmey fisherman died in the decades surrounding the Spanish invasion.

The fisherman's emphasis on the dead having committed suicide was also an everyday archaeology with a political purpose. It complicated church doctrines that since the 1570s had declared non-Christian ancestors populating the coun-tryside to be "sinners," "burning in Hell," whose past veneration marked them for extirpation.[16] Instead, the fisherman interpreted the millennia of Indigenous cemeteries and tombs as evidence for a belief that historian Alberto Flores Galindo called the "Andean Utopia" of fertile and just Inca rule: an idealized kingdom that had supported many more than under the Spanish. Huarmey's many bodily remains represented that fertility, but also the political ability to defy, via suicide, the cataclysm of colonial violence, disease, or more "natural" causes of death.[17]

The exposed dead also indicated the everyday violence of colonial rule. Since Gonzalo Pizarro burned Viracocha's sacred mummy (yllapa) for its treasure in the 1530s, the mining of huacas (tombs and sacred structures) had become a bureaucratized industry, huaqueo, that also served the religious purpose of undoing the supposedly diabolic commitment of wealth to the "gentile" dead. Digging up their gold and silver recirculated it among the living, and the Crown took a share, theoretically, to help the looted dead's "Indian" descendants. In practice, this was a historic transfer of centuries of wealth, particularly on the northern coast, where Spaniards formed legal partnerships to loot rich tombs of the Moché and Chimú elite. Cities like Trujillo were founded near pre-Hispanic mortuary palaces, and as colonial buildings went up, platform tombs were sliced into for their riches.[18] Andean peoples easily saw through claims that this was for their own religious good; chronicler and artist Felipe Guaman Poma de Ayala, for example, suspected that the highland extirpators of the ancestors were also motivated by "the theft of precious objects belonging to huaca cults."[19] By the 1680s, a century and a half of this legalized grave-robbing left a landscape punctuated by looted elite tombs and more everyday graves, whose disinterred, dried, and fragmented bodies clutched what couldn't be melted down—"broken bows," "Spinning-wheels, and Distaffs" like those Wafer encountered at Huarmey.

The words the fisherman used to describe this dead hints at how grave-opening made new colonial identities. In Wafer's telling, the dead were local "Indians" who had killed themselves rather than be ruled by the Spanish. Yet if the Indians had all died, then who was the fisherman? Wafer deemed him a "Spanish Indian," which suggests the Welshman's perception of his descent and acculturation. But this may not have been how the fisherman understood him-self. When he described the local Indians as all having died, this implied that he may not have seen the dead surrounding him as ancestral. This nuance seems to fly in the face of the modern perception—a politically important one—that living Indigenous peoples are descended from the historic remains surrounding them. It instead underlines how some Andean peoples found political power or escape in describing the surrounding dead as antecessors but not necessarily ancestors—a crucial distinction that refused their racialization as "Indians" descended from a "gentile" dead looted for centuries.[20]

It is also possible that the fisherman, or his Christian ancestors, participated in that dead's looting. In the sixteenth century, Inca and Andean subjects had addressed threats to their bodily integrity by interring themselves in churches, while keeping the pre-Christian dead on the move.[21] Yet the pressure to reveal those wealthy ancestors yielded a surprising compromise, particularly on the coast. Rather than see Spaniards profit from their ancestors' wealth, some Andean lords argued that ancestral interments were theirs to mine, as loyal Christian heirs. Starting in the late 1550s, Andean lords registered huacas with colonial authorities, put their subjects to work looting them, gave the Crown its share, and kept the rest for their own now-inheritable estates.[22] In doing so, the lords tried to wrest back control. By bringing their ancestors' underground economy into circulation, they could also perform as good Christian lords.[23]

This looting also gave Andean grave-openers greater access to the bodies of these lords' sacred ancestors. Spanish authorities feared this possibility—that enlisting "Indians" in huaqueo, in addition to seeming unkind, extended their intimacy with the dead. Viceroys and the church thus periodically tried to prevent native Andeans from being employed in grave-opening, ordering the merciful re-interment of nonidolized "gentiles" to limit temptation.[24] Peruvians of Andean descent continued to participate, however, for which historians propose two explanations beyond straight coercion. One, as explored by Susan Ramírez and Rocio Delibes Mateos, is that grave-opening became a form of covert resistance: after reporting precious metals to the bureaucrats, a community could re-inter venerable human remains by night.[25] The second recognizes that the wealthiest dead were themselves elites and that their looting degraded the authority of their noble descendants, whose community then demanded a share of their "ancient" wealth. One Indigenous community sued their *curaca*, their lord, when he failed to share the proceeds of looting "his" ancestors' huaca; they won the lawsuit, and his family's previously "sacred" wealth was applied to freeing the wider community from the constraints of paying tribute.[26]

To put it another way: not all dead are ancestors, especially within Andean communities whose internal differences and hierarchies had been accentuated by Inca and Spanish imperial rule. Dispossessing the previously sacred elite dead—whose descendants benefited from Inca and Spanish demands for their subjects' "Indian" labor—was an act of broader Andean transformation, even resistance. It turned "ancient" leaders' minelike huacas into a shared resource. Even in the highlands, where interments were not nearly so rich, the decision of some seventeenth-century communities to turn mummified "gentiles" over to extirpators may have been a way of retiring older, elite models of hierarchical ancestor mummies in favor of mountain ancestors whom everyone shared.[27] Andean communities that revolted against colonial rule in the eighteenth century were the heirs to these decisions—radically nonhierarchical Christian communes, whose authority lay in their present commitments, and not the racialized remains the Spanish had abused.[28]

Yet another unintended consequence of colonial grave-robbing was that it let the dead build intimacies with a wider range of actors. Belief in Andean ancestors' damnation was not universal, even among non-Andean Peruvians. In 1572 a Limeña named Ysabel de Porras told friends that "before the Spaniards came to these lands, the Indians who died went to Heaven." In 1579 a priest in Alto Peru—present-day Bolivia—said masses blessing "Inca Indians, their dead, infidel ancestors."[29] By the seventeenth century, some men and women of Andean, Spanish, and African descent even propitiated formerly ancestral remains. They left offerings at huacas to ask permission to collect sacks of bones and objects, whose "gentile" power infused the "hybrid medicine" of their curing and conjuring rituals.[30] In 1699 the Inquisition accused an "Indian" hatmaker in Lima and his wife, Francisca Violanda, of offering coca leaves to a skull in a pot in the corner of their corral. Violanda blamed this "superstition" on a Franciscan brother who had given the skull to Indian draft laborers who slept in the house on Saturdays.[31]

Who did these surreptitious curators of the dead and their objects believe that they were conjuring or propitiating? In some highland places, like Huarochirí, Arequipa, Cajatambo, and Andagua, they remembered or re-encountered the dead as the progenitors of locally sacred lineages and continued soliciting them through the eighteenth century and beyond.[32] But in creolized zones they were said to be antecessors even more epic than the "Indians" of Huarmey: "Inca" skulls and bones, a means of calling upon the "rei gentil" or gentile king, the "rei Indio" or "Indian king," and, dramatically, the "Inca rey" or *Inkarrí*—the fisherman's Ynca King.[33]

That the anonymous dead could become Incas was by no means obvious. The Inca royalty's yllapas had been lost in the Hospital of San Andrés, and in the years immediately after the Spanish invasion, the Incas' former subjects could not have been counted on to memorialize their imperial rule. But time had softened their memory and magnified their non-Christian power. The Incas' most imperial cosmology, that they were sacred "ancestors" of all humanity, became a subversive genealogy—a locally accessible anticolonial identity. Even the Incas' fiercest enemies, the Cañari, came to believe that, when Spain invaded, *Anticristo* (Antichrist) tricked their own now-Inca ancestors into burying themselves with their gold treasures. The anthropologist Frank Salomon suggests that this turning of Incas from enemies to ancestors recognizable in the dead may have been produced by colonial assaults on ancestral burials, creating "a new common condition for Inca and non-Inca peoples alike, that of descendants of destroyed persons."[34]

Grave-opening also made it possible to claim that these broadly ancestral Incas were not quite destroyed—that their skulls were like seeds. By the early seventeenth century, the memory of Atahualpa's strangling in 1533 had been mingled with Tupa Amaru's 1572 decapitation such that both were said—by chronicler Guaman Poma, for example—to have lost their heads to the Spanish. From this commingling grew a belief that the Spanish still possessed the *Inkarri*'s head, which was regrowing a body that when resurrected, Christlike, would herald a new Inca dawn.[35] The politics of knowing this absent "Inca" dead were powerful. In 1742 a Jesuit-educated Indian or *mestizo* (a person of Indigenous and European descent) calling himself Juan Santos Atahuallpa Apu-Inca Huayna Capac launched an uprising that expelled colonial authorities from a patch of the Central Andes. Among his goals, bureaucrats learned, was to "recuperate the crown that Pizarro and the other Spaniards took from him, killing his father (that is what he called the Inca) and sending his head to Spain."[36]

Literally speaking, the heads of Atahuallpa, Huayna Capac, and Tupa Amaru had not gone to Spain. And the mummified bodies surrounding the fisherman at Huarmey were almost certainly not "Indian" suicides. Yet what their exposure and even looting made possible was an everyday intellectual tradition that regarded that dead as possessing radical—rootlike—power. Colonial rule had indeed looted, decapitated, dissected, and dispersed the bodies and hearts of the Inca emperors, and tomb-raiding's bureaucratization made legal what would have struck the first generation of Andean peoples as horrific. Yet the visible landscape of looted skulls and scattered mummified bodies became a way of remembering that past. When historian J. H. Elliott tweaked Marx and Engels to suggest that the "most effective grave-diggers of empire are usually the imperialists themselves," he wasn't being quite so literal.[37] But the Huarmey fisherman's tale suggested that grave-opening's wages went beyond the gold or silver that circulated out to the world; it included the dead whose thirsty roots could be watered by memories of better pasts to grow new futures.

Whether Wafer credited every word of the Huarmey fisherman's explanation mattered less than what he did next, which the buccaneer surgeon related in *A New Voyage and Description of the Isthmus of America, Giving an Account of the Author's Abode there* (1609). On the way back to his ship, Wafer picked up the dry corpse of "a Boy of about 9 or 10 Years of Age." He was "intent to bring him home for *England*." Once there, the preserved boy might help prove Wafer's credibility as an observer of historical and natural reality.[38]

More specifically, the boy's arrival might provide evidence for a dialogue that had developed about whether the Incas had "embalmed" the dead that the sixteenth-century Spaniards displayed in Lima's Hospital of San Andrés. This conversation hinged on the study and translation of Peruvian texts, but also the important question of whether esoteric knowledges might be found in the Americas. European readers debated claims for superior Inca "embalming," given that they implied that the Inca dead were comparable to the mummies of Egypt. This debate continued into the eighteenth century, when comparisons between Incas and Egyptians led to the invention of "Inca mummies"—a recognition of Inca skill but one that made them "ancient" and even more subject to European hierarchies of past and present.

This conversation began with the Spanish invasion. The conquistadors' early report of Huayna Capac and his consort as "two Indians in the manner of embalmed dead" was rapidly translated after its initial publication in Seville in 1534.[39] In the 1550s Venetian cosmographer Giambattista Ramusio included it in his widely read *Navigationi et Viaggi* with Pizarro's secretary's account of Manco Inca's 1534 investiture, when the Inca yllapa and wawqi paraded and Huayna Capac was so whole he "only lacks the tip of his nose."[40] Subsequent chroniclers revealed still more. Pedro Cieza de León (1553) reported that Peruvians preserved their dead en masse in mountain crypts.[41] There were those Peruvians described by Agustín de Zárate (1555), who distilled a "liquor" from a sweet-smelling wood and "if one covers a dead body with it and pours it down that body's throat, never will it corrupt."[42] The most widely read early chronicler of all, Francisco López de Gómara (1554), never visited Peru but popularized the idea that not only did Incas believe in the "resurrection of bodies and the immortality of the soul"—their embalming cast as proto-Christian—but also that in the sierras the dead "are conserved for an infinite time by the cold, and in that way there is much *carne momia*"—mummified flesh.[43]

López de Gómara did not necessarily mean that Peru's dead were "mummies"—a term that only in the sixteenth century came to refer to an Egyptian dead believed embalmed with mumiya, bitumen.[44] Through the seventeenth century *momia* in Spanish also referred more minutely to desiccated flesh.[45] But López de Gómara's extension of mummification's languages beyond the Old World lent itself to embellishment, especially as these early chronicles were translated, muddled, and used to elevate the Incas over other New World peoples. In 1570 French cosmographer François de Belleforest suggested in his *L'Histoire Universelle du Monde* that Peru's "civil enough people" honored their dead in ways that supposed cannibals elsewhere in the New World did not. Mixing Zárate, López de Gómara, and Cieza, Belleforest claimed that Peruvian kings were "embalmed" by a liquor poured down their throats; by their anointing with certain "gums that could be more precious than those of Aloe, or the Myrrh of the Levant"; and by "guarding these bodies within the mountains, because of the cold, which causes the druggists to find an abundance of *bonne Mómie*" throughout the country.[46]

Belleforest's Peruvian "mummy" was no longer merely preserved flesh. "Good *Mómie*" now referred to *mumia secondaria*, the ground-up flesh of the Egyptian and Near Eastern dead that Europeans sought, bought, and sometime swallowed as a powerful materia medica, hoping that it retained the life-extending properties of the original *mumiya*.[47] In this way, Belleforest proceeded from the medical fact of the Spanish conquest—which had yielded new balsams and curing substances—to project a vision of Spanish druggists traveling the Andes, seeking gums "more precious" than those of the Old World, and collecting and grinding up embalmed Peruvians.

There is no evidence that Spaniards used dried Andean flesh in this manner. (Conquistadors in Mexico had used dead Mexicas' fat as a salve for their wounds, but eating Incas—or at least writing about it—may have been a step too far.[48]) "Mumia" was in the cabinets of early-seventeenth-century Peruvian physicians, but its discussion points to Old World origins.[49] Yet from faraway Europe, it was not so wild a speculation, and Belleforest's innovation inspired grander claims. In 1581 French jurist Claude Guichard's *Funérailles*, a Herodotean categorization of Old and New World funerary habits, borrowed from Belleforest to claim that the embalming Peruvians produced both "mummy" and the most "sumptuous tombs & sepulchers" in the world.[50]

This elevation of Inca funerary practices to heights implicitly above those of ancient Egyptians led to the first contemplation—and rejection—of the possibility that the Peruvians made "mummies" too. Mid-sixteenth-century French cosmographer André Thevet had sought to educate fellow learned Europeans on the distinctions between *mumiya* and *mumia*.[51] In 1584 Thevet—who had traveled to Egypt, swallowed its dead as a drug, and described them in a prior tome—used his nine-volume magnum opus, *Les vrais pourtraits et vies des hommes illustres*, to dispute Guichard. A devout Catholic who defended Spanish efforts in the Americas, Thevet dismissed claims of elite Inca mortuary practices as "a manifestly Pantegruelian tale": Guichard was deluded in believing that Spanish druggists had found "a magazine of *Momies*"—mummies, plural. Thevet called upon Guichard "to ask merchants who deal at the Lyon merchant-fairs to enquire whether any of these good Mummies"—those of Peru—"are found by these drug peddlers in these parts and in that case (otherwise I presume that, had he known, he would never have dared publish such a lie) he will learn that there is no trace."[52]

Thevet was therefore the first European to ask whether the Incas "mummified" their dead, but he did so to scorn the possibility. His Atahuallpa was a cannibal-descended tyrant, too savage to have done so. But it was also a matter of evidence.

Fig. 3.1 French cosmographer André Thevet's example of Egyptian mummies—possibly the earliest engraved by Europeans. André Thevet, *Cosmographie de Levant . . . Revue et augmentée de plusieurs figures* (Lyon: Jean Tournes et Guil. Gazeau, 1554), 155. Gordon 1554 .T54. Special Collections, University of Virginia, Charlottesville, VA.

Mummies were things of ancient sophistication from Egypt and the Near East, validated by the medical market. If the Incas were such good embalmers, Thevet sneered, then where was the proof of their work? The Americas' only embalming was metaphorical—that of Pizarro, who put Atahuallpa in chains, by whose efforts "Europe and all the rest of the world are embalmed with the exhalation of heroism, engendered from so many, and happy, conquests."[53]

Thevet's dismissal of Inca embalming aged poorly because Spanish Jesuits like José de Acosta were, at that very moment, investigating the yllapas of Huayna Capac and his cohort. Europeans received news of these New World displays and investigation of "embalmed" Incas in the Hospital of San Andrés alongside the relatively intact Old World mummies only recently arriving to European cabinets of curiosity—a project of knowing human history that culminated in Christianity, but was open to lost knowledges and histories of the "ancients," however idolatrous.[54] Readers did not overlook, for example, that in his *Historia natural y moral de las Incas* (1590), Acosta had marveled at how the Incas had "embalmed" Pachacutic Inca Yupanqui so that he was "so well preserved, and adorned with a certain betún that it seemed alive."[55] Because Acosta's *Historia* was an early European bestseller—fourteen editions were published in six languages—it is possible to trace the reception of his claims for Inca embalming by sampling their translation.[56] In 1614, for example, English cosmographer Samuel Purchas rendered the Jesuit's Incas as having been "preserv[ed]," not embalmed—their more notable mortuary characteristics being their wealth and idolatry.[57]

What later made Acosta's work more credible was his validation by writers of Inca and Andean descent, whose Christian, "Peruvian" testimony argued that

Inca attainments like embalming were even greater than the Jesuit suggested. Whether that made them civilized was the question. Debate in part hinged on whether embalming implied belief in an immortal soul, or a desire to induce idolatry among the living.

Some non-Inca Andeans weighed in on the side of idolatry. Though not widely read in its day, the Indigenous chronicler Felipe Guaman Poma de Ayala's *El primer nveva corónica I bven gobierno* (1616) was a 1,189-page manuscript that distinguished the "ages of the Indians" in part via their mortuary practices. In the "first age," the "Indians" gave their dead "common" and simple interments. In the "fourth age," immediately prior to the Incas, they began to inter their principal dead "very honorably in vaults." In both cases, their interments were with neither "ceremony" nor "idolatry." This was a good thing, in Guaman Poma's eyes; it marked their mortuary rites as closer to the knowledge of God and Christianity than the sacrificing rites that Guaman Poma blamed the Incas for introducing.[58]

Guaman Poma's whole chapter on the various mortuary practices of Peru's peoples under the Incas made clear embalming's accomplishment, but also its danger. All other dead were *aia*, corpses, and Tawantinsuyo's four parts each had their ways of dispatching them, from anthropagy in Antisuyo to preservation with balsams in Kuntisuyo. The interments of Chinchaysuyo, whose lord had been Guaman Poma's grandfather, honored the dead with elaborate ceremonies, but without engaging in the Inca embalming that Guaman Poma framed as inducing idolatry.[59] Only the Incas were "interred and . . . embalmed without disturbing the body," becoming "yllapa," their "eyes and face arranged as if he were still alive," and encouraging their now-idolatrous service. The women and servants who accompanied an Inca were likewise embalmed, and in Guaman Poma's drawings the perfect yllapa—such as the "embalmed" Huayna Capac and his wife, being carried to Cuzco—look as if they were only asleep.[60] In this way, Guaman Poma registered Inca embalming's accomplishment but also its idolatry, given that he was implying that the Incas appropriated the godhood (that of Yllapa) that pious Indians supposedly knew as a three-in-one deity before the Inca conquest.[61]

Guaman Poma's chronicle was not widely read—in the 1660s the Spanish Crown sent his manuscript to Copenhagen, where it was discovered in 1908— but its perfectly preserved Inca kings toured Europe by other means.[62] The most widely read Peruvian chronicler was Garcilaso de la Vega Inca—the young man who had left Cuzco for Spain after touching the hand of the yllapa of his great-uncle Huayna Capac. One of the more powerful chapters of Garcilaso's *Primera parte de los comentarios reales* (1609) recalled the death of the emperor Viracocha, in which Garcilaso embedded his memory of Huayna Capac's hand—a testament to Peru's lost Native kings.[63] But Garcilaso specifically asked how and why Huayna Capac's hand was "like that of a wooden statue, it was so hard and strong."[64] He distinguished between types of Andean preservation, accusing the "terrible and cruel" Mexicans of bringing to Peru the idolatry of drying the "bones and sinews" of the dead "in the sun, setting them atop hills," and offering them sacrifices. Garcilaso's Incas, however, were proto-Christian sun worshippers, whose embalming represented an encouraging belief that the soul's resurrection required bodily incorruption.[65]

Garcilaso's discussion of that embalming would be debated for centuries. Garcilaso argued that Acosta would have been even more impressed had he seen the Inca dead before they left dry Cuzco for humid Lima. He admitted to not having noticed the bitumen that the Jesuit credited, but this was only evidence of the Incas' virtuosity. For "bodies dead for so many years, to be so entire and full of flesh, would not have been possible without some treatment: but it was so subtly done that it could not be discovered." Garcilaso therefore proposed that their bodies were taken up above the snow line until their flesh dried, much as Andeans dried meat to make *charqui* (jerky). It was only then that the dead were treated with Acosta's bitumen, so that the bodies were left "as whole as if they were alive, hearty, and hale, lacking only the power of speech." But he admitted this was speculation. He regretted his "carelessness, that I did not examine them further, because I wasn't thinking to write of them, for if I had, I would have looked for how they were so entire, to discover how and with what they were embalmed, because . . . they would not have denied me, as they have denied the Spaniards." He feared he would never learn the truth. "It has been impossible to get it out of the Indians; this must be because the tradition is now lost."[66]

Their paper selves, at least, were celebrated by Garcilaso's prose, whose translation shaped European perceptions of Peru more than any other text. English cosmographer Samuel Purchas, who had once edited Acosta's work to read that the Incas were "preserved" rather than "embalmed," now excerpted Garcilaso in *Hakluytus Posthumus, or Purchas, his Pilgrimes* (1625) so "that thou mightst heard a Peruan speake of Peru." Purchas reproduced Garcilaso's claim that Incas believed in universal resurrection, that their immortal "soules should raise all that belonged to their bodies forth of the gra[v]es." Their "*embalming* arte" now rendered the dead "Kings" and "Queenes" so perfect "that they seemed ali[v]e."[67]

The years separating Garcilaso and his translators made Inca embalming seem ever more "ancient," demanding comparison with Egypt. Jean Baudouin's 1633 translation of Garcilaso into French was hugely successful; its meditation on the dead as *embaumé* with *bithume* went through at least twelve editions before 1745.[68] When Sir Paul Rycaut translated the entire *Commentarios reales* into English in 1688, he set the embalmed Incas' perfection in even starker relief. In the large-run, handsomely illustrated publication of *The Royal Commentaries of Peru in Two Parts*, Rycaut expanded on Garcilaso's speculations about Inca embalming with "bituminous matter"—"so firm and plump, that they seemed to be living Flesh"—by putting words in Garcilaso's mouth. "And what is more strange," interpolated Rycaut, "these Bodies were more entire than the *Mummies*, wanting neither Hair on the Head, nor Eye-brows, and even the very Eye-lashes were visible."[69]

Like Belleforest, Rycaut was not saying the embalmed Incas were mummies. "*The* mummies" remained from Egypt and the Near East. But to claim that the Incas were "more entire" was notable. The past century had seen Egyptian's dead become highly desired for European cabinets of curiosities. Yet demand for medical *mumia* meant it remained more profitable to grind up the dead, whom sailors and ship captains resisted transporting whole, believing that they could curse a ship.[70] But as European natural scientists explored ways to halt time in their own anatomical collections, they celebrated Egyptian mummies even more, as specimens of both "'naturalia' and 'artifcialia,' God-formed and man-made." In collections from Wroclaw to Leiden, scholars took them as nonidolatrous biblical ancients, whose preservation of the bodies of their "Fore-Fathers" suggested a worthy belief in an immortal soul.[71] To therefore render the Inca dead as better than mummies—which Rycaut's publishers underlined by repurposing a 1596 plate by Theodor de Bry, in which an Inca's perfect body was interred—contested histories of knowledge and antiquity limited to the Old World.[72]

Rycaut's radical proposal was only halfheartedly embraced. Like Mexican "hieroglyphs" that were compared to those of China and Egypt without ceding the latter's supposed sophistication, the South American dead joined a hierarchy in which the Egyptian dead came out on top. This was in part because Egyptian bodies, like their "written" wrappings, could be circulated and examined in ways that the Incas specifically could not.[73] In 1674 a description of the contents of one European royal's curiosity cabinet depicted what was supposed to be a desiccated South American body alongside an Egyptian funerary package. Only the Egyptian was labeled a "mumia."[74] In 1739 an English universal historian included Rycaut's interpolation of the Inca dead as "more entire than the *Mummies*" but averred that he did "not design to impose these things on any readers as articles of faith."[75] Debate over Garcilaso's credibility flourished in the eighteenth century, when many "Enlightened" Northern Europeans doubted that civilization existed anywhere but Europe.[76]

That doubt meant that when French scholars used Garcilaso to expand the category of "mummy," they did so in a way that denied the embalmed Incas any great advantage. In the 1749 volume of the *Histoire Naturelle, Générale et Particuliére*, naturalist and comparative anatomist Louis Jean-Marie Daubenton devoted an essay to "Momies" that, for the first time in European thought, deemed any artificially preserved bodies of great age to be "mummies." The

Fig. 3.2 This 1596 image depicted the material "Magnificence" with which "Princes" and their "Subordinates" were interred with treasure in Peru, and the comfort it gave to "Satan." But its repurposing by the publishers of English translator Paul Rycaut's rendition of Garcilaso de la Vega's *The Royal Commentaries of Peru in Two Parts* in 1688, on the plate facing 193, flipped the image both on its y-axis (typical in the reproduction of engravings) and in terms of its meaning. In a text that Rycaut had burnished to read that the "embalmed" Inca were "more entire than the Mummies," the seeming preservation of the body became a statement of worthy ancient knowledge rather than idolatry. Theodor de Bry, *Ad. Cap. XXII. Principum & Satraparum Indiæ Occidentalis sepulturæ*, from Girolamo Benzoni and Nicolas Challeux, *Americae pars sexta, sive historiae ab Hieronymo B[en]zono Mediolanense scriptae, section tertia*, ed. de Bry (Frankfurt, 1596). Library of Congress, Rare Book and Special Collections Division, The Hans P. Kraus Collection of Sir Francis Drake.

essay's prompt was an Egyptian finger in the Natural History collection attached to the French king's botanical garden, but Daubenton included two non-Egyptian textual examples: the dried bodies of the Guanche of the Canary Islands, observed since the sixteenth century and sparsely collected since the seventeenth, and the embalmed Inca, whom Daubenton knew entirely from a 1744 translation of Garcilaso's 1609 reflection upon Acosta's 1590 description of the yllapa.[77]

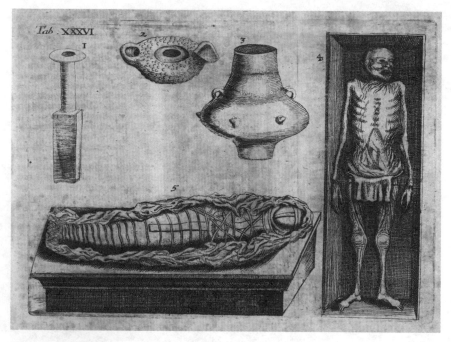

Fig. 3.3 In this illustration of a German cabinet of curiosities, the purported preserved remains of a South American is "4," and an Egyptian "mummy" "5." Adam Olearius, *Gottorfische Kunst-Kammer: worinnen allerhand ungemeine Sachen, so theils die Natur, theils künstliche Hände hervor gebracht und bereitet* (Schleswig, Germany: Auff Gottfriedt Schulzens Kostens, 1674), plate facing 70. Getty Research Institute, Los Angeles (85-B1700).

Nevertheless, this first European recognition that the world beyond Egypt made "mummies" further demoted the Incas from their status as yllapa. Their prior animacy, but also their royalty's possession of lively "embalming," became a matter of the distant past, subject to a comparative project of universal history in which ancient Egypt surpassed Peru, and Europeans surpassed all. In 1767 Daubenton described a French "mummy" found in Auvergne as even "More perfect than those of the Egyptians."[78]

Back in 1687 Wafer picked his way across Huarmey's sands, the mummified boy "dry and light" in his hands. Together they boarded the *Batchelors Delight*. The boy was likely fragile, but that made him even more valuable as a specimen of lost Inca fertility, Spanish injustice, and the Peruvian preservation that embodied those histories. If Wafer were able to give the boy to the Royal Society's scientists in London, he would have the dubious distinction of delivering England's very first "Inca mummy."

Wafer's attempt to do so heralded a shift in how to know and write about not just the Peruvian past but the Americas writ large. This shift sought "new" materials and sources by which early ethnographies of Indigenous culture and antiquity could be debated and remeasured.[79] Andean tombs and the preserved dead and materials they contained became important references, given that each disinterment was a supposedly unmediated revelation of Indigenous America before Europeans' arrival. These glimpses were particularly important in what has been called the eighteenth century's "Dispute of the New World," in which Europeans and American-born Spaniards (creoles) debated whether Indigenous Americans had been limited or degenerated by the New World's climate, their purported race, or Spanish rule. For this dispute, Europeans relied especially on creole Peruvian traditions of disinterring and knowing the Andean dead that cut squarely against the sort of claims that Wafer heard from the Huarmey fisherman. Instead, the dead were interpreted as evidence either of more recent Spanish misrule or of a shallow pre-Hispanic antiquity of limited repute, redeemed by colonial rule. And by shifting scholarly attention from Incas to "ancient Peruvians," and even measuring their skulls, defenders of Spanish rule prepared the Andean dead for their role as one of nineteenth-century Americanist anthropology's foundational subjects.

Like the fisherman's, these reappraisals emerged from the exposure of an increasingly "ancient" and specifically Peruvian dead. In the sixteenth century, that antiquity was most embodied by the Indigenous-Spanish apprehension of the remains of supposedly prehuman giants, in both Mesoamerica and the Andes. In 1555 Spaniard Agustín de Zárate had written of massive skulls found in Santa Elena, in modern-day Ecuador, whose teeth circulated among Spaniards in Peru as evidence of giants destroyed by God. Jesuit José de Acosta extended the theme, and by the seventeenth century these "giant" remains were proposed as a population wiped out by a Noachian flood or by Indigenous Americans.[80]

As the Spanish invasion became ever more distant, the interments of pre-Hispanic Andeans were grandfathered in as well. The extirpatory interests of Peru's clerics made them crucial to this process. In the first half of the seventeenth century, All Saints' Day in Lima was intermittently an occasion for the Inquisition and the viceroy to unwrap Andean funerary bundles, "evoking the admiration of all who were present, at the state of preservation of both the body and the offerings it contained."[81] One Jesuit "amazed" at their preservation was Bernabé Cobo, who disclosed the calabash rind found beneath one cadaver's cheek. Cobo dissected tombs across Peru, searching not for treasure or the idolized bodies of Inca sacrifices, but "Traces of the most antiquity" to compare to Spanish and "Inca historians." Those traces included ossuaries of giants' bones, which led Cobo to believe Andean peoples who said giants built Tiwanaku's monumental constructions, rather than the tribes of Israel or King

Solomon, as others claimed. Crucially, Cobo also asked whether the Andean people of his day were the "same" as those who had ruled and built monuments before the Incas. To learn the answer, he crawled into tombs "as small and narrow as an oven door," to know a people whose possessions, dress, and style of burial revealed their occupations, rank, and group belonging. These ancient non-Inca "Peruvians" took "great care in building and adorning the tombs where they were to be buried, as if all of their happiness resided there," wrote Cobo, showing "more care, style, and skill than any of the other peoples of this New World." Most pointedly, those "who possessed this Kingdom of Peru when the Incas started to rule it are the same as those that inhabit it now."[82]

This claim of "Peruvian" sameness was both historical and increasingly racial. Rather than locating identity in changeable religion, language, and subjecthood, Cobo drew from the colonial claim that "Indian" bodies and minds were distinct from those of Europeans and needed the latter's guidance. Because of their bodies, "Indians" remained the same no matter how they dressed, what language they spoke, what rituals they learned, or whose children they bore. As historian Jorge Cañizares has argued, this location of identity in inherited biological difference preceded similar articulations by northern Europeans: Spanish Americans like Cobo were developing "ancient Peruvians" as living Indians' preserved and observable historical racial set.[83]

This racialization's historical stakes were also political. If the "Indians" whom Spain ruled were Peru's original peoples, then the supposedly tyrannical Incas had usurped their sovereignty. Cobo and the fellow priests who opened tombs could thereby contradict tales circulating among Andean subjects like Huarmey's fisherman that claimed that the dead were Inca subjects who committed suicide or had been murdered by conquistadors. Cobo's archaeology could be put to reactionary ends, clearing the Spanish of charges of misrule.

Over the next century, foreign travelers and elite Spanish subjects joined Cobo in suggesting causes of death for Peru's "ancients" that absolved the Spanish of violence. Between 1712 and 1714, near Arica—a southern port city whose cemeteries were millennia old—French engineer and traveler Amédée-François Frézier witnessed the digging of "Bodies almost entire with their Cloaths, and very often Gold and Silver Vessels." Locals told Frézier the "receiv'd Notion" that these were Indians who died in terror after Atahuallpa's death, having fled west to the edge of the Sea, hiding themselves "to implore Mercy of the Sun, whom they thought they had greatly offended, since he brought upon them such cruel and powerful Enemies." Spaniards "freely acknowledge[d] the Cruelties they exercis'd on the *Indians* at the Time"—suggesting an awareness of claims that the dead were victims of the Spanish—but believed the coastal tombs belonged to superstitious sun worshippers who buried themselves to be near their supreme deity.[84] Later travelers recorded further versions: that the exposed dead at

Arica represented the mass sacrifices undertaken upon the death of an emperor, or suicides from the moment that *Atahuallpa* had usurped the empire.[85] Peru's exposed landscape of death was to be blamed on tyrannical Incas, not Spanish colonialism.

Removing Peru's preserved dead to the precolonial past was also useful to Europeans because they could be used to test the cultural and civilizational attainments of American peoples prior to Columbus, escaping the supposed biases of sixteenth-century Iberian and Indigenous sources.[86] In 1735 the Spanish-French Geodesic Mission left for Peru.[87] This scientific collaboration is best known for its measurement of the Earth at the Equator, but expedition members were also reassessing Garcilaso's claims of Inca sophistication.[88] Spanish naval officers Antonio de Ulloa and Jorge Juan did so by drawing upon local efforts to know Andean huacas and tombs in a more antiquarian vein. Their book, published after Ulloa's return to Europe, credited a Dominican friar in Ecuador for "his talent in opening many huacas throughout the course of his life," sending their contents "to the *Provincial* of his order, and likewise to other Personages of Quito." Ulloa commissioned an engraved plate detailing the method of these huacas' T-shaped excavation and the artifacts they contained. In the majority, "only the skeleton of the person interred was found," with ceramic vessels, copper axes, and stone hand mirrors whose level of artifice could be judged as "of little value, although of great curiosity, and worthy of estimation for their great antiquity."[89] They reflected that human habitation of the Andes may have been old—and the Incas were Indigenous to the Americas, contrary to speculations to the contrary—but that Garcilaso's claimed Inca utopia was a fiction. Pre-Hispanic material deficiencies instead supposedly justified Spain's lasting intervention upon the "miserable" Indian present.[90]

This plate was Europe's first visualization of how a precolonial tomb was opened, whose contents then became important to the "Enlightened" debate over race and civilization in the Americas.[91] In 1749, the year after Ulloa and Juan's book was published, French natural historian Georges-Louis Leclerc, Comte de Buffon published his "Varieties of the Human Species" in the very same volume of the *Histoire Naturelle* that admitted the Incas as mummy-makers. Buffon's essay is known for its theorization of humanity's physical and societal variations, arguing that migration between altitudes and climates produced bodily differences. One of his most important examples for the Americas was Peru and its Peruvians. Buffon argued that Peru and Mexico were the "temperate" and "civilized" high altitudes from which other Indians literally descended, migrating to lower, colder, humid regions, like North America, and in the process biologically degenerating; "Mexico and Peru must therefore be regarded as the *most ancient lands* of the continent," "*the most anciently peopled*, given not only their elevation but also the fact that they were the only ones in

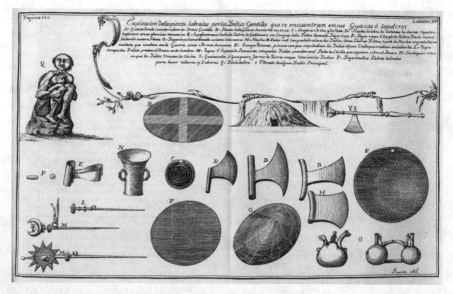

Fig. 3.4 Lamina XV, "Explanation of the pieces artificed by the Gentile Indians that are found in their *huacas* or sepulchers." "B." is an overhead T-shaped plan for opening Andean huacas, or monumental tombs ("A."). "Q.," upper left, represents a "Gold Idol," with a telling resemblance to a crouched and mummified ancestor. As the first such "excavation" schematic for pre-European Indigenous graves in the Americas, this image was influential, and was used by subsequent writers (like William Robertson) to judge those Americans' material attainments. Jorge Juan and Antonio de Ulloa, *Relacion historica del viage a la America Meridional hecho de Orden de S. Mag.* Parte primera, Tomo segundo (Madrid: Antonio Marin, 1748), Libro VI.

which man was found [by Europeans] united in society"—though neither as united or as old as some claimed.[92]

This was an exceedingly important series of claims. In a two-year period, Spanish and French *ilustrados* (enlightened ones) and *philosophes* had argued that Peru possessed mummies like those of Egypt; that it was one of two anciently peopled lands in the Americas, whose inhabitants were societally "temperate"; and that—unlike Mexico, whose larger "sacrificing" reputation was a strike against it—these facts might be tested through the preserved graves and active grave-opening culture that Peru's living inhabitants made accessible. This meant that Peru and its "ancients"—as described and depicted by Ulloa, Juan, and Garcilaso—caught particular fire in the subsequent dispute of Buffon's theory. According to that theory, if Garcilaso was right, and the material possessions depicted by Ulloa and Juan were more sophisticated than those of the Indigenous present, this was evidence either that the New World's climates degenerated all societies, or that Native peoples' present misery was the result of Spanish malfeasance. If those material possessions were understood as worse than those of the present, then it implied that the Incas and Peruvians were noble but never as unified or civil as Garcilaso claimed, and that their development had been unlocked by Christianity and European rule.[93]

In the 1760s and 1770s, following the translation of Ulloa and Juan's work, Dutch clergyman Cornelius de Pauw and Scottish historian William Robertson took the latter tack, savaging the Peruvians. They used Garcilaso's words against him and took Ulloa and Juan's depictions of South American tombs and possessions as evidence of sacrifice, idolatry, cannibalism, and some metallurgical ability, but not civilization. Bodily preservation was no measure of religious complexity, de Pauw claimed, and was sometimes just an accident of nature. De Pauw also rejected out of hand stories of greater and more vigorous antiquity. If giant remains really existed, he charged, then why hadn't Spain brought them to Europe?[94]

While de Pauw and Robertson doubted, Spanish-American excavations in Peru drew attention to a "new" source: Indigenous human remains whose internal racial difference could be quantified in novel ways.[95] Ulloa was the hinge of this "discovery," having returned to Peru as an administrator in 1758 before serving as West Louisiana's first Spanish governor from 1766 to 1768. These postings made him one of a few Europeans who claimed personal and scientific experience of both North and South America's Indigenous peoples. He did so by using the Andean dead to argue for the essential unity, historicity, and inferiority of the "Indians of the two Americas." His *Noticias Americanas* (1772) asserted an essential biological similarity for all Indigenous American peoples based on their skulls' characteristics. Amid discussing Indians' supposed endurance of pain—an old prejudice used to justify all sorts of abuse—he pointed to crania taken from "ancient sepulchers" in Peru that were thicker than that which was "regular." By Ulloa's rhetorical sleight of hand these Peruvian skulls became American ones, with a thickness of "6 to 7 *lineas*; the same [sort of thickness] is noticed in the skin" of living Americans, he continued, as observed via "operations of Surgery and in the *Skeletons* that are removed from the Sepulchres."[96] In this way, Ulloa went from estimating Indigenous civilization via Andean gravegoods to measuring their skulls, bones, and skin, making him one of the first Europeans to do so.[97]

Having asserted the Peruvians' "Indian" representativeness, Ulloa projected them back in time, using them to estimate the antiquity of all American peoples. In a discussion of Indigenous mortuary practices, he observed that Louisiana—his proxy for North America—possessed two mounds one hundred leagues above New Orleans that "leave no doubt of being Sepulchers" like the "huacas" of Ecuador and Peru, housing "*Indios* of the greatest consideration." He then cited Peru's dead "to conjecture regarding the antiquity of the *Pueblos*" before Spain's invasion—a proxy for the antiquity of Indigenous presence in the

Americas overall, if Mexico and Peru were presumed to host the Americas' most ancient societies, per Buffon. Ulloa turned to spurious calculation: because Peru's huacas each contained "about 30 to 40 skulls," and "supposing that each family is six people, and of these die four over the course of 25 years, it would come out to be 250 years, and this is the antiquity of the Pueblos before the conquest." There was thus no need for Garcilaso or Inca histories. The "*Memorias* of the *Indians* of *Peru*, before their Conquest, are preserved in the Settlements, Buildings, and Walls of the *Guacas*, or burials, and in those things that they used."[98] And if Peru stood in for the Americas, then it meant that all Indigenous Americans had reached the continent only 250 years before the Europeans.

Ulloa was one of the most influential scholars of the colonial Americas in his day, and his Peruvian interventions—measurements of Indigenous crania and tombs to give low estimates for Indigenous historic presence in the Americas—became a fundamental basis of eighteenth- and nineteenth-century anthropology.[99] Other scholars would similarly date the Incas. Voltaire thought the first Inca emperor, Manco Inca, arrived via the Canary Islands; Alexander von Humboldt believed he was a peripatetic brahmin from Asia.[100] These suggestions retained Ulloa's political edge, fact-checking histories that Indigenous peoples and their sympathizers crafted to explain the preserved dead around them. In 1772 Ulloa aimed at the fisherman's narrative, noting it was "widespread opinion in these parts that certain more resolute Nations of Indians, or of greater courage than others, upon seeing those Countries subjected to a foreign people, took the desperate measure of burying themselves alive with their families," fleeing to the coast to do so. Ulloa was skeptical. If true, tombs throughout the Andes were more accessible means of mass suicide. Yet he quibbled with the story's fundamental logic. To commit suicide by interment, the "Indians" needed someone to seal them in. And if they all died, then who was that?[101] Ulloa's matter-of-fact proposal hid a colonizing power: the not-so-ancient Peruvians had died of natural causes, and not the historical events of the conquest.

———

European scholars had to trust Ulloa's word for the same reason that Wafer's Huarmey tale was taken on faith: until the early nineteenth century, the only place these embodied knowledges could be known was Peru. Wafer's crewmates aboard the *Batchelors Delight* were not pleased to be transporting the mummified boy, and their reaction helps clarify why almost no Indigenous remains were collected outside of the Americas prior to the nineteenth century. Like other sailors of their day, they believed dead bodies were bad luck at sea—a "difficulty" that was cited in attempts to collect Andean mummies and skulls through the 1830s. The "prejudice existing with sailors and even officers against anything of the kind being brought on board ship" was often too great, and Wafer's experience suggests why many collectors didn't even try.[102] As Wafer complained to his readers, "[I] was frustrated of my purpose by the Sailors; who having a foolish Conceit, that the Compass would not traverse aright so long as a dead Body was on board, *threw him overboard*, to my great Vexation."[103]

In the century to come, still greater violence was visited upon the Inca sovereignty that the boy embodied. In 1780, after decades of local rebellions in the Andes, an Andean leader from the highlands south of Cuzco named José Gabriel Condorcanqui executed a Spanish official, launching the largest Native uprising against colonial rule in American history. Condorcanqui believed himself Tupac Amaru II, descended from Manco Inca's final son, the decapitated Tupa Amaru. Though the Crown and Cuzco's Incas denied that claim, his grievances were not solely personal. Condorcanqui, a close reader of Garcilaso, protested that Spanish officials had broken the contract of fair imperial rule. Higher tribute requirements and sales taxes were the breaking point for Condorcanqui's followers. To draw communities to his revolution to restore Inca sovereignty, Condorcanqui spoke in their towns' Christian cemeteries, validated by his dead and their own.[104]

In response, colonial authorities excommunicated Condorcanqui and threatened his followers with the same—in effect, a denial of Christian burial to those rebels who would be killed. With the help of Cuzco's loyal Inca nobility, the authorities captured Condorcanqui and in May 1781 executed him. His body was quartered and displayed as a monument of apostate "Indian" rebellion. Speaking Quechua was prohibited, as were the reading of Garcilaso, and the use of Inca solar symbols, portraits, plays, conch trumpets, and clothes to mourn "their deceased monarchs."[105] These measures missed their mark—who could ban Quechua?—and the revolution burned until 1783 because communities in the southern Andes fought less for an Inca than for their own radical collective sovereignty. Nevertheless, Spanish authorities painted Tupac Amaru II's fight for Inca sovereignty, and the southern Peruvian's communities' fight for hyperlocal democracy, as an atavistic race war. The repression and counterrepression killed one hundred thousand, cooling the ambitions of elite Peruvians of Spanish descent who might have otherwise struck for independence.[106] Creole support for non-Indigenous patriarchal rule became the order of the day.[107]

One counterintuitive way that creole elites rebuilt that rule was by appropriating the traditions that claimed to explain and avenge the exposed royal dead. In 1791 doctor and natural scientist Hipólito Unanue—the most influential Peruvian ilustrado of his generation—contributed an essay on the "Monuments of Ancient Peru" to an early issue of Lima's *Mercurio Peruano*, a new publication dedicated to celebrating and improving Peru. The essay denounced conquistador Gonzalo Pizarro for immolating the "cadaver of that Monarch"

Viracocha Inca, bringing "desolation to the sepulchers," and rebelling against the Crown. Unanue pinned these acts upon an "execrable hunger for gold," claiming that this mortuary violence was an early excess of conquest that royal authority reformed. In Unanue's account, Xâxâbuana, where Viracocha burned, and Jaquijahuana, where the president of Lima's *audiencia*, Pedro de la Gasca, executed Gonzalo, became a single place: Sacsahuana. This allowed Unanue to make the remarkable claim that la Gasca "cut off [Gonzalo's] Head next to the very grave that he had violated so vilely." By delivering justice on behalf of one of Peru's mummified sovereigns, la Gasca "washed out the stains of the [Spanish] Nation," justifying their right to ongoing rule.[108]

In November the following year, in a speech celebrating the inauguration of Lima's first anatomical theater, Unanue asserted that Spanish creoles like himself honored the preserved Peruvian dead by studying them. Fittingly, the theater was in the Hospital of San Andrés, where the Incas' yllapas were once displayed. The setting reinforced Unanue's call to restore sciences like anatomy that had served the Peruvian past and could help his fellow ilustrados cultivate Peru's past "genius" as a "sovereign, self-sufficient country."[109]

Among Unanue's examples of anatomical genius were the Incas' "*momias*," which seems to be the first time the "embalmed" Inca royals were called "mummies" in Peru. Unanue likely encountered Daubenton's mummy essay in the original French *Encyclopedie* or its 1788 Spanish translation, but he repurposed it to critique Old World claims to medical or scientific superiority, insisting that the Incas' scientific heirs were Peruvian ilustrados like himself. "If the progress that the ancient Peruvians made in that science had been measured by the preparation and conservation of cadavers, which requires a certain skill and intelligence, without a doubt they would gainsay the precedence given to the Egyptians," he declared. Like famed Dutch embalmer Frederik Ruysch, "the Peruvians perpetuated the life of their mummies, while the Egyptians only prolonged the death of their own."[110]

Like Ulloa, however, Unanue believed that those mummies belonged to the Andean past and could be explained in ways that avoided hatred of Spain. Forgetting the excesses he had pinned upon Gonzalo Pizarro, Unanue denied that the Andean dead suffered at Spanish hands or in violent protest of the conquest. He denied that their bunched-up fetal positions reflected agony or unnatural death. Rather, "The sepulchral mummies indicate through their intactness and posture their being men who died naturally, who were interred under the peaceful ceremonies of their Religion." The claim may have been inspired by excavations in the 1780s in Trujillo by Bishop Jaime Martínez Compañón; his artists were the first to depict the layering of Indigenous tombs in the Americas, painting the dead as if sleeping, their bodies wholly intact. What Peruvian preservation most revealed, then, was ritual repose and lack of injury—deaths by natural causes, and not at the hand of the "illustrious" Spanish "dominators of the New World."[111]

Unanue's pride on this point—using excavation to exonerate his ancestors of the violence and colonial mismanagement that Huarmey's fisherman knew from that dead—distilled these more "scientific" approaches to Peru's dead. Knowing the Inca yllapas as embalmed mummies claimed their "science" for the creole present. Likewise, by denying the belief that the exposed Peruvian dead were suicides or murder victims of Spanish rule, Ulloa and Unanue and their cohort formulated a pre-Hispanic dead whose remains could be read as "ancient" racial objects, and not as subjects of a colonial horizon extended every time a shovel opened their graves. The potency of this invention was registered in the many "enlightened" visitors who ventured outside of Lima or dropped anchor along the coast to open a tomb as part of their scientific duties.[112]

The assumptions of this more "scientific" Peruvian approach to the Americas' dead were foundational to what became known as "archaeology." The field's ability to connect or delimit identities in the "ancient" past was a necessary precedent for its more heralded methodologies of identifying cultural discontinuities and transformations through time.[113] Its distillation in this late-eighteenth-century American moment, both colonial and revolutionary, also clarifies the politics of sciences that identify the Indigenous dead as of the past, rather than subjects moving through time. By asserting that the dead's history and agency were fixed upon interment, these sciences deny ancestors' ability to indict those who rotate them into the present.

These assumptions shape how we may feel about the Huarmey boy's loss. Wafer likely assumed his readers would share his outrage at the sailors' "superstitions," and feel that something was destroyed by tossing the boy overboard, denying his arrival, collection, and learned discussion in London. But it was also a fate averted. From the vantage of the Huarmey fisherman, the violence of the boy's story had begun long before, and Wafer's collecting made him just as much as party to it as the sailors. And from the perspective of those sailors, the boy remained dangerous, forcing their hands. This led the sailors to an action functionally indistinguishable from burial at sea, despite its fundamentally different meaning. They presumed the boy's proper place was at rest, whether beneath the soil or beneath the waves—that the dead were not meant to travel.

Wafer left the story there, not recording what happened next. Perhaps it was too obvious, that the dried boy would have bobbed in the water for a moment, before sinking into the ocean, lost but released. A century and a half later, however, Peruvian independence and a new field named American anthropology delivered his countrymen a different fate.

PART 2

EXPORTING, 1780–1893

The "Inca mummy" that South American revolutionary José de San Martín sent to King George IV in London, in 1822, after declaring Peru's independence. Thomas Joseph Pettigrew, *A History of Egyptian Mummies* (London: Longman, Rees, Orme, Brown, Green, & Longman, 1834), Detail from Plate V. Courtesy of University of Pennsylvania Museum Library.

Trading Incas

San Martín's Mummy and the Peruvian Independence
of the Andean Dead

In early 1822 the South American patriot José de San Martín sent an "Inca mummy" from Lima to London. The general had declared Peru's independence the previous year, but Spanish forces refused to cede the colony. So when one of San Martín's colonels sent the "Protector of Peruvian Independence" two bodies unearthed from a northern tomb, San Martín put them to work. The first, a mummified child, went to the not-yet-established Museum of Buenos Aires, which could have made the child the museum's founding accession.[1] San Martín had a more concrete destination for the second. He had the male "Inca mummy" boxed up for Thomas Hardy, commodore of Britain's South American naval station. Hardy gave the box to Captain Basil Hall, who ferried it aboard the *HMS Conway*. Hall's "shriveled" charge spent the trip to Portsmouth, England, in the same painful position: bone poking through one shoulder's skin, "knees almost touching his chin, the elbows pressed to the sides, and the hands clasping his cheek-bones." Finally, in 1823 Hall passed "my friend the Inca" to independent Peru's first diplomats to Europe, who gave the body to San Martín's intended recipient, King George IV of Britain.[2]

The mummy came bundled with San Martín's high hopes. He hoped that Britain would recognize Peru's independence diplomatically; that one of George's brothers, the Duke of Sussex, would become Peru's constitutional monarch; and that George would deposit his sovereign Inca counterpart in the British Museum.[3] All three hopes were dashed. Britain sent a consul to Peru later that year but delayed formal recognition out of sensitivity to Spain. The Duke of Sussex would not become Peru's new monarch, not least because public opinion in Lima shifted to favor a republic, and a constituent Congress swept monarchy off the table.[4] And rather than transfer the "Inca mummy" to the British

Empires of the Dead. Christopher Heaney, Oxford University Press. © Oxford University Press 2023.
DOI: 10.1093/oso/9780197542552.003.0005

Museum, where he would have joined the antiquities of Egypt, the Crown gave his body to the Hunterian anatomical museum of London's Royal College of Surgeons. There he became a specimen of curious preservation gifted "by his Majesty King George the Fourth," not San Martín, before disappearing in the late nineteenth century.[5] San Martín's plan to have Peru's ancient sovereignty recognized by sharing it with England was lost in translation across the Atlantic.

Yet to take San Martín's "Inca mummy" as a quixotic diversion from Peru's republican destiny ignores all that this first national scientific object of independent Peru symbolized.[6] Its collection and export claimed that Peru's original rulers and ancestors of the nation were dead but redeemed from their Spanish repression by the patriots. Like the libraries, museums, and "republics of knowledge" San Martín and his army established, the study of "Inca mummies" liberated literal Peruvian sovereigns and their South American "sciences" of embalming from the supposedly benighted colonial legacies of Spanish rule.[7]

San Martín's Inca was only the first. Over the coming decades, Peru's scholars and National Museum displayed and exported "Inca mummies," arguing for their particular use in the project of knowing the Americas' past and its resources. Foreign collectors extended this scientific republic of the Andean dead by digging, buying, selling, and donating their bodies and artifacts to museums from Sydney, Australia, to St. Petersburg, Russia. "Digging Up the Dead a Regular Industry in Peru," declared one North American newspaper.[8]

This chapter excavates the matrix for that diaspora of bones: the landscape of open tombs and adopted ancients whose preservation and appropriation were "sciences" that republican actors claimed as an act of nation-building.[9] At first, these sciences continued to study the nature of the Peruvian dead's "embalming" and the debatable history that it preserved. Did Peruvian mummies reveal an Andean utopia whose loss indicated Spanish violence and Inca resistance? Or did they preserve a precolonial "Indian" past whose heights and antiquity were neither as high nor as deep as the Incas claimed? Both narratives cast Andean remains as symbols of a restored "Peruvian" science of sovereignty, whose original possessors were either dead or in need of further liberation. In either case, the power to redeem the precolonial dead supported creole (American-born) patriots' claim to better lead Peru than their fellow Indigenous citizens, let alone the Inca families carrying on in republican Cuzco.[10] Even "if the Incas were erected as ancestors of the nation," observes historian Maude Yvinec, "that did not mean that the Indians of the 19th century were recognized as their worthy descendants."[11]

Mounting interest in Inca and ancient Peruvian mummies shifted their meaning as the century continued. Later archaeologists and historians would emphasize an early republican failure to halt the huaqueo (tomb-raiding) and the "squandering" export of pre-Hispanic tombs, bodies, and artifacts. "Wealthy mummies had awakened from their centuries-old dream to travel to another, unsuspected world," lamented the great Peruvian historian Jorge Basadre: "Europe or the United States."[12] These narratives overlook how, following San Martín, Peruvian natural historians and collectors helped foreigners open tombs, export their contents, and discuss the "ancient" historical and natural resources that Peru's dead uniquely embodied. More than symbols of sovereignty, Andean "mummies" became mobile laboratories for the study of precolonial Peruvian history, anatomy, and the natural resources that preserved them. Like the guano (bird excrement) and nitrate fertilizers whose export to Great Britain and the world made Peru's leaders fantastically rich, this project of studying Peru's "ancient" bodies of nature and culture sowed their bodies in multiple scientific fields.[13] And to germinate them, foreign scientists cited republican Peruvian debates over whether the Inca and other ancient dead were mummified by Inca embalming or by more "natural" resources of climate and soil that might profit Peru and the world. This was body-collecting as a project of postcolonial nation-making and foreign export, and it made scientific commodities of the Andean dead.

The unintended consequences of national grave-opening were many. Everyday republican grave-openers and antiquarians ventured into the countryside. They dug for artifacts, skulls, and mummies sold internally and abroad, undoing millennia of Andean women's mortuary labor. But the republican state's retreat made space for rewrappings as well. The once-ancestral dead remained capable of revealing treasure, curing climates, and cursing the living, and Andean communities with the room to renew relations with the "little grandparents" competed with foreign collectors for that dead's possession. What the transatlantic collection and export of "Inca mummies" could not destroy were the descendants who still wanted to know them.

———

As a political and scientific symbol, San Martín's mummy stood in for the many other Inca bodies believed to have been lost to Spanish colonialism. For Andean individuals like Juan Santos Atahuallpa, the head of the Inca king that conquistadors supposedly took to Spain had been a reason to revolt.[14] Enlightened Peruvians, however, wished that more mummified bodies traveled. In 1792 Limeño scholar Hipólito Unanue responded to Dutch clergyman Cornelius de Pauw's charge that if South American tombs had produced remains evidencing pre-Christian civilization or antiquity or vigor, then the Spanish would have collected them.[15] Wanting to prove de Pauw wrong, Unanue lamented that Peru's Inca "mummies" hadn't been sent to Spain. "It would have been worth paying their weight in gold to conduct them to the Cabinet of Natural History" in Madrid, Unanue wrote in the pages of the *Mercurio Peruano*, Lima's learned journal.[16]

Instead, illustrations of the dead traveled in their place. In 1788 Madrid's cabinet received bishop Jaime Martínez Compañón's collection of antiquities, which included watercolors depicting the layering of northern Peru's huacas (sacred tombs) and its uncannily whole and outstretched Chimú dead. The first portrayal of the American dead in line with increasingly anatomical conventions of "true to nature" illustration was also from Peru—the sketches of Felipe Bauza, a geographer attached to Spanish naval officer Alessandro Malaspina's scientific expedition to the Pacific, which in 1790 dropped anchor at Arica. There, Bauza and the corvette's lieutenant came upon an "infinity of pits and human bones" and opened tombs to disprove anti-Spanish tales of Andean suicide. Bauza's illustrations brought a more "naturalistic" antiquity to Madrid's royal cabinets of science in lieu of their fragile fragmentary bodies.[17]

Fig. 4.1 Sketch of a human torso and leg of a body encountered by the Malaspina expedition in 1790 at the viceroyalty of Peru's bay of Chacota, belonging to the port city of Arica (today, Chile). Attributed to Felipe Bauzá, it represents the first "scientifically" illustrated Andean remain, drawn to fragmentary life. Museo de América, Madrid, 02203.

Unpublished after their arrival in Spain, these "paper" mummies did little to answer de Pauw's critique. Unanue therefore referred northern European readers to a preserved and monumental South American he believed was already in their possession. In 1793, on the occasion of a visit to Lima of Basilio Huaylas, a seven-foot-two "Indian," Unanue told the *Mercurio Peruano's* readers that Huaylas was prefigured in Peruvian history.[18] On top of "ancient traditions" that a race of giants once populated Ecuador, Unanue noted that the Natural History Cabinet of Lima's Sociedad de Amantes del País had a 15-pound molar of a giant "Mummy" from southern Peru. To this "Mummy," Unanue appended an extraordinary footnote, claiming that

> A respectable and truthful elder, who was the owner of the aforementioned molar, assures us that the cadaver from which it was pulled had been conducted from Tarija to Cuzco at the cost of much money and solicitude by the celebrated Don Joseph Pardo de Figueroa, the Marques de Valle-umbroso, and this individual then sent it on to Madrid; but that in the voyage there it fell prey to the English, who carried it off to London. If the *Mercurio* happens to reach there, those Gentleman will be able to review their collections, and see if it is true that the pillaged Giant lacks said molar, dignifying us with a reply through the medium of the Philosophical Transactions of the Royal Society.[19]

Biopiracy is rarely so literal. Unanue believed England not only had stolen a prodigious body from Peru's preserved past, but that an appeal to the age's collective empiricism might induce London's natural historians to match Lima's molar to the Royal Society's mummy, corroborating his claims.[20]

In a surprising turn of events, Unanue's plea reached its intended destination, but it was received unkindly. In 1793 the British captured the Spanish galleon *Santiago*, in whose hold was a run of the *Mercurio Peruano*. An English doctor named Joseph Skinner bought the journal's run at auction and in 1805 he published some of its "intellectual treasures" as *The Present State of Peru*, including Unanue's essays on Peru's "multitude of mummies which, after a lapse of so many years, indeed, of so many ages, are to be found entire in the catacombs."[21] If any search for Huaylas's ancestor was made, the Royal Society made no public note of it, but one reviewer ridiculed Unanue's claims. The "word mummy should not have been used," he opined, claiming that Inca preservation seemed less elaborate than that of Egypt. As for whether the supposed giant "wants the tooth in question," he added, "Was there ever so prodigious a fable so circumstantially related?" Unanue was out of step with a growing consensus that "giant" bones belonged to far older and larger fossilized beasts. Spanish-American claims to knowledge seemed like the uninformed pretension of conquerors over abused Indian subjects, the reviewer charged. Skinner's translation even seemed a dangerous attempt to interest England in territorial buccaneering in Spanish America. "What madman dreams of subduing Peru?"[22]

When Napoleon's invasion of Iberia the following year made such dreams seem slightly less mad, the idealized Inca dead served as a guide. In 1808 King Ferdinand VII abdicated the throne, and in his absence Spain's cities and territories elected delegates to a Cortes, an assembly in Cádiz to draft new terms for the empire's rule. Although some American provinces declared outright independence, liberal delegates from loyalist territories saw it as a chance to make Spain's empire more just. One of Peru's deputies, Dionisio Inca Yupanqui, spoke as an "Inca, Indian, and American," calling upon the Crown and the Cortes to relieve their people's oppressions. Cádiz's resulting Constitution of 1812 was among the most liberal in the Atlantic world, enfranchising a far wider range of society than in the United States. It retained the monarchy but limited its powers; put Spain's global citizens—regardless of ethnicity or location—on supposedly equal legal footing, essentially eliminating Indigenous tribute in the New World; and established universal suffrage for male community members, as long they were not enslaved.[23]

In Peru, the Cortes stirred memories of Tupac Amaru II's revolution. Elites in some cities rapidly elected delegates to resist the extension of the franchise to people of Indigenous and African descent. Some Andean communities welcomed the reduction in tribute; others kept paying it, not wishing to lose that claim upon royal authority. When Ferdinand VII returned to power in 1814 and scrapped the Constitution, even some loyalists became radicalized. Mateo Pumacahua was an Inca noble and brigadier who helped repress Tupac Amaru II. Now, even he turned to insurrection, supported by creole allies who proposed an Inca Empire. The viceroy executed Pumacahua and his allies, but lower-class and Indigenous militias outside of Cuzco continued to mobilize.[24]

The dead and dethroned Incas were nonetheless used to assuage creoles nervous at the prospect of armed Andeans and people of color. Instead their symbol was used to promote an independent South American monarchy that could take revenge for the Incas and unite a diverse society, but keep creoles at its head.[25] In his 1812 poem "Enslaved Peru," for example, Peruvian revolutionary Benito Laso sought vengeance for the unjust "crime" of the execution of Atahualpa and the first Tupac Amaru, but made no reference to living Inca heirs. "The dethroned Inca," wrote another patriot in 1821, "appears to have raised the stone of the sepulcher [tomb], and raising his bloodstained head told us with courage: Peruvians, avenge me."[26] Peruvian conservatives later marked the irony of this claimed inheritance. In 1846 priest Bartolomé Herrera ridiculed how "Peruvian independence and the reconquest of the Inca Empire were reclaimed as one and the same thing," persuading "many American Spaniards" to believe "that they belong to the Inca Empire; that they are Indians; and that the European Spaniards conquered them and did them harm."[27]

The revolutionary Inca mantle stretched beyond Peru. News of José Gabriel Condorcanqui reached Saint-Domingue almost immediately, for example.[28] One novel cast the Peruvian dead as interred in Saint-Domingue soil, and Haitian revolutionary Jean-Jacques Dessalines dubbed his army of free Blacks "Incas."[29] Venezuelan revolutionary Francisco de Miranda sought an independent Spanish America under one or two titular "Incas"—hereditary or elected executives chosen from elite creoles, not actual Inca nobility.[30] Inca suns were common on revolutionary flags, such as in Río de la Plata, present-day Argentina, where resurrected Incas were especially noisy.[31] "The Inca is roused in his tomb," went the national anthem of 1813—"Ardour reanimates his bones." Its Congress even considered uniting the southern Andes under Juan Bautista Tupac Amaru— Condorcanqui's half-brother, who remained in exile in Spain and Morocco. San Martín offered nothing quite so dramatic as his army advanced upon Peru itself, but his proposal that an English prince become Peru's constitutional monarch mixed both Inca and British history. The Inca dead had become a past precedent for the restoration of American empire—not the ancestors of a living people in Cuzco. The "successors of Manco, sent forth from their tombs," accompanied San Martín into Lima in 1821, one Chilean poet wrote.[32]

The poet's words were more accurate than he knew: Peru's new political situation radically transformed the terms of the Inca dead's study. In securing Peru's countryside, South American revolutionaries examined "mummies" and other bodies claimed to be "Incas" killed by Spain. English doctor James Paroissien, for example, collected "antiquities, dug up from the sepulchres of the Indians before the establishment of Christianity" while assisting an attempted liberation of Peru in 1812.[33] In 1820 he was with San Martín's army when it disembarked at the Bay of Paracas where, two millennia before, communities had interred hundreds of their finely wrapped ancestors. By then Paroissien had embraced the narrative that took that the dead as evidence of all that Spanish colonialism ruined. "This country must have been extremely populous in the time of the Incas," he wrote in his journal: "all the country from [Pisco] to Chincha is covered with Guacas or burying places, and in Chincha itself the ruins of a city cover the extent of several miles in circumference."[34]

Paroissien's comrades liberated that dead populace through grave-opening. In 1821 Tomás Heres, a Venezuelan colonel, learned of a northern huaca believed to be "the site of a voluntary sacrifice of the life of a *Curaca*, one of an order of nobles, immediately following in dignity the members of the blood royal." Knowing "the ancient Peruvians" were buried with possessions, Heres had the huaca opened, revealing three brightly wrapped "mummies": a male, a female, and—in her arms—a one-year-old with a ball of camelid wool tucked under their arm. The female "crumbled into dust on exposure to the air," but Heres sent the male, the child, and her textiles to San Martín, whose Minister of the Interior Unanue had asked London's Royal Society to search their collection for a giant "mummy" three decades earlier.[35]

It was this child and this man whom San Martín sent to the Museum of Buenos Aires and the British Museum, the latter in the care of Paroissien. This made them diplomatic gifts, meant to endear both Río de la Plata and England to Peru's cause: in the case of England, they were evidence of the sovereign "Inga" antiquity Peru had enjoyed, that San Martín hoped the royalty of "Inglaterra" (England) might restore. But they also addressed the doubt that continental scholars had directed at preserved Inca bodies, corroborating the claims of Garcilaso, Unanue, and others. This made them scientific objects as well, Peruvian counterparts to the Egyptians whom San Martín likely saw in the British Museum in London in 1812.[36] Once in the British Museum, they might enlist other foreign scholars and doctors—like Paroissien, one of Peru's first diplomats—to lift the intellectual veil the Spanish had dropped on the Incas and their history.[37]

The fact that these mummies were the very image of death was also part of their message: Peru's Indigenous kings were gone. On December 13, 1821, San Martín showed them to officers of Britain's Royal Navy breakfasting in the viceroy's former palace. "The tradition with respect to this and other similar bodies," wrote Basil Hall—who ferried "my friend the Inca" to Portsmouth—"is that, at the time of the conquest, many of the Incas and their families were persecuted to such a degree, that they actually allowed themselves to be buried alive rather than submit to the fate with which the Spaniards threatened them." In the "countenance" of the Inca before him, Hall saw "an expression of agony."[38] This was the radically anticolonial way of reading the Andean dead that Lionel Wafer learned from Huarmey's fisherman, now wrapped up with San Martín's Inca. But in independence that narrative had new meaning. Rather than fueling dreams of Inca return, Peru's mummies showed that the country's original sovereigns were so extinguished that new leadership was needed. As the nation's first scientific object, the Incas' "mummies" deserved a place in the British museum, the world's most famous collection of antiquities—but their supposed suicide had vacated Peru's throne.[39]

Mariano Eduardo de Rivero y Ustáriz imagined that republican Peruvian science would excavate that throne and redeem its dead. Rivero was a mining engineer trained in Europe, a "technocrat" member of Alexander von Humboldt's scientific circle, and the founding director of Peru's National Museum.[40] Sometime after

1826, when Spain vacated its fortress at Lima's port city Callao, Rivero ventured into the depths of Chavín de Huantar, an underground temple in Peru's Central Andes. Two thousand years earlier, Andean leaders had snorted hallucinogenics before navigating Chavín's snaking galleries, seeking the obsidian-illuminated stone deities whose shadowy mouths growled with the sound of water and priests' conch-shell trumpets.[41] Rivero instead explored Chavín by candlelight, crawling through deep subterranean chambers where "ancient" artifacts and the "skeleton of a seated Indian" had been found. Afterward he sat upon a carved monolith at the confluence of Chavín's two rivers, letting his "imagination, like a lightning bolt," flash over the ancient places he had been, whose dead were now fellow Peruvians killed by Spain. "I saw the sad images of the blights committed by our ancient oppressors," he wrote. "Three centuries have been unable to erase the memory of the infinite ills suffered by the peaceful and simple inhabitants of the Andes, and I still seemed to be able to see in the water of the small rapids, the dye of the blood of the victims; that the debris of its banks were mountains of corpses on which fanaticism sat and erected its throne to tyranny." Rivero "gave thanks to Heaven for having achieved the work of its destruction."[42]

Rivero's mourning was a performance of sorts.[43] But as the National Museum's director he also knew how literal the work of recollecting of the Andean dead could be. Rivero justified the trespass of these places of "eternal rest" because it bypassed histories of the Spanish conquest, whose glimpses of pre-Hispanic grandeur were framed in "sad portraits of vengeance, petty passions, and the itch to destroy." Peruvians should instead "preserve the precious relics of our ancestors," he believed, so that "future generations cannot accuse [us] of being indolent, destructive, or ignorant."[44]

For that reason, the museum he had founded in Lima displayed four Andean mummies, which he and his fellow learned Peruvians used to discuss, unwrap, and even dissect these predecessors of the nation.[45] These encounters were akin to the anatomical examination of Egyptian mummies happening in Europe, and they presented Peru's dead as important vessels for research into American history and resources. Through this research some scholars recast Inca embalming as a shared heritage of all ancient Peruvians—and thus the modern nation—while others like Rivero credited Peru's nature and soil, whose chemical and climactic characteristics might profit the republic. Both positions were extended by transatlantic collectors who gathered the Andean dead to test three centuries of Peruvian scholarship regarding the "embalmed" superiority of its ancients.[46]

The mummies' display in the museum, however, was not inevitable. In 1822 San Martín's right-hand man, Bernardo de Monteagudo, propagated a decree claiming national ownership of the country's huacas and their "antiquities." Those excavated for export without a license would be confiscated for a national museum.[47] But that museum did not yet exist, and the pre-Hispanic dead were not included among "antiquities" protected and owned by Peruvian law until 1929. Rivero was likewise ambivalent about their presence. Like the institutions he visited in Europe, Rivero imagined a working museum of natural history and eminently practical sciences, complete with a botanical garden, chemistry lab, and a working collection of minerals, animals, insects, shells, and scientific books, where European professors would educate Peruvians in "practical" sciences like agriculture, manufacture, chemistry, zoology, conchology, mathematics, physics, mineralogy, and geology. His initial call for donations for the museum, founded in 1826, meticulously described how patriots and regional officials might prepare minerals, plants, and animals for transport but dispatched "antiquities" in a single sentence.[48]

Yet Rivero's framing of the museum as correcting the "conduct of our stupid oppressors, [who] deprived us of scientific establishments . . . contributing to our lack of knowledge of the merit of the treasures that have been extracted to enrich foreign museums"—meant that it would receive "treasures" unique to Peru.[49] In 1828, amid donations of gold and Inca "idols" on which Rivero began to publish, he received boxes of "figures and curious instruments" that the museum's keeper, Francisco Barrera, had newly dug from tombs at Chancay, a coastal settlement north of the capital.[50] By 1829, when the museum moved into the former hall of judgment of Lima's Inquisition—a symbolic gesture, if there ever was one—four expensive glass cases in the corners of the new exhibit space displayed mummies from the highland region of Cajatambo: two male, two female, their red and green textiles in varying states of undress.[51] These mummies reconsecrated the site of the Inquisition, the terrifying colonial instrument of Christian discipline and bureaucracy, as a republican temple to national Peruvian science and history, whose four new pillars were the "ancient Peruvians" Spain repressed but Rivero redeemed.[52]

To outsiders, the Andean dead were one of the museum's defining features. Foreign visitors were less impressed with the institution's minerals and other "natural" holdings but remarked on these mummies' incredible "state of preservation."[53] Some enjoyed believing they were "Incas." French-Peruvian freethinker Flora Tristan told readers that the museum had "four mummies of the Incas, whose forms have suffered not one alteration, although they appear to be prepared with less care than that of Egypt."[54] In the 1860s, one North American enjoyed the frisson of staring at all that "remains of the once magnificent Atahualpa, last king of the Incas." Whether he truly believed it was Atahuallpa mattered less than its rhetorical claim: that republican science had made Peru's most infamous sovereign into a specimen.[55]

Every Inca under glass was a tomb undone, of course, and the museum's curators went even further in unwrapping them, to reveal and debate the science they contained. Francisco Barrera sought that knowledge with a knife.

Fig. 4.2a and b These lithographs represented two of the four Cajatambo mummies in the four corners of the "Museum of Lima," Peru's first national museum, which opened in 1826 in the former quarters of the Inquisition. D. Leopoldo Müller, Plates III and IV of Mariano Eduardo de Rivero and Johann Jakob von Tschudi, *Antigüedades Peruanas* (Vienna, 1851).

After delivering the three boxes of antiquities from Chancay, Barrera became the museum's "keeper," sometimes serving as director when Rivero was out of favor with shifting national governments in Lima.[56] Barrera knew the collections intimately, and in 1828, in Rivero's science journal, he published the first detailed narration of an Andean funerary bundle's dissection.

In describing Peru's ruins and antiquities, Barrera offered a breathy celebration of how Peru's "professors" of "embalming" preserved, wrapped, and interred these "mummies prepared by art." Like the Egyptians, these Peruvian professors had a "good understanding of anatomy," which Barrera thought was evidenced by the packing of the skull's cavities with cotton; he believed that brains were removed through the nose. The "professors" then sliced open the perineum, removing the viscera, which Barrera corroborated—he believed—by dissecting at least one mummy himself. He saw no organs but found a "subtle powder," "the color of liver, which exuded a slight smell of turpentine." He experimented with the powder. Dropped in cold water, it effervesced, which Barrera believed revealed it to be lime, mineral earth, and the resin of the Peruvian pepper tree *Schinus molle*. The body's "tanned leather" skin owed to the "anointing of the face with an oily liquid, orange-colored." Finally, Barrera reconstructed the process of wrapping the body, describing the textiles, objects, cotton, and fragrant

LAST DAY AT LIMA.

Fig. 4.3 "Once magnificent Atahualpa, last king of the Incas. 'Alas, poor Yorick! To this complexion must we come at last." The drawing represents one of the remaining "Inca mummies" in Peru's first National Museum. The mummy's blackened "complexion" may owe to its treatment with a preservative bitumen by the museum itself. George Washington Carleton, "Last Day at Lima," *Our Artist in Peru: Fifty Drawings on Wood: Leaves from the Sketch-Book of a Traveller during the Winter of 1865–6* (New York: 1866), 50.

plants whose placement with "prolixity and art" culminated in ritual installation. This dissection re-collected something "history's pages have silenced," Barrera claimed: a skill at embalming observable in the mummies of all "ancient Peruvians," not just the Incas. This achievement presumed an immortal soul, required embalming with materia medica, minerals, and textiles, and did Peruvians "justice in the face of an Enlightened age."[57]

Barrera's dissections were nonetheless comparable to those done to Egyptian mummies on the other side of the Atlantic, and just as destructive. As historian Christina Riggs observes of the Egyptians: "Unwrap a mummy and what emerges is rarely the lifelike corpse of gothic film and fiction but a collapsing, crumbling stratigraphy of textile, resin, skin, muscle, organs, and skeleton."[58] This was doubly true of the South American dead, which, when removed from dry interments to become specimens, were even more affected by the conditions that induce decay, especially when dissected.[59]

This Egyptian comparison also helps explain why San Martín's Inca went to the Royal Anatomy Museum in London. In Peru, disarticulating the dead had been part of their study since the Jesuits. In Europe, loose remains were still ground up for "mummy" medicine and paint, but mummies wrapped with hieroglyph-covered bandages seem to have been immune through the eighteenth century, given that to dissect them would destroy their arcane illegibility.[60] In 1792, however, Göttingen anatomist Johann Blumenbach broke the spell. Blumenbach sought skulls for a research project that asserted the historic divisions of what he believed were humanity's five races—American, Ethiopian, Malayan, Mongoloid, and Caucasian, whom he came to believe were ancestors of all.[61] But when he unwrapped three small mummies in the British Museum he found they were possibly fakes. Human bones, linen scraps, and debris were bundled with ancient linen to meet European collectors' expectations of what "mummies" looked like.[62]

Unwrapping Egyptian mummies to reveal their identity became a scientific performance, and it displaced them from their original antiquarian settings. By 1811, British Museum curators viewed mummies as "a harbor for dirt . . . only fit to be destroyed," donating several to London's Royal Academy of Surgeons, where San Martín's Inca would also be sent.[63] From the 1820s on, surgeons like Augustus Bozzi Granville and Thomas Joseph "Mummy" Pettigrew unwrapped Egyptians for popular and learned audiences, explaining the nonmystical means of their embalming, exposing their sex, and sometimes dissecting them to ascribe their "race." These unwrappings tore through the layers that made the dead sacred, instead diagnosing their mortality and means of preservation.[64]

Barrera's dissection of an "ancient Peruvian" and the diversion of San Martín's Inca to the Royal Academy of Surgeons were thus part of a shared story. Mummies were submitted to a way of knowing in which they ceased to be a relatively self-evident antiquity and instead became a corpse for scholars and anatomists to demystify. Their comparison also allowed different types of mummification to be ranked. Once in the Hunterian Museum, San Martín's Inca was too rare to be dissected—at least at first—but was displayed as a specimen whose preservation could be judged alongside that of a "perfect" Egyptian mummy—"an excellent example of the mode of embalming practiced in ancient Egypt"—and the body

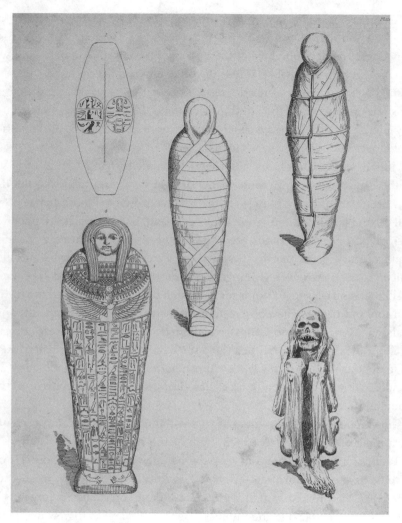

Fig. 4.4 This plate compared San Martín's "Inca mummy" to his Egyptian counterparts, presenting the former as an example of "natural" mummification, and the latter as "artificial." Thomas Joseph Pettigrew, *A History of Egyptian Mummies* (1834), Plate V. Courtesy of University of Pennsylvania Museum Library.

of an Englishwoman whose dentist husband "embalmed" her upon death.[65] In 1834, in his *History of Egyptian Mummies*, "Mummy" Pettigrew distinguished between mummies "naturally" preserved by climactic or mineral conditions, and those that were "artificial"—embalmed by human hands. The distinction was itself artificial, given that the Andean decision to entrust the dead to a spirited and preserving landscape made more complex arrangements unnecessary; it was Pettigrew who saw humans, "nature," and the sacred as separate. But Pettigrew found it useful. While allowing for Garcilaso de la Vega Inca's memory of "his royal ancestors," Pettigrew deemed San Martín's mummy an example of how Peru's salt, sand, dry air, and chalky soil made "dried (for it is really not proper to call them embalmed) bodies."[66]

Identifying nature as the Andean dead's agent of preservation was nonetheless powerful in Peru, where commodified natural resources were an avenue for republican development. This was the tack that Rivero, Barrera's supervisor, took in the debate. As a trained mining engineer, Rivero was primarily concerned with the nation's material and technological growth; an adherent of Humboldt's claim that the original Inca leader, Manco Capac, was an "Oriental sage," Rivero believed that overestimating the Incas' achievements made Peru's actual resources hard to see.[67] Rivero thus submitted Barrera's claim for widespread ancient Peruvian embalming to his own experience and training in chemical analysis.[68] In the 1841 edition of his *Antiguedades Peruanas,* Rivero referred to the National Museum's four Cajatambo bodies, noting that in "none of these *Mummies* . . . has it been possible to discover herbs, resins, or other preservatives with which they were interred."[69] Their preservation, then, owed not to a romantic past of embalmers but to Peru's natural conditions—its dry air and desiccating earth whose minerals and nitrates Rivero promoted.[70]

The Andean dead's export carried these Peruvian debates across the Atlantic. Foreign visitors spoke with the National Museum's keepers, Rivero and Barrera, and then ordered mummies for collections of their own or experimented with digging up the dead themselves. In the early 1830s, for example, Prussian naturalist Franz Julius Ferdinand Meyen believed the National Museum's mummies were the country's "greatest rarities," the most expensive to acquire.[71] Meyen brought four to Lima, two of which were destined for the Anatomical Museum of Berlin, where he promoted them using Barrera's "interesting" essay. While disagreeing with some of Barrera's claims, Meyen credited him for at least establishing elite Inca embalming. Moreover, Meyen celebrated how Peruvians were studying the dead rather than ransacking them—"gathering the remnants of the creative industries of that half-extinct nation."[72] Citing Barrera and Meyen, scholars in Denmark, France, Italy, Great Britain, Chile, and the United States referred to a "Peruvian mode of embalming" well into the next century. They tested Barrera's theory of evisceration and resinous embalming by dissecting South American mummies exported for their own museums and anatomical cabinets.[73]

Other scientific travelers and collectors followed Rivero, celebrating the wondrously "mummifying nature of [Peru's] climate" over Barrera's "zealous" vision of an ancient nation of embalmers. Swiss naturalist Johann Jakob von Tschudi returned to Europe from Peru in 1843 and delivered a collection of Peruvian mummies and skulls to Blumenbach's collection at the Physiological Institute of Göttingen.[74] The final pages of his *Travels in Peru during the Years 1838–1842* were devoted to their interpretation, citing Acosta and Garcilaso to claim that the "ancient Peruvians were acquainted with the art of embalming, but . . . employed it only for the bodies of their kings." Tschudi "deplored" how Spanish "fanaticism" destroyed the Inca "mummies." Tschudi then combined his own exhumations and exports of the Peruvian dead from the coast and sierra with Rivero's observations in *Antiguedades Peruanas* to assert that the wider "process [of embalming] never had any existence, save in the imagination of Barrera," who—Tschudi hinted—projected Egyptian embalming upon "Indians" at large. Tschudi instead credited the coast's hot sun and nitrate-rich sand and the mountains' "pure atmosphere" and "peculiarly drying" wind—characteristics of "Nature's bounteously favoured land" so "adverse[ly]" affected by "Spanish dominion."[75]

It was a telling end to his book. Spain had repressed both Inca mummies and Peruvian nature, but Peru's natural and historical bounty was unlocked by collaborations between foreign and republican scientific actors. In 1851 in Vienna, Tschudi worked with Rivero to bring out an expanded edition of Rivero's *Antiguedades Peruanas*. The book's promotion of Peruvian history and pre-Hispanic antiquities was a major event. Its frontispiece "entombed" the portraits of the Inca kings in the Sun-gate of Tiwanaku, claiming them as the foundations of "Peruvian civilization." Its lavish plates depicted the contents of Peru's National Museum, making it a mobile counterpart to the opening of a salon for American antiquities at the Louvre in Paris the previous year.[76]

Rivero and Tschudi's text was also important for the anatomical and mortuary knowledges it expressed. The majority of the book displayed Rivero's wide knowledge of both Andean tombs and colonial sources. This included the archbishop of Lima's 1649 instructions on how to investigate and extirpate the "idolatries" of Peru's peoples, by which Rivero introduced "mallki," a preserved and venerated ancestor, to the international lexicon. The book's dedicated chapter on the mummified dead also drew from Tschudi. Generalizing from the "hundreds of these corpses" both men uncovered on the coast and sierra, they referred readers to Rivero's failure to find evidence of "herbs, or other preservatives" in the four Cajatambo mummies in the National Museum. They allowed for embalming among "a certain class of Incas," but dismissed Barrera as having composed the recipe of its wider practice "according to the method which the Egyptians used to prepare their mummies"—a "mere play of fancy."[77] The first five plates of the book's volume of lithographs unbundled the National Museum's Cajatambo mummies for the viewer, highlighting their preservation and decay into racialized skulls (see plates 5a and 5b, and figure 4.5).

Rivero and Tschudi also agreed that the method of the Peruvian dead's preservation was unknowable without new chemical analyses. This was impossible for the long-lost Inca royalty, but not for the rest of the Andean dead. Like

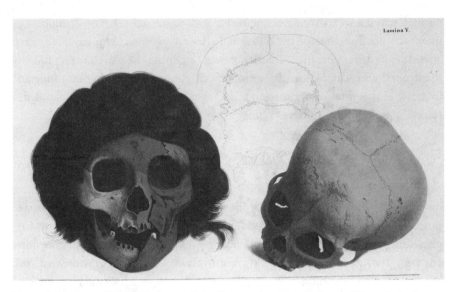

Fig. 4.5 Rivero and Tschudi depicted the disarticulated head of a pre-Hispanic Andean mummy, with hair and preserved skin, alongside a skull with the scalp removed, to reveal their shared cranial form. D. Leopoldo Müller, Plate V, in Mariano Eduardo de Rivero and Johann Jakob von Tschudi, *Antigüedades Peruanas* (Vienna, 1851).

Barrera, Rivero and Tschudi had cut the dead open, but saw no evidence of evisceration or "preservatives." They found a "brown or blackish mass" in Andean skulls—that in Egypt's mummies was believed to be resin—and sent it to a chemical pathologist at the University of Giessen, in Germany. "Chemical and microscopical analysis" showed it "was composed of cerebral fat and globules of dried blood . . . [lacking] the slightest vestige of a vegetable substance."[78]

Their trump card was horrific. They described how in 1841 they—though possibly just Tschudi—had found "the mummy of a pregnant woman, perfectly preserved," in "a cave of Huichay, two leagues from Tarma," and cut her open to extract her "foetus, which is now in our possession, mummified." In Europe, the fetus was examined by a German obstetrician, who said it was seven months in gestation. Rivero and Tschudi commissioned an illustrated plate depicting the fetus which, with a reference to another mummified woman who had died in childbirth and whose mummified infant was still crowning, were presented as "conclusive" "proofs which militate against an artificial mummification."[79]

In the name of knowing "ancient Peruvian" bodies in a way that Spain supposedly repressed, Rivero, Tschudi, and Barrera extended their disarticulation. Barrera's goal was to elevate the sciences of the Peruvian past; Rivero celebrated those of the present. Continental collectors sought Rivero's particular expertise to explain the "infinite number of Peruvian mummies" that were now making their way to collections beyond Peru.[80] But the translation of both by European natural scientists, anatomists, chemists, and obstetricians like Tschudi—all men—undid the labor of the "ancient Peruvian" women who cared for their ancestors and descendants. That labor was not limited to the preservation of the dead; it was also the literal planting of generations—a mother bundling and interring a daughter and grandchild. What Barrera, Rivero, and Tschudi dissected, in the name of understanding mummification, was love.

———

Scholars were also interested in how Inca or "Indian" Peruvians related to these mummies and their belongings. Some republican actors advised and assisted in exhuming these "gentiles," extending their own labors as Christian and republican grave-openers. Others opened graves to reinvent old relationships, engaging the "gentiles" and "grandparents" to heal the temporal present. Still others kept the dead hidden, hoping to avoid their offense. Outsiders collected their reasons for doing so, bundling them with the uncanny bodies and objects whose export shaped Peruvian law.[81]

In the first several decades after independence, these outsiders sought the former Incas themselves. In 1825 Venezuelan "liberator" Simón Bolívar had abolished Peru's hereditary titles of nobility, including those of the Incas and their fellow Andean lords. Although the ideal of a past "Inca" empire remained politically useful, particularly in Cuzco and southern Peru, living Inca descendants found themselves subject to an antiquarian culture that treated their ancestry as antiquity, their knowledge as folklore, and their material culture as museum objects.[82]

Some heirs joined the conversation. Don Justo Apu Sahuaraura was a church canon and supporter of independence who was also an Inca heir. In 1837 he wrote to the *Museo Erudito*, a periodical in Cuzco devoted to antiquarianism, literature, and science, to correct a recent article about how Gonzalo Pizarro had looted and burned the mummy of Viracocha. Sahuahaura explained that, during his childhood under the Spanish, his grandmothers spent evenings discussing the "heroic actions of their grandparents, the sovereigns," and how they were described by Garcilaso. His grandmothers told him that Viracocha and his fellow sovereigns had been disemboweled and embalmed with odiferous herbs before being brought to the snow-covered peak of Pachatusan, to the northeast of Cuzco, where they dried in such a manner that they seemed alive. After this they were placed in the Temple of the Sun.[83]

Sahuahaura had surpassed Garcilaso. The detail that the Inca dead went to Pachatusan was singular, a piece of unique ethnohistorical memory passed down by his grandmothers, or a claim based on their understanding of the surrounding landscape. Sahuaraura's family continued to interpret their genealogical past, which Sahuaraura and fellow former Incas like him hoped to contribute to the journal, "providing insight into our antiquities" and, in Sahuaraura's case, to seek a pension from the nation.[84] Sahuaraura was successful in the former, though not the latter. He died in 1848 unsupported by the state, but in 1857 a member of France's Academy of Sciences who had traveled to Peru cited both Rivero and "don Justo Sahuaraura of Cuzco, descendant of the ancient Incas" to explain a mummy the Academy acquired. "In the many conversations that this worthy canon had with one of us, [we were] easily convinced that the body of the greatest of the Incas of Peru must have been placed in the Temple of the Sun in Cuzco" and had not been burned.[85] While Barrera dissected and Rivero displayed, Sahuaraura gave his grandmothers' knowledge of Viracocha new life.

The non-Inca dead remained accessible, however, especially as republican bureaucracies gradually lost interest in governing grave-opening. A casual economy of opening "sepulchers" and collecting its "ornaments" was centuries old; by independence it was a profession.[86] San Martín's advisers observed professional grave-openers as they marched on Lima, and their 1822 decree claiming huacas for the nation, forbidding the export of their contents, could be understood as an attempt to seize the Crown's old share of grave-opening's profits but also the funds that everyday Peruvian grave-openers were taking for themselves.[87]

Contrary to assumptions that the republic's attempts at regulation were a failure, evidence exists that they were occasionally applied. In 1828 an "old *Aduanero*," a customs agent, halted a collection of antiquities that the US Consul in Lima hoped to send from Trujillo to Philadelphia, calling it "contraband." The consul's factor hoped to "get around him"—and he seems to have done so, which suggests smuggling, if not bribery. If there was one aduanero willing to halt the flow of Peruvian antiquities outside of the country, there were likely more.[88]

Yet this protectionism conflicted with liberal experiments in developing Peru's economy and knowing and sharing its past.[89] Grave-opening became a way for the rural poor to survive independence's economic contractions, as well as a semiscientific entertainment among the middling and upper classes. By the 1830s, parties of men and women, Peruvian and foreign, ventured from coastal cities—Lima, Trujillo, Arica—into Peru's countryside to disinter the dead "by way of amusement."[90] In 1837 a minister lamented that "with the exception of two or three people, no one has asked for permission [to excavate], and it's public knowledge that [artifacts] are continuously exported to Europe."[91] In November 1839 Peru's Congress opted for deregulation, decreeing that "all Peruvians that might desire to work in the discovery of hidden treasure, commonly known as *huacas*, could do so freely without being obliged to pay" as "required by the older laws," whose inordinate demands were presented as inimical to the discovery of "curious things that might be possessed."[92] The Peruvian past was to be developed like other national resources, encouraging locally patriotic excavations.

These shifts helped give grave-opening and antiquarianism their republican values, only some of which were economic. The 1840s and 1850s saw male and female elites make antiquarian friendships by supporting each other's collections. In Cuzco, local notables founded the city's first Archaeological Museum.[93] In Lima, flush with guano money, the National Museum received a wave of donations: "gold idols," ceramics found by mining engineers, "antediluvian bones," "crania of the ancient Indians," a new "mummy."[94] Stoking foreign scientific interest was also the point. Before collaborating with Tschudi, Mariano Eduardo de Rivero had worked with natural scientists like Joseph Barclay Pentland, whose interest in guano and Andean skulls brought both to Great Britain.[95] This was grave-opening as national improvement, connecting local and international objects and knowledges that Spain had sought to control.

These collaborations also sought the knowledge of "Indians" who during the late viceroyalty were believed to be mourning the Incas and expressing regret at their looting.[96] In April 1821 British diplomat Alexander Caldcleugh traveled with a Spanish general to La Magdalena, a historically Indigenous community outside of Lima surrounded by "Indian huacas or graves." While investigating them, "an Indian passed by, who was asked by [the general] what the mounds were, or if they contained any thing [sic]? He made no reply, but slowly proceeded with sorrow and regret strongly marked on his countenance." When Caldcleugh procured a huaco, a portrait ceramic, another "Indian" he met in Lima "instantly said the Cacique in front of it"—that is, the sculpted face—"was nearly related to him.[97]

This perceived continuity between Indigenous citizens and the forebears whose looting they lamented was in part a trope—a repeated tale bound up in the early republican invention of the ideology of indigenismo, which sought to rescue "the Indian" symbolic of the nation from an abyss of colonial history. Art historian Natalia Majluf ties this process to painter Francisco Laso's Inhabitant of the Cordilleras of Peru (1855), in which a dignified but "poor Andean" in a black poncho—which creoles claimed Indians wore in mourning for the lost Inca—cradles a battered pre-Hispanic Moche vessel.[98] Yet Laso's painting was also misread as a depiction of investigation. When Laso submitted the painting to the Universal Exhibition of 1855 in Paris, a French artist recently returned from Peru read it as representing a rural "archaeologist," who had recently discovered the ceramic "in some sepulture of the ancient Peruvians."[99]

That interpretation misrepresented Laso's artistic intentions but had a logic of its own, given that some Andean peoples through independence also dug for the dead and were sought as experts in their uncovering. Through the late eighteenth century, descendants of the Chimu had covered their tribute to the Crown

Fig. 4.6 Francisco Laso's painting purported to depict an "Indigenous" Peruvian holding a pre-Hispanic ceramic, mourning the original Andean sovereigns ravaged by Spanish rule. One French critic misperceived the painting as depicting an "archaeologist." Francisco Laso, *Habitante de las cordilleras* (1855). Photographed by Yutaka Yoshii. Pinacoteca Municipal Ignacio Merino. Municipalidad Metropolitana de Lima.

by looting mortuary palaces.[100] After independence, travelers claimed that living "Indians" on the coast "look upon the ransacking of these monuments of their ancestors with a stoical indifference" and that they were even expert in how to dig them up.[101] The "ordinary method," reported one English visitor to the ruins of Chan Chan on Peru's northern coast, was to "employ an Indian who, from experience, is pretty expert in guessing at good situations; he probes the hillock with an iron rod"—a long *sonda*, or probe—"and as soon as he finds a hollow, the party commences digging, and is usually rewarded according to the rank of the

Indian whose tomb they have invaded."[102] In Arica, an American surgeon asked an "Indian" fishing along the shore for methods to "discover" ancient graves. He "told us that there were none, except to stamp upon the ground, and dig where it sounded hollow. We pursued this plan with considerable success."[103]

The problem with wholly accepting these visions of inscrutable "Indians" lamenting or facilitating looting is that outsiders used both to justify science's salvage of the dead.[104] Both claims also presumed that those being collected, and those being asked to collect, *were* "Indians," rather than the more complex identities produced by three hundred years of Spanish rule. For centuries, individuals had left Andean communities to avoid taxes, labor requirements, and the abuse of being labeled "Indian."[105] Learning Spanish, changing their dress, and finding partners of non-Indigenous descent, they confounded categorization.

Peruvian independence made those identities even more complex. In 1825, Simón Bolívar had abolished "Indian" tribute, but also communal land ownership—a "colonial" vestige that nonetheless gave some Indigenous groups protection against those who would steal their land. The Peruvian Congress's subsequent resurrection of the "Indian" head tax as an Indigenous "contribution" made even more clear that colonialism's race-based exploitations continued.[106] Individuals or communities therefore had something to gain by acting in ways that "Indians" did not—such as digging up the dead whose "gentility" marked them as outside the community's or state's Christian body politic.

Digging the non-Christian dead was therefore a mark of modernity inherited from the conquest. The colonial dead—Spanish, African, Andean—were protected by church interments and cemeteries, but also by officials who ensured the reinterment of "remains . . . of the venerable and exemplary, and those of the common faithful" if they were disinterred by new constructions, as happened when Lima's Convento Supremo de San Juan de Dios was destroyed to build Peru's first railroad station.[107] The "Inca" and "gentile" dead, however, had less luck. French naval captain Abel Aubert du Petit-Thouars, knowing "the great valley covered with sand situated to the south of the Morro of Arica had been a burial place of the ancient Peruvians," "asked the governor of Arica for authorization to carry out some excavations in this valley of tombs." A quarter-century later he still remembered the response. "He answered me with great politeness that, since all those dead had not been baptized, I could do what I wanted."[108] What distinguished the grave-opener who held the sonda from the skull smashed in by its probe was that the latter was not believed to be Christian—a distinction that may have mattered more than an identity as "Indian."

Nonetheless, the violence aimed at the dead suggests more was at play. In the late 1850s Italian-Peruvian geographer Antonio Raimondi traveled Peru collecting human remains for the University of San Marcos's Faculty of Medicine, and assaying Peru's resources for the national government. Raimondi came to blame everyday grave-openers for how their looting and destruction thwarted scholarly attempts at collection (namely his own). Yet the aggression he registered was bracing. Raimondi lamented that "peons" in one region "crushed almost all the crania" of skeletons they found. A rich *gobernador*, a district governor, even boasted of "crush[ing] with his own hands close to three thousand skulls."[109] Whether the pleasure the gobernador took in his violence was because they were non-Christian or understood to be Indigenous is unclear.

That aggression was likely also related to a belief that the dead remained powerful, requiring grave-opening's ritualization, as travelers often noted. As under Spanish rule, some Peruvians treated "Inca" or "gentile" huacas as spirited beings, to be appealed to for financial support when looted or encountered in fields or countrysides. If handled or improperly approached, the "gentile" dead could be jealous and vengeful, sickening the living with spiritual and physical maladies called *chacho, chullpa usu, humpe, mal de huaca*, or *Mochuscca*, that "little by little dried one up." If they were appeased, the rewards included skulls and huacos (empowered funerary ceramics) that could become part of healing ceremonies or, placed above doorways, protect a home. Like metal ornaments, these objects could be sold to antiquarians in times of economic hardship, as could the knowledge of how to dig for a dangerous "ancient" dead that might smile upon the living.[110]

That knowledge also led some Peruvians to warn against looting by outsiders. In the 1830s in a tavern in coastal Lambayeque, for example, a friar named Tomás bragged of looting "graves of the children of the sun" and drinking corn beer from their vessels. A "tall Indian" listening to the conversation interjected that a huaca in question was "enchanted" and should not be dug. Whether or not the individual would have identified as an "Indian," he was demanding that this particular huaca be respected as an agential being—a suggestion that the friar rejected. "It is no such thing—thou knowest nothing," Tomás snapped. "Don't you believe him," he told an American surgeon and skull-hunter listening to the exchange.[111]

As creole and foreign grave-openers followed the railroads from coastal cities to highland settings, their collecting increasingly registered these "Andean" ritual knowledges.[112] Geographer Raimondi encountered Timoteo Condor, from the rural community of Pumamarca, who had "found in his *chacra* [fields] a great quantity of ancient skeletons," but Raimondi "couldn't get him to show me the site, even when I offered to pay him a *peso* for every skeleton that he extracted." Afterward Raimondi learned that "Condor had placed coca leaves in the mouths of some of the cadavers and gifted cigars to others with the hope that, in gratitude, they would show him a buried treasure."[113] During his grave-opening travels, Swiss collector Tschudi employed a man from Huari named Hatun Huamang, whom he perhaps had in mind when wondering at how, "when a Peruvian on a journey falls in with a mummy, he, with timid reverence, presents to it some coca leaves as his pious offering."[114]

The coastal republic's relative lack of interest in rural communities' well-being even seems to have allowed some communities to renew "religious rituals away from the watchful eye of would be 'civilizers' and nation-builders."[115] In Huarochirí—where seventeenth-century Spanish priests had confiscated so many sacred Yauyo ancestors—those rituals once again included the use of "ancient" remains to manipulate life-giving waters. In 1861 Raimondi followed the Rimac River into the mountains east of Lima, where he learned that Ayamachay, a nearby "cave with mummies of the ancient Indians," was being used by "Indians" around the town of San Mateo to ensure the right amount of water for their crops. The "*Indios* firmly believe that they can stop the rains by bringing down a mummy of the ancient *judios* that they refer to as *abuelitos*"—that is, the "ancient Jews that they refer to as the little or beautiful grandparents."[116]

If calling mummies little or beautiful grandparents is understandable, their description as *judios* might be less so. The editor who later transcribed Raimondi's papers could have mistaken "*yndio*" ("Indian"), written in cursive, for "*judio*." Yet both possibilities underline how Andean communities continued to access interments to understand or heal the present. Some Andean communities approach the "ancient" inhabitants of nearby chullpas (mortuary towers) as precolonial "Indian" or "gentile" dead that exist in "the pre-Christian, diabolic space of pagan Romans and perfidious Jews who, in Spanish accounts of Christ's passion tried and failed to kill Christ." This nonetheless makes them cosmically and historically essential.[117] As Jews and pagans were to Christians, "ancient Indian" mummies were to villagers: antecessors—not ancestors—from an earlier age of humanity, honorary if not always literal "grandparents" whose proper treatment could yield fortune, treasure, or rains. Offered coca, removed from their tombs, and carried through the landscape to communicate with water-yielding mountains, they remained powerful, despite three centuries of claims to the contrary.[118] For Raimondi, these mummies' parade was an "Indian" superstition. For the community, it was an independent knowledge of their interdependence with the past, the cosmos, and time itself.

Over the next half-century, these parallel ways of opening tombs and engaging with "ancient" remains as agential beings and scientific objects would connect and compete. The knowledge that some communities still ritualized the Andean dead even made them more compelling and authentic as collectors' items. In 1851 an Irish sea captain named George B. Duniam explained to the Australian Museum in Sydney why he wanted £200—$25,100 in today's money—for two

Peruvian mummies he was selling. In addition to Peruvian laws against export, the "native inhabitants venerating the dead to an extreme would not hesitate to commit the greatest violence on the party attempting to remove them from the soil." He had therefore incurred "great risk . . . in digging them up (which could only be done at night) and getting them off the coast." This was likely an exaggeration to procure a higher price given that Duniam's mummies came from Arica, where a laissez-faire attitude to grave-opening reigned.[119] But the frisson of theft enriched the body's value. For the rest of the century speculators used these stories and Peru's formal prohibitions on export to drive up the price of the objects and mummies they collected.[120]

In the decades since San Martín's Inca crossed the Atlantic as a unique diplomatic gift, "ancient Peruvian" and "Inca" mummies" had become commodities whose value came from a specific understanding of Indigenous history and Peruvian science.[121] An Englishman in Tacna had a large collection of Arica mummies by 1833, "which he is constantly increasing; for a pair of these mummies, when perfect, he pays a doubloon."[122] The following year, Prussian naturalist Meyen observed that "It happens very rarely that a well-preserved mummy arrives" to Europe, but his own subsequent deliveries helped teach European scholars that enterprising sea captains and businessmen could "obtain any quantity of mummies at Arica, or some other seaport town."[123] By the 1880s, mummies were perceived as "so common . . . that they can be dug up almost anywhere, or can be purchased for four or five dollars a piece."[124]

The mummies were less shelf-stable than the "antiquities" that more generally fueled disinterment, but their perceived accessibility encouraged their collection by scientific institutions worldwide. San Martín's Inca gave England an early start. In 1846 London's Ethnological Society posed the question of whether "the ancient Peruvians embalmed the dead" to Great Britain's wider scientific community: "there being some Peruvian mummies in this country, it would doubtlessly soon be set at rest by examination."[125] By 1848 there were at least fifteen mummies in British museums large and small, including four from Arica at the British Museum—one found embedded in the guano whose trade tied England and Peru together. At least two roamed the countryside in traveling fairs.[126] One promoter's claim that his was "the only specimen of the kind ever exhibited in England" was met with derision.[127]

Andean mummies became such an object of speculation that collectors with the barest knowledge of Peruvian history tried to foil their foreign counterparts. In 1839 London learned that an agent for Russia's Imperial Academy of Science was in Peru and negotiating "for the PURCHASE of the lately discovered MUMMY (supposed to be that of Montezuma)." Knowing that Peru's "Montezuma"—despite being an Aztec emperor—could travel to Russia via Britain, directors of the British and Foreign Medical Institution placed an advertisement above the fold of London's *Morning Chronicle*, offering an incredible "advance of £100 (in addition to the sum then offered for it)," as well as expenses, if it were instead delivered to the institute.[128] (By comparison, an Egyptian mummy in the mid-1830s could be had at Sotheby's for £36 15s.[129])

The gambit failed. By the early 1850s St. Petersburg's Imperial Academy had an Andean mummy, and counterparts were found in France's National Museum of Natural History in Paris, Copenhagen's Royal Chamber of Curiosities, Sweden's Stockholm Museum, Chile's National Museum in Santiago, Bavaria's Scotch College in Ratisbon, Hanover's Physiological Institute of Göttingen, Australia's National Museum in Sydney, and a number of museums in the United States. Belgium's Museum of Natural History had seven. By the 1860s at least twenty Andean mummies from northern Chile and Peru had gone where Huayna Capac's mummy had not: Spain itself.[130]

Once installed, these mummies were displayed and discussed as antiquities; as mobile laboratories for the testing of anatomical preservation along the lines debated by Barrera, Rivero, and Sahauraura; and as racialized specimens supposedly revealing who "Indians" were before colonialism and admixture. But they also could include the anticolonial messages that Ulloa and Unanue had tried so hard to disprove. The Hunterian Museum, for example, retained the narrative that accompanied San Martín's Inca—that he was from among the Inca or Andean lords who had killed or sacrificed themselves rather than "submit to the fate with which the Spaniards threatened them."[131] "There is every reason to consider the history of this figure as extraordinary as its appearance," read one London guidebook. Though this "painful-looking figure raised upon a high pedestal" let viewers feel superior to the "dreadful instance of the lengths to which man's wild imagination will carry him," that history's retention extended the story that some Andean peoples told to make sense of their antecessors' protest of Spanish rule.[132] Even Tschudi transmitted without comment the belief that the mummified dead represented the "great number of Indians [that] committed suicide in despair" of the conquest.[133]

This narrative was useful to republicans and outsiders interested in distinguishing themselves from both the Spanish and those Peruvians who ritualized "abuelitos" to cure the rain. Nevertheless, the Andean dead's mummified yet fetal forms also transmitted an uncanny liveliness that challenged attempts to read them as wholly scientific objects.[134] In 1859, geographer Raimondi sent the Civic Museum in Milan (his birthplace) a "natural mummy" from coastal Chincha. The following year, the museum's curator, Emilio Cornalia, published as nuanced and sensitive an appreciation of the Peruvian dead as any in the nineteenth century. He pronounced the body before him as "not just rare but very rare," given how Peruvian mummies were even more easily broken than those of Egypt. Fascinated by its preservation, he sampled its muscles and ligaments to soak in water. Examined by microscope, they seemed like the flesh of "a day-old corpse." Cornalia cited and rejected Barrera's claim that Peruvians had embalmed the dead exactly like the Egyptians, given that this mummy's viscera were visible through a hole in its side—but he argued that their mummification was still artificial, even as it drew from Peruvian nature: "The ancient inhabitants of [Peru] knew the singular property of their land and drew from it by entrusting to it the corpses of their loved ones, whom that ground, not voracious for human bodies, mercifully preserved."[135]

The insight was a rare recognition of how the Andean use of sacred environments was itself knowledge-based, which in this case had become a cultural technology to mourn the dead and reproduce society. Yet it also meant that there were limits in how far Cornalia took this mummy's study. Like those who had encountered the Andean dead before him, Cornalia was struck by their seated, seed-like pose, the face cradled by their hands. "Ambe le mani pel dolor mi morsi," Cornalia wrote, trusting Italian readers to recognize a count's lament in the Eighth Circle of Dante's *Inferno*, for having eaten his sons: "I bit both my hands in grief." Cornalia was thus loath to do anything that might break the spell, namely dissection. "I did not dare, as much as I would have liked, to look into the skull for the cerebral matter," he admitted, fearing the mummy would have fallen apart. Instead, he commissioned an illustration whose incredible detail mapped the body's sea of preserved flesh (see plate 6).[136] This sort of illustration saved the dead from the Peruvian grave-openers that—as Raimondi told his journal—had covered "piles of earth with thousands of human crania and bones belonging to the ancient Indians."[137] But it was also a sentence of another sort, committing its subject to an inferno of permanent grief.

Collectors would put those piles of "ancient Indian" skulls left behind to a very particular use. But their exposure also administered a test: whether these would-be speakers for the dead were aware of their own place in this landscape. The Scotch College's two bodies, for example, were sent by a Dr. Reid of Aberdeen. Reid had found these "Peruvian mummies" bodies in the northern Chilean site of Chiu Chiu, in the Atacama desert, amid five hundred or six hundred other mummified bodies—men, women, and children—whom Reid described as emerging from the sands, seated in a semicircle, staring forward. Reid believed, like the Huarmey fisherman, that it was "probable that they buried themselves." The "fact of their being all in the same position, and with an expression of pain, which is yet visible on their countenances, may serve to shew that these miserable creatures withdrew themselves from the ravages of the Spaniards, and, in despair, sought death in this awful wilderness." But Reid also looked in the mirror. "One imagines himself altogether in another world, and asks, 'What seek you here?' "[138]

5

Mismeasuring Incas

Samuel George Morton and the American School of
Peruvian Skull Science

Sometime in the late 1830s a North American surgeon named Samuel George
Morton decapitated a mummified woman from ancient Peru. Unearthed in the
Atacama Desert, this "Inca" woman arrived in Philadelphia in 1835 with a man
and a child. Together, they were the first three "Peruvian" mummies to go on
display in the United States, in the nation's first successful public museum, the
Philadelphia Museum.[1]

The mummies' display owed to the museum's efforts at broadening its South
American holdings, but also to Peru's own promotions of the Andean dead.
Since the death of its founder, Charles Willson Peale, in 1827, the museum
had looked to explorations and exchanges with republican sisters, like Peru's
National Museum in Lima. In April 1831 its trustees sent a box of specimens
to the Lima museum's director, Francisco Barrera, who had championed the
Peruvians' dissection some years before.[2] Whether the man, woman, and child
in Philadelphia were Barrera's reciprocal offering is unclear, but they certainly
embodied the "embalmed" ancient science that he and his museum's founder,
Mariano Eduardo de Rivero, debated. At a time when Peale's museum was
struggling financially, the Peruvians' display with several "heathen idols of for-
midable appearance and curious workmanship" helped "attract much attention."
By the early 1840s, visitors met the mummies "as a family of the Incas of Peru,
preserved by embalming, like the mummies of the ancient Egyptians, and, like
them, wrapped in cloths saturated with the embalming substances."[3]

By then, Morton had disarticulated the family's supposed mother for a science of another sort. He had help from the museum's curator, Titian Peale,
the founder's son. The collector of some 550 zoological specimens of his own
in Colombia, Titian made the museum available to scholars who shared his

Empires of the Dead. Christopher Heaney, Oxford University Press. © Oxford University Press 2023.
DOI: 10.1093/oso/9780197542552.003.0006

interest in expanding American knowledge.[4] The first use of the "Inca family" in this way came shortly after their Philadelphia arrival. The museum unbundled their bodies, revealing that the woman had a small bag of bone tools and copper fishhooks. Another body was wrapped with coca leaves and lime, for chewing, "small bags of *Indian corn meal*, and *one ear* of *Indian corn*." A Philadelphia lawyer, Peter Arrell Browne, experimented with the corn. Citing it as evidence that maize was Indigenous to the Americas, Browne convinced Titian to provide a few of the ear's kernels to plant so that he could test the temporal limits of dried corn's ability to germinate.[5] In a similar collaboration, Peale allowed Morton— who believed the study of skulls revealed their character and civilization—to strip the mummified woman's head of her "very long" hair, which "had lost none of its natural black color," along with her skin.[6] Morton registered her skull's dimensions and angles. He filled her cranium with white pepper seed, to quantify her capacity.

In doing so, Morton took the Incas' measure.

Browne's centuries-old corn almost certainly never germinated, whereas Morton's experiment seeded his methods and conclusions far and wide. Morton was writing his first monograph, *Crania Americana* (1839), which amassed and measured skulls to quantify differences between humanity's five supposedly separate and unequal races. The book became the seminal text of the "American School" of ethnology, helping shift interest in Indigenous peoples from the comparative study of language and culture to their increasingly quantified bodies and skulls. The Smithsonian's first physical anthropologist later deemed Morton the "father of American anthropology."[7] Seen from the twenty-first century, Morton's theories of separate human origins are glaringly racist. In his time, they rationalized white supremacist settler colonialism and chattel slavery. They shaped eugenic thought for generations, and their methods inspired white surgeons, anthropologists, and ethnologists on both sides of the Atlantic to measure the skulls and skins of nonwhite peoples, accumulated through increasingly violent means.[8]

Yet Morton's contribution to American anthropology's beginnings was also Peruvian in its origins.[9] The Andean dead were *Crania Americana*'s cornerstone— the primary and essential set whose numbers and historical reputation allowed Morton to mount statistical arguments regarding his supposed science's ability to measure racial continuity and difference over time.[10] The first "American" skull to enter Morton's collection was from Peru; the earliest written pages of *Crania Americana* were an exploration of the "Ancient Peruvians" to whom it belonged, for which Morton immersed himself in centuries of Peruvian scholarship. He examined and collected more "Ancient Peruvian" and "Inca" skulls than any other group, such that the largest single population in his lifelong collection of 867 human crania—the largest and most influential worldwide, when he died in 1851—were the "Ancient Peruvians."[11]

Morton's use of Peru's dead has been recognized, but largely as an object of North American racism. Popular historian of science Stephen Jay Gould claimed in *The Mismeasure of Man* that Morton collected a "major overrepresentation of an extreme group—the small-brained Inca Peruvians"—for the same reason he sought skulls worldwide: as extrinsically useful tools in a project to "plummet" his averaged measurements of nonwhite crania across time.[12] Under Morton's supremacist assumptions, these lower averages marked nonwhite peoples as physically and mentally deficient, rationalizing their displacement, enslavement, colonization, and their collection by an expansionist Euro-American society.

This chapter instead makes Morton a phenomenon of the Peruvian dead's prior empire of study and collection. It argues that their preponderance in his skull collection and those he inspired was the result of Peru's own ways of knowing and embodying the past. "There is nothing natural about systematically collecting and studying the dead," as historian Samuel J. Redman notes.[13] Yet between the late eighteenth century and mid-nineteenth century, anatomists went from ascribing racial and national types to individual skulls ("a Caucasian," "a Cherokee") to seeking cranial series, whose scientific usefulness was proportional to their collection's size. This chapter shows how Peru's earlier promotion of "embalmed," "Ancient Peruvian," and "Inca" bodies was the necessary precondition for Morton's anthropological project of systematically collecting and studying the racialized dead.[14] As historians Mark Thurner and Miruna Achim have observed, Morton's use of Peruvian and Spanish American materials shaped his project's intellectual frame.[15] His private papers show why he, like other North Americans before him, specifically looked to the Peruvian dead as the reputed earliest and most "civilized" of Americans. Morton grasped that their antiquity could be combined with the Peruvian dead's large numbers to assist in quantifying and mapping "race" over time; he could measure their preserved skin, hair, and skulls to compare them to their historical reputation in Spanish-American sources and to living Native North Americans.[16] The Andean dead became America's "ancient" racial baseline—but also possibly its peak, from which the Native living had tumbled.

This shift in the Andean dead's collection transformed racializing sciences more generally. In Peru, the dead continued to matter for how their preservation allowed debate over their origins, cause of death, religious beliefs, "embalming" abilities, and Peru's wider resources and climate. In their translation north, Morton quantified and racialized them as "American" and in doing so attempted to move them—and Native peoples in general—from Peru's realm of history to the realm of North Atlantic biology and ethnology. In Morton's hands, Peru's dead came to symbolize inevitable inferiority and extinction—the presumed fate of "all Indians." His next book, *Crania Aegyptiaca*, then applied these methods to "ancient Egyptians" and African peoples and was used to defend modern slavery.[17]

Finally, Morton's use of the Andean dead shaped both North and South American bio-racism, with tremendous consequences for Indigenous people at large.[18] In Peru, where a more cultural understanding of race reigned, Peruvian scholars ridiculed Morton's conclusions, as did other foreign ethnologists.[19] Yet to argue with him, scholars sought large, statistically useful collections of their own. They similarly took advantage of Peruvian tomb-opening, making the Andean dead the largest single population at museums like the Smithsonian and Harvard's Peabody, the first dedicated anthropology museum in the Americas— a core around which the skulls of living Native peoples were collected en masse as well. In this way, Americanist anthropology began with a foot in Andean graves, extending the violence and science that began with the Spanish confiscations of the Inca ancestors to other Indigenous populations worldwide.[20]

A direct answer to how "Ancient Peruvians" defined Morton's collection begins with the fact that his contemporaries had a capacious understanding of "early America."[21] This vastness was geographical, temporal, and societal, and assumed, as did Thomas Jefferson in 1787, that "the antient [*sic*] part of American history is written chiefly in Spanish." That history's embodied remains were believed to be best preserved in the monumental tombs of "Ancient Peruvians," whose priority to Columbus promised a lack of admixture with Europeans, making possible the supposed measure of their civilization.[22] Their comparison with Native North Americans might then determine whether the attributed civility of the "Ancient Peruvians" was a shared or limited American heritage.

Put another way, Peru was America's Egypt and the "Ancient Peruvian" dead were America's first accepted "pre-Columbian" remains—a means of testing Native Americans' antiquity, civility, and racial unity. As Morton noted in lectures and the earliest written section of *Crania Americana*, Peru's ancients used their climate to preserve their dead so well that "the lifeless bodies of whole generations of the former inhabitants of Peru may now be examined, like those from the Theban catacombs, after the lapse of hundreds, perhaps thousands of years." He thus came to desire "a series of crania from the Peruvian sepulchers [tombs], in order to ascertain, if possible, whether they present indications of more than one great family; or, in other words, to inquire whether among them I could trace such departures from the well known type of the American race, as would lead to the supposition that this continent was formerly inhabited by a plurality of races."[23]

Morton came to that desire for two reasons. First, he benefited from millennia of Andean mortuary innovation in the embodiment of time, place, and ancestry in the dead, which he knew via the three centuries of colonial and republican grave-opening whose knowledges had circulated in the Atlantic world. Peruvian texts describing Andean embalming and the mortuary landscape all figured in Morton's reading. Moreover, he knew them from the Peruvian-centric "Dispute of the New World" initiated by the third volume of France's *Histoire Naturelle* (1749), in which the Inca dead were admitted as "mummies," and in which Georges-Louis Leclerc, the Comte de Buffon argued that Mexico and Peru were the Americas' "temperate," "ancient," and civilized heights, whose peoples degenerated by migrating to more typically humid American zones.[24]

What brought that racialization of American history to Morton was European scholars' repurposing of its Peruvian evidence to argue that Indigenous American inferiority was essential, not climactic. To do so, they relied on Spanish natural historians Jorge Juan and Antonio de Ulloa's descriptions of the well-preserved corporeal remains and objects found in Peru's monumental tombs, published in 1749, arguing that they showed that Garcilaso had overesteemed the pre-European Americas' most "civil" peoples, the Incas. American peoples' supposed inferiority, then, was a matter of race rather than climate or abuse by Europeans. Ulloa was particularly useful in that regard. He used the *lineas* of "thickness" of skulls from Peru's "ancient sepulchers" to claim, in 1772, that all Native Americans were cowardly and brutish. This was a crucial moment in the history of racializing sciences in the Americas and the Atlantic world. Early physical anthropology's methods are usually traced to Petrus Camper, an eighteenth-century Dutch comparative anatomist who began racializing the angle of faces. Camper never measured a Native American skull, however, making Ulloa's claim the first documented reference to European-measured Indigenous skulls. This set the stage for a racialized American history in which Peru and its bodies were the prime referent.[25]

The reason American anthropology is more associated with Morton and the United States, not Ulloa and Peru, owes in no small way to Thomas Jefferson. Jefferson's desecration of a Monacan burial monument in Virginia in 1783 is often taken as the beginning of scientific excavation in North America. His description of that act in *Notes on the State of Virginia* (1787) in fact responded to Ulloa, as well as to Europeans like Buffon who saw North American climates as degenerative. To counter Ulloa's Peruvian-centric evidence, Jefferson used local Native cultures, languages, and mortuary evidence to assert that Virginia was the measure by which American nature and history should be judged. Within that history Native Americans were vigorous and brave but incapable of building monuments.[26]

Jefferson was far from the first white North American to assault Indigenous remains with Incas in mind. Partially inspired by early accounts of Peruvian grave-robbing, England's settlers, soldiers, and early republican heirs had disinterred Indians since the late sixteenth century. Settlers took scalps, and displayed and sometimes dissected Native peoples in "semiscientific spectacles," asserting their passage to history.[27] After independence some patriots celebrated the Incas as a contrary model for American illumination, but Jefferson considered them a distraction.[28] "Of the Indian of South America I know nothing," he wrote in his *Notes on the State of Virginia*, "for I would not honor with the appellation of knowledge, what I derive from the fables published of them. These I believe to be just as true as the fables of Aesop." To French inquiries regarding "Indian monuments," he replied that he "kn[e]w of no such thing . . . for I would not honour with that name arrow points, stone hatchets, stone pipes and half-shapen images." To that end, the sacred earthwork he opened was an "abandoned" burial "mound," not a "monument." Challenging the Monacan claim that earthworks originally honored singular leaders, Jefferson believed they revealed a jumbled, unstratified dead showing neither degeneration of a barbaric boldness whose "original character" was best sought in North America, nor any evidence of a degenerated Peruvian civility. The deficiencies Ulloa observed, Jefferson speculated, owed to Spanish rule.[29]

The Peruvians outlasted Jefferson's oblique assault because the supposed disjuncture of their early "American" past and the Indigenous present remained useful. In 1792 the *American Museum*, a Philadelphia journal, presented Ulloa's meditations on the sameness of Indian skins or skulls in Peru or Louisiana as an interesting puzzle, given that Incas seemed to have sprung from "some race more enlightened than the other tribes of Indians, a race of which no individual seems to remain in the present times."[30] US antiquarians extended this sentiment to the North American interior, arguing that the Native peoples who continued to curate these monuments were squatters, unrelated to Peruvian, Viking, or Israelite "moundbuilder" predecessors. The Native Americans could be extirpated, the latter appropriated as settler ancestors. As Andrew Jackson told Congress, defending the Indian Removal Act of the 1830s, the "monuments" and "fortresses" were "memorials of a once powerful race, which was exterminated or has disappeared to make room for the existing savage tribes," making way for "our extensive Republic."[31]

By then the Peruvian example was used to justify not just "tread[ing] on the graves of extinct nations"—per President Jackson—but opening, knowing, and profiting by them.[32] In 1799 the American Philosophical Society published Benjamin Smith Barton's proposal that Ohio's monuments were

made by "Toltecas," who—citing Mexican Jesuit Francisco Javier Clavijero—
were "ancestors of the Peruvians." By cross-multiplication, then, "the ancient
inhabitants of North-America were as polished as the nations of South-America."
Barton called upon fellow republicans to "open the tombs of the ancient
Americans" to "throw some light upon the[ir] ancient history. . . . If we are not
sufficiently animated by the love of science, let us remember, that in the tombs
of the Mexicans and Peruvians, the Spaniards have discovered treasures of gold,
of silver, and of precious stones."[33] Barton saw Peruvian grave-opening as a repli-
cable science of empire: the republic would profit from making ancient Andean
and Native deathways into "American" history.[34]

Yet when it came to skeletal remains—the data that racializing sciences increasingly sought—North America initially came up short. For one thing,
Native North Americans had, since the sixteenth century, challenged settlers
who disturbed their ancestors. Forced west, some carried remains with them,
while others, like prominent Choctaw Peter Pitchlynn, revisited sacred mounds
"composed of the bones of my ancestry."[35] The second, more material reason was
that North America's wet climate made "ancient" remains rare. Of his 1783 excavation, Jefferson noted the "sculls were so tender that they generally fell to pieces
on being touched."[36] Later scholars did little better. By 1799 Barton had examined
only a piece of a thigh bone and tibia of one inhabitant of a monument that
Cincinnati's settlers had bisected with a street; other bones were "mouldered."[37]
Barton later seems to have received a skull from Illinois, near Cahokia, that he
sent to German anatomist Johann Friedrich Blumenbach, who used that skull,
described as a "Cherokee," and four heads collected in the upper Orinoco and
Brazil by Alexander von Humboldt, to "prove" that humanity had five varieties
descended from Caucasians, one of them "American."[38] These exports nonetheless proved a rule of singular examples, which through 1820 were compared in-
conclusively to other singular examples stolen from living Native Americans.[39]

What changed was Peru's independence from Spain and its presentation as an
emporium of preserved American anatomical antiquity. In 1821, the same year
that José de San Martín declared independence and opened diplomatic relations
with England by sending an "Inca mummy" for the British Museum, British diplomatic secretary Alexander Caldcleugh sent Johannes Blumenbach in Göttingen
an "Inca skull." The German anatomist thereby became the first to illustrate
"Ancient Peruvian" crania, including what became their hallmark feature: an unusual shape and length. Blumenbach credited its form to the cranial modifications
first noted by the Spanish—that some Andean peoples used binding boards and
bandages to alter their children's skulls, to signal group belonging and elite status.[40]
Like Morton after him, this was the beginning of what also became the largest
American population in the German anatomist's collection. After Blumenbach
died in 1840, ten of his forty-three Indigenous skulls were from Peru.[41]

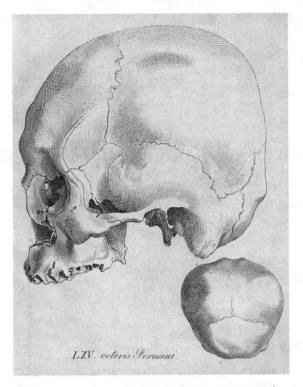

Fig. 5.1 This was the first skull of a *veteris Peruani* ("ancient Peruvian") to be illustrated, having been sent to the comparative anatomist Blumenbach by British diplomat Alexander Caldcleugh in Lima during the last days of Spanish rule. Blumenbach believed it showed that skull's artificial shaping. Johannes Blumenbach, *Nova pentas collectionis suae craniorum diversarum gentium* (Göttingen: 1828) as Plate LXV. The Library Company of Philadelphia.

Others found this newly available and seemingly atypical dead interesting as well. In 1826, after exploring with Mariano Eduardo de Rivero of Lima's National Museum, British natural scientist Joseph Barclay Pentland sent six skulls from "sepulchral monuments" near the ruins of Bolivia's Tiwanaku to the Museum of Comparative Anatomy in Paris. There, German anatomist Friedrich Tiedemann endorsed Pentland's theory that, in contrast to Blumenbach, the Bolivian skulls' "peculiarity of shape depends on a *natural* conformation" so different from any skull "now existing" that they "belonged to a race of mankind now extinct," that may have fallen to "Asian emigrants" (as Humboldt had described the Incas).[42] Also in 1826 the surgeon's mate of the USS *Franklin* delivered ten skulls of "Indian[s] from [the] south-west coast of Peru" to an anatomy professor at the University of Pennsylvania. By 1832 the Peruvian dead at the university outnumbered that of Native North America by nearly four to one.[43]

In a single decade, this rapid diaspora of a single population of "ancient" human remains from the Andes had reshaped the evidence available for humanity's historic forms, concentrating them in a few key places: Göttingen, Paris, and especially Philadelphia. This diaspora made it possible to rephrase Buffon's question, asking whether the bodies of America's oldest peoples were so different as to suggest the climactic or social degeneration of their modern heirs. But Pentland's and Tiedemann's terms added another pair of questions: Were their differences so great as to evidence separate human origins for wholly distinct "races" (or "polygenism")? And if so, could those "races" then go "extinct"? Charles Darwin, among others, was a partisan of the latter question for the Peruvians. In 1838 he jotted in his notebook that "When two races of men meet, they act precisely like two species of animals.—they fight, eat each other, bring diseases to each other &c, but then comes the more deadly struggle, namely which have the best fitted organization, or instincts (ie intellect in man) to gain the day.—The peculiar skulls of the men on the plains of Bolivia['s Tiwanaku]—strictly fossil . . . have been exterminated on *principles* strictly applicable to the universe."[44]

The racializing science that seeped from these speculations is associated with the "American School of Ethnology," and not Darwin, because of the Andean skulls planted in Philadelphia. Besides the University of Pennsylvania's collection, there were also two skulls that a US consul in Peru had "taken up" from an "Indian burying place near Quilca," south of Lima, and sent to a Philadelphia surgeon named Richard Harlan. Harlan was Samuel George Morton's mentor. When Morton sought to build his own collection of crania to lecture upon, he sought those Peruvian skulls as well—though he wasn't yet all that discerning.[45] In 1832, the thirty-three-year-old anatomist asked a US naval surgeon headed to the Pacific for "skulls of Native Indians—or Ancient Peruvians—or South Sea Islanders—anything in the shape of a skull will be a treat to me, for I have paid considerable attention to comparative ~~Anatomy~~ Craniology" [*sic*].[46] Shortly thereafter, Morton, who had previously struggled to even borrow skulls for his lectures, received an "Ancient CHIMUYAN from the ruined city near Truxillo," Peru. This was Morton's first "American." He thought the skull "splendid" and began a memoir about it.[47]

This Peruvian memoir became *Crania Americana*'s earliest section.[48] Morton pulled from three centuries of "Peruvian" mortuary scholarship to write it, from Andean chroniclers like Garcilaso to continental counterparts like Blumenbach and Tiedemann, who were debating Peru's skulls in Europe. He extended that scholarship by making the "Ancient Peruvians" his largest data set. These entanglements between American bio-racism and Andean grave-opening make their consequences even more important. The numbers and prior study of the "Ancient Peruvians" made them a historic population that could be measured, averaged, and compared with living Native North Americans to determine whether America had been populated by one race. If so, that might confirm Morton's polygenist belief in separate origins and histories for humanity's five supposed races. Perhaps most surprisingly, these entanglements meant that Morton at first believed in Indigenous American "civilization." *Crania Americana* took for granted that Peru had civilizations equal to those of the Old World, disproving Eurocentric claims of American inferiority. By proceeding from this widening foundation of Peruvian skulls, Morton offered a new methodology in both anatomy and global history. This means of not just comparing "ancient" skulls to modern ones (as Blumenbach had done), but quantifying and averaging their similarity and distance, permitted generalizations on the stability, transition, and extinction of racial types worldwide over time.

Morton's contextualization of his "Chimuyan" skull took him to the centuries-old literature in which the embalmed Peruvian dead embodied American civilization. The footnotes of *Crania Americana*'s second section, a thirty-seven-page essay devoted to the "Ancient Peruvians," offer a who's who of early modern "Peruvian" historians, chroniclers, and enlightened scholars whose America was more "ancient" than any corresponding Anglo-American text: Cieza de León, Acosta, Antonio de la Herrera, Garcilaso de la Vega el Inca, Wafer, Ulloa, even Hipólito Unanue's *Mercurio Peruano*.[49] Morton used recent travelers' descriptions of the monuments in which Peruvian dead and their artifacts were interred to corroborate those earlier claims of ancient sophistication.[50]

The "Ancient Peruvian" skulls that Morton further acquired were his true data, however, and in amassing them he benefitted from the republican Peruvian projects that had made the "ancient" or Inca dead into collectible specimens of national history. The same regional tomb-raiding (huaqueo) and antiquarianism that made artifacts of mummies and grave-goods left behind a surfeit of skulls. Morton's collectors followed their trail, leaving Lima's National Museum to find the grave-openers who might lead them to these crania unearthed by prior digging, and who could teach them how to dig skulls themselves. Morton dedicated *Crania Americana*'s US edition to the naval surgeon W. S. W. Ruschenberger, who, after visiting the National Museum's mummies, learned from "an Indian, who was fishing with a cast net," how to stomp on the ground to find tombs at sandy Arica. Duly educated, Ruschenberger "dug up with [his] own hands" the dead of "eight or ten graves," then dissected them for their skulls.[51] From the sands of Pachacamac, the massive shrine south of Lima that had been looted since the 1530s, Ruschenberger gleaned a further twenty-three skulls for Morton.[52]

Ruschenberger's skulls were useful to Morton because the surgeon could confirm that some came from "monuments." Morton could also compare them to mummified Andeans entering other American collections, like the Philadelphia Museum's Inca "mother," whom Morton decapitated and defleshed.[53] These first American collections of Andean mummies seemingly confirmed Peruvian claims of Inca embalming, which some North Americans had previously doubted. Morton thought an "embalmed head" that reached Boston in 1837— sent by a chemist with a collection of four mummies and a number of other skulls and artifacts from the "vicinity" of Arica—was "the most perfect instance of embalming, among the American nations, that has come under my notice."[54] They also preserved what he presumed was an "American" racial phenotype: a brown complexion with lank black hair.[55]

When *Crania Americana* was complete, these mummified "American" heads were but two of nearly 100 "Ancient Peruvians" whom Morton boasted of examining, of which he measured 33. The Peruvian dead haunted more than a fifth of *Crania Americana*'s pages and eighteen of the volume's seventy-eight plates—far more than any other group. Of the first 106 skulls in Morton's larger collection, 10 belonged to individuals of African descent and 22 were scattered among other Native American peoples; 29 were from Peru.[56] No prior

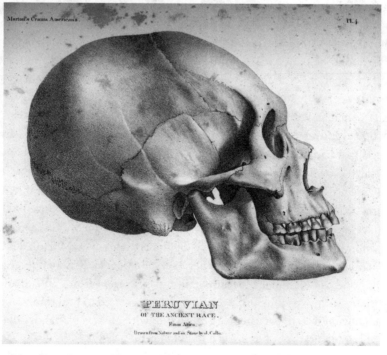

Fig. 5.2 "Peruvian of the Ancient Race" depicts a skull that Ruschenberger had extracted from a mummy bundle and that Morton cast as the prime racial example of the unadulterated "ancient Peruvian" type. John Collins, lithographer. Samuel George Morton, *Crania Americana* (1839), plate 4.

work of anatomy boasted so large a non-European set, and Morton used it, and Peruvian history, to stake a surprisingly radical claim regarding American skulls and civilization. Morton agreed with European counterparts like Pentland and Tiedemann that the "greatly elongated" and "sloping" skulls of "Ancient Peruvians" represented an "extinct race of natives who inhabited upper Peru above a thousand years ago, and differing from any mortals now inhabiting our globe." But he believed that both they and the Incas who succeeded them were families of the same larger American race. And because of the Peruvian texts that explained the dead, Morton was sure that "civilization existed in Peru anterior to the advent of the Incas"—that the "ancient" branch, despite having "heads so small and badly formed," possessed civilization and built monuments.[57]

The Incas then clinched the case. Morton concurred with Barton that they were originally Toltecas, "the most civilised nation of ancient Mexico," and had migrated around 1050 CE to the Andes. Morton's addition was that they then conquered the "Ancient Peruvians" but, in homage to their achievements, shaped their own skulls to resemble the naturally sloping, small-skulled, and now-extinct "primitive civilized Peruvians" ("primitive" here meaning "orig-inal"). These were Garcilaso's glorious Incas: idolatrous without bloody sacri-fice, preferring arts to arms, and architects whose achievements at least equaled the "seemingly superhuman efforts of the Egyptians." "What most excites our admiration in the one, must be also conceded to the other," Morton demanded.[58]

This identity mattered because Morton believed it transferred north. Morton claimed that the Toltecas also became the refined rulers of North America's common class of "barbaric" Indians—visible in skulls from monuments in Mexico and Wisconsin that Morton believed were identical to those he attributed to Incas.[59] The book's frontispiece depicted the still-living "Ongpatonga [Big Elk], Chief of the Omawhaws," but its first "cranial" plate was the "Embalmed Head from the Peruvian Cemetery at Arica."[60] Fourteen plates of "Ancient Peruvian" crania followed, then another sixty-two plates, three of which were also Peruvian. This was a chain of native being that linked Peru's monumental antiquity to America's racialized present.

Finally, if Peruvian history was American history, then in celebrating "Ancient Peruvians" and Incas Morton believed he was elevating the New World. The con-nection of American mounds to the skulls of the Incas showed, he believed, a general Indian capacity for civilized complexity that stretched throughout the continent, disproving Jacksonian claims that the "mound"-builders were giants, Mongols, Hindus, Jews, or Scandinavians.[61] Given "the preceding facts," Morton declared,

> how idle is the assertion of Dr. [William] Robertson, that America contained no monuments older than the conquest! How replete with ignorance are also the aspersions of [John] Pinkerton and [Cornelius]

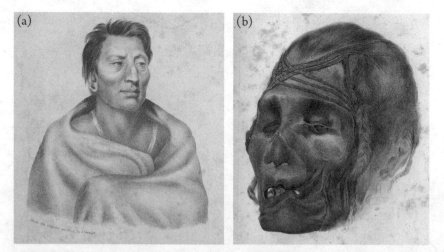

Fig. 5.3a & b "Ongpatonga [Big Elk], Chief of the Omahas" and "Embalmed Head from the Peruvian Cemetery at Arica" suggested a chain of racial phenotype linking the Indigenous living (Ongpatonga) to the "Ancient Peruvian" dead whose "embalming" preserved their hair and skin color. Ongpatonga: T. Sinclair, lithographer (from a drawing by M. S. Weaver, from an original painting by J. Neagle). Embalmed head: John Collins, lithographer, Samuel George Morton, *Crania Americana* (1839), frontispiece and Plate I.

> De Pauw! Two of these authors, who wrote expressly on American his-
> tory, are unpardonable for such gross misrepresentation. They appear to
> have veiled the truth in order to support an hypothesis. It is vain longer
> to contend against facts; for however difficult it may be to explain them,
> they are nevertheless incontrovertible. Whence the Peruvians derived
> their civilization, may long remain a mooted question; that they pos-
> sessed it, cannot be denied.[62]

Morton's praise for past Peruvian achievement was of course backhanded. Like Hipolito Unanue or Francisco Barrera's celebration of Inca embalming, it lacked appreciation for the Native living and defined "civilization" in narrow terms. But by studying Peru, Morton had nonetheless ended up a "patriotic epistemolo-gist" "defend[ing] 'American civilization' against European cynics," historian and anthropologist Mark Thurner observes.[63] In this largest sense, Morton's con-stellation of Andean history, "Ancient Peruvian" skulls, and racializing science tried to pull the Americans' reputation up, not down.

Samuel George Morton is not remembered for this celebration of Indigenous civilization because he almost immediately renounced it. The problem was that

Morton himself highlighted a supposed contradiction: he believed that the size and elongated shape of the "Ancient Peruvian" cranial type was wholly "natural," and not due to head binding; yet he also believed that the original owners of these skulls were nonetheless "civil," despite possessing an internal cranial capacity "probably lower than that of any other people now existing." In *Crania Americana*'s final pages, he diminished the finding—which is only contradictory if cranial size or shape corresponds to civility and intelligence, which they do not—by hinting that proportions and shape might matter more than absolute size.[64] This further suggested that civility's correspondence to cranial measurement could be relative, not absolute.

Morton's own allies were the first to point out that this admission opened the door to denying race's singular effect on history. George Combe, the world's leading phrenologist, an "expert" in the "science" of interpreting the size and shape of the head, had written an appendix for *Crania Americana* without having read the whole text. In that appendix, he claimed that measuring "barbarous" and "savage" skulls revealed more of their capabilities "than the hasty impressions of travellers."[65] When Combe got his copy of the book he was indignant that Morton, 150 pages before, contradicted him, privileging travelers' and chroniclers' defense of the Peruvians over the cranial evidence. Combe wrote Morton a hectoring letter. "If the long narrow ancient Peruvian skulls were compressed, I could understand that the anterior lobe was not destroyed, or impeded in its growth, and only thrown back into another part of the skull, but still capable of performing its functions." But if "Ancient Peruvian" skulls were uncompressed, as Morton claimed, "How can we account for the civilization?" "There is no people with heads so rationally deficient as these ancient Peruvians who are civilized or who constructed," Combe frothed. "The ancient Peruvians with such heads, if they be natural, could not, if now living, [create] such monuments, unless they form an exception to all other races." Morton's celebration of "Ancient Peruvians" also contradicted supremacist history's supposed laws: if they were so capable, then their succession by the Incas needed to be explained. "A superior race is never exterminated by an inferior one," Combe thundered. "How came the ancient Race to perish"?[66] Did Morton realize that his portrayal of "Ancient Peruvians" implied that race did not determine history?

In other words, Morton's attempt to add depth and context to American history via the embodied Peruvian past was only acceptable as long as he did not challenge the story that Native peoples were destined to fall because of racial inferiority. His response also illustrates how racist thinking in science changes shape without altering the fundamental presumption that pure races exist and can be studied to clarify the past.[67] Acceding to Combe, Morton admitted that the Peruvian sections were written before the rest of *Crania Americana*. Further, he admitted that he had based his argument regarding the ancient Peruvian "type" on just one of Ruschenberger's skulls. Morton still believed that skull was unaltered, but allowed it was a particularly small "exception to nature." The skulls of "Ancient Peruvians" were thus not so naturally different as they seemed, making their relative civilization an artifact of an original size and shape closer to the larger skulls of "barbaric" Native North Americans.[68]

This racializing search for "natural" likeness disciplined Morton's dalliance with a more varied "American" history told in Peruvian skulls. "I abandon an hypothesis which is at variance with nature & analogy," Morton wrote Combe. "If my work ever goes to a second edition, I will wholly remodel this section."[69] Morton disavowed the point to Benjamin Silliman, the editor of the *American Journal of Science*, to which Combe submitted an anonymous review of Morton's volume identifying its portrayal of the Peruvians as a "discrepancy" defying the coincidence of cranial forms and mental qualities in "every other race, ancient and modern," but that might be explained away through artificial compression.[70] Combe needed Peruvian skulls "deformed" to confirm his phrenology and the universal history of his fellow Scot, Robertson, who cast the Inca "race" as "intelligent and comparatively mild, but superstitious and feeble." Like all barbaric Indians, Combe wrote, "it has been subdued by the Europeans, and lives under their dominion."[71]

Morton spent the rest of his scientific career hewing to this white supremacist position. He also continued to collect Peruvian skulls. For his 1849 catalogue, he measured 155 Peruvian skulls—nearly half his total sample and more than any other indigenous American population. When he died in 1851, of the 867 skulls in his collection—by then the world's largest—at least 201 were Peruvian, still his largest single population. Morton used the intellectual capital lent by their measurement to shore up his claim that they revealed an early America where genius was limited, whose defeat presaged that of all Native Americans.[72] Morton supported his modified theories with Alcide d'Orbigny's *L'Homme Américaine* (1839), based on the French scholar's travels in the region. To Morton's eyes, d'Orbigny's catalogue of Indians' supposed bodily uniformity showed that narrow and elongated crania resulted from artificial compression and that still-living Aymara-speaking peoples were descendants of the "Ancient Peruvians," whose skulls "corresponded" with those found in Ohio's "mounds."[73]

This meant Peru no longer elevated the American race. Instead, the shared "natural" skull of other Indians pulled down the Incas, who, for Morton, were no longer a racial family, but a fleeting ruling class. Although Spanish-American historians like Clavijero claimed "Mexicans and Peruvians yet possess a latent mental superiority which has not been subdued by three centuries of despotism," Morton told the Boston Society of Natural History in 1842, their genius belonged to a privileged few whose moral impulses were no different than those of barbarous tribes. When Spain destroyed "the Inca power," Morton added, "the dormant spirit of the people was again aroused in all the moral vehemence of their race, and the gentle and unoffending Peruvian was transformed in to the wily and merciless savage." Race was thus what connected the privileged Inca handful to the "vast multitude of savage tribes whose very barbarism is working their destruction from within and without." The Incas and that "vast multitude" enjoyed "the fate of the extremes . . . and extinction appears to be the unhappy, but fast approaching doom of them all."[74]

Morton's final theory, published posthumously, was that the "savage" life of barbarous Indians consisted of "sleepless vigilance [and] perpetual stratagem," requiring a larger brain. But because life under the "demi-civilized" Incas and Peruvians consisted of paternalism and dominance, small brains were all their childlike subjects needed. Americans as a whole were thereby put in their place: the average cranial volume of their "collective races . . . [was] only 79 cubic inches"—"13 below that of the Teutonic race."[75] By collecting "Ancient Peruvian" skulls, then, Morton married a long strain of Peruvian scholarship celebrating the dead to Atlantic anatomical science, hoping to yield an American history as vast as the hemisphere. But by squaring that scholarship with racist assumptions regarding the ends of Native peoples, he instead confined Andean skulls to embodying inferiority, inevitable extinction, and subjugation.

This deformation of Peru's dead left an indelible stamp on what became the "American School of Ethnology." Morton's second book extended the lesson of cross-historical cranial comparison to "questions" of white supremacy and chattel slavery. In *Crania Aegyptiaca* (1844) Morton read ancient Egyptian skulls as "Caucasian," emphasizing their supposed difference from those of recently deceased sub-Saharan "Negros." Pro-slavery allies made the implications explicit: that "Negros" had always been inferior to or enslaved by whiter peoples, Egyptians or white Americans.[76] The Andean dead had made American history vast, stretching from Peru to Philadelphia to Egypt, and beyond—and there was always one group that dominated others.

The space opened by understanding the Peruvian dead as foundational to the American School of Ethnology also clarifies how skull collecting became such a systematic, large-scale, and widespread venture. To both imitate and critique Morton, scholars followed him into the Peruvian stream and for the rest of the century collected the remains of Americans and others as racially historicized series, not just singular specimens. Benefitting from Peru's own modernization efforts, agents of science, the military, and commerce collected as many skulls of as many types as possible, which scholars then used to approach the size of the data set of Andean dead upon which Morton staked his claims. They also used those larger collections to debate skull measuring itself—an ongoing scholarly conversation that almost never questioned those collections' ethical or historical cost.

To begin with, Combe's publicizing of Morton's apology in Silliman's journal revealed exactly how to assault *Crania Americana*. Phrenology's skeptics used Morton's admission to challenge those who insisted upon European anatomical superiority, or that skull size or shape correlated to civilization. Two years before *Crania Americana*, Friedrich Tiedemann, an abolitionist, had published an analysis of the brain size of Blumenbach's five "races," finding the "common doctrine, that the African brain, and particularly that of the Negro, is greatly smaller than the European, is false."[77] So if Morton showed that cranial shaping displaced the brain's organs without affecting intellectual facilities—like those that could build an Andean empire—could phrenologists claim any relationship between their size, shape, or position, and a person's or race's abilities? In 1840 a correspondent in the *British and Foreign Medical Review* pounced on Morton's admission that Peru's civilized "national type" was a single uncompressed skull "whose aspect indicates a very low degree of intellectual development." Given its similarity to another skull deemed artificially compressed, "How can their respective mental capabilities be predicated"?[78]

To engage the question, Morton's allies and critics alike built large Peruvian collections of their own. Like Ruschenberger, they went from gleaning skulls left behind by Peruvian grave-openers to actively disinterring sealed tombs. Morton himself shaped the agenda, trading his "Ancient Peruvians" and encouraging scholars to convert other skulls to Peru's "race."[79] Philadelphia's Academy of Natural Science, of which Morton became secretary, specifically encouraged members of the US Exploring Expedition to the Pacific (1838–1842) to seek out "ante Peruvian remains from the tombs."[80] The expedition obliged. Zoologist Charles Pickering scoured the sands around Pachacamac's "Egyptian-like" buildings for skulls left by prior excavators. The expedition disinterred at least three mummies from Arica as well.[81]

These bodies were the foundation of the Smithsonian's Skull Wall. Established in 1846, America's flagship scientific institution received the government's share of the expedition's collection. When expedition member Titian Peale later catalogued the collection, he organized its ethnological materials in the same way that Morton had in *Crania Americana*, by starting America's first dedicated anthropological collection with the Peruvian dead. Objects 1, 2, and 3 of his catalogue were "Mummies of the Ancient Peruvians," from Arica. Objects 4 to 11 were eight "Crania from the ancient city of Pachicamac" [*sic*], followed by the objects and remains of other peoples throughout the Pacific world.[82] By 1859 these eleven Andeans sat in the Smithsonian's upper hall with a Shuar "Headdress" of beetle wings and monkey bones that the US Consul in Guayaquil,

Ecuador attributed to "Atahualpa, the last of the Incas, brought from the Temple of the Sun."[83]

This Shuar headdress was most definitely not Atahualpa's maskaypacha, the fringe of Inca rule, but it showed how unseen Andean antiquarians or merchants were profiting from the sale of ersatz Inca relics to unsuspecting foreigners.[84] Its acceptance at the Smithsonian underscores how the scholarly attempt to salvage a supposedly disappearing Native present often had specific pasts in mind.[85] Like Spanish Americans before them, North Americans like Morton were adopting the Incas as imperial ancestors—as the intellectual and racial betters of the Indians they dominated. This was a religious and cultural project as well. In Nauvoo, Illinois, three months before Joseph Smith's murder sent the Latter-Day Saints further into Indian territory, Brigham Young took the stage as the high priest of the Inca Empire in a Mormon production of the popular English and American play, *Pizarro* (1799), which imagined an Inca-European society replacing and redeeming that of Native Americans. In 1850 Salt Lake City's *Deseret News* published a letter from Don Justo Sahuaraura Inca, calling upon US president Zachary Taylor to give him "protection and shelter."[86]

Such literal empire-adoption seemed less improbable in the wake of the Mexican-American War, when Morton's research shaped the more hemispheric histories that became anthropology's backdrop. Archive-based history in the United States began with William H. Prescott, who used Spanish sources to contrast "old," benighted Spain and "new," progressive America, which happened to be expanding into the former's old "Indian" territories.[87] In 1847, at the height of the Mexican-American War, Prescott published his two-volume *History of the Conquest of Peru*. Its first chapter, an introduction to Inca civilization, used Morton's research to point to a still deeper and racialized past. The chapter culminated with Prescott's claim that the engravings in Morton's "valuable work" revealed that the "crania of the Inca race show a decided superiority over the other races of the land in intellectual power." This, Prescott suggested, was "the principal foundation of their authority."[88]

Prescott's popular and intellectually influential *Conquest of Peru* shaped the Inca supremacism of other important early works in North American anthropology. Lewis Henry Morgan, for example, presented the Haudenosaunee (Iroquois) as having achieved "a more remarkable civil organization, and acquired a higher degree of influence, than any other race of Indian lineage, except those of Mexico and Peru."[89] Prescott also pointed American readers to Peruvian cemeteries to learn more. The origins of "this remarkable race" of Incas remained unclarified by "time and the antiquary," his first chapter ended.[90]

Foreigners working in Peru applied those expectations to the dead they now encountered. The midcentury explosion in Peru's export of guano as a fertilizer attracted new actors to work on the expensive infrastructure projects the guano boom funded. These projects cut through the Peruvian coast and Andes, revealing the remains of past grave-opening efforts and fueling new ones. Railroads especially displaced previously invisible cemeteries, spilling skulls and mummies onto the sand and forcing foreign engineers to respond.[91]

Some of these foreigners tried to "rescue" the Inca and Peruvian dead they disturbed. In 1850, for example, American Anthony Walton White Evans became the chief engineer of the planned British-owned railroad from Tacna to Arica, which began by leveling a hill to fill in Arica's bay. While waiting for work to begin, Evans joined Arica's centuries of grave-opening, "in which business the officers of Spanish ships of war . . . are said to have shown great industry, Peruvian law against removing bodies to the contrary notwithstanding." Evans dug and diagrammed a tomb for a friend in the US Navy, producing a drawing that would be published by the Bureau of Indian Affairs. Evans hoped to "obtain a good mummy," or a head "with good teeth in [it]," but the "skeletons were so much decayed, that most of them fell to pieces, and I threw them away." Evans remained optimistic that the railroad would let him "rescue from oblivion many

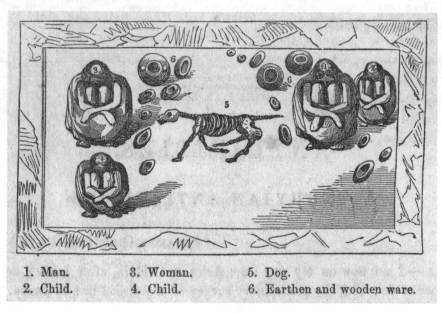

1. Man.   3. Woman.   5. Dog.
2. Child.   4. Child.   6. Earthen and wooden ware.

Fig. 5.4 Top-down view of tomb at Arica by engineer Anthony Walton White Evans. Whether this was a specific tomb or a generalized one is unclear. Evans illustrated these seemingly uniform mummified bodies and their grave-goods before "run[ning them] all into the sea" in railway cars, to help fill the bay. In G. M. Gilliss, "Peruvian Antiquities," in Schoolcraft, ed., *Information Respecting the History, Condition, and Prospects of the Indian Tribes of the United States; Collected and Prepared under the Direction of the Bureau of Indian Affairs, per Act of Congress of March 3, 1847* (1855), 658.

objects of great interest. Should I be able to put my hands on them, instead of the peans [*sic*], I will forward a collection to you, at Washington, for *our* cabinet"—the Smithsonian.[92]

Yet Evan met so many mummies and skulls—"not one [with] a decayed tooth in it"—that it became a problem for the railroad. His solution haunted him for years. When he and the workers "had got into [the hill] some distance," he recounted to Smithsonian curator Spencer Baird three decades later, "we found there was on top an ancient 'Huaca' or burying ground, and as we went in, those Mummies, with all their Pots and Pottery, fishing tackle, corn, beans, dogs . . . came rolling down into the pit." Saving the finest ceramics and arrowpoints, he and his men put the dead and objects that remained to the work at hand. They used them to fill in the bay: "all shoved into Cars and run into the sea." Having recently committed his own son to "the silence of the tomb," Evans seemed haunted by what they had done. "We disturbed the mortal remains of thousands of the ancients at this place and run them all into the sea," he repeated. He recommended that the Smithsonian look to other valleys revealed by railroads, that were "for over twenty-five miles a graveyard [whose] every grave is full of the relics of an age long gone by."[93]

So many skulls and mummies were exposed by the railroad from Lima north to Chancay, a popular bathing spot, that they reached foreign collectors almost unbidden. Construction revealed that Ancón, a small village of "a few native and Italian" fishermen, sat beside a massive burial site, which archaeologists later assigned mostly to the Wari culture (600–1000 CE). Railroad access to the shifting dunes of this "Necropolis" made possible Ancón's looting by moonlight, when treasure was believed closest to the surface. Visitors, pleasure-seekers, politicians, and soldiers came away with huacos, ceramics, largely leaving the disinterred and disarticulated dead on the sands. This enabled foreign anatomists to travel a six- to eight-mile circuit, taking their pick of still mummified "Skulls, legs, arms and the whole anatomy of the human body."[94]

The bodies were so numerous that they overflowed Peru's shores via the often invisible infrastructure of global capitalism. In 1873, San Francisco dockhands were shocked when the bags of ballast they were unloading from a German ship, the *Mathias Meyer*, spilled open at their feet, revealing the skulls and bones of at least six human beings. "Blood-curdling rumors were quickly circulated," and a crowd gathered to argue over the dead's identity. The ship's captain explained that he taken up some 250 tons of sand at Ancón, where Peru's coastal railroads had turned up a dead with "the appearance of mummies," some of which mixed in the bags that sailors brought on to prevent ships from sitting high in the water. A US soldier stationed in the city grabbed one skull, believed to have belonged to a "young woman, with long, heavy, black hair," saying "he would present it to one of the surgeons in the Army."[95]

That the soldier thought to do so—perhaps imagining the skull would end up in Washington's Army Medical Museum, founded in 1862—was another indicator of the Peruvians' multiplying reach.[96] In the decades since the Peruvians' anatomical initiation, skull-collecting had become a far more normalized scientific practice, in part because Morton's Peruvians generated such trans-Atlantic debate.[97] By 1851 Rivero's Swiss collaborator Johann Jakob von Tschudi had added thirty Andean skulls to Blumenbach's collection. He argued—contrary to Morton—there was no one single American type. Peru itself evidenced four types, he claimed—Huanca, Chincha, Aymara, and a "hybrid" of the other three "nations." "Nothing is more variable than the opinions of authors on the shape of the skull of the ancient Peruvians," wrote one French natural historian, endorsing Tschudi as clarifying "the embarrassment and diversity of opinions of ethnographers and naturalists" on the subject.[98]

This was wishful thinking. Four Andean types encouraged the invention of still more types among the many skulls traveling abroad, making the Peruvian dead uniquely useful to collect and debate. Attempts to divide them into "brachycephalic" (a broad, short skull) and "dolichocephalic" (long-skulled) permitted endless reshuffling, dealing "natural" "hybridity" and artificial "deformations" across pre-Inca, Inca, and colonial horizons and geographies. In 1863, fewer than twenty-five years after *Crania Americana*'s publication, an essay in the *Transactions of the Ethnological Society of London* offered footnotes for twenty-six separate studies that focused upon or made use of Andean skulls and mummies since independence. The article's author, Charles Carter Blake, used these citations to ridicule the admission of one of Morton's polygenist followers that "Two skulls of the same type may belong to very different races," a fact that led Tschudi to misclassify an "ancient" Austrian skull as from Peru. Blake believed these proliferating identifications of variations within and across races were a clear argument against Morton's and others' claims for separate "so-called 'species' of mankind."[99]

Morton's critics and fellow travelers responded by stocking anthropological collections with even more Peruvian dead. In 1866, the year Harvard's Peabody Museum was founded, almost half of its 160 skulls were from Peru, owing to a large donation by one of Morton's former collectors, Ephraim George Squier, who drily noted that Peruvian skulls were not uncommon in archaeological cabinets. Another Morton admirer, polygenist Louis Agassiz, swelled Harvard's collection further. By 1873 over 400 of the museum's 684 skulls were Peruvian, along with mummies that Squier and Agassiz's son Alexander collected.[100] Agassiz had gleaned and disinterred 384 "Ancient Peruvians" from Ancón with the guidance of a British consul and surgeon named Thomas J. Hutchinson, who had himself forwarded 150 "Ancient Peruvian" crania to the Anthropological Institute of Great Britain and Ireland in London. Hutchinson's Peruvian skulls were so "numerous" that the institute selected "a sufficient number of typical specimens for

C. C. Blake—*Cranial Characters of Peruvian Races.*   217

paca, South Peru, from Arica, and from near Cobija in Bolivia, and a fourth from Pachacamac, presented by Mr. John Miller, through Mr. Bollaert, to the Ethnological Society.   With a view to identify these skulls, and refer them to their actual ethnic type, my task was to compare them with the extensive collection of Peruvian skulls contained in the Museum of the Royal College of Surgeons, and with the figures and descriptions contained in the works of Owen,* Morton,† Davis and Thurnam,‡ Rivero and Tschudi,§ Nott and Gliddon,‖ Maury,¶ Prichard,** Bellamy,†† Latham,‡‡ D'Orbigny.§§ Meigs,‖‖ Smith,¶¶ Castlenau,*** Retzius,††† Williamson,‡‡‡ Gerrard,§§§ Busk,‖‖‖ Gosse,¶¶¶ Webb,**** Lucae,†††† Barnard Davis,‡‡‡‡ and Wyville Thomson.§§§§

---

* Owen, Catalogue of Osteological Series in Mus. Coll. Chir., 2 vols. 4to, 1853.
† Morton, Crania Americana, folio, Philadelphia, 1839.
‡ Davis and Thurnam, Crania Britannica, 4to. and folio, London, 1856, etc.
§ Rivero and Tschudi, Antigüedades Peruanas, 4to, Vienna, 1851.
‖ Nott and Gliddon, Types of Mankind, 4to, Philadelphia, 1854.
¶ Maury, Indigenous Races of the Earth, 4to, Philadelphia, 1857.
** Prichard, Researches in the Physical History of Mankind, 8vo, London, 1836.
†† Bellamy, Annals of Natural History.
‡‡ Latham, Varieties of Man, 8vo, London, 1850.
§§ D'Orbigny, Voyage dans l'Amérique Meridionale, 4to, Paris, 1834-47.
‖ Meigs, Catalogue of Crania in the Mortonian Museum, 8vo, Philadelphia, 1857 ; Fragmentary Human Skull from Jerusalem, 8vo, Philadelphia, 1859 ; Form of the Occiput in Various Races of Men, 8vo, Philadelphia, 1860.
¶¶ Smith, Archibald, Peruvian Gleanings, Edinburgh New Philos. Journal, 8vo, 1860.
*** Castelnau, Voyage dans l'Amérique Meridionale, 8vo and 4to, Paris, 1851-5.
††† Retzius, Present State of Ethnology with reference to the Form of the Skull, Translated by W. D. Moore, Medico-Chirurgical Review, 1860, p. 503.
‡‡‡ Williamson, Observations on the Crania contained in the Museum of the Army Medical Department, Chatham, 8vo, Dublin, 1857.
§§§ Gerrard, E., Catalogue of Osteological Specimens in the British Museum Collection, 8vo, London, 1862.
‖‖‖ Busk, New System of Craniometry, Trans. Ethnological Society, 1861. Crania Typica, fol., London.
¶¶¶ Gosse, Mémoire sur les déformations artificielles du Crâne, 8vo, Paris, 1855. Sur les anciennes races du Pérou, Bull. Soc. Anthropo., Paris, i, 549. Questions ethnologiques et médicales relatives au Pérou, ii, 86.
**** F. C. Webb, Teeth and Anthropoid Apes, 8vo, London, 1860.
†††† J. C. G. Lucae, Zur Morphologie der Rossen-Schädel, 8vo, Frankfort, 1861.
‡‡‡‡ J. Barnard Davis, Distortions in Crania of Ancient Britons, Natural History Review, ii, 290.
§§§§ Wyville Thomson, Distorted Human Skulls, Nat. Hist. Rev., ii, 397.

Fig. 5.5 Charles Carter Blake, "On the Cranial Characters of the Peruvian Races of Men." Blake's literature review surveyed the twenty-six publications that had addressed Peruvian crania in some way, shape, or form since the 1830s. *Transactions of the Ethnological Society of London* 2 (1863): 217.

permanent preservation in our own Museum," before sending similar representative sets to the University Museums of Oxford, Cambridge, and Edinburgh, with "about a hundred" left over for the Royal College of Surgeons, where they joined San Martín's Inca.[101] French archaeologist Alexandre Bertrand instructed his own collectors to mark Hutchinson's "hundreds of skulls" and follow his "good example."[102]

These Peruvian skulls were used to remeasure Morton's theories or support their critique without abandoning his central presumption—that their study clarified racial difference.[103] The Peabody's first curator, comparative anatomy professor Jeffries Wyman, compared Harvard's Peruvian crania to skulls from mounds in Kentucky and Florida. Like some later critics, he found that Morton's actual measurements were basically correct; it was his extrapolated phrenology that Wyman believed pernicious.[104] Given the Peruvians' historical achievements, "brain measurement cannot be assumed as an indication of the intellectual position of races any more than of individuals."[105] Measuring skulls revealed numbers, not civilization.

Yet these remeasurements, made possible by the expansion of both Peruvian and foreign grave-opening, were no less dehumanizing. While undercutting Morton, Wyman claimed Indian skeletons had "peculiarities which seem to assimilate them to the apes."[106] English anatomist P. F. Bellamy and Swiss natural historian Tschudi identified an interparietal bone believed unique to Andean skulls. Tschudi dubbed it the "Inca bone" and suggested its connection to rodents and marsupials. It was "very curious," he wrote, "that we should find so retarded a formation in a whole race of men, who have exhibited a very inferior degree of the intellectual faculties."[107]

It is not as if Euro-American skull collecting was not already predicated on a violent and racist understanding of humanity. The many crania taken the world over warn against overemphasizing the Peruvian skulls' specific importance to the supremacist history of racializing and dispossessing non-European ancestors.[108] But the Peruvians' study before, by, and after Morton nonetheless transformed this larger process. The Andean skulls' sheer number, their centuries of historicization, their supposed salvage in the face of Peruvian development, and the scientifically attractive *lack* of consensus over their specific meaning made them the single largest population in collections in the United States, fueling the collection of other Native peoples.[109] In return, the wave of collecting that pulled human remains from the Andes returned its racializing debris: Peruvian scholars went from ignoring Morton to building collections of their own—a new, more biologically focused phase in the Andean engagement with the dead.

To begin with, the Andean dead's "rescue" helped promote skull collecting's larger project, rationalizing the violence inherent in disinterring, stealing, or paying for other peoples' children and ancestors. The connection is clearest in the US example. Morton's "closet full of skulls" showed how Americanists with large, historicized series of racialized crania could measure and generalize on the scale needed to wage convincing statistical arguments.[110] In comparison to the Peruvians' numbers, single heads of other Native individuals seemed insufficient to their students. From the mid-1830s on, American settlers' murder of Native

North Americans who resisted the dispossession of their lands, resources, culture, and children made possible the looting of their bodies for scholars like Morton. Claiming that specific tribes needed scientific salvage, Army surgeons dug up or decapitated the skulls of at least one thousand Native North Americans in the 1860s and 1870s, sending them on to the Army Medical Museum, whose forty-five hundred Native dead later went to the Smithsonian.[111]

The hideous irony is that the data wrested from these ancestors were small compared to their Peruvian siblings. Historian of medicine Elise Juzda observes that researchers affiliated with the Army Medical Museum believed that they needed still larger populations to support statistical techniques. This meant that Indigenous skulls were rarely used for the science that supposedly justified their collection. When they were studied, it was either in an Andean light, "arguing . . . for their affinity to the Peruvian race," or in inconclusive terms.[112] One paper at the American Association for the Advancement of Science in 1878, for example, was based on "fifty or seventy-five" whole and fragmentary crania from Iowa, Wisconsin, Illinois, and Kentucky, a low, vague count that Morton's Peruvians had cleared forty years earlier.[113] In the diminishing hope of having enough crania for the sort of science the "Ancient Peruvians" permitted, skull collecting became an American anthropological practice whose exact value was often unclear. "It is most unpleasant work to steal bones from a grave," wrote Franz Boas, often taken as American anthropology's founder. "But what is the use, someone has to do it."[114]

A final measure of the influence of Morton's Peruvian methods was their foothold in Peru itself. At first, Peruvian scientific practitioners ignored Morton's theorizations. This was not for lack of engagement with craniology, phrenology, or the racialization of "Ancient Peruvians" or Incas. Claims for a location of racial difference in the body dated to the seventeenth century in Lima, and the polymath Hipolito Unanue had cited the facial angle studies of Petrus Camper as early as 1806. Although Unanue did so to critique European racializations of Americans as degenerate, enlightened Peruvian scholars still believed that race was a category whose study revealed changes or continuities in time. By 1807 the University of San Marcos's medical students were taught Camper's facial angle.[115] Broader racial thinking flourished after independence, when some Peruvian ideologues attributed immutable traits to "the descendants of the ancient inhabitants of Peru," who, despite intermarriage with Spaniards, "have not modified their race."[116] By 1853 the phrenology of Franz Joseph Gall was positively described in one Limeño journal, and some argued that ancient Peruvian bodies hinted at disappeared races whose presence prefigured whiter Peruvians' rise. Mummies from Chachapoyas were described as having fine and supposedly blonde hair "unlike that of today's indigenes."[117]

Yet belief in racial difference did not mean Peruvians agreed that civilizational hierarchies were more visible in anatomical differences than in culture, history, and language. Peruvian antiquarians' early interest in ceramics and mummies, not skulls, supports the point.[118] Phrenology's insights were therefore first invoked in Peru to reflect upon ideal types and differences between individuals, despite their "same race," rather than diagnosing racial hierarchies.[119] José Mariano Macedo, for example, dismissed Morton, despite being a pathologist and anti-quarian who shied away neither from dissection nor physiognomy. Macedo read the faces of pre-Hispanic portrait ceramics for "the bellicose, religious sentiment dominant in this *raza* of caciques, whose beautiful conformation is proven in the[ir] anatomical proportions."[120] What put Macedo off were Morton's leaps in logic. "If it is true the anatomical character of the indigenous race is inferior, one can't deduce from this that their physiology or intellect would display the nec-essary consequences," he wrote privately, after reading *Crania Americana*. "If the skulls of Cuvier and Byron correspond to the highest scale, that of Dante does not clear the cephalic index but nonetheless does not yield the field to them in intellectual force."[121]

More public censure came from the founder of Peru's National Museum, Mariano Eduardo de Rivero. Rivero and Swiss anatomist Tschudi claimed that their examination of "hundreds of skulls" and their greater familiarity with the history of the Peruvian dead far exceeded Morton's claim to have studied "Inca" crania. The mummies of the royal Inca family had disappeared into the bowels of the Hospital of San Andrés centuries before, they pointed out in *Antiguedades Peruanas* (1851). And didn't Morton know that the Incas had married other peoples? How, then, could Morton be sure he had studied the Inca "race"?[122]

Nevertheless, craniology's methods made their mark in Peru and South America—but via *Antiguedades Peruanas'* European readers, not *Crania Americana*. By the early 1860s Italian-Peruvian naturalist Antonio Raimondi searched the Andes for crania for the collections of Universidad Nacional Mayor de San Marcos in Lima.[123] By 1886 Peruvian doctor Luis Carranza y Ayarza took Aymara or Quechua "races" as craniologically undeveloped and "paralyzed" in their intellect by the trauma of conquest—living "mammoths" who could be matched to ancient skulls collected east of Lima.[124] And in 1890 a young sur-geon and social Darwinist named Manuel Antonio Muñiz returned from two years in Europe studying military health, anatomy, physiology, neuropathology, anthropology, and museums to build what was briefly the largest collection of pre-Hispanic remains worldwide, "something over a thousand" crania.[125] Fellow Peruvian scholars used Muñiz's collection to contradict Morton, underlining how the North American's methods revealed so many counterexamples better explained by continental European anthropology's dolichocephalic and brach-ycephalic types. Nonetheless, Morton's demonstration that large collections of

Andean crania containing those types could be used to debate the racial present and past remained intact, alongside perceptions that cranial variations like "Inca bones" were negative characteristics.[126] These ideas diffused as American and European museums exchanged collections. When Buenos Aires's Museum of Anthropology and Archaeology Museum received "ancient Peruvian" skulls and a mummy from Ancón arrived via Paris, in 1881–1882, they provided a historical and anatomical framework of "notable Peruvian elements" on which the museum could hang the live and murdered bodies of the Indigenous peoples "salvaged" by Argentina's "Conquest of the Desert."[127]

Overlapping histories of colonial and republican mortuary violence against Native peoples in the Americas were thereby entangled and extended far and wide. Peru's "ancient" grave-robbing became cause for Americanist scientific study and civilizational salvage, amplifying similar waves in North America before returning to magnify those in South America. These processes can be easily mistaken as nationally and chronologically discrete, rather than linking specific places, at specific times, via race science's most historic American set.[128] By studying the "Ancient Peruvians," Euro-American scholars came to believe that the proper place for "doomed" Indigenous ancestors was a collection.

The Americas' Native peoples were neither doomed nor destined to remain collected. In the United States, as in Peru, Indigenous individuals and tribes wrested what they could to survive their attempted dissolution or containment. The late-nineteenth and early-twentieth-century Andes saw a widening gyre of Indigenous rebellions, land takebacks, and political organizing against local aristocrats and national government.[129] In North America, reclaiming lost land was more difficult, but Native nations, tribes, and individuals in the late twentieth century regained traction in the realms of economic and cultural sovereignty. With allied scholars they have worked to recover ancestors lost to "scientific" looting. As Pawnee scholar James Riding In explained, "Most Indians view deceased bodies as representing human life, not as scientific data to be exploited for profit and professional development."[130]

But Morton's Andean deformations were lasting. In the short term, Morton reduced the "Ancient Peruvian" dead into more singularly racial "American" skulls. In the medium term, he "proved" the viability of sciences reliant on statistically significant collections of the dead, promising revelations regarding the quantifiable division or unity of "American" races. And in the longest term, because Morton's methods and questions were so widely adopted, criticized, and modified, his primary Andean set remain fixtures of the storage rooms of museums of anthropology, anatomy, and natural history.

This skull-centric approach to the Andean dead obscured much. Even more than their display as "mummies," their collection as skulls removed them from the largely female labor and care of birth, cultivation, and ancestral replanting. Each Peruvian cranium in Morton's collection—which after his death went to Philadelphia's Academy of Natural Sciences, and then the University of Pennsylvania—was a tomb opened, even those gleaned after a looting's initial event in the name of scientific "salvage" and more distant care. It also muted contemporary Peruvian knowledges of the Andean dead as important for their resistance to colonization, their lasting cosmic animacy, and what they revealed of the Inca "science" of embalming.

Finally, the cranialization of Andean ancestors helps explain why only a few mummies sent abroad from Peru before the early 1850s still exist.[131] In 1873, two more "Peruvian mummies" joined San Martín's "Inca" in London's Hunterian Museum, for example, but by the twenty-first century the three were no longer in the Royal College of Surgeons' catalogue.[132] They may have been traded to less "scientific" museums, as happened to Philadelphia's founding "Inca family" of three mummies, who were bought by P. T. Barnum and Moses Kimball with the rest of the Peale family's collection when the Philadelphia Museum's financial problems became insurmountable in 1848. That "entire Family of Peruvian Mummies" went to Kimball's Boston Museum, where they and the "Fejee Mermaid" (a taxidermied baboon, orangutan, and fish) entertained theatergoers between shows. By 1900 the family had disappeared—seemingly not making the transfer with the rest of the Boston Museum's "mummies" to the Museum of Fine Arts. Like the Hunterian, Boston's Museum of Fine Arts today claims no Andean mummies, if it ever did.[133]

The physical state of that group's "mother" at their moment of transfer offers another explanation of their fate, as well as those of the Hunterian. Morton had decapitated and defleshed her skull in the 1830s. The rest of her body could have gradually followed suit: preservation in the Andes was a co-production of care and interment in a preserving climate; disinterment and export often restarted decay. More than a few mummies arrived in Europe and the United States in states of decomposition, requiring more curation than nineteenth-century museums could possibly provide. Researchers complained of their rot and sometimes "salvaged" them by accelerating the process, making bone specimens—a common practice in the natural sciences.[134] Thus transformed, "ancient Peruvians" became more easily manipulable racial and anatomical subjects, as happened at Stockholm's university, which in 1846 anatomized an Andean mummy by removing "the envelope of the skull, without disturbing the lay of the mummy's hair braids," so that the skull could be identified as corresponding to the "well-known forms of the Chincha tribe of Peru."[135]

These transformations make it harder to know which of the many Andean skulls possessed by museums arrived as mummies. The Smithsonian's first three mummies, from the US Exploring Expedition, are no longer identifiable, for example. After being observed in varying states of decay, they seem to have been among the human remains the Smithsonian sent on to the Army Medical Museum in the 1870s.[136] If they survived the trip back to the Smithsonian in the early twentieth century, they were lost in the 1910s when the institution's first dedicated physical anthropologist, Aleš Hrdlička, "macerated" the flesh from nearly all of the collection's Andean remains, making more shelf-stable and measurable crania and bones.[137]

Other Andean bodies escaped the museum altogether. A few mummies arrived so decayed that they were perceived as corpses and immediately de-accessioned. There is an "Inca" mummy in an unmarked grave somewhere in rural Belgium. Like the boy Wafer tried to collect, this was simultaneously an unspeakable loss, a confirmation of the Andean dead's ultimate disposability as racialized specimens, as well as a body's final agency in liberating itself from collection.[138]

Despite these decays—perhaps even because of them, given how specimen loss could motivate museums to seek replacements—more and more "Incas" and "Ancient Peruvians" populated museums worldwide. This diaspora spoke to both the science of their preservation and the supposed races that preservation embodied—Rivero's and Morton's visions combined. Yet what carried the Andean dead's study into the next century was not just race, nor science, but their potential as specimens of ritual. On the most global stage imaginable, the world's fairs in the late nineteenth century, Peruvian technocrats and their North American anthropological counterparts went beyond Rivero and Morton by using the Inca, Peruvian, and "pre-Columbian" dead to embody mourning itself.

6

Mining Incas

The Peruvian Necropolis at the World's Fairs

In 1876 Peru's ancestors celebrated a century of US independence. For six months that year, Philadelphia hosted America's first world's fair, the Centennial International Exhibition, at which thirty-seven countries showcased their natural, agricultural, and industrial wealth in a new 11,644-square-foot hall. Most invited countries dressed their material offerings with culture. Mexico's pavilion was "Aztec" in its trappings but otherwise focused on mineral wealth and knowledge, for example. Peru's pavilion reversed the formula.[1] Its display touted its deposits of silver and guano, but according to one exposition guidebook, what most caught fairgoers' attention was the pavilion's heart, a four-sided glass-fronted showcase of a large collection of Peruvian skulls, grave-goods, and "mummies, taken out of their tombs where they have lain for the last three thousand years."[2]

The collection's owners were Manuel Herrera and Guillermo Colville, who ran an import company in Lima and Callao. The items displayed were from Ancón, the "Necropolis" north of Lima, whose skulls had made their way to San Francisco in ballast. Inhabited for thousands of years, Ancón's interments were revealed when a railroad cut through the cemetery. Daytrippers arrived thereafter, eager to open graves themselves. Some engaged in diversionary looting for objects, leaving behind skulls and mummy fragments that anatomical collectors like Thomas J. Hutchinson had sent abroad for racialized study. Other excavators were more catholic in their interests, assembling antiquarian and anatomical arrays to study or sometimes sell. Herrera and Colville were among the latter. After Philadelphia, their collection went to Paris's Universal Exposition of 1878, where it was sold.[3] In this way, Ancón's millennia-old necropolis diffused around the world.[4]

This semi-industrial diaspora of Andean tombs following Ancón's revelation transformed scholarship on pre-Hispanic Peru and the wider Americas. First,

Empires of the Dead. Christopher Heaney, Oxford University Press. © Oxford University Press 2023.
DOI: 10.1093/oso/9780197542552.003.0007

Fig. 6.1 "Along the hills beyond the bay runs the gradually rising line of the railway intended to connect Lima with the fertile valley of Huacho, but which has been completed only to the town of Chancay." That railway cut through the "necropolis" laid out in the "sandy and gravelly deposits of the old sea bed" of Ancón, unleashing an extraordinary explosion of looting, collection, and export. In the foreground of the bottom image, grave-openers take a break. WIlh. Greve [Lithographer], Plate 2, "The Bay and Necropolis of Ancón," from Wilhelm Reiss and Alphons Stübel, The Necropolis of Ancon in Peru: A Contribution to Our Knowledge of the Culture and Industries of the Empire of the Incas. trans. Augustus Henry Keane, Vol. 1 (Berlin: A. Asher, 1880–1887). Collection Development Department, Widener Library, HCL, Harvard University.

the looting of Ancón and coastal sites like it unearthed an incredible number of ceramics, textiles, and other grave-goods, which Peruvian and foreign antiquarians used to identify and celebrate material cultures more culturally and chronologically distinct than "Inca" or "ancient Peruvian." These objects were sold to foreign museums at a moment when ethnology's evolutionary hierarchies of civilized and savage were breaking down. "Ancient" American objects became "New World Classicals," whose "exotic" aesthetics inspired painters like Gauguin and Picasso. They also yielded the Americas' first articulation of "the concept that what was found in lower strata was of greater antiquity than objects found in more shallow layers." These distinctions made it acceptable to talk of Andean art as more than simply "ancient": as possessing a history, order, and alterity all its own.[5]

Second, while museums do not always emphasize that their Andean "art works" are aestheticized, historicized grave-goods, Americanist archaeology embraced that fact after Ancón. This helped to transform anthropology's understanding of how a burial could be studied. Prior to Ancón, ethnologists, anatomists, and collectors took the resting places of Indigenous ancestors as caches awaiting sorting, whose bodies and belongings were to be separated and measured according to racial scales whose norm was Europe. Less attention was paid to interments as events whose animating ritual could be reconstructed by studying its contents together. Previously, unbundling them was the practice, notes anthropologist Maria Patricia Ordoñez—a stripping for parts that for much of the nineteenth century divided grave-goods from human remains.[6] While the Centennial Exposition was in Philadelphia, for example, another group of Peruvians tried to get four thousand dollars at auction in New York for a collection of antiquities, adult and child mummies, and "fifty heads," all "from tombs discovered by a railroad company in making excavations" (almost certainly Ancón). They got only five hundred dollars for it, the most notable mummy selling for "$11, the purchaser hoping to secure many valuable trinkets with which the remains were supposed to be decked."[7]

Two decades later, anthropology's values had shifted. The largest, most popular display in the anthropology exhibit at Chicago's famed Columbian Exposition of 1893 were some fifty *fardos* (mummies bundled in textiles, or mummy bundles) dug and transported from Ancón by a Harvard graduate student named George Dorsey. The point of their display, besides giving fairgoers something to gawk at, was their scope as historic interments. The Chicago World's Fair was a field-expanding moment for both American history and anthropology, and what Ancón's bundled mummies preserved was their mortuary ritual, the in situ constellation of historicized "American" bodies and their material artifacts. This translated constellation became the object of new archaeological best practices, reflective of anthropology's larger turn "from collecting skulls to studying mortuary customs" and Americanist scholars' shift from taking Latin America as a site of extraction to one of embedded and contextualized evidences.[8] Specifically, Ancón's bundled mummies became the subject of Dorsey's PhD dissertation in anthropology, the first written by an American citizen. The Peruvian dead's empire now took an increasingly North American cast.

Still, Ancón's presentation and methodological transformations at world's fairs like Philadelphia and Chicago remained products of Peruvian history—even when executed by collectors like Dorsey. At the time of Ancón's revelation, Peru's scholars and National Museum presented the Andean dead as ancestors of the modern nation, but also as scientific resources that represented Peru's wealth and history at home and abroad. As such, the dead's export was only accelerated by guano's bust, Peru's 1875 default on its bond payments, and Chile's invasion during the War of the Pacific (1879–1883). During these crises, Peruvian antiquities and human remains became more financially valuable and of even greater interest to foreign museums. The arrival of "scientific" archaeologists sponsored by those museums made the prior Peruvian landscape of republican grave-opening, collection-building, and semi-industrialized mummy-exporting hard to see. But, as historian Stefanie Gänger observes, Andean archaeology was a "cosmopolitan product, a transnational collaboration between Peruvian, German, French, British, and U.S. archaeologists," and Ancón's occupation of Chicago's anthropology building harmonized with Peru's frustrated display plans.[9]

The Americanization of Andean grave-opening nonetheless amplified that dead's horror and care. New archaeological methods relied upon millennia of Andean peoples' investment in the curation, interment, interpretation, and even looting of the ancestral dead, whose re-collection as "mummies" made them attractive to science. When foreign collectors moved from Ancón and the Peruvian coast into the mountains, they also encountered communities less willing to part with active beings that still shaped their fortunes. Forced by Peru's state to surrender these bodies, some communities grieved their loss—a grief that itself became an object of study.

In September and October 1868, some thirty-five thousand people filed through Lima's future Palace of Justice to gawk at Atahuallpa, the Inca killed by Pizarro 335 years earlier. The location of Atahuallpa's actual body remained unknown, but in his place Peruvian artist Luis Montero recast his funeral as the passion play of Peru's foundation. Montero filled a huge canvas (just under fourteen by twenty feet) with the murdered Inca at the right, his mourning wives at left, and Spain's conquistadors and friars in between. Montero had worked on the painting for two years in Italy, and its arrival in Lima after showings in Brazil, Uruguay, and Argentina was a cultural event. *El Comercio*, Lima's newspaper of record, gushed over the realism with which Montero had painted Atahuallpa's "livid" corpse, a "true type of the indigenous race." Peru's Congress bought the painting, ensuring it wouldn't leave the country.[10] (See Plate 4)

By contrast, the Congress did nothing for Atahuallpa's father when he also threatened to appear, not one month later. In late October, excavations in the Hospital of San Andrés turned up a "cadaver" whose "vestments" and the memories of an elderly woman identified it as that of an "insurgent" bishop brought before 1821 to Lima.[11] Yet some Limeños resurrected deeper histories. On November 2—All Souls' Day—*El Comercio* published an unsigned letter naming the cadaver as Huayna Capac, whose mummy had disappeared in that very hospital centuries earlier. The cadaver's clothes, they said, were "the royal vestments of the Inca. Given the system of embalming the Incas possessed, conserving the remains of clothes would have been easy." Now, the author hoped, "patriotism might give him a distinguished sepulcher."[12]

The letter's likely writer revealed himself two days later. Ygnacio Manco Ayllón, secretary of the Society of Artisans, wrote to Peru's Congress as both a citizen and Huayna Capac's descendant, "according to authentic documents I possess." Reviewing the hospital's history, Manco Ayllón asked legislators "to ascertain that the cadaver is that of the Ynca Huayna-Capac"—an "extraordinary event" to which it was "impossible, Sir, to remain indifferent . . . that chance has given us perhaps so that we might show our veneration, via this respectable cadaver, to the so-illustrious chronology of the Inca Emperors that Peru possesses." Given Huayna Capac's "high status and notable civic virtues," Peru owed him a statue like those that other nations erected to emperors, Columbus, and Bolívar.[13]

A Commission on Memorials reviewed Manco Ayllón's petition, but concluded the cadaver was a bishop, and declined to give Huayna Capac a statue.[14] That Peru's Congress nonetheless bought a grandiose depiction of his son's equally absent corpse suggests that more was at play than the cost of paying for a monument. It was perhaps one thing to mourn the Incas as dead in semi-elite spaces; "The Conquest of Peru and the death of the Inca Atahualpa" was a staple drama in Lima, as were performances of "Inca" songs of mourning.[15] It was another to elevate their political bodies in a public plaza in 1877, months after the military had massacred members of a rural Andean movement for having supposedly followed a self-proclaimed "Inca" with plans to "exterminate the Republic's white race."[16]

Yet the "facts" of the matter suggest two further reasons to deny Huayna Capac. The first was that by 1868 Lima's museumgoing elite feasibly knew what a pre-Hispanic mummy like Huayna Capac was supposed to look like, in contrast to a "converted" one, like that of Atahuallpa. Whereas Atahuallpa would have been laid out supine in his original Christian interment, Huayna Capac, as a preconquest mummification, would have been seated like the "mummies" visible in the National Museum and private collections. An extended body— whether of an "insurgent" bishop or not—worked against it being Huayna Capac. Furthermore, the hospital's centuries as a place of healing, medical education, and interment of the bones of thousands of patients led one historian to warn against "the hope that the mummies of the Incas might appear in Lima."[17]

Second, there was little agreement beyond Peru's elite that a pre-Christian Andean body was notable, had it actually appeared. Infrastructural construction and tomb-raiding churned up Andean bodies on a near-daily basis, and "gentile" mummies were met with religious and racial disdain. In 1848 El Comercio described the rural supporters of a presidential aspirant as "Haggard and lean like a mummy from the time of the gentiles, of a greenish color, swinish hair, hyena eyes, grim in aspect, the nose of a Guanaco."[18] "Mummy" by the 1850s was a pejorative, used to dismiss former royalists, Bolivian presidents, outdated laws, republics like Colombia, and the Andean supporters of a regional leader.[19] The decades after independence also saw some Creoles reemphasize their Hispanic heritage and become openly racist regarding the wisdom of celebrating Inca or ancient Peruvian claims.[20] Displayed mummies became objects of irony. "In no short time we won't be able to enter a museum without scaring ourselves," one clergyman said to another in a satirical periodical.[21]

By the 1860s, then, cosmopolitan Peruvians could perceive Andean and "Inca" bodies, ancient and modern, as scientifically knowable, representative of the nation, yet also disposable—three qualities that encouraged the government's sanction of their export to foreign institutions, as San Martín had in 1821. In 1859 geographer Antonio Raimondi, a scientific agent of the Peruvian state, sent Milan's Civic Museum its Dantean mallki. That same year, Austrian natural scientist Karl von Scherzer visited the National Museum in Lima and, having failed to find more than mummified fragments in his own digging, proposed an exchange of duplicate objects with the Imperial Museum of Vienna, which he thought would appreciate "some Peruvian antiquities, like skulls of the ancient Indians and mummies as well," and some "antediluvian bones."[22] The museum's director, Simón Yrigoyen, received the proposal favorably, but his government minders were unwilling to let the "rare and singular" "antediluvian" fossils go. They had no objections to sending Vienna a "Mummy of the gentile ancients of Peru," though.[23] These exchanges of Andean bodies were through official channels, establishing relationships between Peruvian science's local and foreign actors.[24]

Even nature itself seemed to offer up Andean mummies as resources. On August 13, 1868, two months before Lima's reception of Montero's painting, a massive earthquake struck Arica. Survivors who ran for the hills were "met with the appalling spectacle of the grave literally giving up its dead," the foreign press claimed. "The convulsed and writhing earth threw to the surface hundreds of the grim, dried bodies of the Indians who had lived here centuries before, still wrapped in the coarse cerements that the dry and nitrous soil had preserved from decay."[25] British naval officers who assisted in relief efforts also dug the ancient dead. The US consul to Chile, General Hugh Judson Kilpatrick, sent the Smithsonian Institution a mummified infant supposedly taken from among the "five hundred mummies" said to have risen from the sands.[26] Joseph Henry, the Smithsonian's secretary, hoped Kilpatrick might procure still more "as they will be very acceptable presents to several other scientific institutions in the United States."[27] In 1875 a photographer arranged the infant and two adult mummies sent by Peru's most successful railroad builder, Henry Meiggs of Boston, on the lawn outside of the Smithsonian's castle for a stereograph—a doubled photograph that when viewed through a stereoscope gave a three-dimensional view of Washington's most ancient American dead.[28]

Fig. 6.2 Stereograph of three "Peruvian mummies," positioned and photographed on the grass outside the apse of the West Wing of the original Smithsonian Building, on the National Mall of Washington, DC, 1875. Union General J. Kilpatrick sent the Smithsonian the mummified infant in 1869, after the earthquake at Arica. The two adults were sent by the railroad-builder Henry Meiggs in 1872. Publisher: J. F. Jarvis. Courtesy of the Smithsonian Institution Castle Collection, SI.2009.020.

Little was made of these exports in Peru. The 1873 account of those crania carried from Ancón to San Francisco by accident in a ship's ballast was translated in Lima's *El Comercio* without censure: "Incas Transported to Foreign Lands" was an entertaining side effect of Peru's importance to Atlantic and Pacific economies.[29] Peru's National Museum already had its mummies, as did antiquarians in Lima and Cuzco, who described their collections in ways that valued antiquities and ethnological objects over the dead themselves. Surgeon and antiquarian José Mariano Macedo, for example, possessed "four perfectly preserved mummies" in Lima, but in an 1878 letter to an admirer instead lingered upon the ceramics whose antiquity they validated, explaining their provenance, portraiture, and style.[30]

The display of the Andean dead at the late-nineteenth-century's world's fairs therefore made sense. It started in Peru, where the International Exposition of Lima in 1872 celebrated fifty years of Peruvian independence by showcasing the developments funded by opening Peru's natural resources to foreign capital.[31] Among those "resources" were the ancient Indigenous dead from Ancón and elsewhere that represented Peru's "original" race.[32] To that end, the National Museum and its mummies were relocated from the tight quarters of the National Library to a new Palace of the Exposition. They were joined there by collections made by private citizens and regional representatives like Manuel Anatasio Fuentes, who brought a "collection of outfits, mummies, arrows and other objects of the Indians," and Gregorio Durían, who brought a collection of ceramics and mummies from Huanaco.[33]

European traders and travelers imitated these displays with collections of mummies and antiquities of their own. In Lima, after the exposition, "the display of antiquities seemed to be a thing of fashion, and as they were under constant demand, they were retained on all sides." Limeño elites listened to new poetry in the presence of antiquities and oil paintings depicting Peruvian mummies. Even if these elites were willing to sell their collections, foreign ethnologists like Adolf Bastian couldn't afford their prices and so went to the countryside to dig for themselves.[34]

Such was the experience of Austrian collector Charles Wiener, who visited Peru in 1876 on behalf of France's Ministry of Public Instruction. Before arriving, Wiener wrote a flatly racist "historical" thesis condemning the "communist" Incas and arguing that it was in the "wrong-headed, abusive, unhealthy consti-tution of the Peruvians that we must look for the harmful causes of the mum-mification of this country and the degradation of the individual."[35] Mummies, for Wiener, as for some Peruvians, were atavistic throwbacks. Yet upon arrival, after sampling the collections of Lima, Wiener took the train to dig at Ancón and beyond. He confessed to have felt "singularly violent emotions" as he watched mummies come out of the ground. Experiencing "something like a fever" when his workers uncovered a funerary bundle or a "yellowing skull," he leaped down in the hole to "scrape with his fingernails at the soil . . . asphyxiated by the am-monium smell of the mummies." He and his workers found sixty-nine, only five of which were in an "excellent state of preservation" to collect.[36] The rest were left on the sand.

Wiener's collecting fever led him to tombs up the coast, and then into the *cordilleras* and Bolivia. Wiener tallied up his finds as including ten tons of ma-terial from Ancón, 632 Moche objects from the North, and some 500 pieces from highland sites and Andean tombs near Cuzco—where he heard about but failed to visit "Macho-Piccho" and "Huaina-Picchu."[37] He examined and took further mummies of adults and infants along the way. At least ten came with him to Europe, two of which ended up in Denmark, the rest at the Musée d'Ethnographie du Trocadéro in Paris.[38]

Wiener also took a young boy. In Vilque, beyond Cuzco, a Peruvian land-owner named don Gervasio Mercado encouraged Wiener to abduct a living child, "to give those scholarly Europeans an idea of the Indian race." Mercado advised him to find a poor and "horribly alcoholic Indian" mother and give her coins for her "starving" child. Wiener did so, finding a sleeping mother and—he claimed to his readers—making the trade. The boy's name was Juan, and when he realized what was happening he became distraught. In August 1877 Wiener brought Juan to Paris, where he became the model for a statue depicting the "characteristic traits that attest to the purity of the race" that would be displayed in the Peruvian pavilion at the Paris Universal Exposition of 1878. In the sculpture, Juan knelt, hands to his chest like the mummies Wiener displayed as well.[39]

It was a horrific crystallization of the impulses that had shaped the theft of Andean bodies for centuries. An Austrian scholar and Peruvian landowner went from collecting mummies to abducting a child who died an ocean away from his mother—a fate shared by countless other Indigenous people since 1492.[40] The connection was clear and explicit: Wiener had destroyed a family in the name of seeking "pure" and "ancient" Andean bodies.

Other nineteenth-century scholars worried that the public might miss that "context" for what were also corpses on display. This was the case at Philadelphia's Centennial International Exposition in 1876, where Herrera and Colville's massive array of incredible feathered textiles and ceramics were validated by the many skulls and mummies that surrounded them, and vice versa. The Peruvians "wanted to have experts examine them," a Chinese visitor to the fair named Li Gui understood.[41] Those experts who did found their comprehensiveness valuable. In 1877 Smithsonian secretary Joseph Henry regretted having failed to purchase the collection for Washington.[42] A French observer named Saffray explained its value to readers in France, where it was eventually sold: its pouches, boxes, and bundles of bodies, plants, and quipus documented pre-Hispanic botanical knowledge and literacy. But he worried the display's lack of signage prevented the public from appreciating the collection's importance.[43]

Saffray was right to be concerned. Without guidance, fairgoers expecting prizes of world commerce saw the collection for what it also was: an Indigenous cemetery looted and transported, whose corpses subverted Philadelphia's claims to civility.[44] "Their form was enough to shock one," Li Gui reflected.[45] An American guidebook deemed Peru's display a "rather repulsive collection of half-decayed mummies, skulls, skeletons of the aboriginal races . . . taken out of their tombs where they have lain for the last three thousand years[. They] seemed to leer and grin as if in hideous mockery on the surrounding trophies of modern civilization."[46] Another visitor believed the mummies "so hideous in form that we thought how much better to let the 'dust return unto the dust.'" Rumors that they were actually Incas were met with republican irony: "These forms so loathsome to our view were probably royal people."[47] Not even Peru's sister republic in antiquarianism formed a positive impression. A correspondent for Mexico City's El Monitor Republicano sneered at Peru's display of "disgusting mummies, probably Inca, idols and ancient vessels, mostly broken; in a word, a baratillo"—a junk sale.[48] If Peru was supposed to be presenting itself as a source of commodities as other Latin American republics did, for sugar and coffee, they

Fig. 6.3 Centennial Photographic Co. stereoviews of Peruvian mummies and pottery. Image Courtesy of the Free Library of Philadelphia, Print and Picture Collection.

had done a poor job. One American wondered whether "that republic raised only mummies."[49]

Were it up to fairgoers, then, Ancón's dead might not have reprised their performance. In short succession, though, a wave of Ancón-inspired interest from Europe and the United States drew still more attention to the Peruvian dead's potential as scholarly subjects. As importantly, the ravages of Peru's next two decades created greater opportunities for foreign scholars to profit from Andean knowledge, grave-opening, and prior collecting. While Peruvian scholars recovered from the dispersals of war and economic collapse, foreign scholars promoted Peru's tombs as Americanist archaeology's natural field.

These promotions differed from what came before in both scale and object. The dead now remained bundled with the textiles and grave-goods that had accompanied them into their tombs. That shift can best be visualized in the work of German volcanologists Wilhem Reiss and Alphons Stübel, whose grave-opening at Ancón in 1875 for the Royal Museum of Ethnology in Berlin is sometimes considered Peru's first systematic and scientific excavations.[50] As art historian Joanne Pillsbury notes, their illustrations of Ancón's tombs were attentive to strata and relative depths, which later guided their student Max Uhle to excavate and theorize on the principles of stratigraphy and superposition, a

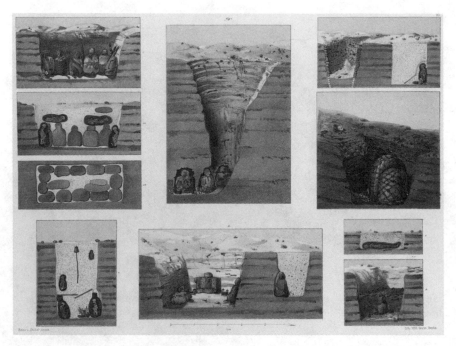

Fig. 6.4 WIlh. Greve [Lithographer], Plate 10, *"Sections of the Graves,"* from *Wilhelm Reiss and Alphons Stübel, The Necropolis of Ancon in Peru: A Contribution to Our Knowledge of the Culture and Industries of the Empire of the Incas.* trans. Augustus Henry Keane, Vol. 1 (Berlin: A. Asher, 1880–1887). Collection Development Department, Widener Library, HCL, Harvard University.

crucial first step in American archaeology's ability to argue that the remains in some tombs and sites were older than others.[51]

Reiss and Stübel's three-volume study of *The Necropolis of Ancon in Peru* (1880 and 1887) was also a guide to the laborers who toiled in those tombs, and the losses they caused. Their 141 plates documented how work proceeded by employing "Indian workmen" who knew where to dig and how to remove "mummy packs" from the tomb (see plate 7). Yet Reiss and Stübel also decried the efforts of those who came earlier. The land was strewn with "Bleached bones, scattered shreds of raiment, bast coverings and cordage used in the careful preservation of the bodies, pottery and other remains of human industry," all pointing "at the contrast here presented between a past breathing a pious feeling of devotion for the departed, and a present betraying nothing but a spirit of vandalism."[52]

Reiss and Stübel's indignation was self-serving, given that their own excavations destroyed as many as two funerary bundles for every one they retrieved.[53] Like the museums of North America, those of Germany were increasingly devoted to the imperial salvage of non-European peoples from their

mixed-race heirs, and by the end of the nineteenth century most German ethnological museums had mummies from Peru.[54] Alongside them should be
imagined the many bundles that the work of collecting left behind (see plate 8).

Reiss and Stübel nonetheless shared Francisco Barrera's project of drawing
attention to the bright textiles and false heads surrounding the body as mean-
ingful original context. To that end, Reiss and Stübel exported them as whole
bundles and illustrated them in meticulous plates. This practical measure—
keeping racialized bodies and ethnographic artifacts associated in transit—
made possible their illustration in their moment of unwrapping in Berlin. More
radically, it let some remain wholly intact, saving them from the dissections that
had marked their collection since the 1820s. Of the 231 mummified remains of
Andean individuals that bioanthropologist María Patrícia Ordoñez Alvarez recently identified in eighteen European museums, only 33 were collected prior to
Ancón's revelation. Of that 33, only 5 remain bundled. By comparison, 87 of the
198 collected in the century since Ancón's revelation remain bundled.[55]

The export and maintenance of these wrapped and seedlike selves also
heralded anthropology's shift in approaching Indigenous American interments
as events with as much complexity and ritual as those of the Old World—an attention that did not equate to respect, spurring their still wider disinterment and
diaspora. This was especially the case in the United States, whose supplanting
of Europe's diplomatic and economic ties with Peru can perhaps be measured in its acquisition of the world's largest collections of Andean remains.[56]
American diplomat and archaeologist Ephraim George Squier neatly tied these
entanglements together, bridging his collaborator Samuel George Morton's interest in Peru to the blockbuster displays of the Andean dead after 1875. In the
late 1840s, Squier had dug the earthworks of Ohio with Prescott's *History of the
Conquest of Peru* in hand. In *Ancient Monuments of the Mississippi Valley* (1848),
the Smithsonian's first published volume, Squier and his collaborator E. H. Davis
argued for the existence of large and advanced North American society indebted
to South America. They claimed that connection using the similarity of a single
skull to those Morton described for the "Toltecan, and of which the Peruvian
head may be taken as the type."[57] Squier went on to excavate in the Yucatán and
in time reached Peru. Charged with settling outstanding guano claims for the
United States, Squier spent much of his time opening "monuments," yielding
the first core of Indigenous dead for Harvard's Peabody Museum in 1866. He
also read the faces of living Peruvian peoples alongside Moche portrait ceramics,
racializing both.[58]

For Squier, these racial continuities were positive. He insisted upon a line of
Indigenous Andean civilization that ran from present peoples back to Inca and
pre-Inca peoples. This was no small thing to maintain in the face of other scholars'
attribution of any American complexity to Old World diffusions or recent Inca

MODERN PERUVIAN HEAD.

Fig. 6.5 "The profile of a servant–boy of mine, having a slight infusion of Spanish blood, as compared with the profiles of two of the huacas" (182). For Squier, this was a positive—and racializing—demonstration that Peru's "ancient" peoples lived on in the modern population, and that their "civilization" was not a result of Old World influence. "Modern Peruvian Head," from Squier, *Peru* (1877), 184.

intrusions, and it allowed Squier to credit the Peruvian scholars who knew those attainments first and best. Squier's final, monumental book, *Peru* (1877) was also a guide to Peru's texts, grave-openers, scientists, and antiquarians: Garcilaso and Rivero; Trujillo's "most experienced, enthusiastic, and persistent treasure-hunter," Colonel La Rosa; Antonio Raimondi, with whom Squier explored Lake Titicaca; and Cusqueña landowner Ana María Centeno de Romaineville, "the collector of the finest and most valuable museum of antiquities in Peru." Squier lamented la Rosa's grave-opening for what it obliterated, but he credited the Peruvians' knowledge of a dead whose historic attainments were like those of the United States. Pachacamac, the massive Inca shrine south of Lima, was "the Mecca of South America," Squier claimed, "the burial-place of tens of thousands of the ancient dead," whose strata could be dug into to reveal and unwrap the modest possessions of what "are loosely called *mummies*." Squier described one "family" of five inhabitants of "what may be called 'an apartment,' or one of the tenement-houses in the ancient city, which were, in some respects, better than ours." Near the end of the book, Squier explained why there were supposedly so few pre-Inca monuments by way of a telling comparison: "The only modern nation that, in its polity, its aggressiveness, its adaptation, and, above all, its powers of assimilation, as well as in its utter disregard of traditions and of monuments, at all comparable to the Incas is our own. Does the most ancient of cemeteries stand in our way?"[59]

Squier's incitement for other Americans to seek their Inca predecessors by undoing Andean tombs acquired new urgency during the War of the Pacific. In 1879 Chile invaded Bolivia's nitrate-rich leg to the sea. When Bolivia's secret defense pact with Peru was revealed, Chile invaded that northern neighbor too, taking mummy-rich Arica. The war went badly for Bolivia and Peru, but Peru's losses were also archaeological. In 1881 the Chilean Army occupied Lima, during which huaqueo at Ancón apparently increased and the National Museum was sacked. What happened to Mariano Eduardo de Rivero's mummies in that moment is unclear, but Chilean officers in general engaged in scientific collecting. When Chile's army withdrew, keeping Arica, all that remained of the National Museum was a single stele that Raimondi had collected from Chavín de Huantar, the underground temple where Rivero had pondered Spain's throne of dead. To survive the economic distress caused by guano's collapse and the war, Peru's antiquarians sold collections abroad to institutions like Berlin's ethnology museum, further dispersing the country's web of scholarship and objects.[60]

US support of Peru during the war allowed North American collectors to present themselves as salvaging what more rapacious counterparts destroyed. In 1882 a collector for the Smithsonian reported being unable to excavate at Catacaos, in Peru's north, because of the "antipathy" of the "natives," who were opposed to "white" excavators after a French professor used gunpowder to blow the top off of a huaca, a sacred structure; he nonetheless delivered what he claimed was "one of the finest collections ever brought by one individual."[61] The following year, railroad engineer Anthony Walton White Evans suggested to the Smithsonian that "it must be a good time to pick up things in Peru as there is much suffering and poverty there now, occasioned by the long and terrible war Chile is more than exacting."[62]

Most prolific of these American collectors was George Kiefer, who came to Peru to help fight Chileans but, on a trip by rail to Ancón, "beheld a wonderful sight. As far as the eye could reach northward the ground was almost white with skulls." By offering "liberal pay" to "native" huaqueros, and assisting other collectors, national and foreign, Kiefer learned how to employ a steel rod to search for graves and distinguish their contents' value. Kiefer became part of the local and self-romanticizing antiquarian scene; he posed for pictures wearing an Andean poncho, cradling a skull.[63]

Fig. 6.6 The American grave-opener and collector George Kiefer sits at left, with Swedish archaeologist Knut Hjalmar Stolpe (center). Standing at rear are the team of expert coastal huaqueros that Kiefer relied upon. The huaqueros hold the tools; the collectors, the "specimens." Photograph by O. B. Ekholm, 1884. The National Museum of Ethnography, Stockholm, Sweden.

It was a forecast of his own mortality. Kiefer sold to Washington's institutions boxes of "peculiar" skulls, antiquities, "Mummies generaly [*sic*] in their wrappings and sometimes entirely nude," and—anticipating US expansion—herbs that "Indians" treated him with, which Kiefer kept for "Uncle Sam if he ever intends sending some of his boys up these valleys." In 1888 alone he sent the Army Medical Museum four mummies from a coastal huaca halfway between Lima and Ancón, plus 129 cranial specimens.[64] In 1889, when Kiefer returned to New York, he told the press that he had dug two thousand graves and handled five thousand skulls. But he died before he could deliver forty-three more Andean skulls to Washington. When his final collection was auctioned off, the Army Medical Museum acquired four mummies for $42 and twenty skulls for $4.10. "To the cost in time and money [Kiefer expended in Peru] must be added that of life itself," the catalogue explained, "for, owing to the irritating dust arising from freshly opened graves, Mr. Kiefer contracted lung desease [*sic*] to which he succumbed."[65]

Limiting the activities of foreign collectors like Kiefer was the least of the Peruvian state's worries. In the wake of the war, coastal creoles scapegoated Peru's Andean population for having supposedly failed the nation in the country's defense. Meanwhile, private networks of foreign and national antiquarians and speculators bought and sold shares in ventures to loot the tombs of those Andeans' ancestors.[66] North American collectors observed they had a freer hand in Peru than in Chile, where officials occasionally limited excavation.[67] US ministers to Peru delivered mummies to collectors and universities back home. American naval officers stationed in Peru made "Inca-hunting" a "favorite pastime." The mummies of "Inca chiefs" and their wives were displayed in New York's stores of exotic foreign wares.[68] The Peruvian dead became a literal consumer good: one Smithsonian employee was rumored to have "found a peanut in the stomach of a Peruvian mummy and ate it. He wanted to see if anything would happen."[69]

It became a "fad among American tourists" in the Andes to "go out and dig open a grave or two just as they visit the Vatican when in Rome or Pere la Chaise in Paris."[70] By the 1890s, American writers translated *huaqueando* as "mummy-mining," advertising that "Digging Up the Dead [was] a Regular Industry in Peru." "It seems a strange thing to deliberately set out on a grave-robbing expedition," admitted American journalist Fannie B. Ward in 1891, "but in this part of the world it is fashionable to go mummy-hunting, and to search the aboriginal cemeteries for the curious articles they may contain besides dead Indians." Ward knew of what she wrote, having collected two mummies at Arica. "Dig anywhere and you cannot go amiss of a grave."[71]

Peru's mummy-mining peaked in 1893 at Chicago's Columbian Exposition. Peru's government hoped to reprise the displays sent to Philadelphia and Paris some years before, but a lack of financial support allowed US anthropologists to steal the show by restaging Ancón's Necropolis at the World's Fair. This was a consequential course in Americanist archaeology—the staging of not just bodies or objects but Indigenous mortuary ceremonies as subjects of knowledge.

The Columbian Exposition celebrating the four hundredth anniversary of Europe's American invasion invited the world's nations to display their peoples and products. In this "white city" made of plaster, the United States presented itself as the polity of the future: an industrialized and expansionist democracy, imperial in its use of Indigenous and Latin American peoples as preface to a Euro-American present. Anthropology and archaeology were crucial: they provided a pre-Columbian "background to the other departments of the Exposition in which will be illustrated the developments made during the past four centuries."[72] Specifically, the United States redeemed the Incas. The director of the fair's Latin American Department—who had bought artifacts from George Kiefer—predicted the United States' "manifest destiny [was] to dominate the

American hemisphere," including those parts occupied by the Incas' heirs. "The remnant of that race whose misfortunes have made the history of Peru pathetic will contemplate the blessings of civil and religious liberty under the shadows of the Bartholdi Statue [of Liberty] and the Washington Monument."[73]

Nevertheless, tremendous labor by Indigenous peoples went into the fair, belying claims to their "pastness." US and Latin American actors represented their nations with art and culture that had been bought, dug, and looted from Indigenous peoples, living and "ancient." Then there were the Indigenous people who worked at the fair, parading its grounds, and whose skulls populated its cases.[74] One scientific speculator built an entire replica "mountain" to display the remains of at least eighty-six Pueblo "cliff dwellers" in various states of mummification and decay. After Chicago the Pueblo display was restaged for audiences in Philadelphia and St. Louis before being bought and divided up by the University of Pennsylvania and the University of California.[75]

No Indigenous peoples were made to give more to the World's Fair than the generations of families who interred their dead in the sands and mountains of Peru. At first, this was Peru's own plan. In the early stages of planning, the US consul to Peru had emphasized the importance of the country's participation, "being one of the most ancient States of the American continent." Flattered, Peru's government promised an incredible one hundred thousand dollars for Chicago, making up for its poor showing at the Paris fair of 1889. As late as 1892 the country planned a large national pavilion, a delegation of Amazonian Indians, and "a large supply of mummies belonging to the Incas," along with a collection of skulls from seventy Peruvian localities. The plan was to display this collection first in a national exposition in Lima and then send it on to Chicago.[76]

Like Mexico, however, the Peruvian government's plan to represent itself was frustrated by the financial shortfalls of the 1890s.[77] The Lima exposition opened late, and its cost made Peru's Congress resist sending nine commissioners to Chicago; Peruvian president Remigio Morales Bermúdez's attempt to decree enough money to "fulfil the 'national desire' of fair participation" was likewise denied by the Supreme Court.[78] So individual agents, not all of them Peruvian, took advantage of the vacuum, with tragic results. American agents and a Bolivian mine operator brought seventeen Aymara miners to New York, billing them as "Inca" and "Peruvian"—the more recognizable Andean brand—but then abandoned the troupe in Philadelphia, after which one fell ill and died.[79]

The Peruvian scholars in attendance—elite, creole, male—were more successful. Most recognizable was the antiquarian display of a Cusqueño *hacendado* and former mayor named Emilio Montes, who believed his Inca ceramics and other objects as elegant as any from the Old World.[80] Montes himself escorted his collection to the fair and at its anthropology congress insisted that the language and facial features of Cuzco's "Quechua" proved they were "the world's oldest race," making Peru "the archaeological point from which progress and civilization first radiated" worldwide—to Mexico, Egypt, and beyond.[81] US counterparts did not buy his argument, but he was able to sell his collection for ten thousand dollars to department store magnate Marshall Field's new Columbian Museum.[82]

Chicago's Peruvian apex, however, was Department M, "Anthropology," whose organizer, Frederic Ward Putnam, used the Andean dead to stage his vision of what Americanist archaeology should be. Putnam, a Harvard professor, in 1886 had called for a new "scientific" foundation for the field, in which collectors excavated not to find singular objects or instructive skulls, but to recover whole interments. These new excavators would then make good notes and drawings of the context of what they found, leaving behind neither flakes of stone nor splinters of bone.[83] Peru was "selected" as an ideal subject "because mummies abound there," Putnam's graduate student George Dorsey told the press. Department M gave Dorsey at least fifty-five hundred dollars for excavations of a scale and attention that no "tourist" could afford.[84] And because Arica's mummy-fields seemed "depopulated," Dorsey would follow Reiss and Stübel to Ancón for mummy bundles and the "Indian workmen" who knew how to find them.[85]

Dorsey wanted to outdo Reiss and Stübel, given "that the great part of the scientific value of their expedition was destroyed when they scattered the objects from the graves and formed them into different groups based on an artificial classification according to art forms."[86] His own venture would discard nothing. His workers would block off fifty-foot squares before digging, to map or photograph the relative position of finds. In theory, interments could then be reconstructed. It was expensive paying workers to excavate this way, Putnam acknowledged, but "unless such work is to be done thoroughly it should not be attempted. Isolated objects, without a record of their source or affiliation, are simply bric-a-brac and are of no scientific importance, however interesting they may be as specimens of ancient art or workmanship."[87] Peru was also promising because Dorsey could focus on "bundles containing bodies" whose internal contexts remained intact in transport. Putnam wanted "the most thorough collection ever brought from Peru, illustrative of the modes of burial and the arts of this ancient people"— ideal vessels for American anthropology's transit from objects and crania to embodied rituals and culture.[88]

Dorsey's hopes rested on the ancestral Andean carework that had made those interments, as well the networks of Peruvian grave-opening, science, government policy, and capital that preceded him. Putnam and Dorsey told patrons this was an American achievement, facilitated by US diplomats in Lima, a collecting partner from the US Navy, Harvard astronomers, and American mining engineers and railroad officials who smoothed Dorsey's way into the countryside. Of the fourteen men Dorsey credited at his work's end, only one was from Peru, Carlos Pezet of Cuzco.[89] Yet Dorsey relied on Peruvians too. He traveled with letters from the Peruvian state ordering officials to facilitate his work and introducing him to antiquarians who guided him to good sites and spoke Quechua with locals who did the digging.

Many workers were of Andean descent. On the coast, "We had no difficulty procuring good Cholo laborers," Dorsey wrote to Putnam, using what was then a slur for a person of Andean origins: "from their frequent work among the huacas or graves [they] are called Huacieros [sic]."[90] At Ancón he employed four to six men at a time: "good native labor" who "invariably had prior experience," and who for seven weeks "operated the search rod" and told him where to dig.[91] "Good native workmen are always readily obtainable who are willing to desecrate the graves for the love of gain," Dorsey claimed, "quieting their consciences by the thought that it can be no sin to rob the 'Gentiles,' 'for,' they say, 'they have no souls.'"[92] Whether this was true is questionable. But to wholly dismiss Dorsey's estimation of Peru's opportunity to an American excavator with pockets full of cash would be to ignore the centuries of forced choices that Andean peoples had made when asked to reveal the "ancient" dead: between torture and survival, between obligation to past leaders or an agent of the state ordering them to dig, between a prior age of ancestors and feeding their own families.

Dorsey offered enough that he was wildly successful. His excavators expanded graves to two to three times their size, then moved their contents onto burlap and heavy canvas bags to be covered in straw and wrapped again. In the end, Dorsey's excavators opened 127 interments at Ancón, from which they extracted 185 bodies, as well as the remains of many past digs.[93] In June 1892 Dorsey sent Putnam sixty-eight boxes of human and cultural remains excavated or bought there or in other zones, like Iquique, Arica, Sierra Gordas, Chancay, Cuzco—forty-four tons of the embodied Peruvian past destined for Chicago.[94]

For context, in just one year Dorsey had shipped only fourteen fewer Andean bodies than would be collected in all of Europe in the entire century after Ancón's revelation.[95] The Chicago press took the arrival of these 185 Andean mummies as something like an invasion. Their packaging allowed them to arrive by train in early 1893 "without attracting so much as a passing notice." They were placed in an unused dairy barn in long rows: a "platoon of mummies," the "advance guard" from those "South American countries that abound in mummies and insurrections."[96]

In June, Dorsey moved them to the Anthropology Building, re-creating "probably the largest burying ground, either pre-historic or modern, in the world."[97] Against one wall of the Anthropology Building, in a central, open area that visitors would easily see, Dorsey made two large enclosures to fence off fifty of the mummies. He covered the floor with eight inches of sand and ridges of gravel to mark the boundaries of "the graves," each of which "included the mummy-pack and all accompanying objects," even the mattings forming each tomb's roof. The goal was not just verisimilitude, but to display "different modes" of another peoples' mortuary practices. "As each grave was complete . . . it was possible to make a comparative study of the graves," maintaining the "original relative position of the objects," showing by "transverse section[s] just how [they] appeared when opened."[98] Mummies from other sites were included, but Dorsey specifically wanted to present the Necropolis. Scattered skulls, long bones, and textiles gave "some idea of the appearance of the surface of Ancon, for thousands of graves have been despoiled by relic hunters and the contents left scattered about."[99] It was a presentation of modern Peru as a land of looted tombs, ready for salvage—a bravura display of what Americanist anthropologists claimed to recover of the rituals wrapping the dead, halfway between their sandy tombs and Chicago.

Although the Anthropology Department itself was overshadowed by the fair's more lively attractions, within its walls the Necropolis "attracted more attention than any exhibit in the building." It outshone the displays of subsequently famous anthropologists like Franz Boas, who complained that his own looted skulls from British Columbia were lost in a corner.[100] Dorsey, not Boas, had

ANCIENT PERUVIAN BURIAL GROUND

Fig. 6.7 One-half of the fifty Andean mummies that F. W. Putnam and George Dorsey staged in the Anthropology Building of Chicago's Columbian Exposition of 1893 to re-create the "Necropolis" of Ancón. The 185 mummies that Dorsey brought were later redistributed between Harvard's Peabody Museum, Chicago's Field Museum, and the American Museum of Natural History. Hubert Howe Bancroft, *The Book of the Fair* (1893), 633.

executed Putnam's "scientific" ideal. Though less showy than the Pueblo cliff-dwelling outside, it still excited the public. On July 4, 1893, twenty-five thousand to thirty thousand fairgoers spent the holiday visiting Ancón, drawn in by *The Book of the Fair*'s description of the Anthropology Building's "most uncanny collection."[101] Following the cues of North America's ethnologists, the press took the fair's Andean collections—including those of its Peruvian collectors—as the key to American antiquity. The Puebloan mummified remains in the pseudo-mountain were of interest because they showed that the story of early humanity also "unfolded here in America, to take its place beside and confirm the Peruvian record of the early life of man on this continent."[102] Another reporter took the Peruvian dead as evidence of America's precedence over the Old World, as Emilio Montes had insisted: more ancient "than any spice-embalmed and cloth-swathed corpse ever exhumed in Egypt," advertising "the crude methods of the old-time American undertaker."[103] Most telling were two cartoons for the *Sunday Chicago Herald* by William Wallace Denslow, the original illustrator for L. Frank Baum's *The Wonderful Wizard of Oz*.[104] In one, two seated mummies face each other, playing a "A Pre-Columbian Shell Game." In another, a Peruvian mummy plays pots like a battery of timpani drums while a smoking monkey, mammoth, octopus, human and animal skeletons, fossils, a totem pole, and even an Egyptian statue await their cue. It was as if all science and ancient history at the fair danced to an uncanny Andean beat.

Since the heady first days of independence, when José de San Martín sent an "Inca mummy" for the British Museum, the country's leaders and republican scholars had advertised Peruvian sovereignty, history, science, and resources by turning a dry face to the world. Publications, exchanges, and collaborations with foreign researchers encouraged the Andean dead's study, fueling scholarship that took them as a singular window onto American civilization, race, and culture. Andean mummies, skulls, and artifacts thereafter populated national and foreign collections, connecting Peruvian debates over Inca mummification to American anthropologists' perception that Andean bodies and tombs were their natural subject. For that reason, and because of Peru's economic hardships, scholarship on the Andean dead by 1893 no longer seemed so obviously Peruvian. Yet it nevertheless sat atop centuries of collection-building, grave-opening, and ancestor-making in the Andes. In Chicago, Dorsey's Ancón could seem like what historian Sven Schuster calls intellectual "imperialism, through which North American institutions tried to merge, and ultimately dominate, the pre-Columbian past by replacing it with the more inclusive concept of 'American prehistory' in the context of a growing informal imperialism."[105] Seen from Lima, however, Dorsey

A PRE-COLUMBIAN SHELL GAME FROM PERU.

Fig. 6.8a and b These cartoons by William Wallace Denslow—who later did the original illustrations for L. Frank Baum's *The Wonderful Wizard of Oz*—depicted three of the 185 Ancón mummies at Chicago's World's Fair. "A Pre-Columbian Shell Game from Peru" and "Sept. 11—Anthropological Building," *Sunday Chicago Herald*, 17 September 1893, from the collection of Curtis Hinsley.

and Putnam had paid for the display that the Peruvian republic itself hoped to build, in which Andean ancestors embodied a past foundational to republican monetizations of a no-longer-solely Indigenous present.

Raising an Andean graveyard at American anthropology's crossroads had consequences for the field's direction in the United States.[106] After the fair, Putnam, Dorsey, and others articulated the importance of Andean "archaeology" as a model project of excavation, salvage, export, and display. They used it to build American museums' largest anthropological collections and reiterate what a more "scientific" archaeology of Peruvian mummies was good for: not simply identifying layers of "prehistory," but capturing the rituals specific to each epoch's cultures. And because of their perceived proximity to their subject, Peruvian antiquarians continued to shape anthropology's future.[107]

The move was most visible in Dorsey's work, particularly his "An Archaeological Study Based on a Personal Exploration of over One Hundred Graves at the Necropolis of Ancon, Peru"—again, the first PhD dissertation in anthropology written by a US citizen. Read today, Dorsey's dissertation is often vague. As archaeologist Nicole Slovak observes, his field notes were, at worst, as flat as his predecessors, hindering reconstruction today of the identities of those whom he collected. His brief, unillustrated descriptions of tombs foreshadowed his later encouragement of assistants and correspondents to steal what Indigenous communities refused to sell.[108]

This made those spots where the dissertation departed from such terse practices all the more notable, as when Dorsey's attention to ritual complicated racialist hierarchies of human civilization. At their best, his notes deemphasized objects and skulls to document and theorize interments as reflective of social relations, "culture," and environment. The resulting portrait was ambivalent. "If civilization rests on the ability of a people to acquire territory at the expense of their neighbors," he wrote, "and that rests on the possibility of an artificial food supply, then the people of Ancon and of the entire coast were savages, for such an artificial supply was impossible." But complicating that "if" was a "quietness and refinement" showing "much enlightenment." Dorsey sidestepped body-centered approaches that took mummification or cranial capacity as civilization's proxy. Instead, he described six kinds of burial, attending to internal similarities that suggested that "the position of woman at Ancón was not inferior to that of man." The "painstaking care shown on every side in their mortuary customs," he wrote, "shows a tenderness and reverence and a degree of affection which is not always found even among civilized communities."[109] The dissertation's hundred-plus photos documented that care, and its disinterment.

Dorsey never published his dissertation, but his popular writings and collecting broadcast Peru's archaeological opportunities.[110] The exposition's Peruvian mummies ended up in three separate museums. The majority of Ancón's mummy bundles joined Montero's ceramics at Marshall Field's Columbian Museum—today, the Field Museum—where Dorsey became the first curator in anthropology.[111] About a quarter went to Harvard's Peabody Museum, per the collecting agreements set up by Putnam. When Putnam became a curator of the American Museum of Natural History (AMNH) in New York, he sent some of Dorsey's mummies there to anchor a new Peruvian Hall. *Peruvian Mummies and What They Teach* (1907), a guide to that exhibit (on display through 1965), asserted that "the history of the Andean Peruvian must to a large degree be read in their graves, since they left no written customs and the Spanish conqueror destroyed many of their cities and suppressed their customs."[112] The display of the interments of a millennia-old people in these three museums promoted an Americanist archaeology that celebrated the museum display of Indigenous mortuary culture, whose apex remained Peru.

Putnam's colleagues took note. The five years after Chicago's Ancón display saw incredible competition between US and European museums for Andean collections.[113] In the United States, it resulted in two of the more important museum "expeditions" to the Andes: that of German archaeologist Max Uhle for

Fig. 6.9 Two intact mummy bundles from Ancón displayed alongside a less fortunate counterpart in the Peruvian Hall of the American Museum of Natural History, New York, ca. 1907, identified as excavated by George A. Dorsey in 1891. Charles W. Mead, *Peruvian Mummies and What They Teach* (1907).

the University of Pennsylvania's new museum, and that of Swiss-American archaeologist Adolph Bandelier for financier Henry Villard and the AMNH. Uhle,
who worked at the coastal solar temple of Pachacamac, is often credited with
giving American archaeology its "scientific" start, using stratigraphic excavation to establish chronological orders.[114] Bandelier, by contrast, is remembered
for an attention to material remains and their context that questioned assumed
chronologies, such as a "complete MUMMY" collected near Arica and bundled
with a papal bull printed in 1578 in Madrid. Bandelier warned colleagues that
Andean tombs thus revealed colonial changes, and could not be presumed to be
simply "ancient" or pre-Hispanic.[115]

Both Uhle and Bandelier's work was shaped by Chicago's Peruvian lessons,
however. The University Museum's patron Sara Yorke Stevenson reached out to
Uhle in the fall of 1893, having seen the Necropolis at the fair. Because Stevenson
asked Uhle to likewise "construct" a "good burial," he began his excavations and
purchases at Ancón, sending 3,848 items to Philadelphia, including two mummy
bundles and over two hundred skulls, mummified heads, and other human remains. He continued that work of collection-building at Pachacamac, sending
Penn the ninety-plus interments unearthed for his stratigraphically revolutionary Pachacamac (1903).[116]

The connection was more explicit at the AMNH. When Putnam took up the
anthropology curatorship in 1894, he was taken aback by Bandelier's collecting
practices to date. Putnam believed that Bandelier aggressively mined interments
for "complete" and exemplary objects, destroying their more fragmentary context. Putnam was shocked to read of six skulls Bandelier collected and then lost,
and about partially opened mummy bundles ruined in transit—"fifty mummies
which dropped to pieces" and were scavenged for parts, some abandoned altogether. "Why could he not have saved the skeletons in those mummy bundles?"
Putnam wrote to the AMNH's secretary; rather than just "types," "skulls should be
collected by the hundreds from every locality that he explores."[117] In 1895 Putnam
pointed Bandelier to the "new scientific practice" of Dorsey's work. He asked him
to photograph and map all interments before excavating, to send mummy bundles
intact. At Chicago, this "gave the public a pretty good idea of the burial customs as
shown by our exploration of that necropolis," permitting consideration on their
own terms—a culture no longer comparable to that of Europe.[118] Bandelier got the
message, ultimately collecting some twelve hundred Andean skulls from Peru and
Bolivia, adding to the AMNH's largest Indigenous series.[119]

From Putnam's displays the idea traveled. By the mid-twentieth century,
anthropology and natural history museums across the United States featured
Peruvian or South American Halls like that of the AMNH, anchored by duos or
trios of Andean mummies—one or two bundled, one stripped bare.[120] American
collectors were portrayed as rescuers, salvaging Andean cemeteries from

huaqueros, Indian "superstition," and governments whose laws were supposedly venal in motivation.[121] But behind every pair of mummies on display were others torn apart, left in place, or moldered for lack of documentation or care. The "largest mummy bundle" Dorsey unearthed in his time in Peru crumbled into a "pile of garments, leaves and flowers" when he and his workers moved it from its deep Chancay tomb.[122] The orphaned mummy fragments, textile scraps, and ceramic vessels that also represent the Andes in museums worldwide are the evidence of this sort of grave-opening, which made knowledge with the right hand and unmade tombs with the left.

For that reason Dorsey's 1893 display might strike the modern observer as the truest depiction of the uncanny work of knowing the Andean dead. Viewers certainly felt that frisson at the time. For all that Dorsey hoped to educate fairgoers regarding Ancón's culture, this was still a chance to gawk at another people's dead in the moment of their abject exposure, drawing attention to anthropology's blurring of graverobbing and science. The "ghastliness about the display" disquieted one reporter for Chicago's *Daily Inter Ocean*, who noted that night watchmen apparently felt themselves "haunted by the restless spirits of the people who lived hundreds or thousands of years ago, and whose bodies are now the mummies on exhibition."[123] *Cosmopolitan's* writer found Peru's "hideous mummies, swathed and unswathed, [who] sat in ghastly groups making blood-curdling faces at each other . . . unpleasantly suggestive. There was one blackish-brown squatter, in particular, who pursued me for a week in my dreams. His face was screwed up into an expression of heart-rending mirth, with a fascination of horror in it which would have made it a find to E. T. A. Hoffmann or Edgar Allan Poe. He, too, had his instructive side, no doubt; or he would not have been there."[124]

Cursed mummies and vengeful Native ghosts sold. But the literalism of Peru's mummified ancestors provoked particularly existential questions, if not guilty terror at viewing these disinterred "uncanny bundles"—open-mouthed heads cradled in hands, so far from home.[125] Long before Chicago, Flora Tristan had written about the "Inca" mummies of Lima's National Museum; four decades later, Tristan's grandson, French-Peruvian painter Paul Gauguin, was inspired by a stunning mummy from the Chachapoyas region. Collected in 1877 and later installed at Paris's Musée d'Ethnologie du Trocadéro, the mummy appeared in a number of Gauguin's works, including as humanity's mother *Breton Eve*, seated in a "fusion of birth and death."[126] Because Gauguin's Norwegian admirer Edvard Munch may have seen the same mummy during his Paris sojourn, one art historian suggests their pose inspired *The Scream* (see plate 9).[127] If true, Munch made Peru's ancestors the most invisibly famous mummies in history.

There is no need to speculate about what Andean peoples closest to the ancestral dead may have felt about their disinterment and translation. Since Morton,
foreign collectors had claimed that "Cholos, or native people tell you that the
ancient inhabitants were Gentiles and have no souls, and although in many cases
they realize the fact that they are disturbing the remains of their ancestors ... they
are so accustomed to it that they have absolutely no scruples in assisting you in
your work."[128] Yet Dorsey and his cohort knew the truth was more complicated,
especially as they left Ancón. In following the railroads into the Andes they met
communities that might abuse or avoid "gentile" remains but also gave them
offerings, or chased would-be excavators away. Most powerfully, at least one
Huarochirí community paraded the "little grandparents" again.[129] To navigate
these lived realities, collectors asked museums, diplomats, and financial interests
for letters of "protection" from Peru's president and ministers. These letters ordered regional prefects to release soldiers to escort them and, if needed, force
"superstitious Indians of the interior" into disinterring the dead for outsiders,
once again.[130] In doing so, the Peruvian state helped make communities into
accomplices in their antecessors' kidnapping.

The distress these coercions produced was itself of interest to anthropology.
For Dorsey, it marked a community's cultural proximity to the past. In March
1892, before returning to the United States, Dorsey made the thirty-four-day
mule ride to Cuzco to see the capital of Peru's most famed empire of the dead
and do some collecting in the Incas' heartland.[131] To smooth his way, Dorsey
acquired letters from Cuzco's prefect, the regional representative of the national
government, commanding "all Gobernadors in the Province to place ... men at
our disposal." Dorsey also connected with "a well educated gentleman" named
Corbacho, who spoke Quechua "perfectly, and was as well acquainted with the
legends and traditions of the present Indians as he was with the hidden tombs
of their ancestors."[132]

Together they rode to Huarocondo, a Quechua-speaking community on a
tributary of the Urubamba River, which connected Huayna Capac's former royal
estates at Yucay with Pachacuti's retreat at Huayna Picchu. It was a day's travel by
mule, and Corbacho took Dorsey to the village priest when they arrived. The priest
summoned the town's Quechua-speaking gobernador to explain that they needed
laborers the following day to disinter the dead. The gobernador, despite being the
central government's representative, bravely objected: "the people of that district
would not disturb the tombs in the valley as they contained the remains of their
ancestors, and to remove them would be sacrilege." But Corbacho countered with
the prefect's letter, which "had the desired effect." The next morning the village's
men met Dorsey and Corbacho and escorted them to a series of cave tombs in
cliffs beneath them, fifteen hundred feet above the river. The men would have to
climb down to unbrick the stones that sealed the ancestors in.[133]

Huarocondo's men fettered their mules and got out ropes and candles. But before Dorsey could propose descending, Corbacho explained "we should be obliged to wait until our Indians went through with their customary ceremony." He gave them corn beer, aguardiente (hard sugarcane liquor), and coca bought for that very purpose. Huarocondo's men "removed their hats and ponchos, bowed and knelt, and in unison began the following invocation, which was addressed to the supposed spirits beneath them," a "ceremony" Corbacho purported to transcribe in Quechua and translate to Spanish for Dorsey.[134]

"*Intip churin,*" it began: "Son of the sun, you and we are brothers, sons of the great Pachacamac. You only know this, but we know that three persons exist, the Father, the Son, and the Holy Ghost. This is the only difference between you and us." "*Intip churin,*" they continued, "Son of the sun, we have not come to disturb your tranquil sleep in this, your abode. We have come only because we have been compelled by our superiors; toward them may you direct your vengeance and your curses."[135]

Spreading coca on a poncho, they each chose three perfect leaves on which to blow, buried some, and burned a handful more: "Take this coca, perhaps it may comfort you." From a cup they flicked aguardiente north, east, south, and west: "Take some aguardiente, be drunk." Each man poured some on the ground and drank the rest, doing the same with corn beer. Then, asking Huarocondo's snow-capped sacred mountain "Sancahuara," or Sinqa, to witness their invocation, they "drained several cups of chicha [corn beer], filled their mouths with coca, and were ready to go to work."[136] The men secured the ropes, prepared the candles, and went over the cliff for ancestors who had escaped even the Spanish. They procured "eight mummies in good condition" that Dorsey transported to Chicago with about six skulls. After the fair, they were acquired by the Field Museum, where they are today. Only one remains a mummy, a child. Two of their number were displayed as "Inca" skeletons. The rest were reduced to crania.[137]

Dorsey also collected "the ceremony" that mourned them, sharing it in the *Journal of American Folklore.* He believed it revealed continuities between "a once proud and powerful race" and "pure descendants" who "had not forgotten their 'brothers,' and, more remarkable still, acknowledged their allegiance to their ancient religion, in spite of nearly four centuries of Catholic rule, and called themselves children of the sun and worshippers of the great Pachacamac."[138]

Which is one way to look at it, if the villagers said exactly what Dorsey believed they did.[139] Another is that, without Dorsey, Corbacho, the village priest, the Peruvian state, and nearly four centuries of coercive grave-opening, this "ceremony" would not have taken place. The men from Huarocondo were not locked "in an impossible museum" of their study.[140] They had spent centuries in transformation, taming a Christianity and its burial practices, a knowledge of the Trinity, and a relationship to the state that promised afterlives more secure than those of their sleeping "brothers" nearby. But the destroyed tranquility of those *Intip churin* remained something to lament, redirect, even cure. Their "ceremony" was thus thoroughly modern and centuries old—a counterknowledge to the imperial sciences that forced them to collaborate in their antecessors' loss. Dorsey, Corbacho, Harvard, the World's Fair, the Peruvian state, Americanist anthropology—all who made a museum of Huarocondo's mourning and anger—were party to a condemnation that sought to bear fruit.[141] It could take years, decades, a century or more, but by grieving their "brothers" anew Huarocondo planted what could someday become a seed for their recovery.

PART 3

HEALING, 1863–1965

SUPERIOR ASPECT OF CRANIUM 1, FROM HUAROCHIRI

The Chuicoto Skull, from Huarochirí, collected by Julian Tello, the father of Huarochirí anthropologist Julio César Tello, ca. 1890, which later became part of the collections of the Bureau of American Ethnology and the Smithsonian. Manuel Antonio Muñiz and W. J. McGee, "Primitive Trephining in Peru" (1897), Plate 1.

Trepanning Incas

*Ancient Peruvian Surgery and American Anthropology's
Monroe Doctrine*

The broken cannot always be mended. The lost can be forgotten. But holes are also openings through which the old can be glimpsed and the new can grow.

For the three centuries since conquistadors reported that the yllapas of Huayna Capac and his consort were "like embalmed ones," outsiders read Andean ancestors as a dead beyond healing and certainly incapable of curing the living. Even anti-imperial tales of these "mummies" emphasized their death— that they were suicides or victims of Spanish rule. Outsiders like George Dorsey knew that communities like Huarocondo met their disinterred "Intip Churin" brothers as still present, but gave little actual credence to the "old ceremonies" that redirected their wrath. That the "dead" may have also had healing powers was out of the question.

Present-day students of the Andes, however, respect its peoples' ability to heal and be healed, even by seemingly inanimate or nonhuman ancestral beings. Anthropologists and ethnohistorians approach these capabilities with nuance, understanding their goals as sometimes distinct from so-called Western medicine. Ritual healings are no less "authentic" for being executed with coca leaves or a huaco (ancient, lucky ceramic) on a textile "mesa" (a healer's table) by a tourist-oriented "shaman."[1] Scholars also study how healing knowledges in the Andes responded to the pressures of colonialism. Afro-Peruvians and less elite creoles adapted Andean cures, sometimes calling upon dead Incas to assist them in their medicine—but also adopting Indigenous herbalism.[2] Andean healers, meanwhile, learned to mitigate the effects of Old World diseases by experimenting with the bark of the cinchona tree, whose malaria-fighting agent would later be isolated as quinine.[3]

Empires of the Dead. Christopher Heaney, Oxford University Press. © Oxford University Press 2023.
DOI: 10.1093/oso/9780197542552.003.0008

This chapter shows how scholars began attending to the "ancient Peruvian" roots of these Andean healing abilities via the discovery of "prehistoric" trepanation or trephination—a surgery that cuts or drills into crania to relieve injuries or maladies threatening the brain.

European and American scientists previously ascribed holes in "ancient" crania to "savage" violence or superstition. But in Cuzco, in 1863, a Peruvian collector and a US archaeologist discussed an "Inca" skull whose fifteen-by-seventeen-millimeter quadrilateral hole suggested another cause.[4] This cranium,

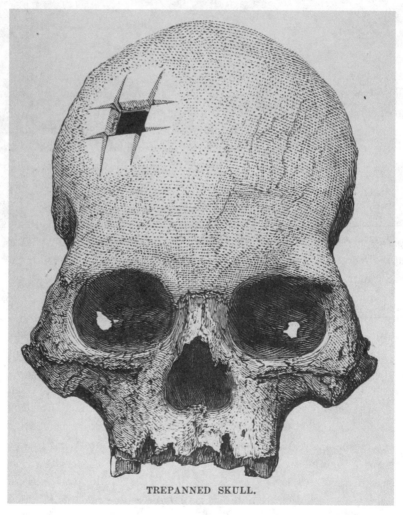

TREPANNED SKULL.

Fig. 7.1 The Yucay skull from Peru, found near Huayna Capac's old estate, whose collection in Cuzco by the antiquarian and surgeon Ramón Matto, and the museum-builder and landowner Ana María Centeno de Romaineville, launched the global study of trepanation's antiquity. "Trepanned Skull," Ephraim George Squier, *Peru* (1877), 457.

found near Huayna Capac's estate, Yucay, was the first specimen of its type worldwide, and its travels beyond Peru initiated a global search for others like it.

Whether that search would be embraced was another matter. Trepanation has proven as old as the Neolithic Era. Though its uses include freeing or connecting to supernatural forces, humans used it diagnostically and curatively as well—to address pressure caused by traumatic head wounds and pooled blood; to cure epilepsy; and to palliate "invisible" conditions, from headaches to mental disorders. In the wake of the Yucay skull's revelation, trepanation's students declared it humanity's oldest surgical operation and—because it is practiced today as craniotomy—its longest lasting. Trepanation was "perhaps the boldest feature of modern surgery," wrote one American anthropologist of Andean skulls in the 1890s, "and it may be characterized as the only feature of modern surgery which is known to be of great antiquity. Accordingly, trephining may be considered to represent the trunk of the genetic tree of surgery, and the history of trephining may fairly be considered to represent the history of surgery" itself.[5]

To claim that surgical history for "ancient" Andean peoples turned global hierarchies of science, civilization, and savagery on their head. Although many Peruvian, American, and French collectors and scholars believed its practice medical, others deemed it "superstitious" at best and barbaric at worst. To debate the existence of medical trepanation in the Andes, anthropologists and surgeons sought further examples. The stakes were high. Examples of nonmedical skull-opening could be used to keep America's Native peoples in what anthropologist Michel-Rolph Truillot insightfully called anthropology's savage slot, as violent or primitive peoples without history.[6] But pre-Hispanic Andean "surgeons" challenged American anthropology to see how Indigenous peoples viewed skulls with an expertise of their own—as subjects to heal via high-risk medical operation.

In the decades after 1863 this debate culminated in the transformation of Andean anthropology, as practiced in Peru, into something more than the grave-opening that had so shaped Americanist anthropology. Andean remains were still appropriated under this new regime, but no longer solely as mummified avatars of a dead Inca nation. They were entertained as healing ancestors as well, whose re-interment in Peruvian museums promised a new science based upon curing and care. In claiming Andean healers as "Peruvian surgeons," anthropologists and museums simplified manifold concerns of the body, the climate, and the cosmos into something to display. But finding that a non-European people like the Incas were more skilled at trepanation than nineteenth-century Euro-Americans was as consequential to anthropology as the Andean dead's recapture of context at Chicago in 1893. Peruvian scholars and Andean anthropologists would reinterpret skulls beyond racial essentialism, reading them for malnutrition, disease, and violence and those forces' healing via trepanation and mummification. This reading hinted at a new ethics of their care, shaped by the Andean ancestors themselves. Their healing would be visible not only in Peru but also in the Smithsonian's Hall 25.

Knowledge rarely moves in a straight line, however. This chapter focuses on Andean trepanation's initial denial—a transnational process whose politics supported both Peruvian and US colonial projects.[7] Some Peruvian and US scholars met the Yucay skull's implications with a resistance that was only in part a matter of evidence. Even when further examples were found, anti-Indigenous prejudice shaped their study, and in debating "ancient" trepanation, Peruvian surgeons asserted their own medical knowledges over those of the innovative Andean healers upon which many Peruvians still rely.[8] These prejudices also climaxed at the Chicago World's Fair of 1893, where, separate from Ancón's mummies, a Peruvian surgeon named Manuel Antonio Muñiz educated his North American colleagues with a collection of nineteen trepanned skulls. But when Muñiz's counterpart at the Bureau of American Ethnology in Washington got his hands on the skulls, he reversed their meaning.

In this first phase, anthropology's collection of Andean healing practices was riddled with holes.

Unlike the Inca mummification practices that the Spanish equated with Old World embalming, Andean trepanation escaped the conquistadors' notice. Nevertheless, bioanthropologist John Verano today estimates that an astounding 75.3 percent of people who were trepanned and interred at Ollantaytambo, a royal estate of the Inca emperor Pachacutic, showed signs of long-term healing. And long-term healing suggests they survived a surgery that killed almost that exact proportion in nineteenth-century Europe and the United States.[9] The only possible example of the practice in written sources is Pachacutic himself—that "pedrada" on the head of his yllapa, observed by the Jesuit José de Acosta in the 1580s. Acosta's failure to see this possible example meant that a two-thousand-year-old Andean operation, in which accomplished surgeons used coca leaves as analgesics, and employed bronze and obsidian knives to remove damaged bone, relieve pressure, or excise tumors, went unrecognized. It may have also gone underground. If trepanation also had a ritual component, then its practitioners may have tried to keep it from Spanish eyes, lest it be read as one of the "superstitions" that priests sought to quash.[10]

Nevertheless, skull surgery remained in healers' repertoire. Violence in the Andes changed, from Inca maces and Spanish swords to the slower imperial poisons of mining mercury and silver for the global economy. But physical abuse and "natural" accidents still happened. In 1895 Swiss-American anthropologist

Adolph Bandelier learned of a hacienda administrator who "had known a man near Cuzco who had been trephined for skull-fracture and who wore a piece of gourd inserted in the orifice." Bandelier inferred "that both the operator and the man on whom the operation was performed were Indians," and in Bolivia he himself met two individuals successfully operated upon by "Indian medicine-men." One of those healers—Paloma, an "Aymará" from "Hachacache"—was so famed that "members of the medical faculty at La Paz, learning of his successful operations with such clumsy implements, presented him with a box of surgical instruments which, it is stated, he never used, preferring his own primitive way." Paloma had "acquired the art empirically and through training by other and older shamans," but had died a few years earlier. Although Bandelier was unable to find another "medicine man," he believed it an active practice that survived colonialism.[11]

Bandelier was also looking for trepanned pre-Hispanic skulls, hoping to replicate the example that had launched "prehistoric" trepanation's global study. This was the Yucay skull, found before 1863 in an "Inca cemetery" near Yucay, Huayna Capac's former estate in the Urubamba Valley. The first phase of this skull's transformation from embodied ancestor to specimen must be imagined. Its earliest known collector was Ramón Matto, a surgeon, landholder, and antiquarian in Cuzco. It is unclear whether Matto found the skull himself or if it was found by an individual attached to his property, Paullo Chico, just upriver from Yucay; Matto could have sent a dependent of Paullo Chico into an "Inca" cave for antiquities and mummies, as Dorsey would at Huarocondo decades later.[12]

Or the Yucay skull may have been the product of more local ways of knowing. Historian Stefanie Gänger observes that Cuzco's antiquarians possessed things found not through excavation, but via purchase or acquisition from "Indians" who maintained that item via "continued use."[13] Given that the earliest reference to contemporary trepanation was near Cuzco, per Bandelier, it can at least be speculated whether the Yucay skull's earliest re-collection was by a local healer who understood the skull as the patient of a fellow practitioner. It may have then been spotted by Matto, who, a surgeon himself, perhaps recognized the import of the four perpendicular cuts in the skull's frontal bone and sought to celebrate ancient Cuzco's Indigenous precedence in Peru's medical history.[14] In the hands of Cuzco's antiquarians it became a specimen of surgical knowledge—but this may have overlaid its earlier life among descendants of Pachacutic's own healers, who were now marginalized by nineteenth-century medical elites.[15]

Next, Matto gifted the skull to Cusqueña landowner Ana María Centeno de Romaineville, "the collector of the finest and most valuable museum of antiquities in Peru." Praise for that collection—and specifically the Yucay skull—came from North American archaeologist and diplomat Ephraim George Squier, who visited Centeno in 1863. Squier was impressed by "this important relic," believing it "the most remarkable evidence of a knowledge of surgery among the aborigines yet discovered on this continent." "Zentino [sic]," Squier claimed, "was kind enough to give [it] to me for investigation."[16] Matto's prior ownership of the skull thereby disappeared—at least to non-Peruvian interpreters.

Peruvian scholars later questioned Squier's acquisition and elision of Matto but celebrated its subsequent debate. Although Squier had in 1866 provided Harvard's Peabody Museum with its early core of Andean dead, he retained property of the "Zentino skull." He believed that it showed that ancient Peruvians practiced a relatively complex surgery, one that demonstrated the originality of Inca and American civilization, free of European influence. From New York he circulated the skull to reignite the referendum on ancient Peruvian development that Morton had foresworn.

At its first stop, doctors at the New York Academy of Medicine in 1865 debated whether the bones showed signs of healing, which would prove the operation had occurred while the patient was alive. If there was no healing, the hole could be dismissed as "barbarous" postmortem trophy-taking. The doctors were divided. "Dr. Post stated that he did not see any of the evidence of the reparative process sufficiently marked to decide positively that the operation was not performed after death." Dr. August K. Gardner, who exhibited the skull for Squier, disagreed, responding that the signs of reparation "were more easily discernible during the daytime than by gaslight."[17]

The skull was better received by France's famed anthropologist and surgeon Paul Broca, who was dismantling phrenology's correlations of skull size and shape to intelligence by studying the functions of the brain. Squier sent the skull to Broca, who gave it a celebrated showing at the Société d'Anthropologie de Paris in 1867.[18] Broca began by asserting the bona fides of this "entirely new fact": Squier was the "first archaeologist in America," he declared, and the skull's thick walls "could only belong to an Indian of Peru"—a pre-Hispanic one, found in an "Inca cemetery." Broca highlighted the cuts on the skull's surface. The bone had started to heal, which indicated that the operation occurred while the patient was alive; its halt indicated that the patient died a week or two later. Broca deemed it trepanation, speculating that a bronze instrument or knife had been used.[19]

Broca then made an extraordinary leap, rewriting global medical history in light of Peruvian precedent. He observed that there was no evidence of premortem fracture or fissure—a fact that some interpreters took as trepanation's nonmedical or shamanic mark. Broca instead saw it as "astonish[ing]" evidence that the pre-Hispanic surgeon had diagnosed an intracranial lesion invisible on the skull's exterior, and had operated to evacuate blood pooling beneath. "This idea, an entirely new one, is not without interest in American anthropology," Broca declared with scholarly understatement.[20] His presentation launched

Plate 1 The "Skull Wall" in the Smithsonian Institution's first permanent Hall of Physical Anthropology, ca. 1965, in which 160 Andean crania embodied the population growth of all humanity. This photograph cuts off the bottom row of nine skulls, which were only visible when a museumgoer approached the display. Smithsonian Institution Archives, Image No. MNH-1646A.

Inca skull surgery was a form of body modification.

Plate 2 For at least two thousand years, Andean healers practiced trepanation, a skull surgery in which the world's most successful practitioners prior to the late nineteenth century belonged to the Inca Empire. This photograph depicts the exhibition of Alton Tobey's "Inca trephination mural" in the first Hall of Physical Anthropology at the Smithsonian's National Museum of Natural History after 1965. Tobey's painting depicts the Incas trepanning at famous Machu Picchu, though the display qualifies its medical achievement by suggesting "Inca skull surgery was a form of bodily modification." Smithsonian Institution Archives, Image No. 75-2104.

Plate 3 "The burial of the Inga: Inca Yllapa Aia Corpse." At right sit the yllapas (mummified sacred bodies) of the Sapa Inka (Inca emperor) and Coya (the Inca empress, or paramount wife). The seventeenth-century Andean chronicler Felipe Guaman Poma de Ayala illustrates their bodies as so perfectly embalmed that after at least a year they look identical to their attendants, at left, serving them aqha, corn beer. Felipe Guaman Poma de Ayala, *El primer nueva corónica y buen gobierno* (1615/1616), 287 [289]. Royal Danish Library, GKS 2232 4°.

Plate 4 Luis Montero, *Los Funerales de Atahualpa* (1865–1867). Painted while in Italy, Luis Montero's massive scene imagined the funeral of the Inca emperor Atahuallpa (for whom Montero used a fellow Peruvian artist as model) as a foundational moment of the Peruvian past—a worthy interment of a pitiable sovereign by noble Christian priests and conquistadors, mourned by Atahuallpa's (notably Italian-looking) wives. In reality, Atahuallpa's partisans rescued his corpse from a shallow Christian interment and brought him to Ecuador for his transformation into a cosmic ancestor. Pinacoteca Municipal Ignacio Merino. Metropolitan Municipality of Lima; in custody of the Museo de Arte de Lima.

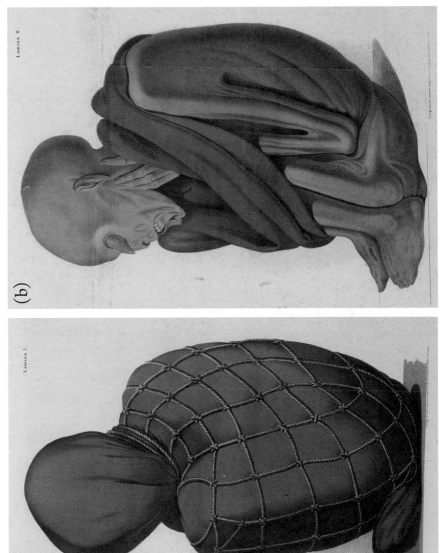

Plate 5 a and b These lithographs represented the first two of the four Cajatambo mummies—one bundled, one unwrapped—in the four corners of the "Museum of Lima," Peru's first National Museum, which opened in 1826 in the former quarters of the Inquisition. D. Leopoldo Müller, Plates I and II of Mariano Eduardo de Rivero and Johann Jakob von Tschudi, *Antigüedades Peruanas* (Vienna, 1851).

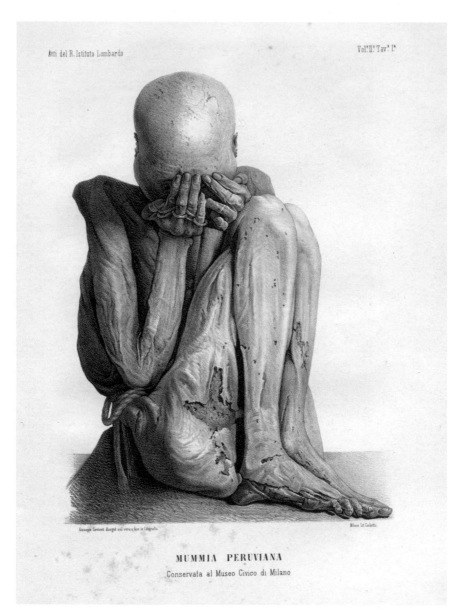

MUMMIA PERUVIANA

Conservata al Museo Civico di Milano

Plate 6 "I bit both my hands in grief." The Italian-Peruvian scientist Antonio Raimondi sent this Andean mummy to the Civic Museum of Milan, whose curator took it as an example of ancient Peruvian knowledge of both artificial and natural methods of mummification. The curator was loathe to dissect its supposedly Dantean form. "Mummia Peruviana Conservata al Museo Civico di Milano." Lithographic plate, Emilio Cornalia, "Sulla Mummia Peruviana del Civico Museo di Milan . . . Letta nella tornata del 21 Aprile 1859," *Atti del Reale Istituto lombardo di scienze, lettere ed arti*, Vol. 2 (Milano: Tipogradia Bernardoni, 1860), opposite 26. Courtesy of Yale University Library.

Plate 7 "In order to give a better idea of the proportions, two Indian workmen are introduced, as engaged in the work of exhumation. One of them is in the act of withdrawing the body of a mummy already devested [sic] of its cerements." Opposite Plate 6, *"Exposed Graves with Mummies of a Simple Type,"* from Wilhelm Reiss and Alphons Stübel, *The Necropolis of Ancon in Peru: A Contribution to Our Knowledge of the Culture and Industries of the Empire of the Incas.* trans. Augustus Henry Keane, Vol. 1 (Berlin: A. Asher, 1880–1887).

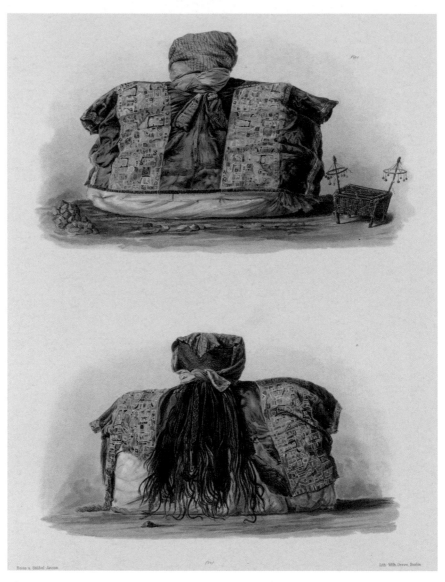

Plate 8 In a shift important to archaeology, art history, and the status of Andean remains in museums today, many of the "mummy bundles" that Reiss and Stübel collected were never undone and remain intact today. WIlh. Greve [Lithographer], Plate 16, "Sumptuous Mummy Pack," demonstrating the double-headed Ancón type, from Wilhelm Reiss and Alphons Stübel, *The Necropolis of Ancon in Peru: A Contribution to Our Knowledge of the Culture and Industries of the Empire of the Incas*, trans. Augustus Henry Keane, Vol. 1 (Berlin: A. Asher, 1880–1887).

Plate 9 a, b, and c a) The Peruvian mummy in the Musée de l'Homme, as depicted in E. T. (Ernest Théodore) Hamy, *Galerie américaine du Musée d'ethnographie du Trocadéro; choix de pièces archéologiques et ethnographiques, décrites et publiées par le dr E.-T. Hamy . . .* 2 vols., (Paris, E. Leroux, 1897), *Vol. 2*, pl. XXXIII. Courtesy of Beinecke Rare Book and Manuscript Library, Yale University. b) and c) Two paintings the mummy likely inspired: the French-Peruvian artist Paul Gauguin's *Breton Eve* (1889) and Edvard Munch's *The Scream* (1893). Gaugin: Courtesy of McNay Museum, San Antonio Texas. Munch: National Museum, Oslo, Norway. Free use (Creative Commons—Attribution CC-BY).

Plate 10 This image reproduced Tello's "Man of Paracas" mannequin from his National Museum of Archaeology. Robert Thom. "Trephining in Ancient Peru," for Parke, Davis, and Company, ca. 1952. From the collection of Michigan Medicine, University of Michigan, Gift of Pfizer, Inc., UMHS.3.

Plate 11 The final burial of Julio César Tello (1880–1947), in the rear patio of what is today the Museo Nacional de Arqueología, Antropología y Historia del Perú in Pueblo Libre, Lima. Photograph by author.

Plate 12 Rascar Capac calls down a ball of lightning to liberate himself from a private collection in Belgium. Hergé, *The Adventures of Tintin: The Seven Crystal Balls* (1948). © Hergé/Moulinsart, 2022.

a search for comparable French examples, reclassifying holes in Neolithic European skulls previously believed injuries. Debate continued over whether these interventions were thaumaturgic—a taking of cranial amulets, *rondelles*, from the skulls of the notable or the trophied dead, for magical cures. But Broca continued to pay Peruvians the highest of compliments. Using a new method of localizing specific cerebral phenomena, he popularized medical trepanation with modern instruments, which, with the introduction of aseptic techniques, gradually reduced the 75 to 90 percent of patients who previously had died after trepanation in nineteenth-century Europe and America.[21]

This was the life-extending side of the foreign collection of the Andean dead—the literal reverse of that haunting Peruvian mummy in the Musée d'Ethnologie du Trocadéro that inspired Gauguin's art, and possibly Munch's *Scream*. When viewed from behind, this mummy from Chachapoyas—where later scholars also observed a higher incidence of mummification, trepanation, and even the extension of trepanation's methods to other bones—shows that the individual died while a massive operation was underway.[22]

That the Incas practiced trepanation at all remained in doubt in the Americas, however. Broca sent Yucay's skull back to the United States, where scholars were particularly resistant to the idea that Native Americans were surgeons too. Instead, Americans like Henry Gilman described ten to fifteen skulls taken from mounds in Michigan, portraying their perforated vertices as evidence of post-mortem display—not trepanation.[23] With only one specimen to Gilman's dozen, Squier struggled to respond. In *Peru*, he argued that the Yucay skull's operation addressed an injury made invisible by the trepanation itself. To that end, Squier cited Josiah Nott, a southern surgeon who had argued that Morton's racial "evidence" justified slavery. Nott hypothesized that the obliterated wound could have been due to a small perforating weapon, whose possibility Squier tried to corroborate by observing that pre-Hispanic spears and arrows had long, sharp bronze tips. He had one such lance-head and had found, amid skeletons in the ruins of Chan Chan, "a skull thus perforated, with a bronze arrow still sticking in it . . . with no radiating fissures." His readers, though, had to take his word, for this "interesting specimen was lost, with other valuable relics, on its way to the United States."[24]

It was Squier's last comment on the matter. America's champion of Andean civilization had had a mental breakdown and was committed to an asylum. *Peru* was only published with his brother's help. When Squier died in 1888, his archaeological collection was bought by New York's American Museum of Natural History, where the Yucay skull still sits.

Other North Americans allowed for trepanation's existence but inverted its value. The second confirmed trepanation in the Americas was also from Peru—a skull collected for the Smithsonian by W. H. Jones, a surgeon on the USS

Fig. 7.2 The reverse of the Peruvian mummy in the Musée de l'Homme, revealing its trepanation, as depicted in E. T. (Ernest Théodore) Hamy, *Galerie américaine du Musée d'ethnographie du Trocadéro; choix de pièces archéologiques et ethnographiques, décrites et publiées par le dr E.-T. Hamy . . . 2 vols.* (Paris, E. Leroux, 1897), vol. 2, Plate XXXIII.

Wachusett. In November 1884 Jones left Lima and climbed to Chaclacayo, the westernmost folds of Huarochirí where, at four thousand feet, he found three wrapped mummies and a number of artificially shaped skulls—one trephined.[25] A section had been removed from that skull's frontal bone, but the furrowed work led the ethnologist who studied it in Washington to declare it more violent than healing. "The work seems to have been done in the most bungling manner," Otis T. Mason claimed in the *Proceedings of the U.S. National Museum*. Adding insult to injury, he theorized that the bone, once harvested, begot

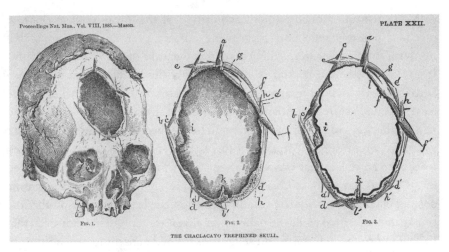

Proceedings Nat. Mus., Vol. VIII, 1885.—Mason.   PLATE XXII.

FIG. 1.   FIG. 2.   FIG. 3.

THE CHACLACAYO TREPHINED SKULL.

Fig. 7.3 The "Chaclacayo Trephined Skull," whose 1884 collection and study in Washington led to its dismissal as "bungling" and a prelude to violence. *Proceedings of the U.S. National Museum*, Vol. 8 (1885), Plate XXII.

further warfare. The removed fragments were likely "wrought into some useful thing, like the point of an arrow or spear. Instances are not wanting among peoples of low civilization where human bones have been considered to have great potency."[26]

American mummy-miners watched out for further trepanations, but the going was hard. In 1888, a year before dying of mummy dust, collector George Kiefer also made "perilous ascensions" to Huarochirí in search of one, but none of the eighty-eight skulls he sent to the US Army Medical Museum that June were trepanned. He nonetheless hyped a connection. Kiefer observed that some of the skulls showed "cuts" in the face, "leaving a groove which gives us an idea [of] the kind of instrument they must have used in trephining as the marks are similar. I wish I was so fortunate as to find some of their surgical instruments as so far I have never seen any. I have found plenty of instruments to kill but none to cure."[27]

Peruvians succeeded where Kiefer had not. They collected new examples of Andean trepanation out of frustration that their prior contributions had been elided. In 1886, Broca's 1867 paper was translated by the Sociedad Fernandina of Lima—a new society of the University of San Marcos's medical school. Among its members was David Matto, a surgeon employed by Lima's police. On the occasion of the translation, Matto told the society that Centeno had been given the Yucay skull by his father, Ramón, whom Squier had entirely forgotten.[28]

Matto also questioned Squier's acquisition of the Yucay skull in the first place—a possible reflection of growing anxiety over the collections that Peruvian antiquarians were selling abroad in the wake of the War of the Pacific. In the case of the Yucay skull, Matto seemingly alluded to a claim made by a British-American photographer named Augustus le Plongeon who, before leaving Lima to search for Atlantis in the Yucatán, spread a rumor that Centeno had lent her keys to Squier, at which point he "robbed" the Yucay skull.[29] Matto was more circumspect. "We don't know the means that Sr. Squier employed to acquire an object that was very esteemed by Sra. Centeno," who had died in 1874. But having raised his eyebrows, Matto credited Centeno's scientific cosmopolitanism and Squier's and Broca's appreciable demonstration that the trepanation occurred while the patient was alive: "we can assume, however, that this lady of such intelligence and selflessness would consent to give up the curious cranium for the noble reason that it might be examined by the European savants to whose study Sr. Squier later submitted it."[30] The rest of Centeno's museum followed: in 1887 her sons sold her collection to Berlin's Ethnological Museum for £2,000.[31]

It would go too far to say that the loss of the Yucay skull sent Peruvian collectors and scholars in a more self-consciously national direction. But it was an opportunity to highlight the diagnostic abilities of both "ancient" and republican Peruvian surgeons and scholars, who sought the more anthropological credit they believed they were due. In Lima, members of the Sociedad Fernandina and the Sociedad Geográfica de Lima—decreed into existence in 1888 by the government of Andrés Avelino Cáceres—married the country's republican antiquarianism to modes of anthropology and racialized hygiene honed by reading Morton, Broca, and others during European sojourns. This engagement with more anatomically permanent notions of bodily difference bridged colonial and postcolonial racism in Peru. By 1890 the Sociedad Fernandina possessed a requisite mummy from Cuzco, but its members were collecting dolichocephalic "Aymara" skulls, which they declared backward and quiescent, and brachycephalic "Quechua" skulls, seen as smarter but more docile.[32]

That racism, combined with scholarly skepticism, made some Peruvians no more willing than North Americans to ascribe medical talent to a few cranial holes—especially if it threatened their own medical specialization in the face of a proliferation of less elite competitors.[33] The Sociedad Fernandina kept up with foreign research on trepanation and in 1890 hosted a presentation by Antonio Lorena, a physician and member of Cuzco's archaeological society who would go on to teach anthropology, legal medicine, and physiognomy at the University of Cuzco.[34] Lorena claimed some authority on Inca medical customs "conserved almost in their primitive originality" in various populations in the department of Cuzco—and used it to pit trepanation against the ancient Peruvians' purported skill at mummification. Lorena claimed that ancient Peruvians extracted the dead's viscera from natural openings, not incisions. This prevented them from trepanning "as Indo-European surgeons conceived of it," Lorena claimed. "The medicine born with man's first pain could not have been advanced among peoples that looked at human cadavers as sacred and untouchable." Instead, Lorena argued that the heights of pre-Hispanic medicine were no higher than "small islands that persist like the remains of a submerged Continent," perceptible in the Andean living. *Laîcca* or shaman (*brujos*) possessed a "confused and monstrous mix of superstitions and empirical knowledge," he claimed. Their "single instrument, a small fragment of silex or obsidian," seemed to him insufficient for cutting bone. Squier and Broca were thus credulous, ill-informed outsiders. Lorena added racism to evidentiary doubt: "Meek and unsure, with that timidity that is the characteristic trait of the nature of the indigenous race of Peru, they no doubt would not have dared to have opened the cranium, when they would not even open the abdomen of their dead."[35]

Finally, one skull was insufficient to "affirm a fact," Lorena insisted. Cuzco's collectors had what Lorena believed were contrary specimens. He revealed photographs of hundreds of "perforated" skulls found in the tombs of Calca, Pomacanchi, and Silque and sent by Ramón Nadal, representative of the province of Urubamba, to the house of Dr. Teodicio Rosas and the museum of Dr. Cáparo Muñiz, president of Cuzco's Sociedad Arqueológica. Lorena claimed these photographs instead showed that pre-Hispanic violence and sexuality produced these holes: "perpetual war" by skull-crushing weapons, and necrotic syphilis caused by Inca toleration of prostitution. Any smoothing of wounds was postmortem. Given the sheer number of holes found by Cusqueños, Inca surgeons would have been so skilled at trepanation as to make it as common as the "strike of a lancet," which Lorena would not accept. "Wouldn't trepanation have been preserved along with the many other *authentic* techniques that persist in isolated towns in the Sierra that, as I've already said, still live the life of the Incas, [for whom] the three centuries that separate us from the fall of the empire of *Tahuantinsuyo* haven't passed at all?" Perforations, not medical trepanations, were the wages of inherited Indigenous barbarity.[36]

Lorena did not speak for all, though, and the Sociedad Fernandina told him so. This was a contest between Limeño and Cusqueño authority over Andean bodies and their attributed past. When Lorena finished, doctors Leonardo Villar, Celso Bambarén, and Manuel A. Muñiz, a twenty-nine-year-old surgeon, countered. They observed that Lorena's own photographs showed a cranial excavation that had been abandoned—a hint that the skull's manipulator was not smoothing preexisting holes but beginning new ones, halting when a patient died. Had Lorena just given a presentation on hundreds of trepanations? Lorena yielded. In an addendum to his talk's publication, he admitted the Incas clearly possessed procedures for opening the cranial vault and that the holes might have been tried to relieve compression.[37]

Muñiz took advantage of the opening, changing trepanation's landscape in Peru and abroad. He was an apt representative of the positivism and technocratic elitism that took hold after the War of the Pacific. When Chile invaded Peru, Muñiz had been in medical school; during the conflict he was a surgeon in a hospital improvised in Lima's Palace of the Exposition, where Rivero's mummies had been. For siding with General Avelino Cáceres during an ensuing Peruvian civil war, Muñiz was exiled to Chile, where he ensconced himself at Santiago's National Library, rich with books looted from Lima's National Library. Muñiz began to study the Peruvian history of diseases and hygiene, a field he credited with making "peoples and nations strong, rich and respected."[38] When Cáceres won his war and in 1886 won the presidency, he made Muñiz, just twenty-five years old, surgeon general of Peru's army. Muñiz used his platform to emphasize epidemiology's importance for present policy, and in 1888 he was sent to Europe to study military health, anatomy, neuropathology, hygiene, and criminal anthropology. When he returned two years later, he applied his learning by assisting Lima's police by profiling accused criminals using bodily measurements learned in France.[39]

Muñiz believed these state interventions on Peru's multiethnic bodies were well founded in history. Like other members of the Sociedad Fernandina, Muñiz believed "ancient Peruvians" had diagnosed and depicted syphilis, goiters, and other diseases on their ceramics, which could be studied as new documents in the history of medicine and science.[40] Unlike Lorena, Muñiz emphasized what he claimed was Inca regulation of prostitution. In elitist and racializing terms, Muñiz contended that Inca knowledge of their "Indian" subjects' supposedly bestial sexual practices begat the empire's medical ingenuity and state control.[41] Muñiz and his fellow surgeons inherited that Inca knowledge and control but surpassed them with European training. In 1891, in Lima's cathedral, Muñiz used these skills to autopsy Peru's decidedly non-Inca "mummified" ancestor: Francisco Pizarro, "Conqueror of Peru, founder of Lima."[42]

This re-collection of Peru's medical history returned Muñiz to Andean trepanation. Like other doctors, Muñiz collected artifacts from tombs. What set him apart was his series of "something over a thousand" "ancient" crania—the world's largest collection of pre-Columbian skulls at the time—which he loaned to fellow scholars interested in discussing Peru's cranial types.[43] Muñiz built it using his position as Peru's surgeon general, opening huacas and graves in the Andes and the coast during his travels. But like Dorsey in Huarocondo, he also enlisted the help of others, like Pérez Albela and, more consequentially, local authorities and Andean grave-openers like Julián Tello García, a gobernador in

Huarochirí, that highland region east of Lima that for three hundred years had been reputed for its ancestors.[44]

Those grave-openers enabled Muñiz to build an anthropological collection that racialized "Indian" skulls but judged them medically—specifically, whether they practiced surgery.[45] Muñiz didn't have just one trepanned pre-Columbian Peruvian skull. He had nineteen, from sites across the country: from Cañete and the shrine of Pachacamac, near Lima; from Tarma; from near Cuzco; and eleven from Huarochirí, including at least one found in "Chuicoto" by one Julián Tello. Muñiz marked them as his own, labeling their frontal bones and detailing the village near where they were found. He arranged them to show trepanation's arc as a therapeutic surgery with a range of approaches, from rectilinear marks to careful circular apertures to bravura performances. One Cuzco skull had an enormous aperture, four inches long and an inch wide, which apparently was found covered with a silver plate. The majority showed signs of healing. One was trepanned three times, revealing surgical skill and patient survival. At least one was still covered with mummified flesh, more a decapitated head than skull. Muñiz supplemented the collection with pre-Hispanic tools he believed to have been used by Peru's "trephiners."[46]

Muñiz chose the grandest possible stage to present this Peruvian medical knowledge. In 1893 Peru's government dispatched Muñiz to attend the Pan-American Medical Congress in Washington, DC, to study US military hospitals and collect data on the North American health system. Beforehand, however, Muñiz decided to bring his nineteen skulls to the Columbian Exposition in Chicago, helping to take the place of Peru's unfunded official delegation.[47] There, they would embody Peruvian science and then return to Peru, triumphant. Or so Muñiz planned.

———

Muñiz unveiled his nineteen skulls in a morning session of the fair's Congress of Anthropology in August. The Peruvian surgeon drafted an explanation of the skulls' importance; George Dorsey, the collector of the Fair's Ancón Necropolis, translated it for their assembled colleagues. While Dorsey spoke, Muñiz stood beside the skulls, likely lifting them to highlight their features.[48] The presentation answered doubts regarding Andean trepanation's medical purpose, as well as objections that it was singularly Inca. Muñiz showed that trepanation occurred while patients were alive, and that examples were found throughout the Andes and Peruvian coast—a shared surgery addressing traumatic lesions of the cranium and certain cerebral diseases.[49]

Other presentations provoked more discussion but this was in part because Muñiz's collection and authority as a Peruvian surgeon and anthropologist soared over the initial burden of proof. Frederic Ward Putnam, the exposition's planner, was convinced of the collection's value. In his account of the anthropological congress, W. H. Holmes of the Bureau of American Ethnology (BAE) praised Muñiz's collection as "the richest ever made." Muñiz then took the skulls to the Pan-American Medical Congress in Washington, where his collection was considered so valuable that he was offered large sums to leave it in the United States.[50]

Muñiz demurred. He wanted the collection to return to Peru. But he also found a way to diffuse Peruvian anthropological knowledge in the United States while ensuring he received proper credit. The BAE's self-titled ethnologist in charge, W. J. McGee, had offered Muñiz the last three annual Smithsonian reports in exchange for the collection. Although scientists often exchanged publications and specimens to diffuse results and build relationships, McGee's offer was a lowball bid. Muñiz negotiated for something far more valuable. He returned to Peru but temporarily left the collection with McGee. In exchange, McGee would make a series of forty to fifty quarto- or "full-sized" photographs to become the centerpiece of a BAE publication that would include Muñiz's paper from the fair and a new study by McGee. Two skulls would then stay permanently with the BAE and the Army Medical Museum. The other seventeen, the published volume, a set of photographs, and other Smithsonian publications would then go to Lima, to be divided between Muñiz's library and the Sociedad Geográfica's museum.[51] McGee was gleeful, but Muñiz perhaps got the better deal. Peru's surgeons and scholars would be recognized by anthropology's larger community, resulting in a lavish publication that Peru's government could ill afford, while the majority of the skulls would return to their country of origin.

What instead happened was a gradual transfer of the skulls and their interpretation to the Bureau of American Ethnology. The BAE, founded in 1879, followed ethnologist Lewis Henry Morgan's evolutionary paradigm, which interpreted Native Americans as socially "retarded" but not biologically inferior, meaning they could be educated to become farmers while ethnologists salvaged and studied their abandoned tools and arts. This meant that the BAE initially left the collection and study of Indigenous human remains to the Army Medical Museum.[52] But the BAE was getting into anthropometry, collecting bodily measurements from Indian children forcibly sent to federal schools to ascend Morgan's ethnocidal ladder. Muñiz's collection provided an even more natural way for the BAE to extend its tool-based evolutionary ethnology to bodies, measuring the techniques of Peruvian skull-opening.[53]

This expanded the Bureau's geographical ambit too. After years of focus on Native North Americans, the Smithsonian and the BAE were following Harvard and the Peru-centric exposition at the World's Fair into the theorization of a more vast America.[54] John Wesley Powell, the BAE's director, articulated what one

British anthropologist lamented as a "'Monroe doctrine' of American anthropology": that because America's peoples developed independently of Europe and Asia, they required American eyes, much like President James Monroe's 1823 dictum against further European intervention in the Americas.[55] In practice, this anthropological Monroe Doctrine was, like its namesake, affected by neighbors' projects, like Mexico's National Museum, which asserted its own influence over BAE agents' projects.[56] But the bureau had free rein with materials in Washington like the skulls left by Muñiz, whose claim that some "Indians" practiced an extraordinary surgery warranted testing, Powell believed, "in so far as this is necessary for the explanation of the methods and ideas of the aboriginal practitioners."[57]

Muñiz advocated for this sort of hemispheric corroboration, likely confident that his conclusions would win out.[58] McGee at first gave no signs to the contrary. Muñiz and Federico Elguera, the secretary of Lima's Sociedad Geográfica, let McGee present on the skulls. At Washington's Anthropological Society, Baltimore's Medical Historical Society, and Philadelphia's College of Physicians and Archaeological Society, McGee reproduced Muñiz's line exactly.[59] He advanced the centuries-long tradition that those at the apex of Indigenous America were the "most highly cultured" Peruvians, whose "native genius . . . fertilized by the intelligence of the mysterious Manco Capac and his consort, bore fruit in one of the most remarkable cultures recorded in history." Peru's tillers, quarrymen, weavers, growers, civil engineers, astronomers, and architects were "remarkable," as evidenced in Muñiz's collection, whose "19 specimens may be arranged in such order as practically to tell their own story." McGee had previously belonged to the school that thought trepanning was solely postmortem and thaumaturgical, "after the manner of the primitive 'medicine' of the American Indians"—that is, those of North America—but Muñiz had opened his mind. Where there was no obvious trauma, McGee agreed that trepanation could have been employed to relieve epileptic conditions. "If these inferences be true," McGee explained in relation to one skull, "it will follow that the operation in this case was not only surgical but parallel with the traumatic trephining of modern practices, thus indicating a considerable advance in medical knowledge and surgical skill."[60]

McGee's diffusion of Muñiz's findings caused no small sensation across the scientific world. A writer for *Scientific American* suggested the ancient Peruvians had "surpassed their Spanish conquerors," perhaps even modern medicine. Trephining was nearly always fatal in Paris and Vienna, still killing three out of four patients in Great Britain and thirty-eight of forty-nine in New York.[61] The presentations also excited a "desire to obtain specimens from the collection," as Muñiz and McGee anticipated—a desire partially fulfilled by sharing the "full-sized" photographs that communicated Muñiz's data to scientific collaborators.[62]

Muñiz also gave the BAE permission to make plaster copies of the 19 skulls—a series of casts "painted to represent closely the originals."[63] McGee kept one set, sent two to the Smithsonian, and gave a fourth to the Army Medical Museum. Another was gifted to Chicago's Field Museum and another to archaeologist and philanthropist Sara Yorke Stevenson, who had seen Muñiz's collection at Chicago; hers would end up in the University of Pennsylvania's museum. It was also a moneymaking venture: Philadelphia's College of Physicians paid seventy-three dollars for their copies, today on display at the Mütter Museum. In years to come, copies would be ordered, exchanged, or sold to institutions in London, Paris, and elsewhere in Europe.[64] Muñiz's 19 became 38, 76, then 152, winging his Peruvian message across the anthropological world—to the BAE's profit.

But in 1895 this Peruvian-led anthropology went up in smoke. That year, Muñiz's patron, Cáceres, returned to power via an election in which he was the sole candidate. When anger at this second term exploded, Muñiz and his science were caught in the crossfire. On March 17, 1895, Nicolás de Piérola—who had seized the country's leadership during the war with Chile—attacked Lima with a column of revolutionaries, fighting street by street until a thousand lay dead and Cáceres was exiled. The next day, a "mob" set Muñiz's home on fire. He and his family survived and were exiled to Buenos Aires, but they lost everything, including Muñiz's thousand ancient Peruvian crania. "My house was sacked and burned, and I lost my library, collections, etc," he wrote to McGee, distraught.[65] Muñiz's colleagues believed that his crown jewels, the trepanned skulls, were lost as well. McGee assured Muñiz of their safety in Washington, "in a fireproof building, subject to your order at any time."[66]

The order never came. McGee had encouraged Muñiz to give the skulls to Washington, "where it would be accessible to the largest number of individuals," bringing Peru and the United States "into closer relations and more complete harmony."[67] In 1896 Muñiz accepted the offer, hoping to start again. "Partly by reason of desire to enrich his library, partly because of the feeling that his unique collection of trephined crania is safer in this country," McGee explained to the US surgeon general, Muñiz proposed to exchange the collection for a series of its plaster casts, for books in anthropology and ethnology, and for assurance that the original crania would be labeled so "as to indicate his instrumentality in collecting." McGee sent Muñiz as complete a set of BAE reports and bulletins as he could muster and sought scientific publications from the chief of engineers, the commissioner of education, and the Smithsonian, lest this collection "of the highest scientific value" instead go to a Russian collector rumored to be offering Muñiz two thousand dollars (fifty-three thousand dollars today).[68] Washington would get Muñiz's treasures, while Lima's first dedicated anthropological collection and library would be rebuilt in a North American image.

Even that was not to be. If Muñiz ever received the books or casts of the nineteen Andeans who built his international career, he had only months to enjoy them. In 1897, while founding a new mental asylum in Lima, Muñiz died suddenly at age thirty-six. He never got to read McGee's final thoughts on his collection. He would have been shocked had he done so.[69] His fellow Peruvian surgeons believed Muñiz's legacy was one of "Ciencia y Patria," but his American counterpart thought that Muñiz's love of country had corrupted his science.[70] McGee had decided that what Peru's trepanners actually represented was butchery and barbarity.

Muñiz and McGee's "Primitive Trephining in Peru" was a Frankenstein's monster of a publication. The lead study in the BAE's long-delayed *Sixteenth Annual Report* (1897), its sixty pages promised the most extensive treatment of trepanation in the New World yet. After an introduction by John Wesley Powell, noting that Muñiz's skulls were the property of the US government, came Muñiz's celebration of Peruvian surgery to the Congress of Anthropology in 1893.[71] But the main text revealed the awkward seams between Muñiz's vision and that of McGee, who now disagreed with his former collaborator.

Rather than make much of the nineteen skulls' shape and size, McGee trained his attention on the ancient Peruvians' skill as surgeons. Their success rate was impressive, he acknowledged—thirteen survivals out of twenty-four operations on the nineteen skulls, "a percentage value quite as high as that of modern practice"—but he buried that fact in the essay's conclusion. Instead, McGee claimed the skulls told a story of violence, from the "desperate wounds" of weapons and warfare to the efforts of the trepanners. He argued the surgeons had botched the procedures of those patients who died under the knife. He dwelled on an operation that ended with twenty abandoned incisions. His estimation of Cranium 14, an almost entirely mummified head from Huarochirí, was scathing. He thought that a slingstone or a club had fractured the left frontal bone. McGee claimed the wound went untreated for several hours, after which a "clumsy operator" opened the scalp and commenced scraping, the instrument supposedly slipping from the surgeon's hands until the patient died "on the table."[72]

McGee's conclusions reflected as badly upon Muñiz's interpretations as they did on the work of the original surgeons. There were "many indications that the operators were (1) inexpert in manipulation, (2) ignorant of physiology, (3) skilless [*sic*] in diagnosis and treatment, and (4) regardless of the gravity of the operations performed." Muñiz had seriated the skulls to show a refinement of technique; McGee thought them organized "from the more clumsy to the less." Under ethnology's tool-based hierarchies, McGee also saw no evidence of anything more sophisticated than stone implements "found among nearly all primitive peoples, including the ancient Peruvians." He speculated that these implements—perhaps even spearpoints—had torn the intracranial tissues, a "highly indefensible procedure apparently growing out of ignorance concerning the delicacy of brain and meninges."[73]

McGee's last testament to Muñiz's exploration of ancient Peruvian medical skill was a tombstone: "Thoughtless hacking, with no indication of diagnosis or intelligent adaptation of means to ends . . . Utter incompetence . . . Peruvian trephining, as exemplified in the Muñiz collection, can only be regarded as crude in plan and bungling in procedure; and study of the procedure only occasions surprise that the results were not worse."[74] McGee questioned whether there was any indication that Peruvian trepanation was therapeutic. He proposed that they claimed to practice "thaumaturgy" or magic, relieving mental disorders by extracting an "evil 'mystery,'" requiring no "physiologic knowledge and etiologic skill."[75]

This was a stunning subjugation of Peruvian science to American anthropology's "Monroe Doctrine," as practiced by the BAE. Four years after Muñiz and Dorsey put "ancient Peruvians" at the heart of anthropology's conversation, McGee dismissed them as "uncivilized." Neither crania, nor instruments, nor operations showed anything "to indicate noteworthy intellectual development," McGee concluded. Instead, these skulls revealed a "remarkable record of accident indicat[ing] that the individuals lived eventful albeit short lives, and were inured to blood and pain and accustomed to facing danger." Their "ill-planned, clumsy, and extravagant" operations were a primitive stage in trepanation's historic development, untouched by "refined methods of civilization." If Peru was America's pre-US heights, as McGee himself once claimed, the ceiling was savagely low.[76]

McGee's Peruvian epitaph for Americas' Native peoples was wrong, as his own facts regarding success rates revealed. But the American ethnologist made his literal mark: McGee inked each cranium with its point of origin, only occasionally reproducing the location on Muñiz's labels. McGee fulfilled Muñiz's request that his "instrumentality" be recognized, adding the Peruvian surgeon's name below the BAE numbers each cranium received. But McGee then added his own name, indexing each skull to its corresponding photographic plate in the report. The mummified head from Huarochirí, supposedly killed by a "clumsy operator," challenged him. It was all mummified skin, no bone. The American ethnologist, who with Franz Boas soon took up their field's flagship journal, *American Anthropologist*, instead improvised. He found a dry spot of flesh above the neck and wrote "McGee."[77]

The re-collection of Andean bodies by nineteenth-century Americanist anthropology helped turn a field materially invested in the collection of racialized
specimens to one also interested in culture, ritual, and the historicity of the
Indigenous past. While the cost of those re-collections was borne by the Andean
ancestors and local peoples who remembered them, Peruvian scholars and
grave-openers profited, their reputations mostly rising as the century went on.
McGee's study of Muñiz's trepanned skulls, however, threatened another shift.
The global history of trepanation began with contemporary Peruvians' appropriation and display of pre-Hispanic surgery's embodied past. Squier's transfer
of the Yucay skull to the United States and Europe extended these studies, and
their recycling back to Peru encouraged younger surgeons and scholars to advocate for Peruvians' ancient and modern importance to global knowledge. Muñiz
did so, leading a celebration of Peruvian science, ancient and modern, before
the collection that was his legacy—the largest gathering of Andean ancestors
in the Americas—caught fire. His North American colleague McGee then
reduced Muñiz and his trepanning Andeans to nothing more than a primitive
link in a chain of collection and experimentation that only became "science" in
Washington, DC. A bolder dispossession of meaning and ownership is hard to
imagine.

But it turned out that American anthropology was also subject to revision.
Five years after McGee and Muñiz's publication, a young man from Huarochirí
named Julio César Tello was working in Peru's National Library when he came
upon the *Report*. Tello was studying to become a surgeon at the University of San
Marcos, defying those who dismissed him as "Indio."[78] While flipping through
the *Report*'s pages, he saw something that promised him a still older identity. The
book's first plate depicted a skull labeled "Chuicoto, Pueblo Huarochirí, Lima."
Tello realized, with a jolt of recognition, that he had once held this skull in his
own hands. His late father, Julián, was the gobernador who had first found and
displayed the "Chuicoto" skull in his small store before sending it on to Muñiz.[79]
In that moment, Tello saw how his family had contributed to the hemispheric
science of Andean healing—but also how the contribution of these ancestral
surgeons, and his own family, had been effaced by both Muñiz and McGee.
From the dark folds of that doubly absent scientific ancestry flared a radical idea.
Tello decided to change his life, becoming an anthropologist of another kind.

8

Decapitating Incas

Julio César Tello and Peruvian Anthropology's Healing

On an August day around 1890, a young Julio César Tello watched in horror as Francisco Pizarro removed the Inca emperor's head. Recalling the scene decades later as an anthropologist with a museum full of heads of his own, Tello knew it had been for show. His hometown of Huarochirí, in the province by the same name in the mountains east of Lima, was three and a half centuries and 350 miles from Cajamarca, where Atahuallpa was garroted—not decapitated—and recovered by his partisans to become an ancestor. *The Death of Atahuallpa* was a popular drama staged by Huarochirí's adults each year during the festival of Santa Rosa de Lima. One group of adults dressed as Pizarro and his men, and another as Atahuallpa and his people. Each side danced and twirled, finally facing each other for Atahuallpa's killing—the Incas' head lost to the colonizer, the sovereign disarticulated, a sharper passion play of Peru's foundation.[1]

In Tello's hand, this memory braided centuries of disarticulated Inca bodies and Andean identity into his career's common thread, explaining why he left for Lima soon after to study medicine, but was discriminated against as an "Indio"; why in 1909 he began studying anthropology at Harvard; and why he returned to found Peru's first three archaeology museums.[2] Tello was conscious of his place in history. The first half of his career, through 1927, saw a surge in Peru of both indigenismo, an honest and cynical concern for Indigenous peoples, as well as a recommitment to Inca and pre-Hispanic patrimony. In 1912, farmers and intellectuals had resisted President Augusto B. Leguía's facilitation of Yale University's excavation and export of Machu Picchu's tombs. When Leguía returned to the office in 1919, he cloaked his authoritarianism in the indigenismo, Inca symbology, and museum-building that, ironically, his own prior pro–North American tendencies had incited. Because Tello, sometimes dubbed the "Father of Peruvian Archaeology," benefitted from these turns, it is

Empires of the Dead. Christopher Heaney, Oxford University Press. © Oxford University Press 2023.
DOI: 10.1093/oso/9780197542552.003.0009

tempting to take his memory of Atahuallpa's head as he perhaps intended—as a primal national trauma that his science sought to heal.[3]

There is also a way of reading the memory in which Tello became the decapitator. His institution-building and creative interpretations relied upon Atahuallpas of his own—from a huge collection of crania he traded abroad to fund his studies, to a cohort of 429 fardos (bundled mummies) dug from the dry peninsula of Paracas. In doing so, Tello extended the grave-opening, export, and displays that shaped Peruvian museums and American anthropology since independence, fueling the Andean dead's last massive diaspora to the Smithsonian and Harvard. To some countrymen, Tello's trafficking in "beautiful grandparents" allied him with national and imperial outsiders upon whom the dead would have revenge.[4] Like other proclaimed renovators of national Indigenous identity, Tello's actions on behalf of the living can seem inadequate.[5]

Yet Tello believed that "this favorite science of unearthing cadavers interred centuries back," as he put it in 1925, was a liberating gesture.[6] Tello collected Andean bodies to celebrate them—an anthropology that threatened the hierarchies of US colleagues and anti-Indigenous Peruvian intellectuals. While working with North Americans, Tello secretly turned Peruvian bureaucracies

Fig. 8.1 Dr. Julio C. Tello (left) and Alfred L. Kroeber, 1926. Waldo Schmitt Papers, 1907–1977. Smithsonian Institution Archives.

against them, trying to hinder their ability to excavate and export collections. Most importantly, his first great intellectual project lay in convincing skeptical colleagues that trepanation was medical and not exclusive to Incas who, for Tello, were only the last pre-Hispanic wave of an older and nonimperial Peruvian culture, whose ancestral sciences included surgery and mummification. And the place for the avatars of these twin cornerstones of Peru's scientific excellence was a museum—a conviction that stoked the "racial prejudice" against him, historian Jorge Basadre believed.[7]

In that sense, Tello positioned himself as inheritor of Peru's most ancestral "sciences": the trepanation that defied anthropology's Eurocentric suprem-acism; the colonial and republican efforts to disinter, collect, and export the "ancient Peruvian" dead to the world; and the curing and curation of the dead, mummification, whose pausing of time promised a history free from the colonial past. Yet these knowledges retained an imperial edge. Tello honed it by taking other Peruvians' ancestors for his own.

Tello was born on April 11, 1880, in Huarochirí, the steep highland province whose trepanning Yauyo people believed themselves the children of Pariaqaqa, the 18,865-foot-tall snowcapped sacred mountain. Huarochirí was where the seventeenth-century extirpations of sacred ancestors began, and where its people afterward struggled but survived as small-scale farmers and herders. The region's community ayllus (descendant clan groups) maintained their pre-Hispanic canals and reservoirs. Through the early twentieth century they kept track of members' work using cord-record khipus. Huarochirí was where Antonio Raimondi observed villagers parading with ancestral mummies to ma-nipulate the rains, and where Tello's father, Julián Tello García, had collected the trepanned "Chuicoto" skull that traveled to Chicago and Washington, DC, with Peru's surgeon general Manuel A. Muñiz. Shortly before Tello's birth, the Peruvian state labeled Huarochirí 100 percent "indio."[8]

By the 1930s Tello had embraced that inheritance. His was an ancient family, he told North American journalist Blair Niles, and "according to a tradition" they were descended from Pariaqaqa himself. His father was from Huarochirí's lower ayllu of leaders, the "ancient lords of Lurín Yauyo, named Nina Willka." His mother, María Asunción Rojas Erikes (Erqes), was illiterate but belonged to a proud family of herders and weavers from the upper ayllu of "Anan Yauyo named Yaksha Willka," descendants of Huarochirí's last lords under the Inca Empire. Tello told Niles of dancing in harvest festivals as a child, his whole town "dressed and adorned in Inca fashion."[9] His maternal grandmother, he told another American, was "an Indian, who still maintained with great veneration all of the idolatrous practices of the ancient ones."[10]

In Tello's childhood, his identity may have felt more complicated. Colonialism and republican transformation had strained communal solidarities and Andean identities in Huarochirí.[11] The fortunes of Tello's family, for example, may have faltered in the early republic, when liberal laws chipped away at communal landholding rights—but by maintaining access to what communal property remained, while combining family resources like Maria's llama pens at the heights of Llampilla, they amassed capital to purchase new, individual parcels of land. In the late nineteenth century, anthropologist Frank Salomon observes, Huarochirí's inhabitants started to "regard themselves as progressive *campesinos* (peasants) of Peruvian nationality, not as members of an indigenous 'race.'"[12] Julio's father defended Huarochirí from Chile during the War of the Pacific, and then translated that military service into a position as the central government's gobernador of Huarochirí proper, a relatively large town of fifteen hundred. He founded a school after 1890, when Peru's Constitution was amended to make Spanish literacy a requirement for the right to vote. The school was an object of patronage, and Julián's store in Huarochirí, where he bought and sold coca, was a node of economic and political power.[13]

It was in the family's "little coca store," Julio later remembered, that his father displayed the trepanned Chuicoto skull, before it went to Surgeon General Manuel A. Muñiz. The labels Muñiz pasted to his skulls revealed that eleven originated in Huarochirí: in Kilkamachai, Santa Eulalia; Paramina, Matucana; and Chuicoto, the ancient settlement from which the Spanish resettlement of Huarochirí was made. These labels hid that it had been the Tellos and people like them who first gathered these "beautiful grandparents" or "gentiles." Places like Julián's store, where Julio first held the Chuicoto skull, might be considered small museums of local and republican belonging, displaying "gentile" antecessors, as well as the Tellos' power in handling them without falling ill.[14]

Like the Chuicoto skull, the Tellos sent their son Julio to Lima, to make further inroads with the coastal elites who governed what historians sometimes call the Aristocratic Republic. During this period of relative peace, Peru's government was all but dominated by the Civilista party, whose projects included the solution of the so-called Indian problem through education and white immigration. Julio understood his arrival through that lens. He and his father traveled to Lima by mule two days after his thirteenth birthday. Once there, Julio was enrolled in the prestigious Colegio Labarthe, paid for with his mother's gold and silver "antiquities." He likely also benefitted from his family's political connections. Julio, the only one of twelve siblings to receive a Lima education, had been encouraged by his paternal aunt María. María was a servant in the Lima home of Manuel Pardo y Lavalle, Peru's first civilian president. Tello later called María an "eugenicist [who] wanted all *serranos* to marry 'superior people.'"[15]

In Lima, Julio saw how others read his cleverness and education as contradicting his skin color and highland origins. In one of Lima's poorest, most historic neighborhoods, Cinco Esquinas, he rented a room from *morenos*, "brown-skins." Shortly after Julio started school, his father died, putting Julio at the mercy of the city. He sold newspapers to survive, ran errands, and competed with other children at railway stations to carry travelers' bags. "I wandered the streets of Lima, in those days where there was no compassion for *indios*." But he thrived in his classes and found a patron in a classmate's father, Ricardo Palma, the director of the National Library, who recognized Tello's intelligence and gave him a job in the library that would support him when he went on to study surgery at the University of San Marcos's medical school.[16]

It was in that library that Julio saw his father's photographed Chuicoto skull, staring out at him from the Bureau of American Ethnology volume containing Muñiz and McGee's "Primitive Trephining in Peru." Given how Tello periodically returned to this moment, it is hard to overstate its importance.[17] It was as if he had discovered a lost family album with empty pages left for his future. The skull linked his own medical studies to "ancient" predecessors who were also "Indian" surgeons from Huarochirí. But it also revealed that he was part of a chain of Americanist anthropological knowledge anchored in Peru, by which Peruvian scholars and collectors—his father included—had entangled foreign researchers in local sciences, but had been hidden in turn. If he pulled on those ties, would they pull back?

———

It was the question of the moment. Despite growing economic links to the United States, science in Peru's Aristocratic Republic remained oriented toward European positivism, under which most Peruvian elites assumed there was nothing to learn from Andean peoples.[18] Muñiz's trepanation research tweaked those assumptions slightly—trepanation was a past knowledge, interpreted by European-trained elites like himself. But there was also a perception that foreign scientific interest in Peru was destroying historic resources. In 1905 the president of the Historical Institute of Peru complained of foreign museums' possession of so many Peruvian collections, including that of Muñiz. "We are tired of seeing any old traveler take a gang of peons and throw themselves into digging up mummies and objects, without anyone's permission, as if they were in their own house, leaving nothing but a memory of their passage," he thundered. The institute called on the government to regulate excavation, prohibit exports, and establish a Museum of National History.[19]

That museum opened in the Palace of the Exposition with a foreigner at the helm: Max Uhle, who had excavated at the necropolis of Ancón and the sun temple of Pachacamac for the University of Pennsylvania and Peru's northern coast for the University of California. This hire was a coup for the new institution. Uhle's use of vertical stratigraphy on Peru's huacas and cemeteries was archaeology's cutting edge. By showing how pottery styles shifted and how complex architecture existed layered beneath "Inca" layers, Uhle provided a chronology that disproved the idea that societies climbed through evolutionary stages. Uhle also demonstrated a deep layering of discrete cultures and styles unbound by racialized "Quechua" or "Aymara" cross-temporal identities.[20] The "well-ordered cases" of Uhle's museum made the colonial and republican epochs just later historical layers, preceded by "row upon row of those strange seated mummies, whose knees touch their chins and whose faces are covered with masks of gold, silver, or vicuña cloth."[21]

Uhle was nevertheless an odd spokesman for an institution meant to make Peruvian archaeology a more national venture. In November 1905 he told his US

IN THE MUSEUM, EXPOSITION BUILDING

Fig. 8.2 Mummy Bundles as mounted by Max Uhle "In the Museum, Exposition Building," Lima, ca. 1911. Annie Peck, *The South American Tour* (New York: George H. Doran and Company: 1913), 78.

colleague Frederic Ward Putnam that a collection of ceramics Uhle sent to San
Francisco would be "the last collection of antiquities that will leave Peru legally."
From then on, "No more can be shipped from Peru, nor will any foreigners be
allowed to excavate here. Or, if they do so all the objects secured by them must
go to the National Museum of this country."[22] Uhle himself drafted a law to make
state property of "all pre-Hispanic huacas, monuments, and cemeteries, as well
as their contents, found on public, church, and private lands," absolutely banning
their export.[23]

Uhle's proposal languished, but its spirit—that Peru's Andean past belonged
to Peru's scientific present—burned within Tello. A friend translated "Primitive
Trephining in Peru" for Tello. Upon learning that McGee denied Muñiz's
contributions, claiming that the trepanned skulls showed a lack of Peruvian
medical and scientific expertise, Tello sought to prove the American wrong.[24]
He spent vacations at home and in surrounding regions—Lurín, Chillón,
Yauyos—collecting stories and plants that suggested Huarochirí's importance
to ancient and modern Andean medical and botanical knowledge. His first publication used linguistics, ethnobotany, and eighteenth-century Spanish natural
history to argue for Huarochirí's connection to the kallawayas, the famed traveling healers of Bolivia.[25]

He also began to collect ancestors. In 1903 Tello took charge of Antonio
Raimondi's museum at San Marcos's medical school, but its mummies in
glass cabinets and cranial collection were not nearly as numerous as those that
Muñiz lost to fire in 1895.[26] So Tello returned to his homeland to gather the
dead with the help of his family and "local peons." A classmate who worked with
them recalled that the eldest would gather the group in a circle to pray to the
"ancestors" to reveal their remains. These prayers (which may have also fended
off grave-opening's malign consequences) were efficacious: they rode back to
Lima with six to eight mules at a time, laden with the dead.[27] Tello saw himself
as becoming both ancient and new. "The first time I had in my hands the skull of
an Inca mummy to study, I felt a profound emotion," Tello told a student. "That
skull, honored by the centuries, connected with my heart and made me feel the
message of the race whose blood ran through my veins. From that moment I became an anthropologist."[28]

Tello later claimed that he built a collection of ten thousand to fifteen thousand crania and mummies. Surpassing Muñiz's nineteen, Tello identified four
hundred skulls as indicating trepanation.[29] On May 4, 1906, he lectured at Lima's
Geographic Society on the surgical skills of the Yauyos. Uhle attended, along
with doctor and linguist Pablo Patrón, the National Library's archivist Carlos
Romero, the library's director Ricardo Palma, and Tello's professors and fellow
students, male and female. Behind a table covered with thirty trepanned skulls
and mummies, Tello described Huarochirí as a wonderland of curing knowledge.

He distinguished successful surgical styles from those that only accelerated death. He may have even described his own attempt to reproduce the operation with a skull and *tumi*, a pre-Hispanic bronze knife. Contrary to McGee, he declared the operation flatly medical: "With trepanation, Peru achieves first place in prehistoric surgery throughout the world."[30]

Tello extended his studies to other areas of pre-Hispanic medical knowledge. In his thesis he argued that ancient Peruvians had known, diagnosed, and depicted syphilis in their ceramics, and that trepanation had partly developed to heal it. It was a controversial claim, but his advisers secured its publication and a government scholarship to enable him to continue his studies abroad. Other promising young students used similar grants to study in Europe; Tello differed in choosing to go to the United States—specifically, the anthropology program at Harvard, which offered him free tuition.[31]

The departure was bittersweet. Tello's ambitions marked him in his countrymen's eyes. Tello remained close to his relatives for the rest of his life, but his beliefs had changed. On one visit home, he failed to convince his "Indian" grandmother that a child's deformity was not a spiritual punishment for a father's thieving ways, but spinal bifida.[32] His collecting underlined his difference. In Yauyos, a town's gobernador who was suspicious of prying questions jailed Tello and two helpers. It may have been worse in Huarochirí, where Tello collected the dead. Oral traditions gathered by anthropologist Frank Salomon emphasize Tello's "aggressive emptying of burial caves . . . shocking to local sensibilities."[33]

In Lima, Tello was also subjected to old prejudices. A story circulated that his neighbors reported him to the police as a *brujo*, a witch or shaman who brought home the skulls of victims, talked to them, cut them to pieces, and then burned them to forge pacts with the devil. The gossip denounced his Harvard plans as the pretensions of a "cholo," a person of specious Andean origins. "Have you all noticed what is happening to the cholo Tello? They say that he is now a doctor and plans to travel abroad! Don't you remember that he was one of so many *serranitos* who lived poorly and people said he was a 'witch' because at night he chatted with 'skulls' and 'bones of pagans'? Don't you all remember that the police took his skulls to see if he was 'crazy' or 'possessed' like the newspapers said in Lima?"[34] A person of Andean heritage who studied the dead, like Tello, had to struggle to be respected as a scientist.

The racism Tello experienced gave him a painful double consciousness regarding his desired identity. At a banquet shortly before his departure, he suffered in silence as his mentor, Palma, toasted him as one of his generation's three leading lights. The wealthy young whites in attendance suspiciously eyed the "*cholito*," the little cholo. Tello was mortified. "That day I went back to my room and I wept," he later recounted. "I wept like I hadn't wept since the morning that my mother gave me the faja and bag she had stitched, and two handfuls of roasted corn" the morning he left home for Lima.[35] In 1942 his memory was even more precise: "I wanted to bury myself like a mummy."[36]

⸺⸺

Instead, Tello went to Harvard—likely the university's first Peruvian student. And from Harvard he had an unheralded effect on American anthropology's entanglement with Peruvian archaeology. He at first struggled to be seen as more than an Indigenous informant, collector, or go-between, but he achieved credibility on the ancestral sciences of the Yauyos. He ultimately did so by manipulating the ebbs and flows of the empires of the dead shaping his career. The skulls he brought with him inspired a final wave of North American collecting that benefited his own work.

Tello later looked back fondly at his time at Harvard. His professors invited him home to practice his English.[37] Gatherings with other Spanish-speaking students in Cambridge led him to refer to himself as "latino." After a conversation with Franz Boas, who was planning an International School of Americanist Archaeology in Mexico City, he marveled at the "incredible" importance that North Americans saw in Peru and Mexico.[38]

Tello's struggle to be recognized as a scientist honed his sensitivity to a field that still treated Native peoples as primitive informants.[39] Since 1907 he had corresponded with Albert S. Ashmead, a physician from Philadelphia interested in ancient New World surgery and disease. In July 1909, before Tello even arrived at Harvard, Ashmead began summarizing Tello's thesis in his own publications. Ashmead's reasons were unflattering: Tello's diagnosis of syphilis on pre-Hispanic ceramics contradicted their diagnosis by Ashmead as a disease named "uta." Ashmead ridiculed Tello's argument that Huayna Capac died of pre-Hispanic syphilis as well as his claim that every syphilitic cranium he recovered in the countryside was pre-Hispanic. Swiss-American archaeologist Adolph Bandelier had only just reminded North American scholars that nonchurch Andean burials lasted well past the sixteenth century.[40]

This fact had tremendous import for the thousands of skulls exported from Peruvian tombs to North American collections: because they were no longer automatically "pre-Columbian," they could not be presumed to be "untainted" by Old World intermarriage or disease. But Ashmead and other North American colleagues used that fact to denigrate Tello, whose self-defense revealed his awareness of the racism that chased him. "The labor to which I dedicated myself out of affection and care for my *raza* [race] was without any pretension," he wrote to Ashmead.[41] "As you will understand, when one works in an environment like that in which I've worked, and in which one doesn't have the sufficient preparation, one doesn't attempt to climb so high, without being a target of ridicule."[42] Ashmead was unmoved. He published Tello's correspondence—and photographs Tello had loaned without giving permission to print—in further articles criticizing his theories.[43]

Ashmead's public attacks nonetheless advertised Tello's success as an anthropological collector, especially in the realm of trepanation. By late 1909 Tello's massive collection of skulls was a matter of American knowledge. Tello and an associate "have drawn out with their own hands from graves near Huarachiri (very ancient burial place) [*sic*] trepanned mummies still with the bandages put on them at the time of the surgical intervention," Ashmead explained.[44]

Early the following year, a physical anthropologist named Aleš Hrdlička acted on Tello's success. Hrdlička is a controversial figure in the history of his field. When he was thirteen he had moved with his family from Bohemia to the United States, where he trained as a doctor before studying anthropometry in Paris. In 1903 he became the Smithsonian's first physical anthropologist—one who believed in finding simple averages in large collections of different "races," rather than employing statistics. His bigotry toward people of color, his sexism, his rapacious collecting on the Smithsonian's behalf, and his gatekeeping regarding what he believed was Native Americans' shallow antiquity are well documented.[45] Less obvious has been why Hrdlička did so much collecting in Peru. The perceived accessibility of its human remains is one answer—a useful quality for an opportunistic scholar building bone-rich collections and displays.[46] Another is the fact that, since Morton, the US Army Medical Museum and the Bureau of American Ethnology had built large collections of Andean mummies and skulls, almost all of which joined the Smithsonian following Hrdlička's appointment in 1903. In turning to Peru, Hrdlička was extending American anthropology's foundational reliance upon centuries of Peruvian grave-opening, mortuary knowledge, and circulating bodies.

Yet the most pressing reason Peru interested Hrdlička was Tello's massive collection of skulls, many trepanned, which by mid-1910 he wanted to acquire.[47] He hoped to do so as part of a larger tour of South America intended to debunk Argentine anthropologists' claims to have uncovered the world's oldest human remains. Disgusted by the "miscegenation" and "mixbreed[s]" he saw on the way to Peru, Hrdlička arrived in Lima, possibly unaware that Tello had already left for the United States.[48] Hrdlička instead turned to Max Uhle, the German head of Peru's National Museum, for help collecting.

Despite earlier promises to halt foreign excavation and exportation in Peru, Uhle obliged. Uhle was disillusioned. His proposed law had not been adopted, and he had alienated allies by blaming the country's looting on Peru's "ignoramuses of the *pueblo*, the vultures of national antiquities." In 1909 the government declined to send Uhle and Tello to investigate the Inca site of Choquequirau, then believed to be the site of Manco Inca's resistance to Spanish rule. A similar proposal by the National Library's archivist, Carlos Romero, that Uhle be sent to search for Manco's actual "last cities" also went unheeded. So, feeling "condemned to eternal inactivity" in Lima, Uhle helped Hrdlička collect twenty-two hundred skulls and bones disinterred by prior excavators at Pachacamac, the massive huaca complex to Lima's south. At the museum, Uhle helped pack the skulls into thirty hogshead barrels bound for the Smithsonian.[49]

Hrdlička believed they were "salvaging" the remains of Peruvian looting and that the exportation of human remains was not illegal. What ensued, however, revealed that there were Peruvians who increasingly viewed such collections as belonging in Peru. The barrels of skulls "aroused a lot of talk, which reached the police and from there other authorities," Hrdlička complained. The health officer at the port of Callao tried to stop the barrels' departure, charging that "the moving and exporting of such remains was against the law, which stipulated that no bodies or skeletons could be moved without a due permission of the health authorities, and that the permission could only be given on the basis of due information as to the person to whom the bones had belonged and the cause of his death; and that therefore a permission for the exportation of the material to America [could not] be granted until it [was] stated what the separate people to whom the bones in question belonged had died of!"[50] In other words, that they were a matter for Peruvian forensics, not North American anthropology.

This attempt to thwart Hrdlička using Lima's health bureaucracies failed. Indignant, Uhle told the health officer that the bones all belonged to "pre-Columbian Indians, and all had died of natural death; . . . moreover the whole thing was done with the authorization of his Government to which was referred." As the barrels traveled to Washington, Hrdlička expanded his collection at a hacienda in the Chicama Valley, whose owner, an important antiquarian named Victor Larco Herrera, welcomed Hrdlička to "his village" by leading him onto a narrow street his "peons" had "lined on both sides with skulls" left over from prior grave-openings—an almost hallucinatory example of how North American anthropology followed the paths blazed by Peruvian antiquarianism and racialized labor. Larco spent the next two weeks sending his "peons" to bring "basket after basket" of skulls and bones to his hospital, where Hrdlička packed up "specimens of prospective value to science." The "rest returned to the sands there to be reburied." Hrdlička's selections were loaded onto a freighter at Larco's private dock, uninterrupted by customs officials. Hrdlička then returned to Washington with thirty-four hundred crania and more than six thousand long and other bones, instantly doubling the Smithsonian's physical anthropology holdings. He believed the Pachacamac collection was "the most valuable reliably pre-Columbian study series in existence."[51]

The use of "pre-Columbian," rather than Peruvian, was an assertion of American anthropology's superiority in knowing the Indigenous dead. Despite meeting Peruvians like a wealthy gentleman who insisted that the black residue rattling about in skulls was balsam—and thus evidence of artificial mummification, not naturally mummified brain—Hrdlička saw no irony in telling his journal that "No one [in Peru] took the least interest" in the Peruvian dead, and "nothing had been taken for which anybody in the country had any use."[52] Hrdlička called upon the Anthropology Society of Washington to pass a resolution denouncing the "destruction of antiquities . . . and the associated skeletal parts of man himself" in Peru, whose remains "are of great value to science."[53] In his journal he was flatly racist. "So things go on—[Peru], rich in natural resources, rich exceedingly for the explorer, is miserable with human ignorance and degeneration."[54]

Hrdlička may have also been annoyed that the collection he most wanted had escaped his grasp: Tello's skulls, which doubly belied Hrdlička's claims of Peruvian ignorance and degeneration. On his way to Lima, Hrdlička learned that Tello, then at the end of his first year at Harvard, had brought a thousand trepanned and diseased skulls from his collection to Cambridge. Tello said the export was temporary—he wanted to demonstrate his efforts as a scientist, and thereby encourage the Peruvian government to buy the collection for its National Museum—but Hrdlička, who had returned to the United States without a single trepanned skull of his own, felt thwarted. The "great collection of Trephined skulls from Lima has been secured by the Peabody Museum," he told the Smithsonian. "I wish it were ours!"[55]

By 1911, however, Tello's needs had changed. His grant from the Peruvian government was running out, and to support himself, he sought an American buyer who would credit him as the collection's original researcher. Hrdlička was thrilled to have a chance to consolidate Washington's status as the world's premier site for studying pre-Columbian medicine. But he negotiated by dismissing the collection's value. He objected that there was no proof that Tello's skulls were pre-Columbian; it could have been Spanish influence that produced the trepanations. "It is not enough that I tell him that I extracted them with my own hands," Tello complained.[56] Privately, Hrdlička enjoined Tello's professor at Harvard, Curtis Farabee, to "not permit this collection to leave the country" by buying it, "and if you cannot buy it, I shall do the best I can to raise the money."[57] In February 1911 Tello and Hrdlička made a gentleman's agreement. It was Tello's understanding that he would bring the skulls to the Smithsonian, where he would be employed and mentored by Hrdlička while the two of them studied the collection together.[58]

Tello then learned what Hrdlička actually intended. He read in a newspaper that Hrdlička was about to solve "numerous problems considered unsolvable until today" using trepanned skulls from Peru. Given that Hrdlička had found no such skulls in 1910, Tello realized that the Smithsonian anthropologist had given the newspaper the story presuming that he would be sole interpreter of Tello's collection. Tello was shocked by Hrdlička's "pretensions" and wrote to clarify the terms of his employment. He asked for guarantees that his collection would bear his name if it ended up at the Smithsonian and that whatever book they published would bear his name first. Hrdlička replied that all he wanted was to buy his skulls. Tello realized that he was just a laborer in Hrdlička's eyes, there to "complete the collection that he [Hrdlička] had brought *from* Peru," he wrote to a friend. "I told him I was not a *comerciante*," a trafficker, but a scholar at Harvard, and "my collection would only be studied by me."[59] On the condition that he would be first to publish on them, Tello sold his skulls to a wealthy Harvard alumnus, who gave them to the university's Warren Anatomical Museum, which would later pass on the vast majority—with Tello's name permanently attached—to the Peabody Museum.[60]

Hrdlička was furious. Likely embarrassed that he had publicized findings he could not deliver, he began a whisper campaign against Tello. Tello was dishonest and venal, Hrdlička told colleagues for three decades; his thesis was "thoroughly unreliable, and should best be consecrated to oblivion."[61] Tello believed Hrdlička's fury was behind his denunciation of looting in Peru.[62]

Tello and Hrdlička's conflict crystallized tensions over whether the Andean dead were specimens or possessions, as well as where American science resided. In 1910 Hrdlička believed their natural home was Washington, where he was building the world's largest collection for the study of embodied pre-Columbian history; that a supposedly peripheral Peruvian scholar had made and sold an even more valuable collection marked Tello as a trafficker in Hrdlička's eyes. Tello had indeed made the return of his collection to Lima and its sale to Peru's National Museum impossible. But he did so to ensure that the knowledge generated by his collection was associated with him and his emerging anthropological style—not pre-Columbian and American, but self-consciously Yauyo and Peruvian. Unlike his father, he would not be left out.

Tello chose wisely. With the money from the sale, he finished his master's degree at Harvard and continued his studies in Europe with anthropologists like Félix von Luschan. At the Eighteenth International Congress of Americanists in London in 1912, he delivered his revised paper, "Prehistoric Trephining among the Yauyos." With Hrdlička attending, Tello explicitly challenged the Washington consensus of Andean trepanation as savage and superstitious. Projecting slides of his collection, Tello argued that ancient Peruvian skull surgery was medical, civilized, and sophisticated. He explained the range of techniques, in which signs of healing in the bone suggested trepanation's surgical nature. He used his medical training to argue that the surgery addressed a range of trauma and

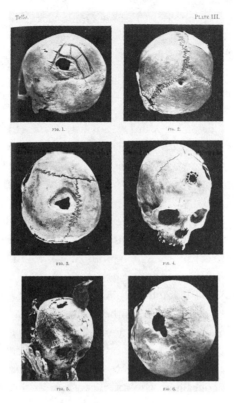

Fig. 8.3 Tello's array of the range of trepanation methods and their healing, from the Tello collection now at Harvard. Tello, "Prehistoric Trephining among the Yauyos of Peru" (1913), Plate III.

illnesses—including lesions of a syphilitic nature, a claim he was loath to give up. Of his 400 skulls, 250 showed that patients at least temporarily survived. The Yauyos thus carried out so risky an operation "due to an inherited empiricism, to the rational knowledge acquired by previous practice which had resulted in success": the patient's healing.[63]

Tello's performance of Andean science in the name of an anthropology that saw healing in skulls, not racial deficiency, was a turning point in trepanation's international study. His paper was published and widely distributed. Hrdlička himself registered in the congress's record that Tello demonstrated Peruvian medical capability in trepanation: that the young South American had made a "most careful study of his excellent collection," having not yet "received the credit for his work to which he was entitled."[64] It went unsaid that Hrdlička had wanted that credit for himself. Other scholars in the Americas and Europe pressed Tello for more details, as well as trepanned skulls of their own.[65] Most importantly, those skulls would be interpreted more in light of Tello's scholarship than that of McGee. At Yale, anthropologist George Grant MacCurdy credited Tello. "In sickness or in health, in peace or in war, the ancient Peruvians of the highlands were a cephalocentric race," MacCurdy quipped.[66]

The hundreds of skulls in MacCurdy's possession may have begged to differ. This collection was the result of Yale historian Hiram Bingham's expeditions to Machu and Huayna Picchu and their environs between 1911 and 1916. To excavate the royal Inca estate, Bingham combined local antiquarian and campesino labor and knowledge, US corporate funding and State Department influence, and the support of Peru's national government and gendarmes. In doing so, he made "Machu Picchu" famous—but also a lightning rod for local resistance to foreign excavators.[67] Yet this watershed moment was also a failed attempt at collaboration by Tello, who hoped to join his knowledge and training to Bingham's ambitions and funding. The tomb-opening that both men then undertook, with Hrdlička's continued work for the Smithsonian, was the apogee of the transnational collection of human remains in the Andes, spurring Peruvian intellectuals to again call for a total ban on the export of scientific collections. Publicly, Tello wasn't one of them, and his dance between North American anthropologists and elitist Peruvian colleagues who racialized him as the gringos' "Indian" in Peru provides a story more complicated than the Yale expedition's apparent drama of US cultural imperialism and local Peruvian resistance. Tello's relationship to Bingham and Hrdlička instead illustrates how cosmopolitan intellectuals could turn US imperial ambitions to their own ends, which included fighting local racism.

To begin with, Tello was indirectly responsible for Peruvian archaeology's most neo-imperial moment. In 1909 Augusto B. Leguía, Peru's gringophilic president, got Bingham to Choqquequirau, an Inca site that Uhle and Tello had been boxed out of excavating. Bingham doubted it was Manco Inca's final redoubt, as local antiquarians claimed. Tello confirmed those doubts. Late in 1910 Tello sent Bingham the Peruvian archivist Carlos Romero's proposal for the more likely locations of the Incas' "last cities." Inspired, Bingham planned what became the first Yale Peruvian Expedition. In early 1911, however, Tello asked Bingham via an intermediary, the head of anthropology at Yale's Peabody Museum, whether he might be the expedition's "archaeological representative." Keeping the glory for himself, Bingham declined the offer. In June 1911 he left for Peru, where Tello's lead—and extraordinary permissions from President Leguía—set him on the road to Machu Picchu, without Tello.[68]

This was a mistake. The backlash was immediate and again, Tello was partly responsible. For years, it had been rumored that Max Uhle had done more than help colleagues like Hrdlička "salvage" the human remains of looting—that he had actively collected for foreign institutions even while directing Peru's National Museum. In 1911 Tello was asked about those rumors. In a letter, Tello noted that Uhle's rival, Bandelier, believed them true. Tello's letter was shown around Lima just as Bingham was traveling to Machu Picchu. Two things happened in short succession. First, a new Society to Protect Monuments pushed Leguía's government to decree that all artifacts found via excavation belonged to the Peruvian state, that every excavation would be monitored, and that artifacts' export was "absolutely prohibited" until Peru's Congress passed a full law protecting antiquities. Second, Peru's government declined to renew Uhle's contract. Uhle left for Santiago, where he was hired by Chile's National Museum.[69]

In the medium term, Bingham tried to turn this attempted reform of Peruvian archaeology to his advantage. In 1912, with the encouragement of Leguía, the US State Department, and his North American funders, Bingham proposed a concession that would make Yale responsible for all Peruvian archaeology and give the university possession of half of all he excavated. Leguía agreed, and with his imprimatur Bingham used Peru's national gendarmes to force campesinos at Machu Picchu and surrounding areas into disinterring the estate's dead.

Those campesinos resisted this labor in ways large and small, from setting fires that almost killed Bingham's subordinates to not coming to work. The bigger threat came when Leguía unexpectedly lost that year's presidential election to Guillermo Billinghurst, a populist who saw the proposed concession as an embarrassment to Peruvian sovereignty. Intellectuals in Cuzco and the Peruvian press joined in, attacking the coastal oligarchy's apparent capture by US corporate and diplomatic interests. "It would be the final indignity if our government had to send Peruvians to North America to study what it now has in its own country. We're not sucking our thumbs anymore," one Peruvian wrote to Lima's *El Comercio*. "Do you understand, North America?" Humiliated, Bingham withdrew the deal, not telling Yale that the new government allowed ninety-three boxes containing the human remains and artifacts of some 173 individuals from Machu Picchu's tombs to leave Peru only on the condition that Yale send them back when asked. This was a watershed moment after nearly a century of the relatively free export of Andean ancestors and their belongings.[70]

In other words, Tello's attempt at one transnational anthropological collaboration, while sharing doubts regarding another, yielded both the most overtly neo-imperial moment in Peru's republican history of archaeology and its museums, as well as its repudiation. Alone, that repudiation could not stop the grave-opening and trade in antiquities that later let Bingham smuggle artifacts to Yale's permanent collection.[71] But it meant that in 1913 Tello—and Hrdlička—returned to a changed Peru. Tello hoped to run Peru's National Museum; Hrdlička was collecting for the Panama-California Exposition in San Diego in 1915, hoping to reproduce Tello's "great" trepanation collection at Harvard, which he had finally examined.[72] Resenting what "Bingham spoiled," Hrdlička promised Peru's Ministries of Education and Foreign Relations he would collect no antiquities. He thought this would keep him clear of the new decree's requirements.[73] He procured a letter from the director of health in Lima—whose department had given him such trouble in 1910—requesting that personnel in all of Lima's ports help him with his "prehistoric bones."[74] With a gendarme to ensure local compliance, Hrdlička went straight to Huarochirí, wanting to outdo Tello and "his native friends."[75] At Cinco Cerros (Five Peaks) he found a chullpa (a stone house of the dead) two feet deep with bones and skulls. The first he grabbed "was a trephined one, well worthy fifty dollars." Many more were inside, and he slept among them, shivering in the cold tomb. "Then, at last, I was where these Treasures, at least, were not despoiled!"[76]

Hrdlička thought the tomb had already been tossed by prior "treasure hunters"—a self-serving claim, given that chullpas were secondary interments where semi-disarticulated Andean ancestors were revisited and manipulated by descendants. When he came down, Hrdlička got a rude awakening as to how

Fig. 8.4 One of the chaukallas or chullpas at Cinco Cerros, Huarochirí, where the region's people once interred their ancestral dead. The Smithsonian physical anthropologist Aleš Hrdlička began the process of emptying these specific structures of their skulls in 1913. Photograph by author.

his own tomb-raiding looked amid Peru's new legal norms. To fulfill the new decree's terms, Tello had asked to be assigned as Hrdlička's monitor. It fell to Tello—"an intelligent young man, looking more than half Indian," Hrdlička grumbled—to ensure he "take nothing but duplicates," only skulls similar to what Peru's museums already possessed.[77]

Hrdlička tried to make the best of it, benefitting from the Tello family's local knowledges. At Lupo, Hrdlička saw how "natives provided themselves with ample quantities of coca and cigarettes, supposed to antagonize the injurious effects resulting from the showing and especially handling the old human remains," before making a "perilous descent" to empty nine "burial houses" of their mummies and skulls.[78] The honeymoon ended when Hrdlička realized that Tello was collecting for himself as well.[79] In early March, at a graveyard exposed and looted by railroad-builders in Huacho, north of Lima, Hrdlička started "at one end of a burial site and [Tello] would go to the other and [each would] work as hard as he could for their own collection." Heads to the sand, backs to the sky, the American and the Peruvian beetled toward each other, a century of mutual American-Peruvian parasitism in the matter of the Andean dead becoming an outright race.[80]

Tello's vigilance got him his promotion. After Huacho, Peru's Ministry of Education acknowledged "the awkwardness of the arrangement" to Hrdlička—but hired Tello for the National Museum, making him its first designated curator of anthropology and archaeology. Tello immediately threw his weight around. On his way out of the country, Hrdlička saw two of his collections temporarily halted by medical and customs officials, in Callao and Lomas. Hrdlička suspected that Tello was involved—and indeed he was. Tello told Peru's consul in America that he had tried to keep Hrdlička's bones from traveling to the United States, believing them important Peruvian scientific resources.[81]

Hrdlička nonetheless got what he wanted, taking credit for their shared work, whose "ancient Peruvian" yield positioned the Smithsonian as the world's leading collection in "American" specimens.[82] Moreover, of the forty-eight hundred crania he exported to the United States, sixty were trepanned skulls, "something that could not be bought for five thousand dollars," Hrdlička wrote the Smithsonian.[83] These trepanned skulls and "natural mummies from Peru" became the culmination of the San Diego exposition's anthropological display, *The Story of Man through the Ages*. If not exactly the "first [fair] to truly place human remains . . . at center stage," it was certainly the most ambitious since Dorsey did so with Ancón's dead in Chicago. The exhibit's last room was "a systematically organized mass grave," explains historian Samuel J. Redman—one overwhelmingly Peruvian in nature.[84] Hrdlička used the Peruvians to cast the Americas' pre-Columbian history as only two thousand years old, embodied by violence, disease, but also healing. Yet in his publication on the collection, he thanked Tello's family but not the anthropologist himself. From these skulls and mummies, a major portion of which became San Diego's Museum of Man, Hrdlička claimed to have "learned conclusively [that trepanations] were performed for purely surgical reasons." The US navy's surgeon general clarified the message: "Science" had "evolved" among these "early *American* surgeons," however "savage."[85]

Ironically, the full scholarly purpose of Hrdlička's massive collection of Andean remains was never fulfilled, as he never completed their description and publication.[86] He was more successful in his private vendetta against Tello. He publicly told Washington's anthropologists that Peru's protections were shameful, but privately boasted of smuggling out two ancient feather "ponchos" bought from an Afro-Peruvian looter in Nazca.[87] Peru had "two or three first-class archaeological collections, which could be bought and I think, on the quiet, exported," Hrdlička told Edgar Lee Hewett, who had made the US Antiquities Act a reality. Hrdlička convinced those who read his words that Tello was "corrupt," rather than his watchdog.[88] "Tello . . . is very pleasant always in conversation with you and can even be helpful," Hrdlička wrote to Bingham, "but you can not be too careful that this help should not go beyond a certain point, for underneath all, he is a 'Peruvian for the Peruvians,' regardless of everything else. . . . Do everything in your power to prevent them from imposing upon you a 'companion,' and if you already must have one, let it be someone else than T."[89]

To this Peruvian for the Peruvians, though, Hrdlička was all smiles, aware of the power Tello wielded at the National Museum. Hrdlička applauded him on that appointment and got him invited to the Second Pan-American Scientific Congress in Washington in 1915. But the edge remained. Hrdlička's letters made offers that he thought Tello too hypocritical or hungry to refuse. He told Tello he would buy whatever any future skeletal materials "which you would be willing to dispose of and which you could get safely on board of one of the ships for U.S." Tello wrote back, complaining that Hrdlička's public observation that Tello had sold his collection to Harvard in 1911 had caused him trouble in Peru. "The matter was surely no secret," Hrdlička replied, "and the mention is very simple— merely giving due credit where it belongs." Nevertheless, foreign colleagues were valuable, and when Tello needed cash, in November 1915, he wrote to Hrdlička for advice. Hrdlička recommended that Tello offer skulls he collected "to some scientific institution" abroad. Just how cheaply could he sell them?[90]

Tello needed cash because he had quit his position at the National Museum. He spent the following decade between institutions he joined or founded, shaped, and left—rarely by choice. The partial cause of these departures was that Tello's whiter colleagues claimed he was an "Indian," "difficult" to work with, and ironically, a pawn of North American anthropologists like Hrdlička. But these conflicts also owed to his commitment to what amounted to an anti-racist anthropology that cast the pre-Hispanic dead as revealing a Peruvian history larger than Incas, Spaniards, and "Indians." These commitments affected his politics. But they were most movingly expressed in the museums he dedicated to celebrating Indigenous Andean cultures of science, healing, and time. That he did so by displaying the human remains of his claimed ancestors is only a paradox if we see Tello's anthropology as separate from the millennial empire of Andean mortuary creativity that earlier museums tried to contain.

Tello began by trying to use elite Peruvians' interest in foreign science against their own internal racism. In March 1913 he published a manifesto in Lima's *La Prensa* insisting that at Harvard he learned that *all* races had the potential for greatness—a statement as forceful in Peru as it was in the United States. A more detailed report for the director general of education argued for Americanist anthropology's specific potential in Peru. Citing English biostatistician and eugenicist Karl Pearson, Tello declared it was time to use science to shape Peru's modern citizens via a national anthropology museum that would convince the ignorant of Indigenous Andean culture's precedence and value.[91]

These positions put Tello in conflict with Emilio Gutiérrez de Quintanilla, an art critic whose political connections gained him the directorship of the National Museum. To Tello's horror, Gutiérrez had muddled Uhle's finely sliced cultures and chronologies back into the broadest of generalizations: "Mountain" Indians, "Savage Tribes," "Archaeological Objects." Tello proposed their deliverance in a new research-oriented national museum of anthropology informed by the plans of Harvard's George Brown Goode and the Smithsonian's William H. Holmes. There, active investigations in archaeology, linguistics, culture, and somatology—physical anthropology's study of the body—would yield publications and displays. To inculcate national pride, Peru's populace would be schooled in Indigenous communal organizations, the dangers of racial prejudice, and—unironically—the negative influences of immigrant races.[92]

Tello's very presence as the National Museum's curator of anthropology and archaeology galled Gutiérrez, who denigrated Tello as "*el indio.*" Gutiérrez believed that the remains "contained in our sepulchral archives" could not go to a rural scholar with foreign anthropological ties.[93] Playing the Inca card, he claimed publicly that Tello was setting himself up as the museum's "Manco Capac," threatening "to belittle and close off the history of colonial and independent Peru" by crushing it with the "somatological and folkloric weight of a ridiculous imperialism exercised by mummies."[94]

Gutiérrez's choice of words was striking. Historians have focused on how imperial museums and anthropological actors claimed other peoples' beloved ancestors as ahistorical specimens of racial doom—Samuel Morton's transformation of "ancient Peruvians" into harbingers of Indigenous American extinction being one clear example. Gutiérrez's fears show how a museum project built around Indigenous remains, when curated by a scientist read as "Indian," was also a radical provocation. Gutiérrez framed it as a problem of hygiene and history; he charged that a group of mummies that Tello had collected, from Rinconada de Ate, were rotting, their odor filling an entire room of the museum. The "young archaeologist," Gutiérrez sneered, said that the smell was imaginary given that mummies were "aseptic after so many centuries." But Gutiérrez believed that the "nose trumps science," charging that Tello's tables of mummies turned the museum into a public clinic for the wounded, a cemetery, the Last Judgment. For Gutiérrez, this "caricature" of a museum, imitative of those Tello had trained in abroad—was an "imperialism" exercised by an Americanist anthropology that cared more for dead Andeans than for Spanish colonists and patriot heirs. "We, the fatherland whose grandness we are obliged to promote, come first," Gutiérrez protested; "afterwards come the mummies and their mummifiers."[95]

But the American anthropology culture in which Tello trained was of course "Peruvian" already, in its imitation of the grave-opening, knowledge production, and museums that since 1821 had made "mummies . . . mummifiers" and their necropoli into avatars of historical and scientific knowledge. Tello's translation of that mortuary empire back to its Peruvian context was not radical vis-à-vis the Andean communities that Tello—like his North American counterparts—induced to reveal tombs and ruins. But it at least made explicit how Peruvian and American history and its colonizing sciences had always demanded knowledge from Indigenous tombs, skulls from bodies, objects from ancestors. Curation had been sepulchral, violent, medical, and desacralizing since the sixteenth century, when Spaniards dissected sacred ancestors, yllapas, and mallkis, in the name of knowledge, faith, and imperial rule. Tello's provocation was that curation could also care for that dead in the name of a better, more proudly Indigenous nation.

Gutiérrez won, for the moment. He refused to let Tello see the inventory that might unscramble Uhle's collection. He accused Tello of hiding books, changing locks, stealing sofas, and cleaning in such a way that dust got on his paintings.[96] Lacking funds, Tello sold property he owned in Huarochirí and called in debts from friends and relatives before finally resigning in March 1915.[97] Paraphrasing Goode, Tello accused Gutiérrez of having let the museum become scientifically paralyzed, "a dead museum, a cadaver condemned ultimately to mummification or putrefaction."[98] With Tello out, Gutiérrez seems to have accelerated the anthropology collection's rot, despite submitting a law to Congress that positioned himself as the protector of Peruvian antiquity. In 1915 the final Yale Peruvian

Expedition confronted Peru's government with rumors that Gutiérrez was selling off skulls Tello had collected.[99]

The gesture helped Tello little. In 1915 he and Daniel Alomía Robles,
composer of the anti-imperial operetta *El Condor Pasa*, tried to visit the Yale
expedition's house in Ollantaytambo, filled with the trepanned mummies and
skulls from nine of the region's burial caves. Hoping to collaborate, Tello was
instead turned away at the door. Alomía Robles reported that Bingham and
his team were excavating without oversight and secreting some artifacts out
of the country—true on all counts. Cusqueño intellectual Luis E. Valcárcel
investigated, learning that the region's campesinos believed Yale was smuggling
mummies to Chile *to reanimate them against Peru*. The expedition was ultimately
able to export the two tons of material it had collected to New Haven, but temporarily; Yale anthropologist George Grant MacCurdy had only a few years to
interpret the collections' trepanned skulls in light of Tello's work.[100] Bingham
abandoned work in Peru. At least some of his North American colleagues re-
solved to be "conciliatory in the future . . . going to Peru now with the obvious
intention of obeying their regulations and respecting their wishes."[101]

Meanwhile, Tello's money troubles exposed him to larger hazards. He collected for others, sending Harvard inventoried collections of pathological skulls,

Fig. 8.5 Yale Peruvian Expedition of 1914–1915 members pose with the dead. Yale
expedition engineer Ellwood C. Erdis (left) steadies a trepanned mummy from the
tombs near Machu Picchu, whose seated pose a Peruvian expedition member reproduces
(center). At right another North American expedition member, likely David E. Ford,
holds a skull. An accompanying picture, taken by Ford of the same scene but with only
one expedition member holding skulls, features a trepanation. Photographer:
J. J. Hasbrouck. National Geographic Society Image Archives 786237.

paying his way to US conferences by selling artifacts and specimens. Those choices caught up with him when he was denounced for excavating in Nazca without a license. Most dramatically, he coordinated a Peruvian zoological expedition for Harvard; Tello later complained that he had been denied adequate remuneration or intellectual credit for his work—a slight compounded by how Tello had engaged in ethically, physically, and spiritually hazardous work in Harvard's name. When an "unseasonable rain" followed Tello's collection of seven "mummies" near the northern town of Huancabamba, residents confronted Tello, saying "that the rain will continue until the mummies are put back in their graves." The boxed bodies made it to Harvard nonetheless.[102]

Tello's complicity in the transfer reflected his commitment to grave-opening's science. His own precarity, however, highlighted his connection to those from whom he stole. In 1915 he tightened that connection, becoming a member of the Asociación Pro-Indígena, decrying the exploitation of Peru's "Indians." In 1917 he won Huarochirí's seat in the Chamber of Deputies (*diputados*) of Peru's Congress, promoting literacy, fighting alcoholism, and celebrating the character "inherited from our *antecesores indígenas*"—a clever phrase that could be heard as "indigenous predecessors" or "indigenous ancestors," pointing to continuities without necessarily racializing them. When a wealthy family contested the election, Tello led over fifteen hundred Huarochiranos into Lima to convince the Supreme Court to validate his win.[103]

Was Tello's bundling of national politics and ancestral sciences apt or opportunistic? In 1917 José Carlos Mariátegui, South America's first Marxist theorist, hinted that the cultural politics Tello promised could be both revolutionary and reactionary. "If we lay our eyes on a display case, we find ourselves facing a mummy," he observed. "The huacas are opened so that the shades of the emperors of Tahuantinsuyo might fly out."[104] Because Tello's fortunes rose further with Augusto B. Leguía's 1919 return to the presidency, it has been easy to take him as an emblem of the statist *indigenismo* of Leguía's eleven-year-rule. As a diputado, Tello authored important reforms of secondary- and university-level instruction, opening institutions to rural students. He secured a highway to Huarochirí, bridges, schools, aqueducts, and telephones, all built by his countrymen. He helped create the Patronato de la Raza Indígena, which recognized Indigenous communal land holdings for the first time since the 1850s but often ruled on the side of landholders.[105]

Tello was no Incanist, however, and his anthropology questioned politics that made Andean peoples into objects rather than individuals capable of, for example, founding the Peruvian Society for the Advancement of Science, as Tello did in 1920.[106] He also contrasted with the indigenistas of his time. In late 1917 he spoke against proposed educational policies for "Indians," "as if they were of a race distinct from Peruvians." The label itself was problematic, originating in the Spanish colonialism that extracted their labor. "From a scientific standpoint," he told Congress, "there is no essential difference, not just between an Indian and a white, but also between a black and a white."[107] Tello observed that "white proletarians," the descendants of Spaniards, were also labeled "Indians." The so-called Indian problem, then, was the fault of circumstantial socio-political divisions laid upon Andean peoples since the European conquest, in which their exploitation was justified by their ascribed but not actual race.[108]

Tello's critique of racism as Peru's great problem shaped a self-consciously "Peruvian" anthropology whose primary concern was history, culture, and class, not biology. In 1918 Tello received his doctorate at the University of San Marcos for a thesis on mummified trophy heads. He then founded the university's first archaeology museum with objects from the central Andean site of Chavín de Huantar, where Rivero had dreamed of the dead throne of Spanish tyranny. Tello, by contrast, saw Chavín as a fertile place—as the three-millennia-old "matrix" of an autochthonous Peruvian culture whose forms moved across the Andes. In that museum, Tello taught his students an anthropology that questioned Americanists' beliefs that Peru's cultures were foreign imports. In 1921 Tello characterized both Hrdlička's and Uhle's theories to that end as "polygenist," compounding Samuel George Morton's error in dividing humanity based on cranial differences that Tello called insignificant. Tello instead declared himself a "monogenist," arguing that Peru was "a single geo-ethnic region" before colonialism and mestizaje racialized and divided Incas and Indians into separate classes "degenerated by . . . alcohol, coca, diseases and religious fanaticism." Tello instead identified a deeper basis for Peru—an "Indigenous pedestal" from which "Science" could overcome "men's selfishness, to establish the economic equilibrium of the social classes and thus to build up the nation."[109] One did not need to be Inca to deserve respect. And being Indigenous was no cause for pity.

Tello turned the racist reaction his proposals received into his greatest victory yet. In 1922 his enemy Emilio Gutiérrez de Quintanilla published a race-baiting memoir calling Tello a "false prophet of his race," whose *indigenismo* "extinguish[ed] the splendor of the white race." This "living imitation of Huaina Capac," Gutiérrez frothed, "loot[ed] huacas while high on coca."[110] Tello read the offending passages in the Chamber of Deputies, observing that Gutiérrez's libel was published with government money. Gutiérrez was beaten, and agreed to sign over the National Museum's artifacts to Tello. In 1924 Tello folded them into a new National Museum of Archaeology he directed, housed in a neo-Tiwanakoid building built by Victor Larco Herrera—the antiquarian who paved Hrdlička's way with skulls. They were joined there by the potsherds that Bingham's Yale expedition exported in 1916, but not the human remains, which Tello believed Gutiérrez had "sent to the dump heap as soon as [they] arrived to the National Museum in Lima."[111]

Tello's speech at the museum's opening was a sop to Leguía, associating the president with the collective labor of the "national" and "socialist government of the Incas." But his own personal historical vision also prevailed. This museum would be a "general Archive of Peruvian Prehistory and History," where all that had been removed from the "great archive of the pre-Columbian cemeteries" could be re-indexed. What Peruvian tombs guarded, Tello claimed, was not "race" but the "history of a soil that guards the sacred ashes of our fathers"— shades of Viracocha's and Huarochirí's mallkis, burned by the Spanish. What their scientific investigation achieved was a better understanding of the "children of indigenous mothers" whose future was a Peru whose ancestors deserved care in their own museum.[112]

Finally, Tello brought this museum the discovery that, in the words of his friend and high-altitude physiologist Carlos Monge, "closed his chapter" on pre-Hispanic trepanation "with a masterly hand."[113] In July 1925 Tello and a fellow graduate of Harvard's anthropology program, Samuel K. Lothrop, drove south seeking a pre-Hispanic cemetery whose long, beautiful, textiles were being looted for collectors. They found it at the bay of Paracas where José de San Martín and his revolutionaries had landed in Peru, 105 years earlier. US anthropologists William Curtis Farabee and Alfred L. Kroeber had recently visited the region without realizing what lay beneath their feet. With Lothrop's money, Tello paid off the right person, a tomb-raider (huaquero) named Juan Quintana, "el Sordito"—"the little deaf one"—who had been digging and unwrapping mummy bundles since the early 1900s.[114]

Quintana led them to the discovery that Tello's work had been building toward—two mass interments at the neck of the Paracas peninsula, on the north-facing slope of Cerro Colorado. Tello and Lothrop had been on the trail of textiles, but what most struck Tello, Lothrop remembered, were "the deformed crania, scattered across the surface, many of which exhibited enormous trepanations." "Doctor Tello began to shout and make exclamations." He collected forty-five skulls for his museum, twenty-five of which showed signs of surgery. Because there was no room in their car, Tello and Lothrop tied the skulls to the running board, "the first collection of Paracas." They drove back to Lima in the rain, wondering what the "people on the road thought to see us pass by with our fantastic car loaded" with the trepanned Peruvian dead.[115]

It was as much because of those skulls as the site's textiles that Tello sent his team back to dig, expecting the site would add to his thesis that ancient Peruvians were scientific and medical actors, knowable from the holes they left behind. Through 1928 in this graveyard peninsula—which Tello rightly dated as beginning long before 1 CE, Hrdlička's shallow horizon for Indigenous American settlement—his excavators pulled 429 conical funerary bundles, wrapped and rewrapped in fine, long textiles. All 429, some of them massive, were transferred to Tello's museum, and for the rest of his life Tello curated them. From their selective opening he distinguished the dead of "two periods, and two generations," cultured and scientific. The second group, from what Tello called the "Necropolis of Wari Kayan," has garnered more attention for their stunning textiles, considered the finest in the pre-Hispanic Americas. But a full 40 percent of the dead of the first group ("Cerro Colorado") showed traces of cranial operations, Tello believed. Even more notably—and this was what fellow scientist Monge thought closed this chapter of Tello's life—they found "a packet containing obsidian knives complete with their respective sleeves stained with blood, together with a spoon or curette made of a sperm whale's tooth," cotton, bandages, and thread. Tello told the press this was nothing less than the operating kit of an ancient "surgeon"—a healing Peruvian ancestor who had himself been cured, given that the cavern's bodies showed signs of having been mummified over a low, slow flame, Tello claimed.[116] This made Paracas's people the Americas' oldest trepanners and mummifiers.

One disgruntled colleague would dispute the evidence for trepanation, and Tello proved wrong regarding their mummification. In fact, arrested

Vista panorámica de la Gran Necrópolis de Cerro Colorado en la que se vé los fardos de las momias tal como fueron halladas. (Según el modelo del Museo de Arqueología Peruana).

Fig. 8.6 "Panoramic view" of the Museum of Peruvian Archaeology's model of the Gran Necrópolis of Cerro Colorado, depicting its funerary bundles as they were found. Julio C. Tello, *Antiguo Peru. Primera Epoca* (Lima: 1929), Lamina VI.

decomposition had caused the bodies' carbonization, and seven-thousand-year-old mummies would be recognized at Arica.[117] But this perceived conjunction of trepanation and mummification nonetheless led Tello to a conviction regarding Paracas he held to his death. As his student and institutional heir Rebeca Carrión Cachot explained, Paracas's "first [generation] was one of surgeons, experts in cranial trepanations; the other was one of priests or dignitaries that, according to Dr. Tello, ought to have had in their care the worship and the computation of *tiempo*"—time and the weather, the seasons.[118] For Tello, Paracas was nothing less than a wellspring of Peru's sciences of healing, death, and temporality. His most essential point—that these sciences were far older than Americanist colleagues allowed—was borne out.

Tello's claimed inheritance of that legacy lay within his name for the second set of tombs: "Wari Kayan." In Quechua, "Wari" or "Huari" can be glossed as "The Originals of the Land." "Kayan," in Huarochirí, were those plazas in pre-Hispanic "old towns" where postconquest peoples sorted labor obligations, argued over justice, and heard announcements validated by the *colca* surrounding the plazas—"tiny lodgings" like storehouses containing the mummified bodies of the village's founders and "lesser holy objects."[119] Tello's Wari Kayan, then, was a place where Paracas's ancestral scientists and Huarochirí's modern heirs met, legitimacy emerging from the bodies around them.

Tello rewrapped that connection using the mummies' textiles. If evidence of trepanation linked them to the Yauyos—and himself—then their textiles' artistic motifs linked them to Chavín de Huantar in the central highlands, which he believed was the transregional wellspring of Peruvian civilization. If the Incas were Peru's Romans, Tello told his students, then this "Chavin-Paracas Civilization" were the Greeks, whose republican greatness now covered their postimperial heirs.[120] Believing that the Paracas bundles' best textiles were actually robes, he had the National Museum of Archaeology's workers drape them over mannequins modeled after living Peruvians, as at Henry Fairfield Osborn's American Museum of Natural History.[121] In New York, these mannequins extended a diorama effect to the world's "primitive" non-European peoples.[122] But context matters. In Lima, the mannequins of Tello's museum re-embodied the dead in the living, bundling Tello, his museum collaborators, and their claimed ancestors in a mantle of science and history.[123]

There were hard years to come. In 1930 Peru's military overthrew President Leguía, Tello's patron. With no evidence, new revolutionary newspapers accused Tello of building a fortune for Leguía by looting archaeological sites. Tello was stripped of the directorship of his museum but kept control of the

Fig. 8.7 "Reconstruction of a Man of Paracas with authentic dress of the period."
Mannequin from National Museum of Archaeology, ca. 1929. Julio C. Tello, *Antiguo Peru.*
Primera Epoca (Lima: 1929), frontispiece.

four hundred or so Paracas funerary bundles still unopened.[124] Marginalized by subsequent governments, Tello returned to North American networks to seek help maintaining the bundles against Lima's damp humidity. He found it in another new museum, the Museum of Anthropology and Archaeology among the huacas of La Magdalena, the "Pueblo Libre" where San Martín declared Peruvian independence in 1821.

In that museum, Tello reenacted what death's empires had long assaulted: a longstanding Andean culture in which even non-Inca remains received curation, study, display, and respect. This complexity was hard earned, born of Andean bodies' looting and racialization by colonialism, Americanist anthropology, and elite Peruvian antiquarianism. But by following those bodies abroad and back again, Tello had built a place of radical if self-serving insistence: an anti-racist anthropological and museum project founded in millennia-old Andean sciences of curing and curation, trepanation and mummification. This project did not celebrate a de-Indianizing racial mixture or idealize "pure" Indigenous farmers at arms' length.[125] Instead, it embraced the Andean dead's ability to collect their many heirs, who survived where even Inca emperors had not. "Soy Indio," he told his anthropology students: *I am Indian*—and a scientist as well.[126]

The Three Burials of Julio César Tello

Or, Skull Walls Revisited

On May 22, 1947, a notary visited Julio César Tello to record his final will and testament. Sixty-seven years old, Tello was dying. The doctors caring for him in a clinic in San Isidro, Lima, believed it was Hodgkin's lymphoma, whose cancer cells had spread throughout his body and overtaken its functions. His fellow Huarochiranos might have begged to differ. Decades later, some told anthropologist Frank Salomon that it was Tello's work that laid him low; by disinterring the mummified neighbors of his home and putting them into museums, Tello had incurred their ire, making him ill.[1]

Either way, his hour of death had come, and Tello determined to set the course of his afterlife in ways distinct from Huayna Capac centuries earlier. His will began like others. The notary recorded the facts of Tello's birth in Huarochirí, the names of his parents, his wife, and their four children—two already deceased—and a son born out of wedlock before 1909. Tello divided his earthly goods between them, making special provisions for his daughter Elena Tello Cheesman's education, and for his library and archive to go to his alma mater, the Universidad Nacional Mayor de San Marcos.[2]

The next six provisions spoke to his intellectual legacy and victories as a champion of Native Peru. He explained how he had stewarded many of Lima's museums "guided by the purest scientific devotion." His revelation of the "archaeological sources" of Peruvian culture—"Chavín, Paracas, Pachacamac, Nepeña"—clarified the "antiquity and contents of our old and autochthonous civilizations." And in "accumulating such valuable documentation of some of the grandest civilizations of America," he continued, "I believe I have rendered a deserved homage to the creative genius of the indigenous Peruvian, the basis of our nationality."[3]

Yet so much remained undone. Tello lamented having been unable to analyze "in a definitive way all of the immense documentary material uncovered and

Empires of the Dead. Christopher Heaney, Oxford University Press. © Oxford University Press 2023.
DOI: 10.1093/oso/9780197542552.003.0010

accumulated" sitting in the deposits and exhibits of the Museum of Anthropology and Archaeology, his last, opened in La Magdalena in 1937. Tello directed his former students Rebeca Carrión Cachot and Toribio Mejía Xesspe to carry on the publication of his findings, fulfilling the promise recognized by his allies: Harvard, which welcomed and propelled him, Tello remembered; American petroleum heir and philanthropist Nelson Rockefeller, who in the late 1930s supported the La Magdalena museum's preservation of the Paracas *fardos* (mummy bundles); and the Peruvian politician Germán Luna Iglesias, who donated land for that final museum's storehouses of the dead.[4]

In remembering this transnational assistance to his life's work in digging up and curating the Andean dead, Tello's last will and testament made explicit the circulations of mortuary knowledge set in motion by Huayna Capac's own determinations some four centuries earlier. And like Huayna Capac, he was concerned with his body's final disposition. Tello's eleventh provision asked that his body's rest be in keeping with the life he lived. Tello entrusted his corpse to his executor, Alberto Arce Pari, reminding him that "I have received enough honors in life to satisfy whatever my compatriots might want to give me in death." For that reason, he went on, "I make a special recommendation to my executor that the inhumation of my mortal remains be undertaken as a strictly private act and, if possible, that I might be given sepulcher in the soil, in a place singularly welcome to me that my executor knows, and that above my tomb be erected a replica of the Chavín Obelisk."[5]

No Christian cross would mark his grave. Instead, he would be guarded by a replica of a two-and-a-half-meter-tall stone deity from Chavín de Huantar, the two-millennia-old underground temple where the first curator of Peru's National Museum Mariano Eduardo de Rivero had contemplated colonialism's dead. Farmers had at some point dragged the obelisk to the atrium of their town's church. Against the protests of the church's priest, Tello had sought an order from the national government to move the obelisk to his museum in Lima, having decided it was the principal deity of the wellspring of Andean civilization.[6] A replica of this devouring, defiant, and life-sustaining god would instead rise—serpentine, feline, knifelike, germinating, both masculine and feminine—from Tello's body into the open sky.[7]

The dying man listened as the notary read his afterlife back to him. Tello ratified it, and he and three witnesses signed the document.[8] Two weeks later, after a failed final surgery, after his museum's employees gave him their donated blood, Tello joined the dead he had studied. His final words, according to one newspaper, were "Conferences, Museum."[9]

Tello's afterlife did not go as planned—at least not at first and never exactly how he envisioned. Instead, he and his legacy were buried three times over, thousands of miles apart. This chapter takes these interments as revelatory of three destinations of Peru's empire of the dead, all still in place today.[10] One kept Tello at the service of the state, interred in a largely Christian and Spanish pantheon of national heroes, racializing him as a dead "Indian" when it didn't ignore his ethnicity entirely. The next hid him within an Americanist physical anthropology whose history was claimed by white US scholars, not those of Peru. The last, however, placed him at the very heart of the Indigenous expertise-based anthropology Tello had sought to craft, which celebrated scientific ancestors by installing them in museums.

Church burials these were not. But all three responded to Tello's most vaulting claims: that the history of knowing and curing ancestors was among Peru's most powerful lessons, and that to be a speaker for that dead—in Quechua, a mallkipvillac—was a way of doing science that defied the claimed universalities of the supposed West. These burials presented museums and nations as possible solutions to colonialism, rather than just its products—a contradictory ancestry that Tello and his heirs embraced.

————

The first interment claimed Tello's authority as an "Indian" archaeologist for the Peruvian state, extending the national appropriation of ancestral remains that Tello both crafted and contested. Tello's desire to see the state adequately fund, protect, and study archaeological "remains" was longstanding, despite his own pragmatic use of huaqueros' knowledge and his occasional export of graves' contents. In 1929, in one of his final efforts as a diputado to Peru's Congress, Tello helped put the finishing touches on Law 6634, which established a Patronato Nacional de Arqueología to monitor all excavations in the country, allowing the state to expropriate lands marked by "whatever constructions, remains, or residues of human labor" preceding the colonial era, including burials. The overlapping, contradictory decrees that had defined state policy on huacas and export since independence were cut away. The state also claimed definitive ownership of whatever those constructions contained. First on the list were "human remains."[11]

This law, which Tello and his followers later identified as one of his chief legacies, claimed more than any prior colonial or republican legal regime.[12] It gave the Peruvian state possession of its Andean predecessors: a preemptive owning of not just their wealth, monuments, or land, but their very bodies as well. It was thus a law prone to the sort of state overreach that Tello himself experienced. Also in 1929 President Leguía's Ministry of Foreign Relations confiscated six

Paracas mummies from Tello's museum, sending them to Spain to inhabit Peru's neo-Inca pavilion in the Exposición Ibero-Americana in Seville. This was its due, the ministry believed, for state funding of excavations at Paracas, but Tello delivered them with "tears in his eyes," historian Jorge Basadre claimed. Though the contents of four bundles were returned, he and his museum long advocated for the return of the other two.[13]

Tello was most disturbed by his lack of control, rather than the export itself. When Leguía was overthrown, and governmental opinion turned against Tello and slashed his financial support, he faced even harder decisions. A decade later, "in return" for that five thousand dollars to support Tello's expeditions and the Paracas bundles' preservation, Nelson Rockefeller told Tello it would be "highly useful" if he gave Rockefeller "four or five" of the mummies. Tello acquired government permissions to send four, which Rockefeller gave to the American Museum of Natural History and Harvard's Peabody Museum for unwrapping and display. Grateful, Tello used the funds to open his last museum in La Magdalena, the National Museum of Anthropology and Archaeology. He had traded away four Paracas ancestors to save the rest.[14]

The conversion of Tello's claimed ancestors into national diplomats foreshadowed Tello's own first interment. He did not get the "strictly private" inhumation he asked for. Rather, his death on June 3, 1947, initiated a year of mourning, supported by the state that benefited from his labor for thirty-five years but only sporadically supported him. Now, a year after anthropology's institutionalization as a Peruvian university discipline, the democratizing government of president José Luis Bustamante y Rivero (1945–1948) sprang to action. Condolences arrived from the University of San Marcos, Peru's YMCA, the Ministry of Public Education and National Museum of History, the National Tourism Corporation, Lima's Geographical Society of Lima, colleagues in the United States, Tello's own National Museum of Anthropology and Archaeology, and the community of San Mateo in Huarochirí.[15] The constellation of his work and origins unleashed panegyrics ranging from the profound, to the profoundly racializing, to the literally overheated. "The eminent Archaeologist has been immolated in a holocaust of science," read one tribute. Another praised his "bronze" skin, "unruly" hair, and "good Indian" arrival to Lima. The dead Tello uncovered were even enlisted in his mourning. "He will no longer visit . . . the Paqarinas that yesterday followed him, listening for how he might communicate with our ancestors. . . . The Nascas, the Paracas, whom day and night he worked hard to revive, are in the Museum awaiting his return."[16]

What was meant by that "return" might have been lost on casual newspaper readers; their attention was instead directed to the treatment that the body of the "wise Indian" received in the hours after his death.[17] This was the sort of Indigenizing language Tello himself sometimes trucked in, especially later in life, when his explicit goal was the conversion of archaeology from a "dead science" to a "militant" one that demonstrated that the Americas' many futures lay in Indigenous people like himself.[18] In 1932 one of Tello's anthropology students offered a paternalistic exam answer declaring that the Peruvian state owed it to Indians to return them to farming. In response, Tello's red pencil challenged, "And why can he only be a farmer?"[19]

Tello was relatively privileged, though, in declaring himself an "Indian" scientist, given that *indio* remained an insult for those not of his education and status. After his death, his colleagues and friends expanded his lionization, enlisting the state in Tello's postmortem wishes. After one of his artists made a death mask of Tello's face, his body was sent to the Institute of Pathology, where his friends and longtime medical collaborators Pedro Weiss and Carlos Monge autopsied and embalmed him with an eye to his near-permanent preservation. To honor him, they kept his heart in a jar.[20] Peru's Congress, meanwhile, declared a moment of national mourning—one that Lima's press helped to carry out. Newspapers explained how this "total Indian," fluent in "the funereal and pomp-filled message of mummies," was placed in an ebony coffin and laid in state in the Paracas rotunda of his museum, surrounded by three rings of Peruvians. The outermost "guard of honor" were Tello's textile-draped mannequins and mummies of Paracas. Next came "Indian sentinels in steel helmets"—soldiers detailed by Peru's president. The closest ring were twenty of his "disciples," who watched him overnight. There, in the museum where Tello delved his "hand in the subterranean cosmos of Peru's prehistory," disturbing "the peace of the necropolis so its mummies could speak," he now "slept, beside the steel-helmeted Indian sentinels and the warriors, princesses, and priests of the prodigious Peru at its apogee."[21]

This temporary interment, far from the private ceremony Tello requested, diverged in still other ways. A crucifix hung above him, and La Magdalena's parish priest said a prayer. On June 6, a camera crew filmed his coffin being carried out of the museum, so his funeral might be seen in movie theaters nationwide. An honor guard of soldiers was followed by a representative of Peru's president; the presidents of the Senate, Chamber of Deputies, and Supreme Court; and his friend Weiss, elected by Tello's family. A slow funeral procession drove him through Lima's streets to the Cementerio Presbítero, a pantheon for statesmen and elites since its founding in 1808 as part of the ilustrados' war on unhealthful church interment.[22] There, led by the Afro-Peruvian confraternity members long relied upon in Limeño funerals, Tello received a full state interment in a burial niche, and the soldiers fired off a salute. Intellectuals and the minister of public education eulogized him. Huarochirí's diputado to Congress imagined the living and dead he had inspired and studied, heralding his transformation. "The grand multitudes that you revived in your arduous life now assemble in ceremony, brandishing their rich arms with dignity, tipping their ritual insignias, while in the milky obscurity of the beyond, the immortal weavers of Paracas lay at your feet their richest mantle, so that you might gently enter your eternity, finding yourself face to face with the mysteries that in life you fought to decipher."[23]

Given that dignified burial in Peru was neither guaranteed nor free, given that Tello was honored in a Lima whose elites were lately receptive to the anti-Indigenous Hispanism that came of admiring Franco's Spain, this first interment was significant.[24] April 11, his birthday, would become Archaeologist's Day in Peru. But this loud celebration of Tello as a national hero made it possible to mute his critique of racism in both his field and Peruvian society at large. Six months later, Rebeca Carrión Cachot, director of his final museum, noted the lasting challenge that Tello's anthropology posed to Peruvian society: that "the supposed inferiority of the *indio* is not ethnic but circumstantial," the result of being "orphaned of all social support, at the margin of justice." But the University of San Marcos rector's words on the same occasion, the dedication of a bronze bust of Tello, suggested the limits of staking Andean dignity upon an exceptional but still-national past. Tello was a "symbol," he declared, as much a "synthesis of the race as is Garcilaso" de la Vega, the Inca-Spanish chronicler.[25] Like the Incas, Tello had become a dead icon—one that schools, streets, and dental clinics could be named after without registering his anti-racist indictment of the creole historical pantheon that now embraced him.[26]

Tello's anti-racist message could be easy to miss, given how easily it was overshadowed by its frequent medium. To generate interest in his work, Tello had made the unwrapping of Paracas mummy bundles into occasional spectacles for fellow Peruvians and foreigners alike.[27] Tello's second burial, abroad, underscores the hazards of such a claim to scientific belonging, showing how easily Andean bodies were appropriated without the messages that Tello and other Peruvian scholars tried to transmit. These occlusions, especially in anthropological contexts whose understanding of "American" was more limited, made the long history of Andean sciences of the dead easier to forget. In Tello's case, his contributions were all but entombed behind the Skull Wall and the Smithsonian's Hall of Physical Anthropology.

That American entombment was far from inevitable. In the years before his death, during the heyday of the Good Neighbor Policy, Tello was celebrated in the United States for his science and Indigenous heritage. As anthropologist Marisol de la Cadena notes, in 1942 the influential North American geographer Carl Ortwin Sauer deemed Tello not just the "cornerstone of social science in Peru," but "the greatest archaeologist in the New World."[28] Tello was profiled that same year in *Builders of Latin America*, a US textbook that educated high schoolers on twenty-two of their most notable "Good Neighbors." Of them, eighteen were dead, Simón Bolívar and Atahuallpa included. Of the four still living, only Tello was flagged as Indigenous, and the book detailed his incredible rise.[29] Two years later, North American anthropologist Alfred L. Kroeber, Tello's sometime collaborator, likened Tello to Heinrich Schliemann, the archaeologist who claimed to have discovered Troy, if Schliemann had also been "a mountain Indian, risen from the ranks."[30]

Tello was likewise celebrated in death, with his racialized identity presented as relevant to his achievements. Reports of his passing were wired from Lima the day he died. The *New York Times* published Tello's obituary the next day; later letters to the editor remembered the mummy unwrappings he performed for visitors in the 1930s and 1940s.[31] Samuel K. Lothrop, who had accompanied Tello to Paracas, wrote a seven-page obituary for *American Antiquity*, noting that "Tello was of almost pure Indian blood, of which he was proud." It was "inspirational," Lothrop said, "that an Indian from Huarochirí was buried in state with the notables of the land attending amid salvos of artillery and that his countrymen rank him high in their history with Garcilaso de la Vega and Tupac Amaru."[32]

It was the least Lothrop could have said. In the late 1930s Tello had enlisted Lothrop, Kroeber, and their American colleagues to form a collaborative inter-American center for Andean research that Tello hoped to direct, with international financing. The North Americans moved the idea forward, but took over the leadership of the resulting Institute of Andean Research, making Tello adviser on local logistics. They sent Tello their students to learn his findings that, for lack of time and funding, he taught, lectured upon, and wrote up for public audiences but had yet to publish with a full evidentiary apparatus.[33] The North Americans' more frank perspective on Tello was reflected in Kroeber's confidential report on Peruvian archaeology in 1942, in which he noted that Tello was "disliked by many Peruvians, who consider him egotistic, domineering, greedy, jealous, ruthless, and (often) unscrupulous," and that "among American archaeologists, dislike prevails in half, tempered admiration in the others." Kroeber was mostly of the latter camp. Tello would have been cut to the quick to know that Kroeber believed him "not a scientist in his interpretations." But Kroeber nonetheless respected him. Tello "has done more for Peruvian archaeology than any one else, except possibly Uhle, its scientific founder," he wrote privately. Likening Tello and his energy to that of his own mentor, Kroeber concluded that "Tello is the grand old man in his field, and still going strong—the Boas of Peru."[34]

Yet Boas would be remembered in ways that Tello would not. In the two years after Tello's death, those American colleagues mounted a conference rethinking Peru's archaeology; they proposed historical, cultural "horizons" traceable across geographies—arguments that "seem to have implicit antecedents in

Tello's thinking" but gave no credit to his influence, archaeologists Ann Peters and Alberto Ayarza observe. Several conference publications critiqued Tello's theories and his nonacademic publishing. After the conference, a new Berkeley school of Andean archaeology developed under John H. Rowe. It addressed sites and questions Tello pioneered but published almost exclusively in the United States, and it used "Tello's data but without citing his works, except as a source of photographs."[35]

Even more symbolic was the burial of Tello and his self-consciously Peruvian science at the Smithsonian, where Aleš Hrdlička's estimation of Tello as a "corrupt" actor—sometimes not even worthy of being named—still affects histories written from Hrdlička's archives.[36] When the Hall of Physical Anthropology opened in 1965, Tello's legacy was there, hidden in the hall behind the Skull Wall, whose 160 Peruvians came from the thousands that Hrdlička had exported and that Tello had tried to stop.

After having toured Hall 25, a visitor could have been forgiven for thinking that the exhibit used the ancient dead because they had *not* been valued by living Peruvians—that the Smithsonian had salvaged its many ancient Peruvians from local looting and neglect, making them American anthropology's most reliably insightful quarry. In that hall, Peruvian skulls illustrated how Indigenous Americans expressed group belonging with cranial shaping. They illustrated how physical anthropologists observed ancient fractures and "prehistoric" diseases in skeletons. Even the "differentiation" of physical traits over time and space were illustrated by the Peruvians, from the cranial variety that contrasted with the "generalized Asiatic mongoloids" that the Smithsonian said had migrated over the Bering Strait, to "The 'Inca' bone" or *os incae*, the cranial interparietal bone that Tschudi used to liken Andean peoples to marsupials.[37]

Returning to Hall 25's two most memorable displays shows how ambivalent the Smithsonian's anthropologists remained about studying Peru's dead as more than objects—as subjects embodying knowledges that were extended by their heirs. In Unit 23, "Mummies," visitors met the seated ancient Peruvian whose presence was as much an outcome of Spanish appropriations and Garcilaso's translations as the late-nineteenth-century American who sent the body to Washington—George Kiefer, the collector who died of mummy dust. The centuries-long fight to assert Inca embalming over the sacred meaning of Inca and Andean ancestors, however, was elided: the unit's script reserved artificial preservation for the display's recumbent Egyptian, presenting the Peruvian body as a "prehistoric Indian" "naturally preserved" by Peru's "dry desert," and certainly nothing sacred.[38]

That agnosticism extended to the most surprising fact the Smithsonian's anthropologists claimed to have learned from Peruvian skulls: the antiquity of trepanation (skull surgery) in the Americas. Early scripts presented it as "a type of quackery." The final exhibit dropped that old ambivalence in favor of Tello's line, that "Ancient Peruvians excelled in Skull Surgery." And if the skulls with five, even seven holes, failed to impress, then Alton S. Tobey's mural of an Inca surgeon at work at Machu Picchu clinched the experience (see Plate 2).[39]

In both cases, what a visitor would not have seen was just how Peruvian their study had been, nor how Inca and American—imperial in both cases—their presentation had become. This was partly due to new popularizations of science, in which the desire to titillate American visitors trumped any exploration of the cultural reasons for curing and collecting the living and the dead. ("What do you think?" the exhibit's visual coordinator wrote to Tobey regarding the trepanation mural: "More gore?")[40] But it was also a matter of how the archives of North American science incline both students and critics to histories of the field in which intellectual initiative, positive and malign, begins and ends in the United States. The exhibit closed with a tribute to the NMNH's contributions to physical anthropology, crediting Hrdlička in particular. There was no place in the narrative for how Hrdlička replicated the labors of his Indigenous rival Tello, whose exports of the trepanned Andean dead extended nineteenth-century Americanist anthropology's historic reliance upon Peruvian grave-opening and its knowledges.[41]

Yet Tello and his embodied history of knowing the dead as healing, scientific ancestors were still in the exhibit, if a visitor knew how to look. For the mural depicting an Inca surgeon at work, Stewart had directed Tobey to look at a prior visualization of Peruvian trepanation: one of eighty-five "great moments" in the history of medicine and pharmaceutics that Robert A. Thom had painted for Parke, Davis, and Company's industry magazine *Modern Pharmacy* in the 1950s. Boxed sets of prints of these paintings went to physicians throughout the United States and Canada for display in waiting rooms. Of those eighty-five "great moments," only two depicted Indigenous peoples from the Americas, and one of them was "Trephining in Peru."[42] Stewart told Tobey to attend to it (Plate 10), which was nothing less than a restaging of Tello's surgeons of Paracas. Overlooking them was the exact textile-draped mannequin Tello had mounted at his last museum (see Fig. 8.7), who then guarded him at his wake—a beautifully garbed Paracas ancestor monitoring a patient, relieving their pain.

Stewart, however, wanted the scene restaged at Machu Picchu, which was more recognizable to American visitors via its association with its American "discoverer," Hiram Bingham. Stewart thought it could be done without loss of any interest. "Highland costumes are different from those of Paracas used by Thom," Stewart noted, "but can be almost equally colorful."[43]

This was no small edit. Tello had devoted his research on trepanation to proving that healing and civilization were general in Peru, not just limited to the imperial Incas, and that the people of Paracas, or the Yauyo peoples who inherited their skills—himself included—were as sovereign and scientific as an Inca. Over the course of his funeral procession, from the hospital to his embalming, from his last museum to the cemetery, he had been watched over by many such non-imperial Peruvians—including, in the Paracas rotunda, the very mannequin copied by Thom. The Smithsonian's restaging of what in some sidelong way was Tello's own final operation and wake, replacing a Paracas surgeon with Incas, and Tello's less imperial landscapes with Machu Picchu, was a burial, whether Stewart knew it or not. Hall 25 entombed not just the centuries-long argument over the Peruvian dead's forced contribution to the global history of human sciences; it buried Tello's conviction that what redeemed it all was showing how Andean Peruvians could know, heal, and preserve in the present, just as they had done for millennia.

Tello's third burial, however, rededicated his body to that cause, seeking a longevity for his anthropology that his nearest counterparts could not. In suggesting Tello was the "Boas of Peru," Alfred Kroeber captured a similarity—not least of which was that both began their career by collecting the Native dead. But there was a good reason that Boas never had a chance of becoming the Tello of America. Tello did what Boas did not: remember and protect the dead that built his career. Unlike Boas, whose emblematic turn to cultural anthropology and a university setting forestalled American anthropology's reckoning with the collections of Indigenous skulls that his generation left in North American museums, Tello buried himself among them. The place where Tello asked to be interred, the "place singularly welcome to me that my executor knows," was the rear patio of his final museum, close to the Paracas mummies he celebrated.

Tello had known that burial in the backyard of his museum would take some time, requiring government permission—and, perhaps, his embalming. His executor made his wishes known. *El Comercio,* on the day after Tello died in 1947, championed his desire, arguing that to do so "would repeat the example of [Louis] Pasteur, whose body rests in the Institute carrying his name in Paris."[44] *La Tribuna* reached for an Andean example: in wanting to "sleep" in his museum, Tello was "like the ancient Peruvians: the tomb beside the home."[45] By the day Tello was carried to the cemetery, the government had agreed, decreeing that his remains could return to the museum when a suitable tomb was constructed. "In your Museum you will be relic, guardian, and director without wane," promised geographer Javier Pulgar Vidal, "because it was there that you lifted up the man you had seen humiliated and battered so that he might be respected; that he might be lord and not servant; that he achieve a status worthy of your honor guard."[46]

And so, a year to the day after his death, Tello got the burial he wanted. On June 3, 1948, he was disinterred and carried back to La Magdalena. He laid in state in his museum's Paracas rotunda one night more. Candles flickering, he was surrounded by the trepanned skulls he had made into Huarochirí's ancestors, the "surgeons of Paracas" whose scientific descendants—the students and employees from Lima and Huarochirí that Tello trained—again watched over them all. The next morning, museum employees and representatives from Huarochirí carried him from that rotunda to the rear patio of the museum. There, in a marble tomb topped by a replica of the Chavín Obelisk carved by the museum artist Luis Ccosi Salas, Tello was laid to rest with an "amphora" filled with earth from the nineteen districts of Huarochirí, his homeland (see plate 11).[47]

A burial this personal, this self-consciously scientific and ancestral—whose yearlong process was redolent of the purucaya ceremony by which the Incas' embalmed yllapas were paraded back to Cuzco a year after their death—blurred past and present. It spurred his survivors to extraordinary rhetorical heights. Tello was "the soldier who requests that they bury his cadaver in the field of battle that was his greatest victory," observed Germán Luna Iglesias, who paid for the tomb—"the poet that seeks return to the bosom of the earth, wrapped in the sweet serenity of the countryside that most delighted his eyes." Here, in his "spiritual home," "the bones of the great Indian" reposed beneath the replica of the Chavín monolith "he exhumed, covered in symbolic figures and mysterious drawings, that will seem like a strange tree of granite, sinking its roots of eternity in the sarcophagus of he who was also a sturdy monolith, with stony determination and flintiness against adversity."[48]

Tello's burial also sought to ensure his museum's longevity. Over time, governments might find it harder to scatter an institution with a modern burial at its heart. Like the Paracas cemetery Tello had dubbed a Wari Kayan, the museum was now even more clearly a place where the living conversed and claimed legitimacy in the presence of the first owners of the land. Unable to reassemble the generations of tombs and remains that centuries of grave-robbing and export had scattered, or the Inca yllapas who had vanished in a patio of a prior "museum of medicine," some three hundred years before, Tello instead reenacted their interment: the museum as burial and ancestral promise. Rebeca Carrión Cachot was grateful that he could "repose alongside the remains of his ancestors, who forged with their labors and wisdom the Peru of yesterday and of forever." Now an ancestor himself, Tello and his tomb would illuminate and guide this "great Museum of America."[49]

The tomb was closed, the candles extinguished. This "great Museum of America," today the National Museum of Peruvian Archaeology, Anthropology and History, was cleared of dignitaries. But the next day, and the day after that, and the day after that, the former mallkipvillac remained at work, embalmed and surrounded by the fellow archaeologists, doctors, conservators, and artists who carried on the curation of the ancestors who had demanded nothing less of Julio César Tello than his afterlife.

Epilogue

Afterlives: Museums of the American Inca

There is no single end to a five-century history of how Andean and Inca ancestors became mummies, skulls, and specimens, scattered in museums around the world. Their absence and presence, however, continue to seed new beginnings.

In her 2021 book, *Huaco retrato* (Huaco Portrait), Peruvian writer Gabriela Wiener describes walking through the Americas hall of Paris's ethnographic museum, the Musée du Quai Branly, and finding an empty case labeled "Momie d'enfant"—an infant's mummy, collected by Charles Wiener, who took a boy named Juan to Paris's Universal Exposition of 1878. "Something in this blank space sets off an alarm in me," Wiener writes. "That it's a burial. That it's a burial of an unidentified child. That the display is empty. That it is, after all, an open or reopened burial, infinitely desecrated, shown as part of an exhibit that tells the triumphant history of one civilization over others. Can the denial of the eternal rest of a child tell that story?"[1]

Wiener imagines the child's absence as an "indictment of its disappearance"—an invitation to ponder "the idea of theft, of relocation, of repatriation," as well as the recent history of all those Peruvians disappeared by the military and Maoist rebels in the 1980s and 1990s. "If I didn't come from a land of forced disappearance," she continues, "in which there are unburials and, above all, clandestine burials, perhaps that invisible burial behind glass wouldn't speak to me." The absent child is also from Chancay, near where Wiener was born, and she sees her own "shadow trapped behind glass, embalmed and exposed." She imagines what would happen if the child was present: "someone—which would be me—giving in to the impulse to take the momie d'enfant in my arms, the baby huaqueada by Wiener, wrapped in a textile with two-headed snake designs and ocean waves bitten by time, then start running toward the quay, leaving the museum behind, heading toward the Eiffel Tower with no fixed plan other than to get as far away as possible from there, firing shots in the air."[2]

Empires of the Dead. Christopher Heaney, Oxford University Press. © Oxford University Press 2023.
DOI: 10.1093/oso/9780197542552.003.0011

Fig. E.1 Rascar Capac's mummy avenges his theft from Peru and export to Belgium. Hergé, *The Adventures of Tintin: The Seven Crystal Balls* (1948). © Hergé/Moulinsart, 2022.

This book's epilogue attends to Wiener's vision of flight, reflecting on what it means to encounter the Andean dead in museum settings today. It emphasizes the legacy of Peru's grave-opening empire for Americanist anthropology. But it also asks readers to take seriously how Peruvian and Andean actors intentionally transformed those fields and their practices: what it has meant that nearly half a millennia of Andean and Peruvian peoples have, like Wiener, "plant[ed their] shovel in the hole of unreality and remove[d] the dirt."[3] Finally, it makes space for how Andean remains themselves challenge us to think harder about ancestry, descent, and the possibilities of reanimation.

This epilogue has conclusions but is not prescriptive. Andean ancestors have received prescriptions enough—five centuries of outsiders limiting their power or that of their heirs, telling them where they should go or "return." Instead, it amplifies this book's refrain: that in spite of imperial, colonial, and republican efforts to name, claim, and display Andean ancestors and remains as more and less than human, they move and transform those who take them up.

———

This book's first conclusion is that the encounter between communities and empires in the Andes laid an embodied foundation for anthropology and its museums in the Americas and the world. That foundation extended from Peruvian history, in which imperial, colonial, and national actors took Inca and Andean ancestors as objects of larger, successively more global, and eventually more racialized histories. These collections—or *re-collections*, given their contingency upon prior collecting regimes—claimed knowledge of Andean ways of knowing and curing, and their appropriation shaped the scholarly fields and infrastructures that placed Andean ancestors in exhibit spaces and storerooms worldwide.

These interventions began with imperial Incas and local ancestors before 1532. In the land the Spanish knew as Huarochirí, for example, healers cut into the skulls of fellow descendants of their paramount mountain ancestor. A patient who expired might become a sacred ancestor cared for by an ayllu, or a speaker for the dead. In the fifteenth century, however, the Incas took particularly powerful ancestors for the empire—collecting them in Cuzco as subjects of the Incas' own mummified yllapa who, like their namesake the lightning, could start and stop the rain. Like trepanation, the skull surgery in which Incas also excelled, this made care into a tool of empire, bracketing communal Andean pasts with an "older" Inca present.

This Inca empire of the dead was re-collected as "Peruvian" after Spain's invasion in 1532. The Spanish looted Tawantinsuyu's curing and collecting ancestors, and later burned many outright, grasping the threat that they might pose to Christian conversion. But the intermediate step was more subtle. The Spanish seized the yllapas of Pachacuti, Huayna Capac, Mama Ocllo, and possibly two others, and in 1559 moved them to a hospital in Lima where they were displayed, observed, and possibly even dissected. These efforts denied the yllapas' still-present cosmic power through supposedly higher knowledge: relabeling them "embalmed" and ancient sovereigns to be judged within Christian hierarchies of time, nature, medicine, and religion. This first encounter of this sort between Europeans and Indigenous ancestors in the Americas displayed Andean bodies as conquered objects of anatomy, history, and "science."

These "embalmed" Andean sovereigns nonetheless shaped the writing of global history, through the efforts of early modern Andean and Inca chroniclers like Felipe Guaman Poma de Ayala and Garcilaso de la Vega Inca. While Guaman

Poma's initially unpublished chronicle agreed with the Spanish in casting the Inca yllapas as an embalmed origin of Andean idolatry, Garcilaso's representation of Inca embalming as a lost and secret art was translated throughout Europe. By the eighteenth century, non-Peruvian scholars debated whether that lost art meant that the embalmed Incas were "mummies," and whether Peru was America's Egypt: an ancient, civilized height, whose preserved tombs and bodies permitted America's pre-Christian measure. Spanish ilustrados like Antonio de Ulloa also showed how quantifying Peru's preserving tombs and skulls might measure Native Americans' historical depths and putative race. Peru's empire of the dead became trans-imperial, an evidentiary basis for what became the racializing sciences of the deep American past, in which mummified Peruvians would be measured and displayed as the ancestral analogs of all Indigenous people.

Yet for Peruvian creoles like Hipólito Unanue, "Inca mummies" were an inheritance of Peruvian sciences more complex than bodily measurement. Their republican collection of the Andean dead likewise shaped the core practices of nineteenth-century Americanist anthropology. San Martín's restoration of Peruvian sovereignty in an "Inca mummy" went astray in an English anatomy museum, but the four Andean ancestors in Peru's National Museum inspired foreign actors to seek mummifying "Incas" for their own national and local museums and anatomical collections. Citing Peruvian scholars, Samuel George Morton specifically made "Ancient Peruvian" crania his default population for the study of the antiquity of Indigenous "race" and civilization in the Americas. He also used the ancient Peruvians to argue for the importance of large series of crania, rather than singular examples—a consequential move for white supremacist skull-collecting worldwide. The resulting diaspora of Andean mummies and skulls made them the largest and most striking population at world's fairs and American museums, which increasingly disinterred the remains of other Indigenous peoples as well.

This trans-imperial array of the "Inca" and Andean dead remains in place. In US museums like the Smithsonian they are still the single largest original population, though Native North Americans, Hawaiians, and Alaskan ancestors are far higher, when counted together. In Peru, their collection continues, as laws claiming national ownership of monuments, tombs, and their contents channel remains to museums in Lima and beyond. These laws make museums resemble charnel houses, protecting human remains tossed by looting, urban sprawl, and a national and global market interested in "pre-Columbian art."[4] Yet when combined with lasting prejudice in Peru toward the Andean present, the national claim upon the Andean past leaves little ground for explicitly Indigenous movements to confront museums, and sometimes encourages grave-opening as a whole.[5] Archaeologist William Isbell suggests that the proliferation of rural teachers fluent in the study of Peru's embodied Indigenous past fueled "yearly excursion[s] with students to an 'old town,'" to dig among ruins for the local school museum. "Few rural schools are without a mummy or two," Isbell wrote in 1997.[6]

The Peruvian state also intermittently encourages the Andean dead's display outside of Peru. After the death of Julio César Tello, Peru's government and allied scholars continued to conduct mummy diplomacy with the remains he and others collected. Some were sent abroad to cement scientific relationships with colleagues in revolutionary Cuba; others were deployed in performances of Peruvian scientific expertise on the capitalist side of the Cold War, such as in New York, in 1949, or at the World's Fair in Knoxville, Tennessee, in 1982, when a Peruvian doctor unwrapped an Inca-era fardo (mummy bundle) for a theater full of fairgoers.[7]

Knoxville's Peruvian organizer claimed that display was the last of its kind—that "No mummies ever will be allowed to leave [Peru] again"—but was proved wrong in 1995, when North American archaeologist Johan Reinhard and Peruvian climber Miguel Zárate found the frozen mummy of a fifteen-year-old adolescent girl atop Ampato, a sacred and semidormant volcano in southern Peru.[8] The girl had died of exposure, installed there by the Incas as a capacocha, one of their "opulent prestations" or sacrifices to the cosmos. President Alberto Fujimori used "Juanita" for cultural diplomacy, permitting her export to the United States, where she was fitted for a climate-controlled case and displayed in the headquarters of the National Geographic Society, which financed Reinhard. Peruvian scholars and politicians, however, protested the child's endangerment in what seemed to be an attempt to distract from Fujiumori's corrupt and authoritarian regime. That the "Lady of Ampato" was displayed in Washington, DC, before being displayed in Peru struck some as imperial. "If this mummy were a person of another race or from another part of the world, they would not put it on display," said historian Mariana Mould de Pease. "Why can't they come here and examine it? I think it's a matter of disrespect, disrespect for Peru"—a claim hardly disproven when then-president Bill Clinton called Juanita a "good-looking mummy."[9]

That a fifteen-year-old whom the Incas killed to communicate with the cosmos was sent to arouse scientific goodwill in a US president is less an irony than an extension of the power long claimed by these trans-imperial re-collections of the Andean dead. That power hums along despite changing norms for the display of human remains outside Peru. In 1990, Native American activists pushed the US Congress to pass the Native American Grave Protection and Repatriation Act (NAGPRA), which required museums receiving federal funding to identify sacred objects and human remains in their collections that could be returned to federally recognized descendants. The law excluded non–North American remains, but many museums erred on the side of sensitivity (or at least self-protection) by removing all Indigenous remains from display.

American institutions have found all sorts of ways to use NAGPRA to avoid actually returning Indigenous ancestors, however; while some institutions have gone beyond the letter of the law, one recent count finds that museums, universities and federal agencies retain over 110,000 ancestors of Native Americans, Hawaiians and Alaskans, over thirty years since NAGPRA's passage. Those retentions often rely on an assertion of "scientific care" for "ancient" and supposedly anonymous remains—a move pioneered in Peru, whose sanction of Andean ancestors' display abroad reinforces the study of the dead in general. In the 1980s, for example, Peru's government apparently protested when the American Museum of Natural History removed its Andean mummies from display.[10] That they are "mummies"—associated with the embodied antiquity that Egyptian tourism and archaeology likewise promote—is a major factor.[11] In the 2010s, not one but two exhibits of Andean and Egyptian mummies traveled the United States, one of which featured bundled bodies that George Dorsey and his huaqueros dug at Ancón for the World's Fair of 1893, that later went to Chicago's Field Museum: twenty-first-century museumgoers could "unwrap" their bundles themselves, using "non-invasive" CT scans.[12] North American and Peruvian scholars have even framed Peru as a NAGPRA-free space to study the dead, because of how Peruvians are said to have inherited the Incas' "ancient" pride in displaying them.[13]

In this way, Peru's re-collections of mummified empire offer some foreign scholars a rope bridge over pointed debates about colonialism and human remains—an invocation of the language of marvel, power, and ancestry that the Spanish re-collected from the Incas in the sixteenth century, and Samuel George Morton collected from republican Peruvians in the 1830s. Understanding Peru as an absent referent in these debates highlights the necessity of attending to histories of museums, anthropology, and human remains that begin in neither Europe nor the United States. Doing so underlines the endurance of those histories' imperial elements—but also the degree to which places like Peru shaped global history.

―――――――

This book's second conclusion is that Peru's peoples re-collected history in "ancient" bodies to remedy the imperial past and restore an Andean present. By doing so they bundled knowledges and relations that complicate assumptions of what "should" be done with the dead. For example, when Juanita or the Lady of Ampato returned to Peru, she and her climate-controlled case were installed in the Museo Santuario Andinos in the city of Arequipa. Since the late 1990s, however, locals from Cabanaconde, on whose lands Juanita was found, have sought her return. They say she "cannot rest peacefully," and that Ampato might cause water-related disasters if not returned.[14] Local authorities also protested that Arequipa profits from Juanita, and so Cabanaconde "constructed a museum that bears her name" to receive and display her to tourists, notes bioanthropologist Matthew Velasco. Peru's cultural agencies refuse their call for Juanita's return, citing a lack of conservation capabilities and supposed profit motives. But Cabanaconde's "Museo Juanita" remains open, and its heart is a replica of Juanita. The museum invites visitors to learn about the community that sought the return and display of a woman who was frozen by empire not once but twice—who had survived in ways that the Incas' yllapas had not.[15]

The Museo Juanita shows how Peru's peoples responded to the most imperial aspects of the Andean dead's mummification, collection, and editing of ancestry by reclaiming some of those functions for themselves, long before decolonization became a goal of foreign museums. As other scholars have shown, these adaptations began in the sixteenth century, when Andean peoples met Spanish looting with grave-opening of their own, sometimes to prove they were good Christian subjects deserving of ancestral wealth that Spaniards might otherwise steal, other times to re-inter ancestors elsewhere, to extend their spiritual efficacy.[16] Some communities may have chosen to give up the mummies of discredited leaders, shifting their cosmic allegiances to more recent Christian ancestors in village churches and cemeteries, and to local ancestral mountains converted with crucifixes. Over time, remains encountered in the countryside became more anonymous "grandparents" or "gentiles"—earlier owners of the land, sometimes beneficent, sometimes dangerous.[17]

Exposing the Andean dead also inspired revolutionary thought. This book has shown how, by the late seventeenth century, some Peruvians claimed that the disinterred dead were *all* Inca—murders and suicides dating to Spain's invasion. Such visions indicted colonial rule, chalking the outlines of lost and defiant Inca kings whose memory then animated resistance.[18] In the 1740s, the rebel Juan Santos Atahualpa referred specifically to the Spanish theft of Inca bodies. While José Gabriel Condorcanqui Tupac Amaru re-embodied the Inca emperors directly, their appropriation as mummified symbols of creole-led independence revealed grave-opening's anti-imperial flexibility. Its small revolutions of the soil revealed new ancestors for the nation.

After independence, the historical power of the accessible dead—mummies and skulls, ancestral or not—was again remade. Under Spanish rule, Andean, creole, and Afro-Peruvian actors had used "Inca" skulls and ceramics in healing ceremonies, attributing to them the ability to cure or sicken the living. Those practices continued into the republic, and while urban elites made private and public museums, some rural communities re-ritualized the distant dead.

In Huarochirí, one community again shouldered the mummified and "beautiful grandparents," carrying and feting them to negotiate with water-giving mountains—a ritualized reciprocity between living and dead that some communities continue to practice.[19] On the coast, even looting huacas was ritualized—a taking and giving that some outsiders denigrated as commercial huaqueo's superstitious cousin.[20]

In the late nineteenth century, grave-openers' knowledge of gentiles and abuelitos as agential beings who harmed or healed was medicalized when surgeons and anthropologists used a skull from Huayna Capac's Yucay estate to identify "prehistoric" trepanation worldwide. Some scholars challenged the resulting claims that Incas were skilled at surgery, while others sought further skulls to argue for the sophistication of Peruvian healers as a whole. Huarochirí's native son Julio César Tello claimed that science for non-Inca peoples: the live legacy of a nation of children with Indigenous parents, and not a dead past knowable only to foreign or elite scholars. Tello's dating of the origins of mummification and trepanation to temporalities earlier than the Incas, to Paracas and his own Yauyos, was part of an anti-racist anthropology that asserted the historical contributions of all Peru's Andean peoples. Tello emphasized neither their biology, nor their supposedly abject position as campesinos, but the knowledge they possessed.

That Tello did so by collecting, displaying, circulating, and sometimes selling the skulls of Andean ancestors—like the large set of trepanations he took to Harvard—underscores how past actors sought respect in ways that may not conform to present ethics. Tello transformed the antiquarian study of Andean remains by celebrating them as cultural and scientific ancestors of the nation, not racial fossils—and these celebrations again rationalized the dead's collection and display. Yet why Tello did so matters: to argue for a pre-Hispanic and pre-Inca history of science and healing as rich and variegated as that of the Old World, to combat what he called the polygenism of some Americanist anthropologists, and to claim space for Andean urban professionals like himself in the face of an elite Hispanicist racism that only accorded respect to dead Incas.[21] Tello has been celebrated as the Americas' first Indigenous archaeologist with good reason.[22] His remembrance outside of Peru might undo the vanishing of his legacy at the Smithsonian, where his trepanning Paracans were re-collected as Incas. Inside of Peru, the re-collection of his radical arguments of belonging is important given ongoing violence towards rural and Andean peoples.[23] Like other Indigenous peoples throughout the Americas, Tello countered the objectifications of anthropology and colonialism with new knowledges of his own.

Still, Tello's love of "this favorite science of unearthing cadavers" starkly contrasts with those Andean communities that protested disinterment. This too is part of Tello's legacy, joining him to the other late-nineteenth-century

Americanist anthropologists whose interest in mortuary ritual and modern "superstitions" pulled "pre-Hispanic" remains from live relationships, such as in Huarocondo, where George Dorsey and his elite Peruvian collaborator forced a community to disinter their "brothers," or in Huancabamba, where Tello slipped mummies out under cover of night. Paying attention to these protests and consequences—for example, the belief that Tello died from mummies' wrath—clarifies why some communities continue to debate anthropology as another ritual of extractive colonialism in the Andes.[24]

Yet it also draws out the importance of understanding all those Andean and Peruvian peoples who have reached for shovels and displays of their own. Some were compelled to do so. Others dug as a means of self-determination, to thwart their racialization as "Indian" vestiges of the past. Others have done so to profit from the wealth of past elites or future tourists. Still others have renovated useful ritual languages or acts of care that they extended to their own more recent ancestors. For example, as of 2016, one descendant of the Inca royal families in Cuzco, Mariano Huamanrimanchi, kept the skulls of his mother, sister, and brother on the mantelpiece next to icons of Catholic saints, as do some families throughout the southern Andes.[25] These sorts of displays in homes, stores, and schools are both more and less than acts of local resistance, or extensions of the empires or polities that claimed their subjecthood. They are rituals of knowing, mourning, and care dependent on specific contexts and constant negotiation— a dialectic older than Tawantinsuyu. Yauyo peoples remembered what happened when their powerful ancestral huaca Ñan Sapa was taken by the Incas to Cuzco. By making a bone mask to re-embody him, his dancing descendants re-collected Ñan Sapa from the empire—much like modern Cabanaconde's replica of Juanita.[26]

But is this what Ñan Sapa, Juanita, and their siblings would have wanted? Or is any re-collection a trespass against them? Modern fictions imagine the Andean dead's ire at their displacement. In 1924 Peruvian writer Ventura García Calderón's short story "The Mummy" ended with a collector discovering his own daughter, mummified, in the tomb he is looting.[27] Belgian comic artist Hergé's boy reporter Tintin faced his own vengeful Inca mummy two decades later. In *The Seven Crystal Balls* (1948), "Rascar Capac" vanishes in a ball of lightning, punishes those who collected him, and haunts Tintin's dreams before liberating himself in a way that the "Incas" in museums who inspired Hergé could not (see plate 12).[28] Other mummies are less fortunate. In 1997, in an episode of the US television show *Buffy the Vampire Slayer,* a vampiric "Inca Mummy Girl" clearly inspired by Juanita hungers for life as an American teenager before dying again at Buffy's hands.[29] The paintings of Gauguin and Munch that hide Andean mummies answer the question less obviously, masking their specific challenge in more universal themes of life, death, and existential angst.

It would be short-sighted to dismiss these visions as fictions written by outsiders: there are no outsiders here. Like tales of Indian or Egyptian curses, these tales reflect a shared awareness of the accusing stares of the lifelike seated Andean dead encountered in the Quai Branly, the American Museum of Natural History, or the countryside of Huarochirí.[30] The violence projected from these remains is proportional to their real dislocations, as Huarochiranos believed in the case of Julio Tello's death-by-tomb-raiding. Even when played for nervous laughs, they suggest an opening of debts, as in the case of two "Inca" mummies gifted to an American mining engineer named Lyman Chatfield in 1916, in northern Chile. "One of them, a young lady, I opened up on the boat coming back, and it fell apart," Chatfield told a writer for the New Yorker in 1942. "I had to throw it into the ocean. I don't know anything about these things." In a box beneath his sofa was the other, a child twenty-two inches long, of "indeterminate sex." The child had been displayed at Southern Methodist University for twenty-six years, and the American Museum of Natural History in New York was interested in borrowing the body, but Chatfield wanted "to get something out of it." He hoped for "two hundred dollars," the New Yorker reported, "but we got an idea you could have it for less."[31]

This final section surveys how some actors in Peru and the United States have answered the accusatory or beseeching stare in recent years—an accounting of the possible obligations created by the Andean dead's entanglement of Peruvian and American museums since the nineteenth century. There are no conclusions here, and the diversity of dialogues over the re-collection of Andean "mummies" and Indigenous bodies from Peru and the many places that the mortuary Inca Empire extended—Argentina, Bolivia, Chile, Ecuador—warn against generalization.[32] But there are nonetheless a number of recent examples that, in the aggregate, show how a half-millennium of encounter yielded an ancestral population that continues to break the bounds of the museums and temporalities that pen them in. The dead themselves continue to create new identities, relationships, and surprising outcomes, from repatriations and collaborations to the transformation of museum spaces in an Andean image. As Gabriela Wiener imagined, these nonmetaphorical skeletons in museums' closets move our sense of obligation.

Julio Tello's ancestralization of all pre-Hispanic remains has been key to this wider shift in perspective. Although researchers continue to seek the remains of the lost Inca yllapas in Lima, Peruvian archaeologists lead efforts at educating more rural communities about the damage done by looting other national "ancestors" for international smugglers.[33] In the other direction, those

communities have taught Peruvian archaeologists that in whisking away finds
to Lima or regional cities like Arequipa, as in the case of Juanita, they might as
well have taken them to New York. One result is the development of "Museos de
Sitio": site museums that keep archaeological finds and human remains close to
local descendants.[34] Since 1992, for example, bio-anthropologist Sonia Guillén
has directed the Centro Mallqui, which conserves mummies exposed by looting,
curating them in museums owned by local communities on the southern coast
and the department of Amazonas.

Some Peruvian anthropologists grapple with how past treatments of Peruvian
ancestors as "mummies" could contribute to a global culture of their objectifi-
cation. " 'Mummy' is a category that erases the subject," writes anthropologist
Sandra Rodríguez. "One says 'mummy' and the person becomes a specimen."[35]
Some anthropologists came to this disquiet amid the political violence of the
1980s and 1990s, when over sixteen thousand Peruvians—many from Andean
communities—disappeared during the Peruvian military's war against Maoist
rebels. Families of the disappeared continue to seek their lost loved ones and
have refused state-led attempts to quell their mourning.[36] Bio-anthropologists
like Elsa Tomasto Cagigao assisted in that postconflict work of identifying remains, and since have reflected upon how putatively scientific displays, rather
than evoking a connection between a public and its ancestors, can literally al-
ienate them.[37] In 2017 Tomasto Cagigao had to debate a Mexican "ufologist"
on Peruvian television, to explain to the public that "Maria," the "mummy" of
a three-fingered and three-toed "humanoid" that the ufologist promoted, was
an Andean ancestor that had been looted, mutilated and powdered eerily white
using diatomaceous earth. "There's a crime here," she had to explain.[38]

That "Maria" was one of several "humanoid" mummies promoted by an esoteric media platform in Boulder, Colorado, is a reminder of transnational
responsibilities for this story. In the United States, public discussions of the
Indigenous dead have affected those of the Andes at least since the 1980s, when
some Native North Americans and Peruvians protested the Andean dead's display at events like the Knoxville World's Fair.[39] NAGPRA's subsequent passage
did not formally affect American museums' possession of Indigenous remains
from outside the United States, but it did lead to many being removed from
display, and it educated anthropologists in both countries regarding widening
differences in national norms. Sonia Guillén protested Juanita's departure, for
example, by observing that "public exhibition . . . in the United States would
be offensive to American Indians, who have opposed the display of indigenous
human remains and religious artifacts."[40]

Public consciousness regarding the return or repatriation of archaeological collections is also a factor. In the late 1990s and early 2000s, Native North
American groups amplified calls to halt popular traveling displays of Andean

mummies.[41] More successful were nationalist efforts like that of Peru, which in 2010, after over a decade of public pressure, convinced Yale University to return the collection taken from the tombs of Huayna Picchu (commonly known as Machu Picchu) by Hiram Bingham in 1912. Although Peruvian discourse centered far more on the Peabody Museum's possession of Machu Picchu's "artifacts" than the human remains of 174 of its largely unfree servants, some of which had been used in Yale anatomy classes, the university returned both to a museum in Cuzco managed by the University of Cuzco. Residents of Machu Picchu's adjacent town were upset, hoping the collection might have gone there instead. The parties involved have described the move as generating future scientific collaboration, such as the use of the Machu Picchu dead's bones and teeth to suggest an earlier date for the site's inhabitation.[42]

Yale studiously avoided the language of repatriation, but other foreign museums have since returned other artifacts believed to be stolen—such as a mummy smuggled out from Peru in 1986 and textiles stolen from Tello's last museum.[43] The possibility of the return of further Andean human remains has been mooted. At an online conference based in Huarochirí in 2021, Peruvian paleopathologist Guido Lombardi delivered a paper written with Bradymir Bravo, a University of San Marcos–trained archaeologist, highlighting the trepanned skulls collected by Tello and Hrdlička. Those skulls are today split between Harvard and the Smithsonian, but also San Diego's Museum of Us (formerly the Museum of Man), which permitted a company named Bone Clones Inc. to make and sell "osteological reproductions" of Andean skulls for $278 each. Lombardi noted that NAGPRA's terms exclude non-US Indigenous remains from consideration but that its spirit might be applied to Andean remains as well.[44] Other Andean ancestors can be specifically retraced. For example, the mummies of Huarocondo and Huancabamba taken by George Dorsey and Julio César Tello, respectively, can be followed to Chicago's Field Museum and Harvard's Peabody Museum.[45]

Where repatriations might go, however, can be neither dictated nor predicted. Lombardi explored the possibility of in situ reinstallation of Huarochirí remains in the tombs from which they were taken, but some communities in the area have relocated many of the remaining skulls and mummies into museums of their own—to protect them from looters, they say. It is also worth noting that some South American anthropologists have been leery of foreign-initiated conversations regarding museums' possession of pre-Hispanic ancestors. "We can handle human remains our way," Lombardi explained on another occasion: "honoring our ancestors appropriately both by studying them, storing them the best we can, and whenever the chance occurs, by displaying them contextually."[46] Not all would agree with the decision to display them "whenever the chance occurs," but it is hard to imagine Peruvian museums dispensing with what Tello imagined as one of their chief functions: care for Andean human remains in the face of looting. "At the very least every museum might incorporate a special place to honor our mallkis, our dead," anthropologist Sandra Rodríguez recently concluded. "Ceremonial spaces where they assume their character as ancestors. Because when we shrink the distance they are simply the grandparents of our grandparents."[47]

Foreign scholars and even some museums are taking the time to understand these conditions. San Diego's Museum of Us, for example, removed its Andean remains from display and is repatriating the Native North American remains in its collection before addressing ancestors collected outside of the United States, such as those of Peru.[48] In early 2023, the Smithsonian announced that it was placing temporary restrictions on research on any human remains in its collection—not just Native North Americans—while it developed an Institution-wide policy for "the appropriate care, shared stewardship or ethical return of human remains."[49] Museums are therefore catching up to the work of scholars in Peru, such as bioanthropologists who are particularly sensitized to how their work intersects with multiple ethical and intellectual needs and national norms. Some feel called to recuperate the context destroyed by the Andean dead's prior looting or racialized analysis. They seek to better understand their mortuary care, cranial modification, pre-Hispanic skull surgery, or experience of layers of imperial violence, including their collection.[50] North American anthropologists and Peruvian colleagues write of not just soliciting government permission to excavate, but going beyond the law by consulting communities, whose desires can be economic and not just patrimonial. Anthropologists are enlisted in rituals for the past and present dead. These collaborations can lead to excavations preceded by payments to huacas or ancestors or dangerous nonancestral beings—a recognition of their lasting temporality in the present.[51]

At the same time, scholars like Frank Salomon and Kathleen Fine-Dare have offered examples that warn against projecting models of North American Indigeneity upon the Andean dead, lest they reproduce anthropology's "race-based" logic.[52] European and American-led efforts at decolonizing museums or anthropology may be challenged by Peru's far older project of decolonizing global history using Andean ancestors. For example, Weltmuseum Wien recently entertained a visit by Peru's new ambassador to Vienna. The ethnographic museum's director asked if Austria could return the Peruvian mummies it had in storage—some still in their earlier display cases. The ambassador's reply? He wanted the Weltmuseum Wien to instead put those mummies *on display* in a Peruvian room of their own, like those dedicated to Mexico and Brazil, where they might provoke discussion.[53]

To look at that reply critically, Andean mummies might still enjoy a kind of "diplomatic immunity" when it comes to Peruvian state interest in their return. As this book has shown, that state has worked hard to move them abroad. Communities adjacent to where these mummies were found might have responded differently. But it also leads us to consider how offers of "return" yield deeper discussions, in which parties can counter with requests of their own: investments more "present" than the return of ancestors, such as research collaboration, help with infrastructure, land claims, or even museums to display those ancestors to potential tourists. They may even ask foreign museums to make their debts more obvious, to assist in further research, or to *remain* responsible for the curation of Andean ancestors abroad. These older ways of escaping the "impossible museum" of Andean history, as written by outsiders, bracket recent Euro-American attempts at de-colonization, such as commitments of US institutions like the Smithsonian, Harvard, and the University of Pennsylvania to review the white supremacist roots of their wider anatomical collections.[54] They are also the product of centuries of efforts of Andean peoples to educate themselves and others about the necessity of understanding their predecessors as subjects who are sometimes ancestral, and sometimes historical, but who remain actors in their own right.[55] Decolonizing Western museums without attending to the Andean dead's lasting power to both help and harm the living can dangerously retrace the colonial and racializing paths that first collected them.

Once again, the Smithsonian has faced these questions before. Since the 1980s, the 160 "ancient Peruvians" that constituted the Skull Wall have been in the National Museum of Natural History's off-display research collection, along with the museum's only extant Andean mummy and another 4,690 lots of human remains from Peru—still the NMNH's largest single population. As more Native and Black American remains are returned, Peru's proportional share of the NMNH collection will get even bigger. The Smithsonian's National Museum of the American Indian (NMAI), however, more actively addressed the non-US human remains it inherited upon its 1989 foundation. In 1996 the NMAI sent thirteen "ancient" Peruvian bones to the area of Ausangate, a mountain being "of great symbolic relevance to its present-day Indian communities" in the Cuzco region. Two father-and-son communicators to Ausangate, or *paqos,* Mariano and Nazario Turpo, then ritually interred the thirteen bones near their town, Pacchanta.[56]

However, as anthropologist Marisol de la Cadena notes, the Turpos did not see this as "repatriation of ancestral remains." Rather, they called it "burying *suq'a* in Pacchanta." And "suq'a are not just bones," De la Cadena explains,

> let alone bones of ancestors that need to be buried in the rightful place, as is the case in North America. Rather, suq'a are remains of beings from a different era; popular wisdom in Cuzco has it that these beings were burned by the sun, an episode that marks the separation between

our era and that of the suq'a. Their current contact with living beings (mostly humans but perhaps also plants and animals) can cause diseases and even bring death. Nazario remembered: *The suq'a was with its body, with its bones; it was in the museum, they brought it here.* He was not too concerned, he said, about this suq'a because he thought they had lost power: *You know, Marisol, there was nothing like petroleum [before], or gas, nor priests to say masses, or holy water. That is why suq'akuna were bold. But now—I do not know if it is because they have been blessed, or because of the gas—they have become tamed, they are not that evil [anymore].*

What the NMAI delivered as the "remains of the ancestors," the Turpos received as suq'akuna, "potentially dangerous entities" that needed several offerings "to prevent and curtail the possible negative effects of bringing suq'a to the village." The NMAI officials there for the occasion "were thrilled to witness what they thought was a celebration of the repatriation." But for the Turpos it was an extension of a far older contest and combination of Andean and Christian temporalities and museum functions. The suq'akuna had been "tamed" by their time away, their blessing by a priest, and possibly even their treatment with gasoline, used by twentieth-century ethnological museums to preserve "specimens" from insects.[57]

This reception was not Nazario's "mistake," de la Cadena notes. It marked the complexity of his stance between the remains and what he called the "Museo del Inka Americano, thus avoiding [Peru's] negative connotation of Indian." When the NMAI later brought Nazario to Washington to consult on an exhibit, only those parts of his life that were "Quechua . . . without mixtures" went on display in a section on ancestral "traditional knowledge." Internationally famous, Nazario then returned to Peru to work in Cuzco's tourism industry as an "Andean shaman."[58]

In sum, this "repatriation" reassured the NMAI, but it also extended a longer, sometimes imperial history of engaging Peruvian bodies and knowledges as distant Indigenous American ancestry. The re-collection of Nazario as a "traditional" possessor of "ancient" knowledge and ancestors made it hard to see how Andean expertise in the dead, the living, and their care has shaped science, museums, and anthropology in Peru and the Americas for centuries.[59] The "return" of remains also laid the burden of the museum's goals upon an individual, rather than engaging the wider communities to which they belong. Quechua is the most widely spoken language in the Americas, linguist Américo Mendoza Mori observes—six to eight million of its speakers reside in the Andes. In the United States, there are over 628,000 Peruvian-Americans who, if engaged, may have their own goals—such as space in the NMAI to honor "grandparents of our grandparents" brought to the United States before them.[60] Yet the suq'akuna had made their way, and Nazario made the best of them, building an even more entangled expertise from the exchange—his status as a "shaman" who could heal suq'akuna and North American consciences alike. He was able to do so because of his right understanding that the Smithsonian was also an outcome of Andean remains and Peruvian history. It was a Museum of the American Inca.

From the sixteenth century to the twentieth, Incas, Spaniards, Peruvians, North Americans, and others used the "ancient" bodies of Andean peoples to craft vast, often imperial histories. Some desecrated them. Others re-collected them in historic and racial terms that overflowed Peru's colonial and republican borders, shaping the scientific practices of other empires and polities. Through American anthropology, these re-collections affected other peoples who saw their own ancestors amassed on scales imitative of Peru. Yet Peru's peoples also wove more complicated stories of the people who preceded them: that they were healers, even suicides who defied imperial rule, people who were only sometimes "dead." To write of American anthropology's Peruvian ancestors is to understand how the bodies of many were re-collected as one and relegated to a racialized past. But it also shows how Peru's peoples crafted and displayed knowledges and histories concerned with care, and how Andean remains continue to act upon the living. These details warn against conclusions that treat Andean remains as problems to "solve" rather than as bundles of actors and intentions who will either outlast the institutions that seek to contain them or, perhaps more radically, will continue their weathering or decay.

For that reason, there is no end to this story. The Andean dead continue to experience looting, as well as dispossession by institutions unknown to their descendants. They also remain collaborators, willing or not, shaping their descendants' understanding of the past. In 2018, for example, archaeologists located a nine-thousand-year-old burial of a woman whose "big-game hunting kit" challenged a basic tenet of archaeologists regarding ancient peoples everywhere—"that males hunted and females gathered." This finding was the result of local collaborator A. Pillco Quispe's discovery of artifacts nearby, but it was also an unforeseen consequence of the woman's interment by her community— an action that extended her personhood and their will.[61] Her excavation undid that interment but rippled her personhood into the collection space where she ended up. It is too easy to dismiss Tello's description of Peruvian museums as temples for the dead as nationalist sentiment. His own burial suggests his heartfelt literalism: that Peru's museums—around the world—are always and already mortuary spaces, claimed by empires, nations, and the Andean ancestors that move us in return. How we respond therefore matters.

Here, then, is one final story about them, and about us. After 2014, a recent American college graduate named Madeleine Fontenot became an edu-
cator at the Corpus Christi Museum of Science and History, her South Texas
hometown's science museum. Fontenot had received her bachelor's degree in
anthropology at the University of Oklahoma, and before being hired, she had
heard that the museum had an "Inca mummy." She was excited to see it during
an onboarding tour, until collections manager Jillian Becquet opened a cabinet
and took down a white archival box.[62]

Inside was a small six- to eight-year-old girl from the Andes, the museum
believed. Bound circumflex in a rope bundle just under twenty inches long, she
had come to Corpus Christi in 1957 with the museum's first permanent director,
Aalbert Heine. Heine came from the American Museum of Natural History,
where he had spent his final month "'pestering' his colleagues at the museum for
spare collection items." Their "gifts" were a museum in miniature: a whale bone,
a moose jaw, spare pottery, and this "Inca mummy," one of over forty brought to
the AMNH by its expeditions, Heine told the *Corpus Christi Times*.[63]

What struck Fontenot, as Becquet opened the box, was how the words "Inca
mummy" hid the reality wrapped in tissue paper before her: a child, "so small, so
out of place," and far from home. At her university, many of Fontenot's professors
and fellow students had been Indigenous. In classes, they had discussed
NAGPRA and the "Ancient One" or "Kennewick Man"—a nine-thousand-
year-old individual found in Washington State in 1996, and only returned to
Columbia Basin tribes by physical anthropologists in 2017. Fontenot realized
that Corpus Christi shared that story. "I was not excited anymore," she recalled.
"I just felt sad."[64]

Becquet had her own misgivings about the museum's possession of the girl.
She explained why she would never again be on display, how she no longer fit
the museum's local mission, and how her study was limited by the lack of documentation with which she arrived. "It's somebody's daughter," she explained.
"It's somebody's sister and they took care of her body. And then somebody took
it and brought her here."[65]

Fontenot and Becquet decided to act. They sought details that might confirm her connection with a country or people, rather than an imaginative "Inca"
label. Becquet was surprised to learn that the AMNH reported no record
of the girl even being in their collection, let alone going to Texas with Heine.
Anthropologists were more helpful, confirming that the rope bundling matched
pre-Hispanic mummies from Peru. A local hospital X-rayed the girl, revealing
disquieting traces of prior display—metal loops in her wrappings, likely used
to hang her from a wall. But they also showed a shape to the skull that, despite
Samuel George Morton, is today understood as indicative of artificial cranial
modification. That, and the rope bundling, were suggestive of pre-Hispanic

Collagua communities from the upper reaches of Arequipa's Colca Valley, whose sacred mountain, Ampato, was where Juanita had been found. "We have remains of yours," Fontenot informed the Peruvian embassy in Washington, DC.[66]

Repatriations take time. In late 2018 the return took place at the Peruvian consulate in Houston. It gave Becquet and Fontenot a moment of pause to learn where the girl was headed next—a museum in Lima's capital. They had a "secret hope," Becquet admitted, that the girl would not have gone to the capital city. Having "grown up around NAGPRA," they had perhaps imagined she would go "close[r] to home," nearer a community. But that was a question for Peru, Becquet explained: "Peruvian hands were the goal."[67]

The moment was nonetheless bittersweet. Despite having done the work to relocate the girl, neither Fontenot nor Becquet attended the ceremony, having been among the staff let go when a new private management company took over the museum. They nevertheless cried together when they heard the news—out of relief, but also disbelief. They had done something so many other American museums had not. It was the proudest moment of Fontenot's career, she later reflected. But she also wanted to know more about where the child went.[68]

The child's destination was Julio César Tello's National Museum of Archeology, Anthropology and History (MNAAH). When the "Inca mummy" girl got off the plane in Peru in February 2019, she was taken there for a press conference presided over by the Ministries of Foreign Affairs and Culture and attended by the museum's new director, Dr. Sonia Guillén, who had protested Juanita's display in the United States and whose Centro Mallqui sought better curations of the Andean dead. The museum's archaeologists told the press what they knew. They confirmed that the child's cranial shaping and funerary bindings seemed to correspond to the cultural practices of elite Collaguas from the Colca Valley. The ministry posited that the child—who was now described as being between two and four years old, and a boy—had possibly been looted before ending up at the AMNH.[69]

The ritual that followed was as dense as any other. The press conference was in the museum's lecture salon, whose walls bore the portraits of Lima's colonial viceroys—the men who had once ruled the Incas in the name of the Spanish Crown—but also a famed painting of South American patriot José de San Martín, the first non-Peruvian to send an "Inca mummy" abroad. Reporters watched two of the museum's anthropologists, two women in surgical masks, open the box that Becquet had taken down from a shelf, revealing the delicate child. The child's new home was, like any museum, precarious in its own way—the Peruvian government was about to start starving the MNAAH of the funds it needed to stay open, spending them on a newer Museum of the Nation whose displays threatened to cannibalize the collections of Peru's most broadly ancestral museum.[70] But not the child, not yet. For the moment, she was a little further along in her odyssey of care, separation, knowledge, and return.

While the press filed their stories, uploading photographs and videos of the event to Facebook, the museum's employees carefully rebundled the child and turned the lights out on the viceroys and San Martín.[71] They carried the box around to the back patio, past the obelisk where Julio César Tello's embalmed body was interred. They unlocked the museum's deposit. They placed the child amid new ancestors. Then, they wrapped up their workday, locked the doors, and went home, to care for loved ones and descendants of their own.

ACKNOWLEDGMENTS

This book has suggested that Andean ancestors have defied their collection by seeding care among the descendants, curators, and visitors who seek them. At some point in the twelve years it took to research and write this book, I was reminded of those seeds when I accidentally flipped a photograph of the Smithsonian's Skull Wall on its head. This simple inversion turned the Skull Wall from an explosion of death to a tree's bottom half—bony roots reaching earthward to support an invisible canopy of branches above. This reminder of still-present life, with its unseen descendants asking for consideration, was perhaps the display's subliminal message all along. Inverting the photograph once again, to write these acknowledgments, I was struck by a second detail I missed in all the years I'd looked at it: there is a plant of some sort reaching toward the Skull Wall from the lower right corner (or down from the upper left corner when inverted). The plant's base is invisible, as is the person who must have planted and watered it. But its leaves are evidence of their care.

I am grateful to be able to thank the many people who cared for this book's roots, even as I mourn those who missed its flower. First, for trusting me with its beginning, I thank my mentors, friends, and colleagues from the University of Texas at Austin, where this book began as a dissertation co-advised by Jorge Cañizares Esguerra and Seth Garfield. I am eternally grateful to Jorge and Seth for their challenging questions and care for me as a person. Seth's rigor, sense of humor, and dedication to long Indigenous histories of survival gave this work a compass. Jorge's capacious insights, unstinting support, and critiques of American history's walls opened its most surprising doors. I thank Susan Deans-Smith, Lina Maria del Castillo, Alison Frazier, Ginny Garrard, Bruce Hunt, Jackie Jones, Jim Sidbury, and Ann Twinam, for helping me grow. José Barragán, Rachel Ozanne, Pablo Mijangos, and Matt Powers—thank you for being such rolemodels for life in and out of this profession. I am grateful to Bruce and Megan Raby for inviting me back to speak on Morton to the History and Philosophy of Science Colloquium, and to Marilyn Lehman and Courtney Meador, who kept me going. I thank Erika Bsumek for her wisdom, friendship, and sense of empathy and perspective. And I thank R. Alan Covey, whose continued thoughts on all things Inca, and many reads of this book's chapters, gave me hope that this book might be useful to anthropology as well.

I am grateful to the many archivists, librarians, curators, and institutional historians whose care for their collections and interest in their accessible and equitable future made this book's research conceivable. In Peru, I thank Maria Eugenia Huayanca Cajigao, Alexander Ortegal Izquierdo, Elizabeth López, and Rocio López de Castilla of the archives of the Museo Nacional de Arqueología, Antropología y Historia in Lima, its former librarian Benjamin Guerrero Ramón, its current director Rafael Varón Gabai, and José Salazar, the museum's former artist; Victor Paredes Castro for his curation of the Tello archive of the Universidad Nacional Mayor de San Marcos's Museo de Arqueologia y Antropologia, and Henry Tantaleán Ynga, its director; all those at the Biblioteca de la Facultad de Medicina de San Fernando, the Archivo General de la Nación in Lima, and the Biblioteca Nacional of Peru, and Ramón Mujica Pinillo, its former director; the archivists of the former Instituto Nacional de Cultura, now the Ministerio de Cultura in Lima, and Fernando Brugue Valcárcel, for encouraging my use of his grandfather's papers; and Ada Arrieta Álvarez and her fellow archivists at the Instituto Riva-Agüero, Lima. In Spain, I think the caretakers of the Archivo General de Indias, and Beatriz Robledo and Encarnación Hidalgo Cámara at the archives of the Museo de América.

In the United States, I thank the UT Benson Latin American Collection's staff, including AJ Johnson and Michael Hironymous, former archivist, and Eric Novotny, Manuel Ostos, and Clara Drummond at the Pattee and Paterno Library at Penn State. Pamela Henson, Ellen Alers, and Tad Bennicoff were generous guides to the Smithsonian Institution Archives and its sister collections at the Archives of American Art, National Museum of Natural History, and National Anthropological Archives, as were Courtney Gray Bellizi, Brian Daniels, David R. Hunt, Daisy Njoku, Marguerite Roby, David Rosenthal, and Richard Stamm. I thank Megan Gibes at the Academy of Natural Sciences Archive; Roy Goodman and Adrianna Link at the American Philosophical Society; Annie Brogan and Anna N. Dhody at the College of Physicians of Philadelphia; Alessandro Pezzati and Clark Erickson at the University of Pennsylvania Museum; David Hurst Thomas and Kristen Mabel at the American Museum of Natural History; Armand Esai, Lauren Hancock, Ryan Williams, and Rebecca Wilke at the Field Museum of Natural History; Chris Weideman and Bill Massa at Yale's Manuscripts and Archives; Patricia Kervick at Harvard's Peabody Museum of Archaeology and Ethnology; and the many other curators at the Historical Society and Library Company of Philadelphia,

Princeton University Rare Books and Special Collections, the Rockefeller Archive Center, the Harvard University Archives, the Center for the History of Medicine Archives at the Countway Library, the American Antiquarian Society, and the US National Archives.

A book with so many archives behind it is the product of incredible privilege, institutional support, and opportunities to air new ideas. I thank the Donald D. Harrington Scholars Program for bringing me to UT Austin, and Carla Yanni, Bill Leslie, and the Social Science Research Council's Dissertation Proposal Development Fellowship Program for broadening my work's foundations. I am grateful to Babak Ashrafi and Simon Joseph at the Consortium for History of Science, Technology and Medicine in Philadelphia. I would not have gotten back to Peru without a Fulbright-Hays Graduate Fellowship and the support of Henry Harman, Marcela Harth, and Julissa Espinoza, or without the help of Pedro Guibovich and Marco Curatola, who lent me an institutional home in the Programa de Estudios Andinos of the Pontificia Universidad Católica del Perú. Audiences at the Asociación Peruana de Historia y Estudios Sociales de la Ciencia, la Tecnología y la Salud, the University of San Marcos, and the Museo Nacional de Arqueología, Antropología y Historia in Lima, and the LAGLOBAL network in Madrid gave me especially crucial feedback. A Barra Postdoctoral Fellowship at the McNeil Center for Early American Studies at the University of Pennsylvania thoroughly transformed my project; I remain grateful for the guidance of Dan Richter and Kathy Brown, and for the inspiration, friendship, and critical reads of Emilie Connolly, Liz Ellis, Nancy Gallman, Emma Hart, Elaine LaFay, Melissa Morris, and Jeremy Zallen. At Penn State, I am thankful to my first dean, the late Susan Welch, and to Clarence Lang, who supported me in a very hard time. I thank John Christman, Lauren Kooistra, and the Humanities Institute at Penn State for the time to worry this project's ramifications. For the opportunity to gain feedback on my work in progress, and the permission to extend that work, I thank the editors and anonymous readers of *Isis: A Journal of the History of Science Society*, the *History of Anthropology Review,* the *American Historical Review*, Yale University Press, and Oxford University Press. I thank Nancy Torres for permission to use her sculpture, *Yachaya*, as this book's cover.

Some of the most important insights in this book have come from the friends, writers, artists, editors, academics, and museum professionals who have taken the time to share research leads, read versions of chapters or proposals, respond to questions, or be encouraging. I am grateful to Claudia Augustat, Fernando Bedoya, Bradymir Bravo, Roberto Chauca, my agent Dan Conaway, Mackenzie Cooley, Jesse Cromwell, Rosanna Dent, Stefanie Gänger, Andrew Hamilton, Curtis M. Hinsley, Kelly Hyberger, Renata Keller, Guido Lombardi, Natalia Majluf, Américo Mendoza Mori, Paul Wolff Mitchell, Lyra Monteiro, Catherine Gilbert Murdock, Barbara Mundy, Linda Newson, Maria Patricia

Ordoñez, Bianca Premo, José Carlos de la Puente Luna, Monica Ricketts, Jordi Rivera Prince, Julia Rodríguez, Miguel Rosas Buendía, Erik Seeman, Sarah Senk, Nancy Shoemaker, Sarah Steinbock-Pratt, Henry Tantaleán Ynga, Mark Thurner, Sarah Van Beurden, Kukuli Velarde, Matthew Velasco, Vanessa Wagner, Charles Walker, Adam Warren, Kerry Webb, Eyal Weinberg, and Isaiah Wilner. I thank Antonio Coello and David Mogrovejo Vidal for key research help. At Penn State, I'm lucky to have colleagues and friends as generous as Jyoti Balachandran, Kate Baldanza, José Capriles, James Doyle, Lori Ginzberg, Michelle Kennerly, Kate Merkel-Hess, Amanda Scott, Christina Snyder, Lior Sternfeld, and the students of "Exhibiting Incas." Michelle Sikes and Abigail Celis were wonderful writing partners. My fellow Latin Americanists, Martha Few, Zachary Morgan, Matthew Restall, and Amara Solari, gave tremendous feedback, as did the wonderful students who reacted to the manuscript. I thank Scott Doebler and Ana Hidrovo for their excellent research assistance in particular. I am grateful to have had a department head as supportive and thoughtful as Michael Kulikowski. I thank Keshia Kennelly, Lynn Monoski, and Amber Thomas. Last, I thank the Peruvian Student Association at Penn State for their confidence in me.

In a special category are those friends and colleagues without whom this book would not have existed. I consider it one of the gifts of my professional life to have learned from Ann Fabian, Pedro Guibovich, Irina Podgorny, and Frank Salomon, between whose brilliant research this book sits. I thank Veronika Tupayachi and the late Donato Amado for orienting me in this work in Cuzco, nearly two decades ago. Benjamin Breen, Brian Jones, Amy Kohout, José Ragas, and Cameron Strang changed the course of this project many times over. They read every word of this book between them, and though any errors are mine I credit their friendship and scholarship for its best stretches. Last, I am so honored to have Susan Ferber as my editor, and Oxford University Press as a publisher. I am grateful to my anonymous readers, and to Susan, a writer's editor, for believing in this book and caring about its prose; her handiwork is on every page.

Then there are those loved ones who kept me alive. I'm lucky to have generous stepparents in Kevin O'Brien and Vivian Heaney, and wonderful in-laws in Nancy Murdock and Randy Selden, John and Elaine Carney, and Janet Murdock. Jess and Doug, you're the best siblings a guy could ask for. Adam Chanzit, Ryan Sison, Nick Spodak, Jared Leboff, Emily Guilmette, Ryan Floyd, Ben Warrington and Katherine Gajewski, Kate Vickery and Kyle Shelton, Brendan Lynaugh, and Annie Avilés: thank you for being there.

To my parents, Brigid O'Brien and William Heaney—I float on gratitude to you for this life that you gave me. Mom, you taught me how to heal, how to tend gardens, and how to remember; also, thank you for not letting me claim that the plant next to the Skull Wall was an Australian umbrella tree. Dad, this book was always a letter to you, written in gratitude for all you valued in anthropology, questioning authority, and embracing the world. Your loss in the pandemic taught me how to mourn. I miss you.

Last, this book is dedicated to my beloved wife, Hannah, and to our wonderful sons, Curtis and Jack. Hannah, you are the warmth in my life, my first and best reader, our laughter. My dear Curtis and Jack, Overfoot and Underfoot: you are my joy.

NOTES

Introduction

1. Exhibit script: Hall of Physical Anthropology, Exhibit Unit No. 2—World Population Explosion, Folder: Hall 25, Box 2, Smithsonian Institution Archives (SIA), Record Unit (RU) 363. Unless noted, all further quotes and descriptions of Hall 25 are drawn from exhibit work orders, scripts, drawings, and photographs archived in Boxes 1, 2, and 28 of SIA RU 363, and the mapped layout of the exhibit in Box 7, Folder—Hall 25—Angel of SIA RU 366. Richard Corrigan, "Visit National History Museum and Have a Real Skull Session," *Washington Post*, 1 July 1965. See also oral history interview with T. Dale Stewart, 14 January, 12 February, 1975, conducted by Pamela M. Henson, 61–64, 135–136, SIA RU 9521 for Stewart's reflections on the scale the exhibit sought.
2. Titian Ramsay Peale, Collection of the United States South Sea Surveying and Exploring Expedition, 1838–1842, Folder 8, Ethnology, Box 1, SIA RU 7186; Aleš Hrdlička, Division of Physical Anthropology annual reports 1910–1911 and 1916–1917, Box 32, SIA RU 158.
3. David J. Hunt, the bio-anthropology collection manager at the NMNH, clarified this point to me, breaking down the modern numbers. Of over 34,000 catalogue records for human remains in the SI bio-anthropology collections in 2014, 4,851 lots of crania, long bones or other skeletal elements are from Peru, about 14 percent. Again, this is far less than the 75 percent that are, geographically speaking, from the United States, whose single largest internal population are 4,500 white and Black Americans in the anatomical skeletal collections of known individuals. "Peruvian" also nationalizes peoples of different culture groups, separated by thousands of years from across the Andes. But again, in the historical terms of their collection, the "ancient Peruvians" remain the largest. The next largest from any one country is Egypt, at about 2.2 percent. Author's correspondence with David R. Hunt, 24 February, 14 April, 16 April, 2014.
4. For how race continued to shape anthropology at the Smithsonian and other museums during the field's attempted anti-racialist shift to questions and displays of migration and culture, see Teslow, *Constructing Race*; Redman, *Bone Rooms*; and Conklin, *In the Museum of Man*.
5. Verano, *Holes in the Head*, 193, and *passim*.
6. See Amado Gonzales and Bauer, "The Ancient Inca Town Named Huayna Picchu," for the site's true name.
7. For "imperial body collecting," see Fabian, *The Skull Collectors*, 171. Maria Rostworowski de Diez Canseco (*History of the Inca Realm*, x) argues that "empire" is an inadequate if not inappropriately Old World term for what Tawantinsuyu sought to do, in attempting to bind together the Andes. It nonetheless functioned—and was at times resisted by its subjects—in ways that make other historians and archaeologists comfortable with speaking of empire.
8. Herrera, "Indigenous Archaeology," 70.
9. In this sense they are like the enslaved and Black women's bodies foundational to the development of American gynecology, per Owens, *Medical Bondage*.

10. I borrow here from the useful formulation for American archaeology's origins proposed in Conn, "Archaeology, Philadelphia, and Understanding Nineteenth-Century American Culture," 166.

11. Stocking, *Race, Culture, and Evolution*; Hinsley, *Savages and Scientists*; Bieder, *Science Encounters the Indian*; Darnell, *Invisible Genealogies*; Redman, *Bone Rooms*; Hinsley and Wilcox, *Coming of Age in Chicago*; Beck, *Unfair Labor?*

12. Achim, "Skulls and Idols"; Kehoe, "Manifest Destiny"; Blackhawk and Wilner, eds., *Indigenous Visions*; Salvatore, *Disciplinary Conquest*. Rodriguez, "No 'Mere Accumulation of Material,'" specifically and insightfully attends to the late-nineteenth-century shift to embedded evidence.

13. Hrdlička, *Physical Anthropology*, 41; Fabian, *The Skull Collectors*, 38. In Morton's last published catalogue before he died in 1851, Peruvian skulls numbered 205 of 867, while the rest of the Indigenous "Americans"—North, South, and Caribbean—numbered 206: Morton, *Catalogue of Skulls*, v–vi. By contrast, Geller, "Building Nation, Becoming Object," 53, reports that "roughly 25% of [Morton's] crania collection (about 250–300) crania were from various regional locations in North America," but the source for this estimate is unclear, and may be based on the collection as it was modified in the century after Morton died. His first posthumous catalogue, (Meigs, *Catalogue of Human Crania* (1857), 9–10), claimed there were 256 Toltecan skulls (Peruvian and Mexican), and 247 from the "Barbarous Tribes scattered across the continent"—which includes 1 "Central American," 7 "Araucanians," 3 "Brazilians," and 1 "Charib"—but are at variance with the accompanying table, where only 177 Toltecans actually appear, of which 25 are Mexican and 152 are Peruvian. This suggests that 79 "Toltecans" are not accounted for. When those 79 are added to the 152, the count becomes 231, better approximating the Peruvians' original value within the larger collection.

14. Wyman, "Report of the Curator" (1868), 5–9; Wyman, "Report of the Curator" (1873), 6.

15. As will be seen, these mummies became a founding collection of Chicago's Field Museum, but also ended up at New York's American Museum of Natural History, whose own largest population when tallied in the 1920s comprise 600 crania from Bolivia and Peru. Moorehead, "Anthropology at the World's Columbian Exposition," 20; Dorsey, "An Archaeological Study"; Redman, *Bone Rooms*, 193. The first PhD in anthropology in the United States was a Canadian named Alexander F. Chamberlain, who wrote his dissertation under Boas at Clark University in 1891; see Bernstein, "First Recipients," 557.

16. Hodgen, *Early Anthropology in the Sixteenth and Seventeenth Centuries*; Pagden, *The Fall of Natural Man*; MacCormack, *Religion in the Andes*; Cañizares-Esguerra, *Nature, Empire, and Nation*; Barrera Osorio, *Experiencing Nature*; Bleichmar, *Visible Empire*; Few, *For All of Humanity*; Norton, "Subaltern Technologies"; Achim and Podgorny, "Descripción densa"; the essays in Kohl, Podgorny, and Gänger, eds., *Nature and Antiquities*, especially Achim, "Skulls and Idols."

17. Degregori, "Panorama de la antropología en el Perú"; Salomon, "Etnología en un terreno desigual"; Sandoval, "Antropología y antropólogos en el Perú." This claim builds upon the literature that emphasizes scientific innovation in "peripheral" Latin America—see Cueto, *Excelencia científica*; Cueto and Lossio, *Innovación en la agricultura*; Gootenberg, *Andean Cocaine*, for Peru—to include more disquieting contributions to the transnational history of surveilled, racialized, or archaeologized bodies, per Peard, *Race, Place, and Medicine*, and Rodriguez, "South Atlantic Crossings." For the specific call to reapproach the history of race from a Latin American or Global South perspective, see Sweet, "The Iberian Roots"; Roque, *Headhunting and Colonialism*; Anderson, "Racial Conceptions in the Global South."

18. See Cueto, *Excelencia científica en la periferia*; Soto Laveaga, *Jungle Laboratories*; and Rosemblatt, *The Science and Politics of Race in Mexico and the United States* for key articulations of this cycle of local knowledges, their national and foreign scientific appropriations as known yet hidden things, and the effect of those appropriations on the subjects and producers of that original research. But see Cadena, *Indigenous Mestizos*, and Gildner, "Indomestizo Modernism," for how these knowledges could reproduce old exclusions of race and class in the Andes.

19. In this, I combine the points of Gould, "Entangled Histories, Entangled Worlds"; Cañizares Esguerra, *Entangled Empires*; and Blackhawk, *Violence over the Land*, to think about how

Anglo-American colonialism—here as intellectual and scientific as it was geographical and economic—benefitted from prior waves of unseen violence against Native American bodies caused by Spanish colonialism. Joseph, Le Grande, and Salvatore, *Close Encounters of Empire*, is likewide foundational to my thinking.

20. This attention to bodily itineraries is inspired by Fabian, *The Skull Collectors*, Chps. 2 and 4; Harries, "Of Bleeding Skulls"; Wagner, *The Skull of Alum Bheg*; Roque, *Headhunting and Colonialism*; and Gänger, *Relics of the Past*. The intellectual genealogy of this approach can be traced to Appadurai, ed., *The Social Life of Things*, esp. Kopytoff, "The Cultural Biography of Things"; Daston, "Introduction."

21. See Scott, *Contested Territory*, for the early presentation of Andean landscapes as rife with hidden knowledges.

22. For those subsequent encounters, see Chaplin, *Subject Matter*; Heaney, "A Peru of Their Own"; Midtrød, "Calling for More Than Human Vengeance"; and Seeman, *Death in the New World*, which usefully labels them "deathways."

23. Pagden, *The Fall of Natural Man*; MacCormack, *Religion in the Andes*; Mumford, *Vertical Empire*; Duviols, *La destrucción de las religiones andinas*; Salomon, "'The Beautiful Grandparents'"; Stephenson, "From Marvelous Antidote to the Poison of Idolatry"; Thurner, *History's Peru*; Brosseder, *The Power of Huacas*.

24. Thurner and Pimentel, "Introduction," in *New World Objects of Knowledge*, 2. See also Mundy, *The Mapping of New Spain*; Cañizares-Esguerra, *Nature, Empire, and Nation*; Bleichmar, *Visible Empire*; Portuondo, *Secret Science*; Few, *For All of Humanity*.

25. Salomon, "'The Beautiful Grandparents.'" For a Mesoamerican example of the extension of cosmologies and ontologies, see Cooley, "The Giant Remains."

26. Eeckhout and Owens, eds., *Funerary Practices and Models in the Ancient Andes*; Shimada and Fitzsimmons, eds., *Living with the Dead in the Andes*; Brosseder, *The Power of Huacas*, 134; Yaya MacKenzie, "Sovereign Bodies"; Cussen, "The Search for Idols and Saints in Colonial Peru."

27. Estenssoro Fuchs, *Del paganismo a la santidad*; Ramírez, *The World Upside Down*; Dean, *Inka Bodies*; Ramos, *Death and Conversion*; Delibes Mateos, *Desenterrando tesoros*; Klaus and Tam, "*Requiem Aeternam?*"

28. Flores Galindo, *In Search of an Inca*; Salomon, "Ancestors, Grave Robbers," "Ancestor Cults and Resistance," and "Unethnic Ethnohistory"; Abercrombie, *Pathways of Memory and Power*, 324–328; Silverblatt, *Modern Inquisitions*, 170–180; Garofalo, "Conjuring with Coca and the Inca"; Gose, *Invaders as Ancestors*. These adaptations might be considered "hybrid healings," per Cueto and Palmer, *Medicine and Public Health in Latin America*, 34–35, as well as Few, *For All of Humanity*, Chp. 2; Crawford, *The Andean Wonder Drug*; Gómez, *The Experiential Caribbean*.

29. For the history of eighteenth- and nineteenth-century political identity formation through the collection of "past" Indigenous sovereignty, see Brading, *The First America*; Estenssoro Fuchs, "Modernismo, estética, música y fiesta"; Méndez Gastelumendi, "Incas sí, Indios no"; Majluf, "De la rebelión al museo"; Cañizares-Esguerra, *How to Write*; Earle, *The Return of the Native*; Díaz Caballero, "Incaísmo as the First Guiding Fiction"; Berquist, *The Bishop's Utopia*; Cabello Carro, "Las colecciones peruanas"; Alcina Franch, *Arqueólogos o anticuarios*; Pillsbury and Trever, "The King, the Bishop, and the Creation of an American Antiquity"; Trever, "The Uncanny Tombs in Martínez Compañón's *Trujillo del Perú*." See Ordoñez, *Unbundled*, and Carter, Vilches, and Santoro, "South American Mummy Trafficking," for excellent past treatments of this diaspora.

30. For epistemes connecting colonial science and medicine to national and regional museum and knowledge projects, see Podgorny, "Fossil Dealers"; Achim and Podgorny, "Descripción densa"; Achim, *From Idols to Antiquity*; the essays in Kohl, Podgorny, and Gänger, eds., *Nature and Antiquities*, especially Achim, "Skulls and Idols"; and, specifically for Peru, Warren, *Medicine and Politics*; Gootenberg, *Andean Cocaine*; Cushman, *Guano*; Gänger, *Relics of the Past*.

31. As Appelbaum, MacPherson, and Rosemblatt, "Introduction," 13, put it more generally, "shap[ing] racialization in both North and South" America.

32. I am inspired on these points by Riggs, *Unwrapping Ancient Egypt*, and "Loose Bodies."

33. Astuhuamán and Tantaleán, eds., *Historia de la arqueología en el Perú del siglo XX*; Tantaleán, *Peruvian Archaeology*.

34. These Indigenous grave-openers were the "invisible technicians" whose expert or artisanal knowledge undergirded what became Andean archaeology: Shapin, "The Invisible Technician"; Gänger, *Relics of the Past*; Cox Hall, "Collecting a 'Lost City' for Science"; Warren, Adam. "Photography, Race, Indigeneity."

35. Tello, "Prehistoric Trephining"; Bastien, *Healers of the Andes*, 14–24; Verano, *Holes in the Head*.

36. See Cadena, *Indigenous Mestizos*; López Lenci, *El Cusco, paqarina moderna*; Heaney, *Las tumbas de Machu Picchu*; Astuhuamán and Tantaleán, eds., *Historia de la arqueología en el Perú del siglo XX*; Tantaleán, *Peruvian Archaeology*; Salvatore, *Disciplinary Conquest*; Cox Hall, *Framing a Lost City*; Asensio, *Señores del pasado*, for the broader frame of these disputes. See Rosemblatt, *The Science and Politics of Race in Mexico and the United States* for a like arc in anthropological interaction.

37. "La craniectomia en el Peru pre-historico," *El Comercio* (Lima), 5 May 1906.

38. Cadena, "From Race to Class"; Burger, ed. *The Life and Writings of Julio C. Tello* ["America's First"]; Astuhuamán and Tantaleán, eds., *Historia de la arqueología en el Perú del siglo XX*; Tantaleán, *Peruvian Archaeology*; Ramón Joffre, *El neoperuano*; Asensio, *Señores del pasado*. Richard Daggett's work on Tello is crucial, especially *An Annotated Tello-Centric History*.

39. Gutiérrez de Quintanilla, *El Manco Capac*, 19.

40. Salomon, "'The Beautiful Grandparents,'" 336.

41. As noted in Fine-Dare, "Bodies Unburied, Mummies Displayed"; Herrera, "Indigenous Archaeology"; Endere, "Archaeological Heritage Legislation and Indigenous Rights in Latin America"; Heaney, "Skull Walls."

42. Atwood, *Stealing History*; Mould de Pease, *Machu Picchu*; Heaney, *Cradle of Gold*; Heaney, *Las Tumbas*; Asensio, *Señores del pasado*; Salomon, "Unethnic Ethnohistory;" Rojas-Perez, *Mourning Remains*; Velasco, "Humans Remain."

43. Thomas, *Skull Walls*; Fine-Dare, *Grave Injustice*; Lonetree, *Decolonizing Museums*; Colwell, *Plundered Skulls*; Hicks, *The Brutish Museums*; Riding in, "Decolonizing NAGPRA"; Blakey, "Archaeology under the Blinding Light of Race"; Dunnavant, Justinvil, and Colwell, "Craft an African American Graves Protection and Repatriation Act."

44. Rodríguez, "Recuperando la mirada, el cuerpo y la voz"; Lombardi and Bravo Meza, "Tello y los restos humanos de los huarochiranos ancestrales"; Wiener, *Huaco retrato*.

45. Flores Galindo, *In Search of an Inca*, 2.

46. Julio C. Tello to M. Toribio Mejía Xesspe, June 1, 1925, in Shady Solís and Novoa Bellota, eds., *Cuadernos de investigación del Archivo Tello, No. 2*, 155.

47. Per Johnson, ed., *Death, Dismemberment, and Memory*; Verdery, *The Political Lives of Dead Bodies*; Brown, *The Reaper's Garden*;; and Laqueur, *The Work of the Dead*, 18, 81 (quotes).

48. For wonderful meditations on "acolonial" Andean things' survival of collection, see Weismantel, *Playing with Things*, Epilogue. For similar meditations on the multiple timescales of the dead in Latin America, see Johnson, ed., *Death, Dismemberment, and Memory*, and Gillingham, *Cuauhtémoc's Bones*.

Chapter 1

1. Salomon and Urioste, eds., *The Huarochirí Manuscript*, 1, 43, 99n44, 128.

2. For Huarochirí's negotiated entry to the Inca Empire, and service in its army, see Spalding, *Huarochiri*, Chp. 3; Hernández Garavito, "Legibility and Empire," 86–89; Mikecz, "Beyond Cajamarca," 205-206.

3. Or he. Gender was no barrier to being a healer or wielding its tools. Andean healers were male and female: Silverblatt, *Moon, Sun, and Witches*; Brosseder, *The Power of Huacas*; Bastien, *Healers of the Andes*, 24.

4. Tello, "Prehistoric Trephining among the Yauyos of Peru." Armus and Gómez, *The Gray Zones of Medicine*, 9, usefully note colonialism's mystique of "seemingly stable medical systems."

5. For the *huañuc* continuum between the living and the dead, see Salomon, "'The Beautiful Grandparents,'" 328–329.

6. This description of trepanation's diagnoses, techniques, and tools, and Huarochirí's healers' success rate (55.6 percent of Huarochirí's trepanned patients completely healed), draws from the work of Julio César Tello, who took this particular man's skull while writing his "Prehistoric Trephining among the Yauyos of Peru," and bioanthropologist John Verano, whose *Holes in the Head*, 60–62, discusses this man's two operations. On breath and Andean healing, see Bastien, *Healers of the Andes*, 16, citing Jorge Flores Ochoa.

7. Salomon and Urioste, eds., *The Huarochirí Manuscript*, 129.

8. Ibid., Chps. 9, 11, 27, 28; Salomon, " 'The Beautiful Grandparents' "; Avendaño, *Sermones*, 44v; Rostworowski, *History of the Inca Realm*, 157–158; Isbell, *Mummies and Mortuary Monuments*, 92–97. It is important to note that the term *mallki* does not appear in the Yauyo-focused Huarochirí manuscript, it being a term that Spanish priests learned in their extirpations elsewhere, but scholars use its logic to explain the crafting of mummified ancestors in general.

9. Hernández Garavito, "Producing Legibility through Ritual"; Salomon, "Turbulent Tombs," 329–334; Verano, *Holes in the Head*, 60, 62.

10. For other informed and responsible narrations of histories and lives either made invisible or cut short by colonialism or violence, see Richter, *Facing East from Indian Country*, and Hartman, "Venus in Two Acts." For reflections on how the specific colonial context of Andean ethnographic sources must be understood to be surpassed, see Salomon, "The Historical Development of Andean Ethnology"; MacCormack, "Ethnography in South America."

11. Salomon and Urioste, *The Huarochirí Manuscript*, 41, 42. Further works directly addressing the Quechua manuscript's creation by an Indigenous intellectual (and use by Ávila) include Arguedas and Duviols, *Dioses y hombres*; Taylor and Acosta, *Ritos y tradiciones*; Salomon and Urioste, *The Huarochirí Manuscript*; Durston, "Notes on the Authorship"; Ramos and Yannakakis, eds., *Indigenous Intellectuals*—in particular, Durston, "Cristóbal choquecasa," and de la Puente Luna, "Choquecasa va a la audiencia."

12. Tello, *La antigüedad de la sífilis en el Perú*, 139; Tello, "Prehistoric Trephining among the Yauyos of Peru"; Verano, *Holes in the Head*, 60, 62.

13. Huan and Cock Carrasco, "A Bioarchaeological Approach to the Search for Mitmaqkuna"; Williams and Murphy, "Living and Dying as Subjects of the Inca Empire"; Velasco, "Ethnogenesis and Social Difference"; Hu and Quave, "Prosperity and Prestige."

14. Yaya MacKenzie, "Sovereign Bodies."

15. As Chapter 6 discusses, the words of American journalist Fannie B. Ward captured that perception best: "Dig anywhere and you cannot go amiss of a grave" (Ward, "Mummies of Peru," 1). Aufderheide, *The Scientific Study of Mummies*, remains a foundational modern text that maintains the natural or artificial distinction.

16. Rivera, "The Preceramic Chinchorro Mummy Complex"; Marquet et al., "Emergence of Social Complexity"; Kaulicke, "Corporealities of Death"; Lau, "Different Kinds of Dead"; Dillehay and Kolata, "Long-Term Human Response."

17. Boone, "Preface," viii, points out how culturally important these environmental conditions must have been.

18. Peters, "The Cemetery of Paracas Necropolis"; Verano, *Holes in the Head*, Chp. 5, though see 234 for trepanned crania from Bolivia that could be older. For solar-hydraulic recycling, see Gose, "Segmentary State Formation."

19. Salomon, " 'The Beautiful Grandparents' "; Abercrombie, *Pathways of Memory and Power*.

20. Conrad, "The Burial Platform of Chan Chan"; Billman, "Irrigation and the Origins"; Dillehay, "Introduction," 5–10; Verano, "Where Do They Rest?," 202; Moore, "The Social Basis of Sacred Spaces"; Huchet and Greenberg, "Flies, Mochicas and Burial Practices."

21. Millaire, "The Manipulation of Human Remains," 371; Buikstra, "Tombs for the Living," 239.

22. Salomon, " 'The Beautiful Grandparents,' " 328–329, and *passim*; Sillar, "The Dead and the Drying." Isbell, *Mummies and Mortuary Monuments*, argues that the ayllu as bundled with ancestral relations is a more recent vintage than Andeanists long argued, dating to the Early Intermediate Period (circa 0–500 CE) and the creation of chullpas. See Hamilton, *Scale & the Incas*, *passim*, but esp. 107 for important insights as to the condensation of power in smaller ancestral selves.

23. Salomon, "Turbulent Tombs," 329–347; Dillehay, "Introduction," 8; Gose, "Segmentary state Formation," 494. The spread of this "Andean funerary package" of an ayllu attached to

artificial mummies has been attributed to encounters with the Wari, an imperial confedera-
tion or culture that expanded from present-day Ayacucho in the southern Andes before its
collapse around 1100 CE: Eeckhout and Owens, "The Impossibility of Death"; Eeckhout,
"Change and Permanency," 151. For thinking with potatoes and the dead, see Allen, "Body
and Soul in Quechua Thought," and Trever, "A Moche Riddle in Clay," which traces the relation of potatoes to the dead to earlier and even more spectacular ends. For appeals to the dead
to heal the living, see Avendaño, Sermones, 44v.

24. Salomon and Urioste, The Huarochirí Manuscript, 99–100; Sharratt, "Steering Clear of the
Dead"; Pérez Fernández, ed., El anónimo de Yucay frente, 142; Arnold and Hastorf, Heads of
State, 223–224 and passim; Lau, Ancient Alterity, 88-89.

25. Salomon, "'The Beautiful Grandparents,'" 321 and passim; Isbell, Mummies and Mortuary
Monuments, 92–97; Chase, "Performing the Past," 14, 177.

26. Salomon, "'The Beautiful Grandparents,'" 346; D'Altroy, "Killing Mummies"; Yaya
MacKenzie, "Sovereign Bodies." See Hyland, "Writing with Twisted Cords"; Salomon, The
Cord Keepers; and Curatola Petrocchi and Puente Luna, eds., El quipu colonial for reflections
on khipus' inscriptive potential. Royal ayllus are frequently referred to as panacas, but Puente
Luna, "Incas pecheros y caballeros hidalgos," 26–35, argues that this term's inherited meaning
was an invention of the Toledan conflict between "Incas by blood" and "Incas by privilege,"
which led the former to codify descent as genealogical rather than the more fluid relationships
of the pre-Hispanic Andes.

27. Bauer, "Pacariqtambo"; D'Altroy, The Incas, Chp. 3; Covey, "The Spread of Inca Power in the
Cuzco Region," 58.

28. Covey, How the Incas Built Their Heartland; Covey, "Inka Imperial Intentions"; d'Altroy,
"Killing Mummies," 415.

29. Julien, Reading Inca History; MacCormack, "History, Historical Record, and Ceremonial
Action," 335; Covey, "Chronology, Succession, and Sovereignty," 174n20, 185–186n53;
D'Altroy, "Killing Mummies," 413; Niles, The Shape of Inca History. For Huayna Picchu being
Machu Picchu's true name, see Amado and Bauer, "The Ancient Inca Town Named Huayna
Picchu."

30. Covey, How the Incas Built Their Heartland, 118.

31. Sarmiento de Gamboa, Geschichte des Inkareiches, 68 [Chp. 31].

32. Hernández Astete and Cerrón-Palomino, eds., Juan de Betanzos y el Tahuantinsuyo, 198–199;
MacCormack, Religion in the Andes, 78; Salomon, "'Beautiful Grandparents,'" 336, 343;
Julien, Reading Inca History, 19; Ramírez, To Feed and Be Fed, 73–76, 191–193; Dean, A
Culture of Stone; Hamilton, Scale & the Incas, 215–221; Lau, "Animating Idolatry." (Also see
Hamilton, 82–87, for the suggestion that Pachacuti's possible development of the purucaya
ceremonies' elements owed to the Inca incorporation of Chimú deathways).

33. Hernández Astete and Cerrón-Palomino, eds. Juan de Betanzos y el Tahuantinsuyo, 198–199;
Silverblatt, Moon, Sun, and Witches, 54–59; MacCormack, "History, Historical Record, and
Ceremonial Action," 338; Covey, "Inca Gender Relations"; Covey, The Inca Apocalypse, 127–
131 ("most powerful" on 129).

34. Eire, From Madrid to Purgatory, explores the "good death" similarly modeled by the Catholic
monarchs in Spain.

35. Hernández Astete and Cerrón-Palomino, eds., Juan de Betanzos y el Tahuantinsuyo, 267–268;
Sarmiento, Geschichte des Inkareiches, 92–94 [Chp. 47]; Cabello Valboa, Miscelánea Antártica,
462–463; Niles, The Shape of Inca History, 37, 62, 105–108; Covey, "Chronology, Succession,
and Sovereignty," 187–188n60; Ramírez, To Feed and Be Fed, 74, 76.

36. Julien, Reading Inca History, 126–129; Chirinos and Zegarra, eds., El orden del Inca por el
licenciado Polo Ondegardo, 208.

37. For ylla/Yllapa, see Cieza de León, Obras Completas, 1:181 (La Crónica del Perú, Part 2,
Chp. 30); Duviols, "Un inédit de Cristóbal de Albornoz," 19; and Guaman Poma, El primer
nueva corónica, 287 [289]. See also Dean, "The After-Life of Inka Rulers," 32–33; Dean, A
Culture of Stone; Covey, The Inca Apocalypse, 115–116; MacCormack, Religion in the Andes,
286; Brosseder, The Power of Huacas, 160–162; D'Altroy, The Incas, 134. My reading of the Inca
yllapa as different from mallki—first recorded by the Spanish as a term in the early seventeenth

century, elsewhere in the Andes—is based on discussions of *ylla, yllapa,* and other words for the dead in contemporary dictionaries (Santo Tomás, *Lexicon,* 107, 141v, 148v; *Arte de la lengua general del Peru,* "Ylla, yllatupa, ditado de Incas señores"; and González Holguín, *Vocabulario de la lengua general de todo el Peru,* 368) and reflections by Flores Ochoa, "Enqa, enqaychu y Khuya Rumi"; Mannheim, *The Language of the Incas,* 184–185; Allen, "When Utensils Revolt," 24; Salomon, "Andean Opulence," 115; Dean, *A Culture of Stone,* 32, 63; Stephenson, "From Marvelous Antidote to the Poison of Idolatry." Joan de Santa Cruz Pachacuti Yamqui Salcamaygua describes a pair of Inca trees as ancestors after 1613 (see Hamilton, *Scale & the Incas,* 107–108, for an important discussion of this) which has encouraged their conflation, but the repeated use of *yllapa* to refer to the nonmetaphorical dead (in the 1540s, 1570s, and 1610s, the latter by Felipe Guaman Poma de Ayala) seems more correct.

38. D'Altroy, *The Incas,* 134.
39. Hernández Astete and Cerrón-Palomino, eds., *Juan de Betanzos y el Tahuantinsuyo,* 198–199, 259–268, 319 ["had him opened"]; Levillier, ed., *Gobernantes del Perú,* Tomo IV, 344–345; Vega Inca, *Historia General del Peru,* 56r; D'Altroy, "Killing Mummies," 411; Sahuaraura Inca, "Artículo remitido." I thank Stefanie Gänger for sharing Sahuaraura Inca's article with me, of which more is said in Chapter 5. For tradition regarding *schinus molle,* see Barrera, "Antigüedades Peruanas," and Cushman, "The Environmental Contexts," 118.
40. Guillén et al., "Three New Mummies"; Cobo, *Historia del nuevo mundo,* 165 ("calabash").
41. Verano, *Holes in the Head,* 193, 234–235.
42. Van Dalen Luna et al., "The Multimodal Chemical Study of Pre-Columbian Mummies"; University of York Research Group, "The Peruvian Mummy at the Towneley Museum."
43. Allen, "The Sadness of Jars," 312; Hernández Astete and Cerrón-Palomino, eds., *Juan de Betanzos y el Tahuantinsuyo,* Chapter 31.
44. Hernández Astete and Cerrón-Palomino, eds., *Juan de Betanzos y el Tahuantinsuyo,* 198–199; Silverblatt, *Moon, Sun, and Witches,* 54–59; MacCormack, "History, Historical Record, and Ceremonial Action," 338; Mac Cormack, *Religion in the Andes,* 144 (Mama Ocllo's womb); Rostworowski de Diez Canseco, *History of the Inca Realm,* 19; Covey, "Inca Gender Relations"; Covey, *The Inca Apocalypse,* 33–36, 123–127; d'Altroy, *The Incas,* 4; Yaya MacKenzie, "Sovereign Bodies," 641.
45. Conrad and Demarest, *Religion and Empire,* 131–136.
46. D'Altroy, *The Incas,* 116; Covey, *The Inca Apocalypse,* 33 ("coca leaf"); also see Hamilton, *Scale & the Incas,* 107.
47. D'Altroy, "Killing Mummies," 411; Hu and Quave, "Prosperity and Prestige."
48. Schjellerup, *Incas y españoles en la conquista de los Chachapoya,* 133-134; Buikstra and Nystrom, "Ancestors and Social Memory," 255; Arnold and Hastorf, *Heads of State,* 213–214.
49. MacCormack, "History, Historical Record, and Ceremonial Action," 353n35; Covey, "Chronology, Succession, and Sovereignty," 174n20; D'Altroy, "Killing Mummies," 414–415.
50. Bongers, "Mortuary Practice," 36.
51. Poma de Ayala, *El primer nueva corónica y buen gobierno,* 186 [188], 189 [191].
52. Bongers, "Mortuary Practice."
53. Salomon and Urioste, *The Huarochirí Manuscript,* 115; Bastien, *Healers of the Andes,* 19.
54. Guillén et al., "Three New Mummies."
55. Ibid.; Buikstra and Nystrom, "Ancestors and Social Memory," 258.
56. Velasco, "Ethnogenesis and Social Difference"; Hernández Garavito, "Producing Legibility through Ritual."
57. As Frank Salomon has noted, the ethnographic present in the Andes helps explain these Khipus found in funerary contexts. One highland community that retains and maintains their khipus today drapes them across the torso of new ayllu presidents: quipus are therefore a "wrapping text," in Salomon's words—"wrapped onto the bodies of its officials at the moment when these men's bodies instantiate the 'body politic' "; see Salomon, *The Cord Keepers,* 12, 18 ("wrapping"), 134–135, 232–233, 274–276. See also Medrano, *Quipus.*
58. Hernández Garavito, "Producing Legibility through Ritual"; Verano, "Where Do They Rest?," 190; Salomon, " 'The Beautiful Grandparents,' " 331–332; Ramírez, *To Feed and Be Fed,* 107–108; Lechtman, "The Inka and Andean Metallurgical Tradition."

59. Poma de Ayala, *El primer nueva corónica y buen gobierno,* 256 [258]. It is notable that for that month's image Guaman Poma selected not an Inca mummy, but one of his own Chinchaysuyu ancestors. See also Kilroy-Ewbank, "Fashioning a Prince for All the World to See," 91.

60. Salomon and Urioste, eds., *The Huarochirí Manuscript,* 99, 120 ("was a human being," "the Inca").

61. Silverblatt, "Imperial Dilemmas," 91, 93 (quote); Salomon, "Turbulent Tombs," 332. See also Moore, "The Social Basis of Sacred Spaces," 84, 95, 101.

62. Lau, *Ancient Alterity in the Andes,* 87. See also Covey, *The Inca Apocalypse,* 113: a "museum to Inca victory."

63. Hernández Astete and Cerrón-Palomino, eds., *Juan de Betanzos y el Tahuantinsuyo,* Chp. 31; Salomon, "'The Beautiful Grandparents,'" 327; D'Altroy, 277; Ceruti, "Human Bodies as Objects of Dedication"; Dean, *A Culture of Stone,* 99. See Hamilton, *Scale & the Incas,* 233–240, for particular nuance.

64. Silverblatt, *Moon, Sun, and Witches,* Chp. 5; Fine-Dare, "Bodies Unburied"; Heaney, "As Peru Heads."

65. Silverblatt, *Moon, Sun, and Witches,* Chp. 5; Covey, *The Inca Apocalypse,* 148–149. For the power to "not let die," see Radin and Kowal, eds., *Cryopolitics.*

66. Salomon, "Turbulent Tombs," 329–335; Salomon and Urioste, eds., *The Huarochirí Manuscript,* 120–121.

Chapter 2

1. Hernández Astete and Cerrón-Palomino, eds., *Juan de Betanzos y el Tahuantinsuyo,* Pt. 1, Chp. 48 ("like leprosy"). Researchers suggest it may have been smallpox. Over the next half-century, as many as 90 percent of the estimated 15.7 million people living in Tawantinsuyu are estimated to have died: Cook, *Demographic Collapse.* It is limiting to attribute the demographic collapse solely to new diseases, however, rather than to the violence and exploitations of Spanish colonialism that worked atop disease; doing so also overlooks how Native peoples managed these changes by innovating different kinds of curing (Crawford, *The Andean Wonder Drug;* Kelton, *Cherokee Medicine*), including, in this case, the dead.

2. Cabello Valboa, *Miscelánea Antártica,* 462–463 (Pt. 3, Chp. 24); Niles, *The Shape of Inca History,* 62, 105–108; Ramírez, *To Feed and Be Fed,* 74, 76; Covey, "Chronology, Succession, and Sovereignty," 187–188n60, and *The Inca Apocalypse,* 138–140.

3. Hernández Astete and Cerrón-Palomino, eds., *Juan de Betanzos y el Tahuantinsuyo,* 198–199, 259–268, 319, 322; de la Vega Inca, *Historia General del Peru,* 56r; MacCormack, "History, Historical Record, and Ceremonial Action," and *Religion in the Andes,* 70, 78, 128, 292, 393; Niles, *The Shape of Inca History,* 78–79, 105–109, 151; Ramírez, *To Feed and Be Fed,* 18. For the crucial catch that the smaller figure on the right is likely one of Huayna Capac's two wawqis, adapted by Guaman Poma to be legible to Europeans, see Hamilton, *Scale & the Incas,* 215–217.

4. Rostworowski de Diez Canseco, *History of the Inca Realm,* 90. Huayna Capac's son Huascar had his father's executors killed when they arrived. D'Altroy, *The Incas,* 108.

5. Covey, *The Inca Apocalypse,* 139–143; Cobo, *Historia del Nuevo Mundo,* 93; Hernández Astete and Cerrón-Palomino, eds., *Juan de Betanzos y el Tahuantinsuyo,* 323 (Pt. 2, Chp. 2); de la Vega Inca, *Historia General del Peru,* 56r. As D'Altroy, *The Incas,* 192 notes, Huascar may have had his father's mummy officially marry Huascar's mother, giving him full genealogical legitimacy.

6. *La Conquista del Perú* (sometimes attributed to Cristóbal de Mena), 110; Lamana, *Domination without Dominance,* Chp. 1, and 104–105.

7. Sarmiento, *Geschichte des Inkareiches,* 102 [Chp. 54], 122–124 (Chps. 66–67).

8. See, for example, Jared Diamond's *Guns, Germs, and Steel,* whose cover is British painter John Everett Millais's *Pizarro Seizing the Inca of Peru* (1846), and many secondary school textbooks, which largely reproduce Diamond's line.

9. Seed, "'Failing to Marvel,'" and Lamana, *Domination without Dominance,* 27–64, are the sharpest guides to rereading the writing surrounding this moment.

10. For a direct rejoinder to the guns, germs, and steel narrative, see Cahill, "Advanced Andeans and Backward Europeans." For the extended military conflict, see Hemming, *The Conquest of the Incas;* Espinoza Soriano, *La destrucción del imperio de los Incas;* Guillén Guillén, *La*

guerra de reconquista Inka; Stern, "The Rise and Fall of Indian-White Alliances." For sacred convergences and contests, see Estenssoro Fuchs, *Del paganismo a la santidad*; Lamana, *Domination without Dominance*; Ramírez, *To Feed and Be Fed*; Ramos, *Death and Conversion in the Andes*. For familial negotiations, see Vicuña Guengerich, "*Capac* Women," and Mangan, *Transatlantic Obligations*. For how Inca and Andean nobilities shaped the Spanish Empire, see Mumford, *Vertical Empire*, and de la Puente, *Andean Cosmopolitans*. See Restall, *When Montezuma Met Cortes*, and Covey, *The Inca Apocalypse*, for similar re-estimations of this period in Mexico and Peru.

11. For dead-body politics, see Verdery, *The Political Lives of Dead Bodies*.
12. For ethnography and rule, see Rowe, "Ethnography and Ethnology in the Sixteenth Century"; Pagden, *The Fall of Natural Man*; Salomon, "The Historical Development of Andean Ethnology"; Julien, "History and Art in Translation"; MacCormack, "Ethnography in South America," and *On the Wings of Time*; Silverblatt, "Imperial Dilemmas"; Whitehead, *Of Cannibals and Kings*; Benton, *Law and Colonial Cultures*, Chps. 2–3; Covey, "Chronology, Succession, and Sovereignty"; Mumford, "Litigation as Ethnography"; Mumford, *Vertical Empire*, 34; Thurner, *History's Peru*; Graubart, "Learning from the *Qadi*." For natural history and rule, see Mundy, *The Mapping of New Spain*; Pimentel, "The Iberian Vision"; Cañizares-Esguerra, *Nature, Empire, and Nation*; Barrera Osorio, *Experiencing Nature*; Bleichmar, *Visible Empire*; Breen, *The Age of Intoxication*; Thurner and Pimentel, "Introduction"; Cooley, *The Perfection of Nature*.
13. See Norton, "Subaltern Technologies and Early Modernity in the Atlantic World," and Cooley, "The Giant Remains," for excellent like examples of Indigenous ontologies and technology's effect on wider understandings.
14. Silverblatt, "Imperial Dilemmas," 97.
15. Morison, ed., *Journals and Other Documents on the Life and Voyages of Christopher Columbus*, 107; Whitehead, *Of Cannibals and Kings*, 17, 33–38. Heaney, "The Pre-Columbian Exchange," Chp. 2, details the legal arc of Spanish grave-opening before Peru. For "deathways," see Seeman, *Death in the New World*.
16. Xerez, "Verdadera relación," 178 (filthy, sepulchers).
17. Hernández Astete and Cerrón-Palomino, eds., *Juan de Betanzos y el Tahuantinsuyo*, 321 [Chp. I]; D'Altroy, *The Incas*, 196.
18. Sarmiento, *Geschichte des Inkareiches*, 102 [Chp. 54], 122–124 [Chps. 66–67]; Covey, "Chronology, Succession, and Sovereignty," 174n20 ("new historical program").
19. See Ziólkowski, "The Inka and the Breviary," 357, for the observation regarding Cajamarca and the Inca calendar.
20. Ramírez, *To Feed and Be Fed*, 74–76; also Herring, *Art and Vision in the Inca Empire*, Chp. 2; Lamana, *Domination without Dominance*, 52.
21. Lamana, *Domination without Dominance*, 61, 81–83; Mikecz, "Beyond Cajamarca," 198, 212–217.
22. *La Conquista del Perú*, 110; MacCormack, *Religion in the Andes*, 124n21.
23. Varela, *La muerte del rey*, 18–20; Ramos, *Death and Conversion in the Andes*, 76. For esteem for the Incas' monarchical, religious complexity, see Pagden, *The Fall of Natural Man*, 59, 78–79; MacCormack, *On the Wings of Time*, 48–49, 90–92.
24. Covey, *The Inca Apocalypse*, 89–91.
25. Hemming, *The Conquest of the Incas*, 74–81, and Lamana, *Domination without Dominance*, 92–94, survey Spanish and Indian rationales for Atahuallpa's death.
26. Ramos, *Death and Conversion in the Andes*, 50, 39; Covey, *The Inca Apocalypse*, 76–77, 180–181.
27. Cieza de León, *Obras completas*, 1:292 (*La crónica del Perú*, Pt. 3, Chp. 54).
28. Cummins, "La fabula y el retrato," 11–12. To Pizarro's first explanation of the execution, Charles wrote that "the death of the Atahuallpa displeased me, as he was a monarch, and especially because it was done in the name of justice" (Cédula Real, Toledo, 21 de Mayo 1534, excerpted in Porras Barrenechea, ed., *Colección de documentos, Tomo III*, 64).
29. Xerez, "Verdadera relación," 240 (quote). See also Sancho de la Hoz, *Relación de la conquista del Peru*, 19 (Chp. 1); Cieza de León, *Obras completas*, 1:292 (*La crónica del Perú*, Pt. 3, Chp. 54).

30. Majluf, "El rostro del Inca," provides the fascinating history of this painting's production. See Chp. 6 of this book for its relationship to mummified "Incas" of the 1860s.

31. Xerez, "Verdadera relación," 241 (Emperor).

32. Vega Inca, *Historia general del Peru*, 36r–36v (Pt. 2, Bk. 1, Chp. 3); Hernández Astete and Cerrón-Palomino, eds., *Juan de Betanzos y el Tahuantinsuyo*, 412 (Pt. 2, Chp. 26); Ramos, *Death and Conversion in the Andes*, 41; Estupiñan Viteri, "El Puxilí de los Yngas."

33. Sancho de la Hoz, *Relación de la conquista del Peru*, 97-98 (Cap. XIX); MacCormack, "History, Historical Record, and Ceremonial Action," 329–331.

34. Pizarro, *Relación del descubrimiento*, 52–54 (Chp. 11). I use the translation of MacCormack, "History, Historical Record, and Ceremonial Action," 342.

35. Acosta, *Historia natural y moral*, 432–433.

36. Sancho de la Hoz, *Relación de la conquista del Peru*, Chp. 12 (1534); Covey, *The Inca Apocalypse*, 189–190.

37. Burns, *Colonial Habits*; Graubart, "Indecent Living," 220–223; Mangan, *Transatlantic Obligations*, Chp. 1; Quispe-Agnoli, "Taking Possession of the New World"; Vicuña Guengerich, "*Capac* Women."

38. Vega Inca, *Historia general del Peru*, 56r [Bk.2, Chp. XXIII].

39. Lamana, *Domination without Dominance*, 136–138 gives a nuanced reading of these exchanges.

40. See Murúa, *Historia general del Perú*, 310, for the yllapa of Manco Inca the Spanish found in Vilcabamba.

41. *La conquista del Perú*, 110.

42. Christian, *Local Religion*.

43. Siraisi, *History, Medicine, and the Traditions of Renaissance Learning*, 225–243; Varela, *La muerte del rey*, 18–20, 40, 77–81; Marinozzi and Fornaciari, *Le mummie e l'arte medica*, 23–40; Bouley, "Papal Anatomy in the News"; Solomon, *Fictions of Well-Being*, 86–88. See Lazure, "Possessing the Sacred," and Cussen, "The Search for Idols and Saints in Colonial Peru," for early modern understandings of bodily sanctity, in Europe, Spain, and Peru.

44. Mundy, *The Mapping of New Spain*; Portuondo, *Secret Science*; Barrera Osorio, *Experiencing Nature* ("early").

45. Barrera Osorio, *Experiencing Nature*, 13–23, 154n15, 154n16.

46. Kole de Peralta, "The Nature of Colonial Bodies," 183–184.

47. Diego de Zárate y Diego Caballero a Su Majestad, 12 August 1536, Archivo General de las Indias (AGI) Indiferente, 1092, N. 156; Carta real a los oficiales de la Casa de la Contratación, 6 November 1536, AGI Indiferente, 1962, L.5, 28–29v.

48. Zárate, *Historia del descubrimiento*, Libro 1, 3f. For the circulation of Zárate's other knowledges of Peruvian wealth, see Heaney, "Marrying Utopia," 95.

49. Rodrigues, *Amati Lusitani Doctoris*, 536–537; Findlen, *Possessing Nature*, 270 (antidote); Marinozzi and Fornaciari, *Le mummie e l'arte medica*, 141; Bastien, *Healers of the Andes*, 145–146. Today, *Myroxylon pereirae* is an ingredient in medicines, dental products, foods, drinks, fragrances, and pesticides. In the Andes it is still used for earaches, urinary tract infections, and wound dressings. For a similar medicalization of "Peruvian" knowledges, see Stephenson, "From Marvelous Antidote," though Newson, *Making Medicines*, Chp. 6, attends to the limits of Spanish adoptions.

50. Morales, "Relación que dió el Provisor Luís de Morales," 81–82; Estenssoro Fuchs, *Del paganismo a la santidad*, 125; Ramos, *Death and Conversion in the Andes*, 64, 194, 297n117.

51. Lamana, *Dominance without Domination*, 212. Vaca de Castro may have had in mind the Crown's profitable reprieve for forcibly baptized Muslims in Spain: by paying a massive tribute, they preserved language, dress, cemeteries, and marriage practices for ten years. See Perry, *The Handless Maiden*, 69, 136.

52. Pérez Fernández, ed., *El anónimo de Yucay Frente a Bartolomé de las Casas*, 142.

53. Hernández Astete and Cerrón-Palomino, eds., *Juan de Betanzos y el Tahuantinsuyo*, 322. Hampe Martínez, "Las momias de los Incas en Lima," 407; Lamana, *Domination without Dominance*, 212–213; and Ramos, *Death and Conversion in the Andes*, 194, 297–298n117, meditate on these multiple losses of Huayna Capac.

54. Salomon, " 'Beautiful Grandparents,' " 334; Ramos, "The Incas of Cuzco."

55. Cieza de León, *Obras Completas*, 1:181 (*La crónica del Perú*, Pt. 2, Chp. 30]; Julien, *Reading Inca History*, 4–5, 11, 53, 163–164; MacCormack, "History, Historical Record, and Ceremonial Action," 331.

56. Hernández Astete and Cerrón-Palomino, eds., *Juan de Betanzos y el Tahuantinsuyo*, 198–199, 259–267, 266, 319–322.

57. Hemming, *The Conquest of the Incas*, 290; Cahill, "Becoming Inca," 261, 267; Vicuña Guengerich, "Inca Women under Spanish rule," 115.

58. Cobo, *Historia del nuevo mundo*, 59. For Polo as ethnographer, see Honores, "El licenciado Polo"; Mumford, *Vertical Empire*, 34–39. For how Ondegardo's king list was unusual (Sapa Inka Tarku Huaman was in no other), see Covey, "Chronology."

59. Vega Inca, *Primera parte de los commentarios reales*, Bk. 5, Chp. 29; Ruiz de Navamuel, "La fe y testimonio," 256; Bauer, *Ancient Cuzco*, 180; Rostworowski de Diez Canseco, *History of the Inca Realm*, 33.

60. Hemming, *The Conquest of the Incas*, 297–298.

61. Hampe Martínez, "Las momias de los Incas en Lima," 408; Guillén Guillén, "El enigma de las momias Incas."

62. MacCormack, "History, Historical Record, and Ceremonial Action," 342.

63. Santo Tomás, *Lexicon*, 107, 141v, 148v. I am indebted to R. Alan Covey for this insight. See Estenssoro Fuchs, *Del paganismo a la santidad*, for the need to understand the religious convergences of this prior period.

64. MacCormack, "History, Historical Record, and Ceremonial Action," 342; Hampe Martínez, "La última morada de los Incas," 109; Ramos, "The Incas of Cuzco."

65. Julien, *Reading Inca History*, 128–129; Chirinos and Zegarra, eds., *El orden del Inca por el licenciado Polo Ondegardo*, 208.

66. Vicuña Guengerich, "Inca Women under Spanish rule," 117; Puente, "Incas pecheros y caballeros hidalgos."

67. Strong, " 'The Devil Was in That Little Bone.' "

68. Ruiz de Navamuel, "La fe y testimonio," 256 ("los cuales hizo enterrar secretamente"); MacCormack, *Religion in the Andes*, 433n82; Ramos, "The Incas of Cuzco," 181.

69. Vega Inca, *Primera parte de los commentarios reales*, 128r–v.

70. Ibid.

71. Firbas, "La momia del Inca," 42; Duviols, *La destrucción de las religiones Andinas*, 122–123.

72. Alcina Franch, *Arqueólogos o anticuarios*, 20. See also Certeau, *The Writing of History*, 3.

73. Chirinos and Zegarra, eds., *El orden del Inca por el licenciado Polo Ondegardo*, 208; Cobo, *Historia del Nuevo Mundo*, 82, 94.

74. Findlen, *Possessing Nature*, Chp. 6 (Museums of Medicine).

75. Bauer and Coello Rodríguez, "The Hospital of San Andrés," 9; Kole de Peralta, "The Nature of Colonial Bodies," 80–90.

76. Warren, *Medicine and Politics*, 31.

77. Acosta, *Historia natural y moral*, 433, 435, 317.

78. Pagden, *The Fall of Natural Man*, Chp. 7; see also MacCormack, *Religion in the Andes*, Chp. 6.

79. See Cooley, *The Perfection of Nature*, Chp. 7, for Acosta's materialist, even quasi-evolutionary approach to the populations of the New World.

80. Acosta, *Historia natural y moral*, 266, 317, 435.

81. Suárez de Figueroa, *Plaza universal de todas ciencias y artes*, 148v; Dannenfeldt, "Egyptian Mumia"; Forbes, *Studies in Early Petroleum History*, 162–168.

82. Verano, *Holes in the Head*, 77–88.

83. Martínez Vidal and Pardo Tomás, "Anatomical Theatres"; Sawday, *The Body Emblazoned*.

84. Pomata, "Observation Rising"; Bouley, "Negotiated Sanctity"; Vidal, "Miracles, Science, and Testimony," 482.

85. Pagden, *European Encounters with the New World*; Cussen, "The Search for Idols and Saints in Colonial Peru"; Johnson, "Stone Gods and Counter-Reformation Knowledges"; Johnson, *Cultural Hierarchy in Sixteenth-Century Europe*, Chp. 6.

86. Acosta, *Historia natural y moral de las Indias*, 435.

87. Cobo, *Historia del nuevo mundo*, 165.

88. Cf. Pagden, *European Encounters with the New World*, and Sawday, *The Body Emblazoned*. Europeans seem to have taken this move toward the Egyptian dead later, in the eighteenth century: Riggs, *Unwrapping Ancient Egypt*, 44–48.

89. Pérez Fernández, ed., *El anónimo de Yucay*, 10–11, 42; MacCormack, "History, Historical Record, and Ceremonial Action," 347–348; Adorno, *The Polemics of Possession*, 58; Julien, "History and Art in Translation"; Julien, "Francisco De Toledo," 244; Mumford, *Vertical Empire*, Chp. 7; Puente Luna, "Incas pecheros y caballeros hidalgos"; Covey, *The Inca Apocalypse*, 412–433 (420: "God's punishment").

90. Covey, *The Inca Apocalypse*, 427.

91. Levillier, *Gobernantes del Perú*, Tomo VI, 313.

92. Murúa, *Historia general del Perú*, 310; Heaney, *Cradle of Gold*, 1–6.

93. Julien, "History and Art in Translation," 75, translating Levillier, ed., *Gobernantes del Perú*, Tomo IV, 344–345; Julien, "Francisco de Toledo," 258–259; Johnson, *Cultural Hierarchy in Sixteenth-Century Europe*, Chp. 6.

94. Lazure, "Possessing the Sacred."

95. Mumford, *Vertical Empire*.

96. Murphy, "Colonial Demography and Bioarchaeology"; Graubart, *With Our Labor*; Vicuña Guengerich, "*Capac* Women."

97. Burns, "Making Indigenous Archives"; Curatola Petrocchi and Puente Luna, *El quipu colonial*; Puente, "That Which Belongs to All"; Puente Luna and Honores, "Guardianes de la real justicia"; Ramos, *Death and Conversion in the Andes*; Ramos, *Andean Cosmopolitans*.

98. Dean, *Inka Bodies*; Amado, *El estandarte real y la mascapaycha*.

99. Salomon, "'The Beautiful Grandparents'"; Gose, *Invaders as Ancestors*, 139, and *passim*; Wernke, "Transformations," 705-707; Hyman and Leibsohn, "Washing the Archive," 432-434.

100. MacCormack, *Religion in the Andes*; Estenssoro Fuchs, *Del paganismo a la santidad*; Duviols, *La destrucción de las religiones Andinas*; Duviols, *Cultura andina y represión*; Mills, *Idolatry and Its Enemies*, 29-33; Duviols, *Procesos y visitas de idolatrias*.

101. Duviols, "Un inédit de Cristóbal de Albornoz," 19; Guibovich, "Cristobal de Albornoz y el Taki Onqoy"; Gose, *Invaders as Ancestors*, Chp. 3.

102. Hyman and Leibsohn, "Washing the Archive," 433.

103. Cobo, *Historia del nuevo mundo*, 272–273; and Guibovich, *El edificio de letras*, 93, 109.

104. By 1597 an Italian writer named Contugo Contugi believed that the Spanish had brought the "embalmed" Peruvian dead to Lima specifically to burn them: see Mattos, "Los retratos de Incas," 382.

105. "Al Excmo. Don Francisco de Borja, Queipo de Llano, Conde de Toreno, Ministro de Fomento," in Jiménez de la Espada, ed., *Tres relaciones de antigüedades peruanas*, 36 ("dry and entire"); Salomon, "Introductory Essay," 27 ("800 years old"). See also Arriaga, *La extirpación de la idolatría*, 21–23.

106. Gose, *Invaders as Ancestors*; see also this book's next chapter.

107. Bauer, *Ancient Cuzco*, 181; Bauer and Coello Rodríguez, "The Hospital of San Andrés," 13.

108. Julien, "History and Art in Translation," 63, 75–77. Conversely, Philip's own death and bodily corruption was presented as a lesson in faith: Eire, *From Madrid to Purgatory*, 255–272.

109. Cf. Greer, Mignolo, and Quilligan, eds., *Rereading the Black Legend*.

110. For reflections on camaquen and its survival of colonization, see MacCormack, *Religion in the Andes*, 408–411.

Chapter 3

1. Howse and Thrower, eds., *A Buccaneer's Atlas*, 180n132.

2. All Wafer quotes are from his *A New Voyage and Description of the Isthmus of America* (1699), 208–210. I am indebted to Ben Breen for alerting me to this source.

3. Breen, "A Pirate Surgeon in Panama."

4. This section offers insights of its own via Wafer's encounter, but also synthesizes the important past work of Flores Galindo, *In Search of an Inca*; Zevallos Quiñones, *Huacas y huaqueros*; Estenssoro Fuchs, *Del paganismo a la santidad*; Ramírez, *The World Upside Down*, Chp. 5; Garofalo, "Conjuring with Coca and the Inca"; Ramos, *Death and Conversion*;

Delibes Mateos, *Desterrando tesoros*; Danwerth, "El papel Indígena en la huaquería Andina (siglos XVI y XVII)"; Silverblatt, *Modern Inquisitions*, 170–180, and Salomon, "Ancestors, Grave Robbers," "Ancestor Cults and Resistance," and "Unethnic Ethnohistory." For a like articulation from the Mesoamerican context, see Hamann, "The Social Life of Pre-Sunrise Things."

5. In thinking through these only-sometimes transportable everyday and experimental knowledges in the Iberian Atlantic world, I am inspired by Cañizares-Esguerra, *Nature, Empire, and Nation*; Barrera Osorio, *Experiencing Nature*; Bleichmar, *Visible Empire*; Breen, *The Age of Intoxication*; Crawford, *The Andean Wonder Drug*; Gómez, *The Experiential Caribbean*; Norton, "Subaltern Technologies"; and Cooley, "The Giant Remains."

6. See Gerbi, *The Dispute of the New World*, 155, and Safier, *Measuring the New World*, Chp. 6, for how the Incas came under particular fire in that debate.

7. For the importance of "new" material evidence to test prior claims, see Cañizares-Esguerra, *How to Write the History of the New World*.

8. This arc from knowing "ancient Peruvian" possessions, cultures, and bodies to claiming that knowledge as in the late viceregal period as patriotic possession is well laid out by Brading, *The First America*; Estenssoro Fuchs, "Modernismo, estética, música y fiesta"; Majluf, "De la rebelión al museo"; Berquist, *The Bishop's Utopia*; Cabello Carro, "Las colecciones Peruanas"; Alcina Franch, *Arqueólogos o anticuarios*; Pillsbury and Trever, "The King, the Bishop, and the Creation of an American Antiquity"; Trever, "The Uncanny Tombs in Martínez Compañón's *Trujillo del Perú*."

9. Grafton, *Bring Out Your Dead*; Hamann, "How Maya Hieroglyphs Got Their Name"; Levine, *The Amateur and the Professional*; Díaz-Andreu, *A World History of Nineteenth-Century Archaeology*; Riggs, *Unwrapping Ancient Egypt*, Chp. 2.

10. Wafer, *A New Voyage*, 208–210.

11. Chauchat, "Early Hunter-Gatherers on the Peruvian Coast," 64; Fung Pineda, "The Late Preceramic and Initial Period," 76; Shimada, *Pampa grande*, 57, 91; Shady Solis, Haas, and Creamer, "Dating Caral"; Shady Solís, *Caral Supe, Perú*; Pozorski and Pozorski, "Early Cultural Complexity on the North Coast of Peru," 611; Dillehay, ed., *From Foraging to Farming in the Andes*; Dulanto, "Between Horizons," 762; Vega Inca, *Primera parte*, Bk. 6, Chp. 32; Verano, "Trophy Head-Taking and Human Sacrifice in Andean South America," 1053.

12. Howse and Thrower, eds., *A Buccaneer's Atlas*, 184. For English interest in pro-Inca (and anti-Spanish) narratives, see Heaney, "A Peru of Their Own"; Garcés, "The Translator Translated"; Yaya MacKenzie, "Tales of Fallen Empires."

13. Frézier, *Relation du voyage de la Mer du Sud*, Tome Second, 311–312.

14. Salomon, "Unethnic Ethnohistory."

15. See Wernke, "Transformations," for an overview of these insights. See also Lequanda, "Continuación de la descripción," 81–83; Bandelier, "On the Relative Antiquity"; Cabello Caro, "Pervivencias funerarias"; Ramos, *Death and Conversion in the Andes*; Hyman and Leibsohn, "Washing the Archive," 432–434.

16. Duviols, *La destrucción de las religiones Andinas*, 42.

17. Flores Galindo, *In Search of an Inca*, Chp. 2. See also Salomon, "Unethnic Ethnohistory" and Hertzman, "Fatal Differences."

18. *Libro Primero de cabildos de Lima, parte tercera*, 71; Bromley, "El capitán Martin de Estete y dona Maria de Escobar," 135; Zevallos Quiñones, *Huacas y huaqueros*; Ramírez, *The World Upside Down*, Chp. 5; Delibes Mateos, *Desterrando tesoros*, 56, 65–79, 327; Luque Talaván, "Los libros de huacas."

19. Salomon, "Introductory Essay," 27.

20. Salomon, "Unethnic Ethnohistory." See also de la Cadena, *Indigenous Mestizos*.

21. For the coast, see Cabello Carro, "Mestizaje y ritos funerarios en Trujillo," 96; Rowe, "On Absolute Dating and North Coast History."

22. Pérez y López, *Teatro de la legislación*, 28:41; Zevallos Quiñones, *Huacas y huaqueros*; Heaney, "The Pre-Columbian Exchange," Chp. 2.

23. Scott, *Contested Territory, passim*, and 66—citing AGI, Lima 569, lib. II[2], 111v–112—confirms that sense of opportunity—but also royal loyalty—with the case of the son of a Huanca lord who traveled to Spain in the early 1560s to petition, successfully, for honors and privileges including a royal letters patent "that permitted him, along with other native leaders

of Jauja and their subjects, to excavate not only mines but also old sites of burial and worship in search of the offerings 'that in ancient times his ancestors used to make.' "

24. Francisco de Toledo, "Instruccion y ordenanzas de los corregidores de naturales, Los Reyes," 30 May 1580, in Lohmann Villena and Sarabia Viejo, eds., *Francisco De Toledo,* Tomo 2, 413–414; Ramírez, *Patriarcas provinciales,* 67; Zevallos Quiñones, *Huacas y huaqueros,* 12, 55–64; Delibes Mateos, *Desterrando tesoros,* 238–239, 270–271.

25. Ramírez, *The World Upside Down,* Chp. 5; Delibes Mateos, *Desenterrando tesoros,* 167. See also Klaus and Tam, *"Requiem Aeternam?"*

26. Danwerth, "El Papel Indígena En La Huaquería Andina (Siglos XVI y XVII)"; Delibes Mateos, *Desenterrando tesoros,* 339–340.

27. Gose, *Invaders as Ancestors,* 102, 115, 159–160, 218.

28. For the revolutionary arc of those communalizations, see Spalding, *Huarochirí;* Thomson, *We Alone Will Rule;* Serulnikov, *Subverting Colonial Authority;* Penry, *The People Are King.* Conversations with Frank Salomon, Gabriel de Avilez Rocha, and R. Alan Covey have refined my thoughts on these communalizations.

29. Schwartz, *All Can Be Saved,* 151, 153–154, 156.

30. Silverblatt, *Modern Inquisitions,* 163–184, 270n18, and Garofalo, "Conjuring with Coca and the Inca," 76–78. For "hybrid medicine," see Cueto and Palmer, *Medicine and Public Health in Latin America,* 34–35.

31. Lowry, "Forging an Indian Nation," 249–250.

32. Salomon, "Ancestor Cults and Resistance to the State in Arequipa, ca. 1748–1754"; Salomon, "The Beautiful Grandparents"; Menaker, "Becoming 'Rebels' and 'Idolaters.' "

33. For *rei gentil* and *rei indio,* see Silverblatt, *Modern Inquisitions,* 177.

34. Fock and Krener, "Los Cañaris del Ecuador y sus conceptos etnohistóricos sobre los Incas," 177–178; Salomon, "Ancestors, Grave Robbers,' " 226, 228; and MacCormack, *Religion in the Andes,* which argues that Inca solar cosmologies became "natural" to the Andean landscape only in the century after 1532.

35. Szeminski, *La utopia tupamarista,* 139–146; Burga, *Nacimiento de una utopia;* MacCormack, "Pachacuti," 963–966; Ramos, *Death and Conversion in the Andes,* 47; Flores Galindo, *In Search of an Inca,* 37.

36. Mills, Taylor, and Graham, eds., *Colonial Latin America,* 302.

37. Elliott, *Empires of the Atlantic World,* 383.

38. Wafer, *A New Voyage,* 210 ("a Boy . . . Intent"); See Breen, "No Man Is an Island," 410, for his like collection of cinchona bark. See Cañizares-Esguerra, *How to Write,* 15–16, and Neill, "Buccaneer Ethnography" for the growing importance of credible material proofs.

39. *La Conquista del Perú,* 110.

40. Sancho de la Hoz, *Relación de la conquista del Peru,* 97.

41. Cieza de León, *Parte primera de la chrónica del Perú,* 33v, 80.

42. Zárate, *Historia del descubrimiento,* Libro 1, 3f.

43. López de Gómara, *La historia general de las Indias,* 161v, 253. For López de Gómara being most widely read beyond Spain, see Roa-de-la-Carrera, *Histories of Infamy,* 1-4, 209–211.

44. Dannenfeldt, "Egyptian Mumia"; Marinozzi and Fornaciari, *Le mummie e l'arte medica,* 103–132.

45. Firbas, "La momia del Inca," 45–48, 57n13.

46. Belleforest Comingeois, *L'Histoire Universelle du Monde,* 286, 296, 298, 300, 301v, 305, 309.

47. Dannenfeldt, "Egyptian Mumia"; Marinozzi and Fornaciari, *Le mummie e l'arte medica,* 103–132.

48. Díaz del Castillo, *The History of the Conquest of New Spain,* 42.

49. Archivo del Real Jardín Botánico de Madrid, Spain, División 1, leg. 17 Prologo. Libro de examen de los simples medicinales Antonio de Robles Cornejo 1617, 660–665. I thank Linda Newson for sharing this source with me.

50. Guichard, *Funérailles,* 437-438.

51. Siraisi, *History, Medicine, and the Traditions of Renaissance Learning,* Chp. 7.

52. Thevet, *Les vrais pourtraits,* 3:641–642v, 643v. I thank Benjamin P. Breen and Julie Hardwick for help glossing this passage.

53. Ibid., 3:374v.

54. In contrast to Egyptian mummies' prior import as pre-ground medicine, the earliest recorded semi-intact specimen may be "one little hand" of a mummy that reached a doctor in Oxford in 1586. See Chaney, "Egypt in England and America," 52; Dannenfeldt, "Egyptian Mumia." For the work of slotting non-European history into Old World frames, see Pagden, *The Fall of Natural Man*; MacCormack, *On the Wings of Time*; Davis, *Periodization and Sovereignty*, 7–8.

55. Acosta, *Historia natural y moral*, 435.

56. For Acosta's publication history, see Harris, "Mapping Jesuit Science," 234n6.

57. Purchas, *Purchas his Pilgrimage*, 879; Heaney, "A Peru of Their Own," 629–630.

58. Poma de Ayala, *El primer nueva corónica*, 52 [52], 69 [69].

59. Ibid., 287 [289]–296 [298]. See Kilroy-Ewbank, "Fashioning a Prince for All the World to See," for how Guaman Poma was positioning his grandfather and Chinchaysuyu's heirs as the true rulers of Peru, a nonidolatrous dynasty that both Incas and Spaniards corrupted, as well as the notable insight (91) that in his illustration for "November, Festival of the Dead," the mummy wears a Chinchaysuyu headdress and rayed collar.

60. Poma de Ayala, *El primer nueva corónica*, 288 [290]–297 [299], 377 [379]–378 [380]. See Adorno, *Guaman Poma*, and Adorno and Boserup, eds., *Unlocking the Doors*.

61. Poma de Ayala, *El primer nueva corónica*, 55 [55]–56 [56].

62. A Franciscan friar named Buenaventura de Salinas y Córdoba may have reviewed Guaman Poma's manuscript while working in the viceroy's secretaria and used it to draft his own manuscript for the Spanish Crown, in which he lined the walls of the Incas' temple of the Sun with the Inca kings and their wives, seated in order of "antiquity," and "embalmed with such art that they seemed alive" (Salinas y Córdoba, *Memoriál de las historias*, 32–33).

63. Firbas, "La momia del Inca," 43, suggests that this was "a profound and secret farewell, a last contact with the bodies" of his mother's royal Inca lineage that gave shape to the entire work.

64. Vega Inca, *Primera parte*, 128.

65. Ibid., 10v–11r. Garcilaso credited the Mexican claim to the controversial Peruvian mestizo Jesuit Blas Valera, who may have also authored the *Relación de las costumbres antiguas de los naturales del Pirú* (after 1595), which sought to clear Inca embalming of any irremediable idolatry while showing a familiarity with South America's wider botanical knowledges: "They removed the intestines from the dead king or lord," read the *Relación*, "and embalmed his entire body with balsam brought from Tolu"—an island north of Colombia—"and with other preservatives, in such a way that a corpse embalmed like this lasted more than four hundred or five hundred years" (Hyland, *Gods of the Andes*, 58–61).

66. Vega Inca, *Primera parte*, 127, 128.

67. Purchas, *Hakluytus Posthumus*, Pt. 4, 4:1454, 1458–1460, 1464. For the reading of Garcilaso in Peru, see Guibovich Pérez, "The Dissemination and Reading of the Royal Commentaries in the Peruvian Viceroyalty."

68. Vega Inca, *Le commentaire royal*, 638–641; on translations and relative popularity in Europe: Garcés, "The Translator Translated."

69. Vega Inca, *The Royal Commentaries of Peru in Two Parts*, 182, 193.

70. In 1593 Jean Bodin wrote of a mummy shipped from Alexandria believed responsible for a storm, which ended when the body was thrown into the sea; Dannenfeldt, "Egypt and Egyptian Antiquities in the Renaissance," 20.

71. Cook, "Time's Bodies," 229–232; Riggs, *Unwrapping Ancient Egypt*, 45 ("'naturalia' . . ."); Grafton, *Bring Out Your Dead*, 56–59; Swan, "Making Sense of Medical Collections," 202; Jorink, "Noah's Ark Restored (and Wrecked)," 162–164; Bureau d'adresse et de rencontre, *General Collection of Discourses*, 183 (Fore-Fathers).

72. For the originally anti-idolatrous message of that plate, see Heaney, "A Peru of Their Own," 629–630.

73. Hamann, "How Maya Hieroglyphs Got Their Name"; Riggs, *Unwrapping Ancient Egypt*.

74. Olearius, *Gottorfische Kunst-Kammer*, 71–75.

75. Salmon, *Modern History*, 3:298.

76. Cañizares-Esguerra, *How to Write*; Safier, *Measuring the New World*, Chp. 6. See Guibovich Pérez, "The Dissemination and Reading of the Royal Commentaries in the Peruvian Viceroyalty," for similar doubt in Peru.

77. Daubenton, "Momies." Méndez Rodríguez, *Momias,* xaxos y *mirlados* details the European-directed process of reading Guanche *xaxos* as mummies.
78. Daubenton, "Une Momie trouvée en Auvergne," 173.
79. Gerbi, *The Dispute of the New World*; Cañizares Esguerra, *How to Write.*
80. Zárate, *Historia del descubrimiento,* Libro I, 3f, 3v. See Cooley, "The Giant Remains," 62–63, and *passim,* for Acosta and wider sixteenth-century debate as reflective of Nahua ontologies. For the late-eighteenth-century shift in apprehending these giants as fossilized megafauna, see Unanue, "Descripción del gigante"; Podgorny, "De ángeles, gigantes y megaterios"; Pimentel, *The Rhinoceros and the Megatherium.*
81. Calancha, *Corónica moralizada,* I, XXXVII, 538–539.
82. Cobo, *History of the Inca Empire,* 16, 85–86, 94–97, 98–101, 123 (Colombina-Cobo [C-C] Bk. 11, Chps. 3, 19; Bk. 12, Chps. 1, 2, 8); Cobo, *Inca Religion and Customs,* 246–248, 250–251 (C-C Bk. 14, Chps. 18, 19). Also see MacCormack, *On the Wings of Time,* 269–271. Cf. the early-seventeenth-century hunt by Hernández Principe for the still-idolized capacocha Tanta Carhua: Silverblatt, *Moon, Sun, and Witches,* Chp. 5.
83. As laid out by Cañizares-Esguerra, *Nature, Empire, and Nation,* Chp. 4, building from MacCormack, *Religion in the Andes,* 383–405. See also Cooley, *The Perfection of Nature,* Chp. 7, for José de Acosta's use of the Andes to think through population variation, and Chaplin, *Subject Matter,* for how colonialism in North America racialized Indigenous bodies as born to die and be replaced by Euro-descended settlers.
84. Frézier, *Relation du voyage de la Mer du Sud,* 311–312; Frézier, *Voyage to the South-Sea,* 177–178.
85. Payen, "Note sur la composition des yeux de momies péruviennes," 7; Gilliss, "Peruvian Antiquities," 658.
86. Cañizares-Esguerra, *How to Write.*
87. Upon the death of the last Habsburg king of Spain, Charles II, the Bourbon's claim to Madrid's global empire initiated the War of the Spanish Succession (1701–1714); the Treaty of Utrecht ended the war by establishing that France and Spain could never unite, but left Bourbon dynasties on both thrones.
88. Safier, *Measuring the New World,* Chp. 6.
89. Juan and Ulloa, *Relación Historica,* Libro VI, Cap. XI, 616-617, 619. For more on the career of Jorge Juan see Pimentel, *Viajeros Científicos.*
90. Thurner, *History's Peru,* 88–89.
91. Starting in 1751, English publications translated Ulloa and Juan's antiquarian pages, republishing the huaca-opening plate to, Isabel Yaya argues, "highlight the perceived commonalities between ancient Britons and ancient Peruvians" (Yaya MacKenzie, "Tales of Fallen Empires," 180).
92. Buffon, "Variétés dans l'espèce humaine," 493, 499, 504, 510–512, 515–516 (quote, italics added). See also Gerbi, *The Dispute of the New World,* 3–34; Poole, *Vision, Race, Modernity,* 61–67; Cañizares-Esguerra, *How to Write,* 22, 46-47.
93. Gerbi, *The Dispute of the New World,* 155; Safier, *Measuring the New World,* 171, 196.
94. Robertson, *The History of America,* 1:255, 2:202–204, 3:253–254, 259; de Pauw, *Recherches philosophiques,* 1:66, 140–141, 2:177, 211–212, 216–217, 290, 292; de Pauw, *Défense des recherches philosophiques,* 166–167.
95. On the importance of these new sources in response to de Pauw and Robertson, see Cañizares-Esguerra, *How to Write.*
96. Ulloa, *Noticias Americanas,* 305, 82. For Ulloa's frustrated work in Louisiana, see Strang, *Frontiers of Science,* 77–83.
97. The German Johann Friedrich Blumenbach, for example, in 1779 divided humanity into five ancient varieties, without an "American" example; his first New World skull arrived around 1790. Cook, "The Old Physical Anthropology," 33; Achim, "Skulls and Idols," 31.
98. Ulloa, *Noticias Americanas,* 337–338, 341, 350. The mounds that Ulloa referred to in Louisiana would have belonged to the millennia-old Native American monument-building traditions of the Mississippian world.
99. For Ulloa's wider intellectual importance, see Mendieta, "Enlightened Readers."
100. Cañizares-Esguerra and Thurner, "Andes," 222–223.

101. Ulloa, *Noticias Americanas*, 342–343.
102. W. S. W. Ruschenberger to Morton, March 3, 1833, Box 2, Series I, Samuel George Morton Papers, American Philosophical Society (SGMP-APS).
103. Wafer, *A New Voyage*, 210–211 (emphasis added).
104. Walker, *The Tupac Amaru Rebellion*, 45, and *passim*; Garrett, *Shadows of Empire*. See Flores Galindo, *In Search of an Inca*, and Guibovich Pérez, "The Dissemination and Reading of the Royal Commentaries in the Peruvian Viceroyalty," for Garcilaso's eighteenth-century Peruvian diffusion.
105. Walker, *The Tupac Amaru Rebellion*, 163–166. See Rowe, "El movimiento nacional Inca en el siglo XVIII," 25-32 for how these measures responded to an "Inca renaissance" in eighteenth century Peru. Again, see Guibovich Pérez, "The Dissemination and Reading of the Royal Commentaries in the Peruvian Viceroyalty," for those measures' relative failure.
106. Thomson, *We Alone Will Rule*; Serulnikov, *Subverting Colonial Authority*; Penry, *The People Are King*; Bonilla and Spalding, "La Independencia en el Perú."
107. Premo, *Children of the Father King* and "Custom Today," 364–368.
108. Unanue, "Idea General de los Monumentos," 203–204n2. I thank R. Alan Covey for pointing out that these Sacsahuanas were not the same location. This was also Acosta's error. For Unanue's shifting use of *nación, país,* and *patria* referred to in this paragraph and the next, see Thurner, *History's Peru*, 84–89. See Guibovich Pérez, "La función de la Historia," for an excellent portrayal of the *Mercurio's* historical vindication of Spain.
109. Thurner and Pimentel, "Introduction," 5. Warren, *Medicine and Politics*, 8–9; Chp. 2 thoroughly reveals this anatomical project.
110. Unanue, *"Decadencia y restauracion del Perú,"* 117. See also Nolasco Crespo, "Carta sobre los monumentos antiguos de los *Peruanos*," 264–265, and Guibovich Pérez, "The Dissemination and Reading of the Royal Commentaries in the Peruvian Viceroyalty," 143. For Unanue's reading: Sánchez-Concha Barrios, "Ideologías del Perú republicano del siglo XIX," 1204.
111. Unanue, *"Decadencia y restauracion del Perú,"* 90—94. Specifically, the word Unanue used, *manes,* referred to domestic and familial deities of Rome—ancestral shades. See also Sanfeliú Ortiz and de Tova Arredondo, *62 meses a bordo,* 98. In 1788 Martínez Compañón sent Madrid's Royal Cabinet of Natural History a "paper museum" of fourteen hundred watercolors depicting Trujillo's riches, among which were ten depictions of the contents of Chimu tombs, nine maps and stratigraphical plans, and over eighty pages illustrating the contents of boxes upon boxes of excavated objects still in Spain today. That collection was known to the ilustrados of Lima, and was described in the pages of the *Mercurio* by the bishop's nephew, Joseph Ignacio de Lequanda, in 1793. Trever, "The Uncanny Tombs in Martínez Compañón's *Trujillo del Perú*," and Pillsbury and Trever, "The King, the Bishop, and the Creation of an American Antiquity," make powerful arguments as to the purposes and effects of these watercolors. Also sees Alcina Franch, *Arqueólogos o anticuarios,* 75, 172–175, 184; Cabello Carro, "Las colecciones peruanas en España"; Berquist, *The Bishop's Utopia*; Thurner and Pimentel, "Introduction."
112. Alcina Franch, *Arqueólogos o anticuarios,* 165, offers a table of fourteen European and Peruvian excavators between 1710 and 1802. Upon landing in Arica in 1787 the astronomer José Joaquin de Ferrer treated the excavation of a tomb as one of his scientific duties: Alcala Galiano, *Biografía del astrónomo Español don José Joaquin de Ferrer y Cafranga,* 10.
113. Schnapp, "Between Antiquarians and Archaeologists," and "Ancient Europe and Native Americans."

Chapter 4

1. The Museum of Buenos Aires was only established on 31 December 1823, and its initial collections focused more on non-human natural history: Podgorny and Lopes, *El diesierto,* 49–58.
2. Thomas Hardy to James Paroissien, 10 March 1822, 23 December 1822, D/DOb C1/11, and Basil Hall to James Paroissien, 22 June 1823, D/DOb C1/29, Records of James Paroissien and the Beuzeville Family (RJP), Essex Record Office (ERO), UK; Hall, *Extracts from a*

Journal, 2:71–73; Pettigrew, *A History of Egyptian Mummies*, 239. I previously addressed this itinerary in "How to Make an Inca Mummy" and "Inca Mummy."

3. James Paroissien to Sir William Knighton, n.d., D/DOb C1/29, RJP; Lynch, *San Martín*, 154–161.
4. Basadre, *El azar en la historia*, 162–164; McEvoy, "El motín de las palabras."
5. Edward Home to Royal College of Surgeons Museum, 27 May 1823, RCS-MUS/5/6/12, Archives of the Royal College of Surgeons of England, London. Its latest register is *Synopsis of the Contents of the Museum of the Royal College of Surgeons of England* (1871), 23–24.
6. For the other Incanist symbols of independence, see Amigo, "Los emblemas en tránsito." In portraying the "Inca mummy" as a "new" scientific object of nationhood, I look to Daston, "Introduction."
7. For San Martín's march as setting up knowledge institutions, see Miller, *Republics of Knowledge*, 15–25. Del Castillo, *Crafting a Republic*, thinks through republican creations of benighted "colonial legacies."
8. "Mines of Mummies," *Quincy (IL) Daily Journal*, 28 May 1892, 3.
9. See Gänger, *Relics of the Past*, for a rich survey of that landscape. For late colonial epistemes' continuity with postcolonial and transatlantic science, see Cañizares-Esguerra, *Nature, Empire, and Nation*, Chp. 6; Achim and Podgorny, "Descripción densa"; Kohl, Podgorny, and Gänger, eds., *Nature and Antiquities*; Achim, *From Idols to Antiquity*, Chp. 1.
10. For the celebration of "dead" Incas, which sometimes ignored both the Inca living and the exclusion of living Indigenous republicans, see Méndez Gastelumendi, "Incas sí, Indios no"; Majluf, "De la rebelión al museo"; Gänger, *Relics of the Past*, Chp. 1; Elward, *Los Incas republicanos*.
11. Yvinec, "Les Péruviens auparavant només Indiens," 19.
12. As quoted by Salvatore, "Progress and Backwardness," 1012. See also Tello and Mejía Xesspe, *Historia de los museos nacionales del Perú*; Tello, *Paracas*, Chp. 2; Ávalos de Matos and Ravines, "Las antiguedades Peruanas."
13. Conceptual motility was precisely their attraction, as "boundary objects" per Star and Griesemer, "Institutional Ecology, 'Translations' and Boundary Objects"; and Van Damme, "The Pillar of Metropolitan Greatness." See Ordoñez, *Unbundled*, and Carter, Vilches, and Santoro, "South American Mummy Trafficking," for excellent past treatments of this diaspora. See Cushman, *Guano*, for their nitrate analogue.
14. This is not so far-fetched as it may appear at first glance. In 1776 in Madrid, one Limeño intellectual claimed that Peru's viceroy had, in 1615, gifted Pachacutec's head to Ana María Coya de Loyola, Huayna Capac's great-great-granddaughter; the head was supposedly in a crystal urn belonging to a marquess in Madrid. Relatives of the marquesate's heir recently told the research Stefan Ziemendorff that their archives possess a "head of a mummified Indian, the size of a large orange, more or less, with long hair and a cord in the nose . . . that my mother used to say belonged to a Jivaro . . . brought from America in the epoch of the Viceroys." Yet this suggests it was a *tsantsa* or "shrunken head" made by the Achuar of the Andes—decidedly not Inca. Ziemendorff, "Los Marqueses de Santiago de Oropesa y las Momias Reales Incaicas," 255 (citing Guillermo Lohmann Villena, "El Señorío de los Marqueses de Santiago de Oropesa en el Perú," *Anuario de istoria del Derecho Español* 19 (1948): 347–458).
15. de Pauw, *Recherches philosophiques*, 2;:290.
16. Unanue, "*Decadencia y Restauracion del Perú*," 117.
17. Sanfeliú Ortiz and de Tova Arredondo, *62 meses a bordo*, 98. For Malaspina's expedition and its part in the "truth-to-nature" shift in scientific "visual epistemology," see Pimentel, *Viajeros Científicos*; Daston and Galison, *Objectivity*; Bleichmar, *Visible Empire*.
18. He was seven-two in Castilian feet and inches, making him a still-tall six-six in English feet and inches.
19. Unanue, "Descripción del Gigante," 293, 294n1. According to Matto de Turner, *Perú*, 27, Don Joseph Pardo de Figueroa, the Marques de Valleumbroso of Oropesa, possessed the *finca* of *Quispicanchi*, to the southeast of Cuzco and died in 1747. He was believed the most enlightened man of Cuzco of his day—a veritable "encyclopedia" with knowledge of Latin, Spanish, Quechua, "Mexican," Portuguese, Italian, French, and Greek. Again, see Guibovich Pérez, "La

función de la Historia," for how the *Mercurio* sought to vindicate Spanish Peruvians in the eyes of Europe.

20. See Daston and Galison, *Objectivity*, for collective empiricism's rise.

21. "Literary and Philosophical Intelligence," *The Christian Observor*, October 1804, 644; Skinner, *The Present State of Peru*, 15.

22. "Art. X. The Present State of Peru . . . ," 50–51, 60. For how other Spanish-Americans were at the forefront of reinterpreting formerly "giant" remains as prehistoric fossils, see Podgorny, "De ángeles, gigantes y megaterios"; Pimentel, *The Rhinoceros and the Megatherium*; Cooley, "The Giant Remains."

23. Eastman, "The Sacred Mantle of the Constitution of 1812," 9; O'Phelan, "Dionisio Inca Yupanqui."

24. Walker, *Smoldering Ashes*, Chps. 3 and 4; O'Phelan, "El mito de la 'independencia concedida' "; Cahill, "New Viceroyalty, New Nation, New Empire"; Sobrevilla Perea, "Loyalism and Liberalism"; Escanilla Huerta, "Las milicias locales."

25. For the Incanist symbology of both loyalism and independence, see Walker, *Smoldering Ashes*; Majluf, "De la rebelión al museo"; Thurner, *History's Peru*; Amigo, "Los emblemas en tránsito"; and Yvinec, "*Les Péruviens auparavant només Indiens*," Chps. 1 and 2. For the debate over whether Peruvian Independence was "conceded"—a conservative move reflective of creole fear of Peruvians of color—or more radical, see Bonilla and Spalding, "La independencia en el Perú"; Contreras and Glave, eds., *La independencia del Perú*.

26. Majluf, "The Creation of the Image of the Indian," 38–39, 40–41.

27. Ibid., 26.

28. Walker, *The Tupac Amaru Rebellion*, 27; Thomson, "Sovereignty Disavowed."

29. Geggus, "The Naming of Haiti." I thank Timothy Vasko for pointing me to this citation.

30. Racine, *Francisco de Miranda*, 106–107, 284n21.

31. Amigo, "Los emblemas en tránsito," 244–249; Yvinec, "*Les Péruviens auparavant només Indiens*," 31–32.

32. Earle, "Creole Patriotism," 131 ("Inca is roused," "successors"); Walker and Clarke, *Witness to the Age of Revolution*; Racine, " 'This England and This Now' " and "Proxy Pasts"; Majluf, "De la rebelión al museo."

33. James Paroissien Journal, 21 January 1812–19 March 1812, D/DOb F1/5, RJP.

34. Humphreys, "James Paroissien's Notes," 262. See also Zevallos Quiñones, *Huacas y huaqueros*, 14.

35. Pettigrew, *A History of Egyptian Mummies*, 239; Hall, *Extracts from a Journal*, 2:72–73. Unanue supported San Martín's approach and negotiated his entry to Lima: Humphreys, "James Paroissien's Notes," 264, 270; Unanue, "Los males de la Guerra civil y el deber de los escritores" (9 de Octubre de 1820), in *Obras científicas y literarias*, 392–393. See Begerock et al., "200 Years a Woman," for our need to question some of these early tales of gendered Andean mummies.

36. Heaney, "A Peru of Their Own"; Lynch, *San Martín*, 26–27.

37. Paroissien to Knighton, n.d., D/DOb C1/29, RJP; Humphreys, *Liberation in South America*, 98–101.

38. Hall, *Extracts from a Journal*, 2:71, 73.

39. This reading is indebted to Majluf, "De la rebelión al museo"; Thurner, *History's Peru*; Hertzman, "Fatal Differences."

40. See Rosas Buendía, "Mariano de Rivero y un diálogo tecnológico," 145, for Rivero as "first technocrat of the republic." For his career before returning to Peru, see del Castillo, "Entangled Fates."

41. Kolar, "Tuned to the Senses"; Rick, "Innovation, Religion and Authority"; Weismantel, "Encounters with Dragons."

42. Rivero y Ustariz, *Antiguedades Peruanas*, 23–24.

43. See Majluf, *Inventing Indigenism*, Chp. 2, for how Peruvian creoles aestheticized melancholy and Inca mourning.

44. Rivero y Ustariz, *Antiguedades Peruanas*, 25–26. See Thurner, *History's Peru*, 109–111, for a less literal interpretation of this passage.

45. See Coloma Porcari, *Los Inicios* for Rivero's first *Antigüedades Peruanas* (1827) as a key turn in criollo interest.

46. For this era's debates over ancient Peruvian and Inca origins, and the genius of Peruvian climate and soil, see Thurner, *History's Peru*, Chp. 4.

47. Decreto Supremo N° 89, Lima, 2 April 1822, in Ávalos de Matos and Ravines, "Las Antiguedades Peruanas," 373. See Amigo, "Los emblemas en tránsito," 251–253, for Monteagudo and an Incaismo stripped of its ethnic character.

48. Mariano Eduardo de Rivero y Ustariz, "Plan para un Museo de Historia Natural," S/f [1826], and "Circular a los Prefectos, Yntendentes, Curas, &c &c de la Republica Peruana," Lima, 3 March 1826, Tribunal de Minería. TM–RE 1, Legajo 52 Archivo General de la Nación, Perú [AGNP], Archivo colonial. Gänger, *Relics of the Past*, 108, and "Of Butterflies" argues for this nonarchaeological vision for the museum.

49. Tello and Mejía Xesspe, *Historia de los museos nacionales del Perú*, 3; Rivero y Ustariz, *Antiguedades Peruanas*, 23–24.

50. Ayllón Dulanto, *El Museo del Perú*, 36; Coloma Porcari, *Los Inicios*.

51. "Ynventario de . . . Museo nacional" (1839), Biblioteca Nacional del Perú Archivos [BNPA], D1957 1846, Documentos pertenecientes al Museo Nacional, 1846–1867, F. 4; Stewart, *A Visit to the South Seas*, 1:179.

52. Rivero y Ustariz, "Noticia de Antiguedades Peruanas."

53. Stewart, *A Visit to the South Seas*, 1:179.

54. Tristan, *Peregrinaciones de una paria*, 484.

55. Carleton, *Our Artist in Peru*, 50.

56. Tschudi, *Travels in Peru during the Years 1838–1842*, 504; Gänger, "Of Butterflies," 289.

57. Barrera, "Antigüedades Peruanas," 106–108, 110, 111. I thank Stefanie Gänger and Miguel Rosas Buendía for sharing Barrera's essay with me.

58. Riggs, "Loose Bodies," 254–255.

59. Heaney, "Dry Subjects."

60. Riggs, *Unwrapping Ancient Egypt*, 44–49; Hamann, "How Maya Hieroglyphs Got Their Name"; Cook, "Time's Bodies."

61. As previously noted, Blumenbach had included "Americans" as one of his races since 1775, but his first New World skull seems to have arrived around 1790. Cook, "The Old Physical Anthropology," 33; Achim, "Skulls and Idols," 31; Niekerk, "Man and Orangutan in Eighteenth-Century Thinking," 479; Gissis, "Visualizing 'Race' in the Eighteenth Century," 91–92.

62. Riggs, *Unwrapping Ancient Egypt*, 48–49.

63. Colla, *Conflicted Antiquities*, 50.

64. Riggs, *Unwrapping Ancient Egypt*, 49–55. See also Latour, "On the Partial Existence," 247–251; Moshenska, "Unrolling Egyptian Mummies"; and Monteiro, "Racializing the Ancient World," Chp. 2.

65. *Catalogue of Contents of the Museum of the Royal College of Surgeons in London. Part VI*, 53–55.

66. Pettigrew, *A History of Egyptian Mummies*, 237–241. French scholar Alcide d'Orbigny, who dug at Arica in the early 1830s, after 1835 also described the bodies he found as "natural mummies" (Riviale, *Los viajeros franceses*, 23). This typology is still used. Arthur S. Aufderheide, who founded the field of paleopathology—dissecting the ancient dead to study the diseases that killed them—as recently as 2003 reproduced Pettigrew's assumptions, writing that "we look in vain . . . for details of [Incas'] mummification methods" (Aufderheide, *The Scientific Study of Mummies*, 124).

67. Thurner, *History's Peru*, 108–109; Rosas Buendía, "Mariano de Rivero y un diálogo tecnológico," 157. See also Gänger, "Of Butterflies."

68. See Coloma Porcari, *Los Inicios*, 35–52, for a review of twenty-three places Rivero seems to have dug or surveyed.

69. Rivero y Ustariz and Schuder, *Antiguedades Peruanas*, 42.

70. Cushman, *Guano*, 32–35, and Chp. 2; Gootenberg, *Imagining Development*.

71. Meyen, *Reise um die Erde ausgeführt*, 2:63.

72. Meyen, "Menschen-Raçen," 22, 23, 24–27, 29, 33.

73. "Antiquités Péruviennes," 186; Joly, "Notice sur une momie américaine," 257; Cornalia, "Sulla Mummia Peruviana," 20, 23; Masson, *The British Museum*, 39 ("Peruvian mode"); Gänger,

"Conquering the Past," 705–706; "Quotations from various authors on b) Peru: Bone Painting copied by C. W. Mead" [1910s]," Folder 6, Box 175, Hrdlička Reprint Archive (HRA), Smithsonian National Museum of Natural History.

74. Wagner, "The Anthropological Collection of the Physiological Institute of Göttingen," 348–349.
75. Tschudi, Travels in Peru during the Years 1838–1842, 504–505.
76. Thurner, History's Peru, 113 ["entombed"]; see Majluf, Inventing Indigenism, 35–37, for the wider aesthetic context of Antigüedades peruanas and the opening of the Louvre's salon.
77. Rivero y Ustariz and Tschudi, Antigüedades Peruanas; Rivero and Tschudi, Peruvian Antiquities, 174, 204–205.
78. Rivero y Ustariz and Tschudi, Peruvian Antiquities, 204–207.
79. Ibid., 36, 207, 208.
80. "Rapport sur un Mémoire de M. Édouard de Rivero," 1199, 1203. Denmark's antiquarian society quickly used Antiguedades Peruanas to interpret some 130 pieces, including the mummy of a woman collected for the Archaeological Cabinet of King Christian VIII. See "Antiquités Péruviennes," 437–438.
81. As Ricardo Roque observed (Headhunting and Colonialism, 178), challenging Michel Foucault's claim that the epistemes of natural history and museums cleaved "knowledge of material things and the knowledge of stories into which things had been entailed." Small histories, biographies of the collected, are there if we look for them.
82. "In a word, archaeology": Gänger, Relics of the Past, 43. See also Majluf, "De la rebelión al museo." For southern Peru's rich Indigenous-shaped republican politics, see Walker, Smoldering Ashes.
83. Sahuaraura Inca, "Artículo remitido," 9–10. Again, I thank Stefanie Gänger for providing me this article.
84. Ibid. See Gänger, Relics of the Past, Chp. 1, for the Cuzco antiquarian scene; 71–76 reads Sahuaraura's intervention in this debate as a matter of familial knowledge and Cusqueño pride. See Majluf, "De la rebelión al museo," 278–289, and Elward, Los Incas republicanos for Sahuaraura and fellow Incas' republican efforts.
85. "Rapport sur un Mémoire de M. Édouard de Rivero," 1207–1208.
86. From the sixteenth century to the 1820s, wills and testaments in northern Peru included objects taken from huacas, not all of which were made of precious metals. Zevallos Quiñones, Huacas y huaqueros, 12–13, 48–53, 60.
87. Ibid., 14, 52–53, 60; Paroissien, 24 September 1820, in Humphreys, "James Paroissien's Notes," 262.
88. John Salkeld to Marmaduke Burrough, 18 October 1828, Folder 9, Box 2, Marmaduke Burrough Papers (MBP), Princeton University Rare Books and Special Collections.
89. For Peru's experiments with protectionist and liberal economic policies, see Gootenberg, Between Silver and Guano. For looking beyond narratives of republican Peruvian failure, see Gootenberg, "Seeing a State in Peru," and Majluf, Inventing Indigenism.
90. "The Peruvian Mummy," The Dublin Monitor, 18 May 1839, 3. See also Ward, "Mummies of Peru," 1.
91. Oficio N° 436. Lima, 26 de Setiembre de 1837, José Mará Galdeano, in Ávalos de Matos and Ravines, "Las Antiguedades Peruanas," 40.
92. "Ministerio de Gobierno y Relaciones Exteriores," El Peruano, 18 Enero 1840, 21.
93. Gänger, Relics of the Past, Chps. 1 and 2.
94. Ministerio de Gobierno, Miguel Cam. to Sr. Ynspector del Ynstituto Nacional, 11 de Setiembre 1845, and Protomedicato Jeneral del Peru al Dir del Museo Nacional, 2 de Julio de 1845, BNPA D1957, 32–35; Tello and Mejía Xesspe, Historia de los museos nacionales del Perú, 25–29.
95. "Remarkable Skulls Found in Peru"; Cushman, Guano, 33–35.
96. Lequanda, "Continuación de la descripción" (1793); Humboldt, Views of Nature, 412; Majluf, Inventing Indigenism, 42.
97. Caldcleugh, Travels in South America, 73-74.
98. Majluf, Inventing Indigenism, 67 ("poor Andean") and Chp. 1, passim, explore this attempt to liberate "the Indian" from past rhetorics of subjection and degradation. See also Gänger, Relics of the Past, 137–138.

99. Charton, "Les Arts au Perou," 102. I thank Natalia Majluf for this reference. See her "'Ce n'est pas le Pérou,'" 881–882, and *Inventing Indigenism* for this episode and further reactions in Paris.

100. Zevallos Quiñones, *Huacas y huaqueros*.

101. Humphreys, "James Paroissien's Notes," 262.

102. Proctor, *Narrative of a Journey across the Cordillera of the Andes*, 195.

103. Ruschenberger, *Three Years in the Pacific*, 340, 341.

104. On portrayals of Indigenous inscrutability, see Majluf, *Inventing Indigenism*, 105–111.

105. Cook, *Demographic Collapse*, 83–88; Albiez-Wieck and Gil Montero, "The Emergence of Colonial Fiscal Categorizations in Peru."

106. For the inclusionary and exclusionary discourses of Andean nation-making regarding Indigenous populations, see Mallon, *Peasant and Nation*; Thurner, *From Two Republics to One Divided*; Larson, *Trials of Nation-Making*; Yvinec, "Les Péruviens auparavant només Indiens."

107. Warren, *Medicine and Politics*, Chp. 5; BNPA D1957, 91, Prefectura del Departamento de Lima al Director del Museo Nacional, 16 Febrero 1850.

108. Petit-Thouars, "Nouveaux renseignements," 737.

109. Raimondi, "Enumeración de los vestigios," 165–166. See also Ravines, *Los museos del Perú*, 37; Villacorta Ostolaza, "Antonio Raimondi"; Bandelier, *The Ruins at Tiahuanaco*, 19, 25. Rodriguez, "No 'Mere Accumulation of Material,'" 64–65, specifically points out the importance of geographical work for Americanist anthropology, focusing on the Mexican context.

110. Raimondi, *El Perú*, I, 47–48; Paz Soldán, *Geografía del Perú*, 214; Wiener, *Perú y Bolivia*, 398, 407; Bastien, *Healers of the Andes*, 18; Gänger, *Relics of the Past*, 138; Herrera, "Indigenous Archaeology," 69, 78–79. See also Gündüz, *El Mundo Ceremonial de los Huaqueros*; Garofalo, "Conjuring with Coca and the Inca," 76–78; Smith, "Looting and the Politics of Archaeological Knowledge in Northern Peru," and for an example of undead agency from Chile, Bacigalupo, "The Mapuche Undead Never Forget."

111. Ruschenberger, *Three Years in the Pacific*, 398–399.

112. For thinking through these engagements as rituals, as formal ways of knowing and engaging sacred or spirited materials, see Salomon, *At the Mountains' Altar*. Bennison, "Waqay," argues more generally that these rituals suggest wider definitions for acting "Andean" than Indigenous descent, Indigenous language use, or ascribed racial characteristics.

113. Raimondi, "Enumeración de los vestigios," 165–166.

114. Tschudi, *Travels in Peru during the Years 1838–1842*, 455.

115. Larson, *Trials of Nation Making*, 45 ("practice religious"), 145–147, 153–154. This could be read as indicative of a nineteenth-century "reindianization" of the countryside, the growth in the perceived "Indian" population. But it was also an articulation of a different sort of Peruvian present, in which communities remodeled rights and rites carried over from the local "republics" they established under Spanish rule. Kubler, *The Indian Caste of Peru*; Gootenberg, "Population and Ethnicity in Early Republican Peru"; Thurner, *From Two Republics to One Divided*, 135–138.

116. Raimondi, "Itinerario," 41. See Salomon, "'The Beautiful Grandparents,'" for the term's depth of meaning. Espinoza Soriano, "Los señoríos de Yaucha y Picoy," 185 and *passim* places Raimondi's observation in the context of San Mateo's fifteenth- and sixteenth-century ethnohistory.

117. Abercrombie, *Pathways of Memory and Power*, 326; Salomon, "Unethnic Ethnohistory."

118. As discussed in this book's conclusion, in the 1990s, at least one Huarochirí ayllu in the village of Tupicocha still propitiated two water deities in the form of two skulls. See Salomon and Niño-Murcia, *The Lettered Mountain*, 104–114.

119. A pawnbroker finally seized the mummies to satisfy a £25 loan to Duniam, and at least one of them seems to have made it to the Australian Museum. Carter, Vilches, and Santoro, "South American Mummy Trafficking," 4 ("native inhabitants").

120. H. Baxley, *What I Saw*, 178; Lummis, *The Gold Fish of Gran Chimú*.

121. Appadurai, *The Social Life of Things*.

122. Ruschenberger, *Three Years in the Pacific*, 340.

123. Meyen, "Menschen-Raçen," 25; Tschudi, "On the Ancient Peruvians," 83.

124. "A Necklace of Mummy Eyes," 240.
125. "Ethnological Society," *Tipperary Spectator*, 3 June 1846, 4.
126. "Royal Society," *Evening Mail*, 31 May 1830, 6; Pettigrew, *A History of Egyptian Mummies*, 238; Pettigrew, "Account of the Unrolling of an Egyptian Mummy," 29; "Cork Scientific and Literary Society," *Southern Reporter and Cork Commercial Courier*, 20 February 1841, 3; *Morning Advertiser* (London) 20 August 1832, 3; Bellamy, "A Brief Account of Two Peruvian Mummies"; "Elgin," *Inverness Courier*, 28 October 1846, 3; "Rosherville Gardens," *The Kentish Independent*, 2 September 1848, 4; "The Annual Fair or Great Market," *Plymouth and Devonport Weekly Journal*, 8 November 1832, 3; "The Pleasure Fair," *Hampshire Advertiser*, 8 May 1841, 2; "Peruvian Mummy," *Chester Chronicle*, 13 May 1842; "A Guano-Embalmed Child," *Leeds Intelligencer*, 30 December 1848, 7; Masson, *The British Museum*, 39. Ordoñez, *Unbundled*, 89, shows that there were two mummies from Colombia brought to the British Museum in this era as well.
127. *The Lancet* (London) 2, no. 4 (22 July 1848): 112.
128. "The Peruvian Mummy," *Morning Chronicle* (London), 29 November 1839, 1.
129. Moshenska, "Unrolling Egyptian Mummies," 13.
130. "Antiquités Péruviennes"; Baquedano, "Al Sr. D. Francisco García Huidobro"; "The Peruvian Mummy," *Morning Chronicle* (London), 29 November 1839, 1; Wagner, "The Anthropological Collection of the Physiological Institute of Göttingen," 348–349; Rivero y Ustariz and Tschudi, *Peruvian Antiquities*, 207–208; "Peruvian Mummies," *The Illustrated London News*, 2 November 1850, 344; Wagner, "The Anthropological Collection," 358–359; Carter, Vilches, and Santoro, "South American Mummy Trafficking"; Riviale, "La marine française," 129, 130; Ordoñez, *Unbundled*, 99, 103, 109–113.
131. Pettigrew, *A History of Egyptian Mummies*, 241; *Catalogue of Contents of the Museum of the Royal College of Surgeons in London. Part VI*, 53–55.
132. Knight, ed., *London*, 6:207.
133. Tschudi, *Travels in Peru during the Years 1838–1842*, 500.
134. Alberti, *Morbid Curiosities*, 193–195, explores how bodies break down the "museum effect" in favor of "museum affect."
135. Cornalia, "Sulla Mummia Peruviana," 20, 23.
136. Ibid., 22, 24.
137. Raimondi, "Ayacucho," 56.
138. "Peruvian Mummies," *The Illustrated London News*, 2 November 1850, 344.

Chapter 5

1. Browne, "An Essay on Indian Corn," 139. "First successful": the Charleston Museum, founded in 1773, only opened to the public in 1824. Pierre Eugene Du Simitiere's Philadelphia museum (founded 1782) was sold after his 1784 death.
2. Meetings of Trustees, 26 April 1831, Philadelphia Museum Company Minutes 1821–1845, 67, American Philosophical Society Mss.507.748.P53.
3. Fuller, "Heathen Idols"; Browne, "An Essay on Indian Corn," 139; Buckingham, *The Eastern and Western States of America*, 1:543; Sellers, *Mr. Peale's Museum*, 260.
4. Sellers, *Mr. Peale's Museum*, 257–280; Uribe Hanabergh, "Titian Ramsay Peale's 1831 'Obscure Expedition to Colombia.' "
5. Browne, "An Essay on Indian Corn," 139, 151.
6. Morton, *Crania Americana*, 107–108. See Begerock et al., "200 Years a Woman," for reason to take mummies' gender with a grain of salt.
7. Conn, *History's Shadow*; Harvey, *Native Tongues*, 196-202 and *passim*. Hrdlička, *Physical Anthropology*, 41.
8. Stanton, *The Leopard's Spots*; Stepan, *The Idea of Race*, 16–17; Bieder, *Science Encounters the Indian*, Chp. 3; Riding In, "Six Pawnee Crania," 105; Riviale, *Los viajeros franceses*, 25–28, 146–147; Menand, *The Metaphysical Club*, Chp. 5; Fabian, *The Skull Collectors*; Painter, *The History of White People*, Chp. 13; Conklin, *In the Museum of Man*, 22–24; Redman, *Bone Rooms*, Chp. 1; Berry, *The Price for Their Pound of Flesh*, 101–112, Chp. 6; Strang, *Frontiers of Science*, Chp. 7; Poskett, *Materials of the Mind*.

9. The search for origins can be a mug's game. Yet questioning American anthropology and archaeology's auto-genealogy of descent from Franz Boas—or, when feeling more self-critical, Thomas Jefferson—is necessary. More than showing how specifically important Morton, skull-collecting, and racism were, it makes clear those fields' debt to prior strains of scholarship and colonial violence—in this case, that of Peru.

10. Per Fields and Fields, *Racecraft*, 1–5, I mostly resist calling Morton's work "race science," which might give exterior solidity to what a set of racist practices that as Fields and Fields observe in *Racecraft* "failed as a science" (4). I've sometimes opted for "racism" to describe Morton's work, but their appellation "bio-racism" is also apt.

11. Fabian, *The Skull Collectors*, 38; Morton to George Combe, 2 March 1840, National Library of Scotland (NLS) MSS 7256/48-49. At least 201 of this 867 were "ancient Peruvian," followed by "ancient Egyptians" (84) and "Negro" skulls (107). Other "Americans" from throughout the hemisphere together were 208. Morton, *Catalogue of Skulls of Man*, v-vi. Morton collected another 100 before dying. When next tallied, his 1,035 human crania included 221 "Peruvians" or replicating casts, still the collection's largest; see Meigs, *Catalogue of Human Crania*, 3, 76–87.

12. Gould, *The Mismeasure of Man*, 89, 99. The Peruvian skulls of Morton and others are also noted by Stanton, *The Leopard's Spots*, 38; Bieder, *Science Encounters the Indian*, 77–78; Delpar, *Looking South*, 12; Fabian, *The Skull Collectors*, 38–39, 189–190; Achim, "Skulls and Idols," 32; and Poskett, *Materials of the Mind*, 102–105. Morton weighted Peruvians equally to other American groups to not distort the shared average, anthropologists have shown, but his decision *to* amass and average them, and his conclusions, illustrate his project's racism: Lewis et al., "The Mismeasure of Science," 3; Mitchell and Michael, "Bias, Brains, and Skulls."

13. Redman, *Bone Rooms*, 277.

14. For "textualization" of racial identities, see Curran, *The Anatomy of Blackness*.

15. Thurner, *History's Peru*, 105–108; Achim, "Skulls and Idols."

16. Peru's dead were the sine qua non of the racialized skull as "authorised object" of physical anthropology, made credible by the historiographical documentation that Roque, "Authorised Histories," identifies as key to the use of human remains "as evidence in support of racial theories, genealogies, and taxonomies" (69).

17. For the American arc of racializing the Egyptian dead, see Trafton, *Egypt Land*; Fabian, *The Skull Collectors*, 105–110; Monteiro, "Racializing the Ancient World," Chp. 2.

18. Appelbaum, MacPherson, and Rosemblatt, "Introduction," 13.

19. For Peruvian indigenism growing from a progressive yet essentializing cultural construct of race, see Majluf, *Inventing Indigenism*.

20. This is to say that "ancient Peruvians" were as foundational to anthropology and remains-based museums as enslaved and Black women's bodies were to American gynecology, per Owens, *Medical Bondage*.

21. Heaney, "Skull Walls," develops these implications at length.

22. Delpar, *Looking South*, 1. Cañizares-Esguerra, *How to Write*, shows why Spanish-American materials and texts were key.

23. S. G. Morton, Lecture (early 1830s), Folder 1, Box 5, Samuel George Morton Papers, Library Company of Philadelphia (SGMP-LC); Morton, *Crania Americana*, 96, 97. For Peru's section being earliest composed, see FN48.

24. See Chapter 3.

25. Cook, "The Old Physical Anthropology," 33.

26. Thomas, "Thomas Jefferson's Conflicted Legacy," 88–89. For his timing of excavation, and use of Ulloa's *Noticias Americanas*, see Wilson, "The Evolution of Jefferson's 'Notes'" 119, 123; Mendieta, "Enlightened Readers"; and Jefferson, Fair Copy MS of *Notes*, 14.

27. Heaney, "A Peru of Their Own"; DeLucia, *Memory Lands*, 53 ("semiscientific"), 54, 70–74, 134–135, 145–147; Midtrød, "'Calling for More Than Human Vengeance.'" See Seeman, *Death in the New World*, for how deathways were also a place of intercultural communication.

28. Wertheimer, *Imagined Empires*.

29. Jefferson, Fair Copy MS of *Notes*, 35.1; Jefferson, *Notes on the State of Virginia*, 36–38, 57, 96; Jefferson to Chastellux, 2 June 1785, in McClure and Looney, eds., *The Papers of Thomas*

Jefferson: https://rotunda.upress.virginia.edu/founders/TSJN-01-08-02-0145. Hantman, *Monacan Millennium*, Chp. 2, reconstructs the Monacan earthwork's sacralization.

30. Ulloa, "Of the Indigenous Inhabitants," 150.

31. Martinko, "'So Majestic a Monument'"; Snyder, "The Once and Future Moundbuilders"; Timmerman, "Contested Indigenous Landscapes," 79; Jackson, Second Annual Message to Congress, x. Portrayals of Indians as not indigenous to the Americas (as descended from Japheth, a lost tribe of Israel, or a pre-Noachian people) were given explanatory force by Acosta's theories of migration by land, and renewed by Humboldt, who posited that the first Incas were in fact east Asian. Lucius, "A Few Observations"; Humboldt, *Views of the Cordilleras*, 10–11.

32. Jackson, Second Annual Message to Congress, x.

33. Barton, "Observations and Conjectures," 184, 201, 211–212, 215. Also, Henry M. Brackenridge to Thomas Jefferson, Baton Rouge, 25 July 1813, in McClure and Looney, eds., *The Papers of Thomas Jefferson*: http://rotunda.upress.virginia.edu/founders/TSJN-03-06-02-0269. For Clavijero's importance as a creole patriot epistemologist, see Cañizares-Esguerra, *How to Write*, 235–249.

34. For early republican science as a matter of imperial knowledge, see Strang, *Frontiers of Science*. As Gould, "Entangled Histories," 784, observes, the US nineteenth-century imperial arc was largely completed not just at the expense of Indigenous polities but also at the expense of Spain and its successor Indo-*mestizo* republics.

35. Heaney, "A Peru of Their Own," 631–643; Seeman, *Death in the New World*; See DeLucia, *Memory Lands*, 147; Morton, *Crania Americana*, 81; Fabian, *The Skull Collectors*; Strang, *Frontiers of Science*, Chp. 7; Snyder, "The Once and Future Moundbuilders," 108–111 (quote: Peter Pitchlynn, 111).

36. Jefferson, *Notes on the State of Virginia*, 158–159.

37. Barton, "Observations and Conjectures," 211–212, 215. See Smith, *A Museum*, 23, for lamentations to that end.

38. Cook, "The Old Physical Anthropology," 33; Achim, "Skulls and Idols," 31. See Poole, *Vision, Race, and Modernity*, 70–78, for Humboldt perceiving colonialism and admixture as thwarting his attempt to read "Indian" physiognomy.

39. Drake, *Natural and Statistical View*, 207–208; Atwater, *Description of Antiquities*, 171, 185, 209–210.

40. Caldcleugh, *Travels in South America*, 73–74; Blumenbach, *Nova pentas collectionis*, 10–11. See this book's previous chapter for San Martín's Inca. Velasco, "Ethnogenesis and Social Difference," offers a most nuanced interpretation of cranial modification.

41. Most came at the end of his life or were added posthumously by Tschudi. Wagner, "The Anthropological Collection," 351, 355.

42. "Remarkable Skulls Found in Peru," 477 ("now existing"); Tiedemann, "Nachricht über merkwuurdige Menschel-Schädel aus Peru," 107–109 (emphasis added). I thank Paul Mitchell for pointing me to Tiedemann.

43. Horner, *Catalogue of the Anatomical Museum*, 40–42.

44. Charles Darwin, Notebook E, 63–65, in Barrett et al., eds., *Charles Darwin's Notebooks, 1836–1844*, 414 (emphasis in original). Desmond and Moore, *Darwin's Sacred Cause*, 149–150, shows that he was referring to Pentland's skulls.

45. Marmaduke Burrough to Richard Harlan, Philadelphia, 28 June 1827, Folder 5, Box 3, MBP. (Marmaduke Burrough was the US consul whose factotum faced off against the dutiful Peruvian customs agent in Chapter 4.) For Morton's extension of Harlan's network, see Fabian, *The Skull Collectors*, 14–15, 20–36.

46. Morton to William Samuel Wauthman Ruschenberger, 28 February 1832, S. G. Morton Letterbook, Princeton University Library Special Collections.

47. Morton, "Account of a Craniological Collection," 18; Fabian, *The Skull Collectors*, 38; Smith, *A Museum*, 29n60.

48. Morton to Combe, 2 March 1840, NLS MSS 7256/48-49.

49. Morton, *Crania Americana*, 99–104, 228.

50. Ibid., 63, 83, 84.

51. Ruschenberger, *Three Years in the Pacific,* 243–244, 340; Ruschenberger to Morton, May 3, 1833, Box 2, Series I, SGMP-APS.
52. Morton, *Crania Americana,* Plates 8–11.
53. Ibid., 108.
54. Ibid., 105. The Boston collection was imported by chemist John Harrison Blake, who believed that some of the Peruvians' preserved flesh "appears to have been subjected to careful"—that is, deliberate—"desiccation, while others, the flesh of which is permeated with resinous substances, are well preserved," an estimation that inspired comparisons to the Egyptians. See Blake, "Notes on a Collection," 277–278, 280–281, 285. By contrast, in 1829 American physician James Haines McCulloh wrote that he had "no reason to believe [that embalming] was ever done by any American people" (*Researches, philosophical and antiquarian,* 117, 380–381).
55. Morton, *Crania Americana,* 108. Morton wasn't alone in this. In 1840 Prince Maximilian, the prince of Wied, referred to the illustration of a Peruvian mummy provided by Prussian physician Meyen, who had so championed Barreda's account of Peruvian embalming. It "perfectly expresses the character of the North American Indians" whom Maximilian during his travels in the North American west. See Thwaites, ed. *Early Western Travels,* 22:218n129.
56. Gould, "Morton's Ranking of Races," 508; S. G. Morton, "Catalogue of Skulls of Man, and the Inferior Animals, in the Collection of Samuel George Morton, M.D.," Annotated Copy, Folder 2, Coll. 30 (Samuel George Morton [1799–1851] Papers), Academy of Natural Sciences Archives, Philadelphia (ANSP).
57. Morton, *Crania Americana,* 97, 98, 99, 101, 105, 108–110.
58. Ibid., 102–103, 113, 116–117, 119.
59. Ibid., *Crania Americana,* 216–230. See Achim, "Skulls and Idols," 33–39, for how Morton mobilized Mesoamerican cranial depictions.
60. Morton, *Crania Americana,* 105. Fabian, *The Skull Collectors,* 80, observes that Morton liked Ongpatonga's portrait because it embraced " 'more characteristic traits . . . than any Indian portrait he had seen."
61. Morton, *Crania Americana,* 229.
62. Ibid., 120.
63. Thurner, *History's Peru,* 107. For creole patriot epistemology, see Cañizares, *How to Write.*
64. Morton, *Crania Americana,* 132, 133, 260–261.
65. Combe, "Appendix," 270.
66. Combe to Morton, 28 February 1840, Box 4, Series I, SGMP-APS. Poskett, *Materials of the Mind,* 99–105, details the exchange.
67. As brilliantly argued by sociologist Karen E. Fields and historian Barbara J. Fields in *Racecraft.*
68. Morton to Combe, 2 March 1840, NLS MSS 7256/48-49.
69. Ibid.; Morton to Silliman, 3 March 1840; Morton to Silliman, 9 March 1840, NLS MSS 7256/45.
70. Morton to Silliman, 9 March 1840 NLS MSS 7256/46-47; Combe to Morton, 13 March 1840, Box 4, Series I, SGMP.
71. Combe, Anonymous Review, 21–22, 28–29.
72. Morton, *Catalogue of Skulls of Man,* v-vi. It had surpassed Blumenbach's 245: Wagner, "The Anthropological Collection," 348.
73. Morton, "Some Remarks on the Ancient Peruvians." See Poole, *Vision, Race, and Modernity,* 78–81. When excavator Ephraim G. Squier sent sketches of the first whole skull he retrieved from mounds in Ohio, Morton gushed that it was the *"perfect* type" of a "truly *aboriginal* skull" because of how "admirably" the Peruvian heads of his *Crania Americana* "correspond[ed] with yours." Nelson, *National Manhood,* 294–295n33.
74. Morton, *An Inquiry,* 7, 19.
75. Morton, "Physical Type of the American Indians," 329, 331; N[ott], "Aboriginal Races of America," 68. See also "Excerpt from Morton's Inedited Manuscripts," in Nott and Gliddon, *Types of Mankind,* 325.
76. Trafton, *Egypt Land;* Fabian, *The Skull Collectors,* 105–110; Monteiro, "Racializing the Ancient World," Chp. 2.
77. Mitchell and Michael, "Bias, Brains, and Skulls"; Tiedemann, "On the Brain of the Negro," 511.

78. Combe to Morton, 20 August 1840, Box 4, Series I, SGMP-APS; Morton, "*Crania Americana . . . ,*" 476, 479, 484.
79. William Cooper to Morton, 5 February 1837; John Edwards Holbrook to Morton, April 1837; S. Wood to Morton, 5 August 1837, Box 3; J. Kearny Rodgers to Morton, 28 December 1838, Box 4, Pentland, Note relative to aborigines of Peru [undated], Box 5, Series I, SGMP-APS.
80. Benj. H. Coates, to the Committee of the Academy of Natural Sciences, 26 September 1836, Letters, 1836, ANSP Coll. 39—U.S. Exploring Expedition, 1838–42; Joyce, *The Shaping of American Ethnography*, 17–22, 38.
81. Wilkes, *Narrative of the United States Exploring Expedition*, 1:278–281; "Original Invoices of Miscellaneous Specimens," 37–38, Folder 5, Box 2, SIA RU 7186, United States Exploring Expedition Collection, 1838–1885.
82. Titian Ramsay Peale, Collection of the United States South Sea Surveying and Exploring Expedition, 1838–1842, Folder 8, Box 1, SIA RU 7186.
83. Rhees, *An Account of the Smithsonian Institution*, floor plan, 69, 71–72.
84. The headdress was later reclassified as having been made by Shuar or "Jivaro Indians." Accession 135, 10 October 1842, Atahualpa's Headdress, Box 17, SIA RU 7508, National Institute. See Bruhns and Kelker, *Faking the Ancient Andes*, for a consideration of the "fake" antiquity trade.
85. On white Americans' belief that Indigenous peoples were passing from history, and that their culture needed to be salvaged, see Conn, *History's Shadow*; O'Brien, *Firsting and Lasting*; Redman, *Prophets and Ghosts*, Chp. 1.
86. Jeremy Ravi Mumford, "The Inca Priest on the Mormon Stage," *Common-Place* 5/4 (July 2005), http://commonplace.online/article/the-inca-priest-on-the-mormon-stage/; "Through the Politeness," *Deseret News*, June 22, 1850, 11–12. See also Deloria, *Playing Indian*, though Mumford makes the observation that white Americans may have adapted wider pseudo-Indian rituals specifically from *Pizarro*.
87. Kagan, "Prescott's Paradigm"; Delpar, *Looking South*, Chp. 1.
88. Prescott, *History of the Conquest of Peru*, 1:39.
89. Redman, *Prophets and Ghosts*, 18, quoting Lewis Henry Morgan (1851).
90. Prescott, *History of the Conquest of Peru*, 1:39.
91. Whether to call these actors neo-imperial is a longstanding object of debate. Peru is where theories of informal economic empire get footnoted to death, given foreign investors' relative inability to get Peruvian policymakers to recoup investments following guano's bust. We risk misapprehending local power and initiative when we assign neocolonialism and neo-imperialism sole explanatory force, ignoring local Peruvian wealth and agency. See Miller, "The Making of the Grace Contract"; Gootenberg, *Between Silver and Guano* and *Imagining Development*. For a like example of how a foreign scientific actor initially presumed to be imperial was schooled by Peruvian epistemic norms, see Lossio, "British Medicine in the Peruvian Andes."
92. Evans to Gilliss, 9 July 1852, in Gilliss, "Peruvian Antiquities," 658–659. Emphasis in original.
93. Evans to Baird, 22 June 1883, and Evans to Baird, 30 November 1883, Acc 13687; Evans to Baird, 22 February 1883, Acc 13028, SIA RU 305.
94. Dorsey, "An Archaeological Study," iv, 15; Hutchinson, *Two Years in Peru*, 2:88; Hutchinson, "Explorations amongst Ancient Burial Grounds," 8. The archaeologist John Rowe took the railroad's construction as the start of large-scale looting in Peru: Daggett, *An Annotated Tello-Centric History*, 82n78.
95. "Discharging Human Remains," *The San Francisco (Evening) Bulletin*, 14 November 1873, 1; "Transplanted Incas," *The Weekly Alta California*, 22 November 1873, 6.
96. For the Army Medical Museum's founding and contradictions, see Fabian, *The Skull Collectors*, Chp. 5.
97. For how scholars across the Atlantic more generally responded to Morton, see Stepan, *The Idea of Race*, 16–17; Riviale, *Los viajeros franceses*, 25–28; Conklin, *In the Museum of Man*, 22–24; Poskett, *Materials of the Mind*.
98. Joly, "Notice sur une momie américaine," 253n1; Wagner, "The Anthropological Collection," 349.
99. Blake, "On the Cranial Characters of the Peruvian Races of Men," 220, 216–231.

100. Wyman, "Report of the Curator" (1868), 5–9; Wyman, "Report of the Curator" (1873), 6; "Notes by Mr. Alexander Agassiz relating to the Peruvian Collection," Peruvian Collection A. Agassiz, Accession 75-20, Peabody Museum of Archaeology and Ethnology Archives (PMAE); Irmscher, *Louis Agassiz*, 328–329; Menand, *The Metaphysical Club*, Chp. 5. These mummies and skulls can be seen as the ancient anchor for the PMAE's photographs of living Andean "types" acquired by Elizabeth Cary Agassiz, Luis Agassiz's wife, as described in Trever, "Criminal Lines." I further develop this point in Chapter Six. For the PMAE's early history, see Hinsley, "From Shell-Heaps to Stelae."

101. Busk, "Remarks on a Collection of 150 Ancient Puruvian [*sic*] Skulls"; Davis, "On Ancient Peruvian Skulls"; "Report of the Council of the Anthropological Institute of Great Britain and Ireland for 1873," 503. For more on Hutchison and his donation of a mummy to Oxford's Pitt-Rivers Museum, see Ordóñez, *Unbundled*, 123–124, 166–167. By comparison, the fifteen-hundred-skull collection of England's Joseph Barnard Davis by 1867 previously had twenty-five skulls from Peru (see Davis, *Thesaurus Craniorum*). For context on Davis, see Roque, "Authorised Histories."

102. Riviale, *Los viajeros franceses*, 94.

103. In the case of the Anthropological Institute of Great Britain and Ireland, they acceded to Daniel Wilson's critique of Morton and the Peruvians in *Prehistoric Man*, Chp. 20.

104. Lewis et al., "The Mismeasure of Science"; Mitchell, "The Mismeasure of All Things."

105. Wyman, "Report of the Curator" (1871), 10.

106. Ibid., 11, 22. Barnhart, *Ephraim George Squier*, 269–271, and Berry, *The Price for Their Pound of Flesh*, 106, provide more context on Wyman.

107. Tschudi, "On the Ancient Peruvians," 83.

108. See, for example, Roque, *Headhunting and Colonialism*; Wagner, *The Skull of Alum Bheg*; Turnbull, "'Rare Work amongst the Professors'"; Magubane, "Simians, Savages, Skulls, and Sex"; Colla, *Conflicted Antiquities*; Harrison, "Skulls and Scientific Collecting in the Victorian Military."

109. Again, in the terms laid out by Star and Griesemer, "Institutional Ecology, 'Translations,' and Boundary Objects," they were boundary objects, used for multiple scientific conversations at once.

110. Nelson, *National Manhood*, 138 ("closet").

111. Fabian, *The Skull Collectors*, Chp. 5; Lonetree, *Decolonizing Museums*, 13; Kehoe, "Manifest Destiny," 189–193 [186–201]; Strang, *Frontiers of Science*, Chp. 7; Riding In, "Six Pawnee Crania."

112. Juzda, "Skulls, Science, and the Spoils of War," 164.

113. McGee, "On an Anatomical Peculiarity," 459.

114. Franz Boas, 6 June 1888, as quoted in Rohner, "Franz Boas," 172.

115. Cañizares-Esguerra, *Nature, Empire, and Nation*, Chp. 4; Unanue, *Observaciones sobre el clima de Lima*, LXXVII–LXXXIII, XCI; Ziemendorff, Millones Figueroa, and Greenwich Centeno, "Las momias reales incaicas," 172–173.

116. Majluf, *Inventing Indigenism*, 64–65.

117. Vigil, "Estudios Frenológicos. (Continuación)," 26; Thurner, *History's Peru*, 105. For the global search for lost white "races," see Robinson, *The Lost White Tribe*.

118. Gänger, *Relics of the Past*.

119. Vigil, "Estudios Frenológicos. (Continuación)," 26.

120. *Vida y Obras de José Mariano Macedo*, 8, 56; Dávalos y Lissón, "La colección de antigüedades peruanas del doctor Macedo."

121. Macedo, "Memorandum Histórico"; I thank Stefanie Gänger for sharing notes from this source with me; see her *Relics of the Past*, 124, for more on Macedo.

122. Rivero y Ustariz and Tschudi, *Antiguedades Peruanas*, 22, 27, 31–32, 35, 36.

123. Raimondi, "Enumeración de los vestigios," 165–166.

124. Carranza y Ayarza, *Colección de artículos publicados*, 82–83, 93–95; Thurner, *From Two Republics*, 132.

125. Muñiz and McGee, "Primitive Trephining in Peru," 5. Only the Museum of La Plata in Buenos Aires seems to have had more: 138 skeletons and about 1,500 crania. Farro, "Historia de las colecciones," 262–268; Salvatore, "Live Indians in the Museum," 111.

126. La Puente, "Estudios etnográficos de la Hoya del Titicaca," 379, 878; Muñiz, "Vida," 315; D. M. "Dr. Manuel Antonio Muñiz," 193–194; Muñiz, "Correspondencia de Londres," 251; Lorena, "Algunos materiales"; Morales Macedo, "Algunas variaciones anatómicas"; Valdizán, "La delincuencia en el Perú."

127. Farro, "Historia de las colecciones," 107, 135–136, 284 ("notable"); Salvatore, "Live Indians in the Museum," 114–115 and *passim* makes this point explicit.

128. In this, I am inspired by the reflections of Blackhawk, *Violence over the Land*, on how Anglo-American colonialism rode prior waves of unseen violence against Native North American bodies caused by Spanish colonialism, and by Appelbaum, MacPherson, and Rosemblatt, "Introduction," on race's transnational American refinement.

129. For how anthropology and archaeology were mobilized in the Bolivian case, see Gildner, "Indomestizo modernism," Chps. 5–7.

130. Riding In, "Six Pawnee Crania," 102 ("most Indians"); Fine-Dare, *Grave Injustice*; Lonetree, *Decolonizing Museums*; Colwell, *Plundered Skulls*.

131. Ordóñez's excellent *Unbundled*, Chp. 4, located nine from the Peruvian Andes and Chile collected prior to the mid-1850s that were still in European museums. By my count (see Chapter 4), at least twenty-nine went to Europe in that era, fifteen to Great Britain alone.

132. "Miscellanea," 230.

133. Sellers, *Mr. Peale's Museum*, 317; Newspaper advertisement for the Boston Museum, *The Barre (VT) Patriot*, 15 September 1850; Ticknor, "The Passing of the Boston Museum," 394. The natural history collection of the Boston Museum went to the Boston Society of Natural History in 1893 and 1899, after which "some of the specimens were destroyed, but most of them"—of the zoological variety—"were sold in 1900 to Mr. C. J. Maynard." Faxon, "Relics of Peale's Museum," 126.

134. Heaney, "Dry Subjects"; Ordóñez, *Unbundled*, 164–165.

135. "Antiquités Péruviennes," 182–183, 184, 185.

136. Fabian, *The Skull Collectors*, 189–190.

137. Aleš Hrdlička to George Grant MacCurdy, 8 March 1917, Folder: MacCurdy (I), Box 43, Aleš Hrdlička Papers (AHP), National Anthropological Archives (NAA); Heaney, "Dry Subjects."

138. Heaney, "Dry Subjects" and "Death of the Object."

Chapter 6

1. Tenorio-Trillo, *Mexico at the World's Fairs*, 38–40.

2. Ingram, *Centennial Exposition Described and Illustrated*, 486–492.

3. Guillermo Colville also went by Guillaume and William. Albertini, *Le Pérou*, 42–44; Wiener, *Perú y Bolivia*, 58; Quiñones Tinoco, *El Perú en la Vitrina*, 90, 163, 171; Riviale, *Los viajeros franceses*, 237–240, 246, 302.

4. Slovak and Wiegand, "Reconstructing Middle Horizon Mobility Patterns"; Slovak, "Reassembling the Mortuary Assemblage."

5. Rowe, *Max Uhle*; Chapman, "Arranging Ethnology"; Williams, "Art and Artifact at the Trocadero"; Hinsley, "In Search of the New World Classical"; Williams, "Collecting and Exhibiting Pre-Columbiana"; Pillsbury, "Finding the Ancient in the Andes," 59–60 ("the concept"); Gänger, *Relics of the Past*, Chp. 2.

6. There were a few pre-Ancón bundles collected and never unbundled, such as three acquired by Belgium's Royal Museum of Arts and History in 1833, but these were exceptions to the larger rule. Ordóñez, *Unbundled*, 102, and *passim*.

7. "Curiosities," *The Metal Worker*, 8 September 1876, 2; "A Peculiar Auction Sale," *The New York Times*, 20 September 1876, 2.

8. Fabian, *The Skull Collectors*, 198 ("from collecting"); see Rodriguez, "No 'Mere Accumulation of Material'" for the shift in seeing Latin America going from a site of extraction to one of embeddedness. For the importance of the Chicago World's Fair to history and anthropology, see Rydell, *All the World's a Fair*, 47; Hinsley and Wilcox, eds., *Coming of Age in Chicago*; Heaney, "Fair Necropolis."

9. Gänger, "¿La mirada imperialista?," 70. For the imperialism of German ethnographic museums as "[coming] from below, pushed into the museums by the increasingly broad and socially diverse audiences that began frequenting them around the turn of the century," see Penny, *Objects of Culture*, 13. Again, see Gootenberg's "Seeing a State in Peru" for looking past narratives of failure, and Gänger, *Relics of the Past*, and Majluf, *Inventing Indigenism*, for how some nineteenth-century Peruvian intellectuals argued that ancient Peruvians and modern Indians were identical, claiming both for the nation.

10. "Lima. "'Los funerales de Atahualpa,'" *El Comercio* (Lima), 30 September 1868; "Los funerales de Atahualpa," *El Comercio* (Lima), 2 October 1868. For the history of this painting, see Majluf, "El rostro del Inca," 15, which shows how Montero, believing he "needed a dead Indian to symbolize" Atahuallpa, sought out the corpse of fellow Peruvian painter Francisco Palemón Tinajeros.

11. "El cadáver de un Opispo," *El Comercio* (Lima), 29 October 1868; "El cádaver," *El Comercio* (Lima), 3 November 1868; "El Obispo cadáver," *El Comercio* (Lima), 3 December 1868.

12. "Cadáver," *El Comercio* (Lima), 2 November 1868.

13. "Petición presentada por Ygnacio Manco Ayllón a la Cámara de Representantes para que investiguen si los restos encontrados en el Hospital de 'San Andrés' corresponden a su ascendiente el Inca Huayna Cápac," Lima, 4 November 1868, BNPA, D2632; "Sociedad de artesanos," *El Comercio* (Lima), 12 October 1868. Among his hopes was that his Inca lineage would be honored by the state: Manco y Ayllón, *Manco-Capac*. See also Majluf, *Escultura y espacio público*, 316; García-Bryce, *Crafting the Republic*, 143–144; Earle, "*Sobre héroes y tumbas*," 407–408.

14. "El cádaver," *El Comercio* (Lima), 3 November 1868; "El Obispo cadáver," *El Comercio* (Lima), 3 December 1868.

15. Majluf, *Inventing Indigenism*, 84–97.

16. In reality, these campesinos were allied with the policies of the prior liberal president Mariano Ignacio Prado, and mobilized on behalf of the rights they saw themselves as having won as "true citizens of the nation." Jacobsen and Domínguez, *Juan Bustamante*, 57–60, 139–141. Thurner, *From Two Republics*, 139 ("true citizens").

17. Hampe Martínez, "Las momias de los Incas en Lima," 413. Periodic searches for the hospital's Incas nonetheless continued through the twenty-first century. Bauer and Coello Rodríguez, "The Hospital of San Andrés"; Ziemendorff, Millones Figueroa, and Greenwich Centeno, "Las momias reales incaicas."

18. "Facción Dominguejo Eliana," *El Comercio* (Lima), 9 September 1845, 6

19. "Ayacucho," *El Comercio* (Lima), 16 January 1850, 3; "Para Bolivia," *El Comercio* (Lima), 25 November 1850, 5; "Libertad de imprenta," *El Comercio* (Lima), 4 January 1852, 4; "Los rojos granadinos y la republica," *El Comercio* (Lima), 9 June 1852, 3; "Facción Dominguejo Eliana," *El Comercio* (Lima), 9 September 1845, 6. I thank Karin Sánchez Manríquez for noting to me that in Chile today, "momio" (from "momia," mummy) signifies a right-wing conservative.

20. Majluf, "The Creation of the Image of the Indian," 167–169; Majluf, *Inventing Indigenism*, 56.

21. "El R. P. Anselmo y el Hermano Tifas," *El Zurriago* (Lima), 24 June 1848. I thank José Ragas for pointing me to this source. See his "Los 'espejos rotos' de la opinion pública" for more on *El Zurriago*.

22. Karl von Scherzer to Simón Yrigoyen, 31 de Mayo 1859, Lima, AGNP RJ 72.

23. Simón Yrigoyen, Carta al Sr. Ministro de Estado en el Despacho de Instrucción Pública, 6 de Junio 1859; Simón Yrigoyen, "Razón de los objetos duplicados del Museo de Lima q[ue] pueden remitirse al de Viena," June 1859; Carta a Yrigoyen, 11 June 1859, AGNP RJ 72.

24. Ordoñez, *Unbundled*, 95-98 observes that two Andean mummies today in the Wien Weltmuseum came from the Novara expedition, for example. Whether these came from Peru's National Museum, and whether Austrian museums reciprocated, is unclear, and will be an object of future research.

25. "The Great South American Earthquakes of 1868," *Harper's New Monthly Magazine* 38, no. 227 (April 1869): 603–623; see also Hutchinson, *Two Years in Peru*, 1:64–65.

26. "After the Earthquake (by a Naval Officer)," 55; Adams, *Richard Henry Dana*, 2:346–347; General J. Kilpatrick to Joseph Henry, 20 May 1869, SIA RU 26, 85:455–459.

27. Henry to Kilpatrick, Washington, 17 [August] 1869, SIA RU 33, 16:542.
28. Accession 2130, SIA RU 192; Accession 5854, SIA RU 305.
29. "Los Incas transportados a tierras extranjeras," *El Comercio* (Lima), 20 December 1873, 6–7. I thank José Ragas for this article.
30. Dávalos y Lissón, "La colección de antigüedades peruanas del doctor Macedo," 74; *Vida y Obras de José Mariano Macedo*, 112–117, quote on 113. His Cuzco counterpart José Lucas Caparó Muñiz likewise valued mummies for their validation of other objects' antiquity, like a sling of black alpaca wool that "don Pedro Serna, vecino of Quiquijana, took from the body of a mummy that had it wrapped from its shoulder to its hip." "Coleccion de antigüedades peruanas. Descripción de las antigüedades peruanas pertenecientes al Dr. D. José Lucas Caparó. (Conclusion)," *El Comercio* (Lima), 23 May 1878, 3. For more on Caparó Muñiz, see Gänger, *Relics of the Past*, 49–52.
31. Quiñones Tinoco, *El Perú en la vitrina*, 160.
32. This dead was therefore more direct evidence of that "race" than the photographs sought by travelers of living Andean subjects suspected to be degraded by colonialism and intermarriage. See Majluf, *Inventing Indigenism*, 138–139. See Trever, "Criminal Lines," for how the Indigenous racializations of these photographs swept out individual and African-descendant identities.
33. Fuentes, *Catálogo de la Exposición de 1872*, 275; Quiñones Tinoco, *El Perú en la vitrina*, 102.
34. Gorriti, *Veladas literarias de Lima*, 163; Penny, *In Humboldt's Shadow*, 36, 37 ("the display").
35. Wiener, *Perú y Bolivia*, xii, xiii. See Wiener, *Huaco retrato*, for his Peruvian great-great-granddaughter's electrifying reflection on this legacy.
36. Wiener dug at Ancón on two occasions, once for six days with a team of six men, and again for 12 days with teams of twenty men from two French naval cruisers. iener, *Perú y Bolivia*, 44, 46–47 (quotes); 58–59.
37. Ibid., 362. Riviale, *Los viajeros franceses*, 102–110, details these efforts.
38. Ordoñez, *Unbundled*, 114–119. For the project behind the Musée, and its original curation of Peruvian and American materials under Ernest-Théodore Hamy, see Riviale, *Los viajeros franceses*, Chp. 8, and Conklin, *In the Museum of Man*, 35–43.
39. Wiener, *Perú y Bolivia*, 403–404; Majluf, *Inventing Indigenism*, 138–139. Juan may have died in 1880. But see Wiener, *Huaco retrato*, 53–56, and *passim* for a less matter-of-fact way in and through the horrors and survivals of this episode.
40. Starn, *Ishi's Brain*; Podgorny and Lopes, *El desierto*, 176–179, 239; Salvatore, "Live Indians in the Museum."
41. Li Gui, *A Journey*, 117.
42. Henry to Meiggs, 7 May 1877, 55:324, SIA RU 33.
43. Saffray, "Exposition de Philadelphia," 402. It has been suggested that the quipu in question was faked: see Radicato di Primeglio, *Estudios sobre los quipus*, 82.
44. See Alberti, *Morbid Curiosities*, 163, 193–195, for how the uncontrolled affect of the preserved corpse, even in scientific settings, broke down their "museum effect."
45. Li Gui, *A Journey*, 118. See also Shibama, *The First Japanese Embassy*, 56, for a similar response to the Smithsonian's mummies.
46. Ingram, *Centennial Exposition Described and Illustrated*, 490–491.
47. "Trip to the 'Centennial,'" *Neighbor's Home Mail* 3, no. 8 (September 1876), 119–120, quote on 119.
48. "Correspondencia particular para el *Monitor Republicano*. Exposición. Filadelfia, Junio 12 de 1876," *El Monitor Republicano* (Mexico City), 1 July 1876, 2.
49. Sears, "Peru and Its People," 187.
50. Kauffmann Doig, *El Perú Antiguo*, t. I, 68. Wiener met Reiss and Stübel on the way to Peru—another reason he visited Ancón, which he predicted would be important to "science." Wiener, *Perú y Bolivia*, 44 ("science"), 57.
51. Pillsbury, "Finding the Ancient in the Andes," 59-60; Rowe, *Max Uhle*. Also see Gänger, "¿La mirada imperialista?"
52. Reiss and Stübel, *The Necropolis of Ancon in Peru*, Vol. 1 (n.p., opposite Plate 6).
53. Ibid., description for Plate 5, "The Deep Grave of the False-Headed Mummies."
54. Penny, *In Humboldt's Shadow*, 96. See also Begerock et al., "200 Years a Woman."

55. Europe's largest collection of mummified Andean remains is in Berlin, where Reiss and Stübel sent what they believed were the mummified remains of eight individuals from Ancón, six of which remain bundled today. The Ethnological Museum of Berlin has sixty-five individual lots, of which thirty-four remain wrapped. Ordoñez, *Unbundled*, 128, 211, and Chp. 4, *passim*, documents that, after Berlin's Ethnological Museum is the British Museum with twenty-three mummified remains; Madrid's Museo Arqueológico Nacional and the nearby Museo Universitario de Antropología Forense, Paleopatología y Criminalística at the Universidad Complutense have twenty four, twenty of which were collected by Spain's Expedición del Pacífico (1862–1866); Paris's Trocadéro Museum has twenty-two; Vienna's Weltmuseum (which inherited the mummies of the prior Imperial Natural History Cabinet) has the remains of seventeen bundled or unbundled individuals; Oxford's Pitt Rivers has fourteen; the Museum of Natural History in Guimet, in Lyon has thirteen; the Geneva Museum of Ethnography has eleven; the Reiss-Engelhorn Museum of Mannheim has ten (currently traveling as *Mummies of the World*); the Netherlands' Museum of World Cultures (formerly the National Museum of Ethnology) contains eight; the National Museum of Denmark has seven; Belgium's Royal Museum of Arts and History also has seven; the Czech Republic's Náprstek Museum has four; Lisbon's Archaeological Museum of the Carmo Convent has two; the Museum of the Department of Anthropology in the University of Coimbra, Portugal, has two; and two are in the Museum of Ethnology of Sweden. To this accounting should be added those other now-"lost" mummies detailed in this book's Chapters 4 and 5, and others, like the mummy of Marburg: Begerock et al., "200 Years a Woman."
56. For that political and economic story, see Clayton, *Peru and the United States*, Chps. 2 and 3.
57. Squier and Davis, *Ancient Monuments of the Mississippi Valley*, 289; Bieder, *Science Encounters the Indian*, 106, 114–119.
58. See Poole, "Landscape and the Imperial Subject"; Achim, "Skulls and Idols"; and Majluf, *Inventing Indigenism*, 139–141.
59. Squier, *Peru*, 72, 73, 74, 75–81, 116–151, 216, 358, 456, 552, 572–573, 575; Bieder, *Science Encounters the Indian*, 124–128; Barnhart, *Ephraim George Squier*, 247, 254–255, 393. For Centeno's collection, see Gänger, *Relics of the Past*, Chp. 1, and this book's next chapter.
60. Gänger, *Relics of the Past*, Chps. 1, 2, 4. For Chilean looting of Ancón, see "An Ancient Cemetery at the World's Fair," *The Modern Cemetery*, 61, but Gänger "Of Butterflies," 299, cautions there is no register of the reception of Peruvian pieces in Chile's museums from that moment. By contrast, see Guibovich Pérez, "La usurpación de la memoria," for Chile's targeted looting of the National Library. Indeed, collections made in Peru by Chilean soldiers during the war ended up in both Chile and Argentina; see Farro, "Historia de las colecciones," 149, 207.
61. W. F. Lee to Spencer Baird, 9 October 1882, Accession 11867, SIA RU 305; *Annual Report of the Board of Regents of the Smithsonian*, 21.
62. Evans to Baird, April 1883, Accession 13028, SIA RU 305.
63. "Bones of the Incas," *The Topeka Daily Capital*, 30 May 1889; Baird, 3 September 1884, Accession 14978, SIA RU 305; Steinberg and Prost, "Bringing Ethnography Home," 115–116. See Majluf, "The Creation of the Image," 310, for romantic Limeños' adoption of Indigenous dress.
64. Kiefer to Boyton, 23 June 1884; Kiefer to Baird, 3 September 1884, Accession 14978, SIA RU 305; Henry to Meiggs, 7 May 1877, 55:324, SIA RU 33; Kiefer to J. S. Billings, 30 June 1888, Kiefer to Billings, 10 October 1888, US Army Medical Museum Anatomical Section Records Relating to Specimens Transferred to the Smithsonian Institution (USAMMAS), 2838–2874, 2896–2973, 2977–2995, NAA. For US interest in imperial tropical medicine, see Cueto and Palmer, *Medicine and Public Health in Latin America*, 95–101.
65. "Bones of the Incas," *The Topeka Daily Capital*, 30 May 1889; Brns & Son. to Billings, 26 October 1889, USAMMAS, 3232–3241; Fabian, *The Skull Collectors*, 189–190. Billings's copy of *The George A. Kiefer Collection of Peruvian Antiquities, etc. etc.* ("To the cost") is in USAMMAS, 3232–3241, with what he was willing to pay penciled to the right of the items, and final prices penciled to the left.

66. Steinberg and Prost, "Bringing Ethnography Home," 113, 124; Gänger, *Relics of the Past*, 150–153. For the scapegoating of Peru's Andean population after the war, see Larson, *Trials of Nation Making*, 157–159; Thurner, *From Two Republics*.

67. Kiefer to Baird, 22 May 1884; Kiefer to Baird, 25 July 1885, Accession 14978, SIA RU 305.

68. "School and Church," *Knoxville Journal*, 9 March 1891, 2; "Peruvian Mummies on Exhibition," *New York Tribune*, 4 February 1894, 20; "Story of a Necklace," *Afro-American Advocate*, 2 September 1892, 6.

69. "Uncle Sam's Snakes," *Dallas Morning News*, 17 August 1894, 4.

70. "Many Mummies at the Fair," *The Daily Morning Astorian* (Oregon), 12 February 1893, 4.

71. Lummis, *The Gold Fish of Gran Chimú*, 3–4; ""Mines of Mummies," *The Quincy (IL) Daily Journal*, 28 May 1892, 3; Ward, "Mummies of Peru," 1

72. Davis and Putnam, *World's Columbian Exposition*, 8; Hinsley and Wilcox, eds., *Coming of Age in Chicago*; Schuster, "The World's Fairs as Spaces of Global Knowledge"; Rydell, *All the World's a Fair*.

73. Curtis, "United States to Dominate the Hemisphere," 87–88; Kiefer to Baird, 25 July 1885, Accession 14978, SIA RU 305. Also see Coates, "The Pan-American Lobbyist," 34.

74. Beck, *Unfair Labor?*; Fane, "Reproducing the Pre-Columbian Past"; Evans, *Romancing the Maya*, Epilogue; Egan, "Exhibiting Indigenous Peoples"; Hinsley and Wilcox, eds., *Coming of Age in Chicago*; Schuster, "The World's Fairs as Spaces of Global Knowledge"; Uslenghi, *Latin America at Fin-de-Siècle Universal Exhibitions*. Interestingly, Colombia elected to represent its archaeological past at the Columbian exposition of Madrid in 1892 but focused at Chicago on its natural wealth; see Valverde, "Catálogos de objetos prehispánicos."

75. Redman, *Bone Rooms*, 47–50.

76. Morgan, *The Historical World's Columbian Exposition*, 30, 312, 363; Quiñones Tinoco, *El Perú en la Vitrina*, 120–134, 203–204, 218, 220; Beck, *Unfair Labor?*, 187.

77. Tenorio Trillo, *Mexico at the World's Fairs*, 184–186.

78. Schuster, "The World's Fairs as Spaces of Global Knowledge," 88; Quiñones Tinoco, *El Perú en la vitrina*, 127–133, 204–218; Johnson, *A History of the World's Columbian Exposition*, 2:367.

79. Egan, "Exhibiting Indigenous Peoples."

80. Morgan, *The Historical World's Columbian Exposition*, 364; Gänger, *Relics of the Past*, 52–67.

81. Montes, "The Antiquity of the Civilization of Peru," 95, 98.

82. Bauer and Stanish, "Killke and Killke-Related Pottery," 2; Gänger, *Relics of the Past*, 87, 91; Schuster, "The World's Fairs as Spaces of Global Knowledge," 90.

83. Beck, *Unfair Labor?*, 41, 235n47.

84. "Many Mummies at the Fair," *The Daily Morning Astorian* (Oregon), 12 February 1893, 4 ("selected"); Morgan, *The Historical World's Columbian Exposition*, 364; Putnam to W. H. Holmes, 25 June 1894, Folder 1891–1900 Field Columbian Museum, Chicago; Putnam to H. N. Higginbotham, 7 August 1895, Folder 1891–1900 Field Columbian Museum—controversy with Rd Specimens, Box 9, Committee report (1896), Folder 1891–1900, Box 11, HUG 1717.2—Papers of Frederic Ward Putnam, Harvard University Archives (HUA); Beck, *Unfair Labor?*, 66.

85. Dorsey, Report, 2, Folder Misc. Papers—Reports (1), Box 36, HUG 1717.2.

86. Dorsey, "An Archaeological Study," iv.

87. "Instructions for Collectors of Ethnographic Material," 6–7, Folder: Papers—Reports (5), Box 36, HUG 1717.2.

88. Putnam "Report for May," 10 June 1891, Folder: World's Columbian Exposition, Monthly Reports to the Director 1891, Box 35, HUG 1717.2.

89. Dorsey, Report, 5, Folder: Misc. Papers—Reports (1), Box 36, HUG 1717.2.

90. Ibid., 1. For a celebration of *choledad* in the face of its stigmatization, see Avilés, *No soy tu cholo*.

91. "Many Mummies at the Fair," *The Daily Morning Astorian* (Oregon), 12 February 1893, 4; (illegible), *Springfield (IL) Republican*, 13 April 1893; Dorsey, "Archaeology in Peru," 3.

92. Dorsey, "An Archaeological Study," 17–18.

93. "Many Mummies at the Fair": ; Dorsey, "An Archaeological Study," iii, v, 18; Slovak, "Reassembling the Mortuary Assemblage," 84.

94. Putnam to Davis, 8 February 1892, January 1892 monthly report, Folder: World's Columbian Exposition Monthly Reports to Director 1892 Jan–June, Box 35; Dorsey, "Contents of sixty-eight boxes shipped from Callao, Peru, June 8, 1892, via Panama, to New York, consigned to W. E. Curtis, care of Mr. Roosa U.S. Transport Agent," Folder: 1891–1900 Field Columbian Museum Chicago, Box 9; Dorsey, "Report," 4, Folder: World's Columbian Exposition—Misc. Papers—Reports (1), Box 36, HUG 1717.2.

95. Ordoñez, *Unbundled*.

96. "Many Mummies at the Fair.".

97. Moorehead, "Anthropology at the World's Columbian Exposition," 20; Dorsey, "Department Exhibit—Anthropology," 13, Folder: Putnam: World's Columbian Exposition—Misc. Papers—Reports (1), Box 36, FWP, HUG 1717.2.

98. "Many Mummies at the Fair"; Dorsey, "Department Exhibit—Anthropology," 13; [Illegible], *Springfield (IL) Republican*, 13 April 1893; Blueprint Plans of Peabody Museum Exhibitions at World's Columbian Exposition of 1893, PMAE 65-41-10/334.2.2.

99. "Among the Ancients. Life of Extinct Races Revealed by Their Dead," *The Daily Inter Ocean* (Chicago), 2 August 1893, 18. Dorsey, "Department Exhibit—Anthropology," 12.

100. Moorehead, "Anthropology at the World's Columbian Exposition," 20; Redman, *Bone Rooms*, 47. Cole, *Captured Heritage*, details how Boas made that collection via grave-robbing. See Jacknis, "Refracting Images," for anthropological displays at the fair more generally.

101. Putnam to Davis, July 1893 monthly report, 1 August 1893, Folder: World's Columbian Exposition, Monthly Reports to Director General 1893 June–Sept, Box 35, HUG 1717.2; Bancroft, *The Book of the Fair*, 636.

102. Redman, *Bone Rooms*, 50. See "Document F Monthly Report of Mr. Frank Hamilton Cushing: September 1893 (inclusive of July and August)," in Hinsley and Wilcox, eds., *Coming of Age in Chicago*, 220–221, 224, for how the North American ethnologist devoted "a large share of [his] leisure attention" to Peruvian collections, including that of Emilio Montes. Cushing saw "striking analogies" between Andean and US southwestern cultures, but believed its religious iconography so far "advanced beyond the Pueblo phase, that it distinctly constitutes the link between prehistoric religion hitherto so little understood, and the historic religions of the Old World so well recorded."

103. "Among the Ancients. Life of Extinct Races Revealed by Their Dead."

104. I'm grateful to Curtis Hinsley for sharing these cartoons with me, and for identifying Denslow.

105. Schuster, "The World's Fairs as Spaces of Global Knowledge," 75.

106. See Hinsley and Wilcox, eds., *Coming of Age in Chicago*, for the fair as American anthropology's coalescence.

107. As Gänger, "Disjunctive Circles," 408, observes.

108. Slovak, "Reassembling the Mortuary Assemblage," 84; Beck, *Unfair Labor?*, 41. See Steinbock-Pratt, *Educating the Empire*, 96–97, for how Dorsey funded US collecting in the Philippines.

109. Dorsey, "An Archaeological Study," iv, 35, 39, 70, 79–80, 81, 83. See Tantaleán, "Un encargo muy especial," for a like articulation of his dissertation's importance.

110. Dorsey, "Archaeology in Peru."

111. Nash and Feinman, eds., *Curators, Collections, and Contexts*; McVicker, "Patrons, Popularizers, and Professionals," 381.

112. Mead, *Peruvian Mummies*, 7, 12; F. W. Putnam to W. H. Holmes, Curator, Department of Anthropology of Columbian Museum, 25 June 1894, Folder 1891–1900 Field Columbian Museum Chicago; Putnam to H. N. Higginbotham, 7 August 1895, Higginbotham to Putnam, 31 July 1895, Folder 1891–1900 Field Columbian Museum—controversy with Rd Specimens, Box 9, Committee report [1896], Folder 1891–1900 S, Box 11, HUG 1717.2. Photos 81968, 81969 in the Old South American Hall Drawer, in the AMNH's Archives, note on their reverse that mummies and trappings were "excavated by Dorsey."

113. Gänger, *Relics of the Past*, 88–90.

114. Uhle, *Pachacamac*; Rowe, *Max Uhle*.

115. Adolph Bandelier to John Winser, 26 July 1894, Bandelier Accession Record (BAR) 1894—13 (Peru), AMNH Archives; Bandelier, "On the Relative Antiquity." Hyman and Leibsohn think deeply on this bundle's museumification in "Washing the Archive."

116. Sara Yorke Stevenson to Uhle, 10 August 1894, 8 December 1894, 23 November 1895, Folders 1 and 2, American Section Box 6, Expedition Records—Uhle, Penn Museum Archives (PUMA). Box 4 of Uhle's expedition records in PUMA contains Uhle's lists and terse descriptions of what he sent. By my count there are 205 skulls or mummified heads, two mummy bundles, and the otherwise fragmented human remains or "belongings of a mummy" of at least ninety more.

117. Putnam to Winser, 18 July 1894, BAR 1894—13 (Peru). Correspondence in this folder between Winser, the collector of the Port of New York, Bandelier, Villard, and James Terry provides many examples of Bandelier's poor packing habits. This is ironic, given that Hyman and Leibsohn, "Washing the Archive," 425, and Rodriguez, "No 'Mere Accumulation of Material,' " identify how Bandelier himself had called for deeper attention to evidence and context.

118. Putnam to Bandelier, 18 February 1895, Folder 19, Box 2, PMAE 999-24 Frederic Ward Putnam Papers (FWPP); Hinsley, "Anthropology as Education and Entertainment," 7. For the AMNH's diorama and mural display program, see Haraway, "Teddy Bear Patriarchy"; Roy, "Visualizing Culture and Nature." It might be suggested that the Peruvian Hall never got a life-size diorama because it had the mummies already.

119. Bandelier, "Aboriginal Trephining in Bolivia," 440; Redman, Bone Rooms, 193.

120. For example, see the "Two Peruvian mummies, one with original wrappings and accompanied with the associated objects" that a Richard H. Clark donated to the Brooklyn Museum in 1904 (Culin, "Report on the Department of Ethnology," 20). An incomplete list of museums that set up Peruvian or South American Halls through the mid-twentieth century include the AMNH, the Field Museum, Harvard's Peabody, Penn's University Museum, the Brooklyn Museum, and the Denver Museum of Nature and Science.

121. Jesup, "Twenty-Sixth Annual Report," 9; Dorsey, "Archaeology in Peru," 4; Lummis, The Gold Fish of Gran Chimú.

122. Putnam to Director, 9 August 1892, July 1892 monthly report, Folder: World's Columbian Exposition, Monthly Reports to Director 1892 July–Dec, Box 35, HUG 1717.2.

123. "Among the Ancients," The Daily Inter Ocean (Chicago), 2 August 1893, 18. A "low, soothing, crooning sound" apparently came from the "mummy graveyard" each night. When a black cat was discovered snacking on one of the largest mummy bundles, and was killed by a janitor, one of the guards claimed the feline "contained the transmigrated soul of the big mummy." "Anthropological Ghost Is No More," read a headline in The Daily Inter Ocean (Chicago), 28 September 1893, 7. "It Was a Black Cat and It Came Back to Die."

124. Boyesen, "A New World Fable," 183.

125. Ward, "Mummies of Peru," 1. See Boyd and Thrush, "Introduction"; Luckhurst, "Science versus Rumour," 257, for how tales of mummy curses and Indian ghosts hint at colonial guilt. See Bacigalupo, "The Mapuche Undead Never Forget," for a key intervention in vengeful ancestors as social ancestors, provoking reparation.

126. Andersen, "Gauguin and a Peruvian Mummy," 238; Gamboni, "Volcano Equals Head," 97–98.

127. Rosenblum, Modern Painting, 111; Ziemendorff, "Edvard Munch y la Momia." See Williams, "Art and Artifact at the Trocadero," for the influence of South American art upon European artists.

128. Dorsey, "Archaeology in Peru," 4. See also Blake, "Notes on a Collection," 279.

129. Bandelier, The Ruins at Tiahuanaco, 19, 25; W. F. Lee to Spencer Baird, 9 October 1882, Accession 11867, SIA RU 305; Raimondi, "Enumeración de los vestigios," 165–166, and "Itinerario," 41–42.

130. George Kiefer to Spencer Fullerton Baird, 25 July 1885, Accession 14978, SIA RU 305; Heaney, Las Tumbas, Chp. 13.

131. Dorsey, "Report. PART I. The Journey," 4, Folder: Putnam: World's Columbian Exposition—Misc. Papers—Reports (1), Box 36, HUG 1717.2.

132. Dorsey, "A Ceremony of the Quichuas of Peru," 307.
133. Ibid., 307–308.
134. Ibid., 308.
135. Ibid., 307–308. Dorsey transcribed it as "Intic churin," but the Sapa Inka had been described as Intip Churin in primary sources since the mid-fifteenth century. See Sabine MacCormack, *Religion in the Andes*, 114.
136. Dorsey, "A Ceremony of the Quichuas of Peru," 308.
137. Putnam to Davis, 1 July 1892, June 1892 monthly report, Monthly Reports to Director General 1892 Jan–June, Folder: World's Columbian Exposition, Box 35, HUG 1717.2; Accession No. 362, Accession 4:19, Field Museum of Natural History Archives; Historical File for Accession No. 362, Anthropology Department, Field Museum of Natural History; FMNH4246 ["Mummy of child"], FMNH40220, FMNH40221, FMNH40222, FMNH40223, FMNH40224, FMNH40225, FMNH40226, FMNH40227, FMNH40228, FMNH40230, FMNH40231, FMNH40232, FMNH40325, FMNH40345, Field Museum of Natural History (Anthropology) Collection http://collections-anthropology.fieldmuseum.org/ (accessed on 29 November 2022).
138. Dorsey, "A Ceremony of the Quichuas of Peru," 307–309.
139. I am grateful to Américo Mendoza-Mori for thinking with me on Corbacho's transcriptions. The transcriptions are at times inexact, but the larger meaning seems adequately translated. Any errors in reinterpretation are my own.
140. Flores Galindo, *In Search of an Inca*, 2.
141. For thinking through how scholars have superficially engaged with the mourning "rituals" of "others" before becoming susceptible to its emotional depths, I am grateful to Rosaldo, "Grief and a Headhunter's Rage."

Chapter 7

1. Gündüz, *El Mundo Ceremonial de los Huaqueros*; Cadena, *Earth Beings*. See Gómez, *The Experiential Caribbean*, and Armus and Gómez, *The Gray Zones of Medicine*, for recent approaches to healing as ways of knowing, being, and curing that are distinct, yet conversant between cultures.
2. Garofalo, "Conjuring with Coca and the Inca"; Warren, "Dorotea Salguero."
3. Bastien, *Healers of the Andes*; Crawford, *The Andean Wonder Drug*.
4. Or .591 inches-by-.669 inches—anthropological measurement is always metric. To the former point, Finger and Fernando, "E. George Squier and the Discovery of Cranial Trepanation," 353, observes that Morton depicted a trepanned skull in *Crania Americana* without realizing it, believing it instead a battlefield wound.
5. Muñiz and McGee, "Primitive Trephining," 72; Arnott, Finger, and Smith, eds., *Trepanation*; Verano, *Holes in the Head*.
6. Trouillot, *Global Transformations*, Chp. 1.
7. Cf. Sivasundaram, "Sciences and the Global," 156.
8. Extending into the past the sort of competitions laid out by Warren, "Dorotea Salguedo," and Palma and Ragas, "The Miraculous Doctor Pun."
9. Verano, *Holes in the Head*, 11, 193.
10. Brosseder, *The Power of Huacas*.
11. Bandelier, "Aboriginal Trephining," 443, 444. See Bastien, *Healers of the Andes*, 17, for its continued practice in Bolivia.
12. Squier, *Peru*, 577; Matto, "La trepanación en la época de los Incas"; Sales Salvador, "Introducción," 28.
13. Gänger, *Relics of the Past*, 77–81.
14. Notably, the *indigenista* writings of Matto's daughter, Clorinda Matto de Turner, drew sympathy to the status of Peru's "Indian" peoples. See Sales Salvador, "Introducción," 28.
15. Cueto, *Excelencia científica*, 45; Warren, *Medicine and Politics*, Chps. 2 and 5; and Gänger, "Disjunctive Circles," 410–413, meditate on these ruptures.

16. Squier, *Peru*, 455–456; Broca and Squier, "Trepanning among the Incas," *Journal of the Anthropological Institute of New York* 1, no. 1 (1871–1872): 72; Matto, "La Trepanación en la época de los Incas."

17. "Committee Reports of December 6, 1865," *Bulletin of the New York Academy of Medicine* 2 (1862–1866), 530.

18. Finger, *Minds behind the Brain*, 137–154.

19. Broca and Squier, "Trepanning among the Incas," 72–73.

20. Ibid., 75.

21. Verano, *Holes in the Head*, 11; Schiller, *Paul Broca*, 158; Finger and Fernando, "E. George Squier," 371–374; Fletcher, "On Prehistoric Trephining and Cranial Amulets," 10, 23, 29.

22. It was so large that the French at the time suggested that this may have been a postmortem trepanation to remove the brain for mummification purposes. Hamy, *Galerie américaine du Musée d'ethnographie du Trocadéro*, 2:65–66. See Nystrom, "Trepanation in the Chachapoya Region of Northern Perú"; Toyne, "Tibial Surgery in Ancient Peru"; and Buikstra and Nystrom, "Ancestors and Social Memory," for specific research on trepanation and mummification's methods in Chachapoyas.

23. Fletcher, "On Prehistoric Trephining and Cranial Amulets," 25.

24. Squier, *Peru*, 579–580; Barnhart, *Ephraim George Squier*, Epilogue.

25. Jones to Baird, 9 February 1885, Accession 15755, SIA RU 305.

26. Mason, "The Chaclacayo Trephined Skull," 411–412.

27. Kiefer to Billings, 30 June 1888, USAMMAS, 2896–2973.

28. Matto, "La Trepanación en la época de los Incas." Matto was a surgeon, formerly the surgeon of the "Callao" Battalion, and since 1886 the "Médico de la Policía" in Lima.

29. Le Plongeon nonetheless also believed that the US consul in Iquique had acted in Sra. Centeno's name and achieved the skull's return to Peru. See Barnhart, *Ephraim George Squier*, 260–263; Augustus Le Plongeon to Stephen Salisbury, 19 January 1878, Salisbury Family Papers, American Antiquarian Society.

30. Matto, "La Trepanación en la época de los Incas."

31. See Gänger, *Relics of the Past*, 49, 83–98, for the sale of the collections of Centeno and Emilio Montes.

32. Alemenara Butler, "Memoria Leida," 207, 213; La Puente, "Estudios etnográficos de la Hoya del Titicaca," 379, 878. See Wilson, "Indian Citizenship," 166, for this shift "from colonial to post-colonial forms of racism."

33. See Bastien, *Healers of the Andes*, 22, and Palma and Ragas, "The Miraculous Doctor Pun," for similar interest in and dismissal of traveling kallawaya healers and Chinese healers in this moment, and Cueto and Palmer, *Medicine and Public Health in Latin America*, Chp. 2, for the specializations of elite medicine more generally.

34. Cadena, *Indigenous Mestizos*, 61.

35. Lorena, "La medicina," 224–226, 227. As Gänger, *Relics of the Past*, 77–81, argues, the claim that Peruvian elites perceived solely a breach between a glorious Inca past and a brutish native present is overdrawn. Instead, like Morton, some nineteenth-century Peruvian intellectuals saw a continuity between ancient Peruvians, Incas, and contemporary Indians that gave artifacts their value but lowered opinions of both.

36. Lorena, "La medicina," 227–229.

37. Ibid., 230.

38. Muñiz, "Vida," 315; D. M. "Dr. Manuel Antonio Muñiz," 193–194; Eyzaguirre, "La tuberculosis pumonar en Lima," 58.

39. Muñiz, "La Lepra en el Perú," 127, 171; Muñiz, "Correspondencia de Londres," 251; Muñiz, "Estado mental de N . . ."; Aguirre, "Crime, Race, and Morals," 77; Aguirre, *The Criminals of Lima*, 69–70. I thank José Ragas for observing that the chief of police, Pedro Muñiz, was likely Manuel's brother.

40. See also Farro and Podgorny, " 'Pre-Columbian Moulages.' "

41. Lorena, "Etiologia del bócio," 293; Muñiz, "Reglamentación de la prostitución," 457, 17–18; Wilson, "Indian Citizenship."

42. Rios and Muñiz, "Informe antropológico," 155; Covey, *The Inca Apocalypse*, 10–15.

43. Muñiz and McGee, "Primitive Trephining in Peru," 5; La Puente, "Estudios etnográficos de la Hoya del Titicaca."
44. Tello, "El curioso final"; Tealdo, "Julio C. Tello."
45. Muñiz was thus akin to fellow criminologists who avoided the extreme biological determinism and biological racism that would have counted out any hegemonic national project based on Peru's "Indian," while employing "other, more subtle but no less effective forms of discrimination, exclusion, and repression" Aguirre, "Crime, Race, and Morals," 86).
46. Muñiz and McGee, "Primitive Trephining in Peru," 6, 13; McGee, "Primitive Trephining, Illustrated," 3; Tello, "El curioso final."
47. See Schuster, "The World's Fairs as Spaces of Global Knowledge," 89–91, for another recounting of Muñiz's mission.
48. McGee to Francisco de P. Suarez, 14 June 1894, Box 17, Bureau of American Ethnology Papers (BAE), NAA.
49. Muñiz and McGee, "Primitive Trephining in Peru," 11–12.
50. Holmes, "The World's Fair Congress of Anthropology," 425, 428; La Crónica Médica, Año 10–Tomo 10, No. 118 (31 October 1893), 340; McGee to Putnam, 24 October 1893, Box 17, BAE.
51. McGee to Prof. G. Brown Goode, 5 October 1893l McGee to Putnam, 24 October 1893; McGee to Guy Hinsdale, 14 February 1894, Box 17, BAE; McGee, "Primitive Trephining," 2. For McGee's arc as self-proclaimed ethnologist in charge at the BAE, see Hinsley, Savages and Scientists, Chp. 8.
52. Hinsley, Savages and Scientists, 22, 23, 29, Chps. 6 and 7; Bieder, Science Encounters the Indian, 235; Redman, Prophets and Ghosts, Chp. 3.
53. Plan of Operations of the Bureau of American Ethnology for fiscal year 1894–1895, August 1894, Box 17, BAE.
54. Hinsley, Savages and Scientists, 65, 284.
55. McGee to George F. Kunz, 13 April 1898, Box 19, BAE.
56. Powell to Matias Romero, 17 September 1894, Box 18, BAE; Hinsley, Savages and Scientists, 238–239. For more on Mexico's National Museum, see Achim, From Idols to Antiquity, and Bueno, The Pursuit of Ruins.
57. Powell to Albert S. Ashmead, 29 June 1898, Box 19, BAE.
58. For example, Muñiz had proposed the unification of the Americas' maritime and quarantine laws at the Medical Congress in Washington: La Crónica Médica, Año 10–Tomo 10, No. 118 (31 October 1893), 340. Muñiz and Elguera gave Powell and McGee honorary fellowships in Lima's Sociedad Geográfica: McGee to Elguera, 26 February 1894, Box 54, BAE.
59. McGee to Muñiz, 14 February 1894; McGee to Suarez, 14 June 1894, Box 17, BAE.
60. McGee, "Primitive Trephining," 1, 2, 3.
61. Hovey, "Peruvian Trepanning."
62. McGee to Putnam, 24 October 1893; McGee to Robert Fletcher, 3 November 1893; McGee to Sara Y. Stevenson, 6 December 1893; McGee to M. A. Muñiz, 14 February 1894 ("desire to obtain"), Box 17, BAE. Farro and Podgorny, " 'Pre-Columbian Moulages,' " 637, describes photographs as "vehicles for communication of data for comparison and relational objects enmeshed in scientific collaboration networks."
63. McGee to Muñiz, 14 February 1894, Box 17, BAE.
64. McGee to Hinsdale, 14 February 1894; McGee to Hinsdale, 9 June 1894; McGee to Suarez, 14 June 1894, Box 17; McGee to Billings, 21 August 1895, Box 18, BAE; Hrdlička to Holmes, 17 July 1919, Folder: Holmes (ii), Box 31, AHP.
65. Muñiz to McGee, 12 June 1895, Box 110, BAE.
66. McGee to Muñiz, 18 July 1895, Box 18, BAE.
67. McGee to Muñiz, 14 February 1894; McGee to Suarez, 14 June 1894, Box 17; McGee to Ashmead 23 (or 28) February 1895, Box 18, BAE; Hovey, "Peruvian Trepanning."
68. McGee to George M. Sternberg, 15 September 1896; McGee to George P. Merrill, 30 October 1896; McGee to S. P. Langley, 11 July 1896, Box 18; McGee to Muñiz, 11 July 1896, Box 54, BAE.
69. Tello, "El curioso final."
70. D.M., "Dr. Manuel Antonio Muñiz," 193.

71. Powell, "Report of the Director," lxxviii.
72. Muñiz and McGee, "Primitive Trephining in Peru," 66, 64, 30, 31, 42–43. See also Schuster, "The World's Fairs as Spaces of Global Knowledge," 89–91.
73. Muñiz and McGee, "Primitive Trephining in Peru," 30, 60, 61, 62.
74. Ibid., 63.
75. Ibid., 67, 69–70.
76. Ibid., 64, 65, 66, 71–72. For McGee's conforming expectations as almost a caricature of Powell's, see Hinsley, *Savages and Scientists*, 240–242, 256.
77. Muñiz collection, NMNH, Suitland, Maryland; Hinsley, *Savages and Scientists*, 234. See Verano, *Holes in the Head*, for the positive reinterpretation of those same skulls.
78. Mejía Xesspe, "Prólogo," viii.
79. Tello, "El curioso final"; Niles, *A Journey in Time*, 76.

Chapter 8

1. Niles, *A Journey in Time*, 72; Mejía Xesspe, "Apuntes biográficos," 36; Flores Galindo, *In Search of an Inca*, 37–46.
2. Mejía Xesspe, "Prólogo," vii ["indio"].
3. For indigenismo and Leguía, see Cadena, *Indigenous Mestizos*; and Drinot, *La patria nueva*. For archaeology and Tello, see Patterson, "Political Economy and a Discourse Called 'Peruvian Archaeology'"; Salvatore, "Local versus Imperial Knowledge" and "Tres intelectuales peruanos"; Astuhuamán and Daggett, "Julio César Tello Rojas"; Burger, ed., *The Life and Writings of Julio C. Tello*; Heaney, *Las Tumbas de Machu Picchu*; Daggett, *An Annotated Tello-Centric History*; Peters and Ayarza, "Julio C. Tello y el desarrollo de estudios andinos"; Tantaleán, *Peruvian Archaeology*; Ramón Joffre, *El neoperuano*; Prieto Burmester, "Dos forjadores de las ciencias sociales en el Perú."
4. Salomon, "Unethnic Ethnohistory," 479; Salomon, *The Cord Keepers*, 134; Asensio, *Señores del pasado*, Chps. 1–2.
5. Cadena, *Indigenous Mestizos*; Gildner, "Indomestizo modernism."
6. Tello to M. Toribio Mejía Xesspe, 1 June 1925, in Shady Solís and Novoa Bellota, eds., *Cuadernos de investigación del archivo Tello, No. 2*, 155.
7. Jave Calderón, ed., *Jorge Basadre*, 27. In approaching Tello from the history of science, I look to Cueto, *Excelencia científica en la periferia*, which notes Tello's leadership of the Sociedad para el Progreso de la Ciencia (81) in the 1920s; Cadena, "From Race to Class"; and Salvatore, "Tres intelectuales peruanos," which observe how Tello challenged the Incas' centrality in Peruvian life. See Cueto, "Andean Biology in Peru," and "'Indigenismo' and Rural Medicine in Peru" for like cases.
8. Spalding, *Huarochirí*; Salomon, *The Cord Keepers*, 49. Salomon and Niño-Murcia, *The Lettered Mountain*, 18–23, 104–114, 134, and Chps. 2, 5, 7, and 8 of this book.
9. Niles, *A Journey in Time*, 72; Mejía Xesspe, "Apuntes biográficos," 35; Lothrop, "Julio C. Tello," 50.
10. Tello to Ashmead, 20 November 1909, Folder: Tello (i), Box 3, Albert S. Ashmead Collection MSS 2/0029 (ASAC), College of Physicians of Philadelphia.
11. Spalding, *Huarochirí*.
12. Salomon, *The Cord Keepers*, 11.
13. Manuel Tello, "Huarochirí," *El Comercio* (Lima), 8 Abril 1891; Patterson, "Political Economy and a Discourse called 'Peruvian Archaeology,'" 40; Mallon, *Peasant and Nation*, 275; Daggett, *An Annotated Tello-Centric History*, 4, 6, 9; Salomon and Niño-Murcia, *The Lettered Mountain*, 83–84, 134, 126. The Tellos were "poor people," one of Julio's collaborators wrote, "but that sort of poor people who have lands, cattle, and besides, were the ones who gave the orders in Huarochirí" (Salomon and Niño-Murcia, *The Lettered Mountain*, 245, translating Ponce Sánchez, *50 Anécdotas de sabio Tello*, 37).
14. Tealdo, "Julio C. Tello" ("little coca store"); "Con honores de Ministro de Estado Fueron Sepultados ayer provisoriamente en cementerio general los restos del ilustre arqueologo Doctor Julio C. Tello," *La Tribuna* (Lima), 7 June 1947; Mejía Xesspe, "Apuntes biográficos," 41; Mejía Xesspe, "Prólogo," vii; Muñiz and McGee, "Primitive Trephining in Peru."

15. Tealdo, "Julio C. Tello," 8 ("eugenicist"); Mejía Xesspe, "Apuntes biográficos," 38; Mendez Gastelumendi, "Incas sí, Indios no," 218. By "superior people," Tello may have meant the literal eugenics of mestizaje and whitening—see Stepan, *The Hour of Eugenics*; Necochea López, *A History of Family Planning*, Chp. 1; and Gil-Riaño, "Risky Migrations"—but see also Cadena, "From Race to Class," 55n12, on serrano perspectives on Indianness's "relative location *within* the vertical environment of the Andean highlands"—a constantly shifting hierarchy of ethnicity, class, and status rather than a strict coastal-sierra white-Indian dichotomy. Jorge Basadre dubbed 1895 through 1919 Peru's "Aristocratic Republic." Burga and Flores Galindo, *Apogeo y crisis de la republica aristocrática*, remains a key conceptualization of its arc.
16. "Con honores de Ministro de Estado Fueron Sepultados"; Mejía Xesspe, "Prólogo," vii; Cueto, *Excelencia científica*, 96–97. Also, Niles, *A Journey in Time*, 75; Mejía Xesspe, "Apuntes Bnográficos," 38; Carrión Cachot, "Julio C. Tello," 7, 8.
17. Tello, "El curioso final de una polémica arqueológica"; Niles, *A Journey in Time*, 76.
18. Cueto, *Excelencia científica*, 54.
19. Ravines, *Los museos del Perú*, 40.
20. Rowe, *Max Uhle*; but see also Lyman and O'Brien, "Americanist Stratigraphic Excavation," 83, which argues for the importance of Alfred Kroeber's seriation of potsherds on the basis of their frequency, measuring *shifts* in types rather than cultural epochs. See Chp. 6, this book, for Uhle's earlier excavations.
21. Peixotto, "Down the West Coast to Lima," 433.
22. Uhle to Putnam, 22 November 1905, reproduced in Rowe, *Max Uhle*, 111.
23. Daggett, *An Annotated Tello-Centric History*, 188.
24. Tealdo, "Julio C. Tello."
25. Tello, "La Calahuala."
26. Ravines, *Los museos del Perú*, 37, notes there were twenty-two or twenty-four "Indian skulls" in its collection as of 1872; Peck, *The South American Tour*, 82, depicts one of its mummies.
27. Daggett, *An Annotated Tello-Centric History*, 25, citing Ricardo Palma, "Cirugía, ortopedia y cerámica pre-colombina," *El Comercio* (Lima), 26 May 1957, 2.
28. Burger, "The Intellectual Legacy of Julio C. Tello," 69, translating Mejía, "Prólogo," viii.
29. Tello to Ashmead, 24 October 1907, Folder: Tello (i), Box 3, ASAC; Tello, "Prehistoric Trephining," 112–113, 124; and Espejo Nuñez, *Formación Universitaria de Julio C. Tello*, 28–29.
30. "La craniectomia en el Peru Pre-Historico," *El Comercio* (Lima), 5 May 1906 ("With trepanation"); Julio B. Rodriguez, "Examen de Antropología", Archivo Julio C. Tello (AT)-416-2001-MNAAHP, 83–84, Museo Nacional de Arqueologia, Antropologia y Historia del Perú (MNAAHP), Lima; Daggett, *An Annotated Tello-Centric History*, 28–30.
31. Tello, *La antigüedad de la Sífilis*; Peters and Ayarza, "Julio C. Tello y el desarrollo de estudios andinos"; Cueto, *Excelencia científica*, 99–103.
32. Tello to Ashmead, 20 November 1909, Folder: Tello (i), Box 3, ASAC.
33. Mejía Xesspe, "Apuntes Biográficos," 40; Salomon, "Unethnic Ethnohistory," 479; Salomon, *The Cord Keepers*, 134; Padilla Deza, "El concepto y la representación de lo indio," 242.
34. "La Anecdota de Hoy: Un Brujo," *La Noche* (Lima), Martes 25 de Agosto de 1931; Mejía Xesspe, "Prólogo," viii. See also Bennison, "Who Are the Children of Pariacaca?," 125–126. I use here the translation and discussion of Cadena, "From Race to Class," 22, which feelingly attends to how Tello's peers racialized his supposed contradiction. Again, see Avilés, *No soy tu cholo* for a reclamation of *choledad*.
35. "Julio C. Tello, amauta preclaro," *La Tribuna* (Lima), 5 June 1947.
36. Tealdo, "Julio C. Tello," 8–9.
37. Peters and Ayarza, "Julio C. Tello y el desarrollo de estudios andinos."
38. Tello to Ricardo Palma, 18 October 1909, 20 December 1910, BNPA. See Rosemblatt, *The Science and Politics of Race*, 32–34, for Boas's plans.
39. Tello is thus comparable to the doctor Nuñez Butron, who had a similar "Indigenous" awakening while in Spain, and to Arthur C. Parker, who preceded Tello in anthropology in Harvard and established his credentials by excavating for Harvard's Peabody Museum of Archaeology and Ethnology, despite confrontations with his fellow Seneca: Cueto, " 'Indigenismo' and Rural Medicine in Peru," 30; Colwell, *Inheriting the Past*.

40. Ashmead, "Utosic Syphilis"; Bandelier, "On the Relative Antiquity." See also Farro and Podgorny, " 'Pre-Columbian Moulages.' "
41. Tello to Ashmead, 1 October 1909, Folder: Tello (i), Box 3, ASAC.
42. Tello to Ashmead, 28 October 1909, Folder: Tello (i), Box 3, ASAC.
43. Daggett, *An Annotated Tello-Centric History*, Chps. 2 and 3, surveys their relationship at greater length.
44. Ashmead, "Medical and Surgical Testimonies."
45. Oral history interview with T. Dale Stewart, 10, 17 January 1975, conducted by Pamela M. Henson and William A. Deiss, 17–34, SIA RU9521; Blakey, "Skull Doctors"; Thomas, *Skull Wars*, 106; Leonard, "American Indian Yaqui Warriors Laid to Rest"; Redman, *Bone Rooms, passim*, but esp. 53–55, 101–104.
46. Redman, *Bone Rooms*, Chp. 4.
47. Hrdlička to Holmes, 30 June 1910, Folder G, Box 107, AHP.
48. Hrdlička, "My Journeys," 650, Box 163, AHP; for Argentine anthropology and Hrdlička's engagement with it, see Thomas, *Skull Wars*, 137; Podgorny and Politis, "It Is Not All Roses Here"; Podgorny, "Bones and Devices"; Podgorny, "Human Origins in the New World?"; Larson, *Our Indigenous Ancestors*.
49. Heaney, *Cradle of Gold*, 78; Daggett, *An Annotated Tello-Centric History*, 202–210; Hrdlička, "My Journeys," 624, Box 163, AHP.
50. Hrdlička, "My Journeys," 624–625.
51. Ibid., 626, 632, 633–634b.
52. Ibid., 625–628.
53. Michelson, "Proceedings of the Anthropological Society of Washington," 317.
54. Hrdlička, "My Journeys," 630, Box 163, AHP.
55. Hrdlička to Holmes, 30 June 1910, Folder G, Box 107; Farabee to Hrdlička, 19 January 1911, Folder: Farabee, Box 24, AHP. For Tello's side of the export, see Tello to Ashmead, 6 June 1910, 10 July 1910, Folder: Tello (ii), Box 3, ASAC; Curtis S. Farabee to Tello, 15 November 1911, Cuadernillo II, Grupo XXXI: Correspondencia, Folio 191, Archivo Julio C. Tello (JCT), Archivos del Museo de Antropología e Arqueología, Universidad Nacional Mayor de San Marcos, Lima.
56. Tello to Palma, 20 December 1910, BNPA.
57. Hrdlička to Farabee, 13 January 1911, Folder: Farabee, Box 24, AHP.
58. Tello to Palma, 20 April 1911, BNPA.
59. Ibid. See also Asensio, *Señores del pasado*, 71–72.
60. C. G. Weld to William F. Whitney, 28 February 1911, Folder 1, PMAE Accession 56-42.
61. Hrdlička to Farabee, 11 March 1913, Folder: Farabee, Box 24; Hrdlička to Eaton, 26 January 1915, Folder: Eaton, Box 23; Hrdlička to T. Dale Stewart, 29 March 1941, Folder: Stewart, Box 61, AHP.
62. Tello to Palma, 20 April 1911, BNPA.
63. Tello, "Prehistoric Trephining among the Yauyos of Peru," 116, 124.
64. *International Congress of Americanists*, xxxix.
65. Oscar M. Rojas to Tello, 14 April 1914, and Daniel J. Cranwell to Tello, 15 April 1914, Cuadernillo II, Grupo XXXI, 343 and 344, JCT.
66. MacCurdy, "Surgery among the Ancient Peruvians," 387.
67. Salvatore, "Local versus Imperial Knowledge"; Heaney, *Las Tumbas*; Salvatore, *Disciplinary Conquest*, Chp. 4; Cox Hall, *Framing a Lost City* ; Warren, Adam. "Photography, Race, Indigeneity."
68. Heaney, *Cradle of Gold*, 66–67; Heaney, *Las Tumbas*, 104–105.
69. Daggett, *An Annotated Tello-Centric History*, 219–220, 457; Heaney, *Cradle of Gold*, 69, 78, 116, 126; Asensio, *Señores del pasado*, 75.
70. Heaney, *Cradle of Gold*, 146. Chps. 12–15 detail the wider story, including workers' resistance to grave-opening.
71. Ibid., Chp. 17.
72. Hrdlička to William H. Holmes, 22 September 1911 ("great"), 2 October 1911, Folder: Holmes, Box 31, AHP.

73. Hrdlička to Holmes, 27 April 1912, Folder 6, Box 22, SIA RU 45; [US Consul], Lima to Sec of State, 5 July 1912; Justo Perez Figuerola to First Under-Secretary of the Ministry of Foreign Relations, 21 June 1912; Hrdlička to Holmes, 29 January 1913 (quote), Folder [C], Box 58; A. Pezet to Carlos A. Velarde, 31 December 1912, Folder [A], Box 106, AHP; Hrdlička, "Anthropological Work in Peru in 1913," 3.

74. Director de Salubridad Pública, Lima, 25 January 1913, Folder [A], Box 106, AHP.

75. Hrdlička, "Anthropological Work in Peru in 1913," 4, 8–9. For an excellent account of this expedition, see Feldman, "'Miserable San Damian!'"

76. Hrdlička, 4 February 1913, Folder 4, Box 2011–30 6, AHP.

77. Hrdlička, "My Journeys," 656, 671.

78. Ibid., 671; Hrdlička, "Anthropological Work in Peru in 1913," 11.

79. Astuhuamán Gonzáles and Daggett, "Julio César Tello Rojas," 25.

80. Hrdlička, "My Journeys," 687. For "mutual parasitism" and anthropology, see Roque, *Headhunting and Colonialism*.

81. Hrdlička, "My Journeys," 687 ("awkwardness"); Hrdlička to Holmes, 28 March 1913, Folder [C], Box 58; Hrdlička to H. Clay Howard, 9 May 1913, Folder [A], Box 106, AHP; Eduardo Higginson to Tello, 5 May 1913, Hrdlička to Tello, 13 August 1913, Cuadernillo II, Grupo XXXI: Correspondencia, 277, 295, JCT.

82. Hrdlička, "Division of Physical Anthropology Annual Report 1910–1911," Box 32, SIA RU 158.

83. Hrdlička to Holmes, 13 February 1913, Folder C, Box 58, AHP.

84. Redman, *Bone Rooms*, 160, 179, and Chp. 4, *passim*.

85. Hrdlička, "Anthropological Work in Peru in 1913," 56; The Division of Physical Anthropology at the Panama-California Exposition, San Diego, 37, Folder A, Box 58, AHP; Dr. Joseph C. Thompson, "Savage Surgeons Fix Skulls," *San Diego Union*, 11 April 1915 (emphasis added).

86. Oral history interview with T. Dale Stewart, 14 January, 12 February 1975, conducted by Pamela M. Henson, 183–184, SIA RU9521.

87. Folkmar, "Proceedings of the Academy," 479–480; Hrdlička to Holmes, 10 March 1913, Folder [C], Box 58; Hrdlička, "My Journeys," 706–707, 716, Box 163, AHP; Feldman, "'Miserable San Damian,'" brilliantly traces the afterlife of these ponchos, which Hrdlička wrapped around his body, beneath his clothes, before going through customs at Callao.

88. Redman, *Bone Rooms*, 107. The trouble owes to Hrdlička having bought a set of trepanned skulls from one of Tello's relatives that Tello said he had collected. Hrdlička believed Tello was cheating him. See his correspondence with Tello, Otto Holstein, and H. Clay Howard from March through May 1913, Folder [A], Box 106, AHP, but also Higginson to Tello, 5 May 1913, Hrdlička to Tello, 13 August 1913, Cuadernillo II, Grupo XXXI: Correspondencia, 277, 295, JCT.

89. Heaney, *Cradle of Gold*, 174.

90. Hrdlička to Tello, 31 October 1913, 28 January 1914, March 1915, 1 May 1915, 2 November 1915, Cuadernillo II, Grupo XXXI: Correspondencia, 304–306, 328, 382, 390, 431, JCT.

91. Tello, "La ciencia antropológica en el Perú"; Tello and Mejia Xesspe, *Historia de los museos*, 86–92; see also Daggett, *An Annotated Tello-Centric History*, 275.

92. Daggett, *An Annotated Tello-Centric History*, 281–288, 457; Tello and Mejia Xesspe, *Historia de los museos*, 88–92. Asensio, *Señores del pasado*, 75–76, notes Tello "wasn't exempt from the anti-Semitism predominating among the era's Anglo-Saxon academic elites."

93. Valcárcel, *Memorias*, 262; Gutiérrez de Quintanilla, *Memoria del director*, 285, 286, 290–291.

94. Gutiérrez de Quintanilla, *Réplica al panfleto*, 3, 9. See Cadena, *Indigenous Mestizos*, Chp. 2, for how self-proclaimed indigenistas denigrated actual Indigenous politics as Inca-inspired in this era.

95. Ibid., 4, 7–8, 9, 14–15. Also see Daggett, *An Annotated Tello-Centric History*, 288–289.

96. Daggett, *An Annotated Tello-Centric History*, 293–299.

97. Ramón Tello to Tello, 23 Augusto 1914, Cuadernillo II, Grupo XXXI: Correspondencia, 360, JCT.

98. Daggett, *An Annotated Tello-Centric History*, 320.

99. Ellwood C. Erdis to Hiram Bingham, 25 December 1915, Folder 179, Box 12; Erdis Journal, 11 January 1916, Folder 44, Box 21, Yale Peruvian Expedition Papers (YPEP), Yale University Manuscripts and Archives; Heaney, *Cradle of Gold*, 200-201.
100. Heaney, *Cradle of Gold*, Chps. 17-20.
101. Philip A. Means to Hrdlička, 14 October 1916, Folder: Means, Box 45, AHP.
102. William Lorenzo Moss to father, 1 September 1916 ("unseasonable"), Accession 16-5 Mummy Harvard Peruvian Expedition, PMAE; *Report on the Progress and Condition of the United States National Museum for the Year Ending June 30, 1916*, 17; Peters and Ayarza, "Julio C. Tello y el desarrollo de estudios andinos"; Daggett, *An Annotated Tello-Centric History*, Chps. 7, 8, and 418-420.
103. Castillo Morán and Moscoso Carbajal, "El 'Chino' y el 'Indio'"; Mejía Xesspe, "Apuntes biográficos," 43.
104. Ramón Joffre, *El neoperuano*, 30. Given that Mariátegui himself was the object of elite scandal in late 1917 for orchestrating Norka Rouskaya's supposedly sacrilegious dance to Chopin's Funeral March in Lima's cemetery (and in part defended himself by alluding to Peruvian Indian dances in the cemetery; see Stein, *Dance in the Cemetery*, 176-177), his objection was likely less to the elevation of Indigenous history as essential to Peruvian identity—a key aspect of his subsequent project—than the potentially empty symbolic politics of trading one sacred cow for another: Atahuallpas for Pizarros. One of Tello's students later said he accompanied Tello to Mariátegui's house on two occasions; historian Jorge Basadre understood them as sympathetic contemporaries: Jave Calderón, ed., *Jorge Basadre*, 32-38.
105. For Tello's parliamentary output see Padilla Deza, "El concepto y la representación de lo indio." See Cadena, *Indigenous Mestizos*, Chp. 2 for moves against Indigenous politics in this period.
106. Cueto, *Excelencia científica en la periferia*, 81.
107. Padilla Deza, "El concepto y la representación de lo indio," 96-98; Durston, "Quechua Language Government Propaganda in 1920s Peru," 166.
108. "Agasajo al doctor Julio C. Tello," *El Comercio* (Lima), 27 October 1933, 5. See also Daggett, *Julio C. Tello*, 74.
109. Tello, *Introducción a la historia Antigua*, 1-4, 41; Asensio, *Señores del pasado*, 184-186.
110. Gutiérrez de Quintanilla, *El Manco Capac*, 144-145.
111. George Grant MacCurdy to Hrdlička, 15 January 1928, Folder: MacCurdy (ii), Box 43, AHP; Ramón Joffre, *El neoperuano*, Chp. 5; Daggett, *An Annotated Tello-Centric History*, 575-591, 912; Heaney, *Cradle of Gold*, 217-219.
112. Tello, "El Museo De Arqueología Peruana," 20, 23, 26, 27, 28.
113. "Resultó brillante el homenaje tributado al Dr. Julio C. Tello," *La Crónica* (Lima), 27 October 1933. See Cueto, *Excelencia científica en la periferia*, Chp. 5, and "Andean Biology in Peru" for Monge's celebration of Andean biology and his important place in the scientific scene.
114. Daggett, *An Annotated Tello-Centric History*, 993-999.
115. Lothrop, "Un recuerdo del Dr. Julio C. Tello y Paracas."
116. Tello, "En la península de Paracas"; "Actualidad—La ciencia en el Antiguo Peru," *El Comercio* (Lima), 27 March 1948.
117. Daggett, *Julio C. Tello*, 79-80.
118. Carrión Cachot, "Julio C. Tello," 13. Tello's posthumous *Paracas, Primera parte* is a more careful, less speculative rendering of his theorizations. See Peters, "The Cemetery of Paracas Necropolis," for current understandings.
119. Salomon, "'The Beautiful Grandparents,'" 321; Salomon, *At the Mountains' Altar*, 103. Tello may have grown up speaking Spanish, not Quechua or Jaqaru-Cauque, like others in Huarochirí; but Bennison, "Waqay," argues for how Quechua/Andean terms used in supposedly "Spanish" Huarochirí contexts can be "indigenous."
120. Carrión Cachot, "Julio C. Tello," 15, 31.
121. "Una visita al Museo de Arqueologia Peruana: La Exposicion de Arte Pre-Colombino Peruano," *El Comercio* (Lima), 20 Octubre 1929. The textiles were instead woven specifically for the mummies; Peters, "The Cemetery of Paracas Necropolis."
122. Haraway, "Teddy Bear Patriarchy."

123. We see Tello's assistants and artists embrace this discourse in their letters to Tello in the Archivo Tello in the Museo de Arqueología y Antropología of the Universidad Nacional Mayor de San Marcos.
124. Daggett, *Julio C. Tello*; Peters and Ayarza, "Julio C. Tello y el desarrollo de estudios andinos en los Estados Unidos."
125. Cf. Rosemblatt, *The Science and Politics of Race* for the former, in Mexico; Cadena, *Indigenous Mestizos*, for Peru.
126. Castillo Morán and Moscoso Carbajal, "El 'Chino' y el 'Indio,'" 181.

Chapter 9

1. "Fallecimiento del doctor Julio C. Tello," *El Comercio* (Lima), 4 June 1947; Salomon, "'The Beautiful Grandparents,'" 336. See Bacigalupo, "The Mapuche Undead Never Forget," for how to conceive of ancestors and the undead as vengeful actors.
2. Tello, "Testamento del Doctor don Julio C. Tello y Rojas," 137–138.
3. Ibid., 137.
4. Ibid., 137–1388; Expenses, S. American trip of N. A. Rockefeller, Folder 1564, Box 143; Tello to Rockefeller, 11 July 1938, Folder 1566, Box 144, RG 4-NAR, Personal, Ser. A— Activities, Rockefeller Archive Center [RAC].
5. Tello, "Testamento del Doctor don Julio C. Tello y Rojas," 139.
6. Daggett, "An Annotated Tello-Centric History," 507–509, 794–804; see Asensio, *Señores del pasado*, Chp. 3, for Tello's relationship to the in-site museum of Chavín de Huantar.
7. See Weismantel, "Encounters with Dragons," for how the Tello obelisk challenges to our attempts to see it.
8. Tello, "Testamento del Doctor don Julio C. Tello y Rojas," 139–140.
9. "Fallecimiento del doctor Julio C. Tello," *El Comercio* (Lima), 4 June 1947.
10. For the wider story of Peruvian grave-opening in the final years of Tello's career and beyond—an era whose documentary explosion makes synthesis difficult— see Astuhuamán and Tantaleán, eds. *Historia de la arqueología en el Perú del siglo XX*; Tantaleán, *Peruvian Archaeology*; Daggett, *Julio C. Tello*; Asensio, *Señores del pasado*.
11. Ávalos and Ravines, "Las antigüedades Peruanas," 400; "Son de propiedad del Estados los monumentos históricos," *La Prensa* (Lima), 4 September 1929.
12. Tello and Mejía Xesspe's *Historia de los museos nacionales del Perú*, published after Tello's death, builds to this law, contextualizing it with Tello's prior and subsequent museum efforts.
13. "Inventario Descriptivo y numerico de 654 objetos arqueológicos y no arqueológicos de la Colección 'Exposition Iberamericana de Sevilla de 1929,' que no han sido devueltos al Museo, los que se hallan aún en España," Abril 1959, AT-428-2001-MNAAHP; Jave Calderón, ed., *Jorge Basadre*, 23–24 ("tears"); Peters and Ayarza, "Julio C. Tello y el desarrollo de estudios andinos."
14. See the correspondence between Rockefeller, Tello, Albert Giesecke, and US ambassador Fred Morris Dearing, Folder 1564, Box 143, and Folder 1566, Box 144, RAC, RG 4-NAR, Personal, Ser. A—Activities, Box 143. Tello had previously proposed a Paracas mummy bundle for an exchange with Penn's University Museum: J. Alden Mason to Miss Jane McHugh, 24 October 1928, Folder 8, Container 12, Administrative Records, 0044 American Section – Curatorial, PUMA.
15. "Defunciones," "Se rinde homenaje a la memoria del Doctor Julio C. Tello," *El Comercio* (Lima), 5 June 1947; "Condolencia por la muerte del Dr. Tello," *El Comercio* (Lima), 9 June 1947; "Condolencia de la Unión Panamericana a san Marcos por el deceso del Dr. Tello," *La Tribuna* (Lima), 12 June 1947. Unless otherwise noted, all newspaper clippings of Tello's death and interments, here and below, are in AT-334-2001-MNAAHP and AT-351-2001-MNAAHP. For anthropology and indigenismo in this moment, see Degregori and Sandoval, "La antropología en el Perú," 306-308; Sandoval, "Antropología y antropólogos en el Perú."
16. Antonio Flores, "Ha muerto uno de los mas grandes Huarochirianos de Nuestra Epoca," *Resurgimiento* (June 1947), 117; "Relampagos," *La Prensa* (Lima), 5 June 1947; Wancawilla, "El Sabio Antropologo Huarochiriano Julio C. Tello," *Resurgimiento* (June 1947), 116. This focus on Tello's "Indian" rather than possible mestizo identity also reflects the discourse

of Luis E. Valcárcel, now the Minister of Education, who celebrated the former over the latter: de la Cadena, *Indigenous Mestizos*, 166-167.

17. "Homenaje de 'La Tribuna' al sabio Tello," *La Tribuna* (Lima), 7 June 1947.

18. As Tello said in Mexico in 1944, "There will be no Mexicans, Peruvians or Chileans"—only Indigenous Americans like himself. Prieto Burmester, "Dos forjadores," 24–25, citing Luís Spota, "América puede llegar a ser un país de Indios," *Excelsior* (Ciudad de México), 28 January 1944. See Rosemblatt, *The Science and Politics of Race*, for that Mexican context.

19. "Examen de Antropología"—Julio C. Salas D., ca. April 1932, AT-416-2001-MNAAHP.

20. "Fallecimiento del doctor Julio C. Tello," *El Comercio* (Lima), 4 June 1947; author's interview with Uriel García Cáceres and Guido Lombardi, 1 June 2022. The heart ultimately went to the museum in Lima's Arzobispo Loayza National Hospital

21. "Primer plano: Tello y el eterno Peru," *La Tribuna* (Lima), 6 June 1947; "Mañana se realizarán los funerales del eminente arqueólogo Julio C. Tello," *El Comercio* (Lima), 5 June 1947; "Hoy seran Inhumados los Restos del Dr. Tello a quien se le Rendira Honores de Ministro," *La Tribuna* (Lima), 6 June 1947.

22. "Hoy seran Inhumados los Restos del Dr. Tello a quien se le Rendira Honores de Ministro," *La Tribuna* (Lima), 6 June 1947; "Sentida y elocuente manifestación constituyó el sepelio del doctor Tello," *El Comercio* (Lima), 6 June 1947; "Muere un Sabio Peruano," Productora "Huascaran," 1947, https://www.youtube.com/watch?v=9ztHC-YFtxQ&feature=youtu. be; Warren, *Medicine and Politics*, Chp. 5.

23. "Fueron trasladados al Cementerio General los Restos del Doctor Julio César Tello," *La Prensa* (Lima), 7 June 1947; "El sepelio del doctor Julio C. Tello constituyo una imponente manifestacion de duelo," *El Comercio* (Lima), 7 June 1947; "Con honores de Ministro de Estado Fueron Sepultados ayer provisoriamente en cementerio general los restos del ilustre arqueologo Doctor Julio C. Tello," *La Tribuna* (Lima), 7 June 1947.

24. "Tumba inviolable y gratuita," *La Tribuna* (Lima), 30 December 1947; "Conservemos y Prosigamos la Obra de Tello," *La Tribuna* (Lima), 7 June 1947.

25. "San Marcos rindió homenaje a la memoria del sabio Julio C. Tello," *La Tribuna* (Lima), 4 December 1947.

26. Burger, "The Intellectual Legacy of Julio C. Tello," 65, and Prieto Burmester, "Dos forjadores," 3, note the incredible number of clubs, streets, and institutions named after Tello.

27. "Mummy of Woman Described," *The New York Times*, 25 September 1949, E8.

28. Cadena, "From Race to Class," 22.

29. Stewart and Peterson, *Builders of Latin America*.

30. Kroeber, *Peruvian Archeology in 1942*, 5–6, 93.

31. "Dr. J. C. Tello Dies; Archaeologist, 67," *The New York Times*, 5 June 1947, 26; "Mummy of Woman Described," *The New York Times*, 25 September 1949, E8.

32. Lothrop, "Julio C. Tello," 50, 53.

33. Peters and Ayarza, "Julio C. Tello y el desarrollo de estudios andinos."

34. Confidential Report by A. L. Kroeber on Archaeological Trip to Peru, February–May 1942, 13, Henry Allen Moe Papers (HAMP), American Philosophical Society; Heaney, "Seeing Like an Inca."

35. Peters and Ayarza, "Julio C. Tello y el desarrollo de estudios andinos," 73.

36. Redman, *Bone Rooms*, 107.

37. Unit Exhibit Script, Folder: Hall 25, Box 2, SIA RU 363.

38. Ibid.

39. Unit 20 draft script, Folder 3, Box 1, SIA RU 90.

40. Joseph Shannon to Tobey, 19 January 1966, Folder 6, Box 1, Smithsonian Institution, Archives of American Art, Alton S. Tobey Papers (1939–1980).

41. For how postwar American social scientists increasingly treated the work of Latin American colleagues as providing "evidence" rather than conceptual creative theories, see Rosemblatt, *The Science and Politics of Race*, 181–182.

42. The other showed a woman being healed in a Navajo hogan: "Primitive Medicine." Duffin and Li, "Great Moments"; Metzl and Howell, "Great Moments."

43. Unit 19—Tobey Mural, Folder 2, Box 1, SIA RU 90. For how Machu Picchu's repute had been on the rise since the 1940s, see Rice, *Making Machu Picchu*, Chp. 2.

44. "Fallecimiento del doctor Julio C. Tello," *El Comercio* (Lima), 4 June 1947.
45. "Primer Plano: Tello y el Eterno Peru," *La Tribuna* (Lima), 6 June 1947.
46. "El sepelio del doctor Julio C. Tello constituyo una imponente manifestacion de duelo," *El Comercio* (Lima), 7 June 1947.
47. "Con extraordinario Fercor Patriótica se Inhumaron Ayer los Restos del Sabio Peruano Julio C. Tello," *La Tribuna* (Lima), 4 June 1948; "Inauguro El Museo de Pueblo Libre La Exposición de Cirugia Precolombina," *La Tribuna* (Lima), 19 May 1948; "Ayer fueron inhumados los restos del doctor Julio C. Tello en el Museo de Antropologia," *El Comercio* (Lima), 4 June 1948.
48. "Con extraordinario Fervor Patriótica se Inhumaron Ayer los Restos del Sabio Peruano Julio C. Tello," *La Tribuna* (Lima), 4 June 1948; "Primera piedra del mausoleo al Dr. J. Tello," [n.p.], 4 January 1948, 6, in 017-2010, Box 3, Archivo Colección Julio Espejo Nuñez (CJEN), MNAAHP. Luna Iglesias's panegyric was far from atypical. Tello's friend, the incredibly careful historian Jorge Basadre, admitted that he sometimes thought that in Tello there was "a type of reincarnation of some ancestors that lived on in him. that dictated to him, that directed him in his labors, in his investigations, in his works" (Jave Calderón, ed., *Jorge Basadre*, 31).
49. "Con extraordinario Fervor Patriótica . . .";"Ayer fueron inhumados los restos del doctor Julio C. Tello en el Museo de Antropologia," *El Comercio* (Lima), 4 June 1948.

Epilogue

1. Wiener, "Huaco Portrait," 47–48. I use the translation by Gabriela Jauregui for *McSweeney's Quarterly Concern*, No. 65, but the rest of Wiener's *Huaco retrato* is electrifying. Her family knows Charles Wiener as their great-great-grandfather, who romanced and left a Peruvian woman named María Rodríguez. It is María, and herself, that Gabriela Wiener sees reflected in the glass of the hall's Moché ceramic portraits of fifteen-hundred-year-old Andean lords—"that all these figurines that look like me were torn from the cultural legacy of my country by a man whose last name I share" (45). I am reluctantly cutting short my discussion of Wiener's incredible meditation on collecting, race, gender, paternity, and sexuality, in part because I don't want to tread on what her surprising book delicately unfolds. She should be read directly.
2. Wiener: "Huaco Portrait," 47–48, 49, 50.
3. Ibid., 48.
4. Asensio, *Señores del pasado*; Atwood, *Stealing History*.
5. For comparisons of these contexts, see Herrera, "Indigenous Archaeology"; Lonetree, *Decolonizing Museums*; Fine-Dare, "Bodies Unburied, Mummies Displayed"; Endere, "Archaeological Heritage Legislation and Indigenous Rights in Latin America."
6. Isbell, *Mummies and Mortuary Monuments*, 150.
7. Fernández Ortega and Calzada Escalona, "La relación de los investigadores cubanos," 456–457; Heaney, "Mummies Take Manhattan"; Charles Siler, "Mummy Unwrapping to Proceed Despite Indian Warning," *Knoxville News-Sentinel,* 29 July 1982, A-1. I thank Chad Black for sharing the latter source.
8. Siler, "Mummy Unwrapping" ("No mummies").
9. Calvin Sims, "Archeologists in Peru Oppose Loan of Inca Mummy to U.S.," *The New York Times*, 8 May 1996, A5; Pringle, *The Mummy Congress*, 222–241, Clinton on 236. For Fujimori's appropriation of archaeological symbols, see Silverman, "Archaeology and the 1997 Peruvian Hostage Crisis."
10. Nilsson Stutz, "To Gaze upon the Dead," 281. For 110,000 Native American, Hawaiian and Alaskan remains, see Logan Jaffe, Mary Hudetz, Ash Ngu, and Graham Lee Brewer, "America's Biggest Museums Fail to Return Native American Human Remains," *ProPublica*, 11 January 2023, https://www.propublica.org/article/repatriation-nagpra-museums-human-remains.
11. See Colla, *Conflicted Antiquities*; Riggs, *Unwrapping*.
12. Heaney, "Mummies Take Manhattan."
13. Wann et al, "The Tres Ventanas Mummies of Peru," 1027.
14. Seki, "Participation of the Local Community," 111.
15. Peru's cultural agencies even threatened to destroy the Museo Juanita for being built in an archaeological zone without consulting the central government. Velasco, "Humans Remain," 81.

APP América Noticias, "Momia 'Juanita' no regresaría al Colca: museo fue construido sobre zona intangible," 3 January 2014, http://www.americatv.com.pe/noticias/actualidad/momia-juanita-no-regresaria-al-colca-museo-fue-construido-sobre-zona-intangible-n125126; "Juanita, manzana de la Discordia entre autoridades," *VP Semanario*, 19 May 2019; Autoridad Autónoma del Colca y Anexos, "#Museo Juanita abre sus puertos al turismo," Facebook, 24 November 2020, https://www.facebook.com/Autocolca/videos/404397304261707).

16. Ramírez, *The World Upside Down*; Delibes Mateos, *Desenterrando tesoros*.

17. Gose, *Invaders as Ancestors*; Salomon, "Unethnic Ethnohistory." See Cadena, *Indigenous Mestizos*, and Herrera, "Indigenous Archaeology," for how people of Andean descent can complicate "Indigeneity" for its subject position within national racializations.

18. As Flores Galindo, *In Search of an Inca*, previously argued

19. Raimondi, "Itinerario," 41; Salomon and Niño-Murcia, *The Lettered Mountain*, 104–114. For the clearest articulation of some traditional communities' lasting understanding of the reciprocity between living and dead, see Allen, "Body and Soul in Quechua Thought."

20. Réna Gündüz, *El mundo ceremonial*; Smith, "Looting and the Politics of Archaeological Knowledge."

21. No less than the great Peruvian historian Jorge Basadre framed Tello's project as important in its pre-Inca ambitions: Jave Calderón, ed., *Jorge Basadre*, 16–17.

22. Burger, ed., *The Life and Writings of Julio C. Tello*. He has also been given a wonderful bilingual children's book: Brown and Chavarri, *Sharuko*.

23. I complete this epilogue in March of 2023, when media coverage of largely rural protests against the removal of President Pedro Castillo has portrayed protestors—who have been killed by the police—as "savage" and un-Peruvian.

24. Herrera and Lane, "Qué hacen aquí esos *Pishtaku*?"; Turner and Andrushko, "Partnerships, Pitfalls, and Ethical Concerns in International Bioarchaeology"; and Velasco, "Humans Remain," offer moving meditations along these lines.

25. Dan Collyns, "Peru's Royal Pedigree: Direct Descendants Trace Roots to Incan Emperor and Kin," *The Guardian*, 25 October 2016 https://www.theguardian.com/world/2016/oct/25/peru-royal-pedigree-inca-empire-history.

26. Salomon and Urioste, eds., *The Huarochirí Manuscript*, 114–116.

27. Ventura García Calderón, "La Momia," in *La venganza del condor* (1924). I thank Erica Beckman for pointing me to this story.

28. In Hergé's follow-up, *Prisoners of the Sun* (1949), Tintin travels to Peru to meet the Inca descendants who cursed the collectors who disturbed Rascar Capac's tomb. At least three different mummies in Belgian and French are claimed to have inspired Hergé: Ordoñez, *Unbundled*, 99, 103–103; Agence France Presse, "Tintin and the Mystery of the Duelling Mummies," *Bangkok Post*, 14 July 2020, https://www.bangkokpost.com/world/1951336/tintin-and-the-mystery-of-the-duelling-mummies.

29. Also see Fine-Dare, "Bodies Unburied, Mummies Displayed," 107n14.

30. For examples of Indian ghost and Egyptian mummy stories as indices of colonial guilt, see Boyd and Thrush, "Introduction"; Luckhurst, "Science versus Rumour."

31. "For Sale," *The New Yorker*, 7 February 1942, 8–9.

32. For examples of those dialogues, see Fine-Dare, "Bodies Unburied, Mummies Displayed"; Endere, "Archaeological Heritage Legislation and Indigenous Rights in Latin America"; Ordoñez, *Unbundled*; Sardi and Ballestero, "Los cuerpos indígenas entre textos y silencios"; Ballestero, "The Path of the Bodies"; Heaney, "As Peru Heads to the 2018 World Cup"; Lovis, Capriles, and Rodriguez, "La Repatriación de una momia Boliviana."

33. Hampe Martínez, "La última morada de los Incas"; Bauer and Coello Rodríguez, "The Hospital of San Andrés"; Ziemendorff, Millones Figueroa, and Greenwich Centeno, "Las momias reales incaicas."

34. Atwood, *Stealing History*; Smith, "Looting and the Politics of Archaeological Knowledge"; Asensio, *Los señores del pasado*.

35. Rodríguez, "Recuperando la Mirada."

36. Rojas-Pérez, *Mourning Remains*.

37. Akita Maeshiro, "¿Tienen derechos las momias?," 11 July 2014, https://puntoedu.pucp.edu.pe/noticia/tienen-derechos-las-momias/.

38. Heaney, "The Racism behind Alien Mummy Hoaxes." See also Lombardi and Rodríguez Martín, "Fake and Alien Mummies."

39. "Indians Urge Fair Boycott over Mummy," *Los Angeles Times*, 29 July 1982, B4; Fine-Dare, "Bodies Unburied, Mummies Displayed."

40. Sims, "Archeologists in Peru Oppose Loan of Inca Mummy to U.S." See also Guillén, "A History of Paleopathology in Peru and Northern Chile"; Thomas, *Skull Wars*; Fine-Dare, *Grave Injustice*; Lonetree, *Decolonizing Museums*; Riding In, "Decolonizing NAGPRA."

41. Fine-Dare, "Bodies Unburied, Mummies Displayed."

42. Mould de Pease, *Machu Picchu*; Heaney, *Las Tumbas*; Amado and Bauer, "The Ancient Inca Town Named Huayna Picchu"; Hu and Quave, "Prosperity and Prestige"; Burger et al., "New AMS Dates for Machu Picchu."

43. Noack and Grana-Behrens, "Introduction," 10; "In the USA, Peru Recovers Stolen Paracas Textile," *Andino.pe*, 14 January 2015, https://andina.pe/Ingles/noticia-in-the-usa-peru-recov ers-stolen-paracas-textile-539386.aspx.

44. Lombardi and Bravo Meza, "Tello y los Restos Humanos de los Huarochiranos Ancestrales." The non-US loophole is noted by Fine-Dare, *Grave Injustice*, 162; Brown and Bruchac, "NAGPRA from the Middle Distance," 210–211.

45. For the former, I thank Ryan Williams for pointing me to their Field Museum records: Accession No. 362, Accession Vol. IV, 19, Field Museum of Natural History Archives; Historical File for Accession No. 362, Anthropology Department, Field Museum of Natural History; FMNH4246 ["Mummy of child"], FMNH40220, FMNH40221, FMNH40222, FMNH40223, FMNH40224, FMNH40225, FMNH40226, FMNH40227, FMNH40228, FMNH40230, FMNH40231, FMNH40232, FMNH40325, FMNH40345, Field Museum of Natural History (Anthropology) Collection, http://collections-anthropology.fieldmus eum.org/ (accessed 29 November 2022); for the latter, see Accession 16-5 Mummy Harvard Peruvian Expedition, PMAE.

46. Biers, "Rethinking Purpose, Protocol, and Popularity," 245. See also Curtoni, "Against Global Archaeological Ethics," 41–47. See the latter chapters of Asensio, *Señores del pasado*, for the rise of site museums.

47. Rodríguez, "Recuperando la mirada."

48. I thank Kelly Hyberger, formerly of the Museum of Us, now at the Filson Historical Society in Kentucky, for explaining this path to me, 14 March 2023.

49. "Statement on Human Remains at the Smithsonian Institution," 25 January 2023.

50. For example, see ibid.; Guillén, "A History of Paleopathology in Peru and Northern Chile," 313; Arkush, "Violence, Indigeneity, and Archaeological Interpretation in the Central Andes"; Tung, *Violence, Ritual, and the Wari Empire*; Verano, *Holes in the Head*; Slovak, "Reassembling the Mortuary Assemblage."

51. Herrera and Lane, "Qué Hacen Aquí Esos *Pishtaku*?"; Menaker, "Becoming 'Rebels' and 'Idolaters'"; Velasco, "Humans Remain." For how anthropologists' enlistment in mourning and ancestral care can carry over generations, see Heaney, "Living Dead Birds."

52. Salomon, "Unethnic Ethnohistory"; Fine-Dare, "Bodies Unburied, Mummies Displayed."

53. I thank Claudia Augustat, curator for South America at the Weltmuseum Wien, for relating this anecdote to me, 16 March 2023.

54. I discuss this question more amply in Heaney, "Skull Walls."

55. Allen, "Body and Soul in Quechua Thought"; Salomon, "Unethnic Ethnohistory"; see also Chambers, "Little Middle Ground."

56. Edgardo Krebs, "The Invisible Man." *Washington Post*, 10 August 2003, https://www.was hingtonpost.com/wp-dyn/content/article/2007/08/10/AR2007081001366.html; de la Cadena, *Earth Beings*, 211–212.

57. Ibid.; "Preservation of Collections" in Hodge, ed., *Handbook of American Indians North of Mexico*, 2:305–306. I thank Christina Snyder for catching the possible significance of pe-troleum. For how North American tribes have to address contaminated repatriations, see Hemenway, "Trials and Tribulations," 177.

58. Cadena, *Earth Beings*, 221, 226, and Story 6, *passim*.

59. As Fine-Dare, "Bodies Unburied, Mummies Displayed," 82, notes in another case, "The bodies of Peruvian indigenous deceased become an ahistoricized (or inaccurately historicized)

political field for creating pan-Indian solidarity." Using like examples, Lonetree, *Decolonizing Museums*, Chp. 3, challenges the idea that the NMAI is "decolonizing."

60. Mendoza-Mori, "Quechua Language Programs in the United States"; Muschi, "Desarrollo de la informalidad."

61. James Gorman, "Hunter Burial Casts Doubt on Ancient Gender Divide," *New York Times*, 6 November 2020. I thank Janet Murdock for sharing this article with me.

62. Author's interview with Madeleine Fontenot, 2 June 2021.

63. "Museum Director Laden with Collector Items," *Corpus Christi Caller*, 1 August 1957; "Mummy of Inca to Be Displayed," *Corpus Christi Times*, 29 August 1957; Author's interview with Jillian Becquet and Fontenot, 18 October 2017; Author's interview with Becquet, 5 August 2021. To the reader wondering if this was the mummified child that the engineer Chatfield showed to the writer for the *New Yorker*: probably not, given that Chatfield's child was "reclining," not circumflex, and covered "by a mask made of some kind of mud or plaster," which sounds more like a Chinchorro mummy, the world's oldest, from Chile. Still: where did they go?

64. Author's interview with Fontenot, 2 June 2021. See Riding In, "Decolonizing NAGPRA"; Lonetree, *Decolonizing Museums*; Colwell, *Plundered Skulls*, for critiques and reflections upon NAGPRA.

65. Author's interview with Becquet, 5 August 2021.

66. Author's interview with Fontenot, 2 June 2021, and Becquet, 5 August 2021; Corpus Christi Museum of Science and History, Jillian Becquet and Madeleine Fontenot, "Mummy Research—What We Know," unpublished research packet, 2017. For Collagua mortuary styles, see Duchesne, "Tumbas de Coporaque." See Velasco, "Ethnogenesis and Social Difference," for identifications of crania of this type as Collagua.

67. Author's interview with Becquet, 4 August 2021; Meagan Falcon, "Mummy's Home: 2,000-Year-Old Remains Heading Back to Peru after 6 Decades in Texas Museum," *Corpus Christi Caller-Times*, 17 August 2018, https://www.caller.com/story/news/nation-now/2018/08/17/2000-year-old-mummy-leaving-texas-museum-headed-peru/1025583002/.

68. Author's interview with Fontenot, 2 June 2021.

69. "Museo estadounidense devuelve al Perú primera momia infante," *El Peruano* (Lima), 9 February 2019, https://elperuano.pe/noticia/75551-museo-estadounidense-devuelve-al-peru-primera-momia-infante. For a fascinating discussion of the re-gendering of the Andean dead, see Begerock et al., "200 Years a Woman."

70. María Zapata, "Patronato Cívico Cultural de Pueblo Libre cuestiona la eliminación de la memoria histórica del MNAAHP," *LaMula.pe*, 30 May 2021, https://tvrobles.lamula.pe/2021/05/30/patronato-civico-cultural-de-pueblo-libre-cuestiona-la-eliminacion-de-la-memoria-historica-del-mnaahp/tvrobles/.

71. An important line going forward is the social and material history of museums in the Andes, by which they become more than spaces defined by the state and—as I myself am guilty of in the case of the MNAAHP—outspoken individuals like Julio César Tello. They are also physical spaces of contention, dissidence, and care, dependent on employees who maintain their contents, protest their decay, and interact daily with bodies and objects traveling through time. I am grateful that, as this book was going to press, Henry Tantaleán Ynga gifted me the excellent volume he co-edited with Luis Muro Ynoñan, *Arqueologías Subalternas: Voces desde el Perú Pasado y Presente* (Lima: Instituto Peruano de Estudios Arqueológicos and Instituto Francés de Estudios Andinos, 2022), whose essay by Raúl Asensio identifies Tello as crafting a place for social action in Peruvian archaeology. As Ann H. Peters and Gabriel Ramón Joffre have also noted, the politics of Tello's collaborators (many of whom were from the Andes) are an important place to continue.

BIBLIOGRAPHY

Library, Museum, and Archival Collections Cited

PERU

Archivo General de la Nación (AGNP), Lima.
Biblioteca Nacional de Perú Archivos (BNPA), Lima.
Museo de Arqueología y Antropología, Universidad Nacional Mayor de San Marcos (UNMSM), Lima.
  Archivo Tello (JCT).
Museo Nacional de Arqueología, Antropología y Historia del Perú (MNAAHP), Lima.
  Archivo Julio C. Tello (AT).
  Archivo Colección Julio Espejo Nuñez (CJEN).

SPAIN

Archivo General de Indias (AGI), Sevilla
Museo de América, Archives, Madrid

UNITED KINGDOM

Archives of the Royal College of Surgeons (ARCS) of England, London
Essex Record Office (ERO), Essex.
National Library of Scotland (NLS), Edinburgh.

UNITED STATES

Academy of Natural Sciences, Philadelphia, PA (ANSP).
American Antiquarian Society, Worcester, MA.
  Salisbury Family Papers.
American Museum of Natural History (AMNH), New York.
  Bandelier Accession Record (BAR).
American Philosophical Society, Philadelphia, PA.
  Henry Allen Moe Papers (HAMP).
  Samuel George Morton Papers (SGMP-APS).
College of Physicians of Philadelphia, Philadelphia, PA.
  Albert S. Ashmead Collection (ASAC).
Field Museum of Natural History, Chicago, IL. Archives.
  Anthropology Accession Files.
Harvard University Archives (HUA), Cambridge, MA.
  Papers of Frederic Ward Putnam (FWP).

Historical Society of Pennsylvania, Philadelphia, PA.
Library Company of Philadelphia, Philadelphia, PA.
   Samuel George Morton Papers (SGMP-LC).
Peabody Museum of Archaeology and Ethnology (PMAE) Archives, Harvard University, Cambridge, MA.
   Frederic Ward Putnam Papers (FWPP).
Penn Museum Archives, University of Pennsylvania, Philadelphia, PA (PUMA).
Princeton University Rare Books and Special Collections, Princeton, NJ.
   Marmaduke Burrough Papers (MBP).
   Samuel George Morton Letterbook.
Rockefeller Archive Center (RAC), Sleepy Hollow, NY.
Smithsonian Institution
   Archives of American Art, Washington, DC.
   Hrdlička Reprint Archive (HRA), Smithsonian National Museum of Natural History, Washington, DC.
   National Anthropological Archives (NAA), National Museum of Natural History, Suitland, MD.
   Aleš Hrdlička Papers (AHP).
   Bureau of American Ethnology Papers (BAE).
   United States Army Medical Museum Anatomical Section Records Relating to Specimens Transferred to the Smithsonian Institution (USAMMAS).i
   Smithsonian Institution Archives (SIA), Washington, DC.
Yale University Manuscripts & Archives, New Haven, CT.
Yale Peruvian Expedition Papers (YPEP).

Primary Sources

Acosta, José de. *Historia natural y moral de las Indias*. Sevilla: Casa de Juan de Leon, 1590.
Adams, Charles Francis. *Richard Henry Dana: A Biography*, Vol. 2. Boston: Houghton, Mifflin, and Co., 1891.
"After the Earthquake (by a Naval Officer)." In *Mission Life, or The Emigrant and the Heathen*, VI, 48-55. London: William Macintosh, 1869.
Albertini, Luis E. *Le Pérou en 1878: Notice historique et statistique suivie du Catalogue des Exposants*. Paris: Imprimerie Nouvelle, 1878.
Alcala Galiano, Antonio de. *Biografía del astrónomo Español don José Joaquin de Ferrer y Cafranga*. Madrid: J. Martin Alegria, 1858.
Alemenara Butler, Francisco. "Memoria leida por el Presidente de la Sociedad Unión Fernandina en la sesión del 13 de Agosto de 1890." *La Crónica Médica*, Año 7, Tomo 6, No. 80 (Agosto 31 de 1890): 207-213.
Annual Report of the Board of Regents of the Smithsonian Institution, Showing the Operations, Expenditures, and Condition of the Institution for the Year 1882. Washington, DC: Government Printing Office, 1884.
"Antiquités Péruviennes." *Mémoires de la Société Royale Antiquaires du Nord 1845–1849*. Copenhagen: Berling, n.d.
Arguedas, José María [translator], and Pierre Duviols [editor]. *Dioses y hombres de Huarochirí: Narración quechua recogida por Francisco de Ávila (¿1598?)*. Lima: Instituto de Estudios Peruanos / Instituto Francés de Estudios Andinos, 1966.
Arriaga, Pablo José de. *La Extirpación de la Idolatría en el Pirú (1621)*, edited by Henrique Urbano. Cuzco: Centro de Estudios Regionales Andinos "Bartolomé de las Casas," 1999.
Arte de la lengua general del Perú, llamada Quichua. Lima: Casa de Clemente Hidalgo, 1603.
"Art. X. The Present State of Peru . . . . In *The Annual Review and History of Literature for 1805*, vol. 4, edited by Arthur Aiken, 49–60. London: Longman, Hurst, Rees, and Orme, 1806.

Ashmead, Albert S. "Medical and Surgical Testimonies on the Mummy Grove Potteries of Old Peru" (cont.). *Monthly Cyclopaedia and Medical Bulletin* 2, no. 12 (1909): 742–750.

Ashmead, Albert S. "Utosic Syphilis and Some Other Things of Interest to Paleo-American Medicine, as Represented on the Huacos Potteries of old Peru." *American Journal of Dermatology and Genito-Urinary Diseases* 14, no. 7 (July 1910): 329–343.

Atwater, Caleb. *Description of Antiquities Discovered in the State of Ohio and Other Western States*, with new introduction by Jeremy A. Sabloff. New York: AMS Press, 1973 [1820].

Avendaño, Fernando de. *Sermones de los misterios de nuestra santa fe católica en lengua castellana, y la general del Inca*. Lima: Jorge Lopez de Herrera, 1648.

Bancroft, Hubert Howe. *The Book of the Fair*. Chicago: The Bancroft Company, 1893.

Bandelier, Adolph Francis. "Aboriginal Trephining in Bolivia." *American Anthropologist, New Series* 6, no. 4 (1904): 440–446.

Bandelier, Adolph Francis. "On the Relative Antiquity of Ancient Peruvian Burials." Author's Edition, extracted from *Bulletin of the American Museum of Natural History* 20, article 19 (16 June 1904): 217–226.

Bandelier, Adolph Francis. *The Ruins at Tiahuanaco* (Reprinted from the Proceedings of the American Antiquarian Society for October 1911). Worscester, MA: American Antiquarian Society, 1911.

Baquedano, Fernando. "Al Sr. D. Francisco García Huidobro, director de la Biblioteca y conservador del Museo Nacional &c., Lima, 1 de Junio de 1839," *Mercurio de Valparaiso* (Chile), 31 July 1839.

Barrera, Francisco. "Antigüedades Peruanas. Memoria sobre los sepulcros o Huacas de los antiguos peruanos." *Memorial de ciencias naturales, y de industria nacional y extranjera; redactado por M. de Rivero y de N. de Piérola*, Tomo 2, no. 3 (June 1828): 101–110.

Barrett, Paul H., Peter J. Gautrey, Sandra Herbert, David Kohn, and Sydney Smith, eds. *Charles Darwin's Notebooks, 1836–1844: Geology, Transmutation of Species, Metaphysical Enquiries*. Ithaca, NY: Cornell University Press, 1987.

Barton, Benjamin Smith. "Observations and Conjectures concerning Certain Articles Which Were Taken Out of an Ancient Tumulus, or Grave, at Cincinnati, . . . May 16th, 1796." *Transactions of the American Philosophical Society* 4 (1799): 181–215.

Baxley, Willis. *What I Saw on the West Coast of South and North America, and the Hawaiian Islands*. New York: Appleton & Company, 1865.

Bellamy, P. F. "A Brief Account of Two Peruvian Mummies in the Museum of the Devon and Cornwall Natural History Society." *The Annals and Magazine of Natural History* 10 (October 1842): 95–100.

Belleforest Comingeois, François de. *L'Historie Universelle du Monde*. Paris: Chez Gervais Mallot, 1570.

Blake, Charles Carter. "On the Cranial Characters of the Peruvian Races of Men." *Transactions of the Ethnological Society of London* 2 (1863): 216–231.

Blake, John H. "Notes on a Collection from the Ancient Cemetery at the Bay of Chacota, Peru" (Presented 18 February 1878, published 9 September 1878). In *Reports of the Peabody Museum of Archaeology and Ethnology in Connection with Harvard University* 2 (1876–79): 277–304. Cambridge: 1880.

Blumenbach, Johannes. *Nova pentas collectionis suae craniorum diversarum gentium*. Gottingen: Dietrich, 1828.

Boyesen, Hjalmar Hjorth. "A New World Fable." *Cosmopolitan* 16, no. 2 (1893): 1173–1186.

Broca, Paul, and E. G. Squier. "Trepanning among the Incas." *Journal of the Anthropological Institute of New York* 1, no. 11 (1871–1872): 71–77.

Browne, Peter A. "An Essay on Indian Corn." *The Farmer's Cabinet* (Philadelphia) 2, nos. 9 and 10 (1837): 139–141, 150–152.

Bry, Teodoro de. *América. 1590–1634*. Edited by Gereon Sievernich, translated by Adán Kovacsics. Madrid: Ediciones Siruela, 1992.

Buckingham, James Silk. *The Eastern and Western States of America*, 3 vols. London: Fisher, Son, & Co., 1842.

Buffon, Georges-Louis Leclerc, Comte de. "Variétés dans l'espèce humaine." In *Histoire Naturelle, Générale et Particuliére, avec la Description du Cabinet du Roi*. Tome Troisième, 371–530. Paris: de L'Imprimerie Royale, 1749.

Bureau d'adresse et de rencontre. *General Collection of Discourses of the Virtuosi of France, upon Questions of All Sorts of Philosophy, and Other Natural Knowledge Made in the Assembly of the Beaux Esprits at Paris, by the Most Ingenious Persons of That Nation / Render'd into English by G. Havers, Gent*. London: Thomas Dring & John Starkey, 1664.

Busk, George. "Remarks on a Collection of 150 Ancient Puruvian [sic] Skulls, Presented to the Anthropological Institute by T. J. Hutchinson." *The Journal of the Anthropological Institute of Great Britain and Ireland* 3 (1874): 86–94.

Calancha, Antonio de. *Corónica moralizada del orden de San Agustín*, 6 vols. Lima: Ignacio Prado Pastor, 1974 [1638].

Caldcleugh, Alexander. *Travels in South America during the Years 1819–20–21*, 2 vols. London: John Murray, 1825.

Carleton, George Washington. *Our Artist in Peru: Ffifty Drawings on Wood: Leaves from the Sketch-Book of a Traveller during the Winter of 1865–6*. New York: Carleton, 1866.

Carranza y Ayarza, Luis. *Colección de artículos publicados por Luis Carranza, Médico Ia. Serie*. Lima: Imprenta del "Comercio," 1887.

Carrión Cachot, Rebeca. "Julio C. Tello y la Arqueología Peruana." *Revista del Museo Nacional de Antropología y Arqueología* 2, no. 1 (1949): 7–34.

Catalogue of Contents of the Museum of the Royal College of Surgeons in London. Part VI: Comprehending the Vascular and Miscellaneous Preparations in a Dried State. London: Richard Taylor, 1831.

"A Cemetery at the World's Fair." *The Modern Cemetery* 3, no. 6 (August 1893): 61–62.

[Charton, Ernest.] "Les Arts au Perou." *Magasin pittoresque* 24 (March 1856): 101–102.

Chirinos, Andrés, and Martha Zegarra, eds. *El orden del Inca por el licenciado Polo Ondegardo*. Lima: Editorial Commentarios, 2013.

Cieza de León, Pedro de. *Obras completas*, ed. C. Sáenz de Santa María. 3 vols. Madrid: Consejo Superior de Investigaciones Científicas, Instituto Gonzalo Fernández de Oviedo, 1984.

Cieza de León, Pedro de. *Parte primera de la chrónica del Peru: Que tracta la demarcacion de sus prouincias, la descripcion dellas, las fundaciones de las nuevas ciudades, los ritos y costumbres de los Indios, y otras cosas estrañas dignas de ser Sabidas*. Anvers: I. Steelsio, 1554.

Cobo, Bernabé. *Historia del Nuevo Mundo*. In *Obras del P. Bernabé Cobo de la Compañía de Jesus*, Tomo 2, edited by Francisco Mateos. Madrid: Ediciones Atlas, 1956 [1653].

Cobo, Bernabé. *History of the Inca Empire: An Account of the Indian Customs and Their Origin Together with a Treatise on Inca Legends, History and Social Institutions*, edited and translated by Roland Hamilton. Austin: University of Texas at Austin, 1991 [1979].

Cobo, Bernabé. *Inca Religion and Customs by Father Bernabé Cobo*, edited and translated by Roland Hamilton. Austin: University of Texas Press, 1990.

Combe, George. Anonymous review of *Crania Americana: or a Comparative*, etc. *The American Journal of Science and Arts* 2, no. 38 (1840): 1–32.

Combe, George. "Appendix." In Samuel George Morton, *Crania Americana, or, A Comparative View of the Skulls of Various Aboriginal Nations of North and South America: To Which Is Prefixed an Essay on the Varieties of the Human Species*, 269–291. Philadelphia: John Penington, 1839.

"Committee Reports of December 6, 1865." *Bulletin of the New York Academy of Medicine* 2 (1862–1866): 530.

Cornalia, Emilio. "Sulla mummia Peruviana del Civico Museo di Milan . . . Letta nella tornata del 21 Aprile 1859." *Atti del Reale Istituto lombardo di scienze, lettere ed arti* 2 (1860): 20–28.

"Crania Americana . . . ." *The British and Foreign Medical Review* 10 (1840): 474–485.

Culin, Stewart. "Report on the Department of Ethnology." In *Museums of the Brooklyn Institute of Arts and Sciences; Report upon the Condition and Progress of the Museums for the Year Ending December 31, 1904*. Brooklyn, NY: Printed for the Museum, n.d.

Curtis, William Eleroy. "United States to Dominate the Hemisphere" [1893]. In *Today Then: America's Best Minds Look 100 Years into the Future on the Occasion of the 1893 World's Columbian Exposition*, edited by David Walter, 87–88. Helena, MT: American and World Geographic Publishers, 1992.

Daubenton, Louis Jean-Marie. "Momies." In *Histoire Naturelle, Générale et Particuliére, avec la Description du Cabinet du Roi*. Tome Troisième, 282–296. Paris: de L'Imprimerie Royale, 1749.

Daubenton, Louis Jean-Marie. "Une Momie trouvée en Auvergne." In *Histoire Naturelle, Générale et Particuliére, avec la Description du Cabinet du Roi*. Tome 15, 165–173. Paris: de L'Imprimerie Royale, 1767.

Dávalos y Lissón, Ricardo. "La colección de antigüedades peruanas del doctor Macedo." *El Comercio* (Lima), 16 February 1876.

Davis, George R., and F. W. Putnam. *World's Columbian Exposition; Chicago, U.S.A. 1893. Plan and Classification, Department M. Ethnology, Archaeology, History, Cartography, Latin-American Bureau, Collective and Isolated Exhibits*. Chicago: World's Columbian Exposition, 1892.

Davis, Joseph Barnard. *Thesaurus Craniorum: Catalogue of the Skulls of the Various Races of Man in the Collection of Joseph Barnard Davis*. London: n.p., 1867.

Davis, Joseph Barnard. "On Ancient Peruvian Skulls." *The Journal of the Anthropological Institute of Great Britain and Ireland* 3 (1874): 94–100.

de Pauw, Cornelius. *Défense des Recherches philosophiques sur les Americaines*. Berlin: n.p. 1770.

de Pauw, Cornelius. *Recherches philosophiques sur les Américains, ou Mémoires Intéressants Pour Servir à l'Histoire de l'Espèce humaine*, 2 vols. Berlin: Goerge Jacques Decker, Imp. du Roi, 1768.

Díaz del Castillo, Bernal. *The History of the Conquest of New Spain*, edited by Davíd Carrasco. Albuquerque: University of New Mexico Press, 2008.

D. M. "Dr. Manuel Antonio Muñiz." *La crónica médica*, tomo 14, no. 204 (Junio 30 de 1897): 193–196.

Dorsey, George A. "An Archaeological Study Based on a Personal Exploration of Over One Hundred Graves at the Necropolis of Ancon, Peru." PhD diss., Harvard University, 1894.

Dorsey, George A. "Archaeology in Peru." *The Archaeologist* 2, no. 1 (January 1894): 1–5.

Dorsey, George A. "A Ceremony of the Quichuas of Peru." *The Journal of American Folklore* 7, no. 27 (October–December 1894): 307–309.

Drake, Daniel. *Natural and Statistical View, or Picture of Cincinnati and the Miami Country, Illustrated by Maps*. Cincinnati: Looker and Wallace, 1815.

Duviols, Pierre. "Un inédit de Cristóbal de Albornoz: La instrucción para descubrir todas las Guacas del Perú y sus camayos y haziendas." *Journal de la Société des Américanistes* 56, no. 1 (1967): 7–39.

Espejo Nuñez, Teofilo. *Formación Universitaria de Julio C. Tello*. Lima: Editora Médica Peruana, 1959.

Eyzaguirre, Rómulo. "La tuberculosis pulmonar en Lima: Tratamiento Higiénico Sanatoria: Tésis para el Bachillerato en Medicina." *La Crónica Médica* tomo 14, no. 196 (Febrero 28 de 1897): 51–58.

Faxon, Walter. "Relics of Peale's Museum." *Bulletin of the Museum of Comparative Zoology at Harvard College* 59, no. 3 (1915): 119–148.

Fletcher, Robert. "On Prehistoric Trephining and Cranial Amulets." *Contributions to North American Ethnology*, Vol. 5. Washington, DC: Government Printing Office, 1882.

Folkmar, Daniel. "Proceedings of the Academy and Affiliated Societies: The Anthropological Society of Washington." *Journal of the Washington Academy of Sciences* 3, no. 17 (1913): 479–480.

Frézier, Amédée-François. *Relation du Voyage de la Mer du Sud aux Cotes du Chili, du Perou, et du Bresil, Fait pendant les années 1712, 1713, & 1714*, Tome Second. Amsterdam: Chez Pierre Humbert, 1717.

Frézier, Amédée-François. *Voyage to the South-Sea and along the Coasts of Chili and Peru, in the Years 1712, 1713, and 1714*. London: Christian Bowyer, 1735.

Fuentes, Francisco A. *Catálogo de la Exposición de 1872. Edición Oficial por Francisco A. Fuentes, secretario de la Comisión Central.* Lima: Imprenta del Estado, 1872.

Fuller, Zelotes. "Heathen Idols." *Southern Pioneer and Philadelphia Liberalist* 5, no. 11 (17 October 1835): 87.

The George W. Kiefer Collection of Peruvian Antiquities, etc. etc. New York: Geo A. Leavitt & Co., October 25, 1889.

Gilliss, G. M. " Peruvian Antiquities." In *Information Respecting the History, Condition, and Prospects of the Indian Tribes of the United States; Collected and Prepared under the Direction of the Bureau of Indian Affairs, per Act of Congress of March 3, 1847,* Part V, edited by Henry R. Schoolcraft, 657–659. Philadelphia: Lippincott, Grambo & Co., 1855.

González Holguín, Diego. *Vocabulario de la lengua general de todo el Peru llamada lengua Qquichua, o del Inca: Corregido y renovado conforme a la propriedad cortesana del Cuzco.* 1608.

Gorriti, Juana Manuela. *Veladas literarias de Lima, 1876–1877.* Buenos Aires: Imprenta Europea, 1892.

Guichard, Claude. *Funérailles, et diverses manières d'ensevelir des Romaines, Grecs, et autres nations, tant anciennes sur moderns.* Lyon: Jean de Tournes, 1581.

Gutiérrez de Quintanilla, Emilio. *El Manco Capac de la arqueolojía peruana, Julio C. Tello (señor de Huarochirí) contra Emilio Gutiérrez de Quintanilla autor de este folleto.* Lima: n.p., 1922.

Gutiérrez de Quintanilla, Emilio. *Memoria del director del Museo de Historia Nacional; Esfuerzos I Resistencias 1919–1921,* 2 vols. Lima: Taller Tipográfico del Museo, 1921.

Gutiérrez de Quintanilla, Emilio. *Réplica al panfleto presente y futuro del Museo Nacional.* Lima: Imprenta Comercial de H. La Rosa & Co, 1913.

Hall, Basil. *Extracts from a Journal, Written on the Coasts of Chili, Peru, and Mexico, in the Years 1820, 1821, 1822.* 2 vols. Edinburgh: Archibald Constable and Co. Edinburgh, 1825 [1823].

Hamy, Ernest Théodore. *Galerie américaine du Musée d'ethnographie du Trocadéro; choix de pièces archéologiques et ethnographiques, décrites et publiées par le dr E.-T. Hamy. . . .* 2 vols. Paris: E. Leroux, 1897.

Hernández Astete, Francisco, and Rodolfo Cerrón-Palomino, eds. *Juan de Betanzos y el Tahuantinsuyo: Nueva edición de la* Suma y narración de los Incas. Lima: Fondo Editorial de la Pontificia Universidad Católica del Perú: 2015 [1550s].

Hodge, Frederick Webb, ed. *Handbook of American Indians North of Mexico,* 2 vols. Washington, DC: Government Printing Office, 1912.

Holmes, W. H. "The World's Fair Congress of Anthropology." *American Anthropologist* 6, no. 4 (October 1893): 423–424.

Horner, William E. *Catalogue of the Anatomical Museum of the University of Pennsylvania: With a Report to the Museum Committee of the Trustees.* Philadelphia: Lydia R. Bailey, 1832.

Hovey, H. C. "Peruvian Trepanning." *Scientific American Supplement* 985 (17 November 1894): 15743–15744.

Howse, Derek, and Norman J. W. Thrower, eds. *A Buccaneer's Atlas: Basil Ringrose's South Sea Waggoner; A Sea Atlas and Sailing Directions of the Pacific Coast of the Americas.* Berkeley: University of California Press, 1992.

Hrdlička, Aleš. "Anthropological Work in Peru in 1913." *Smithsonian Miscellaneous Collections* 61, no. 18 (1914): 1–69.

Hrdlička, Aleš. *Physical Anthropology, Its Scope and Aims; Its History and Present Status in the United States.* Philadelphia: n.p., 1919.

Huan, Susan J., and Guillermo A. Cock Carrasco. "A Bioarchaeological Approach to the Search for Mitmaqkuna." In *Distant Provinces in the Inka Empire: Toward a Deeper Understanding of Inka Imperialism,* edited by Michael A. Malpass and Sonia Alconini, 193–220. Iowa City: University of Iowa Press, 2010.

Humboldt, Alexander von. *Views of Nature: or Contemplations on the Sublime Phenomena of Creation; with Scientific Illustrations.* London: Henry G. Bohn, 1850 [1807].

Humboldt, Alexander von. *Views of the Cordilleras and Monuments of the Indigenous Peoples of the Americas*, edited and translated by Vera M. Kutzinski and Ottmar Ette. Chicago: University of Chicago Press, 2012 [1813].

Hutchinson, Thomas J. "Explorations amongst Ancient Burial Grounds, Chiefly on the Sea Coast Valleys of Peru" [Second part]. *The Journal of the Anthropological Institute of Great Britain and Ireland* 10 (February 1874): 2–12.

Hutchinson, Thomas J. *Two Years in Peru, with Exploration of its Antiquities.* 2 vols. London: Sampson Low, Marston, Low, & Stern, 1873.

Hyland, Sabine. *Gods of the Andes: An Early Jesuit Account of Inca Religion and Andean.* University Park: The Pennsylvania State University Press, 2011.

Ingram, J. S. *Centennial Exposition Described and Illustrated: Being a Concise and Graphic Description of the Grand Enterprise Commemorative of the First Centenary of American Independence.* Philadelphia: Hubbard Bros., 1876.

International Congress of Americanists. Proceedings of the XVIII Session, London, 1912, Part 1. London: Harrison and Sons, 1913.

Jackson, Andrew. "Second Annual Message to Congress, December 7, 1830." *Congressional Globe: Register of Debates in Congress*, 21st Cong., 2nd sess., vol. 7, appendix. Washington, DC, 1831.

Jefferson, Thomas. Fair Copy MS of *Notes on the State of Virginia* (1783–1784), 14, Massachusetts Historical Society, http://www.masshist.org/thomasjeffersonpapers/notes/nsvviewer. php?page=14.

Jefferson, Thomas. *Notes on the State of Virginia.* London: John Stockdale, 1787.

Jesup, Morris K. "Twenty-Sixth Annual Report." *The American Museum of Natural History: Annual Report of the President, Act of Incorporation, Constitution, By-Laws and List of Members for the Year 1894*, 7–15. New York: Wm. C. Martin Printing House, 1895.

Jiménez de la Espada, Marcos, ed. *Tres relaciones de antigüedades peruanas.* Madrid: Imprenta y Fundición de M. Tello, 1879.

Johnson, Rossiter. *A History of the World's Columbian Exposition*, 4 vols. New York: D. Appleton and Company, 1897–1898.

Joly, Nicolas. "Notice sur une momie américaine, du temps des Incas, trouvée dans la Nouvelle-Grenade." *Mémoires de L'Académie Nationale des Sciences, Inscriptions et Belles-Lettres de Toulouse*, Quatrième Série, Tome 1 (Toulouse: Jean-Matthieu Douladoure, 1851): 251–261.

Juan, Jorge, and Antonio de Ulloa. *Relación historica del viage a la America meridional hecho de orden de S. Mag. para medir algunos grados de meridiano*, Parte primera, Tomo segundo. Madrid: Antonio Marin, 1748.

Knight, Charles, ed. *London*, 6 vols. London: Charles Knight, 1841–1844.

Kroeber, Alfred L. *Peruvian Archeology in 1942.* New York: Viking Fund Publications in Anthropology, 1944.

La Conquista del Perú, Llamada la Nueva Castilla (Sevilla, 1534) [possibly Cristóbal de Mena]. In *Crónicas iniciales de la conquista del Perú*, edited by Alberto M. Salas, Miguel A. Guérin, and José Luis Moure, 65–118. Buenos Aires: Editorial Plus Ultra, 1987.

La Puente, Ignacio. "Estudios etnográficos de la Hoya del Titicaca; Novena Conferencia dada en la Sociedad Geográfica de Lima . . . el 28 de Diciembre de 1893." *Boletín de la Sociedad Geográfica de Lima* 3, nos. 10, 11, y 12 (1894).

Lequanda, Joseph Ignacio de. "Continuación de la descripción de geográfica de la ciudad y partido de Truxillo." *Mercurio Peruano*, Tomo 8, no. 252 and 253 (1793): 81–83, 84–91.

Levillier, Roberto, ed. *Gobernantes del Perú. Cartas y papeles. Siglo XVI*, 14 vols. Buenos Aires: Biblioteca del Congreso de Argentina, 1924.

Libro primero de cabildos de Lima, parte tercera: Documentos. Paris: Imprimerie Paul Dupont, 1900.

Li Gui. *A Journey to the East: Li Gui's A New Account of a Trip around the World*, translated and with an introduction by Charles Desnoyers. Ann Arbor: University of Michigan Press, 2004.

Lohmann Villena, Guillermo. "El Señorio de los Marqueses de Santiago de Oropesa en el Perú." *Anuario de istoria del Derecho Español,* 19 (1948): 347–458.

Lohmann Villena, Guillermo, and María Justina Sarabia Viejo. *Francisco de Toledo: Disposiciones gubernativas para el virreinato del Perú,* 2 vols. Sevilla: Escuela de Estudios Hispano-Americanos: Consejo Superior de Investigaciones Científicas: Monte de Piedad y Caja de Ahorros de Sevilla, 1986, 1989.

López de Gómara, Francisco. *La historia general de las Indias, con todos los descubrimientos, y cosas notables que han acaesido enellas, dende que se ganaron hasta agora.* Anvers: Iuan Sellsio, 1554.

Lorena, Antonio. "Algunos materiales para la antropología del Cuzco." *Boletín de la Sociedad Geográfica de Lima,* Tomo 24, Año 19, Trim. 2 (30 Junio de 1909): 164–173.

Lorena, Antonio. "Etiologia del Bócio y Cretinismo en la hoya del 'Vilcamayo.'" *La Crónica Médica,* Año 3, Tomo 3, no. 32 (31 Agosto de 1886): 293–297.

Lorena, Antonio. "La medicina y la trepanación incásicas" (delivered Lima, 13 Agosto 1890). *La Crónica Médica* Año 7, Tomo 6, no. 80 (31 Agosto de 1890): 224–230.

Lothrop, Samuel K. "Julio C. Tello, 1880–1947." *American Antiquity* 14, no. 1 (July 1948): 50–56.

Lothrop, Samuel K. "Un recuerdo del Dr. Julio C. Tello y Paracas." *Revista del Museo Nacional de Antropología y Arqueología* 2, no. 1 (1949): 53–54.

Lucius. "A Few Observations upon the Western and Southern Indians." *American Museum; or, Repository of Ancient and Modern Fugitive Pieces* (Philadelphia), Vol. 5 (January 1789): 144–147.

Lummis, Charles F. *The Gold Fish of Gran Chimú.* Boston: Lamson, Wolffe, and Company, 1896.

MacCurdy, George Grant. "Surgery among the Ancient Peruvians." *Art and Archaeology* 7, no. 9 (November–December 1918): 381–394.

Macedo, José Mariano. "Memorandum Histórico." 1880. Colección Manuscritos de José Mariano Macedo, Lima.

Macedo Morales, Carlos. "Algunas variaciones anatómicas de los antiguos cráneos Peruanos." *Boletín de la Sociedad Geográfica de Lima,* Tomo 24, Año 20, Trim. 4 (31 Diciembre de 1910): 361–449.

Manco y Ayllón, Ignacio. *Manco-Capac, sus sucesores en el imperio y sus descendientes en las diversas lineas.* Huanuco: Imp. Oficial, 1881.

Mason, Otis T. "The Chaclacayo Trephined Skull." *Proceedings of the US National Museum* 8 (1885): 410–412.

Masson, David Mather. *The British Museum, Historical and Descriptive, with Numerous Wood-Engravings.* Edinburgh: William and Robert Chambers, 1850.

Matto, David. "La trepanación en la época de los Incas," *La Crónica Médica,* Año 3, Tomo 3, No. 29 (31 May 1886): 183–186.

Matto de Turner, Clorinda. *Perú. Tradiciones cuzqueñas. Leyendas, biografías y hojas sueltas.* Arequipa: Imprenta de "la Bolsa," 1884.

McClure, James P., and J. Jefferson Looney, eds. *The Papers of Thomas Jefferson, Digital Edition.* Charlottesville: University of Virginia Press, 2008–2021. https://rotunda.upress.virginia.edu/founders/TSJN.html.

McCulloh, James Haines. *Researches, Philosophical and Antiquarian, concerning the Aboriginal History of America.* Baltimore: Fielding Lucas Jr., 1829.

McGee, W. J. "On an Anatomical Peculiarity by Which Crania of the Mound Builders May Be Distinguished from Those of the Modern Indians." *The American Journal of Science* 116 (1878): 458–461.

McGee, W. J. "Primitive Trephining, Illustrated by the Muñiz Peruvian Collection." *Bulletin of the Johns Hopkins Hospital* 5, no. 37 (January–February 1894): 1–4.

Mead, Charles W. *Peruvian Mummies and What They Teach: A Guide to Exhibits in the Peruvian Hall.* New York: American Museum of Natural History, 1907.

Meigs, J. Aitkin. *Catalogue of Human Crania in the Collection of the Academy of Natural Sciences of Philadelphia: Based upon the Third Edition of Dr. Morton's "Catalogue of Skulls," &c..* Philadelphia: J. B. Lipponcott & Co., 1857.

Mejía Xesspe, M. Toribio. "Apuntes Biográficos sobre el Dr. Julio C. Tello." *Revista del Museo Nacional de Antropología y Arqueología* 2, no. 1 (1948): 35–49.

Mejía Xesspe, M. Toribio. "Prólogo." *Julio C. Tello, páginas escogidas*. Lima: Universidad Nacional Mayor de San Marcos, 1967.

Meyen, Franz Julius Ferdinand. "Menschen-Raçen." *Nova Acta Physico-Medica Academiae Caesareae Leopoldino-Carolinae Naturae Curiosum* T. 16. Supplement Breslau: n.p., 1834.

Meyen, Franz Julius Ferdinand. *Reise um die Erde ausgeführt auf dem Königlich preussischen Seehandlungs-Schiffe Prinzess Louise, commandirt von Capitain W. Wendt, in den Jahren 1830, 1831 und 1832*, 2 vols. Berlin: Sander'schen Bucchandlung, 1835.

Michelson, T. "Proceedings of the Anthropological Society of Washington." *American Anthropologist, New Series* 13, no. 2 (1911): 313–319.

"Miscellanea." *British Journal of Dental Science* 16, no. 203 (May 1873): 230.

Montes, Emilio. "The Antiquity of the Civilization of Peru." In *Memoirs of the International Congress of Anthropology*, edited by C. Staniland Wake, 95–99. Chicago: Schulte Publishing Company, 1894.

Moorehead, Warren King. "Anthropology at the World's Columbian Exposition." *The Archaeologist* 2, no. 1 (January 1894): 15–24.

Morales, Luís de. "Relación que dió el Provisor Luís de Morales sobre las cosas que debían proveerse para las Provincias del Perú." In *La Iglesia de España en el Perú. Colección de documentos para la historia de la iglesia en el Perú*, Vol. 1, no. 3, edited by Emilio Lissón Chávez, 81–82. Seville: Católica Española, 1943–1947.

Morales Macedo. "Algunas variaciones anatómicas de los antiguos cráneos Peruanos." *Boletín de la Sociedad Geográfica de Lima*, Tomo 24, Año 20, Trim. 4 (31 Diciembre de 1910): 361–449.

Morgan, Horace Hills. *The Historical World's Columbian Exposition and Chicago Guide*. St. Louis: James H. Mason & Co., 1892.

Morgan, Lewis Henry. *League of the Ho-dé-no-sau-nee, or Iroquois*. Rochester: Sage & Brother, Publishers, 1851.

Morison, Samuel Eliot, ed. *Journals and Other Documents on the Life and Voyages of Christopher Columbus*. New York: Heritage Press, 1963.

Morton, Samuel George. "Account of a Craniological Collection; with Remarks on the Classification of Some Families of the Human Race." *Transactions of the American Ethnological Society* 2 (1848): 216-222.

Morton, Samuel George. *Catalogue of Skulls of Man and the Inferior Animals in the Collection of Samuel George Morton, Ph.D., Penn. And Edinb.*. Philadelphia: Merrihew & Thompson, Printers, 1849.

Morton, Samuel George. *Crania Americana, or, A Comparative View of the Skulls of Various Aboriginal Nations of North and South America: To Which Is Prefixed an Essay on the Varieties of the Human Species*. Philadelphia: John Penington, 1839.

Morton, Samuel George. *An Inquiry into the Distinctive Characteristics of the Aboriginal Race of America. Read at the Annual Meeting of the Boston Society of Natural History, Wednesday, April 27, 1842* (Boston: Tuttle & Dennett, 1842).

Morton, Samuel George. "Physical Type of the American Indians." In *Information Respecting the History, Condition, and Prospects of the Indian Tribes of the United States; Collected and Prepared under the Direction of the Bureau of Indian Affairs, per Act of Congress of March 3, 1847, Part 2*, edited by Henry R. Schoolcraft, 315–335. Philadelphia: Lippincott, Grambo & Co., 1853.

Morton, Samuel George. "Some Remarks on the Ancient Peruvians." *The Edinburgh New Philosophical Journal* 33 (1842): 335–338.

Muñiz, Manuel Antonio. "Correspondencia de londres" (11 Julio 1888). *La Crónica Médica* año 5, tomo 5, no. 55 (31 Julio de 1888): 251.

Muñiz, Manuel Antonio. "Estado mental de N . . . ." *La Crónica Médica* año 14, tomo 14, no. 199 (15 Abril de 1897): 101–106.

Muñiz, Manuel Antonio. "La lepra en el Perú." *La Crónica Médica* año 3, tomo 3, nos. 28, 29 (Abril 30, 31 May 1886): 127–129, 171–186.

Muñiz, Manuel Antonio. "Reglamentación de la prostitución: Tesis leída y sostenida al optar el grado de doctor por Manuel A. Muñiz." *La Crónica Médica* tomos 4–5, no. 48–49 (31 Diciembre de 1887, 31 Enero 31 de 1888): 455–461, 17–23.

Muñiz, Manuel Antonio. "Vida. Animismo—vitalismo—materialismo." *La Crónica Médica* año 1, tomo 1, no. 8 (August 31 de 1884): 315.

Muñiz, Manuel Antonio, and W. J. McGee. "Primitive Trephining in Peru." *Sixteenth Annual Report of the Bureau of American Ethnology to the Secretary of the Smithsonian Institution 1984-95*, no. 17, 11–72. Washington, DC: Government Printing Office, 1897.

Murúa, Martín de. *Historia general del Perú*, edited by Manuel Ballestros. Madrid: Historia 16, 1987.

"A Necklace of Mummy Eyes." *Scientific American* 53, no. 16 (17 October 1885): 240–241.

Niles, Blair. *A Journey in Time: Peruvian Pageant*. Indianapolis: Bobbs-Merrill Company, 1937.

Nolasco Crespo, Pedro. "Carta sobre los monumentos antiguos de los *Peruanos*." *Mercurio Peruano* 5, vols. 170, 171 (19 Agosto 1792, 23 Agosto 1792): 254–261, 264–265.

Nott, Josiah C. "Aboriginal Races of America." *The Southern Quarterly Review* 8 (1853): 59–92.

Nott, Josiah C., and Geo. R. Gliddon. *Types of Mankind: or, Ethnological Researches, Based upon the Ancient Monuments, Paintings, Sculptures, and Crania of Races, and upon Their Natural, Geographical, Philological, and Biblical History: Illustrated by Selections from the Inedited Papers of Samuel George Morton, M.D. . . . and by Additional Contributions from Prof. L. Agassiz, LL.D.; W. Usher, M.D.; and Prof. H. S. Patterson, M.D.* Philadelphia: Lippincott, Grambo & Co., 1855.

Olearius, Adam. *Gottorfische Kunst-Kammer: worinnen allerhand ungemeine Sachen, so theils die Natur, theils künstliche Hände hervor gebracht und bereitet*. Schleswig, Germany: Auff Gottfriedt Schulzens Kostens, 1674.

Payen, Anselme. "Note sur la composition des yeux de momies péruviennes." In *Comptes rendus hebdomadaires des séances de l'Académie des sciences*. T. 43, 707–709. Paris: Mallet-Bachelier, 1856.

Paz Soldán, Mateo. *Geografía del Perú, obra postuma*, edited by Mariano Felipe Paz Soldan. Paris: L. M. A. Durand, 1862.

Peck, Annie. *The South American Tour*. New York: George H. Doran and Company, 1913.

Peixotto, Ernest. "Down the West Coast to Lima." *Scribner's Magazine* 53, no. 4 (April 1913): 421–438.

Pérez Fernández, Isacio, ed. *El anónimo de Yucay frente a Bartolomé de Las Casas: Estudio y edición crítica del parecer de Yucay, anónimo. Valle de Yucay, 16 de Marzo de 1571*. Cuzco, Perú: Centro de Estudios Regionales Andinos Bartolomé de Las Casas, 1995.

Pérez y López, Antonio Javier. *Teatro de la legislación universal de España é Indias*, vols. 20, 27, 28. Madrid: En la impr. de Don Antonio Espinosa, 1797, 1798.

Petit-Thouars, Abel Aubert du. "Nouveaux renseignements sure les momies péruviennes du Morro d'Arica." *Comptes rendus hebdomadaires des séances de l'Académie des Sciences* 43 (juillet–décembre 1856): 737–738.

Pettigrew, Thomas Joseph. "Account of the Unrolling of an Egyptian Mummy, with Incidental Notices of the Manners, Customs, and Religion, of the Ancient Egyptians." *Magazine of Popular Science, and Journal of the Useful Arts* 2 (London: John W. Parker, 1836): 17–40.

Pettigrew, Thomas Joseph. *A History of Egyptian Mummies: And an Account of the Worship and Embalming of the Sacred Animals by the Egyptians; with Remarks on the Funeral Ceremonies of Different Nations, and Observations on the Mummies of the Canary Islands, of the Ancient Peruvians, Burman Priests, &c.*. London: Longman, Rees, Orme, Brown, Green, and Longman, 1834.

Pizarro, Pedro. *Relación del descubrimiento y conquista de los reinos del Perú*, edited by G. Lohmann Villena and Pierre Duviols. Lima: Pontificia Universidad Católica, 1978 [1571].

Poma de Ayala, Guaman. *El primer nueva corónica y buen gobierno*. 1615/1616. http://www.kb.dk/permalink/2006/poma/info/en/frontpage.htm

Ponce Sánchez, Hernán. *50 anécdotas de sabio Tello*. Lima: Editorial "La Universidad" Libreria, 1957.

Porras Barrenechea, Raúl, ed. *Colección de documentos inéditos para la historia del Perú, Tomo III: Cartas del Perú. 1524–1543*. Lima: Sociedad de Bibliófilos Peruanos, 1959.

Powell, John Wesley. "Report of the Director." In *Sixteenth Annual Report of the Bureau of American Ethnology to the Secretary of the Smithsonian Institution 1984-95*, no. 17. Washington, DC: Government Printing Office, 1897.

Prescott, William H. *History of the Conquest of Peru, with a Preliminary View of the Civilization of the Incas*. Vols. 1–2. New York: Harper and Brothers, 1847.

Proctor, Robert. *Narrative of a Journey across the Cordillera of the Andes and of a Residence in Lima and Other Parts of Peru, in the Years 1823 and 1824*. London: Archibald Constable and Co., 1825.

Purchas, Samuel. *Hakluytus Posthumus, or Purchas His Pilgrimes. In Five Bookes. The Fourth Part*. London: Printed by William Stansby for Henry Fetherstone, 1625.

Purchas, Samuel. *Purchas His Pilgrimage: Or Relations of the World and the Religions Observed in All Ages and Places Discourered, from the Creation unto This Present: In Foure Parts: This First Containeth a Theological and Geographical Historie of Asia, Africa, and America, with the Ilands Adiacent*. London: William Stansby for Henry Fetherstone, 1614 [1613].

Raimondi, Antonio. "Ayacucho. Itinerario de los viajes de Raimondi en el Perú" [1862]. *Boletín de la Sociedad Geográfica de Lima* 5, nos. 1–3 (30 Junio 1895): 1–57.

Raimondi, Antonio. "Enumeración de los vestigios de la antigua civilización entre Pacasmayo y la Cordillera." *Boletín de la Sociedad Geográfica de Lima* 13, Trim. 2 (30 Junio 1903): 159–171.

Raimondi, Antonio. "Itinerario de los viajes de Raimondi en el Perú de Lima a Morococha (1861)." *Boletín de la Sociedad Geográfica de Lima* 6, nos. 1, 2, 3 (30 Junio 1896): 16–43.

Raimondi, Antonio. *El Perú, Tomo I*. Lima: Imprenta del Estado, 1874.

"Rapport sur un Mémoire de M. Édouard de Rivero, relatif' aux momies du Pérou." *Comptes rendus hebdomadaires des séances de l'Académie des Sciences* 44 (Janvier–Juin 1857): 1197–1208.

Reiss, Wilhelm, and Alphons Stübel. *The Necropolis of Ancon in Peru: A Contribution to Our Knowledge of the Culture and Industries of the Empire of the Incas*, 3 vols., translated by Augustus Henry Keane. Berlin: A. Asher, 1880–1887.

"Remarkable Skulls Found in Peru." *Dublin Journal of Medical and Chemical Science* 5, no. 15 (1834): 475–480.

"Report of the Council of the Anthropological Institute of Great Britain and Ireland for 1873." *Journal of the Anthropological Institute of Great Britain and Ireland* 3 (1874): 499–527.

Report on the Progress and Condition of the United States National Museum for the Year Ending June 30, 1916. Washington, DC: Government Printing Office, 1917.

Rhees, William J. *An Account of the Smithsonian Institution, Its Founder, Building, Operations, Etc., Prepared from the Reports of Prof. Henry to the Regents, and Other Authentic Sources*. Washington, DC: Thomas McGill, 1859.

Rios, José de los, and Manuel Antonio Muñiz. "Informe antropológico por los Doctores Don José A. de los Rios y Don Manuel Antonio Muñiz del acta oficial relativa á la ceremonia de que fueron el 26 objeto los restos del conquistador Francisco Pizarro fundador de Lima." *La Crónica Médica* 8, tomo 8, no. 90 (30 Junio de 1891): 149–155.

Rivero y Ustariz, Mariano Eduardo de. *Antiguedades Peruanas. Parte primera*. Lima: Jose Masia, 1841.

Rivero y Ustariz, Mariano Eduardo de. "Noticia de Antiguedades Peruanas." *Memorial de Ciencias Naturales y de Industria Nacional y Extranjera* 1, no. 2 (Enero 1828).

Rivero y Ustariz, Mariano Eduardo de, and Johann Jakob von Tschudi. *Antiguedades Peruanas*. Vienna: Imprenta Imperial de la Corte y del Estado, 1851.

Rivero y Ustariz, Mariano Eduardo de, and Johann Jakob von Tschudi. *Peruvian Antiquities*, translated by Francis L. Hawks. New York: George P. Putnam & Co., 1853.

Robertson, William. *The History of America*, 3 vols. London: Printed for W. Strahan; T. Cadell, in the Strand, and J. Balfour, at Edinburgh, 1777–1778.

Rodrigues de Castelo Branco, João (Amato Lusitano). *Amati Lusitani Doctoris Medici Prarestantissimi Curationum Medicinalium Centuriae quatuor*. Basileae: Frobenius, 1556.

Ruiz de Navamuel, Alavaro. "La fe y testimonio que vá puesta en los cuatro paños, de la verificacion que se hio con los Indios, de la Pintura é Historia dellos" [1572]. In *Memorias Antiguas Historiales y Políticas del Perú, por el Licenciado D. Fernando Montesinos, Seguidas de las Informaciones Acerca del Señorio de los Incas, Hechas por Mandado de D. Francisco de Toledo, Virrey del Perú. Coleccion de Libros Españoles Raros o Curiosos*. Tomo 16. Madrid: Imprenta de Miguel Ginesta, 1882.

Ruschenberger, William Samuel Wauthman. *Three Years in the Pacific; Including Notices of Brazil, Chile, Bolivia, Peru*. Philadelphia: Carey, Lea & Blanchard, 1834.

Saffray. "Exposition de Philadelphia." *La Nature*, no. 182 (Novembre 1876): 401–407.

Sahuaraura Inca, Justo Apu. "Artículo remitido." *Museo Erudito o los Tiempos y las Costumbres* 1, no. 7 (5 June 1837): 9–10.

Salinas y Córdoba, Buenaventura de. *Memoriál de las historias del Nuevo Mundo Pirú*. Lima: Universidad Nacional Mayor de San Marcos, 1957.

Salmon, Thomas. *Modern History, or, The Present State of All Nations*. Vol. 3. London: Printed for Messrs. Bettesworth and Hitch, 1739.

Salomon, Frank, and George L. Urioste, eds. *The Huarochirí Manuscript: A Testament of Ancient and Colonial Andean Religion*. Austin: University of Texas Press, 1991.

Sancho de la Hoz, Pedro. *Relación de la onquista del Peru*, edited by Joaquin García Icazbaleta. Madrid: Ediciones José Porua Turanzas, 1962 [1534].

Santeliú Ortiz, Lorenzo, and Antonio de Tova Arredondo. *62 meses a bordo: La expedición Malaspina según el diario del Teniente de Navío Don Antonio de Tova Arredondo, 2o. Comandante de la "ATREVIDA" 1789-1794*. Madrid: Editorial Naval, 1943.

Santo Tomás, Domingo de. *Lexicon*. Valladolid: Francisco Fernandez de Cordova, 1560.

Sarmiento de Gamboa, Pedro. *Geschichte des Inkareiches von Pedro Sarmiento de Gamboa* [1572], edited by Richard Pietschmann. Berlin: Weidmannsche Buchhandlung, 1906 [1572].

Sears, Alfred F. "Peru and Its People." *The Chataquan* 17, no. 2 (May 1893): 185–192.

Shady Solís, Ruth Martha, and Pedro Novoa Bellota, eds. *Cuadernos de investigación del Archivo Tello, No. 2: Arqueología del valle de Asia: Huaca Malena*. Lima: Museo de Arqueología y Antropología, Universidad Nacional Mayor de San Marcos, 2000.

Shibama, C. *The First Japanese Embassy to the United States of America*. Tokyo: The American-Japan Society, 1920.

Skinner, Joseph. *The Present State of Peru: Comprising Its Geography, Topography, Natural History, Mineralogy, Commerce, the Customs and Manners of Its Inhabitants, the State of Literature, Philosophy, and the Arts, the Modern Travels of the Missionaries in the Heretofore Unexplored Mountainous Territories, &c. &c*. London: Printed for Richard Phillips, 1805.

Squier, Ephraim George. *Peru: Incidents of Travel and Exploration in the Land of the Incas*. New York: Harper and Brothers, 1877.

Squier, Ephraim George, and Edwin H. Davis. *Ancient Monuments of the Mississippi Valley: Comprising the Results of Extensive Original Surveys and Explorations*. Smithsonian Contributions to Knowledge 1. Washington, DC: Smithsonian Institution, 1848.

Stewart, Charles Samuel. *A Visit to the South Seas in the U.S. Ship Vincennes, during the Years 1829 and 1830; with Scenes in Brazil, Peru, Manila, the Cape of Good Hope, and St. Helena*, 2 vols. New York: John P. Haven, 1831.

Stewart, Watt, and Harold F. Peterson. *Builders of Latin America*. New York: Harper & Brothers, 1942.

Suárez de Figueroa, Christóbal. *Plaza Universal de Todas Ciencias y Artes, Parte Traducida de Toscano y parte compuesta por el Doctor Christoval Suarez de Figueroa*. Madrid: Luis Sanchez, 1615.

Synopsis of the Contents of the Museum of the Royal College of Surgeons of England. London: Taylor and Francis, 1871.

Taylor, Gerard, and Antonio Acosta, ed. And trans. *Ritos y tradiciones de Huarochirí del siglo XVI*. Lima: Instituto de Estudios Peruanos / Instituto Francés de Estudios Andinos, 1987.

Tealdo, Alfonso. "Julio C. Tello." *Turismo* (Mayo 1942): 8–9.

Tello, Julio César. *La antigüedad de la sífilis en el Perú.* Lima: Universidad Mayor de San Marcos, Sanmartí y Ca. 1909.

Tello, Julio César. *Antiguo Perú. Primera época.* Lima: Comisión Organizadora del Segundo Congreso Sudamericano del Turismo, 1929.

Tello, Julio César. "La Calahuala." *La Prensa,* 25 September 1905.

Tello, Julio César. "La ciencia antropológica en el Perú." *La Prensa* (Lima), March 23, 1913.

Tello, Julio César. "El curioso final de una polémica arqueológica." *La Crónica* (Lima), 12 January 1915: 13.

Tello, Julio César. *Introducción a la historia antigua del Perú.* Lima: Editorial Euforion, 1921.

Tello, Julio César. "El Museo de Arqueología Peruana: Discurso pronunciado en la ceremonia de inauguración del Museo El 13 de Diciembre de 1924." In *Presente y futuro del Museo Nacional.* Lima: Instituto Cultural "Julio C. Tello," 1952.

Tello, Julio César. *Paracas, Primera parte. Obra complete,* vol. 1. Lima: Clásicos Sanmarquinos, UNMSM, 2005 [1959].

Tello, Julio César. "En la Península de Paracas se han Hallado Yacimientos Arqueológicos de tres Culturas Precolombinas Diferentes," *La Prensa* (Lima), 8 June 1926.

Tello, Julio César. "Prehistoric Trephining among the Yauyos of Peru" (1913). In *The Life and Writings of Julio C. Tello: America's First Indigenous Archaeologist,* edited by Richard L. Burger, 112–124. Iowa City: University of Iowa Press, 2009.

Tello, Julio César. "Testamento del Doctor don Julio C. Tello y Rojas." *Histórica* 7, no. 1 (Julio 1983): 135–140.

Tello, Julio César, and Toribio Mejía Xesspe. *Historia de los museos nacionales del Perú, 1822–1946.* Lima: Museo Nacional de Antropología y Arqueología e Instituto y Museo de Arqueología de la Universidad de San Marcos, 1967.

Thevet, André. *Les vrais pourtraits et vies des hommes illustres grecz, latins et payens, recueilliz de leurs tableaux, livres, médalles antiques et modernes.* 9 vols. Paris: Veuve J. Kervert & Guillaume Chaudiere, 1584.

Thwaites, Reuben Gold, ed. *Early Western Travels 1748–1846.* Vol. 22, Part 1 of Maximilian, Prince of Wied's Travels in the Interior of North America, 1832–1834. Cleveland: Arthur H. Clark Company, 1906.

Ticknor, Howard Malcom. "The Passing of the Boston Museum." *New England Magazine* 28, no. 4 (June 1903): 379–396.

Tiedemann, Friedrich. "Nachricht über merkwuurdige Menschel-Schädel aus Peru." In Friedrich Tiedemann, Gottfried Reinhard Treviranus, and Ludolph Christian Treviranus, *Zeitschrift für Physiologie* 5, 107–109. Heidelberg: August Osswald, 1833.

Tiedemann, Friedrich. "On the Brain of the Negro, Compared with That of the European and the Orang-outan." *Philosophical Transactions of the Royal Society of London* 126 (1836): 497–527.

Tristan, Flora. *Peregrinaciones de una paria,* translated by Emilia Romero. Lima: Flora Tristán; Fondo Editorial UNMSM, 2006 [1838].

Tschudi, Johann Jakob von. "On the Ancient Peruvians." *Journal of the Ethnological Society of London* 1 (1848): 79–85.

Tschudi, Johann Jakob von. *Travels in Peru during the Years 1838–1842: On the Coast, in the Sierra, across the Cordilleras and the Andes, into the Primeval Forests.* London: David Bogue, Fleet Street, 1847.

Uhle, Max. *Pachacamac: A Reprint of the 1903 Edition,* introduction by Izumi Shimada. Philadelphia: University Museum of Archaeology and Anthropology, University of Pennsylvania, 1991.

Ulloa, Antonio de. *Noticias Americanas: Entretenimientos Phisicos-Historicos Sobre La América Meridional, y la Septentrianal Oriental.* Madrid: Don Francisco Manuel de Mena, 1772.

Ulloa, Antonio de. "Of the Indigenous Inhabitants of Both Parts of America." *American Museum; or, Repository of Ancient and Modern Fugitive Pieces* (Philadelphia: 1787–92) 12 (July–September 1792): 44–49, 148–152.

Unanue, Hipólito. *"Decadencia y restauracion del Perú.* Oración inaugural, que para la Estrena y Abertura del Anfiteatro Anatómico, dixo en el Real Universidad de San Marcos el día 21 de Noviembre de 1792." *Mercurio Peruano* 7, nos. 218–222 (1793): 82–89, 90-97, 98–109, 110–117, 118–127.

Unanue, Hipólito. "Descripción del gigante que acaba de ser conducido á esta Ciudad de la de Ica." *Mercurio* 4, no. 138 (1792): 293–297.

Unanue, Hipólito. "Idea General de los Monumentos del Antiguo Perú, é introducción á su Estudio." *Mercurio Peruano* 1, no. 22 (1791): 201–208.

Unanue, Hipólito. *Obras científicas y literarias del doctor D. J. Hipólito Unanúe,* tomo 2. Barcelona: Tipografía la Académica, de Serra Hermanos y Russell, 1914.

Unanue, Hipólito. *Observaciones sobre el clima de Lima y sus influencias en los seres organizados, en especial el hombre.* Madrid: En la Imprenta Real de los Huérfanos, 1806.

Valcárcel, Luis E. *Memorias,* 1st ed. Lima: Instituto de Estudios Peruanos, 1981.

Valdizán, Hermilio. "La delincuencia en el Perú." *La Cronica Medica* (Lima), Año 27, Tomo 27, no. 514 (31 Mayo de 1910).

Vega Inca, Garcilaso de la. *Le commentaire royal, [or] l'histoire des Yncas, Roys du Perou [. . .] Escrite en langue Peruvienne par l'Ynga Garcilassfmiho de la Vega.* translated by Jean Baudouin. Paris: Chez Augutin Covreé, 1633.

Vega Inca, Garcilaso de la. *Historia general del Perú.* Cordoba: Viuda de Andres Barrera, 1616.

Vega Inca, Garcilaso de la. *Primera parte de los commentarios reales, que tratan del origen de los Yncas, Reyes que fueron del Peru, de su idolatria, leyes, y gobierno.* Lisbon: Pedro Crasbeeck, 1609.

Vega Inca, Garcilaso de la. *The Royal Commentaries of Peru in Two Parts,* translated by Paul Rycaut. London: Miles Fletcher, 1688.

Vida y Obras de José Mariano Macedo (1823–1894). Lima: Sanmarti y Cia. S. A. Impresores, 1945.

Vigil, Benigno G. "Estudios frenológicos. (Continuación)." *La Ilustración: Periodico Científico, Moral, Estético y Religioso* (Lima), no. 3 (Mayo 18 de 1853): 26.

Wafer, Lionel. *A New Voyage and Description of the Isthmus of America, Giving an Account of the Author's Abode There.* London: James Knapton, 1699.

Wagner, Rudolph. "The Anthropological Collection of the Physiological Institute of Göttingen." In *The Anthropological Treatises of Johann Friedrich Blumenbach,* edited by Thomas Bendyshe, 347–355. London: Longman, Green, Longman, Roberts, & Green, 1865.

Ward, Fannie B. "Mummies of Peru." *The Pittsburg Dispatch,* March 29, 1891.

Wiener, Charles. *Perú y Bolivia: Relato de viaje,* translated and edited by Edgardo Riviera Martínez. Lima: Institute Francés de Estudios Andinos and Universidad Nacional Mayor de San Marcos, 1993 [1880].

Wiener, Gabriela. "Huaco Portrait," translated by Gabriela Jauregui, *McSweeney's Quarterly Concern,* no. 65, edited by Valeria Luiselli, with Heather Cleary (2021): 45–60.

Wiener, Gabriela. *Huaco retrato.* Barcelona: Penguin Random House Grupo Editorial, 2021.

Wilkes, Charles. *Narrative of the United States Exploring Expedition, during the Years 1838, 1839, 1840, 1841, 1842.* 2 vols. London: Wiley and Putnam, S. Sherman, 1845.

Wilson, Daniel. *Prehistoric Man: Researches into the Origin of Civilisation in the Old and the New World,* 2nd ed. London: Macmillan, 1865 [1862].

Wyman, Jeffries. "Report of the Curator." *First Annual Report of the Peabody Museum of American Archaeology and Ethnology* (Cambridge: Press of John Wilson and Son, 1868): 5–9.

Wyman, Jeffries. "Report of the Curator." *Fourth Annual Report of the Peabody Museum of American Archaeology and Ethnology* (Boston: A. Kingman, 1871): 1–24.

Wyman, Jeffries. "Report of the Curator," *Sixth Annual Report of the Peabody Museum of American Archaeology and Ethnology* (Cambridge, MA: Salem Press, 1873): 1–23.

Xerez, Francisco de. "Verdadera relación de la conquista del Perú y Provincia del Cuzco [1534]." In *Crónicas iniciales de la conquista del Perú,* edited by Alberto M. Salas, Miguel A. Guérin, and José Luis Moure, 147–251. Buenos Aires: Editorial Plus Ultra, 1987.

Zárate, Agustín de. *Historia del descubrimiento y conquista de las provincias del Peru, y de los successos que en ella ha auido desde que se conquistò hasta que el Licenciado de la Gasca Obispo de Siguença boluio a estos reynos.* Libro I. Antwerp: 1555.

Secondary Sources

Abercrombie, Thomas A. *Pathways of Memory and Power: Ethnography and History among an Andean People*. Madison: University of Wisconsin Press, 1998.

Achim, Miruna. *From Idols to Antiquity: Forging the National Museum of Mexico*. Lincoln: University of Nebraska Press, 2017.

Achim, Miruna. "Skulls and Idols: Anthropometrics, Antiquity Collections, and the Origin of American Man, 1810–1850." In *Nature and Antiquities: The Making of Archaeology in the Americas*, edited by Philip L. Kohl, Irina Podgorny, and Stefanie Gänger, 23–46. Tucson: University of Arizona Press, 2014.

Achim, Miruna, and Irina Podgorny. "Descripción densa, historia de la ciencia y las prácticas del coleccionismo en los años de la revolución, la guerra y la independencia." In *Museos al detalle: Colecciones, antigüedades e historia natural, 1790–1870*, edited by Miruna Achim and Irina Podgorny, 15–26. Rosario: Prohistoria Ediciones, 2013.

Adorno, Rolena. *Guaman Poma: Writing and Resistance in Colonial Peru*. Austin: University of Texas Press, 2000 [1986].

Adorno, Rolena. *The Polemics of Possession in Spanish American Narrative*. New Haven, CT: Yale University Press, 2007.

Adorno, Rolena, and Ivan Boserup, eds. *Unlocking the Doors to the Worlds of Guaman Poma and His Nueva Corónica*. Copenhagen: Museum Tusculanum Press, 2015.

Aguirre, Carlos. "Crime, Race, and Morals: The Development of Criminology in Peru, 1890–1930." *Crime, Histoire & Sociétés / Crime, History & Societies* 2, no. 2 (1998): 73–90.

Aguirre, Carlos. *The Criminals of Lima and Their Worlds: The Prison Experience, 1850–1935*. Durham, NC: Duke University Press, 2005.

Alberti, Samuel J. M. M. *Morbid Curiosities: Medical Museums in Nineteenth-Century Britain*. Oxford: Oxford University Press, 2011.

Albiez-Wieck, Sarah, and Raquel Gil Montero. "The Emergence of Colonial Fiscal Categorizations in Peru. Forasteros and Yanaconas del Rey, Sixteenth to Nineteenth Centuries." *Journal of Iberian and Latin American Studies* 26, no. 1 (2020): 1–24.

Alcina Franch, José. *Arqueólogos o anticuarios: Historia antigua de la arqueología en la América Española*. Barcelona: Ediciones de Serbal, 1995.

Allen, Catherine J. "Body and Soul in Quechua Thought." *Journal of Latin American Lore* 8, no. 2 (1982): 179–196.

Allen, Catherine J. "The Sadness of Jars: Separation and Rectification in Andean Understandings of Death." In *Living with the Dead in the Andes*, edited by Izumi Shimada and James L. Fitzsimmons, 304–328. Tucson: University of Arizona Press, 2015.

Allen, Catherine J. "When Utensils Revolt: Mind, Matter, and Modes of Being in the Pre-Columbian Andes," *RES* 33 (1998): 18–27.

Amado Gonzales, Donato. *El estandarte real y la mascapaycha. Historia de una institución inca colonial*. Lima: Fondo Editorial PUCP, 2017.

Amado Gonzales, Donato, and Brian Bauer. "The Ancient Inca Town Named Huayna Picchu." *Ñawpa Pacha: Journal of the Institute of Andean Studies* 42, no. 1 (2022): 17–31.

Amigo, Roberto. "Los emblemas en tránsito y el incaísmo emancipador." In *Arte imperial Inca: sus orígenes y transformaciones desde la conquista a la independencia*, ed. Ramón Mujuca Pinilla, 238–269. Lima: Banco de Crédito del Perú, 2020.

Andersen, Wayne V. "Gauguin and a Peruvian Mummy." *Burlington Magazine* 109, no. 769 (April 1967): 238–243.

Anderson, Warwick. "Racial Conceptions in the Global South." *Isis: A Journal of the History of Science Society* 105 (2014): 782–792.

Appadurai, Arjun, ed. *The Social Life of Things: Commodities in Cultural Perspective*. Cambridge: Cambridge University Press, 1986.

Appelbaum, Nancy P., Anne S. MacPherson, and Karin Alejandra Rosemblatt. "Introduction." In *Race and Nation in Latin America*, edited by Nancy P. Appelbaum, Anne S. MacPherson, and Karin Alejandra Rosemblatt, 1–31. Chapel Hill: University of North Carolina Press, 2003.

Arkush, Elizabeth A. "Violence, Indigeneity, and Archaeological Interpretation in the Central Andes." In *The Ethics of Anthropology and Amerindian Research: Reporting on Environmental Degradation and Warfare*, edited by R. J. Chacon and R. G. Mendoza, 289–309. New York: Springer, 2012.

Armus, Diego, and Pablo F. Gómez, eds. *The Gray Zones of Medicine: Healers & History in Latin America*. Pittsburgh: University of Pittsburgh Press, 2021.

Arnold, Denise Y., and Christine A. Hastorf. *Heads of State: Icons, Power, and Politics in the Ancient and Modern Andes*. Walnut Creek, CA: Left Coast Press, 2008.

Arnott, Robert, Stanley Finger, and C. U. M. Smith, eds. *Trepanation: History, Discovery, Theory*. Lisse; Exton, PA: Swets & Zeitlinger, 2003.

Asensio, Raúl. *Señores del pasado: Arqueólogos, museo y huaqueros en el Perú*. Lima: Instituto de Estudios Peruanos, 2018.

Astuhuamán, César W., and Richard E. Daggett. "Julio César Tello Rojas, una biografía." In *Paracas, Primera parte. Obra completa*, Vol. 1, 17–52. Lima: Clásicos Sanmarquinos, UNMSM, 2005.

Astuhuamán, Cesar W., and Henry Tantaleán, eds. *Historia de la arqueología en el Perú del siglo XX*. Lima: Instituto Francés de Estudios Andinos, 2013.

Atwood, Roger. *Stealing History: Tomb Raiders, Smugglers, and the Looting of the Ancient World*. New York: St. Martin's Press, 2004.

Aufderheide, Arthur C. *The Scientific Study of Mummies*. Cambridge: Cambridge University Press, 2003.

Ávalos de Matos, Rosalía, and Rogger Ravines. "Las antiguedades Peruanas y su proteccion legal." *Revista del Museo Nacional* (Lima), no. 40 (1974): 459–470.

Avilés, Marco. *No soy tu cholo*. Lima: Debate, 2017.

Axtell, James. "Europeans, Indians, and the Age of Discovery in American History Textbooks." *American Historical Review* 92, no. 3 (1987): 621–632.

Ayllón Dulanto, Fernando. *El Museo del Perú: Historia del Museo del Congreso y de la Inquisición*. Peru: 2014.

Bacigalupo, Ana Mariella. "The Mapuche Undead Never Forget: Traumatic Memory and Cosmopolitics in Post-Pinochet Chile." *Anthropology and Humanism*, 43, no. 2 (2018):1–21.

Ballestero, Diego. "The Path of the Bodies: Provenance Research and Repatriation of Human Remains at the Museo de La Plata (Argentina)." In *From "Bronze Rooster" to Ekeko: Impulses toward Ethnological Provenance Research in University Collections and Museums*, eds. Daniel Grana-Behrens and Karoline Noack, 33–44. Bonn: University of Bonn / BASA Museum, 2020.

Barnhart, Terry. *Ephraim George Squier and the Development of American Anthropology*. Lincoln: University of Nebraska Press, 2005.

Barrera Osorio, Antonio. *Experiencing Nature: The Spanish American Empire and the Early Scientific Revolution*. Austin: University of Texas Press, 2006.

Basadre, Jorge. *El azar en la historia y sus límites: Con un apéndice, la serie de probabilidades dentro de la emancipación peruana*. Lima: Ediciones P. L. V., 1973.

Bastien, Joseph W. *Healers of the Andes: Kallawaya Herbalists and Their Medicinal Plants*. Salt Lake City: University of Utah Press, 1987.

Bauer, Brian S. *Ancient Cuzco: Heartland of the Inca*. Austin: University of Texas Press, 2004.

Bauer, Brian S. "Pacariqtambo and the Mythical Origins of the Inca." *Latin American Antiquity* 2, no. 1 (1991): 7–26.

Bauer, Brian S., and Antonio Coello Rodríguez. "The Hospital of San Andrés. Lima, Peru and the Search for the Royal Mummies of the Incas." *Fieldiana. Anthropology*, New Series, no. 39 (August 15, 2007): 1–31.

Bauer, Brian S., and Charles Stanish. "Killke and Killke-Related Pottery from Cuzco, Peru, in the Field Museum of Natural History." *Fieldiana. Anthropology*, New Series, no. 15 (December 31, 1990): i–iii, 1–17.

Beck, David R. M. *Unfair Labor? American Indians and the 1893 World's Columbian Exposition in Chicago*. Lincoln: University of Nebraska Press, 2019.

Begerock, Anna-Maria, Isabel Martínez Armijo, Christiane Clados, Mercedes González, and Nina Ulrich. "200 Years a Woman, 1000 Years a Man: The Case of the Marburg Mummy." *Revista de Arqueologia Pública* 16, no. 1 (2021): 6–25.

Bennison, Sarah. "Waqay: A Word, Water, and the Andean World in a Twentieth-Century Spanish Manuscript from Huarochirí (Peru)." *Anthropological Linguistics* 61, no. 4 (Winter 2019): 459–490.

Bennison, Sarah. "Who Are the Children of Pariacaca? Exploring Identity through Narratives of Water and Landscape in Huarochirí, Peru" PhD diss., Newcastle University, 2016.

Benton, Lauren. *Law and Colonial Cultures: Legal Regimes in World History, 1400–1900.* Cambridge: Cambridge University Press, 2002.

Bernstein, Jay H. "First Recipients of Anthropological Doctorates in the United States, 1891–1930." *American Anthropologist* 104, no. 2 (June 2002): 551–564.

Berquist, Emily Kay. *The Bishop's Utopia: Envisioning Improvement in Colonial Peru.* Philadelphia: University of Pennsylvania Press, 2014.

Berry, Daina Ramey. *The Price for Their Pound of Flesh: The Value of the Enslaved, from Womb to Grave, in the Building of a Nation.* Boston: Beacon Press, 2017.

Bieder, Robert E. *Science Encounters the Indian, 1820–1880: The Early Years of American Ethnology.* Norman: University of Oklahoma Press, 1986.

Biers, Trish. "Rethinking Purpose, Protocol, and Popularity in Displaying the Dead in Museums." In *Ethical Approaches to Human Remains: A Global Challenge in Bioarchaeology and Forensic Anthropology*, edited by Kirsty Squires, David Errickson, Nicholas Márquez Grant, 239–263. Switzerland: Springer, 2019.

Billman, Brian R. "Irrigation and the Origins of the Southern Moche State on the North Coast of Peru," *Latin American Antiquity* 13, no. 4 (2002): 371–400.

Blackhawk, Ned. *Violence over the Land: Indians and Empires in the Early American West.* Cambridge, MA: Harvard University Press, 2008.

Blackhawk, Ned, and Isaiah Wilner, eds. *Indigenous Visions: Rediscovering the World of Franz Boas.* New Haven, CT: Yale University Press, 2018.

Blakey, Michael L. "Archaeology under the Blinding Light of Race." *Current Anthropology* 61, supplement 22 (October 2020): S183–S197.

Blakey, Michael L. "Skull Doctors: Intrinsic Social and Political Bias in the History of American Physical Anthropology, with Special Reference to the Work of Aleš Hrdlička." *Critique of Anthropology* 7, no. 2 (October 1987): 7–35.

Bleichmar, Daniela. *Visible Empire: Colonial Botany and Visual Culture in the Eighteenth-Century Hispanic World.* Chicago: University of Chicago Press, 2012.

Bongers, Jacob. "Mortuary Practice, Imperial Conquest, and Sociopolitical Change in the Middle Chincha Valley, Peru (ca. AD 1200–1650)." PhD diss., University of California, Los Angeles, 2019.

Bonilla, Heraclio, and Karen Spalding. "La independencia en el Perú: Las palabras y los hechos." In *La independencia en el Perú*, edited by Heraclio Bonilla and José Matos Mar, 15–64. Lima: Instituto de Estudios Peruanos, 1972.

Boone, Elizabeth Hill. "Preface." In *Tombs for the Living: Andean Mortuary Practices*, edited by Tom D. Dillehay, vii–viii. Washington, DC: Dumbarton Oaks Research Library and Collection, 2011 [1995].

Bouley, Bradford. "Negotiated Sanctity: Incorruption, Community, and Medical Expertise." *Catholic Historical Review* 102 (2012): 1–25.

Bouley, Bradford. "Papal Anatomy in the News: Bodies and Politics in the Early Modern Catholic World." *Sixteenth Century Journal* 49, no. 3 (2018): 643–662.

Boyd, Colleen E., and Coll Thrush. "Introduction: Bringing Ghosts to Ground." In *Phantom Past, Indigenous Presence: Native Ghosts in North American Culture and History*, edited by Colleen E. Boyd and Coll Thrush, xv–xix. Lincoln: University of Nebraska Press, 2011.

Brading, D. A. *The First America: The Spanish Monarchy, Creole Patriots, and the Liberal State, 1492–1867.* Cambridge: Cambridge University Press, 1991.

Breen, Benjamin. *The Age of Intoxication: Origins of the Global Drug Trade*. Philadelphia: University of Pennsylvania Press, 2019.

Breen, Benjamin. "No Man Is an Island: Early Modern Globalization, Knowledge Networks, and George Psalmanazar's Formosa." *Journal of Early Modern History* 17, no. 4 (2013): 391–417.

Breen, Benjamin. "A Pirate Surgeon in Panama," *The Appendix* 2, no. 2 (April 2014).

Bromley, Juan. "El capitán Martin de Estete y doña María de Escobar 'La Romana,' fundadores de la Villa de Trujillo del Peru." *Revista Histórica* (Lima) 22 (1955–1956): 122–141.

Brosseder, Claudia. *The Power of Huacas: Change and Resistance in the Andean World of Colonial Peru*. Austin: University of Texas Press, 2014.

Brown, Michael F., and Margaret M. Bruchac. "NAGPRA from the Middle Distance: Legal Puzzles and Unintended Consequences." In *Imperialism, Art & Restitution*, edited by John Henry Merryman, 193–217. Cambridge: Cambridge University Press, 2006.

Brown, Monica, and Elisa Chavarri. *Sharuko: El Arqueólogo Peruano / Peruvian Archaeologist Julio C. Tello*. New York: Children's Book Press, 2020.

Brown, Vincent. *The Reaper's Garden: Death and Power in the World of Atlantic Slavery*. Cambridge, MA: Harvard University Press, 2008.

Bruhns, Karen O., and Nancy L. Kelker. *Faking the Ancient Andes*. Walnut Creek, CA: Left Coast Press, 2010.

Bueno, Christina. *The Pursuit of Ruins: Archaeology, History, and the Making of Modern Mexico*. Albuquerque: University of New Mexico Press, 2016.

Buikstra, Jane E. "Tombs for the Living . . . or . . . for the Dead: The Osmore Ancestors." In *Tombs for the Living: Andean Mortuary Practices*, edited by Tom D. Dillehay, 229–279. Washington, DC: Dumbarton Oaks Research Library and Collection, 2011 [1995].

Buikstra, Jane E., and Kenneth C. Nystrom. "Ancestors and Social Memory: A South American Example of Dead Body Politics." In *Living with the Dead in the Andes*, edited by Izumi Shimada and James L. Fitzsimmons, 245–266. Tuscon: University of Arizona Press, 2015.

Burga, Manuel. *Nacimiento de una utopia: Muerte y resurrección de los incas*. Lima: Instituto de Apoyo Agrario, 1988.

Burga, Manuel, and Alberto Flores Galindo. *Apogeo y crisis de la república aristocrática*. Lima: Ediciones Rickchay, 1980.

Burger, Richard. "The Intellectual Legacy of Julio C. Tello." In *The Life and Writings of Julio C. Tello: America's First Indigenous Archaeologist*, edited by Richard L. Burger, 65–82. Iowa City: University of Iowa Press, 2009.

Burger, Richard, ed. *The Life and Writings of Julio C. Tello: America's First Indigenous Archaeologist*. Iowa City: University of Iowa Press, 2009.

Burger, Richard L., Lucy Salazar, Jason Nesbitt, Eden Washburn, and Lars Fehren-Schmitz. "New AMS Dates for Machu Picchu: Results and Implications." *Antiquity* 95, no. 383 (2021): 1265–1279.

Burns, Kathryn. *Colonial Habits: Convents and the Spiritual Economy of Cuzco. Peru*. Durham, NC: Duke University Press, 1999.

Burns, Kathryn. "Making Indigenous Archives: The Quilcaycamayoc of Colonial Cuzco." *Hispanic American Historical Review* 91, no. 4 (2011): 665–689.

Cabello Carro, Paz. "Las colecciones peruanas en España y los inicios de la arqueología andina en el siglo XVIII." In *Los Incas y el antiguo Perú. 3000 años de historia*, 466–485. Madrid: Sociedad Estatal Quinto Centenario, Lunwerg Editores, 1991.

Cabello Carro, Paz. "Mestizaje y ritos funerarios en Trujillo, Perú, según las antiguas colecciones reales Españolas." In *Iberoamérica Mestiza: Encuentro de pueblos y culturas*, 85–102. Madrid: Seacex, 2003.

Cabello Carro, Paz. "Pervivencias funerarias prehispánicas en época colonial en Trujillo del Perú: Nueva interpretación de los dibujos arqueológicos de Martínez Compañon." *Anales del Museo de América* 11 (2003): 9–56.

Cabello Valboa, Miguel. *Miscelánea Antártica*, edited by Isaías Lerner. Sevilla: Fundación José Manuel Lara, 2011 [1586].

Cadena, Marisol de la. *Earth Beings: Ecologies of Practice across Andean Worlds.* Durham, NC: Duke University Press, 2015.

Cadena, Marisol de la. "From Race to Class: Insurgent Intellectuals *de provincia* in Peru, 1910–1970." In *Shining and Other Paths: War and Society in Peru, 1980–1995,* edited by Steve Stern, 22–59. Durham, NC: Duke University Press, 1998.

Cadena, Marisol de la. *Indigenous Mestizos: The Politics of Race and Culture in Cuzco, Peru, 1919–1991.* Durham, NC: Duke University Press, 2003 [2000].

Cahill, David. "Advanced Andeans and Backward Europeans: Structure and Agency in the Collapse of the Inca Empire." In *Questioning Collapse: Human Resilience, Ecological Vulnerability, and the Aftermath of Empire,* edited by Patricia Ann McAnany and Norman Yoffee, 207–238. Cambridge: Cambridge University Press, 2010.

Cahill, David. "Becoming Inca: Juan Bustamante Carlos Inca and the Roots of the Great Rebellion." *Colonial Latin American Review* 22, no. 2 (2013): 259–280.

Cahill, David. "New Viceroyalty, New Nation, New Empire: A Transnational Imaginary for Peruvian Independence." *Hispanic American Historical Review* 91, no. 2 (2011): 203–235.

Cañizares Esguerra, Jorge, ed. *Entangled Empires: The Anglo-Iberian Atlantic, 1500–1830.* Philadelphia: University of Pennsylvania Press, 2018.

Cañizares-Esguerra, Jorge. *How to Write the History of the New World: Histories, Epistemologies, and Identities in the Eighteenth-Century Atlantic World.* Stanford, CA: Stanford University Press, 2001.

Cañizares-Esguerra, Jorge. *Nature, Empire, and Nation: Explorations in the History of Science in the Iberian World.* Stanford, CA: Stanford University Press, 2006.

Cañizares-Esguerra, Jorge, and Mark Thurner. "Andes." In *New World Objects of Knowledge: A Cabinet of Curiosities,* edited by Mark Thurner and Juan Pimentel, 217–224. London: University of London Press, 2021.

Carter, Christopher, Flora Vilches, and Calogero M. Santoro. "South American Mummy Trafficking: Captain Duniam's Nineteenth-Century Worldwide Enterprises." *Journal of the History of Collections* 29, no. 3 (November 2016): 395–407.

Castillo Morán, Miguel Angel del, and María Moscoso Carbajal. "El 'Chino' y el 'Indio': Pedro S. Zulen y Julio C. Tello, una amistad del novecientos a través de su correspondencia, 1914–1922." *Arqueología y Sociedad* no. 14 (2002): 165–188.

Certeau, Michel de. *The Writing of History,* translated by Tom Conley. New York: Columbia University Press, 1988.

Ceruti, Constanza. "Human Bodies as Objects of Dedication at Inca Mountain Shrines (Northwestern Argentina)." *World Archaeology* 36, no. 1 (2004): 103–122.

Chambers, Sarah C. "Little Middle Ground: The Instability of a Mestizo Identity in the Andes, Eighteenth and Nineteenth Centuries." In *Race and Nation in Latin America,* edited by Nancy P. Appelbaum, Anne S. MacPherson, and Karin Alejandra Rosemblatt, 32–55. Chapel Hill: University of North Carolina Press, 2003.

Chaney, Edward. "Egypt in England and America: The Cultural Memorials of Religion, Royalty and Revolution." In *Sites of Exchange: European Crossroads and Faultlines,* edited by Maurizio Ascari and Adriana Corrado, 39–75. Amsterdam: Rodopi, 2006.

Chaplin, Joyce. *Subject Matter: Technology, the Body and Science on the Anglo-American Frontier, 1500–1676.* Cambridge, MA: Harvard University Press, 2001.

Chapman, William Ryan. "Arranging Ethnology: A. H. L. F. Pitt Rivers and the Typological Tradition." In *Objects and Others: Essays on Museums and Material Culture,* edited by George W. Stocking Jr., 15–48. Madison: University of Wisconsin Press, 1985.

Chase, Zachary J. "Performing the Past in the Historical, Ritual, and Mythological Landscapes of Huarochirí, Peru (ca. AD 1400–1700)." PhD diss., University of Chicago, 2016.

Chauchat, Claude. "Early Hunter-Gatherers on the Peruvian Coast." In *Peruvian Prehistory: An Overview of Pre-Inca and Inca Society,* edited by Richard W. Keatinge, 41–66. Cambridge: Cambridge University Press, 1988.

Christian, William A. *Local Religion in Sixteenth-Century Spain*. Princeton, NJ: Princeton University Press, 1981.

Clayton, Lawrence A. *Peru and the United States: The Condor and the Eagle*. Athens: University of Georgia Press, 1999.

Clifford, James. *Returns: Becoming Indigenous in the Twenty-First Century*. Cambridge, MA: Harvard University Press, 2013.

Coates, Benjamin, A. "The Pan-American Lobbyist: William Eleroy Curtis and U.S. Empire, 1884–1899." *Diplomatic History* 38, no. 1 (2014): 22–48.

Cole, Douglas. *Captured Heritage: The Scramble for Northwest Coast Artifacts*. Vancouver: University of British Columbia Press, 1995 [1985].

Colla, Elliott. *Conflicted Antiquities: Egyptology, Egyptomania, Egyptian Modernity*. Durham, NC: Duke University Press, 2007.

Coloma Porcari, César. *Los inicios de la arqueología en el Perú, o, "Antigüedades Peruanas" de Mariano Eduardo de Rivero*. Lima: Instituto Latinoamericano de Cultura y Desarrollo, 1994.

Colwell, Chip. *Inheriting the Past: The Making of Arthur C. Parker and Indigenous Archaeology*. Tucson: University of Arizona Press, 2009.

Colwell, Chip. *Plundered Skulls and Stolen Spirits: Inside the Fight to Reclaim Native America's Culture*. Chicago: University of Chicago Press, 2017.

Conklin, Alice L. *In the Museum of Man: Race, Anthropology, and Empire in France, 1850–1950*. Ithaca, NY: Cornell University Press, 2013.

Conn, Steven. "Archaeology, Philadelphia, and Understanding Nineteenth-Century American Culture." In *Philadelphia and the Development of Americanist Archaeology*, edited by Don D. Fowler and David R. Wilcox, 165–180. Tuscaloosa: University of Alabama Press, 2003.

Conn, Steven. *History's Shadow: Native Americans and Historical Consciousness in the Nineteenth Century*. Chicago: University of Chicago Press, 2004.

Conrad, Geoffrey W. "The Burial Platform of Chan Chan: Some Social and Political Implications." In *Chan Chan, Andean Desert City*, edited by Michael E. Moseley and Kent Day, 87–118. Albuquerque: University of New Mexico Press, 1982.

Conrad, Geoffrey W., and Arthur A. Demarest. *Religion and Empire: The Dynamics of Aztec and Inca Expansionism*. Cambridge: Cambridge University Press, 1984.

Contreras, Carlos, and Luis Miguel Glave, eds. *La independencia del Perú: ¿Concedida, conseguida, concebida?* Lima: Instituto de Estudios Peruanos, 2015.

Cook, Della Collins. "The Old Physical Anthropology and the New World: A Look at the Accomplishments of an Antiquated Paradigm." In *Bioarchaeology: The Contextual Analysis of Human Remains*, edited by Jane E. Buikstra and Lane E. Beck, 27–71. Burlingon, MA: Elsevier, 2006.

Cook, Harold J. "Time's Bodies: Crafting the Preparation and Preservation of Naturalia." In *Merchants and Marvels: Commerce Science and Art in Early Modern Europe*, edited by Pamela H. Smith and Paula Findlen, 223–247. London: Routledge, 2002.

Cook, Noble David. *Demographic Collapse: Indian Peru, 1520–1620*. Cambridge: Cambridge University Press, 2004 [1981].

Cooley, Mackenzie. "The Giant Remains: Mesoamerican Natural History, Medicine, and Cycles of Empire." *Isis: A Journal of the History of Science Society* 112, no. 1 (2021): 45–67.

Cooley, Mackenzie. *The Perfection of Nature: Animals, Breeding, and Race in the Renaissance*. Chicago: University of Chicago Press, 2022.

Covey, R. Alan. "Chronology, Succession, and Sovereignty: The Politics of Inka Historiography and Its Modern Interpretation." *Comparative Studies in Society and History* 48, no. 1 (2006): 169–199.

Covey, R. Alan. *How the Incas Built Their Heartland: State Formation and the Innovation of Imperial Strategies in the Sacred Valley, Peru*. Ann Arbor: University of Michigan Press, 2006.

Covey, R. Alan. *The Inca Apocalypse: The Spanish Conquest and the Transformation of the Andean World*. New York: Oxford University Press, 2020.

Covey, R. Alan. "Inca Gender Relations, from Household to Empire." In *Gender in Cross-Cultural Perspective*, 6th edition, edited by Caroline B. Brettell and Carolyn F. Sargent, 70–76. Saddle River, NJ: Pearson, 2013.

Covey, R. Alan. "Inka Imperial Intentions and Archaeological Realities in the Peruvian Highlands." In *The Inka Empire: A Multidisciplinary Approach*, edited by Izumi Shimada, 83–96. Austin: University of Texas Press, 2015.

Covey, R. Alan. "The Spread of Inca Power in the Cuzco Region." In *The Oxford Handbook of the Incas*, edited by Sonia Alconini and R. Alan Covey, 55–69. New York: Oxford University Press, 2018.

Cox Hall, Amy. "Collecting a 'Lost City' for Science: Huaquero Vision and the Yale Peruvian Expeditions to Machu Picchu, 1911, 1912, and 1914–15." *Ethnohistory* 59, no. 2 (Spring 2012): 293–321.

Cox Hall, Amy. *Framing a Lost City: Science, Photography, and the Making of Machu Picchu.* Austin: University of Texas Press, 2017.

Crawford, Matthew James. *The Andean Wonder Drug: Cinchona Bark and Imperial Science in the Spanish Atlantic, 1630–1800.* Pittsburgh: University of Pittsburgh Press, 2016.

Cueto, Marcos. "Andean Biology in Peru: Scientific Styles on the Periphery." *Isis* 80, no. 4 (1989): 640-658.

Cueto, Marcos. *Excelencia científica en la periferia: Actividades científicas e investigación biomédica en el Perú, 1890–1950.* Lima: Grupo de Análisis para el Desarollo GRADE, Consejo Nacional de Ciencia y Tecnología CONCYTEC, 1989.

Cueto, Marcos. "'Indigenismo' and Rural Medicine in Peru: The Indian Sanitary Brigade and Manuel Nuñez Butrón." *Bulletin of the History of Medicine* 65, no. 1 (Spring 1991): 22–41.

Cueto, Marcos, and Jorge Lossio. *Innovación en la Agricultura: Fermín Tangüis y el Algodón en el Perú.* Lima: Universidad del Pacífico, Centro de Investigación; Cosapi, Organización Empresarial, 1999.

Cueto, Marcos, and Steven Palmer. *Medicine and Public Health in Latin America: A History.* New York: Cambridge University Press, 2015.

Cummins, Thomas. "La fabula y el retrato: Imágenes tempranas del Inca." In *Los incas, reyes del Perú*, edited by Thomas Cummins, 1–41. Lima: Banco de Crédito, 2005.

Curatola Petrocchi, Marco, and José Carlos de la Puente Luna, eds. *El quipu colonial: Estudios y materiales.* Lima: Fondo Editorial Pontificia Universidad Católica del Peru, 2013.

Curran, Andrew S. *The Anatomy of Blackness: Science and Slavery in an Age of Enlightenment.* Baltimore: Johns Hopkins University Press, 2011.

Curtoni, Rafael Pedro. "Against Global Archaeological Ethics: Critical Views from South America." In *Ethics and Archaeological Praxis. Ethical Archaeologies: The Politics of Social Justice*, edited by Cristóbal Gnecco and Dorothy Lippert, 41–47. New York: Springer, 2015.

Cushman, Gregory. *Guano and the Opening of the Pacific World: A Global Ecological History.* New York: Cambridge University Press, 2014.

Cushman, Gregory. "The Environmental Contexts of Guaman Poma: Interethnic Conflict over Forest Resources and Place in Huamanga, 1540–1600." In *Unlocking the Doors to the Worlds of Guaman Poma and his* Nueva Corónica, edited by Rolena Adorno and Ivan Boserup, 87–140. Copenhagen: Museum Tusculanum Press, 2015.

Cussen, Celia L. "The Search for Idols and Saints in Colonial Peru: Linking Extirpation and Beatification." *Hispanic American Historical Review* 85, no. 3 (2005): 417–448.

Daggett, Richard E. *An Annotated Tello-Centric History of Peruvian Archaeology*, Vol. 1, (ca. 1825)–1925. https://www.academia.edu/28070329/A_Tello-Centric_History_of_Peruvian_Arc haeology_part_1.

Daggett, Richard E. *Julio C. Tello, Politics, and Peruvian Archaeology 1930–1936.* Orono: University of Maine, 2016.

D'Altroy, Terence. *The Incas*, 2nd edition. Malden, MA: Wiley Blackwell, 2015.

D'Altroy, Terence. "Killing Mummies: On Inka Epistemology and Imperial Power." In *Death Rituals, Social Order and the Archaeology of Immortality in the Ancient World*, edited by Colin Renfrew, Michael J. Boyd, and Iain Morley, 404–422. New York: Cambridge University Press, 2016.

Dannenfeldt, Karl H. "Egypt and Egyptian Antiquities in the Renaissance." *Studies in the Renaissance* 6 (1959): 7–27.

Dannenfeldt, Karl H. "Egyptian Mumia: The Sixteenth-Century Experience and Debate." *Sixteenth-Century Journal* 16, no. 2 (1985): 163–180.

Danwerth, Otto. "El papel indígena en la huaquería Andina. Siglos XVI y XVII." In *Muchas Hispanoaméricas: Antropología, historia y enfoques culturales en los estudios latinoamericanistas*, edited by Thomas Krüggeler and Ulrich Mücke, 87–104. Madrid: Iberoamericana, 2001.

Darnell, Regna. *Invisible Genealogies: A History of Americanist Anthropology*. Lincoln: University of Nebraska Press, 2001.

Daston, Lorraine. "Introduction: The Coming into Being of Scientific Objects." In *Biographies of Scientific Objects*, edited by Lorraine Daston, 1–14. Chicago: University of Chicago Press, 2000.

Daston, Lorraine, and Peter Galison. *Objectivity*. New York: Zone Books, 2007.

Davis, Kathleen. *Periodization and Sovereignty: How Ideas of Feudalism and Secularization Govern the Politics of Time*. Philadelphia: University of Pennsylvania Press, 2008.

Dean, Carolyn J. "The After-Life of Inka Rulers: Andean Death before and after Spanish Colonization." *Hispanic Issues On Line* 7 (Fall 2010): 27–54.

Dean, Carolyn J. *A Culture of Stone: Inka Perspectives on Rock*. Durham, NC: Duke University Press, 2010.

Dean, Carolyn J. *Inka Bodies and the Body of Christ: Corpus Christi in Colonial Cuzco, Peru*. Durham, NC: Duke University Press, 1999.

Degregori, Carlos Iván. "Panorama de la antropología en el Perú: Del studio del Otro a la construcción de un Nostoros diverso." In *No hay país mas diverso I. Compendio de antropoogía peruana*, edited by Carlos Iván Degregori, 20–73. Lima: Instituto de Estudios Peruanos, 2000.

Degregori, Carlos Iván, and Pablo Sandoval. "La antropología en el Perú: del Estudio del otro a la construcción de un nosotros diverso." *Revista Colombiana de Antropología* 43 (2007): 299-334.

del Castillo, Lina. *Crafting a Republic for the World: Scientific, Geographic, and Historiographic Inventions of Colombia*. Lincoln: University of Nebraska Press, 2018.

del Castillo, Lina. "Entangled Fates: French-Trained Naturalists, the First Colombian Republic, and the Materiality of Geopolitical Practice, 1819–1830." *Hispanic American Historical Review* 98, no. 3 (2018): 407–438.

Delibes Mateos, Rocio. *Desenterrando tesoros en el siglo XVI. Compañías de huaca y participación indígena en Trujillo del Perú*. Sevilla: Editorial Universidad de Sevilla, 2010.

Deloria, Philip J. *Playing Indian*. New Haven: Yale University Press, 1998.

Delpar, Helen. *Looking South: The Evolution of Latin Americanist Scholarship in the United States, 1850–1975*. Tuscaloosa: University of Alabama Press, 2008.

DeLucia, Christine. *Memory Lands: King Philip's War and the Place of Violence in the Northeast*. New Haven, CT: Yale University Press, 2018.

Dent, Rosanna. "Whose Home Is the Field?" *Isis: A Journal of the History of Science Society* 113, no. 1 (2022): 137–143.

Desmond, Adrian, and James Moore. *Darwin's Sacred Cause: How a Hatred of Slavery Shaped Darwin's Views on Human Evolution*. Boston: Houghton Mifflin Harcourt, 2009.

Diaz-Andreu, Margarita. *A World History of Nineteenth-Century Archaeology: Nationalism, Colonialism, and the Past*. Oxford: Oxford University Press, 2008.

Díaz Caballero, Jesús. "Incaísmo as the First Guiding Fiction in the Emergence of the Creole Nation in the Provinces of Río de la Plata," *Journal of Latin American Cultural Studies* 17, no. 1 (2008): 1–22.

Dillehay, Tom D. "Introduction." In *Tombs for the Living: Andean Mortuary Practices*, edited by Tom D. Dillehay, 1–26. Washington, DC: Dumbarton Oaks Research Library and Collection, 2011 [1995].

Dillehay, Tom D., ed. *From Foraging to Farming in the Andes: New Perspectives on Food Production*. New York: Cambridge University Press, 2011.

Dillehay, Tom D., and Alan L. Kolata. "Long-Term Human Response to Uncertain Environmental Conditions in the Andes." *Proceedings of the National Academy of Sciences* 101, no. 12 (2004): 4325–4330.

Drinot, Paulo, ed. *La patria nueva: Economía, sociedad y cultura en el Perú, 1919–1930*. Raleigh, NC: Editorial A Contracorriente, 2018.

Duchesne, Frédéric. "Tumbas de Coporaque. Aproximaciones a concepciones funerarias collaguas." *Bulletin de l'Institut français d'études andines* 34, no. 3 (2005): 411–429.

Duffin, Jacalyn, and Alison Li. "Great Moments: Parke, Davis and Company and the Creation of Medical Art." *Isis: A Journal of the History of Science Society* 86, no. 1 (March 1995): 1–29.

Dulanto, Jalh. "Between Horizons: Diverse Configurations of Society and Power in the Late Pre-Hispanic Central Andes." In *Handbook of South American Archaeology*, edited by Helaine Silverman and William H. Isbell, 761–782. New York: Springer, 2008.

Dunnavant, Justin, Delande Justinvil, and Chip Colwell. "Craft an African American Graves Protection and Repatriation Act." *Nature* 593, no. 7859 (2021): 337–340.

Durston, Alan. "Cristóbal Choquecasa and the Making of the *Huarochirí Manuscript*." In *Indigenous Intellectuals: Knowledge, Power, and Colonial Culture in Mexico and the Andes*, edited by Gabriela Ramos and Yanna Yannakakis, 151–169. Durham, MC: Duke University Press, 2014.

Durston, Alan. "Notes on the Authorship of the Huarochirí Manuscript." *Colonial Latin American Review* 16, no. 2 (2007): 227–241.

Durston, Alan. "Quechua Language Government Propaganda in 1920s Peru." In *Indigenous Languages, Politics, and Authority in Latin America: Historical and Ethnographic Perspectives*, edited by Alan Durston and Bruce Mannheim, 161–180. Notre Dame, IN: University of Notre Dame Press, 2018.

Duviols, Pierre. *Cultura andina y represión*. Cuzco: Centro de Estudios Rurales Andinos "Bartolomé de las Casas," 1986.

Duviols, Pierre. *La destrucción de lLas religiones Andinas. Conquista y colonia*. México: Universidad Nacional Autónoma de México, 1977.

Duviols, Pierre. *Procesos y visitas de idolatrias. Cajatambo, siglo XVII. Pontificia Universidad Católica del Perú*. Lima: Fondo Editorial e Institute Frances de Estudios Andinos, 2003.

Earle, Rebecca. "Creole Patriotism and the Myth of the 'Loyal Indian.'" *Past & Present* 172, no. 1 (August 2001): 125–145.

Earle, Rebecca. *The Return of the Native: Indians and Myth-Making in Spanish America, 1810–1930*. Durham, NC: Duke University Press, 2007.

Earle, Rebecca. "Sobre Héroes y Tumbas: National Symbols in Nineteenth-Century Spanish America." *Hispanic American Historical Review* 85, no. 3 (2005): 375–416.

Eastman, Scott. "The Sacred Mantle of the Constitution of 1812." In *The Rise of Constitutional Government in the Iberian Atlantic World: The Impact of the Cádiz Constitution of 1812*, edited by Scott Eastman and Natalia Sobrevilla Perea, 1–18. Tuscaloosa: University of Alabama Press, 2015.

Eeckhout, Peter. "Change and Permanency on the Coast of Ancient Peru: The Religious Site of Pachacamac." *World Archaeology* 45, no. 1 (2013): 137–160.

Eeckhout, Peter. "The Impossibility of Death: Introduction to Funerary Practices and Models in the Ancient Andes." In *Funerary Practices and Models in the Ancient Andes: The Return of the Living Dead*, edited by Peter Eeckhout and Lawrence S. Owens, 1–11. Cambridge: Cambridge University Press, 2015.

Eeckhout, Peter, and Lawrence S. Owens, eds. *Funerary Practices and Models in the Ancient Andes: The Return of the Living Dead*. Cambridge: Cambridge University Press, 2015.

Egan, Nancy. "Exhibiting Indigenous Peoples: Bolivians and the Chicago Fair of 1893." *Studies in Latin American Popular Culture* 28, no. 1 (2010): 6–24.

Eire, Carlos M. N. *From Madrid to Purgatory: The Art and Craft of Dying in Sixteenth-Century Spain.* Cambridge: Cambridge University Press, 1995.

Elliott, John H. *Empires of the Atlantic World: Britain and Spain in America 1492–1830.* New Haven, CT: Yale University Press, 2006.

Elward Haagsma, Ronald. *Los Incas republicanos: La élite indígena cusqueña entre asimilación y resistencia cultural (1781–1896).* Lima: Fondo Editorial del Congreso del Perú, 2020.

Endere, Maria Luz. "Archaeological Heritage Legislation and Indigenous Rights in Latin America: Trends and Challenges." *International Journal of Cultural Property* 21, no. 3 (2014): 319–330.

Escanilla Huerta, Silvia. "Las milicias locales y la bandolerización de la guerra de independencia en el Perú (1820–1822)." *Historia Caribe* 15, no. 36 (2020): 105–136.

Espinoza Soriano, Waldemar. *La destrucción del imperio de los incas: La rivalidad política y señorial de los curacazgos andinos.* Lima: Mantaro, 2012 [1973].

Espinoza Soriano, Waldemar. "Los señoríos de Yaucha y Picoy en el abra de medio y alto Rimac." *Revista Histórica* (Lima) 34 (1983–1984): 157–279.

Estenssoro Fuchs, Juan Carlos. "Modernismo, estética, música y fiesta: Élites y cambio de actitud frente a la cultura popular en el Perú, 1750–1850." In *Tradición y Modernidad en los Andes*, edited by Henrique Urbano, 181–195. Cuzco: Centro de Estudios Regionales Andinos Bartolomé de las Casas, 1992.

Estenssoro Fuchs, Juan Carlos. *Del paganismo a la santidad. La incorporación de los indios del Perú al Catolicismo, 1532–1750*, translated by Gabriela Ramos. Lima: Instituto Francés de Estudios Andinos, Pontificia Universidad Católica del Perú, Instituto Riva-Agüero, 2003 [1998].

Estupiñán Viteri, Tamara. "El Puxilí de los Yngas, el ayllu de la nobleza incaica que cuidó de los restos mortales de Atahuallpa Ticci Cápac." *Revista de Historia de América*, no. 154 (Enero–Junio 2018): 37–80.

Evans, R. Tripp. *Romancing the Maya: Mexican Antiquity in the American Imagination 1820–1915.* Austin: University of Texas Press, 2004.

Fabian, Ann. *The Skull Collectors: Race, Science, and America's Unburied Dead.* Chicago: University of Chicago Press, 2010.

Fane, Diana. "Reproducing the Pre-Columbian Past: Casts and Models in Exhibitions of Ancient America, 1824–1935." In *Collecting the Pre-Columbian Past: A Symposium at Dumbarton Oaks: 6th and 7th October 1990*, edited by Elizabeth Hill Boone, 141–176. Washington, DC: Dumbarton Oaks Research Library and Collection, 1993.

Farro, Máximo Ezequiel. "Historia de las colecciones en el Museo de la Plata, 1884–1906: Naturalistas viajeros, coleccionistas y comerciantes de objetos de historia natural a fines del Siglo XIX." PhD diss., Universidad Nacional de la Plata, 2008.

Farro, Máximo, and Irina Podgorny. "'Pre-Columbian Moulages': Huacos, Mummies and Photographs in the International Controversy over Precolumbian Diseases, 1894–1910." *Medicina nei secoli* 27, no. 2 (2015): 629–651.

Feldman, Joseph. "'Miserable San Damian—But What Treasures!': The Life of Aleš Hrdlička's Peruvian Collection." *History and Anthropology* 27, no. 2 (2016): 230–250.

Fernández Ortega, Racso, and Anderson Calzada Escalona. "La relación de los investigadores cubanos en la arqueología peruana (1953–2008)." In *Historia de la Arqueología en el Perú del Siglo XX*, edited by Cesar Astuhuamán and Henry Tantaleán, 443–468, Lima: Instituto Francés de Estudios Andinos, 2013.

Few, Martha. *For All of Humanity: Mesoamerican and Colonial Medicine in Enlightenment Guatemala.* Tucson: University of Arizona Press, 2015.

Fields, Karen E., and Barbara J. Fields. *Racecraft: The Soul of Inequality in American Life.* London: Verso, 2014 [2012].

Findlen, Paula. *Possessing Nature: Museums, Collecting, and Scientific Culture in Early Modern Italy.* Berkeley: University of California Press, 1994.

Fine-Dare, Kathleen S. "Bodies Unburied, Mummies Displayed." In *Border Crossings: Transnational Americanist Anthropology*, edited by Kathleen S. Fine-Dare and Steven L. Rubenstein, 67–118. Lincoln: University of Nebraska Press, 2009.

Fine-Dare, Kathleen S. *Grave Injustice: The American Indian Repatriation Movement and NAGPRA.* Lincoln: University of Nebraska Press, 2002.

Finger, Stanley. *Minds behind the Brain.* New York: Oxford University Press, 2000.

Finger, Stanley, and Hiran R. Fernando. "E. George Squier and the Discovery of Cranial Trepanation: A Landmark in the History of Surgery and Ancient Medicine." *Journal of the History of Medicine and Allied Sciences* 56, no. 4 (October 2001): 353–381.

Firbas, Paul. "La momia del Inca: Cuerpo y palabra en los *Comentarios Reales." Revista de Crítica Literaria Latinomericana* 35, no. 70 (2009): 39–61.

Flores Galindo, Alberto. *In Search of an Inca: Identity and Utopia in the Andes*, translated by Carlos Aguirre, Charles F. Walker, and Willie Hiatt. New York: Cambridge University Press, 2010 [1986].

Flores Ochoa, Jorge. "Enqa, enqaychu y Khuya Rumi: Aspectos mágico-religiosos entre pastores." *Journal de la Societé des Américanistes* 63 (1974): 245–262.

Fock, Niels, and Eva Krener. "Los Cañaris del Ecuador y sus conceptos etnohistóricos sobre los Incas." In *Amerikanistische Studien: Festschrift für Hermann Trimborn*, vol. 1, edited by Roswith Hartmann and Udo Oberem, 170–181. St. Augustin: Haus Völker und Kulturen, Anthropos-Institut, 1978.

Forbes, R. J. *Studies in Early Petroleum History.* Leiden: E. J. Brill, 1958.

Fung Pineda, Rosa. "The Late Preceramic and Initial Period." In *Peruvian Prehistory: An Overview of Pre-Inca and Inca Society*, edited by Richard W. Keatinge. Cambridge: Cambridge University Press, 1988.

Gamboni, Dario. "Volcano Equals Head Equals Kiln Equals Phallus: Connecting Gauguin's Metaphors of the Creative Act." *RES: Anthropology and Aesthetics* 63–64 (2013): 93–107.

Gänger, Stefanie. "Of Butterflies, Chinese Shoes, and Antiquities: A History of Peru's National Museum, 1826–1881." *Jahrbuch für Geschichte Lateinamerikas* 51, no. 1 (December 2014): 283–301.

Gänger, Stefanie. "Conquering the Past: Post-War Archaeology and Nationalism in the Borderlands of Chile and Peru, c. 1880–1920." *Comparative Studies in Society and History* 51, no. 4 (2009): 691–714.

Gänger, Stefanie. "Disjunctive Circles: Modern Intellectual Culture in Cuzco and the Journey of Incan Antiquities, c. 1877–1921." *Modern Intellectual History* 10, no.1 (August 2013): 399–414.

Gänger, Stefanie. "¿La mirada imperialista? Los alemanes y la arqueología peruana." *Histórica* (Lima) 30 (2006): 69–90.

Gänger, Stefanie. *Relics of the Past: The Collecting and Study of Pre-Columbian Antiquities in Peru and Chile, 1837–1911.* Oxford: Oxford University Press, 2014.

Garcés, María A. "The Translator Translated: Inca Garcilaso and English Imperial Expansion." In *Travel and Translation in the Early Modern Period*, edited by Carmine G. DiBiase, 203–225. Amsterdam: Rodopi, 2006.

García-Bryce, Iñigo L. *Crafting the Republic: Lima's Artisans and Nation Building in Peru, 1821–1879.* Albuquerque: University of New Mexico Press, 2004.

Garofalo, Leo J. "Conjuring with Coca and the Inca: The Andeanization of Lima's Afro-Peruvian Ritual Specialists, 1580–1690." *The Americas* 63, no. 1 (2006): 53–80.

Garrett, David T. *Shadows of Empire: The Indian Nobility of Cusco, 1750–1825.* Cambridge: Cambridge University Press, 2005.

Geggus, David. "The Naming of Haiti." *NWIG: New West Indian Guide / Nieuwe West-Indische Gids* 71, no. 1/2 (1997): 43–68.

Geller, Pamela L. "Building Nation, Becoming Object: The Bio-Politics of the Samuel G. Morton Crania Collection." *Historical Archaeology* 54, no. 1 (2020): 52–70.

Gerbi, Antonello. *The Dispute of the New World: The History of a Polemic, 1750–1900,* translated by Jeremy Moyle. Pittsburgh: University of Pittsburgh Press, 1973 [1955].

Gildner, Robert Matthew. "Indomestizo Modernism: National Development and Indigenous Integration in Postrevolutionary Bolivia, 1952-1964." PhD diss., University of Texas at Austin, 2012.

Gillingham, Paul. *Cuauhtémoc's Bones: Forging National Identity in Modern Mexico.* Albuquerque: University of New Mexico Press, 2011.

Gil-Riaño, Sebastián. "Risky migrations: Race, Latin eugenics, and Cold War development in the International Labor Organization's Puno– Tambopata project in Peru, 1930–60." *History of Science* 60, no. 1(2022): 41–68.

Gissis, Snait B. "Visualizing 'Race' in the Eighteenth Century." *Historical Studies in the Natural Sciences* 41, no. 1 (Winter 2011): 41–103.

Gómez, Pablo F. *The Experiential Caribbean: Creating Knowledge and Healing in the Early Modern Atlantic.* Chapel Hill: University of North Carolina Press, 2017.

Gootenberg, Paul. *Andean Cocaine: The Making of a Global Drug.* Chapel Hill: University of North Carolina Press, 2008.

Gootenberg, Paul. *Between Silver and Guano: Commercial Policy and the State in Postindependence Peru.* Princeton, NJ: Princeton University Press, 1989.

Gootenberg, Paul. *Imagining Development: Economic Ideas in Peru's "Fictitious Prosperity" of Guano, 1840–1880.* Berkeley: University of California Press. 1993.

Gootenberg, Paul. "Population and Ethnicity in Early Republican Peru: Some Revisions." *Latin American Research Review* 26, no. 3 (1991): 109–57.

Gootenberg, Paul. "Seeing a State in Peru: From Nationalism of Commerce to the Nation Imagined, 1820–80." In *Studies in the Formation of the Nation-State in Latin America,* edited by James Dunkerly, 254–274. London: Institute of Latin American Studies, 2002.

Gose, Peter. *Invaders as Ancestors: On the Intercultural Making and Unmaking of Spanish Colonialism in the Andes.* Toronto: University of Toronto Press, 2008.

Gose, Peter. "Segmentary State Formation and the Ritual Control of Water under the Incas." *Comparative Studies in Society and History* 35, no. 3 (1993): 480–514.

Gould, Eliga. "Entangled Histories, Entangled Worlds: The English-Speaking Atlantic as a Spanish Periphery." *American Historical Review* 112, no. 3 (June 2007): 764–786.

Gould, Stephen Jay. *The Mismeasure of Man.* New York: W. W. Norton & Company, 2006 [1981].

Gould, Stephen Jay. "Morton's Ranking of Races by Cranial Capacity: Unconscious Manipulation of Data May Be a Scientific Norm." *Science* 200, no. 4341 (5 May 1978): 503–509.

Grafton, Anthony. *Bring Out Your Dead: The Past as Revelation.* Cambridge, MA: Harvard University Press, 2001.

Graubart, Karen B. "Indecent Living: Indigenous Women and the Politics of Representation in Early Colonial Peru." *Colonial Latin American Review* 9, no. 2 (2000): 213–235.

Graubart, Karen B. "Learning from the *Qadi:* The Jurisdiction of Local Rule in the Early Colonial Andes." *Hispanic American Historical Review* 95, no. 2 (2015): 195–228.

Graubart, Karen B. *With Our Labor and Sweat: Indigenous Women and the Formation of Colonial Society in Peru, 1550–1700.* Stanford, CA: Stanford University Press, 2007.

Greer, Margaret Rich, Walter Mignolo, and Maureen Quilligan, eds. *Rereading the Black Legend: The Discourses of Religious and Racial Difference in the Renaissance Empires.* Chicago: University of Chicago Press, 2007.

Guibovich Pérez, Pedro. "Cristobal de Albornoz y el Taki Onqoy." *Histórica* (Lima), 15, no. 2 (1991): 205–236.

Guibovich Pérez, Pedro. "The Dissemination and Reading of the Royal Commentaries in the Peruvian Viceroyalty." In *Inca Garcilaso & Contemporary World-Making,* edited by Sara Castro-Klarén and Christian Fernández, 129–153. Pittsburgh: University of Pittsburgh Press, 2016.

Guibovich Pérez, Pedro. *El Edificio de Letras: Jesuitas, Educación y Sociedad en el Perú Colonial.* Lima: Universidad Pacífico, 2014.

Guibovich Pérez, Pedro. "La función de la Historia en el 'Mercurio Peruano,' 1790–1795." *Cuadernos de Estudios del Siglo XVIII* 31 (2021): 235–261.

Guibovich Pérez, Pedro. "La usurpación de la memoria: el patrimonio documental y bibliográfico durante la ocupación chilena de Lima, 1881–1883." *Jahrbuch für Geschichte Lateinamerikas* 46 (2009): 83–107.

Guillén, Sonia E. "A History of Paleopathology in Peru and Northern Chile: From Head Hunting to Head Counting." In *The Global History of Paleopathology: Pioneers and Prospects*, edited by Jane Buikstra and Charlotte Roberts, 312–328. Oxford: Oxford University Press, 2012.

Guillén, Sonia, Andrew J. Nelson, Gerald Conlogue, Ronald Beckett, Jaime Sosa, and John Topic. "Three New Mummies from Huamachuco, Perú: A New Location for the Pattern of Mummification Demonstrated at Laguna de los Cóndores, Perú." Paper presented at the First Bolzano Congress on Mummy Studies, Bolzano, 19 March 2009.

Guillén Guillén, Edmundo. "El enigma de las momias Incas." *Boletín de Lima* 28 (1983): 29–42.

Guillén Guillén, Edmundo. *La guerra de reconquista inka: Historia épica de como los incas lucharon en defensa de la soberanía del Perú o Tawantinsuyo entre 1536 y 1572*. Lima: E. Guillén Guillén, 1994.

Gündüz, Réna. *El mundo ceremonial de los Huaqueros*. Lima: Editorial Universitaria Ricardo Palma, 2001.

Hamann, Byron Ellsworth. "How Maya Hieroglyphs Got Their Name: Egypt, Mexico, and China in Western Grammatology since the Fifteenth Century." *Proceedings of the American Philosophical Society* 152 (2008): 1–68.

Hamann, Byron Ellsworth. "The Social Life of Pre-Sunrise Things." *Current Anthropology* 43, no. 3 (2002): 351–382.

Hamilton, Andrew. *Scale & the Incas*. Princeton, NJ: Princeton University Press, 2018.

Hampe Martínez, Teodoro. "Las momias de los Incas en Lima." *Revista del Museo Nacional* (Lima) 46 (1982): 405–418.

Hampe Martínez, Teodoro. "La última morada de los Incas: Estudio histórico-arqueológico del Real Hospital de San Andrés." *Revista de Arqueología Americana* 22 (2003): 101–135.

Hantman, Jeffrey L. *Monacan Millennium: A Collaborative Archaeology and History of a Virginia Indian People*. Charlottesville: University of Virginia Press, 2018.

Haraway, Donna. "Teddy Bear Patriarchy: Taxidermy in the Garden of Eden, New York City, 1908–1936." *Social Text*, no. 11 (Winter 1984–1985): 20–64.

Harries, John. "Of Bleeding Skulls and the Postcolonial Uncanny: Bones and the Presence of Nonosabasut and Demasduit." *Journal of Material Culture* 15, no. 4 (2010): 403–421.

Harris, Steven J. "Mapping Jesuit Science: The Role of Travel in the Geography of Knowledge." In *The Jesuits: Cultures, Sciences, and the Arts, 1540–1773*, edited by John W. O'Malley, S.J., Gauvin Alexander Bailey, Steven J. Harris, and T. Frank Kennedy, S.J., 212–240. Toronto: University of Toronto Press, 1999.

Harrison, Simon J. "Skulls and Scientific Collecting in the Victorian Military: Keeping the Enemy Dead in British Frontier Warfare." *Comparative Studies in Society and History* 50 (2008): 285–303.

Hartman, Saidiya. "Venus in Two Acts." *small axe* 26 (June 2008): 1–14.

Harvey, Sean P. *Native Tongues: Colonialism and Race from Encounter to the Reservation*. Cambridge, MA: Harvard University Press, 2015.

Heaney, Christopher. *Cradle of Gold: The Story of Hiram Bingham, a Real-Life Indiana Jones, and the Search for Machu Picchu*. New York: Palgrave Macmillan, 2011 [2010].

Heaney, Christopher. "Death of the Object: or, the 'Inherent Corruption' of a Peruvian Mummy and the Microhistory of Things." Paper presented at the Annual Meeting of the American Historical Association (AHA), Washington, DC, 6 January 2018.

Heaney, Christopher. "Dry Subjects: The Collection of 'Artificial' and 'Natural' Mummies from Peru in the Nineteenth-Century History of Science." Paper presented at the Annual Meeting of the History of Science Society, Utrecht, 26 July 2019.

Heaney, Christopher. "Fair Necropolis: The Peruvian Dead, the first American Ph.D. in Anthropology, and the World's Columbian Exposition of Chicago, 1893." *History of Anthropology Review* 41 (2017): http://histanthro.org/notes/fair-necropolis/.

Heaney, Christopher. "How to Make an Inca Mummy: Andean Embalming, Peruvian Science, and the Collection of Empire." *Isis: A Journal of the History of Science Society* 109, no. 1 (March 2018): 1–27.

Heaney, Christopher. "Inca Mummy." In *New World Objects of Knowledge: A Cabinet of Curiosities*, edited by Mark Thurner and Juan Pimentel, 127–133. London: University of London Press, 2021.

Heaney, Christopher. "Marrying Utopia: Mary and Philip, Richard Eden, and the English Alchemy of Spanish Peru." In *Entangled Empires: The Anglo-Iberian Atlantic, 1500–1830*, edited by Jorge Cañizares Esguerra, 85–104. Philadelphia: University of Pennsylvania Press, 2018.

Heaney, Christopher. "Mummies Take Manhattan," *The New Yorker*, April 7, 2017, https://www.newyorker.com/tech/annals-of-technology/mummies-take-manhattan.

Heaney, Christopher. "As Peru Heads to the 2018 World Cup, Its Star Striker Has Three Inca Mummies to Thank." *NewYorker.com*, Elements Blog, 13 February 2018.

Heaney, Christopher. "A Peru of Their Own: English Grave-Opening and Indian Sovereignty in Early America." *William and Mary Quarterly*, 3rd ser., vol. 73, no. 4 (2016): 609–646.

Heaney, Christopher. "The Pre-Columbian Exchange: The Circulation of the Ancient Peruvian Dead in the Americas and Atlantic World." PhD diss., University of Texas at Austin, 2016.

Heaney, Christopher. "The Racism behind Alien Mummy Hoaxes." *The Atlantic*, 1 August 2017. https://www.theatlantic.com/science/archive/2017/08/how-to-fake-an-alien-mummy/535251/.

Heaney, Christopher. "Seeing Like an Inca: Julio C. Tello, Indigenous Archaeology, and Pre-Columbian Trepanation in Peru." In *Indigenous Visions: Rediscovering the World of Franz Boas*, edited by Ned Blackhawk and Isaiah Wilner, 344–376. New Haven, CT: Yale University Press, 2018.

Heaney, Christopher. "Skull Walls: The Peruvian Dead and the Remains of Entanglement." *American Historical Review* 127, no. 3 (2022): 1071–1101.

Heaney, Christopher. *Las Tumbas de Machu Picchu: La historia de Hiram Bingham y la búsqueda de las últimas ciudades de los Incas*. Lima: Fondo Editorial de la Pontificia Universidad Católica del Perú, 2012.

Heaney, William H. "Living Dead Birds: Doing First Fieldwork in the Wahgi Valley, Western Highlands, Papua New Guinea, 1975–1976." In *First Fieldwork: Pacific Anthropology, 1960–1985*. Honolulu: University of Hawai'i Press, 2018.

Hemenway, Eric. "Trials and Tribulations in a Tribal NAGPRA Program." *Museum Anthropology* 33, no. 2 (2010): 172–179.

Hemming, John. *The Conquest of the Incas*. New York: Harcourt Brace, 1970.

Hernández Garavito, Carla. "Legibility and Empire: Mediating the Inka Presence in Huarochirí Province, Peru." PhD diss., Vanderbilt University, 2019.

Hernández Garavito, Carla. "Producing Legibility through Ritual: The Inka Expansion in Huarochirí (Lima, Peru)." *Journal of Social Archaeology* 20, no. 3 (2020): 292–312.

Herrera, Alexander. "Indigenous Archaeology . . . in Peru?" In *Indigenous Peoples and Archaeology in Latin America*, edited by Cristóbal Gnecco and Patricia Ayala, 67–87. Walnut Creek, CA: Left Coast Press, 2011.

Herrera, Alexander, and Kevin Lane. "Qué hacen aquí esos *Pishtaku*?': Sueños, ofrendas y la construcción del pasado." *Antipoda. Revista de Antropología y Arqueología*, no. 2 (2006): 157–177.

Herring, Adam. *Art and Vision in the Inca Empire: Andeans and Europeans at Cajamarca*. New York: Cambridge University Press, 2015.

Hertzman, Marc A. "Fatal Differences: Suicide, Race, and Forced Labor in the Americas." *American Historical Review* 122, no. 2 (2017): 317–345.

Hicks, Dan. *The Brutish Museums: The Benin Bronzes, Colonial Violence and Cultural Restitution*. London: Pluto Press, 2020.

Hinsley, Curtis M. "Anthropology as Education and Entertainment: Frederic Ward Putnam at the World's Fair." In *Coming of Age in Chicago: The 1893 World's Fair and the Coalescence of American Anthropology*, edited by Curtis M. Hinsley and David R. Wilcox, 1–77. Lincoln: University of Nebraska Press, 2016.

Hinsley, Curtis M. "From Shell-Heaps to Stelae: Early Anthropology at the Peabody Museum." In *Objects and Others: Essays on Museums and Material Culture*, edited by George W. Stocking Jr., 49–74. Madison: University of Wisconsin Press, 1985.

Hinsley, Curtis M. *Savages and Scientists: The Smithsonian Institution and the Development of American Anthropology 1846–1910*. Washington, DC: Smithsonian Institution Press, 1981.

Hinsley, Curtis M. "In Search of the New World Classical." In *Collecting the Pre-Columbian Past: A Symposium at Dumbarton Oaks: 6th and 7th October 1990*, edited by Elizabeth Hill Boone, 105–121. Washington, DC: Dumbarton Oaks Research Library and Collection, 1993.

Hinsley, Curtis M., and David R. Wilcox, eds. *Coming of Age in Chicago: The 1893 World's Fair and the Coalescence of American Anthropology*. Lincoln: University of Nebraska Press, 2016.

Hodgen, Margaret. *Early Anthropology in the Sixteenth and Seventeenth Centuries*. Philadelphia: University of Pennsylvania Press, 1971 [1964].

Honores, Renzo. "El licenciado Polo y su informe al licenciado Briviesca de Muñatones (1561)." In *Lecturas y ediciones de crónicas de indias. Una propuesta interdisciplinaria*, edited by Ignacio Arellano y Fermín del Pino, 387–407. Madrid: Iberoamericana, 2004.

Hu, Di, and Kylie E. Quave. "Prosperity and Prestige: Archaeological Realities of Unfree Laborers under Inka Imperialism," *Journal of Anthropological Archaeology* 59 (2020): 1–14.

Huchet J. B., and B. Greenberg. "Flies, Mochicas and Burial Practices: A Case Study from Huaca de la Luna, Peru." *Journal of Archaeological Science* 37, no. 11 (2010): 2846–2856.

Humphreys, Robin A. "James Paroissien's Notes on the Liberating Expedition to Peru." *Hispanic American Historical Review* 31, no. 2 (1951): 253–273.

Humphreys, Robin A. *Liberation in South America 1806–1827: The Career of James Paroissien*. London: University of London, The Athlone Press, 1952.

Hyland, Sabine. "Writing with Twisted Cords: The Inscriptive Capacity of Andean Khipus." *Current Anthropology* 58, no. 3 (2017): 412–419.

Hyman, Aaron M., and Dana Leibsohn. "Washing the Archive." *Early American Literature* 55, no. 2 (2020): 419–444.

Irmscher, Christoph. *Louis Agassiz: Creator of American Science*. New York: Houghton Mifflin Harcourt, 2013.

Isbell, William H. *Mummies and Mortuary Monuments: A Postprocessural Prehistory of Central Andean Social Organization*. Austin: University of Texas Press, 1997.

Jacknis, Ira. "Refracting Images: Anthropological Display at the Chicago World's Fair, 1893." In *Coming of Age in Chicago: The 1893 World's Fair and the Coalescence of American Anthropology*, edited by Curtis M. Hinsley and David R. Wilcox, 261–336. Lincoln: University of Nebraska Press, 2016.

Jacobsen, Nils, and Nicanor Domínguez. *Juan Bustamante y los límites del liberalismo en el Altiplano: La rebelión de Huancané (1866–1868)*. Lima: Asociación Servicios Educativos Rurales, 2011.

Jave Calderón, Noe, ed., *Jorge Basadre: La historia y la política*. Lima: Seminario de Investigaciones y Publicaciones, 1981.

Johnson, Carina L. *Cultural Hierarchy in Sixteenth-Century Europe: The Ottomans and Aztecs*. New York: Cambridge University Press, 2011.

Johnson, Carina L. "Stone Gods and Counter-Reformation Knowledges." In *Making Knowledge in Early Modern Europe: Practices, Objects, and Texts, 1400–1800*, edited by Pamela H. Smith and Benjamin Schmidt, 233–247. Chicago: University of Chicago Press, 2007.

Johnson, Lyman, ed. *Death, Dismemberment, and Memory: Body Politics in Latin America*. Albuquerque: University of New Mexico Press, 2004.

Jones, Jana, Thomas F. G. Higham, David Chivall, Raffaella Bianucci, Gemma L. Kay, Mark J. Pallen, Ron Oldfield, Federica Ugliano, and Stephen A. Buckley. "A Prehistoric Egyptian Mummy: Evidence for an 'Embalming Recipe' and the Evolution of Early Formative Funerary Treatments." *Journal of Archaeological Science* 100 (2018): 191–200.

Jorink, Eric. "Noah's Ark Restored (and Wrecked): Dutch Collectors, Natural History and the Problem of Biblical Exegesis." In *Silent Messengers: The Circulation of Material Objects of Knowledge in the Early Modern Low Countries*, edited by Sven Dupré and Christoph Lüthy, 153–184. Berlin: Lit Verlag, 2011.

Joseph, Gilbert M., Catherine C. Le Grand, and Ricardo D. Salvatore, eds. *Close Encounters of Empire: Writing the Cultural History of U.S.–Latin American Relations*. Durham, NC: Duke University Press, 1998.

Joyce, Barry Alan. *The Shaping of American Ethnography: The Wilkes Exploring Expedition, 1838–1842*. Lincoln: University of Nebraska Press, 2001.

Julien, Catherine J. "Francisco De Toledo and His Campaign against the Incas." *Colonial Latin American Review* 16, no. 2 (2007): 243–72.

Julien, Catherine J. "History and Art in Translation: The Paños and Other Objects Collected by Francisco de Toledo." *Colonial Latin American Review* 8, no. 1 (1999): 61–89.

Julien, Catherine J. *Reading Inca History*. Iowa City: University of Iowa Press, 2000.

Juzda, Elise. "Skulls, Science, and the Spoils of War: Craniological Studies at the United States Army Medical Museum, 1868–1900." *Studies in History and Philosophy of Biological and Biomedical Sciences* 40 (2009): 156–167.

Kagan, Richard L. "Prescott's Paradigm: American Historical Scholarship and the Decline of Spain." *American Historical Review* 101, no. 2 (1996): 423–446.

Kaufmann Doig, Federico. *Historia de la Arqueología Peruana*. Lima: 1961.

Kaufmann Doig, Federico. *El Perú Antiguo. Historia general de los Peruanos*, T. 1. Lima: Peisa, 1980.

Kaulicke, Peter. "Corporealities of Death in the Central Andes (ca. 9000–2000 BC)." In *Death Rituals, Social Order and the Archaeology of Immortality in the Ancient World*, edited by Colin Renfrew, Michael J. Boyd, Iain Morley, 111–129. Cambridge: Cambridge University Press, 2015.

Kehoe, Alice Beck. "Manifest Destiny as the Order of Nature." In *Nature and Antiquities: The Making of Archaeology in the Americas*, edited by Philip L. Kohl, Irina Podgorny, and Stefanie Gänger, 186–201. Tucson: University of Arizona Press, 2014.

Kelton, Paul. *Cherokee Medicine, Colonial Germs: An Indigenous Nation's Fight against Smallpox, 1518–1824*. Norman: University of Oklahoma Press, 2015.

Kilroy-Ewbank, Lauren G. "Fashioning a Prince for All the World to See: Guaman Poma's Self-Portraits in the Nueva Corónica." *The Americas* 75, no. 1 (2018): 47–94.

Klaus, Haagen D., and Manuel E. Tam. "*Requiem Aeternam?:* Archaeothanatology of Mortuary Ritual in Colonial Mórrope, North Coast of Peru." In *Living with the Dead in the Andes*, edited by Izumi Shimada and James L. Fitzsimmons, 267–303. Tucson: University of Arizona Press, 2015.

Kohl, Philip L., Irina Podgorny, and Stefanie Gänger, eds. *Nature and Antiquities: The Making of Archaeology in the Americas*. Tucson: University of Arizona Press, 2014.

Kolar, Miriam. "Tuned to the Senses: An Archaeoacoustic Perspective on Ancient Chavín." *The Appendix* 1, no. 3 (22 July 2013): http://theappendix.net/issues/2013/7/tuned-to-the-sen ses-an-archaeoacoustic-perspective-on-ancient-chavin.

Kole de Peralta, Kathleen M. "The Nature of Colonial Bodies: Public Health in Lima, Peru, 1535–1635." PhD diss., University of Notre Dame, 2015.

Kopytoff, Igor. "The Cultural Biography of Things: Commoditization as Process." In *The Social Life of Things: Commodities in Cultural Perspective*, edited by Arjun Appadurai, 64–92. Cambridge: Cambridge University Press, 1986.

Kubler, George. *The Indian Caste of Peru, 1795–1940; A Population Study Based upon Tax Records and Census Reports*. Washington, DC: US Government Printing Office, 1952.

Lamana, Gonzalo. *Domination without Dominance: Inca-Spanish Encounters in Early Colonial Peru*. Durham, NC: Duke University Press, 2008.

Laqueur, Thomas W. *The Work of the Dead: A Cultural History of Human Remains*. Princeton, NJ: Princeton University Press, 2015.

Larson, Brooke. *Trials of Nation Making: Liberalism, Race, and Ethnicity in the Andes, 1810–1910.* Cambridge: Cambridge University Press, 2004.

Larson, Carolyne. *Our Indigenous Ancestors: A Cultural History of Museums, Science, and Identity in Argentina, 1877–1943.* University Park: Pennsylvania State University Press, 2015.

Latour, Bruno. "On the Partial Existence of Existing *and* Nonexisting Objects." In *Biographies of Scientific Objects,* edited by Lorraine Daston, 247–251. Chicago: University of Chicago Press, 2000.

Lau, George F. *Ancient Alterity in the Andes: A Recognition of Others.* New York: Routledge, 2013.

Lau, George F. "Animating Idolatry: Making Ancestral Kin and Personhood in Ancient Peru." *Religions* 12, no. 287 (2021): 1–18.

Lau, George F. "Different Kinds of Dead: Presencing Andean Expired Beings." in *Death Rituals, Social Order and the Archaeology of Immortality in the Ancient World,* edited by Colin Renfrew, Michael J. Boyd, and Iain Morley, 168–186. Cambridge: Cambridge University Press, 2015.

Lazure, Guy. "Possessing the Sacred: Monarchy and Identity in Philip II's Relic Collection at the Escorial." *Renaissance Quarterly* 60, no. 1 (Spring 2007): 58–93.

Lechtman, Heather. "The Inka, and Andean Metallurgical Tradition." In *Variations in the Expressions of Inca Power: A Symposium at Dumbarton Oaks, 18 and 19 October 1997,* edited by Richard R. Burger, Craig Morris, and Ramiro Matos Mendieta, 313–343. Washington, DC: Dumbarton Oaks, 2007.

Leonard, Tom. "American Indian Yaqui Warriors Laid to Rest." *Daily Telegraph,* November 17, 2009.

Levine, Philippa. *The Amateur and the Professional: Antiquarians, Historians, and Archaeologists in Victorian England, 1838–1886.* Cambridge: Cambridge University Press, 1986.

Lewis, Jason E., David DeGusta, Marc R. Meyer, Janet M. Monge, Alan E. Mann, and Ralph L. Holloway. "The Mismeasure of Science: Stephen Jay Gould versus Samuel George Morton on Skulls and Bias." *PLoS Biol* 9, no. 6 (June 2011): e1001071, https://journals.plos.org/plosbiology/article?id=10.1371/journal.pbio.1001071.

Lombardi, Guido, and Bradymir Bitzen Bravo Meza. "Tello y los restos humanos de los Huarochiranos ancestrales: Hacia la repatriación." Paper presented at the I Congreso Regional de Investigaciones en las provincias de Yauyos y Huarochirí—Ayer, Hoy y Mañana: A doscientos años de nuestra independencia. Online conference, 8 July 2021.

Lombardi, Guido, and Conrado Rodríguez Martín. "Fake and Alien Mummies." In *The Handbook of Mummy Studies,* edited by Dong Hoon Shin and Raffaella Bianucci, 1139–1152. Springer Nature, Singapore Ltd., 2021.

Lonetree, Amy. *Decolonizing Museums: Representing Native America in National and Tribal Museums.* Chapel Hill: University of North Carolina Press, 2012.

López Lenci, Yazmín. *El Cusco, paqarina moderna: Cartografía de una modernidad e identidades en los Andes peruanos (1900–1935).* Lima: Fondo Editorial Universidad Nacional Mayor de San Marcos—Consejo Nacional de Ciencia y Tecnología, 2004.

Lossio, Jorge. "British Medicine in the Peruvian Andes: The Travels of Archibald Smith M.D. (1820–1870)." *História, Ciências, Saúde-Manguinhos* 13, no. 4 (2006): 833–850.

Lovis, W. A., J. M. Capriles, and D. T. Rodriguez. "La repatriación de una momia Boliviana del Museo de la Universidad Estatal de Michigan al Estado Plurinacional de Bolivia." *Revista Textos Antropológicos* 19, no. 1 (forthcoming).

Lowry, Lyn Brandon. "Forging an Indian Nation: Urban Indians under Spanish Colonial Control, Lima, Peru 1535–1765." PhD diss., University of California, Berkeley, 1991.

Luckhurst, Roger. "Science versus Rumour: Artefaction and Counter-Narrative in the Egyptian Rooms of the British Museum." *History and Anthropology* 23, no. 2 (2012): 257–269.

Luque Talaván, Miguel. "Los libros de huacas en el Virreinato del Perú: Fiscalidad y control regio en torno a los tesoros prehispánicos enterrados." In *La Moneda: Investigación y fuentes archivísticas,* edited by María Teresa Muñoz Serulla, 293–311. Madrid: Universidad Complutense de Madrid y Archivo Histórico Nacional, 2012.

Lyman, R. Lee, and Michael J. O'Brien. "Americanist Stratigraphic Excavation and the Measurement of Culture Change." *Journal of Archaeological Method and Theory* 6, no. 1 (1999): 55–108.

Lynch, John. *San Martín: Argentine Soldier, American Hero.* New Haven, CT: Yale University Press, 2009.

MacCormack, Sabine. "Ethnography in South America: The First Two Hundred Years." In *Cambridge History of the Native Peoples of the Americas,* Vol. 3: *South America,* edited by Frank Salomon and Stuart B. Schwartz, 96–187. New York: Cambridge University Press, 1999.

MacCormack, Sabine. "History, Historical Record, and Ceremonial Action: Incas and Spaniards in Cuzco." *Comparative Studies in Society and History* 43, no. 2 (April 2001): 329–363.

MacCormack, Sabine. *On the Wings of Time: Rome, the Incas, Spain, and Peru.* Princeton, NJ: Princeton University Press, 2007.

MacCormack, Sabine. "*Pachacuti*: Miracles, Punishments, and Last Judgment: Visionary Past and Prophetic Future in Early Colonial Peru." *American Historical Review* 93, no. 4 (October 1988): 960–1006.

MacCormack, Sabine. *Religion in the Andes: Vision and Imagination in Colonial Peru.* Princeton, NJ: Princeton University Press, 1991.

Magubane, Zine. "Simians, Savages, Skulls, and Sex: Science and Colonial Militarism in Nineteenth-Century South Africa." In *Race, Nature, and the Politics of Difference,* edited by Donald S. Moore, Jake Kosek, and Anand Pandian, 99–121. Durham, NC: Duke University Press, 2003.

Majluf, Natalia. "'Ce n'est pas le Pérou,' or, the Failure of Authenticity: Marginal Cosmopolitans at the Paris Universal Exhibition of 1855." *Critical Inquiry* 23, no. 4 (Summer 1997): 868–893.

Majluf, Natalia. "The Creation of the Image of the Indian in 19th-Century Peru: The Paintings of Francisco Laso (1823–1869)." PhD diss., University of Texas at Austin, 1995.

Majluf, Natalia. *Escultura y espacio público: Lima, 1850–1879.* Lima: Instituto de Estudios Peruanos, 1994.

Majluf, Natalia. *Inventing Indigenism: Francisco Laso's Image of Modern Peru.* Austin: University of Texas Press, 2021.

Majluf, Natalia. "De la rebelión al museo: genealogías y retratos de los Incas, 1781–1900." In *Los incas, reyes del Perú,* edited by Thomas Cummins, Gabriela Ramos, Elena Phipps, Juan Carlos Estenssoro, Luis Eduardo Wuffarde, and Natalia Majluf, 253–327. Lima: Banco de Crédito, 2005.

Majluf, Natalia. "El rostro del Inca: Raza y representación en los funerales de Atahualpa de Luis Montero." *Illapa* 1, no. 1 (2004): 11–28.

Mallon, Florencia E. *Peasant and Nation: The Making of Postcolonial Mexico and Peru.* Berkeley: University of California Press, 1995.

Mangan, Jane E. *Transatlantic Obligations: Creating the Bonds of Family in Conquest-Era Peru and Spain.* New York: Oxford University Press, 2016.

Mannheim, Bruce. *The Language of the Incas since the European Invasion.* Austin: University of Texas Press, 1991.

Marinozzi, Silvia, and Gino Fornaciari. *Le mummie e l'arte medica nell'evo modern.* Rome: La Sapienza, 2005.

Marquet, Pablo A., Calogero M. Santoro, Claudio Latorre, Vivien G. Standen, Sebastián R. Abades, Marcelo M. Rivadeneira, Bernardo Arriaza, and Michael E. Hochberg. "Emergence of Social Complexity among Coastal Hunter-Gatherers in the Atacama Desert of Northern Chile." *Proceedings of the National Academy of Sciences of the United States of America* 109, no. 37 (2012): 14754–14760.

Martínez Vidal, Alvar, and José Pardo Tomás. "Anatomical Theatres and the Teaching of Anatomy in Early Modern Spain." *Medical History* 49, no. 3 (July, 2005): 251–280.

Martinko, Whitney A. "So Majestic a Monument of Antiquity': Landscape, Knowledge, and Authority in the Early National West." *Buildings & Landscapes: Journal of the Vernacular Architecture Forum* 16, no. 1 (2009): 29–61.

Mattos, Leonardo. "Los retratos de incas y reyes pintados en roma en 1597, con algunas consideraciones sobre Gonzalo Ruiz y Pérez de Alesio." In *Manierismo y transición al Barroco. Memoria del III Encuentrof Internacional sobre Barroco*, edited by Norma Campos Vera, 381–384. Pamplona: GRISO-Universidad de Navarra / Fundación Visión Cultural, 2005.

McEvoy, Carmen. "El motín de las palabras: la caída de Bernardo de Monteagudo y la forja de la cultura política limeña (1821–1822)." *Boletín del Instituto Riva Agüero* 23 (Lima, 1996): 89–139.

McVicker, Donald. "Patrons, Popularizers, and Professionals: The Institutional Setting of Late Nineteenth-Century Anthropology in Chicago." In *Coming of Age in Chicago: The 1893 World's Fair and the Coalescence of American Anthropology*, edited by Curtis M. Hinsley and David R. Wilcox, 374–404. Lincoln: University of Nebraska Press, 2016.

Medrano, Manuel. *Quipus: Mil años de historia anudada en los Andes y su futuro digital.* Lima: Planeta Perú, 2021.

Menaker, Alexander. "Becoming 'Rebels' and 'Idolaters' in the Valley of Volcanoes, Southern Peru." *International Journal of Historical Archaeology* 23 (2019): 915–946.

Menand, Louis. *The Metaphysical Club.* New York: Farrar, Straus and Giroux, 2001.

Méndez Gastelumendi, Cecilia. "Incas sí, Indios no: Notes on Peruvian Creole Nationalism and Its Contemporary Crisis." *Journal of Latin American Studies* 28, no. 1 (1996): 197–225.

Méndez Rodríguez, Daniel. *Momias, xaxos y mirlados: Las narraciones sobre el embalsamiento de los aborígenes de las Islas Canarias (1482–1803).* La Laguna-Tenerife: Instituto de Estudios Canarios, 2014.

Mendieta, Eduardo. "Enlightened Readers: Thomas Jefferson, Immanuel Kant, Jorge Juan, and Antonio de Ulloa." In *Decolonizing American Philosophy*, edited by Corey McCall and Philip McReynolds, 83–110. Albany: State University of New York Press, 2021.

Mendoza-Mori, Américo. "Quechua Language Programs in the United States: Cultural Hubs for Indigenous Cultures." *Chiricú Journal: Latina/o Literatures, Arts, and Cultures* 1, no. 2 (2017): 43–55.

Metzl, Jonathan, and Joel D. Howell. "Great Moments: Authenticity, Ideology, and the Telling of Medical 'History.'" *Literature and Medicine* 25, no. 2 (Fall 2006): 502–521.

Midtrød, Tom Arne. "'Calling for More Than Human Vengeance': Desecrating Native Graves in Early America." *Early American Studies* 17, no. 3 (2019): 280–314.

Mikecz, Jeremy M. "Beyond Cajamarca: A Spatial Narrative Reimagining of the Encounter in Peru, 1532–1533." *Hispanic American Historical Review* 100, no. 2 (May 2020): 195–232.

Millaire, Jean-François. "The Manipulation of Human Remains in Moche Society: Delayed Burials, Grave Reopening, and Secondary Offerings of Human Bones on the Peruvian North Coast." *Latin American Antiquity* 15, no. 4 (December 2004): 371–388.

Miller, Nicola. *Republics of Knowledge: Nations of the Future in Latin America.* Princeton, NJ: Princeton University Press, 2020.

Miller, Rory. "The Making of the Grace Contract: British Bondholders and the Peruvian Government, 1885–1890." *Journal of Latin American Studies* 8, no. 1 (1976): 73–100.

Mills, Kenneth. *Idolatry and Its Enemies: Colonial Andean Religion and Extirpation, 1640–1750.* Princeton, NJ: Princeton University Press, 1997.

Mills, Kenneth R., William B. Taylor, and Sandra Lauderdale Graham, eds. *Colonial Latin America: A Documentary History.* Lanham, MD: SR Books, 2004.

Mitchell, Paul Wolff. "The Mismeasure of All Things: Objectivity and Bias in Stephen Jay Gould's Critique of Samuel G. Morton and the History of Early American Craniometry." MA thesis, University of Pennsylvania, 2014.

Mitchell, Paul Wolff, and John S. Michael. "Bias, Brains, and Skulls: Tracing the Legacy of Scientific Racism in the Nineteenth-Century Works of Samuel George Morton and Friedrich Tiedemann." In *Embodied Difference: Divergent Bodies in Public Discourse*, edited by Christina Jackson and Jamie Thomas, 77–98. Lanham, MD: Lexington Books, 2019.

Monteiro, Lyra. "Racializing the Ancient World: Ancestry and Identity in the Early United States." PhD diss., Brown University, 2012.

Moore, Jerry D. "The Social Basis of Sacred Spaces in the Prehispanic Andes: Ritual Landscapes of the Dead in Chimú and Inka Societies." *Journal of Archaeological Method and Theory* 11, no. 1 (March 2004): 83–124.

Moshenska, Gabriel. "Unrolling Egyptian Mummies in Nineteenth-century Britain." *British Journal for the History of Science* 47, no. 3 (2014): 451–477.

Mould de Pease, Mariana. *Machu Picchu y el Código de Ética de la Sociedad de Arqueología Americana.* Lima: Pontificia Universidad Catolica del Peru, 2003.

Mumford, Jeremy Ravi. "The Inca Priest on the Mormon Stage." *Common-Place* 5/4 (July 2005), http://commonplace.online/article/the-inca-priest-on-the-mormon-stage/

Mumford, Jeremy Ravi. "Litigation as Ethnography in Sixteenth-Century Peru: Polo de Ondegardo and the Mitimaes." *Hispanic American Historical Review* 88, no. 1 (February 2008): 5–40.

Mumford, Jeremy Ravi. *Vertical Empire: The General Resettlement of Indians in the Colonial Andes.* Durham, NC: Duke University Press, 2012.

Mundy, Barbara E. *The Mapping of New Spain: Indigenous Cartography and the Maps of the Relaciones Geográficas.* Chicago: University of Chicago Press, 1996.

Murphy, Melissa S. "Colonial Demography and Bioarchaeology." In *The Oxford Handbook of the Incas,* edited by Sonia Alconini and R. Alan Covey, 721–740. New York: Oxford University Press, 2018.

Muschi, Gianncarlo. "Desarrollo de la informalidad y prácticas alternativas en la comunidad peruana de Paterson, Nueva Jersey." *Antípoda. Revista de Antropología y Arqueología,* no. 43 (2021): 51–73.

Nappi, Carla. "Bolatu's Pharmacy: Theriac in Early Modern China." *Early Science and Medicine* 14, no. 6 (2009): 737–764.

Nash, Stephen E., and Gary M. Feinman, eds. *Curators, Collections, and Contexts: Anthropology at the Field Museum, 1893–2002.* Fieldiana: Anthropology no. 36. Chicago: Field Museum of Natural History, 2003.

Necochea López, Raúl. *A History of Family Planning in Twentieth-Century Peru.* Chapel Hill: University of North Carolina Press, 2014.

Neill, Anna. "Buccaneer Ethnography: Nature, Culture, and Nation in the Journals of William Dampier." *Eighteenth-Century Studies* 33, no. 2 (2000): 165–180.

Nelson, Dana D. *National Manhood: Capitalist Citizenship and the Imagined Fraternity of White Men.* Durham, NC: Duke University Press, 1998.

Newson, Linda. *Making Medicines in Early Colonial Lima, Peru: Apothecaries, Science and Society.* Leiden: Brill, 2017.

Niekerk, Carl. "Man and Orangutan in Eighteenth-Century Thinking: Retracing the Early History of Dutch and German Anthropology." *Monatshefte* 96, no. 4 (Winter 2004): 477–502.

Niles, Susan A. *The Shape of Inca History: Narrative and Architecture in an Andean Empire.* Iowa City: University of Iowa Press, 1999.

Nilsson Stutz, Liv. "To Gaze upon the Dead: The Exhibition of Human Remains as Cultural and Political Process in Scandinavia and the USA." In *Archaeologists and the Dead: Mortuary Archaeology in Contemporary Society,* edited by Howard Williams and Melanie Giles, 268–292. Oxford: Oxford University Press, 2016.

Noack, Karoline, and Daniel Grana-Behrens. "Introduction." In *From "Bronze Rooster" to Ekeko: Impulses toward Ethnological Provenance Research in University Collections and Museums,* eds. Daniel Grana-Behrens and Karoline Noack, 5–18. Bonn: University of Bonn / BASA Museum, 2020.

Norton, Marcy. *Sacred Gifts, Profane Pleasures: The History of Tobacco and Chocolate in the Atlantic World.* Ithaca, NY: Cornell University Press, 2008.

Norton, Marcy. "Subaltern Technologies and Early Modernity in the Atlantic World." *Colonial Latin American Review* 26, no. 1 (2017): 18–38.

Nystrom, Kenneth C. "Trepanation in the Chachapoya Region of Northern Perú." *International Journal of Osteoarchaeology* 17 (2007): 39–51.

O'Brien, Jean M. *Firsting and Lasting: Writing Indians Out of Existence in New England.* Minneapolis: University of Minnesota Press, 2010.

O'Phelan, Scarlett. "Dionisio Inca Yupanqui y Mateo Pumacahua: Dos indios nobles frente a las Cortes de Cádiz (1808–1814)." In *Las independencias desde la perspectiva de los actores sociales*, edited by Juan Luis Orrego Penagos, Cristóbal Aljovín de Losada, and José Ignacio López Soria, 93–104. Lima: Pontificia Universidad Católica del Perú, 2009.

O'Phelan, Scarlett. "El mito de la 'independencia concedida': Los programas políticas del siglo XVIII y del temprano XIX en el Perú y Alto Perú, 1730–1814" [1984]. In *La independencia del Perú: ¿Concedida, conseguida, concebida?*, edited by Carlos Contreras and Luis Miguel Glave, 209–245. Lima: Instituto de Estudios Peruanos, 2015.

Ordoñez, Maria Patricia. *Unbundled: European Collecting of Andean Mummies, 1850–1930.* PhD diss., Universitet Leiden, Ridderprint BV, 2019.

Owens, Deidre Cooper. *Medical Bondage: Race, Gender, and the Origins of American Gynecology.* Athens: University of Georgia Press, 2017.

Padilla Deza, Fernando. "El concepto y la representación de lo indio en la propuesta política de Julio César Tello Rojas (1917–1929)." MA thesis, Universidad Nacional Mayor de San Marcos (Lima), 2018.

Pagden, Anthony. *European Encounters with the New World.* New Haven, CT: Yale University Press, 1993.

Pagden, Anthony. *The Fall of Natural Man: The American Indian and the Origins of Comparative Ethnology.* Cambridge: Cambridge University Press, 1982.

Painter, Nell Irvin. *The History of White People.* New York: W. W. Norton, 2010.

Palma, Patricia, and José Ragas. "The Miraculous Doctor Pun, Chinese Healers, and Their Patients in Lima, 1868–1930." In *The Gray Zones of Medicine: Healers & History in Latin America*, edited by Diego Armus and Pablo F. Gómez, 138–154. Pittsburgh: University of Pittsburgh Press, 2021.

Patterson, Thomas C. "Political Economy and a Discourse Called 'Peruvian Archaeology.'" *Culture and History* 4 (1989): 35–84.

Peard, Julyan. *Race, Place, and Medicine: The Idea of the Tropics in Nineteenth-Century Brazil.* Durham, NC: Duke University Press, 2000.

Penny, H. Glenn. *In Humboldt's Shadow: A Tragic History of German Ethnology.* Princeton, NJ: Princeton University Press, 2021.

Penny, H. Glenn. *Objects of Culture: Ethnology and Ethnographic Museums in Imperial Germany.* Chapel Hill: University of North Carolina Press, 2002.

Penry, S. Elizabeth. *The People Are King: The Making of an Andean Indigenous Politics.* New York: Oxford University Press, 2019.

Perry, Mary Elizabeth. *The Handless Maiden: Moriscos and the Politics of Religion in Early Modern Spain.* Princeton, NJ: Princeton University Press, 2004.

Peters, Ann Hudson. "The Cemetery of Paracas Necropolis: Mortuary Practice and Social Network." In *Tres ensayos sobre Paracas Necrópolis: Historia de la investigación, tecnologías, textiles y prácticas mortuorias*, edited by Carole Sinclaire, Andrea Torres, and José Berenguer, 43–66. Santiago: ArtEncuentro-Museo Chileno de Arte Precolombino, 2016.

Peters, Ann H., and L. Alberto Ayarza. "Julio C. Tello y el desarrollo de estudios andinos en los Estados Unidos: Intercambios e influencias 1915–1950." In *Historia de la Arqueología en el Perú del Siglo XX*, edited by Cesar Astuhuamán and Henry Tantaleán, 43–84. Lima: Instituto Francés de Estudios Andinos, 2013.

Pillsbury, Joanne. "Finding the Ancient in the Andes: Archaeology and Geology, 1850–1890." In *Nature and Antiquities: The Making of Archaeology in the Americas*, edited by Philip L. Kohl, Irina Podgorny, and Stefanie Gänger, 47–68. Tucson: University of Arizona Press, 2014.

Pillsbury, Joanne, and Lisa Trever. "The King, the Bishop, and the Creation of an American Antiquity." *Ñawpa Pacha: Journal of Andean Archaeology* 29, no. 1 (2008): 191–219.

Pimentel, Juan. "The Iberian Vision: Science and Empire in the Framework of a Universal Monarchy, 1500–1800." *Osiris* 15 (2000): 17–30.

Pimentel, Juan. *The Rhinoceros and the Megatherium: An Essay in Natural History.* Cambridge, MA: Harvard University Press, 2017.

Pimentel, Juan. *Viajeros científicos: Jorge Juan, Mutis y Malaspina.* Madrid: Tres Cantos, 2008.

Podgorny, Irina. "De ángeles, gigantes y megaterios: Saber, dinero y honor en el intercambio de fósiles de las provincias del Plata en la primera mitad del siglo XIX." In *Los lugares del saber: Contextos locales y redes transnacionales en la formación del conocimiento moderno,* edited by Ricardo D. Salvatore, 125–158. Rosario, Argentina: Beatriz Viterbo, 2007.

Podgorny, Irina. "Bones and Devices in the Constitution of Paleontology in Argentina at the End of the Nineteenth Century." *Science in Context* 18, no. 2 (2005): 249–283.

Podgorny, Irina. "Fossil Dealers, the Practices of Comparative Anatomy and British Diplomacy in Latin America, 1820–1840." *British Journal for the History of Science* 46, no. 4 (2013): 647–674.

Podgorny, Irina. "Human Origins in the New World? Florentino Ameghino and the Emergence of Prehistoric Archaeology in the Americas (1875–1912)." *PaleoAmerica* 1, no. 1 (2015): 68–80.

Podgorny, Irina. *El sendero del tiempo y de las causas accidentales.* Rosario, Argentina: Prohistoria Editores, 2009.

Podgorny, Irina, and Maria Margaret Lopes. *El desierto en una vitrina: Museos e historia natural en la Argentina, 1810–1890.* Rosario, Argentina: Prohistoria Ediciones, 2014 [2008].

Podgorny, Irina, and Gustavo Politis. " 'It is not all roses here': Aleš Hrdlička's Travelogue and His Trip to Argentina in 1910." *Revista de História da Arte e Arqueologia* 3 (2000): 95–105.

Pomata, Gianna. "Observation Rising: Birth of an Epistemic Genre, 1500–1650." In *Histories of Scientific Observation,* edited by Lorraine Daston and Elizabeth Lunbeck, 45–80. Chicago: University of Chicago Press, 2011.

Poole, Deborah. "Landscape and the Imperial Subject: U.S. Images of the Andes, 1859–1960." In *Close Encounters of Empire: Writing the Cultural History of U.S.–Latin American Relations,* edited by Gilbert M. Joseph, Catherine C. Le Grand, and Ricardo D. Salvatore, 107–138. Durham, NC: Duke University Press, 1998.

Poole, Deborah. *Vision, Race, and Modernity: A Visual Economy of the Andean Image World.* Princeton, N.J.: Princeton University Press, 1997.

Portuondo, María P. *Secret Science: Spanish Cosmography and the New World.* Chicago: University of Chicago Press, 2009.

Poskett, James. *Materials of the Mind: Phrenology, Race, and the Global History of Science, 1815–1920.* Chicago: University of Chicago Press, 2019.

Pozorski, Sheila, and Thomas Pozorski. "Early Cultural Complexity on the North Coast of Peru." In *Handbook of South American Archaeology,* edited by Helaine Silverman and William H. Isbell, 607–631. New York: Springer, 2008.

Premo, Bianca. *Children of the Father King: Youth, Authority & Legal Minority in Colonial Lima.* Chapel Hill: University of North Carolina Press, 2005.

Premo, Bianca. "Custom Today: Temporality, Customary Law, and Indigenous Enlightenment." *Hispanic American Historical Review* 94, no. 3 (August 2014): 355–379.

Prieto Burmester, O. Gabriel. "Dos forjadores de las Ciencias Sociales en el Perú: Sus publicaciones y confrontaciones." *Arqueología y Sociedad* 22 (2010): 1–34.

Pringle, Heather. *The Mummy Congress: Science, Obsession, and the Everlasting Dead.* New York: Hyperion, 2001.

Puente Luna, José Carlos de la. *Andean Cosmopolitans: Seeking Justice and Reward at the Spanish Royal Court.* Austin: University of Texas Press, 2018.

Puente Luna, José Carlos de la. "Choquecasa va a la Audiencia: Cronistas, litigantes y el debate sobre la autoría del Manuscrito Quechua de Huarochirí." *Histórica* (Lima) 39, no. 1 (2015): 139–158.

Puente Luna, José Carlos de la. "Incas pecheros y caballeros hidalgos: La desintegración del orden incaico y la génesis de la nobleza incaica colonial en el Cuzco del siglo XVI." *Revista andina* 54 (2016): 9–95.

Puente Luna, José Carlos de la. "That Which Belongs to All: Khipus, Community and Indigenous Legal Activism in the Early Colonial Andes." *The Americas* 72, no. 1 (2015): 19–54.

Puente Luna, José Carlos de la, and Renzo Honores. "Guardianes de la real justicia: Alcaldes de indios, costumbre y justicia local en Huarochirí colonial." *Histórica* 40, no. 2 (2016): 11–47.

Quiñones Tinoco, Leticia. *El Perú en la vitrina. El progreso material del Perú a través de las exposiciones (1851–1893)*. Lima: Universidad Nacional de Ingeniería, 2007.

Quispe-Agnoli, Rocío. "Taking Possession of the New World: Powerful Female Agency of Early Colonial Accounts of Perú." *Legacy* 28, no. 2 (2011): 257–289.

Racine, Karen. *Francisco de Miranda: A Transatlantic Life in the Age of Revolution*. Wilmington, DE: Scholarly Resources Books, 2003.

Racine, Karen. "Proxy Pasts: The Use of British Historical References in Spanish American Independence Rhetoric, 1808–1828." *English Historical Review* 132, no. 557 (2017): 863–884.

Racine, Karen. "'This England and This Now': British Cultural and Intellectual Influence in the Spanish American Independence Era." *Hispanic American Historical Review* 90, no. 3 (August 2010): 423–454.

Radicato di Primeglio, Carlos. *Estudios sobre los quipus*. Lima: UNMSM, Fondo Editorial; COFIDE; Instituto Italiano di Cultura, 2006.

Radin, Joanna. *Life on Ice: A History of New Uses for Cold Blood*. Chicago: University of Chicago Press, 2017.

Radin, Joanna, and Emma Kowal, eds. *Cryopolitics: Frozen Life in a Melting World*. Cambridge, MA: MIT Press, 2017.

Ragas, José. "Los 'espejos rotos' de la opinion pública: Periodismo y política en el Perú (1845–1860)." *Debate y Perspectivas*, no. 3 (2003): 107–125.

Ramírez, Susan E. *To Feed and Be Fed: The Cosmological Bases of Authority and Identity in the Andes*. Stanford, CA: Stanford University Press, 2005.

Ramírez, Susan E. *Patriarcas provinciales. La tenencia de la tierra y la economía del poder en el Perú colonial*. Madrid: Alianza Editorial, 1991.

Ramírez, Susan E. *The World Upside Down: Cross-Cultural Contact and Conflict in Sixteenth-Century Peru*. Stanford, CA: Stanford University Press, 1996.

Ramón Joffre, Gabriel. *El neoperuano: Arqueología, estilo nacional y pasisaje urbano en Lima, 1910–1940*. Lima: Municipalidad Metropolitana de Lima: Sequilao Editores, 2014.

Ramos, Gabriela. *Death and Conversion in the Andes: Lima and Cuzco, 1532–1670*. Notre Dame, IN: University of Notre Dame Press, 2010.

Ramos, Gabriela. "The Incas of Cuzco and the Transformation of Sacred Space under Spanish Colonial Rule." In *Space and Conversion in Global Perspective*, edited by Giuseppe Marcocci, Wietse de Boer, Aliocha Maldavsky, and Ilaria Pavan, 61–80. Leiden: Koninklijke Brill, 2015.

Ravines, Rogger. *Los museos del Perú: Breve historia y guía*. Lima: Dirección General de Museos, Instituto Nacional de Cultura, 1989.

Redman, Samuel J. *Bone Rooms: From Scientific Racism to Human Prehistory in Museums*. Cambridge, MA: Harvard University Press, 2016.

Redman, Samuel J. *Prophets and Ghosts: The Story of Salvage Anthropology*. Cambridge, MA: Harvard University Press, 2021.

Restall, Matthew. *When Montezuma Met Cortes: The True Story of the Meeting That Changed History*. New York: HarperCollins, 2018.

Rice, Mark. *Making Machu Picchu: The Politics of Tourism in Twentieth-Century Peru*. Chapel Hill: University of North Carolina Press, 2018.

Richter, Daniel K. *Facing East from Indian Country*. Cambridge, MA: Harvard University Press, 2003.

Rick, John W. "Innovation, Religion and Authority at the Formative Period Andean Cult Centre of Chavín de Huántar." In *Religion and Innovation: Antagonists or Partners?*, edited by Donald A. Yerxa, 11–26. London: Bloomsbury, 2015.

Riding In, James. "Decolonizing NAGPRA." In *For Indigenous Eyes Only: A Decolonization Handbook*, edited by Wsziyatawin Angela Wilson and Michael Yellow Bird, 53–66. Santa Fe, NM: School for Advanced Research, 2005.

Riding In, James. "Six Pawnee Crania: The Historical and Contemporary Significance of the Massacre and Decapitation of Pawnee Indians in 1869." *American Indian Culture and Research Journal* 16, no. 2 (1992): 101–117.

Riggs, Christina. "Loose Bodies: Reserve Collections, Curatorial Reservations, and the Ancient Egyptian Dead." In *Museum Storage and Meaning: Tales from the Crypt*, edited by Mirjam Brusius and Kavita Singh, 253–262. Abingdon: Routledge, 2018.

Riggs, Christina. *Unwrapping Ancient Egypt*. London: Bloomsbury, 2014.

Rivera, Mario A. "The Preceramic Chinchorro Mummy Complex of Northern Chile: Context, Style, and Purpose." In *Tombs for the Living: Andean Mortuary Practices*, edited by Tom D. Dillehay, 43–77. Washington, DC: Dumbarton Oaks Research Library and Collection, 2011 [1995].

Riviale, Pascal. "La marine française et l'archéologie du Pérou au xixe siècle," *Bulletin de l'Institut Pierre Renouvin* 2, no. 46 (2017): 123–137.

Riviale, Pascal. *Los viajeros franceses en busca del Perú antiguo. 1821–1914*. Nueva edición [en línea]. Lima: Institut français d'études andines, Fondo Editorial de la Pontificia Universidad Cátolica del Perú, 2000.

Roa-de-la-Carrera, Cristían A. *Histories of Infamy: Francisco López de Gómara and the Ethics of Spanish Imperialism*, translated by Scott Sessions. Boulder: University Press of Colorado, 2005.

Robinson, Michael. *The Lost White Tribe: Explorers, Scientists, and the Theory That Changed a Continent*. New York: Oxford University Press, 2016.

Rodriguez, Julia. "Beyond Prejudice and Pride: The Human Sciences in Nineteenth- and Twentieth-Century Latin America." *Isis: A Journal of the History of Science Society* 104, no. 4 (December 2013): 807–817.

Rodriguez, Julia. "No 'Mere Accumulation of Material': Fieldwork Prctices and Embedded Evidence in Early (Latin) Americanist Anthropology." In *Evidence in Action between Science and Society: Constructing, Validating, and Contesting Knowledge*, edited by Sarah Ehlers and Stefan Esselborn, 60–79. New York: Routledge, 2022.

Rodriguez, Julia. "South Atlantic Crossings: Fingerprints, Science, and the State in Turn-of-the-Century Argentina." *American Historical Review* 109, no. 2 (April 2004): 1–42.

Rodríguez, Sandra. "Recuperando la mirada, el cuerpo y la voz: El cuerpo del 'Otro' en los museos." *Politeama*, 22 September 2019, https://politeama.pe/2019/09/22/recuperando-la-mirada-el-cuerpo-y-la-voz/.

Rohner, Ronald P. "Franz Boas: Ethnographer on the Northwest Coast." *Pioneers of American Anthropology: The Uses of Biography*, edited by June Helm, 149–212. Seattle: University of Washington Press, 1966.

Rojas-Perez, Isaias. *Mourning Remains: State Atrocity, Exhumations, and Governing the Disappeared in Peru's Postwar Andes*. Stanford, CA: Stanford University Press, 2017.

Roque, Ricardo. "Authorised Histories: Human Remains and the Economies of Credibility in the Science of Race." *Kronos* 44, no. 1 (2018): 69–85.

Roque, Ricardo. *Headhunting and Colonialism: Anthropology and the Circulation of Human Skulls in the Portuguese Empire, 1870–1930*. Basingstoke: Palgrave Macmillan, 2010.

Rosaldo, Renato. "Grief and a Headhunter's Rage." In *Death, Mourning, and Burial: A Cross-cultural Reader*, edited by Antonius C. G. Robbin, 167–178. Malden, MA: Blackwell, 2004.

Rosas Buendía, Miguel. "Mariano de Rivero y un diálogo tecnológico con el mundo andino." *Sílex* 7, no. 1 (Enero–Junio 2017): 143–164.

Rosemblatt, Karin Alejandra. *The Science and Politics of Race in Mexico and the United States, 1910–1950*. Chapel Hill: University of North Carolina Press, 2018.

Rosenblum, Robert. *Modern Painting and the Northern Romantic Tradition. Friedrich to Rothko*. New York: Thames and Hudson, 1975.

Rostworowski de Diez Canseco, Maria. *History of the Inca Realm*. Cambridge: Cambridge University Press, 1998.

Rowe, John Howland. "On Absolute Dating and North Coast History." *Memoirs of the Society for American Archaeology*, no. 4 (1948): 51–52.

Rowe, John Howland. "Ethnography and Ethnology in the Sixteenth Century." *Kroeber Anthropological Society Papers* 30 (Spring 1964): 1–19.

Rowe, John Howland. *Max Uhle, 1856–1944: A Memoir of the Father of Peruvian Archaeology.* University of California Publications in American Archaeology and Ethnology 46, no. 1. Berkeley: University of California Press, 1954.

Rowe, John Howland. "El movimiento nacional Inca en el siglo XVIII." In *Tupac Amaru II,* edited by Alberto Flores Galindo, 13–66. Lima: Retablo de Papel Ed., 1976.

Roy, Susan. "Visualizing Culture and Nature: William Taylor's Murals in the Hall of Northwest Coast Indians, American Museum of Natural History." In *Nature and Antiquities: The Making of Archaeology in the Americas,* edited by Philip L. Kohl, Irina Podgorny, and Stefanie Gänger, 145–166. Tucson: University of Arizona Press, 2014.

Rydell, Robert W. *All the World's a Fair: Visions of Empire at American International Expositions, 1876–1916.* Chicago: University of Chicago Press, 1984.

Safier, Neil. *Measuring the New World: Enlightenment Science and South America.* Chicago and London: University of Chicago Press, 2008.

Sales Salvador, Dora. "Introducción." In Clorinda Matto de Turner, *Aves sin Nido,* ed. Dora Sales Salvador, 15-18. Castelló de la Plana: Biblioteca de la Universitat Jaume, 2006.

Salomon, Frank. "Ancestor Cults and Resistance to the State in Arequipa, ca. 1748–1754." In *Resistance, Rebellion, and Consciousness in the Andean Peasant World, 18th to 20th Centuries,* edited by Steve J. Stern, 148–165. Madison: University of Wisconsin Press, 1987.

Salomon, Frank. "Ancestors, Grave Robbers, and the Possible Antecedents of Cañari 'Inca-ism.'" In *Native and Neighbours in South America,* edited by Harald O. Skar and Frank Salomon, 207–232. Goteborg: Etnografiska Museum Goteborg, 1987.

Salomon, Frank. "Andean Opulence: Indigenous Ideas about Wealth in Colonial Peru." In *The Colonial Andes: Tapestries and Silverwork, 1530–1580,* edited by Elena Phipps, Joanna Hecht, and Cristina Esteras Martín, 115–124. New York: Metropolitan Museum of Art and Yale University Press, 2004.

Salomon, Frank. *At the Mountains' Altar: Anthropology of Religion in an Andean Community.* London: Routledge, 2018.

Salomon, Frank. "'The Beautiful Grandparents': Andean Ancestor Shrines and Mortuary Ritual as Seen through Colonial Records." In *Tombs for the Living: Andean Mortuary Practices,* edited by Tom D. Dillehay, 315–353. Washington, DC: Dumbarton Oaks Research Library and Collection, 2011 [1995].

Salomon, Frank. *The Cord Keepers: Khipus and Cultural Life in a Peruvian Village.* Durham, NC: Duke University Press, 2004.

Salomon, Frank. "Etnología en un terreno desigual: Encuentros andinos, 1532–1985." In *No hay país más diverso. Compendio de antropología peruana II,* edited by Carlos Iván Degregori, Pablo F. Sendón, and Pablo Sandoval, 18–97. Lima: Instituto de Estudios Peruanos, 2012.

Salomon, Frank. "The Historical Development of Andean Ethnology." *Mountain Research and Development* 5, no. 1 (February 1985): 79–98.

Salomon, Frank. "Introductory Essay." In *The Huarochirí Manuscript: A Testament of Ancient and Colonial Andean Religion,* edited by Frank Salomon and George L. Urioste, 1-38. Austin: University of Texas Press, 1991.

Salomon, Frank. "Turbulent Tombs." In *Living with the Dead in the Andes,* edited by Izumi Shimada and James L. Fitzsimmons, 329–347. Tucson: University of Arizona Press, 2015.

Salomon, Frank. "Unethnic Ethnohistory: On Peruvian Peasant Historiography and Ideas of Autonomy." *Ethnohistory* 49, no. 3 (Summer 2002): 475–506.

Salomon, Frank, and Mercedes Niño-Murcia. *The Lettered Mountain: A Peruvian Village's Way with Writing.* Durham, NC: Duke University Press, 2011.

Salvatore, Ricardo D. *Disciplinary Conquest: U.S. Scholars in South America, 1900–1945.* Durham, NC: Duke University Press, 2016.

Salvatore, Ricardo D. "Live Indians in the Museum: Connecting Evolutionary Anthropology with the Conquest of the Desert." In *The Conquest of the Desert: Argentina's Indigenous Peoples and the Battle for History*, edited by Carolyne R. Larson, 97–121. Albuquerque: University of New Mexico Press, 2020.

Salvatore, Ricardo D. "Local versus Imperial Knowledge: Reflections on Hiram Bingham and the Yale Peruvian Expedition." *Nepantla* 4, no. 1 (2003): 67–80.

Salvatore, Ricardo D. "Progress and Backwardness in Book Accumulation: Bancroft, Basadre, and Their Libraries." *Comparative Studies in Society and History* 56, no. 4 (2014): 995–1026.

Salvatore, Ricardo D. "Tres intelectuales peruanos: Conexiones imperiales en la construcción de una cultura nacional." In *Ensayos en torno a la república de las letras en el Perú e Hispanoamérica (ss. XVI–XX)*, edited by Carlos Aguirre and Carmen McEvoy, 353–384. Lima: Instituto Francés de Estudios Andinos, Instituto Riva-Agüero, 2008.

Sánchez-Concha Barrios, Rafael. "Ideologías del Perú republicano del siglo XIX." In *Sobre el Perú: Homenaje a José Agustín de la Puente Candamo*, vol. 2, edited by Margarita Guerra Martinière, Oswaldo Holguín Callo, and César Gutiérrez Muñoz, 1203–1222. Lima: Facultad de Letras y Ciencias Humanas, Fondo Editorial de la Pontificia Universidad Católica del Perú, 2002.

Sandoval, Pablo. "Antropología y antropólogos en el Perú: Discursos y practicás en la representación del indio, 1940–1990." In *No hay país más diverso. Compendio de antropología peruana II*, edited by Carlos Iván Degregori, Pablo F. Sendón, and Pablo Sandoval, 18–97. Lima: Instituto de Estudios Peruanos, 2012.

Sardi, Marina, and Diego Ballestero. "Los cuerpos indígenas entre textos y silencios: El caso de una ñina Aché." *Asclepio. Revista de la Historia de la Medicina y de la Ciencia* 72, no. 2 (2020): 1–13.

Sawday, Jonathan. *The Body Emblazoned: Dissection and the Human Body in Renaissance Culture.* London: Routledge, 1995.

Schjellerup, Inge. *Incas y españoles en la conquista de los Chachapoya.* Lima: Fondo Editorial de la Pontificia Universidad Católica del Perú, Instituto Francés de Estudios Andinos, 2005.

Schiller, Francis. *Paul Broca: Founder of French Anthropology, Explorer of the Brain.* Oxford: Oxford University Press, 1992 [1979].

Schnapp, Alain. "Ancient Europe and Native Americans: A Comparative Reflection on the Roots of Antiquarianism." In *Collecting across Cultures: Material Exchanges in the Early Modern Atlantic World*, edited by Daniela Bleichmar and Peter C. Mancall, 58–79. Philadelphia: University of Pennsylvania Press, 2011.

Schnapp, Alain. "Between Antiquarians and Archaeologists—Continuities and Ruptures." *Antiquity* 76, no. 291 (2002): 134–140.

Schuster, Sven. "The World's Fairs as Spaces of Global Knowledge: Latin American Archaeology and Anthropology in the Age of Exhibitions." *Journal of Global History* 13, no. 1 (2018): 69–93.

Schwartz, Stuart B. *All Can Be Saved: Religious Tolerance in the Iberian Atlantic World.* New Haven, CT: Yale University Press, 2008.

Scott, Heidi V. *Contested Territory: Mapping Peru in the Sixteenth and Seventeenth Centuries.* Notre Dame, IN: University of Notre Dame Press, 2009.

Seed, Patricia. "'Failing to Marvel.' Atahualpa's Encounter with the Word." *Latin American Research Review* 26, no. 1 (1991): 7–32.

Seeman, Erik T. *Death in the New World: Cross-Cultural Encounters, 1492–1800.* Philadelphia: University of Pennsylvania Press, 2010.

Seki, Yuji. "Participation of the Local Community in Archaeological Heritage Management in the North Highlands of Peru." In *Finding Solutions for Protecting and Sharing Archaeological Heritage Resources*, edited by Anne P. Underhill and Lucy C. Salazar, 103–119. New York: Springer Science+Business Media, 2015.

Sellers, Charles Coleman. *Mr. Peale's Museum: Charles Willson Peale and the First Popular Museum of Natural Science and Art.* New York: W. W. Norton & Company, 1980.

Serulnikov, Sergio. *Subverting Colonial Authority: Challenges to Spanish Rule in Eighteenth-Century Southern Andes.* Durham, NC: Duke University Press, 2003.

Shady Solís, Ruth. *Caral Supe, Perú: The Caral-Supe Civilization: 5,000 Years of Cultural Identity in Peru.* Lima: Instituto Nacional de Cultura, 2005.

Shady Solís, Ruth Martha, Jonathan Haas, and Winifred Creamer. "Dating Caral, a Preceramic Site in the Supe Valley on the Central Coast of Peru." *Science* 292, no. 5517 (April 2001): 723–726.

Shapin, Steven. "The Invisible Technician." *American Scientist* 77, no. 6 (1989): 554–563.

Shapin, Steven, and Simon Schaffer. *Leviathan and the Air-Pump: Hobbes, Boyle, and the Experimental Life*. Princeton, NJ: Princeton University Press, 2011 (1985).

Sharratt, Nicola. "Steering Clear of the Dead: Avoiding Ancestors in the Moquegua Valley, Peru." *American Anthropologist* 119, no. 4 (2017): 645–661.

Shimada, Izumi, ed. *The Inka Empire: A Multidisciplinary Approach*. Austin: University of Texas Press, 2015.

Shimada, Izumi. *Pampa Grande and the Mochica Culture*. Austin: University of Texas Press, 1994.

Shimada, Izumi, and James L. Fitzsimmons, eds. *Living with the Dead in the Andes*. Tucson: University of Arizona Press, 2015.

Sillar, Bill. "The Dead and the Drying." *Journal of Material Culture* 1, no. 3 (1996): 259–289.

Silverblatt, Irene. "Imperial Dilemmas, the Politics of Kinship, and Inca Reconstructions of History." *Comparative Studies in Society and History* 30, no. 1 (1988): 83–102.

Silverblatt, Irene. *Modern Inquisitions: Peru and the Colonial Origins of the Civilized World*. Durham, NC: Duke University Press, 2004.

Silverblatt, Irene. *Moon, Sun, and Witches: Gender Ideologies and Class in Inca and Colonial Peru,*. Princeton, NJ: Princeton University Press, 1987.

Silverman, Helaine. "Archaeology and the 1997 Peruvian Hostage Crisis." *Anthropology Today* 15, no. 1 (1999): 9–13.

Siraisi, Nancy G. *History, Medicine, and the Traditions of Renaissance Learning*. Ann Arbor: University of Michigan Press, 2007.

Sivasundaram, Sujit. "Sciences and the Global: On Methods, Questions, and Theory." *Isis: A Journal of the History of Science Society* 101, no. 1 (March 2010): 146–158.

Slovak, Nicole M. "Reassembling the Mortuary Assemblage: New Investigations into the Field Museum's Osteological and Artifact Collections from Ancón, Peru." *Ñawpa Pacha* (2020): DOI: 10.1080/00776297.2019.171036.

Slovak, Nicole, and Bettina Wiegand. "Reconstructing Middle Horizon Mobility Patterns on the Coast of Peru through Strontium Isotope Analysis." *Journal of Archaeological Science* 36, no. 1 (2009): 157–165.

Smith, Kimbra L. "Looting and the Politics of Archaeological Knowledge in Northern Peru." *Ethnos* 70, no. 1 (June 2005): 149–170.

Smith, Murphy D. *A Museum: The History of the Cabinet of Curiosities of the American Philosophical Society*. Philadelphia: American Philosophical Society, 1996.

Snyder, Christina. "The Once and Future Moundbuilders." *Southern Cultures* 26, no. 2 (2020): 96–116.

Sobrevilla Perea, Natalia. "Loyalism and Liberalism in Peru, 1810–1824." In *The Rise of Constitutional Government in the Iberian Atlantic World: The Impact of the Cádiz Constitution of 1812*, edited by Scott Eastman and Natalia Sobrevilla Perea, 111–132. Tuscaloosa: University of Alabama Press, 2015.

Solomon, Michael. *Fictions of Well-Being: Sickly Readers and Vernacular Medical Writing in Late Medieval and Early Modern Spain*. Philadelphia: University of Pennsylvania Press, 2010.

Soto Laveaga, Gabriela. *Jungle Laboratores: Mexican Peasants, National Projects, and the Making of the Pill*. Durham, NC: Duke University Press, 2009.

Spalding, Karen. *Huarochirí: Indian Society under Inca and Spanish Rule*. Stanford, CA: Stanford University Press, 1984.

Stanton, William Ragan. *The Leopard's Spots: Scientific Attitudes toward Race in America, 1815–59*. Chicago: University of Chicago Press, 1966.

Star, Susan Leigh, and James R. Griesemer. "Institutional Ecology, 'Translations' and Boundary Objects: Amateurs and Professionals in Berkeley's Museum of Vertebrate Zoology." *Social Studies of Science* 19, no. 3 (1989): 387–420.

Starn, Orin. *Ishi's Brain: In Search of America's Last "Wild" Indian*. New York: Norton, 2004.

Stein, William W. *Dance in the Cemetery: José Carlos Mariátegui and the Lima Scandal of 1917*. Lanham, MD: University Press of America, 1997.

Steinberg, Ellen F., and Jack H. Prost. "Bringing Ethnography Home: Knut Hjalmar Stolpe's Works in Peru (1884)." *Andean Past* 8, no. 13 (2007): 109–143.

Steinbock-Pratt, Sarah. *Educating the Empire: Teachers and Contested Colonization in the Philippines*. Cambridge: Cambridge University Press, 2019.

Stepan, Nancy Leys. *"The Hour of Eugenics": Race, Gender, and Nation in Latin America*. Ithaca, NY: Cornell University Press, 1991.

Stepan, Nancy Leys. *The Idea of Race in Science: Great Britain: 1800–1960*. Hamden: Archon Books, 1982.

Stephenson, Marcia. "From Marvelous Antidote to the Poison of Idolatry: The Transatlantic Role of Andean Bezoar Stones during the Late Sixteenth and Early Seventeeth Centuries." *Hispanic American Historical Review* 90, no. 1 (February 2010): 3–39.

Stern, Steve J. "The Rise and Fall of Indian-White alliances: A Regional View of 'Conquest' History." *Hispanic American Historical Review* 61, no. 3 (1981): 461–491.

Stocking, George W., Jr. *Race, Culture, and Evolution* (with a new preface). Chicago: University of Chicago Press, 1982 [1968].

Strang, Cameron. *Frontiers of Science: Imperialism and Natural Knowledge in the Gulf South Borderlands, 1500–1850*. Williamsburg, VA: Omohundro Institute of Early American History and Culture, 2018.

Strong, John S. "'The Devil Was in That Little Bone': The Portuguese Capture and Destruction of the Buddha's Tooth-Relic, Goa, 1561." *Past & Present* 206, suppl. 5 (2010): 184–198, doi: 10.1093/pastj/gtq024.

Sturm, Circe. *Blood Politics: Race, Culture, and Identity in the Cherokee Nation of Oklahoma*. Berkeley: University of California Press, 2002.

Swan, Claudia. "Making Sense of Medical Collections in Early Modern Holland: The Uses of Wonder." In *Making Knowledge in Early Modern Europe: Practices, Objects, and Texts, 1400–1800*, edited by Pamela H. Smith and Benjamin Schmidt, 199–213. Chicago: University of Chicago Press, 2007.

Sweet, James H. "The Iberian Roots of American Racist Thought." *William and Mary Quarterly* 54, no. 1 (1997): 143–166.

Szeminski, Jan. *La Utopía Tupamarista*. Lima: Pontificia Universidad Catóica del Peru, Fondo Editorial, 1984.

TallBear, Kim. *Native American DNA: Tribal Belonging and the False Promise of Genetic Science*. Minneapolis: University of Minnesota Press, 2013.

Tantaleán, Henry. "Un encargo muy especial: George Dorsey, Las Necrópolis de Ancón y la Exposición Universal de Chicago de 1893." *Latin American Antiquity* (2021): 1–19, doi:10.1017/laq.2021.45.

Tantaleán, Henry. *Peruvian Archaeology: A Critical History*, translated by Charles Stanish. Walnut Creek, CA: Left Coast Press, 2014.

Tenorio-Trillo, Mauricio. *Mexico at the World's Fairs: Crafting a Modern Nation*. Berkeley: University of California Press, 1996.

Teslow, Tracy. *Constructing Race: The Science of Bodies and Cultures in American Anthropology*. New York: Cambridge University Press, 2014.

Thomas, David Hurst. *Skull Wars: Kennewick Man, Archaeology, and the Battle for Native American Identity*. New York: Basic Books, 2000.

Thomas, David Hurst. "Thomas Jefferson's Conflicted Legacy in American Archaeology." In *Across the Continent: Lewis and Clark, and the Making Of America*, edited by Douglas Seefeldt, Jeffery L. Hantman and Peter S. Onuf, 84–131. Charlottesville: University of Virginia Press, 2005 [2004].

Thomson, Sinclair. *We Alone Will Rule: Native Andean Politics in the Age of Insurgency*. Madison: University of Wisconsin Press, 2002.

Thomson, Sinclair. "Sovereignty Disavowed: The Tupac Amaru Revolution in the Atlantic World." *Atlantic Studies* 13, no. 13 (2016): 407–431.

Thurner, Mark. *From Two Republics to One Divided: Contradictions of Postcolonial Nation making in Andean Peru*. Durham, NC: Duke University Press, 1997.

Thurner, Mark. *History's Peru: The Poetics of Colonial and Postcolonial Historiography*. Gainesville: University Press of Florida, 2011.

Thurner, Mark, and Juan Pimentel. "Introduction." In *New World Objects of Knowledge: A Cabinet of Curiosities*, edited by Mark Thurner and Juan Pimentel, 1–8. London: University of London Press, 2021.

Timmerman, Nicholas A. "Contested Indigenous Landscapes: Indian Mounds and the Political Creation of the Mythical 'Mound Builder' Race." *Ethnohistory* 67, no. 1 (2020): 75–95.

Toyne, J. Marla. "Tibial Surgery in Ancient Peru." *International Journal of Paleopathology* 8 (2015): 29–35.

Trafton, Scott. *Egypt Land: Race and Nineteenth-Century American Egyptomania*. Durham, NC: Duke University Press, 2004.

Trever, Lisa. "Criminal Lines, Indian Colours, and the Creation of a Black Legend: The Photographs of 'Los Bandidos de la Halancha,' Bolivia." *History of Photography* 40, no. 4 (2016): 369–387.

Trever, Lisa. "A Moche Riddle in Clay: Object Knowledge and Art Work in Ancient Peru." *Art Bulletin* 10, no. 4 (2019): 18–38.

Trever, Lisa. "The Uncanny Tombs in Martínez Compañón's *Trujillo del Perú*." In *Past Presented: Archaeological Illustration and the Ancient Americas*, edited by Joanne Pillsbury, 107–140. Washington, DC: Dumbarton Oaks Research Library and Collection, 2012.

Trouillot, Michel-Rolph. *Global Transformations: Anthropology and the Modern World*. New York: Palgrave Macmillan, 2003.

Tung, Tiffiny A. *Violence, Ritual, and the Wari Empire: A Social Bioarchaeology of Imperialism and the Ancient Andes*. Gainesville: University Press of Florida, 2012.

Turnbull, Paul. "'Rare Work amongst the Professors': The Capture of Indigenous Skulls within Phrenological Knowledge in Early Colonial Australia." In *Body Trade: Captivity, Cannibalism, and Colonialism in the Pacific*, edited by Barbara Creed and Jeanette Hoorn, 3–23. New York: Routledge, 2013 [2001].

Turner, Bethany L., and Valerie A. Andrushko. "Partnerships, Pitfalls, and Ethical Concerns in International Bioarchaeology." In *Social Bioarchaeology*, edited by Sabrina C. Agarwal and Bonnie A. Glencross, 44–67. Chichester: Wiley-Blackwell, 2011.

University of York Research Group. "The Peruvian Mummy at the Towneley Museum." n.d. [ca. 2007].

Uribe Hanabergh, Verónica. "Titian Ramsay Peale's 1831 'Obscure Expedition to Colombia': Status Quaestionis of the Sketches at the American Philosophical Society." *H-ART. Revista de historia, teoría y crítica de arte*, no. 7 (2020): 287–312.

Uslenghi, Alejandra. *Latin America at Fin-de-Siècle Universal Exhibitions*. New York: Palgrave Macmillan, 2016.

Valverde, Alejandra. "Catálogos de objetos prehispánicos en las exposiciones colombianas de Madrid y Chicago (1892/1893)." In *Historia de escritos Colombia, 1858–1994*, edited by Sergio Mejía and Adriana Díaz, 137–168. Bogotá: Ediciones Uniandes, 2009.

Valverde, Alejandra. *Mallqui, My Friend the Mummy*, translated by Simon Parkinson. CreateSpace Independent Publishing Platform, 2018.

Van Dalen Luna, Pieter, Lukasz Majchrzak, Kamilla Malek, Joanna Kuncewicz, and Pawel Miskowiec. "The Multimodal Chemical Study of Pre-Columbian Mummies." *Analyst* 145, no. 16 (2020): 5670–5681.

Van Damme, Stéphane. "The Pillar of Metropolitan Greatness: The Long Making of Archeological Objects in Paris (1711–2001)." *History of Science* 55, no. 3 (2017): 302–335.

Varela, Javier. *La muerte del rey: El ceremonial funerario de la Monarquía Española: 1500–1885*. Madrid: Turner, DL, 1990.

Velasco, Matthew C. "Ethnogenesis and Social Difference in the Andean Late Intermediate Period (AD 1100–1450): A Bioarchaeological Study of Cranial Modification in the Colca Valley, Peru." *Current Anthropology* 59, no. 1 (2018): 98–106.

Velasco, Matthew C. "Humans Remain: Engaging Communities and Embracing Tensions in the Study of Ancient Peruvian Skeletons." In *The Scholar as Human: Research and Teaching for Public Impact*, edited by Anna Sims Bartel and Debra A. Castillo, 69–92. Ithaca, NY: Cornell University Press, 2021.

Verano, John W. *Holes in the Head: The Art and Archaeology of Trepanation in Ancient Peru.* Washington, DC: Dumbarton Oaks Research Library and Collection, 2016.

Verano, John W. "Trophy Head-Taking and Human Sacrifice in Andean South America." In *Handbook of South American Archaeology*, edited by Helaine Silverman and William H. Isbell, 1047–1060. New York: Springer, 2008.

Verano, John W. "Where Do They Rest? The Treatment of Human Offerings and Trophies in Ancient Peru." In *Tombs for the Living: Andean Mortuary Practices*, edited by Tom D. Dillehay, 189–227. Washington, DC: Dumbarton Oaks Research Library and Collection, 2011 [1995].

Verdery, Katherine. *The Political Lives of Dead Bodies: Reburial and Post-Socialist Change.* New York: Columbia University Press, 1999.

Vicuña Guengerich, Sara. "*Capac* Women and the Politics of Marriage in Early Colonial Peru." *Colonial Latin American Review* 24, no. 2 (2015): 147–167.

Vicuña Guengerich, Sara. "Inca Women under Spanish Rule: *Probanzas* and *Informaciones* of the Colonial Andean Elite." In *Women's Negotiations and Textual Agency in Latin America, 1500–1799*, edited by Monica Díaz and Rocío Quispe-Agnoli, 106–129. London: Routledge, 2017.

Vidal, Fernando. "Miracles, Science, and Testimony in Post-Tridentine Saint-Making." *Science in Context* 20, no. 3 (2007): 481–508.

Villacorta Ostolaza, Luis Felipe. "Antonio Raimondi, Archaeology, and National Discourse." In *Past Presented: Archaeological Illustration and the Ancient Americas*, edited by Joanne Pillsbury, 172–204. Washington, DC: Dumbarton Oaks Research Library and Collection, 2012.

Wagner, Kim. *The Skull of Alum Bheg: The Life and Death of a Rebel of 1857.* New York: Oxford University Press, 2018.

Walker, Charles F. *Smoldering Ashes: Cuzco and the Creation of Republican Peru, 1780–1840.* Durham, NC: Duke University Press, 1999.

Walker, Charles F. *The Tupac Amaru Rebellion.* Cambridge, MA: Harvard University Press, 2014.

Walker, Charles F., and Liz Clarke. *Witness to the Age of Revolution: The Odyssey of Juan Bautista Tupac Amaru.* New York: Oxford University Press, 2020.

Wann, L. Samuel, Guido Lombardi, Bernardino Ojeda, Robert A. Benfer, Ricardo Rivera, Caleb E. Finch, Gregory S. Thomas, and Randall C. Thompson. "The Tres Ventanas Mummies of Peru." *Anatomical Record* 298, no. 6 (2015): 1026–1035.

Warren, Adam. "Dorotea Salguero and the Gendered Persecution of Unlicensed Healers in Early Republican Peru." In *The Gray Zones of Medicine: Healers & History in Latin America*, edited by Diego Armus and Pablo F. Gómez, 55–73. Pittsburgh: University of Pittsburgh Press, 2021.

Warren, Adam. *Medicine and Politics in Colonial Peru: Population Growth and the Bourbon Reforms.* Pittsburgh: University of Pittsburgh Press, 2010.

Warren, Adam. "Photography, Race, Indigeneity, and Ethics in the Yale Peruvian Expedition, 1911-1915." Presentation at the Pennsylvania State University, University Park, PA, 3 February 2020.

Weismantel, Mary. "Encounters with Dragons: The Stones of Chavín. *Res: Anthropology and Aesthetics* 65/66 (2014/2015): 37–53.

Weismantel, Mary. *Playing with Things: Engaging the Moche Sex Pots.* Austin: University of Texas Press, 2021.

Wernke, Steven A. "Transformations: Evangelization, Resettlement, and Community Organization in the Early Viceroyalty of Peru." In *The Oxford Handbook of the Incas*, edited by Sonia Alconini and R. Alan Covey, 701–719. New York: Oxford University Press, 2018.

Wertheimer, Eric. *Imagined Empires: Incas, Aztecs, and the New World of American Literature, 1771–1876.* Cambridge: Cambridge University Press, 1999.

Whitehead, Neil L. *Of Cannibals and Kings: Primal Anthropology in the Americas.* University Park: Pennsylvania State University Press, 2011.

Williams, Elizabeth A. "Art and Artifact at the Trocadero: *Ars Americana* and the Primitivist Revolution." In *Objects and Others: Essays on Museums and Material Culture,* edited by George W. Stocking Jr., 146–166. History of Anthropology 3. Madison: University of Wisconsin Press, 1985.

Williams, Elizabeth A. "Collecting and Exhibiting Pre-Columbiana in France and England, 1870–1930." In *Collecting the Pre-Columbian Past: A Symposium at Dumbarton Oaks: 6th and 7th October 1990,* edited by Elizabeth Hill Boone, 123–140. Washington, DC: Dumbarton Oaks Research Library and Collection, 1993.

Williams, Jocelyn S., and Melissa S. Murphy. "Living and Dying as Subjects of the Inca Empire: Adult Diet and Health at Puruchuco-Huaquerones, Peru." *Journal of Anthropological Archaeology* 32, no. 2 (2013): 165–179.

Wilson, Andrew S., Virginie Cerdeira, Ruth Horry, Sonia Guillén, Karin Frei, Robert C. Janaway, and Ian Barnes. "Sir Henry Wellcome's Legacy to Mummy studies: Seven Mummies with South American Attributes from the Wellcome Collection." Paper presented at the 9th World Congress on Mummy Studies, Lima, 10 August 2016.

Wilson, Douglas L. "The Evolution of Jefferson's 'Notes on the State of Virginia.'" *Virginia Magazine of History and Biography* 112, no. 2 (2004): 98–133.

Wilson, Fiona. "Indian Citizenship and the Discourse of Hygiene/Disease in Nineteenth-Century Peru." *Bulletin of Latin American Research* 23, no. 2 (2004): 165–180.

Yaya MacKenzie, Isabel. "Sovereign Bodies: Ancestor Cult and State Legitimacy among the Incas." *History and Anthropology* 26, no. 5 (2015): 639–660.

Yaya MacKenzie, Isabel. "Tales of Fallen Empires: The Andean Utopia in the Eighteenth-Century British Press." *Bulletin of Latin American Research* 37, no. 2 (2018): 175–190.

Yvinec, Maud. *"Les Péruviens auparavant només Indiens": Discour sur les populations autochtones des Andes dans le Pérou Indépendantn (1821–1879).* Rennes: Presses Universitaires de Rennes, 2021.

Zevallos Quiñones, Jorge. *Huacas y huaqueros en Trujillo durante el Virreinato, 1535–1835.* Trujillo, Perú: Editora Normas Legales, 1994.

Ziemendorff, Stefan. "Edvard Munch y la Momia de un sarcófago de la Cultura Chachapoyas." *Cátedra Villareal* (Lima) 3, no. 2 (2015): 197–212.

Ziemendorff, Stefan. "Los Marqueses de Santiago de Oropesa y las Momias Reales Incaicas: Revisión de la Hipótesis Acerca del Retiro de las Momias del Hospital de San Andrés." *Historia y Cultura* 28 (2016): 243–272.

Ziemendorff, Stefan, Mario Millones Figueroa, and Edwin Greenwich Centeno. "Las momias reales incaicas en el Hospital de San Andrés: Su permanencia e identificación" *Historia y Cultura* 30 (2019): 161–208.

Ziółkowski, Mariusz S. "The Inka and the Breviary, or the Art of Talking with the Huacas." In *Mędzy Drzewem Życia a Drzewem Poznania: Księga Ku Czci Profesora Andrzeja Wiercińskiego,* edited by Mariusz S. Ziółkowski and Arkadiusza Sołtysiaka, 355–367. Warsaw: Uniwersytet Warszawski, 2003.

INDEX

Note: Figures are indicated by an italic f following the page number.